Prejudice and Racism

McGraw-Hill Series in Social Psychology

CONSULTING EDITOR: Philip G. Zimbardo

Leonard Berkowitz:	Aggression: Its Causes, Consequences, and Control
Gary G. Brannigan and Matthew R. Merrens:	The Social Psychologists: Research Adventures
Sharon S. Brehm:	Intimate Relationships
Shawn Meghan Burn:	The Social Psychology of Gender
Steve L. Ellyson and Amy Halberstadt:	Explorations in Social Psychology: Readings and Research
Susan T. Fiske and Shelley E. Taylor:	Social Cognition
Stanley Milgram:	The Individual in a Social World
David G. Myers:	Exploring Social Psychology
Ayala Pines and Christina Maslach:	Experiencing Social Psychology: Readings and Projects
Scott Plous:	The Psychology of Judgment and Decision Making
Lee Ross and Richard E. Nisbett:	The Person and the Situation: Perspectives of Social Psychology
Jeffrey Z. Rubin, Dean G. Pruitt, and Sung Hee Kim:	Social Conflict: Escalation, Stalemate, and Settlement
David A. Schroeder, Louis A. Penner, John E. Dovidio, and Jane A. Piliavin:	The Social Psychology of Helping and Altruism: Problems and Puzzles
Abraham Tesser:	Advanced Social Psychology
Harry C. Triandis:	Culture and Social Behavior
Philip G. Zimbardo and Michael R. Leippe:	The Psychology of Attitude Change and Social Influence

Prejudice and Racism

SECOND EDITION

❖

James M. Jones
University of Delaware

The McGraw-Hill Companies, Inc.
New York   St. Louis   San Francisco   Auckland   Bogotá   Caracas
Lisbon   London   Madrid   Mexico City   Milan   Montreal   New Delhi
San Juan   Singapore   Sydney   Tokyo   Toronto

McGraw-Hill

*A Division of The **McGraw·Hill** Companies*

PREJUDICE AND RACISM

Acknowledgments appear on p. 566, and on this page by reference.

This book is printed on acid-free paper.

2 3 4 5 6 7 8 9 0 FGR FGR 9 0 9

ISBN 0-07-033117-0

This book was set in Palatino by Ruttle, Shaw & Wetherill, Inc.
The editors were Beth Kaufman and Larry Goldberg;
the production supervisor was Annette Mayeski.
The photo researcher was Inge King.
The cover was designed by Karen K. Quigley.
Project supervision was done by Ruttle, Shaw & Wetherill, Inc.
Drawings were done by Fine Line Illustrations, Inc.
Quebecor Printing/Fairfield was printer and binder.

Cover art: Jacob Lawrence: *The Migration of the Negro, Panel No. 49,* 1940–41.
"They also found discrimination in the North although it was much different from that which they had known in the South."
Tempera on masonite.
18 × 12" (45.7 × 30.5 cm).
Acquired 1942.
© The Phillips Collection, Washington, D.C.

Library of Congress Cataloging-in-Publication Data

Jones, James M.
    Prejudice and racism / James M. Jones.—2nd ed.
       p. cm.—(McGraw-Hill series in social psychology)
    Includes bibliographical references and index.
    ISBN 0-07-033117-0 (alk. paper)
    1. Race relations. 2. Prejudices. 3. United States—Race relations. I. Title. II. Series.
HT1521.J65 1997
305.8—dc20   96-34940

http://www.mhcollege.com

About the Author

*J*AMES M. JONES has been Professor of Social Psychology at the University of Delaware since 1982. He earned his bachelor's degree in 1963 at Oberlin College, working with Norman Henderson in behavioral genetics. He obtained a master's degree at Temple University in 1967, working on clinical assessments of skid row alcoholics with Thomas E. Shipley. Jones earned his doctoral degree in social psychology at Yale University in 1970. There he worked with Chuck Kiesler on studies of the role of commitment in conferring resistance to attitude change and with Bob Abelson on psychological implication carried in language and how it affects the formation of attitudes. For his dissertation, he developed a cognitive model of humor based on psychological implication and incongruity resolution. This model demonstrated that humor is structured as an apparent incongruity of ideas or behaviors that violate a psychological implication. The humor enjoyment arose when this incongruity was resolved by replacing a surface expectancy with a deeper one. This interest in humor followed him to Harvard University, where he took his first teaching job in 1970. In 1973, Jones won a Guggenheim fellowship to study humor in Trinidad, West Indies. His studies of calypso, Carnival, and everyday street humor were captured in newspaper articles in Trinidad and in a chapter on calypso humor written with the Mighty Chalkdusk, a calypsonian school teacher in Trinidad named Hollis Liverpool. Also while at Harvard, Jones published the first edition of *Prejudice and Racism* in 1972 and developed the Athletic Profile Inventory (API) to study the attitudes of athletes and how they affect performance. In 1977, Jones moved to the American Psychological Association to direct the Minority Fellowship Program, which he continues to do today. In 1987, Jones became Acting Executive Director of Public Interest at APA and established the Directorate that oversees the applications of psychological knowledge to issues that affect public well-being (AIDS; workplace stress; youth violence; ethnic minority, gay and lesbian, disability and women's issues). Jones's current research interest is in temporal orientation, the focus of attention on the past, present, and future. With his graduate students, he has developed the Temporal Orientation Scale (TOS) to assess individual differences. Current research explores the cognitive, emotional, and behavioral mechanisms that influence and result from variations in temporal orientation. Jones is currently at work on a new book, *Cultural Psychology of African Americans*, that develops his TRIOS idea (*T*ime, *R*hythm, *I*mprovisation, *O*ral expression, and *S*pirituality) as a basis of bicultural evolution of African Americans.

To Olaive, for her generosity and unending love.

Contents

—————— ❖ ——————

ix

Foreword

---------------- ❖ ----------------

*P*rejudice is the perversion of human perfection. Basic to the human condition are the needs to know and to belong. The cognitively based need is essential for understanding our relationship to the environments around us, thereby generating intellectual curiosity and creativity. The socially based need opens us to affiliation with others, thereby generating social support systems and caring communities. Prejudice narrows understanding by biasing our judgments and predetermining what will be discovered from exploring our environment. Such thinking promotes ignorance and demotes knowledge. Prejudice constrains caring for others, it excludes rather than includes. Such negative feelings strain the bonds of the human connection by replacing helping with hurting, by substituting dominating control for democratic sharing.

Racism is the most basic and destructive form that prejudice assumes. Although prejudicial thinking and feeling can extend to any dimension on which individuals evaluate and judge other people, and even things and events in their surround, racial prejudice goes much further. It goes beyond demeaning others to dehumanizing and demonizing those judged as "different." The Unknown Other becomes The Feared Enemy. Enemies are warred against, captured, imprisoned, enslaved, exploited, and executed. Because prejudice thrives on simplistic thought processes, it seeks simple bases for discriminating Self and Us from Others and Them. Across continents and over the ages, skin color has been an easily read discriminanda for such perceptually based (mindless) decisions. When color is not a sufficient criterion for prejudice, then any attributes believed to be associated with it can serve as default values. "Race," as in Hitler's use of the term to extol the "Aryan Race" over the alleged "Jewish Race," comes to be a code term for evaluating people in one's world in terms of good versus bad, desirable versus despicable, worthy versus worthless. Such evaluations not only offer justifications for racial prejudice, they also provide the foundation for racial discrimination—the domination, management, control, and exploitation of the labor, minds, and bodies of those judged as unfit, as inferior, as less human than Us. Such thinking and practices typically give a false sense of superiority to those who dominate through prejudice and discrimination. It may also lower the sense of self-worth of those who accept the negative stereotypes that abound about them. In that way, racial prejudice becomes an insidious force working from within the oppressed to nurture the message of their oppressors.

Prejudice seems to be a fundamental aspect of most human cultures, especially those with any degree of heterogeneity of peoples. We know that even the most minimal of cues can be used as the basis of discriminatory evaluations, of dividing the world into we-folks and them-folks, the acceptable in-group members and the unacceptable out-group members. Midwestern elementary school teacher Jane Elliott demonstrated the ease with which children in her class could come to despise and discriminate against their long-term school friends after she told them that eye color was diagnostic of being a good or bad person, the Blues versus the Browns. And whichever group was on top for the day (she reversed the eye color evaluation on the second day) performed better on math and English tests, while those below performed worse. That provocative demonstration has been witnessed recently in Bosnia and Rwanda, where long-term neighbors have killed one another after they have been labeled as the enemy, as Serbs, Moslems, Croats, Hutus, Tutsis, or whatever. But for generations, castes in India (the Untouchables) and in Japan (the Burakamin), of the same biological status but assigned a different, inferior psychological and social status, have lived their lives within structures that come to justify their imposed subordination. In this sense, individual prejudicial thinking becomes institutionalized as racism and integrated into the functioning of society. The society develops laws, customs, norms, rituals, services, and prisons to deal with its "racial problem." Psychological stereotypes and physical segregation combine to keep the racially discriminated in their place. But curiously, once racism becomes embedded in a society, it is difficult for even thoughtful people not to accept at some level the "kernel of truth" hypothesis behind the stereotype, whether of the mercenary; shrewd Jew; the violent, gangster Italian; or the dumb, dangerous Negro. The racists provide the images that come to color the imagination of both those who are discriminated against and those who are tolerant and should be part of the enlightenment and liberation process.

Let me illustrate the insidious, powerful nature of prejudice and racism, as it affected me in my childhood and adolescence, with several personal accounts of how I suffered because I was discriminated against first for being Jewish, later for being Italian, and finally Negro.

When I was 6 years old, my family moved to a new neighborhood in the South Bronx, and for the first time in my young life I experienced a strange kind of prejudice against me. Every afternoon on the way home from school, the local toughs chased me, yelling curses and epithets I could not understand, like "doityjewbouy." This scenario was replayed each day of the week, and so was my torment and confusion. I could hide in my apartment on Saturday since there was no school I had to attend, but on Sunday, my mother wanted me to go to church, against my better judgment. She asked the janitor's son, Charlie Glassford, if he would show me where the nearest Catholic church was, and was startled when Charlie screamed out, "He can't go to our church, he's a Jew!" "No, he is not, he is a Catholic, we are all Catholics, Charlie," replied my mother. "Well, we've been beating him up because he is a Jew boy, we thought he was a 'dirty Jew boy.'" "Why would you and the other boys think that?" Charlie thought for a moment and replied with the stereotypical wisdom of the mean streets, "He is skinny, with a long nose and blue eyes, that's how Jew boys look." Once it was clear I was not one of the despised group, I was accepted—of course, only after I completed the trials of the gang's elaborate initiation ritual for its 6- to 12-year-old members—but that is another story.

When I was 14 years old, my family moved across the country to live in North Hollywood, California, in part so that my father's extended family could once again all be in proximity. I had become a popular student in all of my Bronx schools, usually elected president of this or that, and also a team leader in my ghetto neighborhood. So, naturally, I had assumed I would soon be welcomed in my new school. Instead, I was shunned. I did not have a single friend for the entire school year. Students would move away when I sat down at a cafeteria table. I could sense them whispering about me, making furtive glances my way, averting their eyes when I tried to make eye contact. Nothing I did made a difference in their total rejection of me. I was dumbfounded, even more so than when the Bronx kids mistook me for their stereotyped version of a Jew. Those were little ignorant kids; these were apparently smarter high school students, and I was clearly a nice, smart, amiable kid, with a proven track record of making friends with almost anyone. I gave up trying in this new vortex of hate. I kept to myself, got all A's, and went directly home at the end of the school day.

I developed asthma, which became so severe that it provided the excuse my family needed to abort our California fiasco, which was making us all miserable, and so we could return to the good old Bronx as soon as school was over. However, before that glorious time came, I made the school baseball team in the spring. But even there I was not integrated into the team comeraderie. One day, on a long bus trip to a game on the other side of the San Fernando Valley, I decided to face up to the beast and ask the left fielder what I had done to be so disliked. "We don't dislike you. In fact, you're not so bad as we all thought you would be, but it's too late to make changes." "What do you mean 'bad'?" "Well, aren't you a New York Sicilian, with Mafia connections?" "Yes and no; yes, New York, and, yes, my family is from Sicily, but, no, neither I nor anyone in my family has ever had anything to do with the Mafia." "Oh, we assumed they all went together." "And you all were frightened of me, me a skinny kid, who never did a single hostile act toward anyone here?" "It don't matter if you're skinny or not, if you carry a gun or a switchblade, does it?"

When I was 21, graduating from Brooklyn College, I decided that Yale was the ideal graduate school for me, relatively close to home, one of the best "Ivory League" schools, as my mother would say, and with a hot-shot psychology department in 1954. Curiously, that was the only school I did not hear anything from in terms of acceptance or rejection letters. So I was prepared to go to Minnesota to work with Stanley Schlachter when I got a call from Yale. The professor asked if I had made my decision yet. I told him my letter of acceptance to Minnesota was on the kitchen table to be mailed out the next day, which was April 15, the deadline for admitted candidates to accept the school of choice. He asked if I would choose Yale instead if there were a position for me. I replied affirmatively, indicating that it was still my first choice. "O.K., then meet me tomorrow morning in the bar of the Statler Hotel on 34th Street at 10 a.m. The Eastern Psychological Association's convention will be going on. I can interview you in person." "That's great! Is there anything I can do in preparation for the interview?" "No, just be prompt!"

After two quick double martinis, routine among male psychologists of that era, he asked me a series of questions about rats. "Have you ever run rats?" "Yes (out of my apartment with a broom, but withheld those details)." "Can you build apparatus?" "Of course (my father can do anything with his hands and would be happy to assist)." "What do you know about exploratory drive?" "A great deal. I have done some work on it, but it's not completed (I never made it all the way to become an Explorer Scout)." "Good, you can be my research assistant. I am authorized to accept you as a new graduate student in Psychology at Yale University, starting in the fall, with tuition paid and a stipend of $1200 a year. I have a grant to study the determinants of exploratory drive in rats, so can pay you to start this summer. Here are a batch of my offprints. Read them and come prepared to work. Don't you want another drink?"

For the next three years, I not only ran rats, hundreds of them, I bred them, nursed them, deprived them, enriched them, cleaned their cages—that I had learned to construct myself—and mopped the lab floors regularly. Now, realize that my graduate school application clearly stated that my primary interest was in studying race relations as a social psychologist, and here I was playing the role of a rat-running behaviorist. But the pay was good and it was, of course, Yale.

After graduation in 1959, I was at my first International Congress in Bonn, Germany, remarking to my former mentor, Harold Kelley, that it must be difficult for American Jewish psychologists to be dealing with their negative feelings about Germany. He blew me away when he said it was probably how I felt knowing that the psychology faculty at Yale thought that I was Black, you know Negro, Colored, and that is why they hesitated so long in accepting me. "Say what?" "We did not know how to deal with your application because some faculty assumed you were a Black ghetto kid because of the circumstantial evidence you presented. Once we had the set to see you that way, it all fell into place naturally." "For instance?"

Let me summarize that evidence: Interests—captain of the track team; Favorite reading—*Downbeat* magazine; Hobbies—listening to modern jazz, Charlie Parker, Lester Young, Dizzy, Miles, Lady Day; Major—sociology-anthropology-psychology, with top grades in The Negro Family in the U.S. and in Race Relations, and a publication on the dynamics of intergroup prejudice between Puerto Ricans and Negroes in the Bronx; Extracurricular activities—secretary of the NAACP chapter; Primary mentor and recommender—Charles Radford Lawrence, well-known Negro sociologist who happened to send his letter on NAACP stationary because he was out of college stationery at home and his letter was late; the Italian name—Roy Campanella, famous Brooklyn Dodger catcher, surely Negro, but also with an Italian name. And so it went. Even the GRE scores fit the stereotype: low math relative to good verbal scores.

Assume black. Then the faculty thinking goes like this: Good letters of recommendation need discounting because they obviously reflected reverse biases. Will have difficulties adjusting to life at Yale since there are none of his kind in the department. Faculty may have difficulty adjusting to him and his lifestyle, especially those from the South (like the professor who interviewed me in New York City). But those with an alternative perspective argued it would be good to take one, even if a token one, and this one was not too bad. In any case, indecision ruled among this august body of intellectuals, and my application was literally shelved, neither accepted nor rejected, nor put on a waiting list. On the next to the last day of the student acceptances, Gordon Bower, the top admittee, deferred to get a master's degree in Philosophy of Science at University of Minnesota, and that Southern professor with the grant and the drive to explore was suddenly without an R.A. Maybe he called those on the waiting list who either did not want to know from running rats or had made a prior commitment elsewhere. That left only me. He calls; I say I am eligible and eager. He comes to New York, asks a few simple questions that I lie to, he sizes me up and offers me the job. Now let's test your detective skills. Why did he have to interview me in person, since I could have answered those same questions during his phone call? In those days, no admitted student went through an interview process. Why did he have to see me before he could offer me his assistantship and thereby admission to Yale? Your call?

Upon my arrival at Yale, some of the faculty were indeed sorry to see that I seemed white when they had hoped I would be their first black, but I don't think my "mentor" saw it that way. In fact, I now think that had he seen me as black, he might have regretfully informed me that the job had just been taken by a more qualified applicant. But maybe I am going too far beyond the data.

But the data that I can add in conclusion is that my mixed-message application and transcript also included the line items that I was Summa Cum Laude, junior year Phi Beta Kappa, fellowship winner, fraternity president, varsity athlete with a Presidential award for distinguished scholarship, and some other goodies thrown in for good measure. All of that was not sufficient to get me a seat on the first-run bus to New Haven, maybe because it was negated by all that circumstantial evidence, which had triggered a cascade of negative stereotypical thinking even among some of the most brilliant scholars and honored psychological researchers in the land.

These three personal vignettes taken together speak to the pain of prejudice felt daily by its untold number of victims. They also point up the ignorance and mean-spiritedness of prejudiced thinking practiced by its untold number of perpetrators. They are also informative of the power of negative stereotypes to construct alternative realities that can come to damage the sense of self-worth of its targets and control their significant life options.

Although I was nearly the first black graduate student in the psychology department at Yale, the author of this wonderful book, James Jones, was indeed the real thing some years later. So it seems altogether fitting that I be the one to extol the virtues of his original contribution to the scholarship of race, racism, and racial relationships since in one sense we are brothers, if not of the same skin, then under the skin—of the same soul, which we all know really matters more.

Many years ago Jim and I also shared the honor of being selected to be authors in the original series of social psychology monographs edited by Charles Kiesler. Both of our books then were slim, trim introductions to our respective areas of attitude change and social influence and of prejudice and racism. Since then, each of our texts has grown in size and depth to reflect our own deeper knowledge of the field and the large body of research now available in those areas.

In this essentially new edition of his successful 1970s book, Jim sets his sights on understanding the individual and social dynamics of prejudice in the broadest of contexts by dealing with personality and societal structure, attitudes and ideologies, biology and culture. This book offers an illuminating social history of prejudice in America, with personal narratives adding vitality to the flow of events and a human dimension to the abstract reality of racial relationships. Our author paints a similarly personal, intense, yet conceptually broad, portrait of race in its many manifestations. He calls on information that spans all of the social sciences, bolstered by historical and biological analyses.

Throughout his unfolding story line, Jim takes his readers on a compelling path of understanding the complex processes underlying the phenomena of prejudice and racism. Its direction is guided by a vision of change, of instilling the concern for figuring out how prejudice can be reduced, how racism and its destructive discrimination can be constrained. He tells us it ain't easy, but any meaningful change will have to be directed by the wisdom that comes from applying the best available conceptual analysis of the social psychological dynamics of prejudice and racism combined with the realities of politics and economics, and a dash of effective "street smarts." I expect that this book will become the classic in the field, comparable to Gordon Allport's earlier analysis of prejudice, with a broader and more personally insightful contribution to the study of race and racism than has ever existed in our literature.

The McGraw-Hill Series in Social Psychology has been designed to celebrate the significant contributions being made by researchers, theorists, and practitioners of social psychology in understanding the social nature of the human condition. Their body of work holds the potential to enrich the quality of our lives through wise applications of their knowledge. This series of texts has become a showcase for presenting new theories, original syntheses, creative analyses, and current methodologies by some of the most distinguished scholars in our field, as well as by promising young writer-researchers. Our authors reveal a common commitment to sharing their vision and expertise with a broad audience, ranging from their colleagues to graduate students and especially to undergraduates with an interest in social psychology. Each of our authors has been guided by the objective of conveying the essential lessons and principles of his or her area of expertise in an interesting style, one that informs without resorting to technical jargon, that inspires others to utilize these ideas at conceptual or practical levels. This book by James Jones clearly does both. It is the best current statement about the nature of prejudice and racism in the United States, based on a deep understanding of basic social psychological and societal processes, and its clearly explicated message will be appreciated by scholars and students alike.

Although each text in our series is designed to stand alone as the best representative of its domain of scholarship, taken as a whole they represent the core of social psychology. Teachers may elect to use any of these texts as in-depth supplements to a general textbook or, ideally, paired with the briefer overview of social psychology found in David Myers's text, *Exploring Social Psychology,* eloquently written for this series. Some teachers have organized their social psychology courses entirely around a judicious selection of these monographs, integrated through their lectures and thereby providing students with a richer background. In either case, if you are interested in giving your students the most exciting presentation of the social psychology of prejudice and racism, this is the text for you and them—James Jones's original contribution to our understanding of this basic aspect of human nature.

Philip G. Zimbardo
Stanford University

Preface

❖

$\mathcal{D}$ale Berra, son of the New York Yankee baseball hall of famer Yogi, was once asked to compare himself with his famous father. He said, "We are a lot alike, only our similarities are different!" Comparing the second edition of *Prejudice and Racism* to the first edition brings Berra's observation to mind.

This edition is organized in three parts, consisting of four, six, and six chapters, respectively. The three-part organization is similar to that of the first edition, but the length, detail, and breadth of coverage are different. Introductory and concluding chapters bind the story together in a book that is nearly three times larger than the first edition.

Part One is a historical review and analysis, included on the premise that the problems of race relations in 1997 cannot be understood without some understanding of events and their consequences that went before. Attitudes, opinions, and beliefs, as well as laws, social policies, and intergroup relations, evolve over time with a continuity between past and present. A person is assumed to carry early childhood memories and experiences that shape his or her personality, attitudes, and behavior forward to adulthood. Similarly, I believe that the collective dynamics of a people and their relations to one another unfold in the crucible of culture over time. We do not reinvent ourselves in each new era, we only extend and modify what was already there.

Another consideration is the connection between what social and behavioral scientists study and write about and what happens to real people in the real world. Thus the social histories are juxtaposed with emergent social and behavioral science research and analysis and, where applicable, major social policy trends in education, intergroup behavior, racial attitudes, legal opinions, and so on. This narrative carries through to 1990, updating the first edition, which ended with the decade of the 1960s. Trends toward social conservatism; ethnic, gender, and racial pride; conflict over affirmative action; and an increase in intergroup antagonisms are traced directly to the aftermath of the 1960s civil rights decade. Social psychological research documents these trends and provides a compelling account of their influence on contemporary social relations.

Part Two summarizes the breadth of research and theorizing on the psychology of prejudice. Requiring but one chapter in the first edition, the voluminous research on racial attitudes, stereotypes, intergroup relations, and prejudice reduction strategies requires six chapters here. The 1970s suspicion that the Civil Rights Act did not eliminate prejudice is given firm scientific credibility by the research in Part Two. We learn how basic and fundamental prejudicial thinking and subsequent behavior can be. Racial attitudes exist at unconscious levels: they have rather automatic influences on perception and judgment and can be traced directly to biasing behaviors.

Also added is a chapter that explores how targets of prejudice react to being singled out and stigmatized. The effects of these biasing behaviors on targets not only tends to undermine their performance and challenge their self-worth, they also motivate these individuals to find strength and positivity in their group status. Thus prejudice not only harms individuals, it also galvanizes group solidarity and thereby increases the likelihood that relations between two people that should be interpersonal are increasingly influenced by group identification and thus become intergroup interactions.

We also explore the broader context of intergroup conflict by considering three major conflicts beyond the black-white United States situation: Rwanda, between Tutsis and Hutus; Bosnia, among Bosnian Serbs, Muslims, and Croats; and Northern Ireland, between Protestants and Catholics. The analysis of these ethnic conflicts shows that patterns of conflict follow similar universal themes. Although our own history of racial conflict may seem uniquely influenced by the circumstances and character of the protagonists, evidence suggests that it may be part of a larger, more universal human tendency toward collective self-interest and the struggle for autonomy and opportunity.

Finally, prejudice is not easy to reduce. The prevailing idea that the best approach is to put different people in contact with one another under a particular set of conditions is shown to have several difficulties. Particularly problematic is the simple admonition to "treat people as if their race doesn't matter—to be colorblind." The research says that we have a very difficult time doing this, and acting as though we can leaves us with a status quo that is affected by race but also a false ideology of racial neutrality. Treating people as though their race *does* matter—but in a positive, not a negative, way—and acknowledging that friendships can arise based on both similarities and differences of experience can encourage the deprovincialization of in-group preferences and increase the likelihood of more positive relations across group boundaries.

Part Three turns to a discussion of racism, making the point that racism is multileveled, historically derived, and culturally embedded. Here it is necessary to go beyond psychology to consider sociology, political science, anthropology, biology, and history. Race itself was discussed as a prelude to understanding racism. The biological basis of race is asserted, and its social and cultural role in support of power arrangements and subsequent consequences defined racism. The biology of race is contrasted with its social construction and cultural propagation over the centuries. The biological view of race is shown to be scientifically bankrupt, and tracing its historical usage and meaning reveals its role in the formation of status hierarchies and the perpetuation of group self-interest. Three levels of racism are identified: individual, institutional, and cultural, which locate problems of what we think race is, how we treat people differentially on the basis of race, and how institutional arrangements and decision-rules sustain and reinforce racial bias. The entire pattern of racial effects is orchestrated and rationalized by a cultural tradition in which race is heavily influenced by values and beliefs that condoned and made racism natural. The levels of racism, and the mechanisms of racialism and racialization that integrate them, are joined with prejudice in a model that delineates how and why race and racism persist, aided and abetted by prejudice and nurtured in a receptive and fertile cultural environment. To balance the approach, we also acknowledge that the forces of racism have always been challenged by the agonistic forces of anti-racism. The struggle and contradictions between extolling liberty and abridging it are an important part of the story of racism.

In 1970, the "American obsession" with race was the engine driving the civil rights movement and concerns with the historical facts of racial bias. The concern was not just race in general, but the peculiarities of black-African and white-European contact that played out in Africa, Latin America, the Caribbean, and the United States. The backdrop to the first edition was the decade of the 1960s, which to many signaled a break from a racially oppressive past and the beginning of a new and more compassionate day. This total story was told in 178 pages comprising six chapters. The present volume suggests that not only has the vision of a racially neutral future not happened, but it may have been Dead on Arrival (DOA).

Prejudice and Racism is conceived as a textbook for upper level undergraduates and graduate students. A textbook is a companion and guide for learning about a subject. I have learned a great deal about prejudice and racism in writing this book. I believe it can be a textbook not only for the students for whom it is intended but also for anyone who is seriously interested in understanding the problems posed by prejudice and racism. *Prejudice and Racism* places both squarely in the core structures and mechanisms of individuals and society. Race relations are by no means perfect, but I believe that in spite of the fundamental and basic nature of prejudice and racism within the species, we have made tremendous progress over the decades. The daily accounts of race-based hateful acts, seemingly small affronts, and statistics that proclaim race-based inequalities in economic, political, social, and educational spheres leave us with the feeling that race relations are the same or maybe even worse than they were twenty-five years ago.

One reviewer praised one of the chapters on racism for its thorough and insightful analysis of the problems, but noted that he was also depressed by it. A solution may seem hopeless when we consider all the forces at work to perpetuate racial bias. But we have made progress, and we historically have done so in response to heightened racial conflict and the contradictions that racial inequality bring to light. That is, progress in race relations has occurred because we tackle the problems of race head-on; we do not sweep them under the rug, pretend they don't exist, or relabel them as something else. It is precisely at those historical moments when racial tension or inequality is most dramatic that we have made the most meaningful progress. It is, of course, at these moments that the problems are most acute and thus command our attention. Our history as well as our social psychological science tell us that we should confront race head-on to make progress. Proposing a "colorblind" approach recalls the ostrich coping with fear by putting its head in the sand.

This book attempts to bring light to the problems of race and racism in the hope that we will learn more about the subject. I hope this book successfully and compellingly illustrates the problems we confront and convincingly provides the evidence that these problems are real. *Prejudice and Racism* does not provide a blueprint for change but does review promising pathways toward change and suggests the broader cultural context in which these problems can be ameliorated. I remain guardedly optimistic that we will continue to make progress and hope that this book will contribute positively to a better future for us all.

Acknowledgments

The second edition of *Prejudice and Racism* benefited greatly from the contributions of many people. Its quality is the direct result of the generous donations of time and expertise by numerous people who care about teaching, learning, and the communication of ideas. I acknowledge and thank everyone who helped make this book happen.

I am grateful to Jim Sidanius, Chuck Stangor, Joe Ponteretto, Jules Harrell, and others who reviewed the first edition and provided very helpful feedback and suggestions on what the second edition should entail. Trish Devine and I shared many hours of stimulating discussion about issues of prejudice and racism and ways to reduce them both. The resulting ideas permeate this book. Several reviewers of early draft chapters made insightful and extremely helpful suggestions that substantially improved the final product. Mark Zanna of University of Waterloo, Russ Fazio of Indiana University, Jack Dovidio of Colgate University, and Victoria Esses of University of Western Ontario reviewed the Introduction and Part Two. Their comments were generously thorough and instructive. They helped me organize the tremendous body of social psychology literature on prejudice. Xeturah Woodley-Tillman of Metropolitan State College of Denver, R. Scott Smith of Utica College of Syracuse University, and Robert E. Steele of the University of Maryland reviewed selected chapters in Parts One and Three. Their comments helped me to see things from an instructor's viewpoint and improved the coverage and clarity of the ideas. Marshall Stevenson of Ohio State University reviewed Part One, corrected flawed historical scholarship, and provided useful direction to current references and lines of argument. Joe Feagin of the University of Florida at Gainesville read Part Three and, in addition to his cogent criticism and helpful suggestions for additional references and interpretations of racism, allowed me to borrow heavily from his important work on living with racism. I also want to thank Russ Fazio's students, Kari Merrill and Jeff Levine, who offered written comments on early drafts of Part Two. In addition, Jenny Crocker, Bill Cross, Claude Steele, Bob Abelson, and Wade Boykin read portions of the manuscript and provided feedback, information, and suggestions that helped me better express ideas. Bill Dorris provided useful information early on that helped me frame the issues in Northern Ireland, and then he and his wife, Mairead Casey, helped me get it straight in the final version of this complex story. Vivian Derryck and Bob Berg helped me to understand issues in Rwanda; and John Perazich helped me to understand the Bosnian issue by sharing his Yugoslavian background and insights. Delbert Spurlock provided great insight into the constitutional origins of this country and some issues they raise for America's future. I also want to thank Henrietta Yuseem, Amelia Palmer, Sara Thompson, Grady Garner, Raven Rowe, A. J. Franklin, and Twana Harris for sharing their stories with me.

My staff at the American Psychological Association, Daisy Clipper, Jo-Anne Fournier, and Diane Rosen, were supportive throughout the long writing process, and Ismael Rivera offered insights and expertise on affirmative action issues as well as assisted me in pulling information off the Internet.

Students and colleagues at the University of Delaware offered support in a variety of ways throughout the process. My colleague Sam Gaertner read versions of several chapters and helped clarify empirical and theoretical points throughout. Graduate students Lisa Banicky and Hilda Speicher read several chapters and gave excellent suggestions for organization and clarity. Hilda also assisted in putting together references and copyediting work. Barbara Parker and Judy Fingerle provided gracious and effective assistance in a variety of administrative and clerical tasks. Terell Lasane helped me formulate and clarify many ideas in his roles as doctoral student working under my supervision, research coordinator of the Summer

Research Institute, and teaching assistant in my Psychological Perspectives on Black Americans course. And students in that course—Chris Black, Paula Chandler-Paramore, Kara Horowitz, Chris Hudson, Tina LaVecchia, Daletha McRae, Audrey Paramito, Mary Prosceno, Earl Shorter, Chris Tenicki, Donna Sarro, Patricia Abrams, and Vera Scabbia—read chapters and wrote helpful critiques. So, too, students from the Summer Research Institute—Gary Bennett, Frank Carvajal, Grady Garner, Paul Jones, Egon Kraan, Nina Seward, and Sassy Wheeler—offered spirited advice on several chapters that made them each better.

I must also acknowledge many people who helped in the editorial and production process. Beth Kaufman, my editor at McGraw-Hill, believed in this project and by her enthusiasm and unconditional support kept me going when it seemed the book would never happen. Inge King was masterful at searching out the photographs and helping me to add a comprehensive visual version of many of the written ideas. Zaza Ziemba conscientiously copyedited the manuscript. Peg Markow at Ruttle, Shaw & Wetherill supervised the production of the book and made it easy for me to complete the final stages of the process. Larry Goldberg was patient and helpful down the stretch as we tried to balance the final writing stages with the beginning of the editorial process. Phil Zimbardo as series editor always saw the importance of this subject and believed in the potential of this book to make a strong contribution. And I am also indebted to Chuck Kiesler, who believed I could write this book in 1970 when he began this series.

Finally, I must thank those closest to me, my family. In the first edition, I noted my daughter Shelly's daily query, "How many more pages, daddy?" Now, she is beginning her residency training in anesthesiology at Johns Hopkins University Hospital and helped to choose the photographs contained in this book. My daughter Nashe was "a cuddly, babbly, and energetic diversion" during the writing of the first edition, and now, as a Microsoft field marketing specialist, provides me with free and extensive technical assistance in preparing graphs and charts and generally getting things done with Windows 95. And my wife Olaive, whose judgment became "the ultimate criterion for the acceptability of a sentence or necessity of a particular point" in the first edition, actually escalated her role in this edition. She read every single chapter and footnote in multiple drafts and provided copyediting advice as well as substantive intellectual and stylistic direction. She literally was a collaborator in the writing, a therapist when I was blocked, and a partner in my life. Without her help, I could not have finished this book. Finally, I express my gratitude to my parents, Arthur and Marcella, and my sister, Judy Stacey, who have always supported my work and my life.

J.M.J.

1

Prejudice and Racism Revisited

———— ❖ ————

Introduction ◆ Whose problem is it anyway? ◆ Defining prejudice and racism ◆
What is prejudice? ◆ *The problem of discrimination* ◆ *What is racism?* ◆ *Three types
of racism* ◆ *Individual racism* ◆ *Institutional racism* ◆ *Cultural racism* ◆ A question of the emphasis on blacks ◆ *Black exceptionalism* ◆ Organization of the book

*I*NTRODUCTION

I began the first edition of *Prejudice and Racism* in June 1970. As I write this introduction, it is August 1995, 25 years later. In 1970, I had just defended my doctoral dissertation some two months earlier. I had a contract for a book with the
working title of *Prejudice* and a host of experiences as a young black man in the
United States to draw on as I embarked on this project. I worried that, although
prejudice was an important focus in attempts of social psychologists to understand
and explain problems of race relations in America, *racism* was emerging as the
more encompassing representation of these problems.

The struggles of the "civil rights decade" (the 1960s) did give way to some
progress in the 1970s. This decade was expected to witness the nation's coming together by race, gender, and age—unity that had been signaled by the civil and voting rights legislation; the organization and implementation of procedures to ensure
their enforcement; and positive changes in attitudes, beliefs, and even behaviors, as
shown by national polls. Yet, as I will suggest in Chapters 4 and 5, this expectation
overestimated the accomplishments of the 1960s and underestimated the complexity and historical legacy of mistrust for the majority by the minority. By the 1970s
the historically disadvantaged minorities (blacks, Indians, and others) and women
had developed a growing desire for self-determination and self-definition. Meanwhile, historically advantaged majorities had retreated behind symbols of Ameri-

1

can traditions that, although truly emblematic of the virtues of the country, were equally symbolic of the conditions that conferred privilege on whites and men. The meanings and realities of whites, blacks, and others, and of men and women were contested now. The moral bankruptcy of the nation's bigotry and bias was also indicted. The political high ground of the civil rights era was relabeled "political correctness," and the battle was on.

Moreover, we were learning in social psychology how deeply the images of race and gender penetrated the mind and directed, *with prejudice,* perceptions, judgments, and behavior with an invisible teleological hand. Racism came into clearer focus and loomed as a large menace to society. And though, in the 1970s, the broader conceptual aspect of racism was emerging, the real significance of the phenomenon can be found in the fact that books on racism outnumber books on prejudice by 10 to 1. Social psychologists often use the terms interchangeably, and some see them as points on a continuum—varying in degree, but not in kind. I believed in 1970 that *prejudice* and *racism* described different phenomena, processes, and points of analysis. I will try to make that point clearly here by exploring and defining prejudice in Part 2 and racism in Part 3.

It seems to us sometimes that race relations are no better now than they were in 1970. I do not believe this is true. Perhaps it is the lofty expectation of peaceful race relations that makes individual acts of race-based violence and intolerance so dramatic. The salience of brutal or disgusting incidents contrasts with the almost unnoticed day-to-day comings and goings of people whose differences may briefly flash into focus, then recede as background to their interaction. Our history is painful, and one event that *represents* that history can bring it *all* back vividly in both emotional and mental terms. Had it not been for cases such as the Emmett Till lynching and Rodney King beating, blacks might have been less suspicious of the Los Angeles Police Department in the O. J. Simpson case. But the history lessons have been well learned, and their conclusions coalesce into a disease whose symptoms are abuse, bigotry, and control. The sickness, like a retrovirus, seems to attach itself to the living cells of possibility and civility, and recreate in its own image the pains and scars of disadvantage and degradation.

The problems signified by prejudice and racism in the United States are not new, not simple, and certainly not gone. Much is different in 1996, yet one thing remains constant: Race is a subject of emotional, volatile, vexing, and frustrating dimension in this society. It seems that no matter how much things change, the *problem* of race remains.

WHOSE PROBLEM IS IT, ANYWAY?

W. E. B. DuBois (1903) foresaw that the issue of the twentieth century would be "the problem of the color line." That constituted the theme of the first three chapters of the first edition of *Prejudice and Racism*. The image that organized the earlier text was that of a horizontal line that divided white (on top) from black (on the bottom). That simple equation symbolized not only the meaning and assumptions underlying both prejudice and racism (white was superior to black and black inferior to white in the minds of most in our society) *but also* the consequences of these beliefs—that is, white advantage and privilege relative to blacks.

The 1970s were the first post-civil rights decade. A young white student from a Midwestern college came to my office in Cambridge, Massachusetts, in 1971, seeking advice on his project—an investigation of "why racial tension and conflict exist now, in 1971." A child of the 1960s, he failed to understand why, after the profoundly egalitarian advances of the civil rights decade, there was still so much racial tension and conflict. The seven years after the passage of the Civil Rights Act of 1964, and the six years after the Voting Rights Act of 1965 seemed like a very long time to someone his age, so perhaps his problem in understanding can be ascribed to the impatience of youth.

But now, in 1996, we grapple with the same set of issues on race. We now have 30 years of experience with the legislative mandate for racial fairness, yet the rhetoric on race seems hardly diminished. Why? Surely we have made substantial progress as a society since 1970, yet sometimes it feels as if things are little changed. This is partly because issues of racial and gender discrimination are always magnified when an incident occurs that draws our attention sharply to them. But surely the day-to-day experiences and opportunities for participation, advancement, and fair consideration for all are better now than they were in the 1950s, 1960s, and 1970s. Maybe we now expect more and so are distressed all the more when reality fails to meet our expectations. Whatever the reason, awareness of the persistence of racial antagonisms and discrimination looms large in our national psyche.

Social psychology has grown increasingly sophisticated in its empirical and theoretical studies on race-related problems of prejudice, stereotyping, and intergroup relations. Perhaps it is this growing sophistication that gives us a clue as to the cause of the persistence of race problems. Race continues to be one of the most salient and significant categories into which we place people in this society. We create these social categories, place people in them, and then treat members of the categories on the basis of the labels we have affixed to them. Sometimes we do this out of self-interest (it is to our advantage to see others as different and somehow less than ourselves). Sometimes it is the result of unconscious and automatic perceptions (arising from notions of history, the social structure, or the subliminal or nonconscious messages of mass media) that subtly but inexorably influence our judgments and alter our behavior. Social psychology has become increasingly better able to detect these subtle influences. As a result, *it has been clearly demonstrated* that biases persist—even when people claim to be unaffected by race or gender considerations.

Events of the year 1995 demonstrated in dramatic terms how salient and deep race-related issues run in the veins of our society. For example, when word first spread that O. J. Simpson's ex-wife and a friend of hers were found murdered in Los Angeles, the first response by most Americans was "No way it could be O. J." Within days, a disheveled, disoriented Simpson appeared, to many, to be someone who perhaps might be capable of such a crime. The bloody glove found at his house, the blood found in his Ford Bronco, the slow-speed chase, an apparent suicide letter, and, finally, his surrender and arrest on June 17, 1994, dramatically and irrevocably changed many people's opinions of his innocence. But this change was not race-neutral. The change occurred primarily for whites in the United States (65% on June 25, 1994, thought him guilty). It did not, for the most part, occur for blacks (63% thought him innocent) (Moore and Saad, 1995). This split between black and white American attitudes persisted throughout the trial. And, when the verdict finally came, after nine months of testimony, the acquittal dramatized what had been there for over a year—a racial divide. Whose problem is it anyway?

In another noteworthy example of a race-related crossroad, Minister Louis Farrakhan of the Nation of Islam organized the Million Man March, which took place on October 16, 1995. The march was billed as an action of atonement for sins and

The agony and the ecstasy: Blacks cheer the acquittal of O.J. Simpson in Times Square; whites watch in grim silence. (Reuters/Archive Photos)

weakness and failure, and in support of unity among black men, who have been the objects of highly negative, widespread racial stereotypes. Standing at the foot of the U.S. Capitol, Minister Farrakhan railed against the white supremacy of the United States as a "sickness" that threatened the well-being of *all* Americans and, specifically, African Americans. The largest demonstration of its kind in the country, it did not petition the U.S. government, as other rallies and marches had done. Rather, it focused inward on black men and their capacity for responsible and uplifting behavior. Whose problem is it anyway?

Senator Sam Nunn of Georgia defended his support of the ban against gays in the military by pronouncing that his views were not *prejudice*, but rational and sound logic. According to Nunn, the military is different from other aspects of life. Gay men and lesbians in the armed forces undermine morale and the fighting preparedness of our military, and it is not in the best interest of the country to be so compromised. Thus, banning U.S. citizens from participation in protecting our country, by this logic, is not prejudice. *Don't ask, don't tell* is a curious pact with the Devil. The official policy of the administration and, now, the military is that a homosexual member of the armed forces may *be* homosexual and not be subject to recriminations, *provided* he or she does not tell anyone. For their part, military leaders are prohibited from *asking* people whether they are homosexual. For example, former Navy lieutenant Paul Thomasson told his superior officer of his homosexual orientation, and this led to his discharge. He sued, and on April 5, 1996, in a 9-4 de-

A million black men and supporters define themselves in positive images as Americans.
(Reuters/Gregg Newton/Archive Photos)

cision the United States Court of Appeals for the Fourth Circuit upheld the Administration policy, stating that it had the right to determine how it would conduct business with military personnel.

If the message of second-class citizenship for gays is not clear from the military's policy, many states have initiated policies that would explicitly deny civil rights to gay men and lesbians (e.g., Amendment Two in Colorado). In fact, because she was a lesbian, a Virginia woman, Sharon Bottoms, lost custody of her own child. Whose problem is it anyway?

In another noteworthy case, the state of California passed an initiative in 1994 that exempts illegal aliens in California from eligibility for social services and free public education. Taking this a step further, the U.S. Congress has considered a bill that would exempt *all* immigrants, legal or otherwise, from eligibility for social services. And on April 2, 1996, two young Mexicans, suspected of being illegal immigrants, were chased down by the California Highway Patrol. Once caught, they were beaten badly. The degree of violence was clear for all to see from a reporter's videotaping, in much the same manner as footage of Rodney King's beating in Los Angeles in 1992 had been shown. Public response varied from outrage at the brutality of the police (one policeman dragged a woman from the car by her hair and then beat her with his nightstick) to a defiant defense of the police by those who choose to ultimately blame the immigrants for crashing our borders.

Many states have passed so-called English only laws. These laws take the view that it is un-American not to speak English and, that as immigrant groups swell, the very core of U.S. life and values is being eroded. The "English only" movement has as a basic objective the denial of full participation in U.S. society to any person who is unwilling to learn how to be a U.S. citizen—a willingness measured by whether or not he or she speaks English. Whose problem is it anyway?

But there is still a massive public awareness and societal representation of these same problems. Absolute progress forward in racial and gender equality is a fact, although relative progress is not so impressive. Over one-half of our population are women, but they account for fewer than 15 percent of U.S. Congress members, fewer than 10 percent of business executives, and fewer than 15 percent of federal judges. Is it because they are not capable of holding these positions? Is it because they don't want them? The answer is surely No to each of these questions. Why, then?

In *Lenses of Gender*, Sandra Bem (1993) provides an explanation. Our culture has created institutional structures and cultural frames that make these outcomes inevitable. They seem right and natural and can be explained as the rational consequences of the natural operation of our society. That is to say, institutional and cultural values are based on and support the unequal participation of racial and gender groups. Specifically, Bem proposes that three psychosocial processes of cultural evolution perpetuate gender disadvantage in the United States:

1 *Androcentrism*: The normative linking of desirable traits and behavior with men.
2 *Gender polarization*: Gender is used to explain and rationalize differences in behavior—for example, "men are from Mars, women are from Venus" (Gray, 1992).
3 *Biological essentialism*: Gender differences are the inevitable consequences of differences in biology.

Thus, the advantage enjoyed by men is created by androcentrism, enhanced by gender polarization, and reinforced and rationalized by biological essentialism. As psychocultural processes, these dynamics affect all of us, men and women, so that we all participate in the practices that ensure gender differences that privilege men over women. We will see that processes of racialism and racialization have operated in similar fashion over the years to create the racial polarization that continues to divide the United States and to maintain "the problem of the color line."

My idea of racism, articulated in the first edition of *Prejudice and Racism*, offers a similar set of propositions and processes. *Eurocentrism* links desirable traits and behaviors with whites, whose "characteristics" become the normative standard of merit. *Racial polarization* links racial differences to behavior, thereby channeling people into racially segregated job niches and opportunities for accomplishment. For example, in *The Bell Curve* Herrnstein and Murray (1994) propose that in the United States a cognitive underclass (disproportionately, but not exclusively containing African Americans) is not capable of performing in major job sectors of America and that its members should be steered to jobs commensurate with their lower cognitive abilities—but, nevertheless, such people should be valued for their work there.[1] Finally, we have *biological essentialism*. This purports to explain ob-

---

[1] We will take a closer and critical look at the data, analysis, and policy recommendations contained in this controversial book in Chapter 16.

served racial differences in biological terms, thereby implying the inevitability of racial inequality (cf. Herrnstein, 1971). Whose problem is it anyway?

John Jay, a student of U.S. jurisprudence, perhaps captured the sense of the problem when he wrote, in the late 1700s, about the virtue of similarity, or like-mindedness:

> Providence has been pleased to give this one connected country to one united people; a people descended from the same ancestors, speaking the same language, professing the same religion . . . similar in their manner and customs . . . . (cited in Schwarz, 1995, p. 62)

The problem of race, prejudice, intergroup conflict, and disadvantage is America's problem. In our society, we believe passionately in the rights of individuals. We believe further in Horatio Alger, in the success that is possible for any person who has the discipline and character to work hard and believe. We can see historically that these possibilities have not been equally available to various racial and gender groups. The case of bias against African Americans was a centerpiece of the first edition. Charting the bias in historical context was a recurring theme and analytical strategy. But, for many in our society, the Civil Rights and Voting Rights Acts changed the tone of the culture. Discrimination on the basis of race or gender was no longer legal. Individual disadvantage based on group membership was ruled impermissible. If that were the end of the story, and the reality conformed to aspiration, there would not be a second edition of *Prejudice and Racism.*

The remainder of this chapter outlines the guiding principles of this revision and contrasts it with the first edition. It further describes the organization of the book, with the aim of illustrating how the analyses and summaries of the problems of prejudice and racism will be brought up to date. First, it would be useful to recount the meanings of *prejudice* and *racism* that were presented in 1972, and related concepts that will recur in this edition.

DEFINING PREJUDICE AND RACISM

Prejudice and *racism* describe ways in which people devalue, disadvantage, demean, and in general, unfairly regard others. In this sense, they refer to negative attitudes about, and negative treatment of, people who belong to other groups. Prejudice and racism are also concepts that encompass the ways in which people value, advantage, esteem, and, in general, prefer and positively regard people who are like themselves or belong to their own group. Therefore, prejudice and racism are processes by which people separate themselves from others who are different in certain ways and attach themselves more closely to people who are like them in certain ways.

These processes work in complementary ways to separate people from one another. These may be quite natural processes in the overall scheme of things. But, in U.S. society and in other cultures around the world, this cleaving of people into separate and distinct groups, with positive value attaching to one and negative value attaching to others, is rendered a problem by the existence of *differential power.* Whether defined numerically, militarily, politically, physically, culturally, or spiritually, differential power makes the distinctions drawn of enormous human consequence.

It is common for us to think of prejudice and racism in their negative dimensions. People are prejudiced toward people they do not like for some reasons, or think this group is inferior to that group, or believe this group possesses qualities that are undesirable. But we will see in the following chapters that both concepts have dual elements, with both positive and negative properties. Disliking people from another group is closely linked to, but not the same as, liking people in your own group. White supremacists assert racial superiority as the driving force behind—and justification for—their antiblack hostility. Others claim that differences in values, character, and social organization explain and justify disadvantages that certain groups have. Both viewpoints rest on the assumption that their group is better than other groups. But the former draws an *explicit* comparison, based on the assumption of the superiority of its own group, and its adherents are emotionally committed to that point of view. The latter *implicitly* accepts the superiority of its own way of life, and its proponents find fault with those who do not *"measure up."* Although the means may differ, the process of setting a standard of comparison centered on one's own group, judging others to be deficient by that standard, and then asserting the validity of the status quo (or whatever course of action ensues) goes to the heart of the problems caused by prejudice and racism.

In the following sections, we will take a brief but closer look at prejudice, discrimination, and racism as we develop working understandings of what they mean and of how these terms will be used in this book.

What Is Prejudice?

We know that the term *prejudice* is used by many people in many different ways. Some use the term to indicate petty, sometimes arbitrary, but generally quite personal dislikes (e.g., H. L. Mencken devoted six volumes to his *Prejudices*) (1927). In other cases, the term can have lethal connotations, as when a Green Beret officer issues orders to "terminate with extreme prejudice" association with a particular individual. A more subtle use of the term came to light in the case of Jack Shaw, a former agent of the Federal Bureau of Investigation (FBI). Having fallen into disfavor with the head of the bureau, Agent Shaw was transferred to Butte, Montana. Rather than face virtual exile, he tendered his resignation to the bureau director, who accepted it *with prejudice*. Because of this prejudicial acceptance, the former agent was unable to get a law enforcement job anywhere in the country.

In the U.S. context, the term *prejudice* has usually been reserved for those attitudes and behaviors that have characterized particular kinds of relations between the white Protestant majority and the racial, ethnic, and religious minorities.[2] This emphasis is captured in the definition offered by Gordon Allport in his classic book on prejudice:

> Ethnic prejudice is an antipathy based upon a faulty and inflexible generalization. It may be felt or expressed. It may be directed toward a group as a whole, or toward an individual because he is a member of that group. (1954, p. 10)

---

[2]For example, we also speak of prejudice against Jews (*anti-Semitism*) and various other kinds of ethnic hostility. The present book is primarily focused on black-white relations. For a general discussion of other kinds of majority-minority relations, see Robin William, *Strangers Next Door* (1964); Selznick and Steinberg, *The Tenacity of Prejudice* (1969); and Simpson and Yinger, *Racial and Cultural Minorities* (1965).

Allport concluded that "The net effect of prejudice, thus defined, is to place the object of prejudice at some disadvantage not merited by his own misconduct" (p. 10).

There are two important elements in Allport's view of prejudice: (1) Prejudice is basically a negative attitude; (2) its existence puts the object of prejudice at an unjust disadvantage. Thus, prejudice is negative, unjust, and a source of disadvantage for its targets.

The psychological position, which emphasizes feelings and attitudes, is in contrast to the sociological position, which emphasizes the primacy of "groupness." For example, Blumer (1958, p. 3) argues that "Race prejudice exists basically in a sense of group position rather than in a set of feelings which members of one racial group have toward the members of another racial group." Although the concept of groupness is not specified at the level of the individual, it is individuals who behave prejudicially. Therefore, if group position is important to prejudice, it is important because people feel something about their group position.

Social psychology has developed the concept of *social identity* to explain how this works (Tajfel, 1969). This concept will be discussed in more detail, but suffice it here to say that group position has a psychological significance that confers feelings of well-being and positive self-esteem on members of groups whose position is believed to be high. The result of these social identity processes is a natural preference for members of your own group, and a tendency to draw distinctions between your group and others. These processes, although based on positive feelings for others like you, is also implicated in the processes of prejudice against others who are unlike you.

Alice Eagly (1995; Eagly and Mladinic, 1989, 1994; Eagly, Mladinic, and Otto, 1991) takes the "positivity view" further by questioning the applicability of this negative attitude toward a group definition of prejudice when it is applied to women. She notes that

> Although there is agreement that many people are . . . prejudiced against women, there is no evidence that the attitude toward women is typically negative in this society, and some evidence that it may even be positive and more positive than the attitude typically held toward men, the more privileged group. (Eagly, 1995, p. 2)

To test this idea, Eagly and Mladinic (1989) had subjects rate men, women, Democrats, and Republicans on semantic differential evaluative measures of attitude (good-bad, positive-negative, valuable-useless, nice-awful, etc.). They also had subjects write down the characteristics they believed were typical of each group, and later evaluated, on a good-bad scale, each of the characteristics assigned to each group. In a second study (Eagly, Mladinic, and Otto, 1991), subjects wrote down emotions they typically felt toward members of several groups, including men, women, Democrats, and Republicans. Results from both studies showed that the most positive attitudes, as well as the most positive stereotypes, were directed at women.

Why is there prejudice when attitudes are so positive? Eagly and colleagues (1991) suggest that it is the nature of the stereotypes that provides the clue. Women who are viewed positively are thought to be warm, helpful, and kind. Men who are viewed positively are thought to be self-confident, active, and decisive. It turns out that women score *a lot better than men* do on the positive feminine traits of warmth, helpfulness, and kindness. So much so that, overall, they come out higher in attitude ratings. Now comes the prejudice. It is not a result of simple, negative attitudes, it is the belief that those stereotypical traits suit group members and consign them to a particular niche in society. When group members seek to move outside that niche, they are resisted. Eagly suggests that

> . . . when times are changing . . . prejudice becomes a social issue. When a group is rising, its members attempt to put themselves in roles in which their group seldom appeared in the past. Because they are then seen as under-qualified, they become victims of discrimination. (Eagly, 1995, p. 8).

While this view is still based on individual-level analysis, it does not limit the concept of prejudice to overt, conscious, and negative attitudes and beliefs. As we will see as we move through the analyses contained in this book, prejudice is a much more complex phenomenon than we may have once thought. It is certainly more complex than I believed when I wrote about it 25 years ago.

To preview our later discussions of prejudice, we offer the following working definition:

> **Prejudice is a positive or negative attitude, judgment, or feeling about a person that is generalized from attitudes or beliefs held about the group to which the person belongs.**

The Problem of Discrimination

Prejudice is a negative attitude toward another person or group; it is based on a social comparison process in which the individual's own group is taken as the positive point of reference. The behavioral manifestation of prejudice is *discrimination*— those actions designed to maintain own-group characteristics and favored position at the expense of members of the comparison group. I agree with Raab and Lipset (1959) when they state that the behavioral manifestation of prejudice creates the social problem. Therefore, behavior is of more concern to us than attitude is.

Discrimination is, in legal terms, *actionable*. Prejudice per se is not. The Civil Rights division of the Justice Department can bring suit when there is strong evidence of discrimination. When a person is treated differently and worse *on the basis of* his or her status (gender, race, age, sexual orientation, etc.), we may presume that the behavior follows from prejudicial attitudes. But the attitudes, when unexpressed, do not cause the problem. When we try to legislate attitudes and their verbal expression—for example, the banning of hate speech—we find the courts relatively unsympathetic. First Amendment guarantees of free speech protect the right to tell individuals that you don't like them and that you think their ancestors were subhuman.

But discrimination is linked specifically to behavior that treats similarly qualified people differently, or dissimilarly qualified people the same. But we discriminate all the time in our society. We may admit a student with comparatively low scores on the SAT to college and reject another with higher scores if the former is the son of an important alumnus. We may hire someone for a job who is the daughter of a prominent family over one who is somewhat more qualified, but not so well connected. We may subsidize an airline that transports wealthy and influential businesspeople and politicians, while rejecting subsidies to community organizations that feed the poor. Discrimination is a fact of our society and is always linked to certain prejudices. When discrimination disadvantages members of certain racial and gender groups, we have the problems of prejudice and racism.

A working definition of *discrimination*, then, can be stated as follows:

Discrimination consists of negative behavior toward a person based on negative attitudes one holds toward the group to which that person belongs, *or*, positive behavior toward a person based on positive attributes one holds toward the group to which that person belongs.

What Is Racism?

Racism builds on the negative-attitude view of prejudice, but includes three other important criteria: First, the basis of group characteristics is assumed to rest on biology—race is a biological concept. Second, racism has, as a necessary premise, the *superiority* of one's own race. Third, racism rationalizes institutional and cultural practices that formalize the hierarchical domination of one racial group over another. Therefore, although racism shares certain aspects of prejudice, it takes on a decidedly broader and more complex meaning.

In describing the basic causes of the wave of race riots that swept the United States in the summers of 1964 through 1967, the U.S. Commission on Civil Disorders, hereafter called the Kerner Commission, made the following observation:

> Race prejudice has shaped our history decisively in the past; it now threatens to do so again. White racism is essentially responsible for the explosive mixture which has been accumulating in our cities since the end of World War II. (1967, p. 203)

Note that history's problems were blamed on race prejudice, while present racial tensions are blamed primarily on white racism. Are *racism* and *race prejudice* interchangeable terms, or is there a discontinuity of history? Or has *racism* generally supplanted *prejudice* as a more inclusive term (Marx, 1971, p. 101) that encompasses, in addition to prejudice, ". . . hostility, discrimination, segregation, and other negative action expressed toward an ethnic group . . ."?

Van den Berghe (1967, p. 101) attempts a rather specific definition of racism when he describes it as follows:

> . . . any set of beliefs that organic, genetically transmitted differences (whether real or imagined) between human groups are intrinsically associated with the presence or the absence of certain socially relevant abilities or characteristics, hence that such differences are a legitimate basis of invidious distinctions between groups socially defined as races.

This suggests that racism is the natural process by which the physical and/or cultural characteristics of one group of people (e.g., black Americans) acquire negative social significance in a racially heterogeneous society.

Racism puts as much emphasis on the positive attributes of one's own race as on the considered negative attributes of the other. As we will see later (Chapters 12 and 13), before we can understand racism, we need to consider what we mean by *race.* Moreover, racism does not follow immediately from what we think about race, per se, but how we attribute certain attributes or characteristics to people who belong to, or are assigned to, different races. And finally, we need to consider how these concepts of race are utilized in the formation and processes of our society. The concepts derived from these considerations are race, racialism, and racialization, respectively. They are defined as follows:

Race (biological):

> . . . an inbreeding, geographically isolated population that differs in distinguishable physical traits from other members of the species. Members of such a population are capable of breeding with members of other populations in their species, but they usually do not do so for some period of time during which the specific physical characteristics of the group emerge from the limited but adaptive gene pool. (Zuckerman, 1990, p. 1298)

Race (social):

> Race is indeed a pre-eminently sociohistorical concept. Racial categories and the meaning of race are given concrete expression by the specific social relations and historical context in which they are embedded. (Omi and Winant, 1986)

Racialism:

> . . . there are heritable characteristics, possessed by members of our species, that allow us to divide them into a small set of races, in such a way that all members of these races share certain traits. (Appiah, 1990)

Racialization:

> . . . the extension of racial meaning to a previously racially unclassified relationship, social practice or group. (Winant, 1994)

Thus, race is based on a belief in biological essences that are imbued with social meaning. Moreover, the biological essences are attached to psychological or behavioral characteristics that are presumed to be heritable. The extension of this thinking to other groups, and the social practices that accompany them, serves to racialize society. All of these beliefs and practices are couched in terms of the racial superiority of one's own group, and the corresponding lesser capacity of others.

To define racism as a singular concept is not an easy task. In fact, it is probably a wrong approach to think that the complexities described above can be reduced to a single definition. Chapter 13 reviews many definitions of racism and offers the viewpoint that racism may better be conceived as a family of *-isms* based on race, or *racisms.* After reviewing these multiple definitions, we have extracted the following as some basic elements of racisms:

1 Belief in racial superiority and inferiority
2 Strong in-group preference and solidarity, as well as the rejection of people, ideas, and customs that diverge from those customs and beliefs
3 A doctrine of a cultural or national system that conveys privilege or advantage to those in power
4 Elements of human thought and behavior that follow from the abstract structures, social structures, and cultural mechanisms of racialism

5 Systematic attempts to prove the rationality of beliefs about racial differences and the validity of policies that are based on them

Three Types of Racism
In the first edition, I distinguished three levels of racism—individual, institutional, and cultural. These correspond to levels of analysis and are distinguished by the interactions among psychological, behavioral, institutional, structural, and cultural dynamics in the unfolding of racialist beliefs and practices.

Individual racism. The first level is most closely aligned with race prejudice. It fits the definition of *racist* given above. Consider the following example, quoted from Abraham Lincoln, which is illustrative of individual racist thinking:

> I am not, nor ever have been, in favor of bringing about in any way the social and political equality of the white and black races; I am not, nor ever have been, in favor of making voters or jurors of Negroes, nor qualifying them to hold office . . . I will say in addition to this that there is a physical difference between the white and black races which I believe will ever forbid the two races living together on terms of social and political equality. And in as much as they cannot so live, while they do remain together there must be the position of superior and inferior, and I as much as any other man am in favor of having the superior position assigned to the white race. (cited in Hay [ed.], 1894, pp. 369–370, 457–458)

Nor is black skin color the only criterion, as the following statement, made in 1909 by California Progressive Chester Powell, indicates:

> [Racial discrimination] is blind and uncontrollable prejudice . . . yet social separateness seems to be imposed by the very law of nature. [An educated Japanese] would not be a welcomed suitor for the hand of any American's daughter [but] an Italian of the commonest standing and qualities would be a more welcomed suitor than the finest gentleman of Japan. So the line is biological, and we draw it at the biological point—at the propagation of the species. (cited in Daniels, 1968, p. 49)

These statements represent what most writers term *individual racism*. Of the three types of racism, individual racism is closest to race prejudice and suggests a belief in the superiority of one's own race over another and in the behavioral enactments that maintain those superior and inferior positions.

Institutional racism. Individual racism and race prejudice do not differ to a major degree. However, the white racism indicted by the Riot Commission (also known as the *Kerner Commission,* after the Illinois governor who chaired it) goes beyond the level of individual racism to the more general, more insidious, and more debilitating institutional racism. Carmichael and Hamilton (1967, p. 4) describe institutional racism as

> . . . [when] five hundred black babies die each year because of lack of proper food, shelter and medical facilities, and thousands more are destroyed and maimed physically, emotionally and intellectually because of conditions of poverty and discrimination in the black community . . . or when black people are locked in dilapidated slum tenements, subject to the daily prey of exploitative slumlords, merchants, loan sharks and discriminatory real estate agents.

Racist institutions are but extensions of individual racist thought in order to achieve racist objectives through manipulation of institutions. Thus, for example, "grandfather clauses" and "poll taxes" can be seen as the manipulation of the political process to achieve individual (or collective) racist ends.

Institutional racism also operates on another, subtler, level. Colleges, graduate schools, and professional schools have for many years relied heavily on standardized test scores as criteria for admission. Black students routinely have received inadequate training in test taking and inadequate familiarization with the content of test materials. Therefore, in many cases the 600 SAT score or 700 GRE score requirement might as well be a "whites only" sign on the gates of the educational institutions.[3] We ask, "How free is free enterprise, how equal is equal opportunity employment, how fair are fair housing statutes"? Is there a difference between de jure inequality and de facto inequality?[4]

Institutional racism, then, has two meanings: (1) It is the institutional extension of individual racist beliefs, consisting primarily of using and manipulating duly constituted institutions so as to maintain a racist advantage over others. (2) It is the byproduct of certain institutional practices that operate to restrict—on a racial basis—the choices, rights, mobility, and access of groups of individuals. These unequal consequences need not be intended, but they are no less real for being simply de facto.

Cultural racism.   The third type, cultural racism, contains elements of both individual and institutional racism. *Cultural racism* can generally be defined as the individual and institutional expression of the superiority of one race's cultural heritage over that of another race. *Culture* is defined in many different ways, but Kroeber and Kluckhohn defined it comprehensively as

> ... patterned ways of thinking, feeling and reacting, acquired and transmitted mainly by symbols, constituting the distinctive achievement of human groups, including their embodiments in artifacts; the essential core of culture consists of traditional (i.e., historically derived and selected) ideas, and especially their attached values. Culture systems may, on the one hand, be considered as products of action, on the other, as conditioning elements of future actions. (1952, p. 181)

Cultures differ on many dimensions. Triandis (1994) emphasizes the individual versus collective dimension, whereas Markus and Kitayama (1991) emphasize independence versus interdependence. I (Jones, 1979; 1986) have emphasized ways in which we view *t*ime, *r*hythm, *i*mprovisation, *o*ral expression and *s*pirituality (TRIOS) as central cultural characteristics in which cultural groups may differ widely.

The point of cultural racism is that, when one group enjoys the power to define cultural values—and the individual forms those values should take—and to reward those who possess them and punish or ignore those who do not, cultural groups

---

[3]Of course, test scores can be "rich only" criteria also. Poor whites, however, have options that blacks may never have, because racism restricts opportunity. Here, as in many other places in this book, the analysis of black problems can be applied to the poor or to other minorities. In the main, the analysis of racism can be applied on a case-by-case basis to other groups.

[4]*De jure inequality* refers to the official, legalized mandate for treating members of one group differently from members of another group. In the South, blacks were forbidden from attending schools with whites *by law*. In the North, residential racial segregation (aided and abetted by discriminatory real estate policies and by discriminatory employment practices) meant that requiring children to go to school within their neighborhoods ensured that racially segregated schooling would persist.

will be marginalized and disadvantaged to the extent that they claim cultural heritage that diverges from these core cultural beliefs. When the diverging cultural group also is defined as a racial group, the basis for bias (culture versus race) is hard to distinguish. Given that racism is feelings of racial superiority reinforced by the power to determine the outcomes for other racial groups that are consistent with one's own group's best interests, then cultural differences are bound up inextricably with racial differences. For this reason, simply asserting that a "colorblind" approach is the best way to eradicate racism is much too simple. We will look specifically at the colorblind strategy for reducing racial prejudice in Chapter 11.

It is cultural racism that has been most apparent to U.S. race relation analysts. It is a matter of cultural racism when the achievements of a race of people are fully ignored in education. It is a matter of cultural racism when the expression of cultural differences is unrewarded or is interpreted negatively. It is not just black people who have been victimized by the myth of the cultural melting pot, but all ethnic minorities. White Western European religion, music, philosophy, law, politics, economics, morality, science, and medicine are all generally considered to be the best in the world.

Within the United States, we are led to believe that black people have contributed absolutely nothing to the national expression of these cultural forms. More significantly, any person, regardless of his or her cultural background, who cannot function well according to the dictates of white Western cultural norms does not have much opportunity for success in this society. Many black Americans are now reacting to cultural racism by asserting their blackness, their African heritage, their cultural uniqueness.

To summarize, racism has three faces. Individual racism is closely akin to race prejudice, but differs from the latter in (1) the importance of biological considerations and (2) the role of behavioral enactments. The concept of institutional racism has gained prominence since Carmichael and Hamilton (1967) and the U.S. Commission on Civil Disorders (1967) sought to clarify and elaborate on it. The term *cultural racism* refers to the intersection of cultural and racial differences, where superiority on both factors is assumed.

A QUESTION OF THE EMPHASIS ON BLACKS

The issue of black-white relations in the United States was the dramatic and critical issue of the 1960s, when the first edition was begun. Some have suggested that this revised text should go beyond the black-white model to make the text more relevant to the changing times brought about by the widening diversity of ethnic, racial, and gender issues in our society. I agree that the scope and usefulness of this book would be significantly expanded if all forms of ethnic bias implicated in prejudice and racism were covered. However, there are several reasons why I have not tried to do so:

1   The first edition was organized around black-white relations, and this text is meant as a revision of that analysis, not as the presentation of an entirely new one.
2   The literature on black-white relations, versus other intergroup relations, is more widely available because that issue has occupied a more central role in the social psychology of race relations and the attendant problems of prejudice and racism.

3   The paradigm of prejudice and racism is fully expressed by the analysis of
     black-white relations. As a paradigm, those generalized elements—albeit devel-
     oped from a black-white analysis—can be applied to other relationships based
     on ethnicity, gender, age, sexual orientation, and so on. However, there are in-
     deed characteristics specific to each group (e.g., immigrant status, language and
     culture, geographical region, the content of stereotypes, differences in group-
     based reactions to stigmatization) that offer opportunities for unique analysis. I
     do not feel confident that I can address both the generalized paradigm of preju-
     dice and racism and the unique aspects that are associated with each of several
     groups that may be implicated in it. My general aim has been to continue the
     primary focus on black-white relations, for three reasons:
     a. They continue to be paradigmatic of intergroup conflict in the United States.
     b. They have generated more research, theorizing, and policy analyses.
     c. They often inspire more intense psychological and emotional reactions—and
        draw more attention—than other forms of intergroup conflict do.

Evidence consistent with this approach is provided by some recent research by
Sears, Citrin, and van Laar (1995) on what they term *black exceptionalism.* As the
United States has become increasingly diverse ethnically, racially, and culturally,
patterns of intergroup competition and conflict, as well as demands for political
power, have grown more complex. Public policy that was conceived to address disadvantage of the sort discussed 25 years ago now confronts a much more complex
social fabric. Policies directed at one group may leave other groups out altogether.
Policies that seek to address the needs of multiple groups may ultimately fail them
all. Sears et al. (1995) suggest that Americans regard the problems aroused by questions of expanding ethnic, racial, and cultural diversity from one of three perspectives. The first, *assimilation,* takes the melting pot as the appropriate way of viewing
diversity and endorses the idea that newer immigrant groups and those considered
disadvantaged should follow the lead of European immigrants. That is, they
should work hard, get educated, marry across ethnic and racial lines, and thus raise
the group socioeconomic standing by assimilating into the mainstream society. A
second view is *black discrimination,* which suggests that the experiences of blacks in
the United States are unique and distinctly different from the experiences of other
racial or ethnic groups. The specific history of African slavery, Jim Crow laws,[5] and
forcible segregation, and the de facto adverse consequences of racial biases and bigotry have undermined blacks' ability to participate in a free-market economy and
to utilize those strategies used by European immigrants (and suggested in the assimilation approach) to advance their collective group position. The only way to
remedy this problem is to address these unique, historically based issues with contemporary social policies. The third perspective is the *multicultural* approach,
which argues that the black discrimination model, and the remedies it endorses,
should be applied to all racial, ethnic, and cultural groups to improve their opportunities and outcomes in this society.

     Therefore, there are two critical questions: (1) Which of these views does a per-
son endorse? (2) What are the consequences of believing in one or the other of these
approaches to social policy?

---

[5]"Jim Crow" laws have been defined as ". . . a broad social system . . . [that] signifies the institutions of
discrimination, segregation, and prejudice . . . [and] connotes the responsibility of white, official America
for the victimization of the colored in all spheres of living." (Conrad, 1947, p. 230)

Black Exceptionalism

Do white Americans in general really think of African Americans as a distinctive, exceptional group, or are the latter now generally seen as just one of the many different ethnic groups here in the United States? The black exceptionalism thesis argues that white Americans' attitudes toward blacks are unique because the black experience in the United States is so unique. Factors contributing to the uniqueness of blacks in the context of U.S. diversity include the forced passage from Africa to America; slavery; legally enforced racial segregation and discrimination based on skin color; rigid, caste-like category boundaries for racial identification; and persistent lower-class status relative to whites and other immigrant groups.

In addition to these basic arguments for black exceptionalism, we can add that blacks have been the largest single minority group, have been highly salient politically, and have been the focal point of legislative (various civil rights acts from 1876 through 1991), political, judicial, and economic systems. If blacks are exceptional in the minds of whites, Sears et al. (1995) argue that (1) racial stereotypes and prejudices should be greater toward blacks than other ethnic minority groups, (2) these racial attitudes should be more highly crystallized or organized for Blacks than other groups, and (3) these stereotypes and attitudes toward blacks should also have more influence on whites' attitudes toward social and public policies when blacks are the targets or beneficiaries. In addition, they argue that attitudes toward blacks are even expected to influence whites' attitudes toward policies more generally directed at other disadvantaged ethnic groups (e.g., immigrants or non–English-speaking minorities), with relatively little relevance to blacks.

To test these hypotheses, surveys were conducted in the early to mid-1990s from which whites' judgments of blacks, Hispanics, and Asians were assessed, along with the former group's opposition to various social policies that (1) targeted blacks *explicitly* (e.g., affirmative action and open housing for blacks, and opposition to the idea that, because of slavery, blacks should get special treatment), (2) targeted blacks *implicitly* (e.g., crime in the streets; death penalty, welfare, and assistance to the poor), or did not directly involve blacks (e.g., group-based quotas, immigration, and multilingualism). The basic question is, (3) to what extent were whites' attitudes toward blacks as a group more negative, well-organized, and related to whites' attitudes toward various social policies that varied in the degree to which blacks were targets or beneficiaries of them? The results are summarized below:

1   Racial attitudes toward blacks were found to be more negative than were attitudes toward Hispanics, Asians, legal immigrants, illegal immigrants, and whites. Specifically, blacks were perceived as lazier, more welfare-dependent, more prone to violence, and less intelligent than all of these other groups.[6]
2   Whites' symbolic racism toward blacks was greater than toward either Hispanics or Asians. *Symbolic racism* refers to the connection of antigroup (e.g., anti-Black, anti-Hispanic, anti-Asian, etc.) feelings and strong support for traditional U.S. values (e.g., individual rights, the Protestant work ethic). Whites rated blacks higher than they rated either Hispanics or Asians on the two questions that assessed symbolic racism:

---

[6]The exceptions were immigrants, for whom information only on laziness was available. Blacks were perceived as lazier than both these groups.

   a. "Do you think that (group members) get much more attention from govern-
      ment than they deserve?"
   b. "Do you think that (group members) are getting too demanding in their
      push for equal rights?"
3 For whites, symbolic racism and stereotypes were highly associated with
   blacks, but were not highly associated with either Hispanics or Asians. This
   high association toward one group suggests that racial beliefs or attitudes toward blacks are more highly organized and crystallized than for other groups.
4. High antiblack symbolic racism scores and belief in the laziness stereotype for
   blacks, but not for Hispanics or Asians, predicted whites' opposition to affirmative action and to open housing for, and special treatment of, blacks. The relationship of antiblack attitudes and stereotypes to social policy opposition was
   not changed by taking into account a subject's political party, liberal or conservative ideology, education, age, or gender. These findings suggest that opposition to social policies that target blacks can be better explained by antiblack sentiment than by adherence to other politically relevant beliefs.
5 High antiblack symbolic racism scores for whites are correlated with whites'
   degree of support of the idea that policemen make streets safe and of the death
   penalty and of their opposition to welfare spending and of assistance to the
   poor. On none of these issues did whites' attitudes toward either Asians or Hispanics affect their positions.
6 Antiblack, but not anti-Hispanic or anti-Asian, symbolic racism predicted
   whites' opposition to group-based quotas. Antiblack *and* anti-Hispanic symbolic racism predicted whites' opposition to open immigration and multilingualism.

In sum, antiblack attitudes among whites are more pronounced, more coherent or
crystallized, and more influential in determining attitudes toward social policies
directed toward blacks as a group (either explicitly, implicitly, or not at all). It seems
that, in matters of ethnic, racial, or cultural rights and the government treatment of
these issues, how one thinks about blacks plays a dominant role in how one thinks
about the whole set of issues. It is as if the black experience is a paradigm for social
justice and social policy beliefs in the United States. If this is true, then, to a large
extent, focusing primary attention on black-white relations offers the most compelling glimpse into the operation of prejudice and racism in the United States.

ORGANIZATION OF THE BOOK

This edition of *Prejudice and Racism* is organized in three parts. Part 1 continues the
first edition's strategy of putting the social science literature in historical context
and juxtaposing this research with significant social dynamics in society. The first
edition ended with a discussion of the decade of the 1960s; this edition reprints the
earlier summaries in lightly edited form in Chapters 2 and 3, and adds chapters on
the 1970s and 1980s. Chapter 4 argues that blacks evolved a racial consciousness in
the late 1960s that was typified by the "black is beautiful" movement, the "cultural
revolution," and the intellectual afrocentrism of black studies. This growing own-
group focus was mirrored in the women's movement and led to a revision of the
well-known "Melting Pot" thesis (Glazer and Moynihan, 1963) toward recognition

of the primacy of *ethnicity* (Glazer and Moynihan, 1975). This trend, coupled with a growing conservative opposition to strategies for implementing the promise of the civil rights gains of the 1960s, presaged a growing racial divide. The 1980s saw a widening of the divide, as the courts rolled back legislative and judicial gains of the 1940s through the 1960s, and further circumscribed the affirmative action—practices instituted with the intent of remedying the inequalities addressed by civil rights legislation. Chapter 5 suggests that the 1980s saw the ascendancy of social conservatism with the election of Ronald Reagan as president of the United States. This conservative trend has persisted. It continues to challenge the moral assumptions of the civil rights era by emphasizing traditional "American" values, such as individualism, and by diminishing the role proposed for government in ameliorating social inequality. Moreover, social research demonstrates that whites and blacks grow further apart in their perceptions of the availability of opportunities and of the role of individuals or government in expanding these opportunities. The ascendancy of the conservative point of view raises questions about the extent to which opposition to social policies endorsed during the civil rights era can be understood as a "principled conservative" point of view, or whether they are actually a symbolic form of "new" racism that combines with antiblack feelings to provide a "legitimate" basis for maintaining the status quo and thwarting the group progress of blacks and of other minority groups and women.

Part 2 offers a detailed discussion of the psychology of prejudice. Whereas the first edition had one chapter on prejudice, this edition has six. After an introductory discussion of prejudice (Chapter 6), we discuss the research and implications of stereotyping (Chapter 7) and intergroup relations (Chapter 8). In an attempt to compare the black-white conflict in the United States with other, similar situations, Chapter 9 describes the conflict in Rwanda between Hutus and Tutsis; in the former Yugoslavia among Serbs, Muslims, and Croates; and in Northern Ireland between Protestants and Catholics. Until recently, one of the important gaps in social psychology has been detailed empirical and theoretical discussion of the predicaments posed for target or stigmatized group members and the nature and consequences of their reactions, coping, and adaptations to prejudice, stigma, and discrimination. Chapter 10 offers a selective review of some recent work that looks at target reactions to prejudice. Finally, Chapter 11 assesses what we know about ways to reduce prejudice and two associated problems—stereotyping and intergroup conflict.

Part 3 recapitulates the three-part concept of individual, institutional, and cultural racism. It begins, though, with a careful consideration of the concept of *race* (Chapter 12). What is race, and what evidence from anthropology and biology can we find for its meaning as a biologically essential way to distinguish human beings? How have societies arrived at a functional meaning and usage of race, and what have been some of the consequences? How does viewing groups in racial terms differ from considering them in their ethnic, national, or religious distinctiveness?

Chapter 13 looks broadly at the concept of racism, or more properly, racisms. A wide range of definitions are presented, and a working definition of racism is selected. Those beliefs about race that organize and drive the unfolding of the connections between racial-category membership and personal characteristics or attributes (racialism) are discussed. Also examined are the implementation of racialistic ideas to the formation of institutions and the ways in which they work (racialization). The chapter relies on first-hand accounts of attitudes, beliefs, and experiences of both whites and blacks. The three-tier approach to racism is examined in the next three chapters. These chapters discuss, in more detail, the defining characteristics of individual racism (Chapter 14), institutional racism (Chapter 15), and cultural racism (Chapter 16). Chapter 17 offers an integration across these tiers and proposes a graphic model of how they interact from the macrolevel (culture) to the microlevel (the individual). Consideration of persistent opposition to racism (antiracism) is offered in a concluding section of the chapter.

Finally, Chapter 18 extracts some general principles from the wide-ranging discussion of the preceding chapters. It then offers some ideas about what we know and how this knowledge may affect intergroup relations in our society. We consider a vision for the twenty-first century that may hold promise for the difficult task of bringing people together and reducing power discrepancies and the negative impact such discrepancies have on opportunity and well-being for so many people. In the end, the fundamental problem of bringing people together while respecting and appreciating their differences is explored in light of how prejudice and racism works and how we may be able to reduce it.

PART ONE

———— ❖ ————

Social and Scientific Developments—1500–1990

Not Gone

The pain from a thousand blows
burns,
and from a thousand slights
turns
into something else.
And then,
and then,
and then,
and even then,
is not gone.

J. M. J.

2

The Problem of the Color Line

❖

Introduction ◆ A concise and selective history of early race relations in America, 1619–1900 ◆ *Racist attitudes, racist behavior—the beginning* ◆ *Regional variations in black oppression* ◆ *The great American lie* ◆ Growth of the problem: 1900–1950 ◆ *The 1900s and 1910s: Eugenics and Jim Crow* ◆ *The first riot report* ◆ *The 1920s: Attitudes, art, and poverty* ◆ *The 1930s: Racial stereotypes and federal bureaucracy* ◆ *The 1940s: Growing civil rights action and attitude change through contact* ◆ *An American Dilemma* ◆ Summary

The problem of the twentieth century is the problem of the color line.
W. E. B. DuBois (1903)

*I*NTRODUCTION

With the twentieth century almost over, there is great evidence that the truth of this simple statement endures. The problem of the color line endures—in stark defiance of all our efforts to contradict its reality or destroy the problem. In 1903 the Wright brothers launched a feeble vehicle and kept it airborne for 59 seconds. Sixty-nine years later we watched men cavorting on the moon. In 1995, Microsoft brought Windows '95 to the world and ushered hundreds of thousands of people into the computer age and onto the "information superhighway." Technological progress is unparalleled, yet DuBois's statement of the problem seems as likely to be true in the twenty-first century as it was when he wrote it a century ago.

23

Every day seems to bring a new story of conflict, charges of racism, and mounting distrust between racial and ethnic groups. In the United States, it seems, there are two story lines, two narratives that describe what it means to be an American. One story is aspirational, a dream—land of the free, land of opportunity; freedom, liberty, and equality; individual rights guaranteed by the Bill of Rights. A second story counters the first and sets certain conditions under which the American dream can be realized. The narrative of opportunity and freedom is juxtaposed, as Gates (1995) suggests, by a *counter*narrative that tells of slavery, oppression, inequality, limited opportunities, and legal infringement on all of those rights extolled by the first cultural narrative—that of promise and possibility.

That *both* stories are true is important. But the truth or applicability of each of these narratives varies across people, groups, and contexts over time. This is not a story simply about black and white. But it is a story that reaches its zenith when the protagonists and antagonists are black and white. The stories that appear daily occur in real time, now. But they derive from a legacy of race relations, cultural evolution, and institutional developments. We cannot understand fully the context of contemporary race relations without some appreciation for the historical patterns that chart their developmental course. Some people despair that we can never transcend the horrible facts of slavery, the decimation of Native Americans, or the legacy of English law that stripped women of basic rights and told them it was for their own good. Such people would have us best forget the past, arguing that we can't change it anyway. But as we shall see in Parts 2 and 3 of this book, these legacies live on in the national psyche, in the images of society, in the institutions that guide our everyday life, and they surface in the values and beliefs that define our most basic cultural tenets and assumptions.

Chapters 2 and 3 "review the bidding" on matters of race. They present the summaries that served as a preamble to the discussion of prejudice and racism in the first edition. This summary and selective history of race-related events introduces some beginning research approaches and conclusions that mark the emergence of a theoretical and empirical basis for our understanding of prejudice and racism. These sections are reprinted from the first edition with only light revisions to correct facts or put a proper context around the points that were made 25 years ago.

The first section of this chapter revisits the time of the earliest contact between Europeans and Africans and considers what they thought of each other. It traces the emergence of racial attitudes and behaviors that build the legacy of racism and give rise to the contradictions between the narrative of opportunity and the counternarrative of oppression, discrimination, and limitation. It ends at the turn of the century with a description of the historical context in which DuBois's statement of the color-line problem was made. The second section moves swiftly through the decades of the first half of this century. We consider some of the social policies and the social sciences that examines them. We hear, first-hand, what some whites think about specific blacks and about blacks in general. We also learn about habits of mind and emotion that accompany the biases attached to skin color.

A CONCISE AND SELECTIVE HISTORY OF RACE RELATIONS IN AMERICA, 1619–1900

As I walk down the main street of a small town in northern Ohio in 1969, I am aware of the curious stares of little children. I watch them tug at their mothers' skirts and point at me as if I had stepped from a TV fantasy. I see their mothers try to suppress this infantile curiosity in the interest of proper public behavior ("It's not nice to point!"). Yet the mothers themselves wait to stare daggers into my back. In 1994, twenty-five years later, I drive my car up beside a school bus on my way to campus. Young children in the bus wave and seem happy when I wave back. One young girl, though, frowns at me and sticks out her tongue. Why, I wonder? Then in 1995, when the verdict acquitting O. J. Simpson of the murders of Nicole Brown Simpson and Ron Goldman is read, a white woman walks out of a campus viewing and exclaims, "I can't believe they let that nigger off!"

Racial tension was probably as high in 1969, as at any time in U.S. history. In 1969 my idealistic undergraduate friend asked, Why now? Why now do black students willfully absent themselves from high schools, segregate themselves in enclaves on predominantly white college campuses, and speak of revolution? Why haven't we righted the obvious wrongs of slavery? Why can't we make peace with our fellow human beings? Why can't we all get along?

When we look around us, we do not find answers, we find only symptoms of a diseased relationship. What do the white rural farmers of southern Illinois know of 12-year-old black children nodding off on 137th Street in Harlem or dying of an overdose in a vacant tenement? What does the President of the United States know of a 15-year-old white girl hanging herself in an upper-middle-class community in northern Ohio? Why is it that, today, a majority of white Americans would not even sign the original Bill of Rights? The country has become quite complex. Each of us is sheltered from the experiences of others by emotional rhetoric, selective reporting on the part of the media, and growing urban sprawl. We cannot know for sure what others feel, why or if they hate, or whether or not there exists a chance for humane interaction. Laws, plans, policies, and programs come churning out of State Houses and federal buildings at a rapid clip, but the problems do not get simpler—they become more complex.

It is difficult—indeed, impossible—to make any sense out of the contemporary social, political, and cultural scene without the benefit of history. History tells different stories to different people. Social discontent in Europe preceded black-white contact in the sixteenth century. Feudalism was proving to be an inadequate basis for economic organization and progress in Europe in the 1300s and 1400s. The Renaissance made a cultural case for individuality and freedom. It not only guided forms of expression such as art, literature and science, it guided the industrial revolution. The industrial revolution, or the rise of capitalism, was a driving force behind exploration of new markets and trade routes. This expansion of European culture led to the contact with Africa that eventuated in the slave trade, and the institution of American slavery.

Although England was a latecomer to the colonial expansion of Europe, it weighed heavily as a contender for a long time. In the sixteenth century, the British were not very familiar with black Africans, and the contrast with ideas of value and beauty, good and bad in England was replicated by a sharp contrast not only of ranges of skin color in the two societies, but of a broadly different cultural sensibility. Black Africans looked strange to the British in 1550, but the white menace evoked its own reaction in the soon-to-be-captive blacks:

> The first object which saluted my eyes when I arrived on the coast was the sea, and a slave ship, which was then riding at anchor, and waiting for its cargo. These filled me with astonishment, which was connected with terror, when I was carried on board. . . . I was now persuaded that I had gotten into a world of bad spirits, and that they were

going to kill me. Their complexions too differing so much from ours, their long hair, and the language they spoke (which was very different from any I had ever heard), united to confirm me in this belief.[1] (Meltzer, 1964, p. 3)

On this score did race relations begin with the white Europeans' shanghaiing of black bodies for the long Middle Passage. Let us now briefly extract the salient aspects of the history of race relations. We are not so much interested in names and dates, or even events; rather, we are concerned with the philosophical, ideological, and attitudinal underpinnings of racial animosity in America.

Racist Attitudes, Racist Behavior—The Beginning

The first fact of history is that the British attitude was predisposed toward racism before any Englishman had ever beheld a black African. The very *color* black had long possessed strong negative meaning and emotional ties. One can well imagine how the British responded to *people* who were that color! Not only was black bad; its opposite, white, was very good. We can label the reactions of white Englishmen to black Africans "racist attitudes." Nonetheless, as with any attitudes, they are of little consequence unless conditions are present that link them to specific, correlated behaviors. The conditions of sixteenth-century England that started the long chain of events leading to the present state of race relations were (1) the social, political, and economic consequences of the Renaissance and (2) the Protestant Reformation.

The Renaissance of the fifteenth and sixteenth centuries represented a formal break from religious domination of life and thought to an intensely individualistic worldview. The measure of a man was his achievements on earth—the more numerous his capabilities, the more impressive his personal worth. Leonardo da Vinci was perhaps the prototypical Renaissance man. The upshot of this individualism was, in the social sphere, the dissolution of the feudal system and a heavy emphasis on individual liberty. However, the poor were not then (as they are not now) able to be free in this so-called free society, and there was widespread thievery, rape, and other evidence of social chaos as well.

In the economic sphere, the accumulation of capital became an attractive way for an individual to become worthy. Also, the adventurism of men such as Hawkins, Drake, and others led to a commercial revolution on the seas. It was not long before one of the principal commodities was black bodies. Politically, the existence of nation-states independent of religious control from Rome led to large-scale nationalistic competition for the world's wealth. Freedom and individualism without social responsibility characterized sixteenth-century England and gave a strong push toward the enslavement of black Africans.

The Protestant Reformation began in 1517, when Martin Luther tacked his 95 theses on the doors of the Catholic church in Wittenburg. More pertinent here, however, is John Calvin, whose doctrines (published as *The Institutes of the Christian Religion,* 1536) put humanity in direct contact with God on one of two levels—saved or damned. How did one know? One looked around at one's fellows—those who led the good life were saved, the "elect"; those who did not were damned. The Calvinist influence prompted the Puritan revolution in England in 1640. The strong

---

[1]From *The Interesting Narrative of the Life of Olaudah Equiano. Gustavus Vassa the African. Written by Himself,* 1791.

Puritan tradition in the New World provided a handy formula for distinguishing between the "elect" and the damned in a socioeconomic order of racist slavery.

In summary, the first significant point of the history of race relations in North America is the predisposition toward racism in British thought, a racism that was realized through the application of social, political, economic, and religious principles of individuality without social responsibility.

Regional Variations in Black Oppression

The second significant historical factor concerns the regional patterns of enslavement and their ideological consequences. It is well-known that slavery in the North (New England and New York, primarily) never attained the large-scale status of that "peculiar institution" in the South (Stampp, 1956). No matter how strongly one emphasizes the economic and geographical reasons for these regional differences in the practice of slavery, the popular impression among Northerners (and Southern blacks) has been a mistaken belief that white racial attitudes have always been more tolerant in the North. It is this belief, perhaps, that has, historically, led many blacks to move North, and that prompted my young college friend to ask, Why now?

Twenty Africans were put ashore in 1619 in Jamestown, Virginia. They were *not* slaves—at least, not technically. They were indentured servants like others before them who were white, or American Indian. As late as 1651, blacks, like whites, who served their period of indenture, were given freedom and even small parcels of land. But American Indians and indentured servants proved inadequate to serve the burgeoning agricultural appetites of tobacco and cotton crops. Virginians began contemplating "perpetual servitude," and by 1661, formalized slavery by statute. Slave codes not only bonded Africans to their white masters in perpetuity, but the codes of enforcement established a social order that ensured that slaves could not enjoy the status of freedom of mind, spirit, or body. Slaves had to have written permission to leave their plantations and, if found off the plantation without such permission, had to be returned. They were hanged if found guilty of murder or rape, and whipped and had their ears cut off if convicted of burglary. For petty offenses they were whipped, branded, or maimed. The subsequent docility about which a master would boast was carefully orchestrated by a code of life that only the strongest and most tough-minded African could endure.

The well-known story of how King Cotton and Queen Tobacco ruled the South needs no recounting here. The interesting and important aspect of Southern slavery is how economic lust and dependence conspired to produce a sociopolitical racial orientation that differed so strikingly from that of the North.

That slavery existed in the North is a fact. That the inhabitants of the Northern colonies felt a certain ambivalence toward slavery is indicated by the following Puritan law of 1641:

> There shall never be any bond-slavery, villenage or captivitie amongst us; *unlesse* it be lawfully captives taken in just Warrs, and such strangers as willingly sell themselves, or are sold to us: and such shall have the libertyes and Christian usages which the law of God established in Israel concerning such persons doth morally require, *provided this exempts none from servitude who shall be judged thereto by Authoritie.* (Jordan, 1969, p. 67; italics added)

Negroes for sale to the highest bidder—commerce in colored bodies. (Archive Photos)

Thus was the spirit of political and legal double-talk given early birth in America. The recognized center of U.S. finance today is Wall Street in New York City. But do you know the original function of the Wall Street Market? It served as a marketplace for the sale of black slaves! To be sure, one could also see advertised in *The New York Times* the sale of "Englishmen, Cheshire cheese, and a few Welshmen," but the predominant commodity at the Wall Street Market in 1711 was African slaves.

For a variety of primarily economic reasons, chattel slavery never flourished in the North. Although some slavery did exist, it was the trading of blacks that was entered in the New England economic ledger. Although they lacked sufficient economic reasons for the wholesale exploitation of blacks, the colonists of the North nevertheless considered blacks (even free ones) to be fundamentally different from themselves, and developed a set of legal, social, political, and educational policies through which—sometimes blatantly, sometimes subtly and insidiously—they perpetuated, reinforced, and widened racial differences. In fact, Jim Crow laws originated in the North, not in the South. Therefore, the ambivalent attitude of Northerners toward blacks has been overshadowed somewhat by the obvious, favorable comparison with Southern attitudes toward blacks. However, as is so abundantly clear now, Northern blacks have never been fully admitted into the mainstream either.

The conspicuous display of inhumanity and moral bankruptcy that characterized slavery in the South has for many years obscured the spiraling attitudinal-behavioral consequences of racial relations. That is, basic attitudes toward African blacks during this country's early history—and possibly up to the invention of the cotton gin—did not vary much between inhabitants of the North and South. Therefore, we must look carefully at how the interaction of sociopolitical structures, attitudes, and behaviors over time has produced such marked regional differences economically, politically, and socially.

The second point, then, is that the regional divergence in race relations has spawned an unwieldy two-ply pattern of attitudes, behaviors, and sociopolitical structures in this country. Therefore, an analysis of prejudice and racism must, in part, be a two-ply analysis. It is only in the past few years that the second ply (i.e., the Northern one) has been given due recognition.

The Great American Lie

Freedom. Equality. Justice. Praise the Lord, and pass the ammunition. Praise America, and lynch a nigger. This country was born in revolution against tyranny and oppression while black people were at that very moment being tyrannically oppressed. The settlers in America sought their economic fortune and freedom, while they enslaved Africans and Indians in the service of these goals. We are taught in school that George Washington was the father of our country. For some blacks, he was probably the father of one of their slave ancestors. There is a place in Philadelphia called Independence Hall where one can go to see the crack in the Liberty Bell. Whose independence? Whose liberty? In Tennessee Williams's *Cat on a Hot Tin Roof*, Big Daddy could smell the mendacity of his children as they vied for his favor. The smell of U.S. mendacity wafts across the land 200 years after independence.

Gunnar Myrdal (1944) spoke of the "American dilemma," that contradiction between the American creed, "All men are created equal," and the facts of racist excesses. Even now, conservative patriots are calling for a reaffirmation of what the United States has stood for—liberty, equality, justice, and individual rights. Historically, these values have been reserved for those with white skin. When black Americans look at what the country has stood for, they see many practices whose reaffirmation they would die to prevent.

We must be aware that some attempt was made to reconcile the spirit of the American Revolution with the practices of the colonists. One can read about the conflicts and inconsistencies that surrounded the drafting of the Declaration of Independence (see Jordan, 1969, pp. 269–311). Many men, such as Thomas Jefferson, had very definite antislavery sentiments; yet the compromise on this issue with the South (e.g., the deletion of an antislavery phrase written by Jefferson) very clearly put the weight of the U.S. government on the side of the white majority in the matter of race. Thus was the U.S. government founded on contradiction and compromise. Widespread slavery was practiced in the land of the free, and the Constitution proclaimed a slave to be three-fifths of a man.[2]

It is important to note that the Declaration of Independence and the Constitution were major determinants of race relations in America. The initial racist attitudes of the English flourished upon the extensive contact with blacks provided by the slave trade and, ultimately, institutionalized slavery. Regional economic necessities resulted in divergent roles for Northern and Southern blacks. The former were trade commodities, the latter were cheap labor. The contradictions in the early ideological and practical foundations of the country continue to exert their effect on the U.S. conscience. The remainder of U.S. history presents us with evidence of the

---

[2]Since slaves were considered property, there was a need to determine how slaves should be counted for taxation and representation purposes. The Constitution concluded that slaves should be "divested of 2/5 the man."

refinement and ramifications of these political, social, economic, and attitudinal dramas. We see North against South, black against white, patriots against "bums," labor against management, wages against profits. Let's now take a brief, whirlwind trip through the nineteenth century of U.S. history and watch some of the racial dramas unfold.

We begin, appropriately enough, with Gabriel Prosser's slave uprising in Richmond, Virginia, in 1801. Prosser's was not the first, nor was it the last, attempt to escape from bondage by force. In 1822, Denmark Vesey conspired to free several thousand slaves in Charleston, South Carolina. Nat Turner went on his famous "tear" in 1831, killing about 60 whites. Ten years later, in 1841, slaves aboard the ship *Creole* overpowered the crew and escaped to the Bahamas, where they were granted asylum and freedom. Thus did blacks resist and strike out against their oppressors.[3]

In 1807 (31 years after the United States had declared that all men were created equal) the slave trade was abolished by Congress, though it continued as a black market operation for nearly 10 more years. By 1816, the American Colonization Society was organized to transport free blacks back to Africa. Some free blacks—for example, the shipbuilder Paul Cuffe—returned to Africa on their own. However, in 1817 Philadelphia blacks organized to protest the prospect of being exiled from their land of nativity. It is important to know that black thought in the United States has always wavered between separatism and integration.

Slavery was not abolished in New York until 1827. In 1831, the year of Turner's rebellion, William Lloyd Garrison's *Liberator*, the voice of the abolitionist movement, first appeared. A year later, the New England Anti-Slavery Society was organized, followed by the American Anti-Slavery Society in 1833. These events greatly exacerbated North-South antagonisms, which reached their peak with the Civil War. But in 1833—even as antislavery activity was escalating—Prudence Crandall, a white woman, was arrested for conducting an academy for black girls (made so because all of the white children withdrew when the first black girl enrolled) in Canterbury, Connecticut. And in 1835, the integrated Noyes Academy in Canaan, New Hampshire, was forced to close by mob violence.

In the 1840s, while Harriet Tubman made her courageous forays to the South to free slaves, Sojourner Truth and Frederick Douglass spoke eloquently against slavery. Nonetheless, in 1850 the U.S. Congress passed the Fugitive Slave Act, requiring free states to return fugitive slaves to their owners. This act was passed as part of a compromise that closed the new Northwest Territory to slavery. However, this restriction on slavery was soon reversed by the Kansas-Nebraska Act of 1854, which left it up to each state to decide whether or not it would allow slavery. In the Dred Scott decision of 1857 the Supreme Court opened federal territory to slavery and denied citizenship to U.S. blacks with Judge Taney's infamous words: "Negroes have no rights that a white man is bound to respect."

In spite of official government complicity in the perpetuation of slavery, tension between the North and South grew. The Civil War erupted in 1861. The war was not precipitated simply by a desire on the part of some to free the slaves; rather, it was a last effort to preserve the Union. Thus, whereas the wish to preserve the Union had worked against blacks in the Revolutionary era, it worked for them in the Civil War era, culminating in the Emancipation Proclamation. But, we have already seen that Lincoln was not free of prejudice himself. It is also important to

[3]There were many slave uprisings. For a complete review see Herbert Aptheker, *A History of Negro Slave Revolts* (1969).

note the frequent immigrant riots against Northern blacks, starting with those of 1830 to the famous "draft riots" of 1863 (when whites rioted against blacks because, ironically, blacks were taking jobs the whites had left in order to fight in the Civil War).

Although blacks were initially not allowed to fight in the Civil War, both the South and the North reconsidered this policy. President Jefferson Davis signed a bill on March 13, 1865, that authorized each state to call up its quota of troops *without regard to their color,* provided that the number of black soldiers did not exceed 25 percent of the able-bodied male slave population between the ages of 18 and 45 (Franklin and Moss, 1994). The North did not rush to allow blacks to fight for the Union, either. But when it was authorized, over 186,000 blacks enlisted. At first, white officers did not want to lead black soldiers in battle. But the African Americans made such outstanding soldiers that, by the end of the war, black companies were distinguished by their bravery and excellence. The movie *Glory* captured this excellence and commitment with passion as it depicted the Fifty-Fourth Massachusetts Regiment, under the direction of Col. Robert Gould Shaw, assaulting Fort Wagner.

This country was founded and grew on the back of black labor. Wave after wave of European immigrants has also grown and prospered by stepping over the backs of blacks.

Reconstruction began with the rapid development of political, educational, and economic institutions and practices beneficial to newly freed *Southern* blacks.

In honor of black fighting men in the Civil War—Robert Gould Shaw and the men of the Fifty-Fourth Massachusetts Infantry. This frieze stands in Boston Common as a monument to the heroic service of this all-black army unit and its commander in the struggle for freedom and the preservation of the Union. The motion picture *Glory* was based on their story. (Bruce Henderson/Stock, Boston)

But, for every forward step taken by blacks, reactionary moves by whites began to accumulate a base for the overthrow of Reconstruction. In 1867, Howard University was opened and dedicated to the first-rate higher education of blacks, and the first national meeting of the Ku Klux Klan was held in Nashville, Tennessee. The meeting symbolized the intention of whites to resist changes in the social order of the South. In 1870, Hiram Revel succeeded Jefferson Davis to the U.S. Senate, and Robert Wood was elected mayor of Natchez, Mississippi. Both Revel and Wood were black. Yet race riots in the South were common during Reconstruction. In 1875 the Mississippi governor *requested* federal troops to protect the rights of black voters.

In that same year Congress enacted the Civil Rights Act of 1875 that gave blacks the right to equal treatment in public conveyances, and at inns, theaters, and other public amusement places. But, alas, 1877 brought yet another compromise. Rutherford B. Hayes secured Southern support for his election to the presidency by promising to withdraw federal troops from the South. Shortly thereafter, in 1879, large numbers of blacks, unprotected from vigilante Klan raids, fled in a mass exodus to the North. In 1883 the Supreme Court greatly assisted Jim Crowism by declaring the Civil Rights Act of 1875 unconstitutional. And, by 1907, Jim Crow stretched his clutching talons throughout the South in a death grip that only began to loosen half a century later.

At this point we break off our historical narrative. Chronologically, we have reached our starting point—the environment that inspired DuBois's statement of "the problem." This brief sketch has outlined the historical foundation for twentieth-century race relations. It is from this background that we begin our analysis.

GROWTH OF THE PROBLEM

Our nation is moving toward two societies, one black, one white—separate and unequal.
U.S. Commission on Civil Disorders, 1967

Deciding the case of *Plessy v. Ferguson* in 1896, the Supreme Court declared racial segregation—the doctrine of "separate but equal"—to be constitutional. The Supreme Court reversed this view in 1954, when in *Brown v. Board of Education of Topeka,* it declared on "modern authority," that "separate" was inherently unequal. In 1967 the U.S. Commission on Civil Disorders stated that the United States is moving toward racial separation without equality. Does this mean that the separation once sanctioned by the Supreme Court had disappeared over the past 70 years but is now threatening to return? Does it mean that racial equality no longer exists? No, the commission's statement is more ominous. It suggests that racial conflict has become so embedded that the long-present inequities are hardening into a racial antagonism more deep-seated and threatening than ever before. The line is drawn, and again we find our thoughts going back to DuBois.

Ours has been a remarkable century. In trying to follow the course of race relations, we find ourselves in a maelstrom of world wars, cold wars, ethnic wars, and undeclared "conflicts." This complexity is compounded by fantastic economic growth, recognition of poverty, and introduction of a national welfare system (and, today, the beginnings of its dismantling), in addition to tremendous upheavals in the relationships among the generations and the sexes. With accelerated social change has emerged the social scientist. Sometimes deftly, sometimes clumsily, this

Charon has attempted to navigate our travel toward understanding the complex network of racial conflicts in the United States. As the federal government has grown more powerful, it has engaged in more and more social engineering of the lives of the people it supposedly represents. In this effort the government appears to rely more and more (although still very little) on its chief informants, the social scientists. Inevitably, social scientists have become an important source of input in the pattern of social relationships they investigate and about which they theorize. In fact, since the mid-1940s, the pattern of U.S. race relations has become increasingly influenced by the research and theory of social scientists.

The 1900s and 1910s: Eugenics and Jim Crow

The first 20 years of this century were ushered in and out with race riots, lynchings, and burnings. Rioting was the North's modus operandi, lynching and burning were the South's. Antiblack riots occurred in New York City (1900); Springfield, Ohio (1904); Greenburg, Indiana (1906); and Springfield, Illinois (1908). One of the worst riots occurred in East St. Louis, Illinois (1917). And, in 1919, the summer of which has been described as "Red Summer," there were no fewer than 26 riots. The following account of the East St. Louis riot captures some of the flavor of this violent period in U.S. race relations:

> When the labor force of an aluminum plant went on strike, the company hired Negro workers. A labor union delegation called on the mayor and asked that further migration of Negroes to East St. Louis be stopped. As the men were leaving City Hall, they heard that a Negro had accidentally shot a white man during a holdup. In a few minutes rumor had replaced fact: the shooting was intentional—a white woman had been insulted—two white girls were shot. By this time, 3000 people had congregated and were crying for vengeance.
>
> Mobs roamed the streets, beating Negroes. Policemen did little more than take the injured to hospitals and disarm Negroes. . . . The press continued to emphasize the incidence of Negro crimes, white pickets and Negro workers at the aluminum company skirmished and, on July 1, some whites drove through the main Negro neighborhood firing into homes. Negro residents armed themselves. When a police car drove down the street Negroes riddled it with gunshot.
>
> The next day a Negro was shot on the main street and a new riot was underway. The authority on the event records that the area became a "bloody half mile" for three or four hours; streetcars were stopped, and Negroes, without regard to age or sex, were pulled off and stoned, clubbed and kicked, and mob leaders calmly shot and killed Negroes who were lying in blood in the street. As the victims were placed in an ambulance, the crowds cheered and applauded.
>
> Other rioters set fire to Negro homes, and by midnight the Negro section was in flames and Negroes were fleeing the city. There were 48 dead, hundreds injured, and more than 300 buildings destroyed. (Rudwick, 1966, pp. 23–53)

As brutal and bloody as race riots were, they took a back seat to lynchings and burnings. In 1918, 64 blacks were lynched; in 1919, the number rose to 83. Perhaps the most brutal act occurred in Valdosta, Georgia, in 1918. Mary Turner, a pregnant black woman, was hung from a tree, doused with gasoline, and burned. As she dangled from the rope, a man in the mob pulled out a pocket knife and slit open her abdomen. Out tumbled her child. "Two feeble cries it gave—and received for answer the heel of a stalwart man, as life was ground out of the tiny form," read one account (see Bennett, 1969, p. 294).

Negro burned alive in 1919 race riot in east St. Louis. A white mob poses for the camera. (Culver Pictures)

Even before white violence against blacks reached such an acute stage, blacks began to organize on their own behalf. In 1905, a group of black intellectuals met secretly at Niagara Falls, Canada. (They were refused accommodations in hotels on the New York side.) There, DuBois and William Monroe Trotter organized what became known as the "Niagara movement." The following year, at its first national meeting, the Niagara Movement publicly demanded "full manhood rights—political, civil, and social." In 1909, a year after the riots in Springfield, Illinois, a group of white liberals headed by Mary White Ovington convened an integrated conference in New York City on the race problem. This conference established the National Association for the Advancement of Colored People (NAACP). A year later, in 1910, the National Urban League was founded to deal with the social problems of urban black Americans.

The uneasy alliance between white liberals and black leaders was shaken when the Ovington group superseded the Niagara movement and took only one black officer, DuBois, from among the leaders of the movement. Trotter angrily withdrew and established his National Equal Rights League. During this period, Jim Crow laws and customs governed many aspects of public life, from transportation to use of restrooms and drinking fountains. By 1915 black ghettos were being established in Northern cities as blacks fled the violence and poverty of the South for the promise of jobs created by the war in Europe. Conditions leading to racial conflict in the 1960s and 1970s existed in embryonic form 50 years earlier.

As race relations underwent violent change in the twentieth century, social thought polarized along the lines of the hoary nature versus nurture–organism versus environment controversy. At the turn of the century the Darwinian emphasis on "survival of the fittest," or natural selection, was the underpinning of U.S. sociological theory. Influenced by Herbert Spencer in England, William Sumner of Yale presented the following U.S. interpretation of Social Darwinism:

> Let it be understood that we cannot go outside of this alternative: liberty, inequality, survival of the fittest; or not liberty, equality, survival of the unfittest. The former carries society forward and favors all its best members; the latter carries society downwards and favors all its worst members. (Quoted in Hofstadter, 1955, p. 51)[4]

The implications of this position for race relations are abundantly clear. The development of the *Eugenics* movement affirms the racism inherent in U.S. Social Darwinist thought. Consider the following illustration:

> The Eugenist believes that no other single factor in determining social conditions and practices approaches in importance that of racial structural integrity and sanity. (Kellicott, 1911, p. 44)

Social psychology developed as an antidote to this natural, biological emphasis. The sociopsychological view rejected the biological analogy and saw the interdependence of the individual personality and the institutional structure of society. Echoing the ideas of colleagues Thorstein Veblen, Charles H. Cooley, and James Mark Baldwin, John Dewey wrote:

> We may desire abolition of war, industrial justice, greater quality of opportunity for all. But no amount of preaching good will or the golden rule or cultivation of sentiments of love and equity will accomplish the results. There must be change in objective arrangements and institutions. *We must work on the environment, not merely on the hearts of men.* (1922, pp. 21–22; emphasis added)

Dewey's statement presages much of the later discussion among social scientists about the best way to deal with racial antagonism. More recently, we have seen legal and legislative attacks on "objective arrangements and institutions," with some notable successes. But, it is important to note that Dewey charted this course early in the century. Although many thought of social action as a good and necessary thing in 1970, it was not always so (nor, apparently, is it considered so by some today). Sometimes social action achieved reprehensible changes. For example, the applied eugenics activities of the National Conference on Race Betterment passed a sterilization law in Indiana in 1907. The intersection of social thought and social action was established early in the century.[5]

---

[4]This idea has been around for a long time. It has recently been recapitulated by Herrnstein (1971) and again by Herrnstein and Murray (1994) in their widely controversial *The Bell Curve.*
[5]In 1972, social action has been reified by proponents of relevance in social science. Social action has not always been a desirable thing, and who knows how history will judge our current social activism. Well, we now (c. 1996) have history to consult and it is a double vision. The appropriateness, necessity, and wisdom of social action depends on who is talking. This story is clearly not over, the values are not set in concrete, and the cyclical nature of government social action is likely to remain the most realistic vision we have.

The First Riot Report

Urban violence between Blacks and Whites has a long history in the United States. In the earlier years (c. 1919–1960), it was whites who rioted against blacks. By the mid-1960s, this trend had changed. Whereas white riots have been a surgical strike to maintain control and been fomented by white racism, black riots seemed to be more result of frustration and anger, directed more at the local symbols of oppression than the perpetrators of it.

> The relation of whites and Negroes in the United States is our most grave and perplexing domestic problem. Our race problem must be solved in harmony with the fundamental law of the nation and with its free institutions. . . . The problem must not be regarded as sectional or political, and it should be studied and discussed seriously, frankly, and with an open mind.

These words could plausibly have been written at any time in this century. In fact, they are found in a report on the causes of the Chicago riot of 1919 (Chicago Commission on Race Relations, 1922). The Chicago Commission stressed the environmental aspects of the racial problem by asserting the innate equality of blacks and whites. It attributed the observed differences to economic and social inequality. Although the Chicago Commission did not forthrightly indict white America (as the Kerner report did 45 years later), it did point out the national scope of the problem and the need for thoughtful reform. The Chicago Commission specified that the 1919 riot was engendered by poor housing, inferior education, mistreatment by police, unemployment, job discrimination, and white prejudice.[6] Its recommendations also sound familiar: better police training for ethnic understanding and riot control; better jobs, housing, and education; equality before the law; integrated neighborhoods; and equal rights in public places. The simple documentation of the ills with the equally simple recommendation to "eliminate them" indicates how little the Chicago Commission knew about the complexities of U.S. race relations.

To summarize, with the "separate but equal" decision of 1896 to uphold them, Southern whites established complete racial segregation *de jure.* With control of all political and economic institutions to support them, Northern whites used systematic racial discrimination to establish almost complete racial segregation *de facto.* When any tendency to challenge the broad line of racial separation emerged, white violence against blacks was the response—riots in the North; lynchings, burnings, and other barbarisms in the South.

The simultaneous emergence of social science and social action as factors in the course of the evolution of race relations in the United States must be noted. For example, early social theory—notably, Social Darwinism—lent itself easily to the perpetuation of racial inequalities. The social action to which that theory gave rise was avowedly racist. The first two decades of the twentieth century were often called the "progressive era," because of the broad advances in social, economic, and polit-

---

[6]The 1919 Chicago Commission report and 1968 Kerner Commission report offer a framework for the concerns of this book. The Chicago report blames, in part, *white prejudice,* while the Kerner report blames *white racism* for racial violence in the United States. We will try, in the remainder of this book, to clarify the different assumptions and perspectives that each of these two terms represents. Between publication of the two reports, riots in 1935 and 1943 in Harlem, and in 1943 in Detroit intervened, with no emergent solution to the problem on the horizon. The recommendations in 1968 were little different from the recommendations in 1919. We may ask ourselves what have we learned over the years, and how much progress in race relations have we made.

ical life in the United States. However, in reality, race relations were in many ways worsening: A white Southerner, Woodrow Wilson, was elected to the presidency and moved to segregate federal offices, *Birth of a Nation* (Griffith, 1915) hailed the rise of the Ku Klux Klan, and riots of whites against blacks signaled a popular determination to maintain white dominance in the country.

The 1920s: Attitudes, Art, and Poverty

In many ways the 1920s represented the lull before the storm. Many of the industrial jobs created by World War I were still available to the blacks who had migrated north, even though blacks were often forced to organize in order to protect their jobs (e.g., A. Philip Randolph organized the Brotherhood of Sleeping Car Porters and Maids and other New York radicals organized the Friends of Negro Freedom). Black businesses increased, as did the number of blacks in white-collar jobs. The Harlem Renaissance in literature (Claude McKay, James Weldon Johnson, Countee Cullen, and Langston Hughes), theatre (Paul Robeson and Bert Williams), dance (Florence Mills), and music (William Grant Still, W. C. Handy) introduced white Americans to black people (albeit often by means of a stereotyped view, as in O'Neill's *Emperor Jones* and *An God's Chillun Got Wings* and Connelly's *The Green Pastures*).

But even as white Americans were being introduced to the "new Negro" (capitalization of the first letter of *Negro* was perhaps the first indication of newness), a West Indian named Marcus Garvey was making plans for blacks to return to Africa. His Universal Negro Improvement Association (UNIA) charted a steamship company called the Black Star Line to carry U.S. blacks back to Africa. In addition, Garvey rejected the "new Negro" image in favor of the tribal African image of warriors and princesses. Although his separatist plans never materialized, he did have several thousand followers. The U.S. government reacted quite strongly to his influence. After being convicted for using the mails to defraud, Garvey was deported to England as an undesirable alien.[7]

The questions of African and U.S. aspects of racial identity, the most appropriate strategies for expressing that identity, and the course that social actions to sustain positive well-being for African Americans were to take was a matter of economic, psychological, political, philosophical, and artistic significance. The Harlem Renaissance captured the spirit of the new Negro as a racial ideology movement of inclusion and integration (cf. Huggins, 1978; Lewis, 1980), whereas Garvey captured the sentiment of self-contained and separatist black society, informed by the traditions and beliefs of an African heritage (cf. Cronon, 1955; Martin, 1976).

In the 1920s New York society made the grand tour of Harlem, siphoning off its pleasures in the evenings and leaving the natives to grovel in their poverty in the morning. (For documentation of how white show business exploited, then dropped, black musicians and entertainers one can read W. C. Handy's autobiography.) No aspect of life was spared racial antipathies.

The 1920s were also crucial for social psychology. As Floyd Allport (1920) began his empirical investigation of social phenomena, the concept of "attitudes" acquired so much importance that social psychology came to be defined as "the sci-

---

[7]Most accounts suggest that although Garvey himself was probably innocent of the charges, other people in his organization had, in fact, used it to personal advantage. Also, many unwise business decisions helped bring about the failure of the enterprise. See E. D. Cronon's *Black Moses* (1955) and Amy Jacques Garvey's *Garvey and Garveyism* (1970).

entific study of attitudes." But the emergence of an attitudinal-behavioral dichotomy assured that any analysis of race relations would be one-sided. That is, attitudes described what people said, or saw, or felt—not *necessarily* what they were likely to do. The empirical positivism of social scientists' focus on attitudes was further advanced with the development of sophisticated statistical techniques by L. L. Thurstone (1927), who declared triumphantly, "Attitudes can be measured." The social scientist was thus fully armed and ready to attack the problem of race relations with a vengeance.

Systematic work on racial attitudes was begun by Emory S. Bogardus (1925; 1928). Interested in measuring the attitudes of one ethnic group toward another, Bogardus developed a *social distance scale*. Respondents were asked to circle one of seven social-distance classifications to which they would be willing to admit a member of a given race. (Bogardus loosely defined *race* to include nationality and ethnic group.) The classifications were ordered by increasing degrees of social distance, from "Would agree to close kinship or marriage" (indicated by a 1) to "Would exclude from my country" (indicated by a 7).

The social-distance scale was administered to a sample of 1,725 native-born Americans, representing 30 ethnic backgrounds. The results of this study are summarized in Table 2.1. Not unexpectedly, black, brown, and yellow peoples were least accepted by the predominantly white Anglo-Saxon sample. In fact, the pattern is so striking that Bogardus subsequently posed a question that was often asked again in the 1960s and 1970s: "Why the extensive social distance between Americans on one hand and Asiatics and Africans on the other?" Bogardus gave a simple answer:

> Where a person feels that his status or the status of anything that he values is furthered by race connections, then racial good will is engendered. But where a person's status or the status of anything that he values is endangered by the members of some race, then race prejudice flares up and burns long after the "invasion" has ceased (Bogardus, 1928, p. 28)

Bogardus wished to portray racial attitudes as clearly and accurately as possible so that agents of social change would know what to do. Social scientific study of racial attitudes was seen as a prerequisite to social action. Furthermore, social action was seen as a means of changing these attitudes and opinions. "The social distance test," Bogardus wrote, "would indicate what changes in attitudes and opinions the native Americans would need to undergo in order to give the immigrants a square deal, what changes the immigrants must make, and where racial conflicts are likely to take place" (1928, p. 256). Bogardus's view of the proper work of a social scientist agrees closely with Rainwater's.

In the same period, Bruno Lasker (1929) was writing about race attitudes from a quite different perspective. As part of a national organization of social, education, and religious workers known as The Inquiry, Lasker produced a study entitled *Race Attitudes in Children*. In researching the subject, Lasker rejected use of the new "sample surveys," preferring to rely on personal reports and testimony. He interpreted much of the observational and reportorial data and left the rest to stand as objective (or subjective) fact. He concluded that everything in a typical white child's environment (e.g., institutions such as family and school, photographs, and public speeches) contributed to the child's negative attitudes toward blacks. Lasker's recommendations were simple: These environmental factors should be changed through education and religion, and by local, state, and federal govern-

TABLE 2.1 SOME SOCIAL-DISTANCE RATINGS OF ETHNIC GROUPS BY WHITE AMERICANS (C. 1925)

1. Reactions of 1,725 White Americans to 14 Different Races by Percentages

Regarding races listed below	1 To close kinship by marriage	2 To my club as personal chums	3 To my street as neighbors	4 To employment in my occupation	5 To citizenship in my country	6 As visitors only to my country	7 Would exclude from my country
English	93.7	96.7	97.3	95.4	95.9	1.7	0.0
Americans (native white)	90.1	92.4	92.6	92.4	90.5	1.2	0.0
Scotch-Irish	72.6	81.7	88.0	89.4	92.0	16.7	0.4
Dutch	44.2	54.7	73.2	76.7	86.1	2.4	0.3
Norwegians	41.0	56.0	65.1	72.0	80.3	8.0	0.3
Spaniards	27.6	49.8	55.1	58.0	81.6	8.4	2.0
Armenians	8.5	14.8	27.8	46.2	58.1	17.7	5.0
Indians	8.1	27.7	33.4	54.3	83.0	7.7	1.6
Jews (Germans)	7.8	2.1	25.5	39.8	53.5	25.3	13.8
Negroes	1.4	9.1	11.8	38.7	57.3	17.6	12.7
Turks	1.4	10.0	11.7	19.0	25.3	41.8	23.4
Chinese	1.1	11.8	15.9	27.0	27.3	45.2	22.4
Mulattoes	1.1	9.6	10.6	32.0	47.4	22.7	16.8
Hindus	1.1	6.8	13.0	21.4	23.7	47.1	19.1

2. Reactions of 202 Native-Born American Negroes and Mulattoes to 9 Races by Percentages

	1	2	3	4	5	6	7
Negroes	96.0	94.0	94.0	90.0	92.0	8.0	0
Mulattoes	52.0	66.0	70.0	70.0	70.0	10.0	2.0
French	32.0	60.0	80.0	76.0	72.0	16.0	2.0
English	16.0	42.0	72.0	72.0	76.0	14.0	0
Americans (native white)	6.0	34.0	66.0	72.0	74.0	0	0
Japanese	6.0	28.0	30.0	34.0	40.0	36.0	8.0
Germans	4.0	22.0	42.0	44.0	34.0	30.0	10.0
Jews (Russian)	2.0	12.0	18.0	24.0	30.0	34.0	10.0
Turks	0	6.0	10.0	16.0	14.0	38.0	26.0

SOURCE: Adapted from Bogardus, *Immigration and Race Relations.* Copyright 1928.

ment. Again, we find current concerns are not new. Rather, they are well-rooted in racial conflict and analysis of earlier decades.

For Southern blacks, the great depression began early. The boll weevil, soil erosion, and a general decline in agriculture hit Southern blacks hard. Those who had not left the South were mired in poverty. The stock market crash of 1929 deepened Southern poverty and exploded the Northern economy—and, as in all hard times, blacks suffered most.

In summary, the 1920s were characterized by three important trends. First, the largest black separatist movement to date was initiated by Marcus Garvey. This separatist trend, with its emphasis on the positive elements of black (primarily African) culture was a precursor to modern developments in black politics and black culture. Second, the rise of blacks in the arts to the point of becoming a class within the black population was highly significant. Then, as now, many of the leading black intellectuals and strategists were artists. Third, social psychology developed primarily as an empirical social science. The development of rather sophisticated measurement pushed social psychology further toward a scientific self-image and the belief that social action could be accurately informed by the results of social scientific investigation. In the next decade, experimental investigations of racial issues would proliferate, and a new dimension would be added to our understanding of the problem.

The 1930s: Racial Stereotypes and Federal Bureaucracy

The great depression struck savagely, fundamentally changing the nation's character. However, for the first time since Reconstruction, black Americans found the federal government sympathetic to their plight. President Roosevelt appointed black advisers in many areas (e.g., Robert C. Weaver in the Department of the Interior, Laurence A. Oxley in labor, Frank S. Horne in housing, Mary McLeod Bethune in youth administration, and Ralph Bunche in the State Department). Black Americans responded to New Deal aid and what seemed to be a sympathetic administration by switching from the Republican to the Democratic party.

In relieving the acute poverty of millions of Americans, the New Deal was a big success. But federal programs such as the CCC and WPA left discrimination and racism essentially untouched. Further, it made millions of black Americans grossly dependent on the federal government. In the nearly 60 years since then, welfare programs have had a cosmetic impact on U.S. society. Moreover, the National Housing Act of 1935 placed public policy squarely on the side of racial segregation in public housing facilities, as administrators of that act followed a principle of racial segregation. It was not until 1948 that this policy was altered. The Federal Housing Administration has also advocated racial segregation, and its discriminatory mortgage policies favored the development of all-white suburban communities. In the 1930s, there was reason for almost anyone to be on welfare. But, as the economy boomed following World War II and two Asian "conflicts," there were fewer (if any) reasons for being on welfare—except simply because one was black.

A belief in the existence of equal opportunity led many whites to attribute the fact that a multitude of blacks were on welfare to the blacks' innate laziness, ignorance, or apathy. Few focused on the interactions of competition and conflict, as well as cultural or racial favoritism.

Racial antagonisms intensified during the 1930s, perhaps, because of the acute competition for the very few available jobs and other necessities. In 1935 Harlem blacks rioted against white merchants and landlords. This was the first of the "modern" riots—that is, by blacks against white property instead of by whites against black people. The Supreme Court showed signs of this same modernity in 1937, when it ruled that the picketing of firms that refused to hire blacks was constitutional.[8] In black communities, "Don't buy where you can't work" programs were started, presaging the mass civil rights activities of the 1950s and early to mid-1960s.

Interest in racial attitudes continued to dominate social science in the 1930s. Katz and Braly (1933) introduced the empirical investigation of stereotyping, although Walter Lippmann (1922) had introduced and analyzed the concept a decade earlier. In an elegantly simple procedure, Katz and Braly listed 84 diverse character traits (e.g., intelligent, superstitious, happy-go-lucky, lazy, artistic, and industrious) and had 100 male U.S. college students (from Princeton) select those traits they believed most characteristic of each of the following 10 groups: (white) Americans, Chinese, English, Germans, Irish, Italians, Japanese, Jews, Negroes, and Turks.

These Princeton men saw Jews as shrewd, mercenary, industrious, grasping, and intelligent. White Americans were seen as industrious, intelligent, materialistic, ambitious, and progressive. Negroes emerged as superstitious, lazy, happy-go-lucky, ignorant, and musical. The authors concluded that the high degree of agreement in stereotyping indicated cultural forces that molded a "public attitude." Prejudiced attitudes, the authors argued, consist of both public and private attitudes. Private attitudes are based on individual feeling and experiences, whereas public attitudes involve acceptance of cultural labels. Stereotypes, then, were seen as deplorable public attitudes, for "to the realist there are no racial or national groups which exist as entities and which determine the characteristics of the group members" (Katz and Braly, 1933, p. 289).

In 1935, Katz and Braly replicated their study of stereotyping with Princeton undergraduates. This time, however, the subjects were given two different tasks. One instruction asked them to identify the traits most commonly used to describe 10 ethnic groups; the second asked for subjects' personal descriptions of these groups. The results were similar to those of the 1933 study. The variation in instructions had virtually no effect, except that Negroes were placed one rank higher in private than in public preferences. The authors concluded that "racial prejudice is, thus, a generalized set of stereotypes of a high degree of consistency which includes emotional responses to race names, a belief in typical characteristics associated with race names, and an evaluation of such typical traits" (Katz and Braly, 1935, pp. 191–192).

By this definition, black college students in 1941 were also racially prejudiced. Bayton (1941) administered the Katz and Braly questionnaire to 100 black college students. Their racial stereotyping differed little from that of the white Princeton subjects of a few years earlier.

Since college attendance in the 1930s and 1940s usually went with middle- and upper-class status (for both blacks and whites), it is possible that the stereotypes were influenced more by class than by race. Dissociating these two variables is dif-

[8]The Court had also shown earlier signs of taking a role in alleviating racial conflict when, in 1917, it struck down the "grandfather clause" and poll tax, identifying them as efforts to disenfranchise black voters.

ficult at every level; hence, assertions about racial factors in attitudes must be evaluated cautiously.[9] In the 1930s, the study of prejudice was primarily the study of attitudes. The belief that the study of attitudes was the first step in the study of prejudice was based largely on the view of attitude as "a disposition to act . . . a broad, generic (not simple and specific) determinant to behavior" (G. W. Allport, 1929). This attitudinal emphasis has had important consequences for the study and progress of race relations in three respects:

First, the attitudinal approach places the burden of blame on the individual. Because of one's culture and experiences one has prejudiced attitudes, and these attitudes describe one's personality and one's behavior. The most extreme result of this approach was *The Authoritarian Personality* (Adorno et al., 1950). These authors concluded that basic personality distinguished prejudiced from supposed nonprejudiced individuals.

Second, and more important, in stressing attitudes, social scientists employed value judgments in their operational definitions of prejudiced attitudes. There was a tendency to consider individuals who answered a question in a certain way not only as prejudiced, but as morally inferior human beings. The task of eliminating prejudice must be seen, in part, as a reorganization of the value systems of prejudiced individuals. That is, the value position inherent in both theory and research in race relations must be recognized.

Third, it was assumed that attitudes were consistently and predictably related to overt behavior. Most of the attitudinal research in the 1930s did not question this assumption. A study by Richard LaPiere (1934) stands out as a warning beacon to all investigators of prejudiced attitudes who assume, as G. W. Allport did, that attitudes are broad, generic determinants of behavior. Between 1930 and 1932 LaPiere traveled across the United States with a Chinese couple. (We know of the negative attitudes toward the Chinese from the Katz and Braly and the Bogardus studies.) LaPiere reported that

> . . . [in] ten thousand miles of motor travel, twice across the United States, and up and down the Pacific Coast, we met definite rejection from those asked to serve us just once. We were received at 66 hotels, auto camps, and 'Tourist Homes,' . . . We were served in 184 restaurants and cafes . . . and treated with . . . more than ordinary considerations in 72 of them. (p. 232)

Six months after his visits, LaPiere sent out a questionnaire asking "Will you accept members of the Chinese race as guests in your establishment?" He got replies from 81 restaurants and 47 hotels. The response was overwhelmingly negative—92 percent checked "No," and the remainder checked "Uncertain, depends upon circumstances." A control group of establishments LaPiere had not visited responded similarly.[10] Therefore, as early as 1934, LaPiere sounded a cautionary note for the true believers of attitudinal research and their paper-and-pencil tests. "It would seem far more worth while to make a shrewd guess regarding that which is essential than to accurately measure that which is likely to prove quite irrelevant," LaPiere advised (1934, p. 237).

---

[9]A later study of stereotyping conducted by Bayton, McAlister, and Hamer [1956] attempted to dissociate the race and class contributions to stereotypic attitudes. In that study, class was found to be a more important determinant of stereotypes than was race.
[10]It might be argued that the same results would not have been obtained had LaPiere traveled with a black couple. That is possible, but later, Kutner, Wilkins, and Yarrow (1952) made a similar study with blacks and got similar results.

Another highly significant contribution to the analysis of race relations was an article on the nature of race and intelligence by Otto Klineberg (1935). In this volume, Klineberg sought to demonstrate the lack of decisive evidence on the innate intellectual inferiority of black Americans. He argued against the hereditary intellectual-inferiority view that pervaded social science at the time. His piece was one of the earliest attempts to reverse the racist inclination that many social scientists had.

Furthermore, while racial attitudes may have buttressed the discriminatory practices responsible for the highly unfavorable position of blacks, the proliferation of bureaucratically run welfare institutions created a vise that tightened year by year on the poorly housed, fed, clothed, and educated black masses. The transparency of individual and institutional racism as basic causes of racial inequality was contributed to by the dominant focus of research on racial attitudes.

The 1940s: Growing Civil Rights Action and Attitude Change Through Contact

As we have seen, the federal government began to make a commitment to easing the plight of the poor, and of blacks, during the 1930s. However, as the great depression lifted with the coming of war, much of the federal bureaucratic maze remained. The numerous jobs that bureaucracy spawned, as well as the wartime labor shortage, gave blacks more economic power. Pressures to eliminate discrimination and segregation in federal agencies forced the U.S. government, for the first time, to face its own involvement in racial strife and inequity.

The growth of black militancy was evident in 1941, as A. Philip Randolph organized the "March on Washington" movement to dramatize demands for fair treatment of blacks in defense industries, the armed forces, and government apprenticeship programs. Rather than face the prospect of a march of 100,000 black Americans, President Roosevelt issued Executive Order 8802, which banned discrimination in war industries and apprenticeship programs, and created the Fair Employment Practices Committee (FEPC), which monitored discrimination in industries with government contracts.[11] Randolph called off his march, but the impact of his organization set the stage for advances in government surveillance of and provision of remedies for racial discrimination in employment (cf. Pfeffer, 1990).

The civil rights movement burgeoned. The Congress of Racial Equality (CORE) was organized in 1943 and staged its first sit-in in Chicago. Further, the black press became so vocal in support of civil rights that the government considered prosecuting black publishers for impeding the war effort.

With the economy booming, as it had during World War I, many blacks migrated north and west to get jobs or simply to escape the oppressive South. However, despite Executive Order 8802, there was still large-scale discrimination in war industries. Moreover, many whites still recovering from the shock of the great depression felt their jobs and neighborhoods threatened by black migration. These tensions exploded into another series of race riots in 1943. The worst was in Detroit, where 25 blacks and 9 whites were killed.

Because of black determination, reaction against Nazi racism, the rise of the third world, and growing recognition of U.S. race-related hypocrisy, segregation

---

[11]It was learned later that Randolph could not really come up with anywhere near that number of people. Nevertheless, this early use of confrontation tactics worked.

Safe at home! Jackie Robinson breaks the color barrier in Major League Baseball, 1948. (UPI-Corbis/Bettmann)

came under frontal attack. In 1945, the year the war ended, a group of black NAACP lawyers decided to implement the teachings of their mentor at Howard University, Charles Houston. Led by Thurgood Marshall, they formulated plans for a direct legal attack on segregation. A year later, President Truman appointed the Committee on Civil Rights, which concluded in its report, *To Secure These Rights,* that racial injustices must be abolished. In 1948 President Truman ordered the integration of the armed services; a year after that, Jackie Robinson became the first black baseball player in the major leagues.[12]

An American Dilemma
Rainwater (1966) suggested that the social scientist's first responsibility was to "tell it like it is." Swedish sociologist Gunnar Myrdal did just that (1944, p. 24).

> The Negro in America has not yet been given the elemental civil and political rights of formal democracy, including a fair opportunity to earn his living, upon which a general accord was already won when the American Creed [rights to Liberty, Justice and Equal-

[12]Prior to Truman's Executive Order, black soldiers were segregated in every branch of the armed services. Some all-black companies did do some fighting. Most black soldiers, however, were given little but cooking and cleaning responsibilities. Racial discrimination in the military has persisted since the early Revolutionary War days. Even though Truman ordered racial integration in 1948, there still exist various forms of racial inequity in the military.

ity] was first taking form. And this anachronism constitutes the contemporary "problem" both to Negroes and to whites.

Thus, in 1944, Myrdal formulated "the problem" posed by DuBois 40 years earlier. In *An American Dilemma,* a massive work of remarkable depth, quality, and insight, Myrdal (1944) and his large and impressive staff documented the character and consequences of racial relations in the United States. The theme of the book is the contradiction between the U.S. creed of equality and opportunity for all, and the general exclusion of black people from its benefits. It is not an exaggeration to say that *An American Dilemma* set the stage upon which the social and behavioral sciences could frame the nature and scope of the problems in race relations and become looked upon as advisors to be consulted as to possible solutions.

Although black writers had written several important books on the plight of the urban black (e.g., DuBois [1973], *The Philadelphia Negro;* James Weldon Johnson [1930], *Black Manhattan;* Claude McKay [1940], *Harlem*), St. Clair Drake and Horace Cayton (1945) presented the most influential sociological study of urban black Americans, *Black Metropolis.* In this lengthy, but highly readable, study of Chicago's South Side, the authors eloquently documented the insights and experiences of Richard Wright's searing novel, *Native Son* (1940). In addition to *An American Dilemma* and *Black Metropolis,* John Dollard's *Caste and Class in a Southern Town* (1937) and E. Franklin Frazier's *The Negro Family in the United States* (1944) broadly reviewed the sociology of race relations. Psychologists and sociologists alike have fed on these sources of information ever since. John Hope Franklin's *From Slavery to Freedom* was first published in 1947, and the importance of his historical narrative on African American life is suggested by the fact that the book was in its seventh printing in 1994.

The interest in attitudes remained, however, and studies continued to affirm the stereotyping data of Katz and Braly (1933, 1935) and the social distance data of Bogardus (1928). The questionnaire approach to attitudes produced copious quantitative data on social distance and stereotyping, but it was unable to capture the intensity of racial attitudes. More illuminating was a collection of interviews with white Americans published in 1946 by the Social Science Institute at Fisk University. In these interviews, conducted between 1940 and 1946, the respondents gave their impressions of and basic orientation toward black Americans. Here are some examples:

White female, age 50, civic and club worker in Philadelphia:

I got along with them first-rate, because I knew how to handle them. They are like children. The only time they get up-ish is when they have too much white blood. These superstitions are one of the worst things they have. . . . That's in the blood. . . . Those in the city, now, are a sassy bunch. I think they should be separated in the schools. Their minds are really not the same. . . . The Japanese are not as repulsive as the Chinese. . . . I am far more tolerant than my mother.

White male, age 50, businessman in Durham, North Carolina:

They are like children; the state of their mental development is low. . . . In spite of all that, I like the darkie. You may think I am prejudiced, and I am, but they are likable. . . . Wits weren't developed in the tropics. . . . I have a feeling of aversion toward a rat or snake. They are harmless, but I don't like them. I feel the same toward a nigger.

White male, age 45, newspaper editor in Durham, North Carolina:

We have no friction, especially on the Negro side, except when outsiders come in and begin to try social equality. . . . There is no disposition on the part of any white people, except the low element, to mistreat the Negro or take unfair advantage of him. . . . A Negro is different from other people in that he is an unfortunate branch of the human family who hasn't had the opportunity, who hasn't been able to make out of himself all that he is capable of . . . Unfortunately, many think of them as a race because they have more of a lower element that we have to keep under subjection because of their animal nature. . . . In a way, we know them less intimately. I believe that I have a better, higher regard because I grant them a certain amount of intelligence. The next generation will go further in this regard. That possibility doesn't alarm me. They will all die out before we get that far.

White male, age 38, newspaperman in Newport News, Virginia:

Our colored people are hard-working, self-respecting, and do not attempt to mix any-where with the whites. There are some who try to butt in with their rights. . . . The best evidence of the fair treatment they get are the public school facilities. They have very ex-cellent nigger schools. . . . The Negro is a black and kinky-haired person from whose body comes a not entirely pleasant odor. He is always regarded as an inferior person and race, mentally and morally, destined by birth and circumstances to serve the white people. . . . I don't understand the northerners. How would they like a nigger to marry their daughter?

White female, age 40, housewife in Little Rock, Arkansas:

As long as you deal with them as your workers, everything is all right. They have no re-sentment. . . . Our cook, here, would just do anything for us. . . . We have several Har-vard graduates here. I can't see where they are any different from the others; they act very humble, and realize that they are still Negroes. . . . Negroes have their own charac-teristics. First their utter lack of responsibility. They have an inborn sense of rhythm and music. As a race, they are not honest. . . . They are not a very stable race; they are here today and there tomorrow. But they are happy, carefree people and get more out of life than any other race. Their morality is low.

White female, age 20, stenographer in Newark, New Jersey:

They aren't different, except for their color. . . . most of the colored people I know are ser-vants or laborers. I never knew any who did skilled work. . . . If I were a monarch and had power to do what I wanted to do with the Negroes, I don't know just what I would do. It would not be a good idea to send them back to Africa. It's necessary for them to mingle with the whites; to learn each other's ways.

This sampling of racial attitudes reveals all of the stereotypes Katz and Braly found and more. Blacks are unfortunate branches of the human family, childlike, lazy, in-ferior intellectually and morally, but are hard-working and good except when they butt in with [talk of their] "rights"! "All men are created equal . . . and are endowed by their Creator with certain inalienable Rights, that among these are Life, Liberty and the pursuit of Happiness." The U.S. creed, the white American creed, did not apply to blacks in 1776, nor did it apply in 1946. The "American dilemma" marches on.

Although the attitudinal studies continued, the lessons of LaPiere (1934) and other investigators led several researchers to seek more general explanations. One of the first such attempts was made at Yale by John Dollard, Leonard Doob, and associates (1939) in *Frustration and Aggression*. The writers argued that prejudice is a form of aggression and that aggression results from frustration. Race prejudice, they suggested, is displaced aggression that results from the frustrations of unemployment and insecure economic conditions. Therefore, their argument ran, the lynching of blacks was not the result of frustration or anger with blacks as blacks, but rather a consequence of generally low and unstable cotton prices.

This approach is known as the *scapegoat theory of prejudice*. It suggests that blacks are the innocent victims of displaced white aggression. This theory seems quite compelling when one observes a pigeon in a conditioning box viciously attacking a dummy pigeon whenever the customary reward is withheld. However, such reasoning applies better to emotional acts of violence than to the years of considered legal, political, social, and economical disadvantage suffered by blacks. It also narrowly focuses on the South, ignoring the physical and psychological oppression to which blacks in the North were and are subjected.

A second approach emphasized basic personality differences between prejudiced and less-prejudiced people. The best known of these studies was *The Authoritarian Personality,* by Adorno and others (1950). This volume reported on three different kinds of questionnaire techniques designed to measure anti-Semitism, ethnocentrism, and antidemocratic feeling (or fascism). The authors felt that prejudice varied so greatly from situation to situation that a broader concept, such as ethnocentrism, would be more relevant.

Adorno and his associates (1950) developed the third of their questionnaires, the F-scale, to measure anti-Semitism and ethnocentrism without mentioning specifically the groups toward which antagonisms were expressed. The F-scale was considered to be more general and more broadly predictive than other scales were. The mental sets or attitudes represented in the F-scale were considered representative of the kind of prejudiced personality often observed in interracial situations. The totalitarian, or prejudiced, personality was delineated as follows (Adorno et al., 1950, p. 228):

Conventionalism: Rigid adherence to conventional middle-class values.

Authoritarian submission: Submissive, uncritical attitude toward idealized moral authorities of the in-group.

Authoritarian aggression: Tendency to be on the lookout for and to condemn, reject, and punish people who violate conventional values.

Anti-intraception: Opposition to the subjective, the imaginative, the tender-minded.

Superstition and stereotypy: The belief in mystical determinants of the individual's fate; the disposition to think in rigid categories.

Power and "toughness": Preoccupation with the dominance-submission, strong-weak, leader-follower dimensions; identification with power figures; overemphasis upon the conventionalized attributes of the ego; exaggerated assertion of strength and toughness.

Destructiveness and cynicism: Generalized hostility, vilification of the human.

Projectivity: The disposition to believe that wild and dangerous things go on in the world; the projection outward of unconscious, emotional impulses.

Sex: Exaggerated concern with sexual "goings-on."

This personality approach tended to slice the world into two types of people—prejudiced and nonprejudiced. Prejudiced people scored high on the F-scale, whereas nonprejudiced people scored low. Rate yourself on these items. Do you score high? Do you consider yourself prejudiced?

This view, like the scapegoat view, tended to obscure very important regional variations in race relations. Both theories spoke directly to Southerners and indicted specific types of individuals. They diverted attention from the North, and from whites who did not fit the characteristics of their theorized prejudiced personality. Pettigrew (1958) later showed that the notion of an authoritarian personality was not a sufficient explanation of prejudiced behavior. He demonstrated that F-scale scores were not higher among a random sample of Southerners than among a similar sample of Northerners.

The generalized-personality approach was given some support by Hartley (1946). Hartley presented a Bogardus social-distance scale to subjects, but added three fictional nationalities (Wallonian, Pirenian, and Danerian). Hartley found that students who showed relatively prejudiced attitudes toward traditional out-groups showed prejudiced attitudes toward the fictional groups. ("I don't know anything about them; therefore, I would exclude them from my country," was one comment.) On the other hand, those relatively tolerant toward traditional out-groups were tolerant of the fictional groups. ("I don't know anything about them, therefore I have no prejudices against them," one such subject noted.)

Although the personality approach traced prejudicial tendencies and prejudices to the heads and hearts of *individuals*, Oliver Cox (1948) made a far more sweeping indictment. Cox concluded:

> Race prejudice is a social attitude provocated [*sic*] among the public by an exploiting class for the purpose of stigmatizing some group as inferior so that the exploitation of either group itself or its resources, or both may be justified. . . . Race prejudice is a socio-attitudinal facilitation of a particular type of labor exploitation . . . .". (1948, p. 939)

The importance of economic exploitation, of course, had been recognized from the time of slavery on. But, in the 1940s, the emphasis on attitudes, personality, and intergroup hostility was so great that the economic interpretation was largely overlooked.

The new emphasis among social scientists on the prejudiced personality suggested strongly that changing people's attitudes was not the way to deal with racial antagonism. Moral appeals and rational argument simply would not work with an authoritarian personality. Other means for dealing with the problems of race had to be discovered—and this brought social scientists back to Dewey (1922), and his emphasis on changing the environment.

Two viewpoints, then, had developed. On the one hand, the personality theorists implied that prejudicial attitudes could not be changed through information and that, therefore, more impersonal institutional means (e.g., legislation) were necessary. On the other hand, the attitudinal approach suggested that changing of *folkways*–or attitudes based on tradition, experience, and social expedience—was a necessary step toward benign intergroup relations. Combined, the two approaches argued strongly for social change through legislation. The rigid personality would not be influenced by moral appeals or rational argument, while the prejudiced, ill-informed attitudes of individuals in a society could be altered only by personal contact. As Bettelheim and Janowitz (1950) stated: "The law and the courts stand within our legal system as an immediate focal point for changing some of the basic norms of interpersonal contact outside the primary groups, including those of inter-ethnic relations" (p. 177).

In the late 1940s most social scientists believed that racial integration was the only possible way to ease racial tensions. They felt that only integration could eliminate the gross educational, social, psychological, and economic disparities between the races.

A few years earlier, Lippitt and Radke (1946, p. 167) had condemned the literature on prejudice for its "narrow emphasis on the surface aspects of the problem." In the late 1940s and early 1950s, social scientists began to emphasize the dynamic elements of prejudice and to outline ways of reducing it.[13] Again and again, social scientists asked whether laws can change customs—whether enforced personal contact can reduce interracial hostility. A well-known social experiment on this subject was conducted by Morton Deutsch and Mary Collins (1951) in the new, federally sponsored public housing.

The authors selected two types of interracial housing projects in which to conduct their study: (1) projects where blacks and whites were assigned living units without regard to race and (2) projects where blacks and whites were assigned to separate sections of the same development. The fully integrated projects were in New York City and the internally segregated projects were in Newark, New Jersey. Projects selected from the two cities were matched according to racial ratio. The Newark project, called Bakerville, with two blacks to every white, was matched with Sacktown in New York, which was 70 percent black. A second matched pair consisted of Frankville in Newark (50 percent blacks and 50 percent whites) and Koaltown in New York, (40 percent blacks and 60 percent whites). Data were obtained through intensive and long interviews (from 1 1/4 to 2 hours) conducted with housewives in their own apartments.

If interracial contact truly ameliorates racial attitudes, the data would show that the racial attitudes of housewives in the integrated projects of Koaltown and Sacktown were more favorable to those of the opposite race than were the attitudes of housewives in segregated Bakerville and Frankville. (See Table 2.2) Because very few of the whites in either the segregated or integrated or internally segregated projects would have picked a project with black families on the basis of their initial attitudes, we can assume that the differences found by Deutsch and Collins were due to the interracial contacts.

White housewives' attitudes toward blacks became more positive in the integrated projects and changed little, if at all, in the segregated project. Deutsch and Collins concluded:

> From the point of view of reducing prejudice and of creating harmonious, democratic intergroup relations, the net gain resulting from the integrated projects is considerable; from the same point of view, the gain created by the segregated bi-racial projects is slight. (1951, p. 155)

Also concerned with the effects of social contact on attitudes, Festinger and Kelley (1951) conducted a field experiment designed to produce desirable attitude changes. In the town studied, hostility had developed toward a public housing project; the townspeople feared it would become a slum. Project residents felt inferior, even though their actual status differential from nonproject residents was quite

---

[13]See, for example, Rose (1947), Williams (1947), and Bettelheim and Janowitz (1950).

TABLE 2.2 INTERRACIAL CONTACT AND ATTITUDES OF WHITE HOUSEWIVES TOWARD NEGROES IN TWO HOUSING PROJECTS

	Integrated Projects		Internally Segregated Projects	
	Koaltown, %	Sacktown, %	Bakerville, %	Frankville, %
1. Closest casual contact:				
As neighbors in the building	60	53	0	0
Outside on benches	46	64	7	21
Shopping in stores on streets around project	12	13	81	60
2. Intimate contact— visiting, helping, clubs, and so on:				
None	61	28	99	96
Once or more	39	72	1	4
3. Type of relations:				
Friendly	60	69	6	4
Accommodative	24	14	5	1
Mixed	7	11	2	3
None	5	0	87	88
Bad	4	6	0	4
4. Feelings expressed:				
Like, desire, friendship	42	60	9	5
Mixed, reserved	30	12	12	27
Avoidant, dislike	28	28	79	68

SOURCE: Adapted from Morton Deutsch and Mary Evans Collins, *Inter-Racial Housing: A Psychological Evaluation of a Social Experiment.* Copyright © 1951 by the University of Minnesota Press. Reprinted by permission.

small. Project residents were also hostile toward each other and anticipated hostility from each other. The goal was to reduce the hostility within and outside the project. Festinger and Kelley reasoned that lessening hostility through interpersonal contact required three types of control:

1 *Motivational control* of attitudes, to be achieved by changing what people want
2 *Perceptual control* of attitudes, to be achieved by changing the person's experience with relevant objects, events, attributes and relationships
3 *Social control* of attitudes, to be achieved by changing the social attitudes and group norms with which the person comes in contact

To lessen hostility, the authors initiated nursery school programs, teenage clubs, and adult softball and crafts activities. The intent was to involve all the members of the community in changing motivational, perceptual, and social systems. The authors found that hostile attitudes lessened only among those people who participated in and had favorable attitudes toward the program. Unfortunately, for the project as a whole the program made matters worse. Festinger and Kelley (1951, p.

76) concluded: "If a group of persons are held together by common interest in community activities, and carry on communication about attitudes and opinions on which they differ, the conditions for attitude-change are present."

The Deutsch and Collins (1951) and the Festinger and Kelley (1951) studies suggest that *social engineering* (i.e., putting people in positions they would not choose themselves, for purposes of social change) may have general usefulness in the area of reducing racial conflict. The Festinger and Kelley study, though, warned that the positive effects of contact may be limited to certain kinds of people and situations. Gordon Allport (1954) later organized the research on interracial contact and extracted from the lave results hypotheses about the optimum contact conditions. We will look at one of these, the contact hypothesis, in greater detail in Chapter 4.

S UMMARY

Race relations in the United States are bound intimately to the facts of history. The enslavement of Africans and Indians, accompanied by rationalizations and the emergent cultural consequences, poisons race relations to this day. Cultural mistrust and collective anger are not easily erased by time. This is especially true when racial events offer a partial reinforcement schedule that sustains the fears, mistrust, and anger born centuries ago. This chapter has selectively reviewed that early history and demonstrated factors of the development of race relations.

In the beginning, color and culture were significant distinctions between Africans and Europeans. They were connected to the unfolding of racial relations of slavery, and the disparate values that were attached to them. The color line was not only a problem of the twentieth century, as DuBois foresaw, but of the sixteenth, seventeenth, eighteenth and nineteenth centuries as well. The conflicts over color and culture went to the heart of the fledgling nation and informed the development of its institutions. The American dilemma captured the contradiction between the freedom yearned for so ardently by the European settlers, and the denial of freedom to those Africans and Indians whom they enslaved or otherwise exploited and subjugated. This dilemma persists in United States society.

Race relations have gone through periods of great conflict since the beginning of the twentieth century, with riots dotting the landscape throughout. Lynching was prevalent in the early years, serving as a reminder of white racial dominance and the penalty for transgression of this status quo. Riots are now associated with African Americans and Hispanics letting out frustration over poor living conditions, feelings of injustice, and an absence of opportunity. But early in this century it was whites who rioted against blacks, burning down their houses and communities, shooting and lynching blacks as they went.

The social and psychological understanding of racial prejudice became a cornerstone of social psychology. Bogardus assessed whites' desire to maintain distance from ethnic and racial minority groups. Katz and Braly tried to understand the content of racial and ethnic stereotypes. Under the direction of Gunnar Myrdal, the whole complex nature of race relations was dissected and its enabling values, beliefs, and processes illuminated.

We end this period with a strong sense of continued racial conflict, which is stitched into the seams of society in both North and South alike, but also with a growing awareness of its costs to the very principles of democracy and freedom on which our society rests.

3

*A*ttacking the *P*roblem

———— ❖ ————

> *It is hereby declared to be the policy of the President that there shall be equality of treatment and opportunity for all persons in the armed services without regard to race, color, religion or national origin (Berman, 1970, p. 118).*
>
> President Harry S Truman
> Executive Order 9981

*I*NTRODUCTION

In terms of race relations, the 1940s had ended on a positive note, with the racial integration of the armed services by President Truman and the racial integration of major league baseball, under the committed and courageous leadership of Brooklyn Dodgers owner Branch Rickey.[1] The 1950s and 1960s were turbulent decades in which the march toward civil rights would not be halted.

---

[1]Rickey's decision to bring Jackie Robinson into the major leagues was a bold and daring example of "affirmative action" (Pratkanis, 1992). Robinson was qualified by his ability, to be sure, but he was not the most qualified (best) player in the Negro leagues. Yet he was selected in a conscious attempt to integrate the major leagues, to give blacks an opportunity to play and to succeed. Many at the time predicted he would fail and assumed he was not qualified to play in the Big Leagues.

In 1954, the U.S. Supreme Court declared racial segregation under the aegis of the "separate but equal" doctrine invalid. In that same year, social psychologist Gordon Allport published *The Nature of Prejudice* (1954), a work of exquisite detail, sensitivity, and understanding. The book captured the depth of feeling, the complexity of cognitive processes, and the complications of the social mores and political processes that underscored the problems of prejudice. Thus, the 1950s began with a declaration that the United States must move toward a racially integrated society, and along with a sociopsychological analysis of the barriers to, and best strategies for, reaching this goal.

The 1960s saw the burgeoning of the civil rights movement. The movement nationwide came of age. It was localized around a bus boycott in Montgomery, Alabama, by Rosa Parks, formalized by sit-ins (at lunch counters), wade-ins (on beaches), sleep-ins (at hotels), and championed with eloquence and vision by Martin Luther King, Jr. The passage of the Civil Rights Act of 1964 and of the Voting Rights Act of 1965 was perhaps the symbolic acknowledgment that the United States must stand *in fact,* for those freedoms that it espoused *in principle.* Those freedoms must extend to every citizen of the country, without regard to race, creed, nationality, gender, or religion. But the legislative intent did not translate immediately to social, political, or economic reality. Riots of the mid- to late 1960s protested the assassination of Dr. King and the country's failure to change at a pace that matched expectations. Students, women, African Americans, and other ethnic and racial minorities joined in demanding more of our leaders and of our citizens.

This chapter follows the course of these events. The seeds of current social policy, the level of expectation against which current reality is compared, were established during the fifties and sixties. What is now labeled pejoratively "political correctness" was, then, a beacon of hope for a more just, compassionate, and caring society. Did we achieve the stated civil rights goals in the 1960s and 1970s? Are social programs now mere pandering to a small minority who lack character? Or have we yet to meet the expectation for what a society can do to support its citizens and to eliminate egregious biases that deny the freedoms proclaimed by our Constitution and our legislators? In the following pages, you will find some bases for assessing where we are now in relation to where we have very recently been.

*T*HE 1950s: CIVIL RIGHTS AND MODERN AUTHORITY

We conclude that in the field of public education, the doctrine of "separate but equal" has no place.[2]

—U. S. Supreme Court, 1954

In 1936, Lloyd Gaines applied for admission to the University of Missouri Law School and was rejected because he was black. He took his case to court and, when the state court upheld the university, he appealed to federal courts and, ultimately,

---

[2]This is taken from the text of the unanimous opinions of the Supreme Court in *Brown v. Board of Education,* and is reprinted in full in Clark (1963, p. 159). This decision came about because an eight-year-old Topeka, Kansas, child was obliged to walk across a railroad track and take a bus to a black school 21 blocks away because her community school was all-white. The social meaning of busing changes, depending on whether it is serving or splitting segregated schools.

to the Supreme Court. In 1938, the Court ruled in Gaines's favor, noting that providing legal education for white state residents but not for black state residents "... is a denial of the equality of legal right to the enjoyment of the privilege which the state has set up ..." (cited in Franklin and Moss, 1994, p. 410). In 1996, federal courts in Texas ruled that preferential admission of black and Latino students to the University of Texas Law School was unconstitutional. The problem of equal access to education has been a major one in this society, and efforts to remedy the discrimination against people who belong to various racial and ethnic minority groups have often been contentious. The critical question is simply put, Granted that, historically, racial discrimination has deprived blacks and other ethnic and racial minority groups of opportunities for higher education, does simply removing discrimination solve the problem?

Contention over access to education was mounting in the 1940s and culminated in the important *Brown v. Board of Education of Topeka* decision, which was handed down on May 17, 1954, and stated:

> Separate educational facilities are inherently unequal. Therefore, we hold that the plaintiffs and others similarly situated for whom the actions have been brought are, by reason of the segregation complained of, deprived of the equal protection of the laws guaranteed by the Fourteenth Amendment.

The immediate importance of *Brown v. Board of Education* was largely symbolic, as the "all deliberate speed" desegregation timetable of a 1955 decision invited ingenious legal procrastination. The full impact of the decision was beginning to be realized in the late 1960s, as the Court's decision was enforced by other judicial decisions and more-vigorous Justice Department activity.

Two months after the Supreme Court decision, the White Citizens' Council was formed in Indianola, Mississippi. "Citizens' councils" began to spring up all over the South, and their members swore to fight integration by every lawful means. Considering the operation of Southern law at this time, they were assured a wide variety of such "lawful means." For example, shortly after the *Brown* decision, a Yale-educated Mississippi circuit judge, Tom Brady, in his book *Black Monday* (1955, pp. 45, 88–89), intoned,

> When a law transgresses the moral and ethical sanctions and standards of the mores, invariably strife, bloodshed and revolution follow in the wake of its attempted enforcement. The loveliest and purest of God's creatures, the nearest thing to an angelic being that treads this terrestrial ball, is a well-bred cultured southern White woman or her blue-eyed, golden-haired little girl. ... We say to the Supreme Court and to the northern world, you shall not make us drink from this cup. ... We have, through our forefathers, died before for our sacred principles. We can, if necessary, die again. (Brady, 1955, pp. 45, 88–89)

Can laws change customs? Deutsch and Collins said Yes; Festinger and Kelley's study said Maybe; Brady said No!

Meanwhile, evidence was accumulated in order to document the negative consequences of being black in white America. E. Franklin Frazier (1944) reported the psychological anguish black Americans experienced in their oppressed role as underclass for a privileged white caste. Kardiner and Ovesey (1951) echoed many of Frazier's observations. When it struck down the separate-but-equal doctrine of *Plessy v. Ferguson,* the Supreme Court noted that segregation had a "detrimental effect on colored children" and cited work by social scientists in support of this claim.

Studies of Racial Identification

Although there were many studies cited in the Court decision, the most famous of these was a study on racial identification in black children by Kenneth and Mamie Clark (1947). The critical question of psychological harm resulting from racial segregation was implied in the Court's conclusion that segregation was *inherently unequal*. The question of whether this harm was due to the internalization of the assumption of racial inferiority implied by segregation or simply to the reduced level of resources for minority schooling or other possible factors was not addressed by the courts. The Court did note, however, that there were many complexities involved in remedying the situation. The Clarks' work focused on the psychological basis for inequality and sought to provide an empirical basis on which to draw conclusions.

One hundred thirty-four black children aged 3 to 7 from racially segregated nursery and public schools in Arkansas, and 119 black children of the same age range from integrated schools in Springfield, Massachusetts, were shown four dolls. The dolls were identical in every detail but skin and hair color. Two were brown with black hair, while two were white with blond hair. With respect to their own skin color, the black subjects were classified as "light" (nearly white), "medium" (from very light brown to fairly dark brown), and "very dark." The experimenter asked each child to give him one doll that:

1	Is a white child	5	You like best
2	Is a colored child	6	Is a nice doll
3	Is a Negro child	7	Looks bad
4	Looks like you	8	Is a nice color

Questions 1 through 4 concern racial identification—that is, "To what extent do the children 'know their race'?" Questions 5 through 8 concern racial preferences—that is, "To what extent do they 'like their race'?" We must recognize that the methodology of choosing a doll of brown or white complexion as a reflection of one's race may be reasonable. As a reflection of racial preference, however, it may require more careful scrutiny. Moreover, the children varied in their own skin color, so that light-skinned children actually resembled the white more than they did the colored doll. The results of the study are organized around these two questions of racial identity and preference.

Racial Identification

The study showed that the black children had a very keen sense of racial awareness. When asked to give the experimenter the white doll, 94 percent chose the white doll; when asked to give the colored doll, 93 percent chose the colored doll; and when asked to give the negro doll, 72 percent chose the colored doll. The authors cautioned, however, that "awareness of racial differences does not necessarily determine a socially accurate racial self-identification" (p. 604). For example, only 66 percent of the children chose the colored doll as resembling them. It was expected that accurate self-identification would have produced 100 percent choice of the colored doll. But if we look at the choice of the doll that looked like them as a function of the subjects' skin color, the presumed inaccuracy of self-identification is questionable. Of the light children (nearly white), 80 percent chose the white doll and only 20 percent chose the colored doll. But, of the dark children, 81 percent chose the colored doll, whereas only 19 percent chose the white doll. The medium-colored black children chose the colored doll at a rate of 73 percent and the white doll at 26 percent. Therefore, the apparently low average of 66 percent's choosing the colored doll is heavily influenced by the *accurate* choices of light-skinned children, of whom only 20 percent chose the colored doll. These data, then, do not provide clear evidence for erroneous self-identification by black children. The Clarks were most interested, though, in the impact of segregation on black children. So, their question was, "If they know their racial identification, 'do they like it'?"

Racial Preferences

The Clarks found that the majority of black children preferred the white dolls. Sixty-seven percent liked the white doll better; 59 percent said the white doll was a nice doll; and 60 percent said the white doll was a nice color. On the other hand, 59 percent of the subjects said the colored doll looked bad.

In general these data are interpreted as an indication of the negative racial self-concept acquired very early by black children. But, because the white dolls in the study had not only white faces but also blonde hair, the preferences of the children could well represent an aesthetic judgment of hair color, or the children's representation of societal norms, or the expectations they perceived of the experimenters.[3]

North-South Differences

If it were true that segregation negatively affects racial identification and preference, one would expect the results for Southern black children to differ strongly from those for the Northern black children. But the Clarks found that "the children in the northern mixed school situation do not differ from children in Southern segregated schools in either their knowledge of racial differences or their racial identification" (pp. 174–175). However, Northern black children preferred the white doll more often than the southern black children did.

Because the results of this study were used frequently in arguments against racial segregation in schools, the lack of difference between segregated Southern and integrated Northern black children's racial attitudes should have been noted. The Northern children showed *less* race-based preference than Southern children did. If the South and its Jim Crow segregation were so significant, why wouldn't children who grew up in those environments have lower racial preferences? This finding suggests that it is not simply racial segregation, but the role requirements and social structural supports that affect how racial attitudes are internalized and expressed. The recent work of Claude Steele (Steele and Aronson, 1995) offers some insights into how these psychological processes might work.

In 1952 Mary Ellen Goodman wrote a sensitive and passionate book, *Race Awareness in Young Children*, in which she portrayed much of the racial dynamics suggested by the Clarks' study. Through interviews and play situations in an interracial nursery school in New England, she found that forms of ugly and insidious race awareness were widespread by the age of 4. Ms. Goodman observed that "four-year-olds, particularly White ones, show unmistakable signs of the onset of racial bigotry . . . and that Negro children not yet five can sense that they are marked, and grow uneasy" (p. 218).

---

[3]For example, Sara Kiesler (1971) showed that black and white children preferred a purple stick figure to others drawn with regular black and blue ink colors. There have been numerous attempted replications and clarifications of this classic study in recent years. We will review several of them in Chapter 10. See Cross (1992) for an excellent review of this early work on racial self-identification.

The children, of course, responded profoundly to the racial attitudes of adults. But to say simply that the children copied or learned the attitudes of the dominant socializing agent (the family) would be very misleading. Ms. Goodman accurately pointed out that each child *"generates his own attitudes* out of the personal, social, and cultural materials that happen to be his." Children respond to the objects they perceive. Ms. Goodman summarizes the meaning children derive from the facts of skin color differences with the following simple fraction:

<u>White</u>
Brown

Once again we encounter the "color line"—a horizontal line separating black from white, with white always on top.

The lawlessness that was sparked by the Supreme Court decision of 1954 was impressive in its own right. In 1955, Emmet Till, a 14-year-old black boy from Chicago, was kidnapped and lynched, and his body mutilated, in Money, Mississippi. In 1956, the home of Dr. Martin Luther King, Jr., who had led a bus boycott in Montgomery, Alabama, was bombed. That same year, a black woman, Autherine Lucy, was admitted to the all-white University of Alabama, but Ms. Lucy was suspended only four days later following a riot at the school. A white mob prevented the enrollment of black students at a high school in Mansfield, Texas. The Tennessee National Guard was called up to quell mobs demonstrating against school integration; the National Guards dispersed a similar mob in Sturgis, Kentucky. The Birmingham, Alabama, home of the Rev. F. L. Shuttlesworth, an aide to Dr. King, was destroyed by a dynamite bomb. The following year, Shuttlesworth was mobbed while trying to enroll his daughters in a white Birmingham school. Also in 1957, in Nashville, Tennessee, an elementary school with enrollment of 1 black child and 38 white children was destroyed by a dynamite blast. In the same year, Governor Orville Faubus of Arkansas led defiance of a federal court integration order, and nine black children had to be escorted into Little Rock's Central High School by the 101st Airborne Division. And, in 1959, Mac Parker was lynched in Poplarville, Mississippi.

The resurgence of violence perpetrated by whites against blacks signified the formers' resistance to change. Under the threat of these whites' hateful and willful disregard for blacks' rights, and in order to secure their own psychological well-being, blacks in the South, and whites and blacks from the North began to fight back. But their weapons were not guns, but moral authority—and, ultimately, belief in the humanity of us all. The six years following *Brown v. Board of Education* saw the perfection of nonviolent tactics such as the boycott; the establishment of militant, yet nonviolent, groups such as Martin Luther King's Southern Christian Leadership Conference (SCLC); and the slow, painful integration of small numbers of Southern white schools.

On December 1, 1955, Rosa Parks took her place at the front of the "colored" section of a bus in Montgomery, Alabama (Parks, 1992). She was tired from a hard day working in the home of her white employer. The bus was fairly full that day and the front (white) section had no room for yet another white patron. The driver approached Ms. Parks and asked her to more further back into the black section, thereby expanding the white section. She had had enough and answered, No! Thus began the Montgomery bus boycott in 1955, and, with it, the rise of its leader, Dr. Martin Luther King, Jr.

Social scientists, meanwhile, continued to expand their efforts to understand

Before busing! Fifteen-year-old Elizabeth Echford walks to school in Little Rock, Arkansas, in 1957, amid the taunts and insults of onlooking whites. Her path was blocked by the Arkansas National Guard, ordered by Governor Orville Faubus to keep her out of the school. (AP/Wide World Photos)

and contribute to improving race relations. Sociologists were concerned with social stratification and proliferation of social roles. Social psychologists remained chiefly interested in how to change attitudes as a means of improving race relations, and in the prejudiced or authoritarian personality as a source of resistance to these changes.

Social Roles in Mass Society

The social role approach was summarized in a brief paper by Lohman and Reitzes (1952), who rejected the stress on attitudes in race relations. Instead, they suggested that behavior is determined mainly by the social role requirements in a given situation. As society has become larger and more differentiated, the authors argued, more and more roles have developed. This has led to greater impersonalization. Therefore, conflict between individuals has been replaced by conflict between social roles enacted by individuals. These roles are determined primarily by social structures. The authors concluded: "Most situations of racial contact are defined by the collectively defined interests of the individuals concerned and do not merely manifest their private feelings toward other races" (Lohman and Reitzes, 1952, p. 241).

Therefore, desegregation in the South can be seen as having created conflict between public officials in their roles as defenders of the Southern way, and the federal government, considered by many Southerners to represent chiefly Northern interests that would challenge and disrupt the Southern way. The conflict, then, was not between the angry whites, led by men like Faubus, and the handful of black children and their parents and supporters who attempted to integrate the schools. Rather, it was between the social ideals of white supremacy and segregation in the South, and the attack on those ideals by the federal government. Recall that Brady (1955) did not issue his challenge to the black people of the South, but to "the Supreme Court and the Northern world." Throughout the 1950s and early 1960s, that hatred of many Southerners for the white liberal who went south to "cause trouble" was at least as great as Southern animosity toward Southern blacks who organized boycotts or defied Jim Crow conventions.

The social-role-based analysis places social structure at the center of the conflict between groups. Groups are in conflict because they compete over valued resources. These resources are not always material (e.g., money and jobs), in fact, these groups are likely to be more contentious when the resources are not material. It seems the most fractious relations occur when two groups differ not on clear-cut, material, or objective bases, but on subjective or personal issues (e.g., values, beliefs, way of life). The later discussions of prejudice (Chapter 6) and intergroup relations (Chapter 8), and cases of intergroup conflict (Chapter 9) will illustrate this tendency.

Interracial Contact

A second major methodology in the attitudinal approach developed from the contact theory of reducing intergroup conflict. In the 1930s, social psychologists had mainly tried to *describe* racial attitudes. By the 1950s, the focus was on how to *change* them.

In his classic monograph on prejudice, G. W. Allport (1954) summarized the characteristics of interracial contact situations. Allport (1954) concluded that prejudice will be diminished when the two groups: (1) possess equal status in the situation, (2) seek common goals, (3) are cooperatively dependent upon each other, and (4) interact with the positive support of authorities, laws, and custom. The South became a major testing ground for contact theory as school desegregation followed, with all deliberate speed, the 1954 Supreme Court's *Brown* decision.

Numerous investigations of the effects of desegregation on black and white children were conducted during the 1950s. As Allport (1954) suggested, interracial contact needs a supportive social milieu in order to effectively diminish racial hostility. It is not very likely that the coercive, emotional atmosphere of the South was supportive of desegregation attempts. For example, E. Q. Campbell (1958) studied the attitudes of 746 white high school students toward blacks six months before and six months after the school was desegregated. He found a large number of both positive and negative changes. Positive changes seemed associated with greater classroom contact and friendship, and negative changes seemed to be influenced more by prevailing parental attitudes. A similar study by Whitmore (1957) found a diminution in prejudiced attitudes, though this change was shown to be unrelated to classroom contact.

The conditions listed by G. W. Allport for positive attitude change as a result of contact are quite stringent compared to the social scientific evidence upon which *Brown v. Board of Education* was partly based. Hence, even if segregation is abolished because of its potentially strong negative impact on black children, it does not follow that merely implementing racial desegregation will diminish racial hostility.[4] The idea that interracial contact can improve race relations is predicated on two assumptions:

1 Interracial hostilities exist partly because of misperceptions of other people's beliefs, attitudes, opinions, and goals. According to this assumption, greater and deeper interracial contact should diminish these perceived discrepancies and thus foster positive attitudes by removing this basis for interracial hostility.
2 Through interracial contact, differences between races will no longer serve to cause derision or animosity, but rather will provide a basis for interesting and varied relationships.

Both of these assumptions are valid, the later presaging the *diversity* or *multicultural* viewpoint widely espoused today. There has been a tendency to emphasize the first, however. (We will review the literature on the effects of interracial contact in more detail in Chapters 4 and 11.) In examining the effects of interracial contact (i.e., racial integration), it is important to consider both the extent to which racial groups share beliefs and purposes and the extent to which their different ethnic backgrounds are major distinguishing characteristics. The only way groups can come together in order to achieve a common purpose is by uniting around those beliefs and goals they share by mutually respecting those differences (inherited and cultural) that they enjoy.

In summary, the events of the 1950s formed a complex backdrop matching the enormous complexities of race relations in the 1960s. The 1954 *Brown* decision intensified racial conflict in the South, while diverting attention from the teeming ghettos and urban crises festering in the North. "What happens to a raisin in the sun? Does it lie there and fester, or does it explode?" (Hansberry, 1959). It also validated the efforts of social scientists as a major force in race relations.[5] The Southern response to the *Brown v. Board of Education* decision anticipated the rise of black demands for equal rights, and the increasing resistance on the part of whites. It also sounded a warning that mere desegregation would not have totally positive effects.

THE 1960s: CONFRONTATION AND THE RELEVANT SOCIAL SCIENTIST

On February 1, 1960, four students from the all-black Agricultural and Technical College in Greensboro, North Carolina (North Carolina A&T), entered a variety

---

[4]As Pettigrew (1971) pointed out, "mere desegregation" should not be confused with "true integration." The optimum conditions for interracial contact do not apply to conditions of mere desegregation. True integration would exist within a supportive social milieu with cooperative racial dependency. Contact theory, then, has not always been adequately tested by school desegregation.

[5]Some of my social science colleagues are pessimistic about their roles as a major "force" in race relations. Whether they are an effective force may be debatable, but there is no question that expert testimony and fact-finding commissions have played increasingly prominent roles in the government's *public* justifications of its policies.

store, made some purchases, sat down at the lunch counter, and ordered coffee. This is clearly not provocative action—at least, not by contemporary social standards—but, in 1960, it was an invitation to a confrontation. The students were refused service because they were black, and they refused to leave. They sat there until the store closed. In Greensboro, and elsewhere in the South, lunch counter sit-ins were staged and people were arrested for trespassing, disorderly conduct, and disobeying police officers. Whites would taunt and jeer, often pouring mustard, ketchup, or sugar on the protesters as they sat peacefully and quietly waiting for service that never came. The sit-in movement replaced the boycott movement as the weapon of choice and ushered in the civil rights decade of the 1960s.

The problem of race relations in the 1960s was so intertwined with other problems of a huge and complex society that one hardly knows where first to turn in discussing the issues. The Student Nonviolent Coordinating Committee (SNCC), which was organized in 1960, led the sit-movement in the South. In 1961, 13 members of CORE took a *freedom ride*—traveling in an integrated bus from Washington southward. In Montgomery, Alabama, crowds of whites pulled the "freedom riders" from the bus and beat them, then overturned the bus and burned it. Attorney General Robert F. Kennedy was obliged to send 600 U.S. marshals to Montgomery in order to restore law and order.[6]

While civil rights workers pushed hard for integration in the South, Elijah Muhammed led the Nation of Islam, or Black Muslims, on a different path. The Black Muslims followed a philosophy similar to that preached earlier by Marcus Garvey. Through Malcolm X, their most popular minister, they proclaimed the beauty of black people and black culture and the horrors of white oppression. They emphasized black pride and self-help, and counseled racial separation as a desirable and necessary means of collective black advancement.

Because the Muslim philosophy offered clear indictments of white people, the group was branded "militant" and generally discredited in the popular press (black as well as white).[7] It was even linked to the Ku Klux Klan. The Black Muslim philosophy is important because (1) it produced a new brand of black hero, typified by Malcolm X (although he was not widely acclaimed by the black community until after his break with the Muslims and subsequent assassination), and (2) it presented in understandable terms the seminal ideas of a black cultural revolution.

The pressure continued to mount, as sit-ins, teach-ins, and freedom rides raised the stakes, and the occasion of the centennial of the Emancipation Proclamation prompted legislative action. The pressure reached its peak on August 28, 1963, when Dr. King led the March on Washington for jobs and freedom. At the Lincoln Memorial, he spoke of his dream for a colorblind society in which all people were judged solely on the basis of who they were, not on the basis of the group to which they belonged.

In 1963, President John Kennedy presented to Congress a new civil rights bill and challenged the nation by stating:

[6]Note that only a short time ago, the phrase *law and order* had very different connotations than it does today. It is now part of the current political shorthand for white conservatism. At that time (the 1960s), it was blacks who sought to appeal for law and order as a means of securing protection from white violence.

[7]In light of recent events, it is interesting that the Black Muslims were seen as so militant and prone to violence. One report linked favorable attitudes toward the Muslims to participation in the Watts riots of 1965 (Cohen, 1970). By current standards, the Muslim philosophy is not militant at all. The Million Man March led by Minister Farrakhan, has again drawn attention to the Nation of Islam as a source of violent and militant rhetoric and philosophy. Yet there is still little real evidence that the group (or its members) have initiated violent actions against whites.

Malcolm X—"By any means necessary" (1963). (UPI-Corbis/Bettmann)

Martin Luther King, Jr.—"I have a dream" (1963). (Archive Photos)

Surely, in 1963, one hundred years after emancipation, it should not be necessary for any American citizen to demonstrate in the streets for an opportunity to stop at a hotel, or eat at a lunch counter . . . on the same terms as any other American." (cited in Franklin and Moss, 1994, p. 502).

President Kennedy was assassinated in Dallas on November 22, 1963. His legislation was tied up in Congress as he was buried at Arlington National Cemetery and the nation mourned his loss. Lyndon Johnson succeeded Kennedy and, in short order, moved the pending civil rights legislation through Congress.

The Civil Rights Act of 1964

Public Law 88-352, the Civil Rights Act of 1964, was passed by the Eighty-eighth Congress of the United States on July 2, 1964. The act contained 11 titles that, in general and in particular, sought to accomplish the following:

> . . . to enforce the constitutional right to vote, to confer jurisdiction upon district courts of the United States to provide injunctive relief against discrimination in public accommodations, to authorize the Attorney General to institute suits to protect constitutional rights in public facilities and public education, to extend the Commission on Civil Rights, to prevent discrimination in federally assisted programs, to establish a Commission on Equal Opportunity. . . . (King, 1965, p. 333)

This sweeping act sought to put the U.S. government on record as opposing discrimination in all forms, finally and irrevocably, and to create official mechanisms for redress when discrimination occurred. It was not an easy victory for its supporters. In fact, the final vote was 73–27 in the Senate and 289–126 in the House of Representatives for a total of 70 percent of voting members of Congress (King & Quick, 1965).

The Civil Rights Acts, as implemented, relied on 13 statutes, referred to as *titles*. The titles constituted prescriptions for proper conduct and corresponding sanctions for noncompliance. *Title I* reaffirmed the fundamental right to vote for all citizens and made illegal any special "tricks" that would have the effect of denying the vote to anyone who was entitled. *Title II* guaranteed "injunctive relief" for anyone who was denied "full and equal enjoyment of the goods, services, facilities, privileges, advantages, and accommodations of any place of public accommodation . . . without discrimination or segregation on the ground of race, color, religion, or national origin.

Title III reaffirmed the right to equal protection of U.S. laws, and empowered the Attorney General to receive and prosecute cases brought to the court under this statute. *Title IV* provided for the same rights regarding public education. However, there is an important statement in section 401(b) that states "Desegregation means assignment of students to public schools . . . *without regard to their race or religion . . .* but it shall *not* mean, the assignment of students to schools to overcome racial imbalance." Mandatory busing came to represent the establishment of racial targets and goals that appear to violate the purposes of this provision.

Title V not only extended the life of the Commission on Civil Rights, it also expanded the Commission's rules and procedures in order to make it more accountable to the public and better able to investigate suits brought before it. President Kennedy (cited in Amaker, 1988, p. 167) referred to the Commission as "the duly appointed conscience of the government in regard to civil rights."

Title VI mandated nondiscrimination in any federally assisted programs, in these words:

> "No person in the United States shall, on the ground of race, color, or national origin, be excluded from participation in, be denied benefits of, or be subjected to discrimination under any program or activity receiving financial assistance." (sec. 601)

This provision was expanded in practice over the years to include the creation of financial set-asides for minorities, either as direct contractors with the government or as subcontractors or workers. Recent decisions have ruled these practices, in the main, unconstitutional.

Title VII is perhaps the most famous—or infamous—title in the act. It provides for equal employment opportunity, as follows:

> *Sec. 703:*
>   (a) It shall be an unlawful employment practice for an employer—
>   (1) to fail or refuse to hire or to discharge any individual or otherwise discriminate against any individual with respect to his compensation, terms, conditions, or privileges of employment, because of such individual's race, color, religion, sex, or national origin; or
>   (2) to limit, segregate, or classify his employees in any way which would deprive or tend to deprive any individual of employment opportunities or otherwise adversely affect his status as an employee, because of such individual's race, color, religion, sex, or national origin.

Paragraph (b) set terms for employment agencies, paragraph (c) set terms for labor organizations, and paragraph (d) extended these statutes to training programs. Paragraph (e) was the most interesting, because it explicitly permitted classification, admission, or employment of persons on the basis of religion, sex, or national origin when these categories constituted a bona fide occupational qualification reasonably necessary to the normal operation of the enterprise. Moreover, religious schools, colleges, or universities were explicitly allowed to exclusively hire and employ employees of their own religion.

Section 705 created the Equal Employment Opportunity Commission (EEOC) and gave it broad powers to litigate civil discrimination suits brought before it. It is the EEOC that has borne the brunt of expectations for redress—and of excoriation for overstepping its bounds. Affirmative action programs and policies are linked to EEOC enforcement of Title VII. We will return to this again in Chapter 4.

The passage of the Civil Rights Act of 1964 was seen by many as the final triumph of civil rights and liberties over the forces of a biased and self-serving status quo. But, as we all know now—and as many understood almost immediately after passage of the act—the story was a long way from over.

The Revolution

By the end of the decade, the Southern civil rights workers' tactics of confrontation and the Muslim's ideology of black pride fused. Accompanying this fusion had been a shift away from a primarily moral thrust (mainly with the end of securing civil rights) to a thrust for power through economic, political, cultural, and quasi-military means. The 1960s witnessed the continuing escalation of the intensity and pace of blacks' efforts to improve their position in this society. From its initial position advocating integration (under John Lewis), the SNCC moved by stages to the enunciation, in 1965, of black power under the leadership of Stokely Carmichael. As early as 1962, Robert Williams had organized armed defense of blacks against marauding Klansmen in North Carolina. In 1964, the Deacons for Defense and Justice in Louisiana used rifles and rode around protecting the black community from rampaging white racists. In Oakland, California, Huey P. Newton and Bobby Seale organized a similar kind of protective vigilante group in 1966, under the name of the *Black Panther Party.* These quasi-military self-protection movements, together with increasingly violent rhetoric, created an ideological conflict for various politically moderate supporters of civil rights activities.

In the mid-1960s explosions ripped open the powderkeg of the black ghettos in the North. Violence exploded in New York City, Philadelphia, and Rochester in 1964; in Los Angeles and Chicago in 1965; Chicago, Cleveland, Lansing, Omaha, and other urban areas in 1966; Cincinnati, Buffalo, Detroit, and Newark in 1967; and in ghettos in dozens of cities throughout the country after the assassination of Martin Luther King in 1968. Most Northern whites had been accustomed to thinking of race relations as a problem of the South. They were rudely jolted by these demonstrations of trouble in their own backyard. With few exceptions (notably the Harlem riots of 1935 and 1943), previous racial riots had consisted of interracial fighting or of the destruction of black communities by white mobs.

As the black struggle widened, everyday black-white relations became more strained, not only because of direct confrontation in the South or violence in the urban ghettos mainly in the North. Rifts also appeared in the ranks of civil rights organizations. In the 1960s a growing sense of dissatisfaction with the prominent— and, for many, too prominent—role of whites in the civil rights movement culminated in the black power position of "Whites to the rear or out." The popular advice to white sympathizers was "go get your white community straightened out." Although it was seen as a new policy at the time, the issues it embodied were not new.[8]

Under Stokely Carmichael's leadership, the SNCC not only enunciated the black power philosophy, but also advised white members that their role would have to be distinctly secondary. After release of the Kerner Commission's report, which cites white racism as the root cause of the riots, charges of racism spread like wildfire, stinging many whites who considered themselves liberals. By 1969, a group of militants, including leaders such as SNCC Chairman James Foreman issued a "Black Manifesto." The militants spoke before a number of white groups and Jewish congregations, calling for monetary reparations for centuries of racism suffered by African Americans.

But just as the leadership tensions were not new, the issues entailed in the racial integration versus separation dispute themselves were not new. The racial

[8]Historically, the major role in the abolitionist movement was credited to William Lloyd Garrison. In 1831, Garrison put out the first issue of *The Liberator.* David Walker, a black man, issued his *Four Appeals* in 1829, calling for blacks to rise up and overthrow their white oppressors. Later, Frederick Douglass, the black abolitionist, was not even on speaking terms with Garrison, the white abolitionist. The NAACP grew out of the all-black Niagara movement of 1905.

problem in this country has not been confined to slavery, segregation, and "red-neck" bigotry. It has tainted nearly every religion, philosophy, movement, and policy. It seems to many that the events of the 1960s were basically different from earlier events, and that the issues of the 1960s were reconstituted on a new level. In an important sense, this view of the newness of the problem is illusory. This text has taken a basically historical perspective in an attempt to demonstrate those elements of the problem that seem to recur generation after generation.

In the 1960s the rhetoric of race changed to the rhetoric of racism, and charges flew in new directions. It is most important to realize that these new perspectives did not reflect newly created problems but recently discovered ones. From the cauldron of race relations in the 1960s, three critical developments are salient:

1 *The use of confrontation tactics in the early phase of the civil rights movement.* Confrontations continued in the late sixties; however, there was a change in tactics, switching from nonviolence to violence.

2 *A sense of black solidarity.* Although by no means totally agreeing on tactics or even goals, black leaders moved steadily toward demanding black power rather than merely equal rights. This ideology was expressed most forcefully by the Black Panther Party (e.g., in the slogan "Power to the people"), but it was evident also in attempts by a variety of black community organizations to exercise control over research, allocation of funds, schools, and so on.

3 *The rampant proliferation of role conflicts.* The importance of this brand of conflict is amply demonstrated in a statement from an organizer of a (white) ethnic working-class symposium in Washington, D.C., in 1970:

> America is not a melting pot. It is a sizzling cauldron for the ethnic American who feels that he has been politically courted, and legally extorted by both government and private enterprise. The ethnic American is sick of being stereotyped as racist and dullard by phony White liberals, pseudo Black militants, and patronizing bureaucrats . . . checked by the political rhetoric of the illusionary funding for Black-oriented social programs, he turns his anger to race—*when he himself is a victim of class prejudice.* (*The New York Times,* June 17, 1970, p. 41; emphasis added)

To many, the growing militancy and assertiveness of blacks validated the philosophy of assertive self-definition and aggressive tactics of inclusion. Although this model of militant insistence was not truly new, it seemed to ride the wave of lowered resistance created by the civil rights gains of the 1960s, and to reflect a growing self-confidence and rejection of the status quo. The paradigm for progress became the assertive demand for rights, the tactics of confrontation, and the celebration of the validity and beauty of one's racial, ethnic, cultural, or gender experience.

This insistence also changed the context of race relations in another way. Generally, whites had acknowledged, in spite of many die-hard pockets of resistance, the legitimacy of equal rights under the law. However, as the demands increased in decibels, their legitimacy began to be questioned by some who had been equal rights supporters. Moreover, some whites began to feel somewhat threatened in that they could no longer determine either the agenda for progress or its timetable. Many of these whites, longtime "friends" of the movement, were asked to step to the rear, and the seeds of an estrangement between white and black activists were sown. The liberalism of whites in the 1960s began to recede, and the conservative reaction gained momentum. The moral correctness granted to the civil rights movement was replaced by a moral legitimacy of the new status quo that rested on the "promise," if not the reality, of equal rights for individuals regardless of race, gender, religion, or national origin.

Reporting on the Status of the United States

One way in which the government has tried to inform its political policies in through large-scale investigations of employment, education, and domestic violence—racial problems of major consequence—by specially appointed social science commissions.

Social and behavioral scientists had been prominent in the analysis of social problems and the formulation of public policy since the early studies of intelligence (cf. Guthrie, 1976) and immigration (Samelson, 1978), the release of Myrdal's *The American Dilemma*, and the government's reliance on social science in reaching the *Brown* decision. In the 1960s, major reports on social issues emanated from the government. They addressed concerns with social welfare (the Moynihan report), education (the Coleman report), and urban violence (the Kerner report). It is 30 years later, but concerns regarding social policy and its effects on welfare, education, and violence remain central to our society—notwithstanding our tendency to look back on history and deem it "old stuff." For example, many believe that the premises of the 1960s are no longer applicable and that we ought to move on to contemporary society. But the problems that were front and center in the 1960s are the same problems we grapple with today. Thirty years is not a long time in any human society, including the United States. The U.S. Congress and the President placed welfare reform on the political agenda in 1995. Concerns with families and children were voiced in the 1960s. These problems have not gone away, and solutions remain elusive (cf. Edelman, 1987, 1992). Riots do not happen as frequently in the 1990s as they did in the 1960s or 1940s, but they do happen. More insidiously, a rise in physical assaults on individuals based on their race, ethnicity, sexual orientation, even age, indicates a level of hate that is criminal. The past is prologue, even the recent past. Accordingly, a review of the major reports on social issues in the 1960s will be useful to our later discussion.

The Moynihan Report
In March 1965, then Assistant Secretary of Labor Daniel Patrick Moynihan (now the Democratic senator from New York) issued a report from the Office of Policy Planning and Research. The purpose of the report, which was entitled *The Negro Family: The Case for National Action*,[9] was expressed in these statements:

> It has to be said that there is a considerably body of evidence to support the conclusion that Negro social structure, in particular the Negro family, battered and harassed by discrimination, injustice, and uprooting, is in the deepest trouble. While many young Negroes are moving ahead to unprecedented levels of achievement, many more are falling further and further behind. . . . At the heart of the deterioration of the fabric of Negro society is the deterioration of the Negro family. . . . It is the fundamental source of the weakness of the Negro community at the present time. . . . A national effort toward the problems of Negro Americans must be directed toward the question of family structure. . . . Such a national effort could be stated thus:

[9]For a full analysis of the contents and history of this report, see Rainwater and Yancey, *The Moynihan Report and the Politics of Controversy* (1967).

> The policy of the United States is to bring the Negro American to full and equal sharing in the responsibilities and rewards of citizenship. To this end, the programs of the Federal government bearing on this objective shall be designed to have the effect directly or indirectly of enhancing the stability and resources of the Negro American family. (Moynihan, 1965, pp. 4–48)

With respect to the black family, Moynihan makes these points:

1   The family structure of lower-class blacks is highly unstable, and in many urban centers it is approaching complete breakdown. The breakdown of the black family is to be contrasted, according to Moynihan, with the stability of the white family. The statistics from the census of 1960 showed that 22.9 percent of urban nonwhite U.S. women, compared to 7.0 percent of urban white U.S. women, had absent husbands or were divorced.
2   Nearly one-quarter of urban black marriages are dissolved. Moynihan buttresses this data with the statistic that 26 percent of female blacks, compared to 10 percent of female whites, who have ever been married are either divorced, separated, or have husbands absent.
3   Nearly one-quarter of Black births are now illegitimate (c. 1965). The report also points out that reported illegitimacy rates have been increasing for all races since the consensus of 1940. Also noted is that, by 1963, the increase had produced a rate of only 3.1 percent among whites, whereas it had produced a rate of 23.6 percent among blacks.
4   In 1965, almost one-quarter of black families were headed by females. This figure is contrasted with the approximately 1 in 16 white families headed by females.
5   The breakdown of the black family had led to a startling increase in welfare dependency. The report points out that a majority of black children receive public assistance under the Aid to Families with Dependent Children (AFDC) program at some point in their childhood. In 1965, the families of 14 percent of black children were receiving welfare, compared to the families of only 2 percent of white children.

The suggested causes of the breakdown of the black family were (1) slavery's systematic destruction of family bonds, recognizing only maternal control for the young; (2) the failure of Reconstruction, closely followed by the institution of Jim Crow laws and customs that robbed the black man of his just place at the head of the family; (3) urbanization, which trapped most blacks in urban ghettos while whites fled to suburbs; (4) the harsh and continuing impact of unemployment and poverty; (5) the wage system, which makes no provision for the size of a person's family (and thereby effectively penalizes blacks, who have, on the average, larger families); and (6) the demographics of dramatic population growth, with a trend toward larger black families and smaller white families.

The report goes on to suggest that the consequence of this breakdown in black family structure is a "tangle of pathology" that has arisen because:

> The Negro community has been forced into a matriarchal structure which, because it is so out of line with the rest of the American society, seriously retards the progress of the group as a whole, and imposes a crushing burden on the Negro male, and in consequence, a great many Negro women as well. . . . Ours is a society which presumes male leadership in private and public affairs. The arrangements of society facilitate such lead-

ership and reward. A subculture, such as that of the Negro American, in which this is not the pattern, is placed at a distinct disadvantage. (p. 29)

The Moynihan report set off a firestorm of reactions and protests because it seemed to lay blame on the "pathology" of black families by suggesting it was the matriarchal family structure that was at fault and that black men were unable to fulfill their roles as breadwinners. His reading of history was not very sophisticated, as detailed work by scholars such as Gutman (1976) showed. Moreover, he underestimated more-general changes in the family in U.S. society as a whole—changes evidenced by soaring divorce rates and a rapid increase in unwed pregnancies among whites. The report explicitly accepted the dominance of men and failed to recognize the pathologies of patriarchy, as well as the corresponding potential for family violence and abuse in this context.

That there was instability in lower-class families in general, and black families in particular, was not the focus of the disputes. What aroused emotions was the attribution of cause and effect. Moynihan's report suggests that the instability of lower-class black families is the *cause* of black problems. Congruent with this analysis, the report advised the federal government to adopt policies designed to enhance the stability of the black family. If the instability of the black family was, in part, an effect of racist discrimination, bias, and oppression (as Moynihan also argued), one might do better to advise the federal government to deal directly with this malady—that is, to eliminate all forms of racism from this society. The report appears to "blame the victim" by focusing on the "tangle of pathology" (Ryan, 1967).

The fact that Moynihan made sweeping conclusions based on rather simple analyses suggests that perhaps he sought to persuade the federal government to adopt a unified and binding commitment to right the wrongs suffered by black Americans. He might also have thought that the best way to appeal to the paternalistic and racially biased thinking of the government was through a report that fostered the notion of gross black pathology and misfortune and stressed the need for federal guidance and intervention. Put another way, the report could be seen as a white liberal politician's attempt to use the language and methods of social scientific analysis in order to shake white moderate politicians into commitment to national action.

Because Moynihan made no specific proposals or recommendations for action, the major impact of his report was to create controversy concerning his diagnosis. Many social scientists rejected the idea that his analysis was uniquely applicable to black Americans, because of more-general social trends that were becoming apparent,[10] as noted earlier. Nevertheless, the publicity and authority of an official government report by a lawyer-politician under the aegis of social scientists had an enormous impact on how Americans thought about race relations.

Until the mid-1960s almost all of the federal government's involvement in civil rights was in response to pressures from blacks or to national crises. The Moynihan report proposed that the federal government take the lead in identifying and dealing with the problems on a national scale. It was this goal, apparently, that guided the writing of the report. However, such an approach can have both positive and negative consequences. Wise and effective federal policies are plainly good in their effects, just an unwise and ineffective ones are plainly bad. However, it is some-

---

[10]Charles Murray (personal communication) notes that the rate of births to unwed mothers among white teenage women is now higher than the rate for blacks, as singled out by Moynihan in 1965.

times difficult to predict which are which when the programs are begun. With several decades of data, there is still no consensus on how a policy can be accurately adjudged wise at its inception.

Perhaps the most important aspect of the Moynihan report was its claim that the poor, in general, represent a substratum within the lower-class stratum of the larger society. It further suggests that people who fall within that economic substratum exhibit a unique set of traits that, collectively, identify a "culture of poverty." The culture of poverty is seen as defective and unhealthy. The problem for black Americans, according to the report, is an overrepresentation in this cultural category.

The general acceptance of this point of view has led many social scientists to argue that black culture is no more than another lower-class culture. Because the problem for the national government is poverty, this focus on the poorest people in the black community has led to the general impression that most black people are products of broken homes, grow up hating themselves, and, early on, learn the ways of crime and immorality. The black child, according to this stereotype, loses motivation to work and just waits until he or she is old enough to get on welfare. This composite picture from several sources (not only the Moynihan report; see also Kenneth Clark [1965], *Dark Ghetto*; Claude Brown [1965], *Manchild in the Promised Land*; and Nathan McCall [1994], *Makes Me Wanna Holler*) portrays the negative characteristics of poor black Americans.

The "defective culture" view of black Americans has dominated social science literature. However, although adaptations to an impoverished socioeconomic condition undoubtedly affect the behavioral and psychological responses of black Americans, this explanation is by no means sufficient to capture all of the ramifications of the black experience in the United States. Research aimed directly at the question of black versus lower-class subcultural characteristics produces equivocal results. For example, investigating a national sample for social-class and race-related differences in value orientation, Rokeach and Parker (1970) suggest that "value differences do distinguish the rich from the poor, but not Negroes from Whites" (p. 97). Johnson and Sanday (1971) interviewed lower-class people in Pittsburgh and concluded: "The data indicate that for the sample studied, there are two subcultures—one Black and one White" (p. 128).

The issue here is that proper programs designed to promote constructive social change must be based on proper understanding of subcultural influences. It is not enough for a politician or an administrator to take a set of census statistics and, on the basis of fairly simple-minded analyses, propose national actions or policies that can affect the lives of millions of people. The community responses of control, participation, and celebration of positive aspects of their experiences are, in part, a reaction to the frequently ill-informed, paternalistic effort of federal organizations.

The Coleman Report

Section 402 of the Civil Rights Act of 1964 requested the U.S. commissioner of education to conduct a survey investigating the lack of equal opportunities for individuals by reason of race, color, religion, gender or national origin in public educational institutions at all levels in the United States. This survey was conducted in late 1965 under the leadership of the sociologist James S. Coleman of Johns Hopkins University. The Coleman report was published by the government in 1966 under the title *Equality of Educational Opportunity*. The purpose of the survey was to determine answers to four questions:

1   To what extent are public schools racially and ethnically segregated?
2   Do schools offer equal educational opportunities in terms of criteria such as quality of buildings and teacher-student ratio?
3   As measured by standardized achievement tests, how much do students learn?
4. How do students' levels of achievement and the kinds of schools they attend relate to one another?

The sketchy social science–based support for *Brown v. Board of Education* was concerned mainly with the psychological effects of segregated schools. But why and how does segregated schooling produce the gross inequalities that are observed? The Coleman report gives some of the answers.

Public school segregation. Segregation is a fact of life in public schools, regardless of the region of the country under consideration. Of all racial groups, white children are obviously the most segregated. In 1966 almost 80 percent of white elementary and high school students attended schools that were from 90 to 100 percent white. Segregation, like prejudice, works both ways. At the same time, 65 percent of all black elementary and high school students attended schools that were between 90 and 100 percent black.

Segregation of teachers showed the same pattern, though not quite so strongly. The average black elementary school student attended a school in which 65 percent of the teachers were black; the average white elementary school student attended a school in which 97 percent of the teachers were white. Again, the pattern of segregation among teachers was most pronounced in the South. Nearly 20 years after the 1954 Supreme Court's Brown decision, the ruling still had had little impact on the actual racial composition of public schools in the United States. Now, over 40 years later, this is still true.

Segregated schools are tantamount to effecting differences in training of teachers, quality of facilities, and the nature and character of the student body on the basis of race. Let us consider how these education factors differ as a function of the racial composition of the school.

The schools and their characteristics. Coleman's data showed considerable variation by race and region; still, some generalizations are possible. For example, facilities that seem related to high academic achievement were underrepresented in predominantly black schools. Such schools had fewer science and language laboratories, fewer library books per pupil, and fewer textbooks. Although these differences prevailed in general across the country, specific regions showed even greater variation. In the metropolitan Far West, 95 percent of black and 80 percent of white high school students attended schools with language laboratories, compared with only 48 and 72 percent, respectively, in the metropolitan South. Predominantly black schools were more frequently located in buildings over 40 years old, and less frequently in ones under 20 years old. Furthermore, black students, particularly in the South, were less likely to attend schools that were regionally accredited, that conducted extensive intelligence testing, or that had well-developed extracurricular programs.

As for instruction, the teachers of black children tended to be slightly less capable, according to such criteria as (1) their scores on verbal tests, (2) whether or not they majored in an academic subject, (3) whether or not their parents attended college, and (4) the highest degree they earned. The differences, however, were very small. And, on several criteria, the teachers of black children scored higher than did the teachers of white children. On the basis of the questions asked by Coleman's team, it seems unlikely that differences in teacher quality and training were ultimately responsible for the differences in quality of education observed between black and white children.

Coleman's team also found that the (white) classmates of white children more frequently had encyclopedias in their homes, had mothers who were high-school graduates, were from small families, were enrolled in college preparatory programs, and had taken more courses in English, foreign languages, and science. These data suggest that white children, more than black children, tend to have classmates who came from environments that fostered achievement in school settings.

So far, we have briefly summarized some of the observations made in the Coleman report that suggest that black children received inferior education compared to the education received by whites. This conclusion describes the education of black children today. Now we will look at the Coleman's findings about student achievement.

Achievement in the public schools. Coleman, in his report, assumes that a main function of schools is to teach children the skills that will be needed in order to successfully compete in schools and in society as constituted and further assumes that standard achievement tests accurately measure a school's success in imparting these skills. On this basis, the report tries to correlate differential achievement with the racial composition of the schools. The report acknowledges that the standard achievement tests upon which these summary data are based are by no means free of cultural bias, but are specifically culture-bound. As does the Moynihan Report—and every other report on U.S. racial relations—the Coleman report takes the characteristics of the dominant and dominating white majority as the yardstick by which to measure the black minority.

Not surprisingly, Coleman found that black Americans scored consistently lower on achievement tests than did whites and that these deficiencies increased as the black child moved through elementary and secondary school. Evidently, whatever the factors producing a difference between black and white children when they enter the first grade, the educational process in public schools increases that disparity. This generalization had a regional qualifier. The differences between black and white first-graders were greatest in the South, and the race-based disparities in the South increased even more rapidly than elsewhere as the children progressed through school. It should be noted also that Southern children scored generally lower than did Northern children, without regard to race.

Relation of achievement to school characteristics. According to the Coleman report, the quality of the facilities, the teachers, and the student body affects black children more than it does white children. Coleman found one of the most important achievement criteria to be the educational background and aspirations of other students. Black students were shown to be more sensitive to this variable. This finding led Coleman (1966, p. 22) to state:

> If a White pupil from a home that is strongly and effectively supportive of education is put in a school where most pupils do not come from such homes, his achievement will be little different than if he were in a school composed of others like himself. But, if a mi-

nority pupil from a home without such educational strength is put with schoolmates with strong educational backgrounds, his achievement is likely to increase. (Coleman, 1966, p. 22)

The report went on to observe that the main difference in school environments of black children and of white children involved the composition of the student bodies and that this composition strongly affects the achievement of black and other minority people. It follows that busing black children to predominantly white schools would raise the children's achievement levels and that busing white children to predominantly black schools would not substantially affect their achievement levels. Therefore, despite its use of considerably more skillful experimental design, data collection, and data analysis than was used in the Moynihan report, the Coleman report ignited a conflagration of opinion and controversy in its turn.

The main thrust of the Coleman report was to show that a majority of public schools were racially and ethnically segregated, and that resultant educational opportunities were grossly unequal. To support its conclusion that public school integration is the best way to insure equality of educational opportunity, the report tried to show that black children in integrated schools achieve more than do black children in segregated schools. The major evidence for this conclusion, however, came not from the report itself, but from the careful analysis of the Coleman data by the U.S. Commission on Civil Rights in 1967.

Relation of integration to achievement. Testing black children in integrated schools indicated minute positive effects of integration. Support for the report's contention that black students do better in integrated schools was underscored by observing that, in every case except one, black students who had been in classes where more than 50 percent of students were white had higher average test scores. We should note, however, that in only two cases did the average score of black children who had attended such classes exceed the average score for those black children who had had no white classmates. This suggests that any positive effect of integration on black students' achievement occurs only if the classes are more than one-half white.

At a time when the proportion of black children in public schools has exceeded 50 percent in some cities (e.g., in Washington, D. C., it is now over 90 percent), it seems highly unlikely that racial integration of public schools will result in most blacks being mixed into classes with a majority of white children. Furthermore, it is highly unlikely that masses of urban blacks can, or should be bused to suburban schools in order to attain the degree of integration recommended by Coleman.[11]

Both the 1966 Coleman report and the 1962 report by the U.S. Commission on Civil Disorders (entitled *Racial Isolation in the Public Schools*) strongly urged the federal government to bring about school integration. The arguments behind these recommendations were straightforward:

1   A student's achievement in school is significantly determined by the social class of his or her fellow students.

---

[11]Pettigrew (1969) offered the concept of a "metropolitan educational park" as a possible solution to racial imbalance in urban-suburban public schools. This plan would create schools districts on the borders of suburban and central city communities. The districts would be pie-shaped, radiating toward the suburbs from a central point in urban centers. This is by far the most reasonable proposal for integration in public schools advanced to date. However, it seems rather unlikely that people in suburban communities will see any advantage in sharing a school district with inner-city black residents.

2 A student's achievement in school is also significantly determined by his or her own social class.
3 The social class of black children in predominantly black schools is considerably lower than the social class of all children in predominantly white schools.
4 Black children in predominantly white schools achieve more than black children in racially mixed or in predominantly black schools achieve.
5 Achievement levels for white children in all-white schools are no higher than those of black children in predominantly white schools.

In contrast to the reception accorded *Brown v. Board of Education*, which had been hailed with a single voice by the black community, the responses to these recommendations of integration were, at best, ambivalent—and sometimes, antagonistic. Black leaders were beginning to cut the shackles of a "We've got to be like *them*" philosophy and were formulating the goals for an educational system that is relevant to black children living in a predominantly white society.

In addition to the issues of community control of schools and to providing a relevant education for black children, educators and researchers were concerned with raising the achievement levels of those black children confined to ghettos and unsatisfactory school situations. Title I of the Elementary and Secondary Education Act of 1965 provided massive funds to improve the educational opportunities within segregated schools. Generally labeled "compensatory education of the culturally deprived," these programs were based partly on the liberal notion that schools should rectify the damage wreaked by socioeconomic inequities. They were also seen as an alternative to the forced desegregation of the public schools. The failure of these programs to produce marked changes in achievement has fed racist arguments concerning racial differences in intelligence and has also pressured the federal government to push harder for integration.

In 1968 another government report looked at a different aspect of the problem of the color line—violence. The National Advisory Commission on Civil Disorders investigated the wave of riots occurring in the summer of 1967. In its report it concluded: "White racism is essentially responsible for the explosive mixture which has been accumulating in our cities since the end of World War II" (National Advisory Commission on Civil Disorders, 1968, p. 203).

The Kerner Report
In 1964 the fuse to the explosive issues of race relations burned down in the North. A white New York City policeman fired a shot, and a black boy lay dead in the street. Four years later, when the cycle of shootings, burning, and looting finally stopped, race relations were more tense and critical than at any other time in this century. In the midst of this period, President Lyndon Johnson established the National Advisory Commission on Civil Disorders, commonly called the "Kerner Commission." In welcoming the commission in the summer of 1967, Johnson said that the American people "are baffled and dismayed by the wholesale looting and violence that has occurred. . . . " It was a rather curious statement. For 350 years, the white-black equation had described American race relations. But, in 1967, President Johnson wanted to know what had happened, and why, and what could be done to prevent it from happening again and again! As had the commissions before it (cf. Chicago Commission on Race Relations (1922). *The Negro in Chicago: A Study of Race Relations and a Race Riot.* Chicago: University of Chicago Press; The Mayor's Commission on Conditions in Harlem (1935). The Negro in Harlem: A Report on Social

and Economic Conditions Responsible for the Outbreak of March 19, 1935. In A. M. Platt (Ed.) (1971) *The Politics of Riot Commissions (pp. 165–182)*. New York: Collier Books; Governor's Commission on the Los Angeles Riots (1965) *Violence in the city—An End or a Beginning?* Los Angeles: Office of the Governor.), the Kerner commission documented the causes of the most recent, blatant manifestation of the problem.

Population redistribution. The first cause of racial unrest cited by the Kerner report was the gross shift in the black population of the United States. In 1910, 91 percent of black Americans lived in the South; 27 percent lived in cities. By 1963, only 55 percent of black Americans lived in the South; 69 percent lived in cities. The problem, the report observed, "has shifted from a Southern rural locus to primarily a Northern urban locus." Between 1900 and 1920, the annual average out-migration of Southern blacks was about 45,000. During the 1920s, after the peak lynching years of 1918–1919, out-migration of blacks increased to 75,000 per year. Slowing down during the great depression, out-migration soared from 1940 on, as the hope of jobs and greater equality in the North and in the West attracted millions of Southern blacks.

In addition to a changing geographical distribution, the black population had risen in both absolute and relative numbers. This increase was due to a decreasing death rate and a rising fertility rate among blacks and other minorities. In 1900, the annual death rate per 1,000 nonwhite Americans was 25; for white Americans it was only 17. However, by 1965 the death rates per 1,000 were 9.6 and 9.4, respectively.[12] The similarity of death rates is even more striking in view of the nearly 2 to 1 black lead in mortality within the first year (40.4 deaths per 1,000 live births for blacks versus 21.5 deaths per 1,000 for whites).

Fertility rates, on the other hand, remained considerably higher for black American women than for white American. (This had been the case since 1900.) In 1965, there were 133.0 births per 1,000 black women 15 to 44 years of age, but only 91.4 births per 1,000 for white women of the same age range. As a consequence, the average age of black Americans was 21.2, whereas the average age of white Americans was 29.1.

We can also note that large numbers of young black Americans were still segregated into small communities, albeit in urban areas. A study by Taeuber and Taeuber (1965) computed a segregation index based on the percentage of blacks who have had to move from their block in order to desegregate the area. The average segregation index in metropolitan areas was 86.2; in only 8 cities was the score below 70; in 50 cities it was above 90. But, as we have noted, segregation in itself does not necessarily harm those who are segregated.[13] We saw, for example, that the most segregated schoolchildren were whites. Certainly most whites, and especially well-to-do ones, live in segregated neighborhoods—segregated according to class even more than to race. The issue again breaks down to basic economic considerations.

Black Americans typically have lower incomes, less well paying jobs, and higher likelihood of unemployment. Furthermore, a higher percentage of black

---

[12]These figures, which include all ethnic minorities, are probably quite conservative when specifically comparing blacks with whites. The trends observed, however, should not be substantially affected.

[13]More recent analyses of racial segregation by Massey and Denton (1993) offer compelling statistics to support the claims that urban ghettos were deliberately constructed by whites, racial discrimination in housing markets persists at high levels, residential segregation on the basis of skin color continues, and that a spiraling in the decay of black neighborhoods is the result of these circumstances.

women are in the labor force. These inequalities are greatest in central cities. In 1968, the Kerner report and large numbers of Americans, black and white, attributed these inequalities to white racism. Racial inequalities persist. Are they still attributed to white racism? We will explore this issue in detail in Part 3.

SUMMARY

From 1954, when social scientists were recognized by the U.S. Supreme Court as a "modern authority," their roles in influencing—indeed, in formulating—government policy have grown. Society has become more complex, and the government's growing involvement in the control of society has given it a greater role in the resolution of race problems. To the extent that government policy is influenced by socio-scientific research, we must pay close attention to that research as we attempt to analyze race prejudice and racism.

We have taken an historical perspective on race relations because the issues that currently garner major attention are complexly related to one another and to issues of the past. The development of these complex interrelations has occurred over nearly 400 years, from the beginning of the slave trade in the colonies to the present. In attempting to unravel the thread of race relations, we need to recognize the constituent strands.

In the 1960s the country came face to face with the moral bankruptcy of racial and gender discrimination, and rejected it as a matter of cultural self-definition. The prescriptions growing out of government reports, though, focused on the pathology of the victims, the need to educate minorities at the side of whites, and the sweeping pathology of white racism. All of these issues and points of view were controversial, and the problems they attempted to solve were recalcitrant subjects. We turn now to the first post–civil rights decade, to see how events unfolded. As we shall see, the legacy of the 1960s is still being written.

4

The Problem II—
Change and Continuity
in the 1970s

───────── ❖ ─────────

INTRODUCTION

The 1970s arrived on the heels of a good news–bad news decade. The sixties saw a tangible measure of success in the civil rights movement with the passage of the Civil Rights Act of 1964, which proclaimed that racial discrimination was illegal, and of the Voting Rights Act of 1965, which bellowed that the fundamental right of citizenship, the right to vote, could not be abridged, compromised, or otherwise violated on the basis of race. The federal government, the Congress, and thousands of citizens black and white alike, proclaimed the immorality of prejudice and racism—whether effected by intention, by deed, or by happenstance. White racism was sniffed out and identified by the Kerner Commission, and steps were taken to eradicate it.

77

Yet, notwithstanding this good news, there were some ominous harbingers of malaise. The engineers of the civil rights victories—John and Bobby Kennedy and Martin Luther King, Jr.—were all dead, all killed by assassins' bullets. The architect of the new order, Lyndon Johnson, was drummed out of office because of another moral imperative, the invalidity of an indefensible war. Malcolm X, hailed by many as a hate monger and divisive force, was also assassinated, but his legacy was only beginning to be realized. Black became beautiful, and black people had a growing sense that their psychological and cultural validity could not be established by legislative vote. Malcolm X perhaps captured the sentiment best when he asserted that "You could not have *Civil* rights until you claim *Human* rights." (cited in Gates, 1991).

Efforts to claim human rights began with a proclamation of self-worth: Black is beautiful. African hairstyles, dress, and names signaled this robust cultural transformation. Maulana Ron Karenga invented a ritual celebration, Kwanzaa, that linked this newfound pride to blacks' African origins while acknowledging their unique experience in this nation. It provided a cultural alternative that both signaled the emergent discrepancy between the racial integration and melting pot togetherness many envisioned and the self-help, self-love approach that suggested a different course of action.

Much of the talk of revolution was surely braggadocio and did not warrant the FBI's paranoid reaction. But the sight of Huey Newton, minister of defense of the Black Panther Party, sitting on his revolutionary throne, rifle at his side in guerrilla dress brought a sense of efficacy and power to many black Americans. It may well have also brought fear to those whites who, looking through a veil of guilt, saw reflected there their own vulnerability. Whatever the visions meant, they were new, vibrant, and vigorous, and they belonged primarily to the young.

The Black Panther party—Bobby Seale and Huey Newton, protectors of the people. (AP/Wide World Photos)

Afro-American studies emerged as the legitimating intellectual and educational force for the new movement. It was a time of migration from south to north of young black Americans, of the opening up of college curricula as a result of the civil rights gains, and the broad-based student activism of the late 1960s. These factors, in tandem with many blacks' massive distrust of educational institutions—given their past use as vehicles for transporting inequality—conspired to make the push for courses on African Americans (and, ultimately, programs and departments of Afro-American studies) a separate movement at the close of the 1960s. Afro-American studies became a key element in the institutionalization of cultural diversity.

Affirmative action was another legacy of the 1960s. The Civil Rights Act proclaimed equal treatment before the law and specified legal penalties for failure to adhere to its dictates. Yet Johnson knew that

> You do not take a person who, for years, has been hobbled by chains and liberate him, bring him up to the starting line of a race and then say, "you are free to compete with all the others," and still justly believe that you have been completely fair. (cf. Franklin and Starr, 1967, p. 226).

He made this observation during the commencement address he gave at Howard University in 1965.

In the remainder of this chapter, we will look in more detail at these dynamic developments and how they have affected race relations. We will first look at the establishment of Afro-American Studies programs and the impact of these developments on campus life, racial attitudes, and the structure of academic activities. We will next review the development of affirmative action as a concept, a policy, and a program. We will consider what the consequences, real or imagined, of affirmative action measures might be for intergroup relations and individual psychological adaptations. We will next consider a major complication in the story line on race, the factor of economics. Finally, we will review the new theoretical and empirical developments in social psychology that have a bearing on race relations. What were we learning about attitudes and behaviors in the 1970s that might provide some guidance to what we might expect to be the course of relations in the subsequent decades?

*A*FRO-AMERICAN STUDIES: NEW IDENTITIES

The creation of Afro-American studies programs or departments followed dramatically different courses across the colleges and universities of the United States. The late Nathan Huggins (1985) chronicled the rise of black studies programs in a report commissioned by the Ford Foundation. He identified three important trends that defined the context in which Afro-American studies came into being.

First, rapid growth of colleges over the decade 1955–1965 saw a total of 3 million students enrolled in college, more than the total number of students enrolled during the previous three centuries of U.S. higher education (Huggins, 1985). This rapid expansion of college enrollment included a substantial increase in black students in Northern colleges, accompanying the black northward migration of the 1940s and 1950s. In 1947, blacks constituted 6 percent of the total college enrollment in this country. By 1971, they constituted 8.6 percent, and by 1976, 10.8 percent.

Prior to the mid-1960s, those black students who attended predominantly white campuses did so in small numbers, with few expectations. They were not treated specially, and they were likely to be called upon to serve as racial standard-bearers, while simultaneously being ignored. Expecting no special treatment—and, sometimes, expecting to be treated less well than others were, they assumed that they had to be better than similarly situated whites in order to be admitted. Overcoming prejudice, disadvantage, and racism was a given for black students.

Second, colleges accepted, as a fundamental approach, that they had a moral role to play in the expansion of social justice for all of the nation's citizens. The civil rights movement had a moral force that caught hold in educational institutions. More money was made available for scholarships, recruiting was a major enterprise, and many universities hired full-time recruiters of black students. These efforts were intended to provide blacks with greater opportunities to attend college, but they did not take into account the transformed expectations of a generation who believed that the legacy of slavery, oppression, and racism had roots in institutions of higher learning. No longer was the opportunity to learn and gain knowledge enough. The ivory tower was no longer universally revered—in fact, it was often scorned. *Relevance* became the measure of worth to many of these youth. Relevance to truth, justice, and lived experience was the metric of the day. While the black student leaders may have believed in this mission to an ever-increasing extent, the vital meaning it took on went well beyond the social relevance they had first envisioned.

Third, the black student movement could be seen as the extension of the SNCC to the campus. The SNCC had been prominent in the civil rights movement. Black students, and numerous white student allies, called for reform. Distrust was the order of the day, and the character of the protest changed from moral petitions for transformation, to aggressive demands for reform. Sit-ins became "takeovers." Petitions became "demands," and, in their most extreme form, they were "nonnegotiable." The earlier silence of the stigmatized individuals or "token" minority students gave rise to the assertiveness and aggressiveness of the critical mass of black students. What isolated individuals had endured silently now became a cause for outrage in the context of a critical mass of like-minded folk. *Militance* became a common term to describe student activism. In 1969, its ramifications were blasted across the consciousness of the nation by *Newsweek* (May 5, 1969) through a cover photograph of three black students at Cornell University holding shotguns at the ready, symbols of this militancy and a changing mood on campuses.

It is against this backdrop that black studies programs were born. Black students had evolved from pawns to power brokers, from an ignored or tolerated presence to a force that had to be reckoned with. It is interesting to make note of the important social psychological finding that may suggest a divergence between black and white students with regard to this activism experience. Rotter (1966) developed the *locus-of-control scale* that indicates the extent to which a person feels that the causes of important experiences in his or her life are under his or her control and the extent to which they are determined by forces in the environment. For example, the belief that "Becoming a success is a matter of hard work, luck has little or nothing to do with it," indicates one has an *internal locus of control*. The belief that "Getting a job depends on mainly being in the right place at the right time," indicates one has an *external locus of control*. Research with this instrument has shown that people with an internal locus of control are more likely to take risks, have higher occupational and educational aspirations, are more goal-oriented. They also formulate plans to a greater degree, participate more in social action, and are more

Let's make a deal! Edward Whitfield, Chair of the Afro-American Society at Cornell University, signs agreement with university officials Steven Muller (Vice President) and W. Keith Kennedy (Vice Provost, partially hidden) that approves all of the black students' demands delivered while occupying the student center at gun-point. The agreement was made April 20, 1969. (UPI-Corbis/Bettmann)

resistant to attempts at persuasion and influence. At least, this is what studies with white students had shown.

Gurin, Gurin, Lao, and Beattie (1969) administered the Rotter scale, along with several other measurement items, to black undergraduates. In addition, the researchers assessed the students' overall level of activism on campus and in the community. Using factor analysis, Gurin et al. found that the simple idea that events were determined either by oneself or by factors external to the self did not adequately represent the complex determinants of behavior. Rather, they found a complex set of relationships represented by six separate factors, as shown in Table 4.1. The first two both reflected a belief in control over events, but differed in terms of *whose* success or failure was at issue. Factor I was labeled the *control ideology* and referred to "people in general"—for example, "No matter how hard you try, some people just don't like you." By contrast, Factor II always referred to the respondent in the first person—for example, "What happens to me is my own doing." Because these are independent factors, one can simultaneously accept the cultural belief in the ideology of control, and recognize that one does not have such control in one's personal life because of prejudice and discrimination. The separation of control into two separate factors is not usually obtained when white subjects are used. This finding suggests that there may be a duality to black experience that is not mirrored in the experience of whites.

TABLE 4.1 DYNAMICS OF CONTROL AMONG AFRICAN AMERICANS

Factor Structure	*Highest Loaded Items*
Factor I: Control ideology	Capable people who fail to become leaders have not taken advantage of their opportunities.
Factor II: Personal control	Trusting to fate has never turned out as well for me as making a decision to take a definite course of action has.
Factor III: Individual versus collective action	*Individual action:* The best way to handle problems of discrimination is for each individual Negro to make sure he or she gets the best training possible for the area in which he or she wants to succeed. *Collective action:* Only if Negroes pull together in civil rights groups and activities can anything really be done about discrimination.
Factor IV: Discrimination modifiability	People may be prejudiced, but it is possible for U.S. society to completely rid itself of open discrimination.
Factor V: Individual versus system blame	*Individual blame:* It is the lack of skill and abilities that keeps many Negroes from getting jobs. It is not just because they are Negro. When Negroes are trained to do something, they are able to get jobs. *System blame:* Many qualified Negroes can't get a good job. White people with the same skills wouldn't have any trouble.
Factor VI: Racial militancy	The only way Negroes will gain their civil rights is by constant protest and pressure.

SOURCE: Adapted from Gurin, P., Gurin, G., Lao, R. C., and Beattie, M. (1969). "Internal-External Control in the Motivational Dynamics of Negro Youth." *Journal of Social Issues* 25: 29–53.

The final four factors were obtained from a set of 14 questions that addressed issues of race directly. Factor III contrasted support for individual versus collective action. While the individual aspect mirrored the typical *internal* locus of control, collective action emphasized the need to go beyond oneself for solutions and suggested more of an *external* dimension. Factor IV distinguished the extent to which respondents believed that racial discrimination *could be* eliminated through a transformation of the U.S. system. Individual action is more likely if the system is incapable of transforming itself to more egalitarian patterns. Factor V located the problems of lower-class status either *within* the individuals (e.g., lack of training, character, or ability) or as characteristics of the social system (e.g., racism, bias, discrimination, or lack of resources). Finally, Factor VI put activism front and center by distinguishing the extent to which students believed that only protest and constant pressure would move society toward greater social justice for African Americans.

With this race-specific approach, Gurin, Gurin et al. (1969) were able to show that, in contrast to the data for whites, among blacks it was the "external" students who were the most active. An external score was associated with a belief that systems were resistant to change, and that only pressure and activism could lead to a more socially just society. When the black students' perception that systems were largely unmodifiable by their own design was balanced with a sense of internal control, or self-efficacy, maximum activism ensued.

The transformation of the campus along racial lines had not been predicted by the civil rights movement nor had it been accounted for in the provisions of the Civil Rights Act. Dr. King's dream saw black children (and all children) judged by the content of their character instead of the color of their skin. What the black student movement was asserting, it seemed, was that content of character and color of skin *were* in fact connected. Posing them in either/or terms bifurcated the racial self into a black self that was stigmatized, and black-less self that had character and honor. Historically, skin color was viewed negatively and tainted all that it was connected to, including individual character. Disconnecting color from character severed this stigmatizing association, but it severed more than that. Eliminating the relevance of skin color or race also severed an aspect of personal and group identity. Blacks had arrived at the point where color was no longer negative and character was a valued expression of color. Academic studies that focused on African Americans, then, sought to illustrate and reinforce this positive association.

Therefore, the institution of Afro-American studies was an academic, political, and psychological assertion of a new identity. This new identity was not only no longer passive, it was aggressively active. Color was not something to ignore; it became a defining property. *Negro* gave way to *black* as black students embraced the symbolic badge of "inferiority," skin color, and gave it new, positive meanings and significance. Cross (1971) made this connection in his classic study of *nigresence*, described as the Negro-to-Black conversion experience.

In Cross's model, the "Negro" could be described as accepting a negative racial status quo, of avoiding race issues because such issues reinforced that negativity. Avoiding race led to a focus on the universal, raceless self and society. However this *pre-encounter* attitude was rudely and abruptly altered by an *encounter* that defined the hazardous consequences of believing that race doesn't matter. The encounter might be an insult, a recognized instance of discrimination, or an attack that is racially motivated. This encounter forces the person to rethink prior beliefs and to modify them racially. The first stage of modification or conversion is *immersion* into a total embrace of blackness. Black is beautiful in every aspect. The corollary to this immersion was a rejection of whiteness. This total immersion, though, eventually became too much and developed its own limitations. Slowly the conversion experience moved toward a stage called *emersion.* Our subject emerged from this total blackness to find a wider range of personal meaning that did not require undiluted fealty to blackness. The final conversion step was to embrace the breadth of humanity while maintaining the newfound love and respect for blackness as a positive force in one's life. This final stage of *internalization* marked the culmination of the conversion process. (This model will be discussed in more detail in Chapter 10). Thus, the societal dynamics of the 1960s gave impetus to a black consciousness that refused to accept old patterns of stigma. This self-awareness demanded self-defining concepts, strategies, and institutional structures that were psychologically nourishing.

*A*FFIRMATIVE ACTION: NEW REMEDY AND NEW PROBLEM

Affirmative action was conceived as a way to enhance justice and opportunity for blacks, women, and other ethnic and racial groups. However, it too became a wedge that divided people along racial lines. In Executive Order 11246, signed September 24, 1965, President Johnson required that all federal contractors "take affirmative action to ensure that applicants are employed, and that employees are treated during employment, without regard to their race, color, religion, sex, or national origin." Enforcement of these provisions fell to the Office of Federal Contract Compliance Programs (OFCCP) in the Department of Labor. The definition of *affirmative action* enunciated in the OFCCP manual is somewhat vague:

> Those results oriented actions which a contractor by virtue of its contracts must take to ensure equal employment opportunity. Where appropriate, it includes goals to correct under-utilization, correction of problem areas, etc. It may also include relief such as back pay, retroactive seniority, make-up goals and timetables, etc. (cited in Holloway, 1989, p. 10)

As noted earlier in this chapter, President Johnson felt that equality must be achieved as a fact and as a result. Therefore *results* play a key role in affirmative action. But if the idea is to create "equal opportunity," how can *opportunity* be equated with *results*? Isn't opportunity just that—not a guarantee, but a chance?

Affirmative action was a means by which past discrimination, racism, and bigotry—and all the lost opportunities they entailed—were to be rectified. Given that prolonged discrimination put its victims at a distinct disadvantage relative to others who had had no such handicap, good-faith efforts would entail more than enforcing a new, race-neutral status quo. They needed to be *affirmative,* it was argued, in order to reverse the cumulative disadvantage and create a truly equal opportunity.

How and in what ways should the federal government extend protection and special opportunities to those disadvantaged persons? Who, after all, were these disadvantaged persons? They were women and ethnic or racial minority group members (blacks, American Indians and Alaskan Natives, Asian or Pacific Islanders, Hispanics). How could these results be achieved? "Offer a carrot, but brandish a stick" was the answer. The *carrot* is that contractors must keep statistics on their workforce, establish goals and timetables for progress, identify problem areas and formulate plans for remediating them, and be open to inspection for compliance if they wished to receive and utilize federal dollars for their enterprises. The stick is simple: Fail to do this would bar them from participation in federal spending programs.

The problem is immediately apparent. If you are a woman of any racial or ethnic group you are protected. If you are a man of any racial or ethnic group, *except white,* you are protected. White men have been the primary beneficiaries of racial, ethnic, and gender biases for years, according to President Johnson's analysis. Therefore, they must now relinquish a degree of that advantage and, as a result, perhaps experience some *disadvantage.* Issues of fairness and justice began to take on new meaning. Remedying historical discrimination against racial, ethnic, and gender groups produces a new experience for some who may have taken their advantage for granted. What had been perceived as a "legitimate" granting of civil rights was beginning to be perceived as an "illegitimate" granting of preference. The social psychology of affirmative action may be simply stated as "Which of these sides does one come down on?" Let's look now at one analysis of affirmative action by the secretary of education under President Reagan, William Bennett.

Numerical versus Moral Equality

Affirmative action creates controversy and differing opinions because of a basic conflict between two principles: equality and equity. *Equality* means what it says, "equal, identical, the same." When applied to opportunities, equality seems to be a fair goal. When applied to outcomes or results, as President Johnson emphasized, it is viewed by some as unfair. *Equity* explicitly links opportunity and outcome by the proportionality principle; that is, each person's inputs (e.g., ability, effort, effectiveness) should be proportional to his or her outcomes (e.g., rewards, salary, admissions, promotions).

Equal opportunity does not mean that the outcomes will be equal. For example, a jump ball in basketball provides equal opportunity for either jumper to tap the ball to his or her teammates. It further provides the opportunity for one team to jump in front of an opponent, even if the ball has been tapped in the opponent's direction. Therefore, equal opportunity is defined simply by the referee's throwing the ball up high enough and in the center of the jump circle so that either jumper has an *equal* chance to tap it. If one jumper is 7 feet tall and the other 6 feet tall, one would argue that the opportunity to win the tap is *equal,* but the likelihood of winning is not. Clearly, equal opportunity does not imply equality of outcome.

But this inequality of outcome is fair. Why? It is fair because height is a *relevant input* to basketball. Being taller or being able to jump higher is usually an advantage that distinguishes more talented players. So winning the jump for a 7-foot-tall player is "fair" because he or she had superior inputs in the situation. It is fair because it is *equitable.*

$$\frac{\text{Input } P_A(7')}{\text{Outcome } P_A(\text{win tip})} = \frac{\text{Input } P_B(6')}{\text{Outcome } P_B(\text{lose tip})}$$

Differential relevant abilities are important in the analysis of equality also. Anyone (now)—regardless of race, ethnicity, gender, or national origin—*may* be admitted to college as long as he or she has scored above 1050 on the Scholastic Assessment Test (SAT). The opportunity to go to college, limited only by test scores (and, of course, money), is made available to all. Suppose a child goes to a school that has no junior SAT administrations, has no preparatory courses, and, by administrative decision, offers no courses relevant to the mathematical portion of the test. This child scores 900 and is not accepted to college. We might argue that the opportunity to pass the test was not equal and that, therefore, the opportunity to go to college was not equal. However, the equity analysis would suggest that the admissions to college were equitable, because the people with the higher scores had higher inputs and, therefore, deserved greater outcomes.

The moral of the story is that affirmative action is basically about the balance struck between equity and equality as definitions of *fairness.* These analyses turn on the point at which opportunity is defined. Is it when the SAT test is taken, or is it when algebra is offered or not offered in the sixth grade? Writing in 1979, William Bennett and Terry Eastland, in their work entitled *Counting by Race,* captured this controversy by the concepts of numerical and moral equality.

Numerical Equality

Eastland and Bennett (1979) define *numerical equality* as the goal enunciated by President Johnson, "equality as a fact and as a result." The idea was that historical discrimination had disadvantaged blacks, Latinos, American Indians, and Asians. Therefore, the desired result would be representation and participation in numbers that would have occurred if discrimination had not held members of these groups back. That number is thought to be roughly equal to the proportion of the given group in the population.

Moral Equality
Eastland and Bennett (1979, p. 9) argue that, morally, each "person should be considered as an individual, not as a member of some racial or ethnic group to which he belongs or says he belongs. . . . Considered as an individual, . . . every person should have his claims evaluated on the same basis as any other person's." Historically, it has been blacks, members of other minority groups, and women who were treated unequally *because of their group membership.* Moral equality now suggests that it is only moral to treat such people now as if their race, ethnicity, or gender didn't matter—that is, to treat everyone equally as individuals.

The effect of this premise of group-based remedies leads Eastland and Bennett (1979) to suggest, by implication, that affirmative action constitutes *immoral equality.* In fact, Carl Cohen (1979) attacked affirmative action in an article titled "Why Racial Preference is Illegal and Immoral." This approach assumes that equality of opportunity is guaranteed simply by treating individuals as individuals. To the extent that their group status has influenced and continues to influence the availability of opportunities, this seemingly moral position may simply perpetuate the biases that have historically operated on the basis of one's group membership. We will consider evidence for these subtle biases in Part 2. For now, let's turn out attention to the charge that affirmative action amounts to group preferences and, thereby, constitutes *reverse discrimination*—that is, discrimination against those that have historically done the discriminating.

Reverse Discrimination?—Acknowledging Ethnicity and Affirming Discrimination

Reverse discrimination describes the belief that affirmative action is a perversion of the principle of individual freedom. A principle that many felt the civil rights movement was designed to achieve for all citizens (Glazer, 1976). In Glazer's view, affirmative action became *affirmative discrimination,* also known as *preferential* affirmative action (Glazer, 1988). What began as an effort to eliminate the cumulative effects of discrimination, in Glazer's view, became a government sponsored program *of* discrimination.

> . . . the Fourteenth Amendment [required] . . . that each individual be judged as an individual, independently of race or national origin or sex. That was the very principle that the advocates of civil rights who succeeded in 1964 were fighting for. When the meaning of true equality of opportunity moved from a color- and sex-blind judgment of the individual to policies that took race into account in making judgments, a key aim of the civil rights struggle had been transgressed. (Glazer, 1988, p. 331)

Glazer suggests that although *preferential* affirmative action violates the individual rights principle of the Fourteenth Amendment, there are clearly advantages to the policy. He suggests that a couple of things need to happen: (1) Groups for whom, as groups, there is no legitimate basis for preferential treatment should not be included under affirmative action. He specifically suggests Asians and those Hispanic groups that are not historically subjected to biases against them (all Hispanic groups *except* Puerto Ricans and Mexican Americans). (2) A time limit should be set for the policies for those groups remaining. Glazer accepts the idea that affirmative action (even *preferential*) is needed to help us move toward equality and that simple *nondiscrimination* would not be enough. How much time is not easily determined, and Glazer even suggests that it could be extended indefinitely. However, it is important to set a time limit because even when we "sunset" the policies, we establish an aspiration for fairness and equality that serves as something to strive for.

The issues of the persistence of discrimination and the proper remedies to its cumulative effects and who should and should not benefit from policies of affirmative remediation have grown in significance over the years. We will see in later chapters that biases are not simply formal and informal rules that maintain separate and unequal opportunities. Discrimination occurs in subtle, automatic, and unconscious ways. Societal structures are *programmed* to take race into account, even when individuals do not personally intend to do so. Prejudice and racism continue to challenge the idea of fairness and equality in our society. Whatever approach we take toward their reduction or elimination, people will be on different sides and so will fundamental principles of our democracy. By better understanding what prejudice and racism are—their history and expression and their consequences—we will be better able to evaluate how to achieve a fairer, more inclusive and diverse society.

Ethnicity
In 1963, Glazer and Moynihan wrote *Beyond the Melting Pot*, which described in general terms, the idea that groups in the United States who were defined by their religious, racial, or cultural histories would, as a condition of advancement and survival in this society, shed the particular features of their groups and "melt into the society." The melting pot metaphor for social relations minimized difference and emphasized similarity. In 1975, Glazer and Moynihan edited a book, *Ethnicity*, which sought to understand this "new" term and its implications for U.S. society. They reached the general conclusion that ethnicity was a label for social groups who feel a distinct sense of difference by virtue of common culture and descent. It is further presumed that such ethnic groups exist within a larger societal structure and possess a complex of traits that distinguish them from other such groups (e.g., language, dress, food, and value).

What was notable about this analysis was that ethnicity was characterized by an ideological or emotional attachment to fellow group members. Just as the movement toward Afro-American studies, Latino studies, women's studies, and Native American studies emerged in the 1970s as self-defining academic structures and intellectual pursuits, ethnicity was acknowledged to be the emergent social consciousness in the country. The perceived emotional, ideological, and political benefits of ethnic attachment were an important indication that intergroup conflict was not on the decline but, quite possibly, on the rise.

Not long after Moynihan and Glazer extolled the fundamental importance of ethnicity and attachment to ethnic groups from a sociological perspective, social psychologist Henri Tajfel (1978) offered a psychological explanation for this phenomenon in his "social identity theory."

Social Identity Theory
For Tajfel (1978, p. 63) *social identity* referred to ". . . that *part* of an individual's self-concept which derives from his knowledge of his membership in a social group (or groups) together with the value and emotional significance attached to that mem-

bership." According to Tajfel (1978, p. 61), social identity is made possible because of *social categorization*—that is, the "ordering of one's environment in terms of groupings of persons in a manner which makes sense to the individual." Thus, people are categorized into groups that make sense to the persons doing the categorizing. What makes sense is not a matter of scientific analysis, only of the psychological, perceptual, or emotional requirements of the person performing the activity.

This theory assumes that individuals tend to stay in groups if doing so confers value upon one's social identity. The following propositions explain how social identity works:

1   An individual will tend to remain a group member or to seek membership in new groups if these groups contribute to the positive aspects of his or her social identity.
2   The individual will tend to leave the group if belonging to it does not satisfy the above requirement, *unless* one of the following holds true.
   a. Leaving the group is impossible for *objective reasons* (say skin color, gender).
   b. Leaving conflicts with important values that are central to his or her self-image.
3   If leaving the group doesn't work—is not an option—two solutions are possible:
   a. Reinterpret the attributes of the groups so that its unwelcome features (e.g., low status) are either justified or made acceptable. ("Black is beautiful" is an example of this process.)
   b. Engage in social action to make the situation more desirable (the civil rights movement and student activism are examples of this.)
4   The determination of positive aspects of social identity, reinterpretation of group attributes, and engagement in social action can only be undertaken in relationship to other groups in society.

The social identity theory provides a compelling link to the trend toward ethnicity. It also provides a dynamic explanation for some of the trends we observe in interethnic relations.

One of the most important elements of this social identity theory is the consequence of social categorization. Tajfel introduced an experimental procedure known as the *minimal group paradigm* to show the effects of mere social categorization on social identity. The procedure is quite simple. First, subjects perform a simple, trivial task, such as expressing a preference for one of two abstract paintings—one by Paul Klee, the other by Wassily Kandinsky. The subjects are then *classified* into one of two groups, based on their preferences for the paintings. Then, working separately in individual cubicles, they are asked to divide points (worth a certain amount of money) between two other subjects, who are also classified in terms of their preference for the Klee or the Kandinsky painting. The question of whether group membership influenced subjects' allocation of points was answered with an unqualified Yes. To illustrate, a subject who was himself a Klee lover, distributed more points to his fellow Klee-ite (21 points) than to the out-group Kandinsky-ite (17 points). This tendency to show higher regard for art lovers that share one's taste in art than is shown to other art lovers was quite consistent.

Thus, we see that the acts of categorizing people into groups and of placing oneself in one group set up a strong tendency to derive positive benefits from belonging to one's own group. It is a tendency that manifests itself in our showing a preference for those in our group *and* selective biases in judgment and treatment of some in our group. So, when we consider the criticism of discriminatory biases against minorities, it is important to recognize that group differences in economic and social standing reflect in-group favoritism among whites as much as they represent out-group discrimination against minority groups.

Affirming Discrimination

Nathan Glazer (1979) wrote *Affirmative Discrimination* to complain that affirmative action policies had gone beyond the intent of the Civil Rights Act of 1964 in that it actually affirmed discrimination through preferential treatment of certain groups. He began his criticism by noting the difficulty posed by the emergence of the ethnic patterns in our society. In his view, the United States had decided, as a nation, that (1) all persons—regardless of national origin, race, or ethnicity—could become members of society and citizens of the country; (2) that no group could establish a separate nation on these shores, and (3) that any group is free to maintain whatever aspects of its national or ethnic heritage it chooses to—but only on a *voluntary* basis.

Th net result of these decisions, according to Glazer, is that, although ethnicity is one of the important building blocks of our society, nowhere in our formal policies and political actions do we have a way of recognizing it. As a society, we believe that rights belong to individuals, not groups. Affirmative action specified that past discrimination against blacks and American Indians, specifically, required specific remedies, as outlined by executive orders and the operations of various branches and agencies of the government, including the OFCCP, EEOC, the Civil Rights Division of the U.S. Justice Department, and the Civil Rights Commission. The Equal Employment Opportunity Commission guidelines required that contractors report on the representation and utilization of employees who were Negroes, Orientals, American Indians, and Spanish Americans (a category later changed to *Spanish surnamed*). In 1973, the *Federal Register* added groups to the list by publishing the following claim:

> Members of various religious and ethnic groups, primarily but not exclusively of Eastern, Middle and Southern European ancestry, such as Jews, Catholics, Italians, Greeks, and Slavic groups, continue to be excluded from executive, middle-management and other job levels because of discrimination based on religions and/or national origin. These [affirmative action] guidelines are intended to remedy such unfair treatment." (*Federal Register*, "Guidelines on Discrimination Because of Religion or National Origin." January 19, 1973, Part (b) of 60-50.1.)

Glazer (1979) makes the same basic argument that Eastland and Bennett (1979) had raised. What had been conceived of as a plan for the establishment of equality of opportunity, he argued, was now operating as a plan for equality of representation (numerical equality). Indeed, Glazer's analysis directly contradicted Title VII of the Civil Rights Act, paragraph 703 (j), which stated that equal employment opportunity provisions should not be construed to allow for preferential treatment as a means of altering racial imbalance in the workplace.[1]

Perhaps you can now see how things are coming together. Ethnicity is emerging as a source of identification, pride, and attachment for individuals in this coun-

---

[1]The text reads "Nothing contained in this title shall be interpreted to require any employer . . . to grant preferential treatment to any individual or to any group because of race, color, religion, sex, or national origin of such individual or group on account of an imbalance which may exist with respect to the total number or percentage of persons of any race, color, religion, sex, or national origin employed by any employer. . . .

try, and affirmative action is practiced in such a way that ethnicity is a lever providing greater access to resources and opportunities. Ethnicity becomes, by this analysis, not only a source of identification but a basis for friction, as its stakes escalate. Designed obviously as a tool to remediate the historical plight of blacks and American Indians, the provisions of Executive Order 11246 now serve to promote the interests of a wide range of groups whose emergent ethnic identification gains power via the new federal policies. Moreover, whites, mainly men, are now largely treated as if they have no ethnicity, and find themselves computed out of the equation. It is ironic that the Civil Rights Act of 1964 ultimately became a rallying cry not only for those who had suffered from discrimination for so long, but also for those acknowledged to be the agents of that discrimination and prejudice for centuries. Moreover, new appeals were heard from immigrants and others who had not been heretofore identified by ethnicity, and from women, who seemed always to be the last ones considered. The cacophony was loud, the confusion and escalating conflict persists to this day.

The Bakke Case
"Our Constitution is Color Blind," said Justice John Marshall Harlan in his dissenting opinion in the 1896 Supreme Court endorsement of racial separation in *Plessy v. Ferguson.* In 1972, Allan Bakke, a white born in South Africa, applied to medical school at the University of California at Davis and was rejected. He applied again in 1974 and was again denied admission. Bakke had very strong "paper" credentials (3.51 GPA; Medical College Admissions Test [MCAT] scores in the 96th, 94th, 97th, and 72nd for the verbal, quantitative, science, and general information sections, respectively). However, the medical school had a special admissions program that reserved 16 of the 100 available slots for black, Hispanic, and American Indian applicants, whose credentials were lower than Bakke's (2.88 GPA; MCAT percentiles of 81, 46, 76 and 24 for the verbal, quantitative, science, and general information sections, respectively). Bakke felt he had been treated unfairly. Therefore, he sued the university, claiming that "reverse discrimination is as wrong as the primary variety it seeks to correct" (Eastland and Bennett, 1979, p. 9).

The arguments presented on Bakke's behalf focused on the Fourteenth Amendment to the Constitution and its requirement for equal protection under the laws, without regard to race. His petition further claimed that Title VI of the 1964 Civil Rights Act, which states that "no person shall be excluded from participation on the ground of race, color or national origin from any program or activity receiving Federal financial assistance," was violated by the UC Davis admissions policy. The California supreme court ruled in favor of Bakke. It held that the special program for minorities was illegal *and* that the consideration of race in admissions policies was impermissible.

In its appeal ruling on the California decision, handed down on June 28, 1978, the U.S. Supreme Court acknowledged the twofold dilemma posed by historical patterns of racial discrimination and the unalterable primacy of individual freedom and liberty. The Court, in a 5-4 decision, *affirmed* the illegality of the separate admissions program by which 16 slots were set aside for minority applicants. It required the medical school to abandon the program and admit Mr. Bakke immediately to the entering medical school class. Both the Fourteenth Amendment and Title VI of the 1964 Civil Rights Act were prominent in the reasoning for this ruling. However, in a second 5-4 decision, the Supreme Court *reversed* the California court decision, that differences in race or color are neither significant nor relevant to the proposition that all people should be treated equally. According to Justice Brennan, race was constitutionally relevant, because the equal protection clause of the Constitution did *not* imply or suggest colorblindness. He concluded that the Davis program had the real effect of overcoming the failings caused by segregation and by bringing the races together. It does not simply advance less qualified applicants, but compensates those applicants who are, without question, fully qualified to study medicine.

Justice Brennan further acknowledged the paradox of using race to eliminate its effects:

> A race-conscious remedy . . . [is necessary to achieve] a fully-integrated society, one in which color of a person's skin will not determine the opportunities available to him or her. . . . If ways are not found to remedy [underrepresentation of minorities in the professions] . . . the country can never achieve . . . a society that is not race-conscious. . . . In order to get beyond racism, we must first take account of race. There is no other way . . . In order to treat persons equally, we must treat them differently." [emphasis added]
> —Justice William Brennan

By the end of the 1970s, affirmative action programs remained, but faced constant attack on legal as well as moral grounds. The Bakke decision was important for two reasons:

1 It legally acknowledged the broad applicability of Constitutional requirements of equal protection guaranteed by the Fourteenth Amendment.
2 It legally acknowledged that, if a group faces discrimination over several centuries, individual members of those groups cannot be assumed to be equal by simply stating it should be so. Remedies to cumulative disadvantage, in other words, *can* take race into account.

The Bakke decision was a virtual Rorschach test. Some hailed it as a victory, offers lamented it as a defeat. In the middle were those who acknowledged the complexity of the issues and felt it was a Solomonic compromise, wisely charting a course that took into account the realities of opposing values and virtues. But, even as the Court provided a window of opportunity for race to be considered in admissions, its demise as a factor in economic opportunity was being proposed.

The Declining Significance of Race?

In 1978, Harvard sociologist William Wilson (then at the University of Chicago) published a book that challenged many of the "facts" and assumed consequences of racism in the United States. Professor Wilson argued that, in contemporary times, one's life chances were affected more by the economic status of the family into which one was born than they were by the color of one's skin or that of one's parents or siblings.

Wilson argued that U.S. race relations could be divided into three stages:

1 *Preindustrial.* This stage comprised the era of slavery and the period right after the end of the Civil War (1619–1875, a period of a plantation economy and racial-caste oppression. Whether slave or free, for nonwhites, one's race was a

badge of inferiority, an occasion of limited opportunity, and a ceiling on expectations, economic, social and political.

2   *Industrial.* The years from the post-Civil War era through World War II (1875–1945) constituted a period of industrialization, growing class conflict, and systematic and informal racial oppression.

3   *Modern industrial*—This stage was characterized by growing sophistication of industrial and information economies, workforce segmentation, and conflict at the class level, more than at the race level.

According to Wilson (1978), the first two stages had in common "overt efforts by Whites to solidify economic racial domination through various forms of juridical, political, and social discrimination." (p. 4)

By the 1960s, not only had the civil rights movement shown a light brightly into the corners of discrimination and illegal bias, but the first of the federal affirmative action policies were beginning to take hold. In the private sector, corporations were beginning to recognize that blacks constituted an important and sizable contribution to the workforce. This fact was reflected in the number of corporations interviewing job candidates on historically black college and universities (HBCUs). In 1960, an average of four campus recruitment visits were made to 21 HBCUs. In 1965, that average had increased to 50; but, by 1970, it was up to 297. Needless to say, job opportunities were expanding in the private sector for college-educated blacks.

But although the effect of corporate America's greater interest in black workers had been reflected in the statistics for 1970, related effects were already evident in the public sector. In 1960, blacks constituted 11.2 percent of workers in the government sector. In 1970, they constituted 12.8 percent, an increase of three-quarters of a million jobs. In the private sector, blacks constituted 10.1 percent of workers in 1960, and only 9.0 percent in 1970. These statistics suggest that the black workforce was increasingly finding employment in the public sector. Perhaps this was attributable to the "great society" programs of President Johnson and the existence of a large bureaucracy that had been created to administer the equal opportunity programs and monitoring procedures.

Although opportunities for higher-paying jobs increased for blacks, educational demands for lower-paying jobs were also raised. The percent educational attainment associated with higher-earning jobs (e.g., professional, technical, managers and administrators, farmers and farmworkers, and sales and clerical workers) increased by an average of 5 percent from 1952 to 1972. Lower-earning jobs (e.g., craftsmen, operatives, and nonfarm and service workers) increased their educational levels by an average of 30 percent! Lack of schooling decreased job opportunities across the board by 1970, not just in the higher-wage positions. This fact is revealed in the unemployment rates as function of education. In 1974, the differential unemployment rate, by race, for men and women combined was 3.2 percent higher for those blacks with fewer than 12 years of education, 4.6 percent higher for those with 12 years, and 2.4 percent higher for those with more than 12 years. But, only a year later, the differentials were 5.3, 6.6, and 2.5 percent, respectively. Thus, for those with education beyond the high school level, the black-white unemployment gap was unchanged from 1974 to 1975. But the gap *increased* by 50 percent for those with only a high school education and by 100 percent for those with less than high school education. So, in the mid-1970s, blacks with a college education were maintaining the pace of employment with whites, but blacks with only high school or less than high school education were beginning to fall behind comparably educated whites at a rapid rate.

This trend signaled another important phenomenon, greater class separation among blacks, as well as an accompanying residential segregation. When segregation was purely racial, blacks lived, by and large, in the same communities—regardless of their level of income. As racial segregation diminished, economic segregation among blacks expanded, as those who could do so moved into neighborhoods that were more affluent. One controversial "spin" placed on these trends was the thesis that race was less important than class. It is clear that higher levels of education are increasingly necessary in order to secure higher-paying jobs. It is also clear that failing to receive that level of education put one at a major disadvantage in competition for jobs, and the number of jobs for which minimal education was required was diminishing rapidly. It did not, however, eliminate the role of race in determining relative outcomes for blacks and other ethnic minority groups. Social psychology was becoming more sophisticated in its methods and offered new insights into the ways in which race continued to have significant influence on behavior.

SOCIAL PSYCHOLOGY MAKES ITS MARK

Against these social, economic, political, and legal developments, social psychologists continued to study prejudice, racism, stereotyping, and discrimination. Social concerns with racial bias in society were focused on affirmative action and its consequences, on racial identity and demands for academic and institutional support, and on the growing evidence of economic disparities between blacks and whites, as well as among blacks. What problems concerned social psychologists?

Racial Attitudes

What do whites think about blacks? What do blacks think about whites? We examined, in earlier chapters, the tendency to accept negative racial stereotypes, to resist residential racial integration, and to believe in white racial superiority. By the 1970s, the development of large-scale survey methods by the National Opinion Research Center (NORC) and the Institute of Social Relations (ISR) made it possible to compare over time and, thereby, to detect trends in racial attitudes. ISR researchers Schuman, Steeh, and Bobo (1985) studied trends in racial attitudes from the 1950s through the 1970s. They focused on racial relations and social standing in U.S. society, examining primarily black-white attitudes. They divided attitudes into two categories: (1) *Broad principles,* which dealt with the major racial issues of the day (i.e., school integration, residential integration, integration of transportation, job discrimination, and racial intermarriage) and (2) *implementation* of those principles that related to the degree to which the government should intervene in order to combat discrimination or segregation, or to reduce racial inequalities in income or status.

White Racial Attitudes

Table 4.2 shows trends in white racial attitudes in the category "broad principles" between 1960 and the late 1970s. On each question of principle, white respondents were more positive in the 1970s than they were in the 1960s. Attitudes were most

TABLE 4.2 TRENDS IN WHITE RACIAL ATTITUDES (1960s–1970s)

Questioning Regarding Principles (Positive response trends)	1960s	1970s	Trend
Blacks and whites should attend same schools. (Yes)	65%	86%	+21%
Blacks should have an equal chance with whites for jobs. (Yes)	85%	97%	+12%
Transportation should be racially segregated. (No)	79%	88%	+ 9%
Blacks have the right to live wherever they can afford and want to. (Agree)	65%	88%	+23%
Blacks have rights to use the same parks, restaurants, and hotels as whites. (Yes)	73%	88%	+15%
There should be laws against racial intermarriage. (No)	38%	71%	+33%
Do you *approve* of interracial marriage? (Yes)	4%	33%	+29%
Do you favor strict segregation, desegregation, or something in between?			
Something in between	48%	60%	+12%
Desegregation	27%	35%	+ 8%

SOURCE: Adapted from Schuman, H., Steeh, C., and Bobo, L. (1985). *Racial Attitudes in America: Trends and Interpretations.* Cambridge, MA: Harvard University Press.

positive on issues of school integration, job equity, and equal access to public facilities and transportation. Further, most whites, in the 1970s, believed that blacks should be able to live where they want (88%) and use public facilities freely (88%). They also felt that there should *not* be laws against intermarriage (71% opposed them), but it is not something of which they generally approved (33%). The desire to maintain 'residential choice' was supported by the small percentage of respondents (35%) who favored residential desegregation. Therefore, although there was an overall trend toward more positive endorsement of racial equality in principle, there remained evidence of boundaries that were not easily erased.

How much did respondents endorse strategies for implementing these principles? Table 4.3 illustrates trends in white respondents' attitudes toward implementation strategies.

Whereas the trends in white's attitudes toward general principles of racial equality were uniformly positive, attitudes toward implementation showed a growing belief that the government should do *less* to achieve the principles of racial equality. This pattern of attitudes among whites suggests some potential problems:

1   Principles of racial equality are positively endorsed, but government intervention to support these principles is becoming less desirable.
2   Social and economic inequality are not best reduced by resolving underlying issues of poverty and unemployment.
3   It is appropriate for government to protect the rights of blacks, but not to promote social arrangements in society.

Embedded in these attitude data are indications that racial groups are not likely to come closer together in practice, although beliefs about the desirability and appro-

TABLE 4.3 WHITE RESPONDENTS' ATTITUDES TOWARD GOVERNMENT ROLE IN IM-
PLEMENTING RACIAL EQUALITY

Questions Regarding Implementation of Racial Equality	1960s	1970s	Trends
Government in Washington should ensure fair treatment fair treatment for blacks (Yes)	38%	36%	− 2%
Would vote for law that forbid homeowners to discriminate in sale of residence on basis of race. (Yes)	34%	37%	+ 3%
Government in Washington should see to it that black and white children go to same schools. (Yes)	42%	25%	−17%
Favor busing of black or white children to another school district. (Yes)	13%	17%	+ 4%
Government in Washington should support the right of black people to go to any hotel or restaurant they can afford. (Yes)	44%	66%	+22%
Are we spending too little on improving the conditions of blacks? (Yes)	27%	18%	− 9%
Should government in Washington make every effort to improve the social and economic conditions of blacks and other minorities? (Yes)	22%	21%	− 1%
The best way to address urban riots and unrest is to correct problems of poverty and unemployment. (Yes)	51%	41%	−10%

SOURCE: Adapted from Schuman, H., Steeh, C., Bobo, L. (1985). *Racial Attitudes in America: Trends and Interpretations.* Cambridge, MA: Harvard University Press.

priateness of such relationships seems clearly to be more positive. The light shines on the desire to *diminish* the role of government as social engineer in the United States.

Social psychologists were interested in understanding more about the behavioral consequences of these trends. A number conducted several investigations of their strength, character, and behavioral representations.

Residential Integration—An Experimental Study

Social psychologists David Hamilton and George Bishop (1976) conducted a series of interviews in 18 all-white neighborhoods into which a family had recently moved. In eight of the neighborhoods, the new family was black, thus integrating the neighborhood for the first time. In the other 10, the new family was white, and these families served as a control group. The researchers were interested in the effect of integration on the white neighbors. Neighbors were assigned to three conditions:

1 *Before and After*: Neighbors were interviewed one to two weeks after the initial purchase agreement was made (usually four to six weeks *before* the family moved in). They were interviewed again two to three months *after* the new family had moved in.
2 *One Month*: Neighbors in this condition were interviewed one month after the new family had moved in.

3   *Three Months*: Neighbors were interviewed three months after the new family had moved in.

In addition, follow-up interviews were conducted in 14 of the 18 neighborhoods one year after the new family had moved in. Interviews were focused on family background (e.g., occupation, length of residence in neighborhood, education), neighborhood interaction (e.g., who were their friends, and with whom and how often they socialized, asked favors of), racial attitudes (e.g., symbolic racism questions such as "members of minority groups have gained more jobs and income recently than they are entitled to"), perceptions of the neighborhood (e.g., how friendly, good for raising children and property values), and finally, information about other families (e.g., how much did they know about other families, particularly the target family). Respondents were selected from a sample of *microneighborhoods*, defined as the target house plus the 2 houses on either side of it on the same side of the street, the 5 closest houses across the street, and the 3 closest houses behind the target house (for a total of 12 houses). The wife was the interview target, but any adult who was home was interviewed.

   Table 4.4 summarizes some of the most important findings. These results show two things: First, a black family moving into the neighborhood was a very salient event, and people were much more likely to know about it before the family even moved in (52% mentioned the new family before they moved in when they were black, only 18% did when they were white). One month after, the differences were not very great, because any new family was still highly visible. The salience of the black family persisted at three months and, though reduced in salience, it was still more frequently mentioned after one year. And what, you might ask, was said about the black families? Before they moved in, any discussion of them was *negative*. After one month, discussions were still mostly negative, but a small percentage became neutral. After three months, neutral and positive discussions now outnumbered negative comments. Finally, after a year, the overwhelming response was positive—42 percent positive compared to 8 percent neutral and 8 percent negative. Therefore, the negativity that came with anticipation of a black family's moving in, only gave way slowly (i.e., over the course of a year) to generally positive feelings. Is this a positive instance of interracial contact? The researchers looked specifically

TABLE 4.4 WHITES TALK ABOUT NEW FAMILIES IN THE NEIGHBORHOOD—RACIAL INFLUENCES

1. Percent mentioning new family when discussing changes in neighborhood:	Before	One Month	Three Months	One Year
Mentioned black family	52%	80%	76%	48%
Mentioned white family	18%	71%	37%	33%
2. Discussion of new black family was:				
None	54%	50%	32%	33%
Negative	27%	25%	29%	8%
Neutral	—	12%	18%	8%
Positive	—	—	21%	42%

Source: Adapted from Hamilton, D. L. and Bishop, G. D. (1976). Attitudinal and behavioral effects of initial interpretation of white suburban neighborhoods. *Journal of Social Issues, 32*, 47–67.

TABLE 4.5   GETTING TO KNOW YOU: INTERRACIAL INTERACTION AND RACIAL ATTITUDES AMONG WHITES

Race of New Family	Did They Interact?	One and Three Months	One Year
1. Percentage of new families "known"*			
Black	Yes	61.33%	66.75%
	No	33.62%	33.72%
White	Yes	68.00%	64.05%
	No	23.31%	15.68%
2. Scores on symbolic racism			
Black	Yes	6.26	6.09
	No	7.10	6.43
White	Yes	4.93	7.17
	No	7.23	9.22

*Indicates whether respondent knew the last name of new family, husband and/or wife's first name, husband's occupation and whether wife worked, where they moved from, what was their church or religious affiliation, how many children there were, and the first names of the children. SOURCE: Adapted from Hamilton, D. L. and Bishop, G. D. (1976). Attitudinal and behavioral effects of initial interpretation of white suburban neighborhoods. *Journal of Social Issues, 32*, 47–67.

at the relationship between the amount of contact respondents had with their new neighbors and their feelings or attitudes about them. Table 4.5 shows these results. These data provide clear support for the effects of interracial contact.

The first finding is that the more interaction respondents had with the new family, black or white, the more they knew about them (61% of black and 68% of white families were "known" when there had been some interaction with them). However, it was also true that respondents knew more about black families when they did *not* interact with them than they did about white families with whom they had no interaction (34% of black families were "known," compared to only 23% of white families when no interaction occurred). How did this happen? Well, it appears that knowledge about the new black families was "communicated" more broadly than was knowledge about the new white families. How reliable was this information, how positive? Table 4.4 shows that 27 percent of the discussion of black families was negative *before* they moved in. One month later, 25 percent was negative and, three months later, 29 percent was negative. Over the first three months, there was little change in the negative attitudes. But by the third month, although negative attitudes remained at the same levels, there began to be positive conversation about some black families (21%), as lack of discussion was replaced by positive attitudes.

What about attitudes toward racially relevant social issues? Symbolic-racism-scale scores were compared for respondents who had and had not interacted with the new families. For the one- and the three-month interviews, those who had interacted had generally lower scores (5.83 vs. 7.17), regardless of the race of the new family. That is, people who attempted to meet and get to know new families were less likely to endorse symbolic-racism items.

A very interesting result occurred after one year. Here, the significant influence was not the amount of interaction, but *whether or not the neighborhood was racially integrated*. That is, symbolic-racism scores were lower for white respondents who had black neighbors than for those with only white neighbors, *whether they interacted with their neighbors or not.* This finding suggests that mere exposure may have the effect of changing attitudes on related issues.

Black Racial Attitudes

The survey researchers at the Institute of Social Research also assessed black racial attitudes during the 1970s. There were signs then of differing viewpoints on racial matters. For example, Table 4.6 shows divergent trends between blacks and whites in responses to questions about the progress of blacks in the United States. Black respondents were nearly unanimous in their endorsement of racially integrated schooling and neighborhoods. Moreover, they were largely in favor of interracial marriages, though not unanimously. However, although desegregation had been favored by 78 percent of black respondents in the 1960s, it was favored by only 39 percent in the 1970s. Desegregation implies bringing races together, and this evidence suggests that it lost some of its appeal among blacks during the 1970s.

   Turning our attention now to the question of implementing strategies to reduce racial inequality, Table 4.7 reveals both disparities and, surprisingly, similar trends between blacks and whites. First, in the 1970s blacks had a much more positive view of the need for action by the government than did whites. This was true in the 1960s, and was still true in the 1970s. For example, 66 percent of whites felt the federal government should support the rights of blacks to go to any hotel or restaurant they could afford. By contrast, 91 percent of blacks believed this should be the case. Blacks believed that the federal government should see to it that black and white children went to the same schools (60%); whites were less likely to support this idea (25%). This general discrepancy reflects the fact that blacks and whites have different expectations for how racial equality can be redressed.

   But the second point these data show is that the trend of the 1970s was for a decline in positive attitudes regarding government's role in creating racial equality by *both* blacks and whites. For example, both black and white respondents reduced their support for the idea that government should make every effort to improve the social and economic conditions of blacks and other minorities—blacks by 21 percent (from 78% agreement in the 1960s to 57% in the 1970s) and whites by 1 percent (from 22% in the 1960s to 21% in the 1970s). Both blacks and whites were less inclined to believe that the way to handle urban riots is to correct problems of poverty and unemployment—both groups showed a 10 percent decline in support. Finally, both blacks and whites showed reduced support for the idea that govern-

TABLE 4.6 TRENDS IN BLACK RACIAL ATTITUDES—1960s–1970s

Questions Regarding Principles (Positive response trends), Blacks	1960s	1970s	Trend
Blacks and whites should attend same schools. (Yes)	96%	98%	+ 2%
Blacks have the right to live wherever they can afford and want to. (Agree)	98%	99%	+ 1%
Do you *approve* of interracial marriage? (Yes)	76%	98%	+22%
Do you favor strict segregation, desegregation, or something in between?			
Something in between	17%	56%	+39%
Desegregation	78%	39%	−39%

SOURCE: Adapted from Schuman et al. (1985).

TABLE 4.7 BLACK RESPONDENTS' ATTITUDES TOWARD GOVERNMENT ROLE IN IMPLEMENTING RACIAL EQUALITY

Questions Regarding Implementation, Blacks	1960s	1970s	Trend
Government in Washington should see to it that black and white children go to same schools. (Yes)	82%	60%	−22%
Favor busing of black or white children to another school district. (Yes)	46%	49%	+ 3%
Government in Washington should support right of black people to go to any hotel or restaurant they can afford. (Yes)	89%	91%	+ 2%
Are we spending too little on improving the conditions of blacks? (Yes)	83%	84%	+ 1%
Should government in Washington make every effort to improve the social and economic conditions of blacks and other minorities? (Yes)	78%	57%	−18%
The best way to address urban riots and unrest is to correct problems of poverty and unemployment. (Yes)	74%	64%	−10%

SOURCE: Adapted from Schuman et al (1985).

ment should see to it that black and white children go to the same schools (black support declined by 22%, white, by 17%).

Therefore, although blacks continued to see things differently in an absolute sense, both blacks and whites were becoming disenchanted with the prospects for, or appropriateness of, federal government intervention in matters of racial equality.

Finally, we may ask about the general view of the progress of black Americans as a result of the efforts made to implement the promise of the civil rights movement in the 1960s? Table 4.8 suggests that "progress may be in the eyes of the beholder."

From 1966 to 1976, blacks and whites had an increasingly different view of progress in equalizing the position of black Americans. With respect to progress itself, whites felt a lot had been accomplished in the 10-year period that ended in 1976. Specifically, 65 percent felt a lot of progress had been made, compared to only 40 percent in 1966, an increase of 25 percent. However, among blacks in 1976, only

TABLE 4.8 PERCEPTION OF RACIAL PROGRESS IS IN THE EYE OF THE BEHOLDER

Questions Regarding Progress for Black Americans	1966	1976	Trend
1. How much real change do you think there has been in the position of black people in the past few years? (A lot)			
Blacks	41%	32%	− 9%
Whites	40%	65%	+25%
2. Do you think that civil rights leaders are trying to push too fast, are going too slowly, or are moving at about the right speed? (Too slow)			
Blacks	22%	40%	+18%
Whites	2%	3%	+ 1%

SOURCE: Adapted from Schuman et al (1985).

32 percent felt a lot of progress had been made, an actual decline of 8 percent from 1966. For whites, the glass of the nectar of progress was filling up and, by 1976, was seen as two-thirds full. For blacks, the same glass was seen as slowly leaking out possibilities and, by 1976, was two-thirds empty!

This feeling among blacks of inadequate progress was reflected by impatience with the pace of change. "Are things moving too fast or are they moving too slowly," the surveyors asked. In 1966, 22 percent of blacks felt that things were moving too slowly, but, in 1976, 40 percent felt this way—an 18 percent increase in impatience. For whites, in 1966, there were almost none who felt things were moving too slowly (2%) and, by 1976, that number had hardly changed (3%).

By the end of the 1970s, blacks were growing frustrated by what they perceived as a lack of progress. They began to endorse strategies that were increasingly being rejected by whites. Whites perceived that progress was being made, that the rate of progress was about right or, at least, not too slow. We will pick up on these diverging trends in the next chapter.

Behavioral Expressions of Racial Bias

Because many of the attitude trends among whites from the 1940s through the 1970s showed consistently positive movement, many came to believe that racial animosities had significantly declined. Some even believed that prejudice was a thing of the past. Although this rosy interpretation of the effects of the civil rights legislation of the 1960s and of the greater residential and educational mobility for blacks was spreading among ordinary people, social psychologists were detecting sinister signs of negativity. Crosby, Bromley, and Saxe (1980, p. 560) summarized several "unobtrusive studies of discrimination" and concluded that "antiBlack prejudice is still strong among American Whites." What unobtrusive evidence led these authors to these pessimistic conclusions?

Aversive racism. When asked to directly state their racial attitudes, whites increasingly expressed egalitarian views. However, when interacting with a black person, whites would often behave more differentially toward the black person than they would toward a white person. For example, Gaertner and Bickman (1976) had black and white experimenters place a call to a wrong number from a pay phone using their last dime and requesting that the called party place a call to a towing service for them. The number of respondents who made the call was taken as an index of willingness to help. The question raised was whether respondents would be more likely to help when the requester was of the same race. The answer was Yes. Whites helped whites more than they helped blacks.

But a subtlety emerged. Several people hung up the phone before they learned that help was needed. These *premature hang-ups* occurred more frequently when the caller was black than when he was white. Those whites who chose to help whites, but not blacks, could be described as "conventionally prejudiced." In-group favoritism is a common attribute of prejudice. But those premature hang-ups exhibited another characteristic, *avoidance*. Gaertner and Bickman (1976) concluded that these people would rather not put themselves in the position of having to either help someone black or decline to do so. By hanging up prematurely, they were able to avoid the conflict and maintain a positive, racially neutral self-image. Gaertner and Bickman (1976) labeled the pattern of racial avoidance described by the premature hang-up results *aversive racism.*

Other illustrations of this phenomenon were also uncovered. Weitz (1972) had

80 white male undergraduates rated as moderately liberal to extremely liberal interact with what each thought was either a black or a white partner over an intercom. Subjects read instructions to the partner and later were asked to make some judgments about him, including how friendly he was, whether they would like to wait with him during an intermission, and how much they liked him. Weitz also had the subjects' speech analyzed in order to assess the degree of warmth, admiration, and other affective qualities. What she found illustrates the aversive-racism pattern beautifully. When subjects thought their partners were black, the verbal rating of friendliness was *negatively* correlated with covert measures of liking. That is, the more they professed to like the black partner, the more negative was the affective tone of their voice. No such relationship was found when the partner was white. Because all of these subjects were self-described liberals, it led Weitz to conclude that self-styled liberals are more prejudiced than they would like to admit.

Self-fulfilling prophesy. Another indication that biases were more evident than surveys of racial attitudes may suggest was illustrated in a clever experiment by Word, Zanna, and Cooper (1974). They reasoned that negative feelings by whites may translate into their differential treatment of blacks. Further, this treatment may result in black behavior that confirms their negative expectations. This self-fulfilling prophesy suggested that whites "create" the behavior they expect in blacks. To demonstrate this effect, they had white Princeton undergraduates meet with and interview black or white high school students. The high school students were confederates of the experimenters and were trained to behave in a standardized manner. The behavior of the white subjects was coded for nonverbal patterns. It was revealed that subjects sat further away, made more speech errors, and terminated interviews sooner for black than for white interviewees. In a second experiment, they had white confederates interview white Princeton undergraduates for a campus job and treat them "as if" they were black or white, based on the pattern of nonverbal interactions obtained in the earlier study. They then had blind judges rate the performance of the white Princeton interview subjects in terms of their suitability for the job. Those white subjects interviewed "as if" they were black were judged to be less qualified for the job. Thus, the authors concluded, prejudicial attitudes can be translated into behaviors that have prejudicial effects.

This brief sampling of experimental research in the 1970s reveals two important things:

1   There was a growing sophistication in the methodologies used by social psychology in order to detect patterns of racial discrimination;
2   White verbal statements of racial attitudes may be susceptible to social desirability that implies a more positive trend than the covert feelings or beliefs warrant.
3   Although compliance with the more egalitarian norms demanded by the civil rights legislation of the 1960s may indeed exist, these egalitarian norms may not be fully internalized in the psychological make-up of many U.S. citizens.

The new subtlety with which racial attitudes can be measured has continued to develop in recent years. We will consider these developments more carefully in Chapter 6.

SUMMARY

This chapter has shown that the seeds of racial divergence were sown in the 1970s. The legacy of the 1960s was believed to be a society of fairness, equality, and racial harmony. Although the 1970s were fairly quiet, compared to the 1960s, with respect to overt racial tensions (e.g., the bombings, riots, assassinations, and protests that had marked the 1960s), there were signs that blacks and whites were not necessarily moving closer together in the 1970s.

Black and Afro-American studies departments were consolidating the black revolution of the 1960s. They began to serve as centers for scholarship, racial and cultural pride, and collective action. This trend was expanding to other groups, including women, Latinos, and American Indians. The pride of one's group led to self-definition of the importance (and value interpretation) of being a racial, ethnic, or gendered person. Rather than apologizing for or seeking to escape one's group membership, people were embracing it.

At the same time, reaction to the role of the government in implementing equality was being rejected by a growing number of whites. This rejection was evidenced by criticism of affirmative action as "reverse discrimination" and an "immoral" disregard for individual rights, and by a dramatic reduction among whites in support for government intervention to secure social and economic opportunities for blacks and other groups. Even blacks themselves were losing patience with government-initiated progress and began reducing their support for government intervention by the 1970s.

Finally, social psychology was developing more sophisticated and elegant ways to detect what people felt about race matters. These techniques suggested that public expressions of positive racial attitudes may mask some underlying, persistent negativity. Surveys that show measured improvement in racial attitudes may fail to capture the growing racial tensions in the United States. The target groups began to show signs that petitioning the government, seeking to integrate with whites as a means of gaining acceptance, became less desirable as an option than did embracing one's racial or ethnic heritage. Studies of social identity captured this emerging ethnic emphasis, and models of racial identity showed dramatically that the years ahead would differ from the decades of the 1940s, 1950s, and 1960s.

5

The Problem II: Conflict and Change in the 1980s

❖

INTRODUCTION

On November 4, 1980, Ronald Reagan was elected President of the United States. His election not only ushered in the decade of the 1980s, it officially proclaimed the ascendance of social conservatism in the United States. There were to be no more apologies for being white, for being American. There were to be no more expressions of guilt for the history of discrimination and oppression against blacks, American Indians, and other people of color. "History cannot be changed, so why beat ourselves up over the past?" was the thought of the day. Reagan longed to return to the "good old days" of the 1930s when, as he recalled it, there was not such racism and race conflict as he saw in 1980. Reagan's election was a call to Americans to feel good again, to feel strong again, to feel moral again.

The 1980s signaled a reversal of figure and ground, a new "null hypothesis." In the 1960s racial discrimination had been declared "officially" wrong, and steps were taken to enforce this belief. The "great society" of Lyndon Johnson declared not only that racial discrimination would be rooted out and prosecuted to the full extent of the law, it set up enforcement agencies (e.g., the OFCCP) to do so. Moreover, resolution of the problems of the poor and the undereducated was not left to the vagaries of invisible societal development and increased self-awareness; the problems were attacked directly. Although Moynihan's view of the black family may have seemed harsh and unfairly critical of the victims of society, that the government had some responsibility for the problem was an important corollary of his view. Similarly, although one may quarrel with the contemporary concept that young ethnic minority children can't learn unless they go to school with middle-class white kids, one must acknowledge that doing something to help the education of these kids was a central theme.

In the 1960s, racial discrimination was not viewed as a hypothetical possibility, but a plausible probability. The null hypothesis, that racial discrimination was gone, was easily rejected by the evidence of bigotry, discrimination, and second-class citizenship. The nation's guilt was easily proved, and, in legal terms, one could say that the moral presumption was that society was "guilty until proven innocent." By contrast, the 1980s ushered in a change of perspective. The new tests for discrimination were more stringent, making rejection of the null hypothesis of nondiscrimination more difficult. The United States was granted a pardon for its racism. The burden of proof now rested, it seemed, with the plaintiff, not the accused. The accused—that is, the United States in general, whites more specifically—were now "innocent until proven guilty." In the 1980s, guilt was no longer to be inferred from racial inequality, but limited to convictions based on evidence of *intentional* racial bias. Institutional racism was not only now harder to prove now, it was viewed by many as an illegitimate charge designed to put white America on the defensive.

It is, therefore, not surprising that differences in these perspectives would lead to conflict in tactics, rhetoric, and support of social policies among the various parties in the racial conflict. Judging the nation to be "guilty until proven innocent" may have been heavy-handed and may have made it too easy to find biases in individual and institutional conduct. The rejection of these post–civil rights strategies was accompanied by a new burden of proof that was based on the conviction that only *individuals* are accountable for their actions. By wiping the slate of a cumulative racist past clean, it was now possible to push for equal rights, individual freedom, and nondiscrimination, a republic that made no distinction between whites and blacks, immigrants and blue bloods, Latinos, and Anglos—all were to be protected by the Civil Rights Act in equal measure.

We Americans have long believed that the problems of prejudice and racism resulted from animosities and hostilities directed by antagonists against targets— usually whites against Blacks. President Reagan by no means suggested that racial animosity *should* be directed at blacks. Rather, he seemed to simply suggest that *we* were okay. *We* in this case were Americans, who could now focus on positive collective esteem, the good things. We would no longer accept the assumption of wrongdoing, of bias, of racism, it would have to be proven. We are no longer guilty by definition, only by deed. Remedies to social inequality could no longer draw sustenance from the ineluctability of past wrongdoing. They had to be contemporary, specific, and real. Unless a person could be caught in the act of degrading, discriminating against, and demeaning another, there could be no claim for redress. The *institutional-racism idea*—that is, that unequal outcomes for racial groups was *ipso facto* evidence of discrimination, independent of evidence of intentional bias—was challenged. Intentionality was key to determining if any wrongdoing had occurred. And, more than that, if wrongdoing were alleged, it must be demonstrated as having a specific, live victim. In sum, *intention* was required in order to prove discrimination, and a *live victim* of discrimination was required in order to bring legal suit.

"Education is the key to opportunity but not necessarily equality" begins an article in the *Washington Post* (Glater, November 2, 1995, p. D13). The article reported a study by the Economic Institute that showed that when you consider only people with college and graduate degrees, African American men and African American women earned more on average than their white counterparts did from the mid-1970s until 1980. Beginning in 1981, the relative salaries reversed, with whites now making more on average than African Americans made (Figure 5.1). This reversal continued through 1993.[1] Reasons for this decline are attributed to weaker unions, greater competition among black men with college degrees, and a lack of enforcement of antidiscrimination laws. There is no doubt that a changed philosophy of discrimination and of the proper role of government in eradicating it is a significant aspect of Reagan's legacy.

The net effect of the "Reagan revolution" was three-fold:

[1]Although there is some suggestion that the salaries of African American men began to approach those of white men beginning in 1991.

FIGURE 5.1

Average Income for Employed Persons with College Degrees and Some Graduate Education, 1977–1993

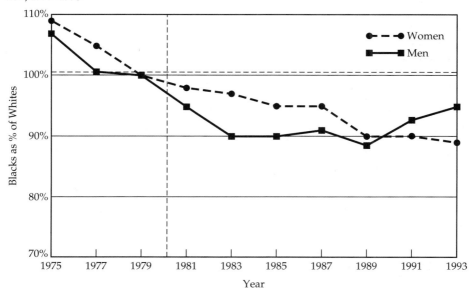

1   The nation's racist past was pardoned;
2   Individualism was affirmed as the driving force of opportunity and merit, and group-based barriers were minimized;
3   Intention was invoked as an escape clause that blunted efforts to remedy persistent and unequal racial outcomes.

As a consequence, the 1980s saw the beginnings of a hardened adversarial relationship between whites and people of color, between social conservatives and liberals. Many white Americans, emboldened by claims of the moral high ground, found it not only permissible but fashionable to be young and conservative. Reclaiming the cultural heritage of white America without shame or guilt was a driving force of this revolution. This reclamation was reiterated in the handling of world affairs as an antidote to the legacy of perceived weakness of the United States under Jimmy Carter's leadership, as well as in the handling of domestic affairs, where taking back the moral high ground and counterattacking the legacies of the "great society" became, for many, affairs of honor.

SOCIAL POLICY VIEWS ON INEQUALITY

In the 1960s, social policy was designed to remedy group-based discrimination through federal institutions and policies, such as the EEOC and affirmative action, respectively. Moreover, it was appropriate in this decade of social activism to utilize instruments of government in order to remedy problems of more private matters, such as single-parent families and unwed parenthood, and even of more fundamental processes, such as public education. By the 1970s, the social action beliefs of the 1960s had been challenged and, in some cases, replaced by more conservative social philosophies. We will consider two here—the conservative views on social welfare argued by Charles Murray in *Losing Ground* (1984) and the critical analyses of the causes and remedies of urban poverty presented by William Wilson in *The Truly Disadvantaged* (1987).

Losing Ground—the Limits of Social Welfare: Charles Murray

Charles Murray (1984, p. 13) considered social policy to be ". . . a loosely defined conglomeration of government programs, laws, regulations, and court decisions touching on almost every dimension of life." The focus of his analyses was social welfare policy. However, in its broader aspects, social welfare policy included federally sponsored jobs programs and efforts to foster better health and housing among the disadvantaged (i.e., the "great society" programs of President Johnson). All of these programs were flawed, according to Murray's analyses. In addition, Murray held that "liberal" decisions by the courts in support of defendant's rights (e.g., the *Miranda* decision), affirmative action policies, and bilingual education programs were also the result of flawed social policies.

Chapter 3 described Moynihan's warning that the breakdown of the black family, signaled by the rise of female-headed households, was a ticking time bomb that must be dismantled. Social policy must do something to address this problem, Moynihan's liberal Democratic soul argued. Writing almost two decades later,

Murray, in his conservative Republican soul, proclaimed Moynihan's prescription a failure. Murray argued that social welfare was the *cause*—not the *cure*—of social problems. He argued that welfare was a disincentive for work, because it provided benefits that exceeded the minimum wage and made it economically more prudent for couples to dissolve a marriage, withdraw from the labor market, and live on welfare.

The basic element of Murray's analysis is that social policy since 1964 failed to appreciate and incorporate in its formulations some basic premises about the nature of people. Murray (1984, p. 146) proposes three core premises about people:

1 People respond to incentives and disincentives. Sticks and carrots work.
2 People are *not* inherently hardworking or moral. In the absence of countervailing influences, people will avoid work and will be amoral.
3 People must be held responsible for their actions. Whether they *are* responsible in some ultimate philosophical sense cannot be the issue if society is to function.

Murray sees people as lazy and immoral by nature, in need of incentives and disincentives to shape them up. He believes they must be held accountable for their actions and their outcomes—even if, "in some sense," they are not. How puritanical is that? In the broad sweep of his analyses, Murray claims that blaming the system and not the person is the fatal flaw in post-civil rights policies. If the "system is to blame," Murray reasons, then we will look to the system for solutions. In Murray's view, the system not only can't solve problems of such personal character flaws (as he sees them), but exacerbates the problems by failing to appreciate the proper role of "the stick" and of "disincentives."

To illustrate his thesis, Murray offered a fictitious case of Harold and Phyllis, an unmarried couple living in "an average city." They were not remarkable people. Although they were poor, they had graduated from a public high school; they were neither industrious nor indolent, intelligent nor dull. They were not motivated to go to college and had no vocational skills. They dated during their senior year of high school and Phyllis now finds herself pregnant. They need to decide whether it is advantageous to them to remain unmarried and for Phyllis to collect Aid for Dependent Children (AFDC) subsidies, or to get married and live on what Harold earns at his minimum wage job. For illustrative purposes, he compared their lot in 1960 and in 1970, and arrives at a different *solution* in the two periods because of (in his view) changes in the nature of social policies.

In Murray's analysis, the AFDC payments alone would have been inadequate to support Phyllis and her child ($23 per week in 1960, equal to $63 in 1980 purchasing power). Moreover, Phyllis cannot get a job because she would thereby lose her welfare benefits, and if she and Harold decided to live together while unmarried, they would have been ineligible even for AFDC. Harold can get a minimum wage job in a dry cleaner that pays $40 per week ($111 in 1980 dollars). In Murray's world, Harold is better off working and Phyllis has little incentive to go on welfare—thus she may herself decide to work. Getting married has no financial benefit, so that the issue would be decided on noneconomic, non-social-policy grounds.

Fast forward to 1970 and , according to Murray, the AFDC income (in 1980 dollars) would be $106 cash, plus another $23 in food stamps, and $5 for health insurance (for a total of $134). Harold may work and live with Phyllis and, as long as he is not legally responsible for the child (i.e., not married to Phyllis), his earnings would not count in determining Phyllis's eligibility. Therefore, when Murray puts himself in Harold's position, he sees a hot, boring minimum wage job in the dry cleaner that would pay him $136 per week (in 1980 dollars) *before* taxes. Notice that Harold can move in with Phyllis, not work, and still have more disposable income. The table below shows Harold's options:

Harold's Status	Unmarried	Married
Employed	$270	$136
Unemployed	$134	$134

If they are married and Harold works, Phyllis cannot collect welfare benefits and either they must live solely on the income from Harold's minimum wage job ($136) *or* they can live on Phyllis's AFDC payments ($134). So if they get married, there is no incentive for Harold to work. By contrast, if Harold chooses to work, there is a disincentive for them to get married, because he can collect his salary ($136) *plus* Phyllis's AFDC ($134) only if they are *not* married. The second option would result in a total income of $270 and represents the best economic choice. Therefore, in Murray's analysis, choosing to work argues against marriage, and marriage argues against work. And it is all the fault of the way social policy is formulated.

This analysis is presented as a *rational* economic choice. Its concluding point is that, social welfare policy, as illustrated by AFDC regulations, made it economically more desirable for many to go on welfare. And, in the hypothesized case, it had the psychological consequence of draining Harold's motivation to work, leaving him with time on his hands to become involved in dubious activities. Therefore, the policy may serve to further erode the viability of the urban poor community.[2]

Murray's trashing of social policies of the "great society" was a bell ringer for social conservatism. It was widely believed that his analysis provided the fuel and rationale for reducing federal spending on social programs like AFDC, Job Corps, and the like. If the 1960s was the decade of the liberal approach to social problems, Murray made a grand claim for the conservative approach in the 1980s.

Murray's analysis was laden with statistics and seemed to support, in compelling fashion, the conservative social policy agenda of President Reagan. The "rational-man analysis" helped make the policy point without resorting to many of the character analyses associated with other conservative critiques that emphasized the link between culture and individual behavior, such as Lewis's (1961) "culture of poverty" analysis. The basic idea of the culture-of-poverty approach is that when people are locked in poverty long enough it becomes their way of life. That way of life perpetuates itself in the values, habits, and life choices that people make, so that even when material conditions improve, these people are unable to take advantage of them. They are thus, in the end, mired in poverty as much by their own doing as by limited opportunities.

This approach blames the poor for their poverty (see Harrington, 1984, for a critique of this view) and rejects government intervention in the belief that it cannot change those personal habits and cultural tendencies that perpetuate poverty and may, in fact, promote them. Moreover, this neoconservative analysis suggests that many government policies themselves exacerbate these tendencies.

Criticisms of Murray's analysis were directed at three issues. First, Murray

[2]Fast forward again to 1995, when a pregnant woman was brutally murdered and her unborn child was "kidnapped" from her dead body in a bizarre crime. Speaker of the House Newt Gingrich suggested that this barbarous act was a reflection of the detrimental effects of welfare programs on the human spirit.

used AFDC benefits in Pennsylvania for his example. During the 1960s, that state's AFDC benefits rose at a rate twice the national average. Therefore, the relative advantage of AFDC benefits (indexed by state) and minimum wage (set by federal policy) was exaggerated as it applied to the country at large. Second, Murray suggested that the changes manifested in 1970 were somehow responsible for a different calculation for welfare beneficiaries. The implication is that the growth in benefits from 1960 to 1970 continued into the 1980s. Evidence suggests that the real benefit of AFDC plus food stamps in fact declined by 16 percent by 1980 and that, by 1984, was 22 percent lower than the 1972 level (Wilson, 1987). If this is a rational choice based on economic benefit, why wouldn't the disincentives to work or marry be even greater in 1980 than in 1970?

Finally, with the enactment of an Earned Income Tax Credit in 1975, it was estimated that, even in Pennsylvania, Harold's minimum wage income plus in-kind transfers would have been one-third higher than the family's welfare payments.

If these calculations are correct, and if Harold and Phyllis still elect to go on welfare, it would strongly suggest that the cumulative social motivational influences dominate their choice, not the cold economic rationality implied by Murray's case example. The bottom line is that "opting" to go on welfare is a bad choice, whether it is facilitated by ill-advised public policies or a consequence of ill-conceived individual or cultural motivational and value systems. Providing assistance that enables otherwise motivated, hard-working people to support their psychological, economic, and physical well-being continues to be necessary in a humane, just, and advanced society such as ours. Beliefs about the relative importance of discrimination, bias, prejudice, and racism in determining socioeconomic status dictate the role of government in ameliorating these disadvantageous conditions. We will consider in more detail the important role responsibility for poor outcomes plays in attitudes toward appropriate social policies. We turn now to Wilson's analysis, which takes issue with both of these *causes* of welfare status.

The Truly Disadvantaged—Universality over Race: William Wilson

If the 1960s offered a liberal social policy to address issues of poverty and race, and the 1980s signaled an abrupt shift toward the opposite direction, William Wilson charted a middle ground in his analysis *The Truly Disadvantaged* (1987). Wilson (1987) takes issue with the liberals who failed to see the mounting social disorganization in urban poor families, particularly among African Americans. He also takes issue with the social conservatives for their tendency to blame the victim either by virtue of cultural shortcomings or individual failings. His analysis suggests that social dislocation in black families is a fact, as the conservatives argue. However, unlike the conservatives, he attributes the problem to patterns of basic economic changes that result in massive inner-city joblessness. In short, according to Wilson, the poor are poor because they do not have jobs!

Joblessness and Social Isolation Cause Poverty

Wilson amasses a very compelling body of evidence to support his idea that "It's jobs, stupid!" Without jobs, all of the basic social and psychological processes are compromised. The following pages document the rise of joblessness among blacks, and the adverse impact of joblessness on basic social processes.

Joblessness
As Figure 5.2 shows, jobs requiring little formal education exited from cities and were replaced by jobs that required education beyond high school. In New York City, Boston, Philadelphia, and Baltimore alone, between 1970 and 1984, there was a decline of 781,000 jobs in industries where the average employee had less than a high school education. At the same time, there was an expansion of 360,000 jobs in industries where employees had, on average, some college education. This is a differential of over 1 million jobs requiring more education. This trend is reflected, as you might guess, in changes in unemployment rates for blacks and whites, who continue to differ in overall educational attainment.

With this shifting educational profile for jobs, it is not surprising that blacks would find it harder to compete for available jobs, as their educational opportunities were demonstrably less than those of whites. Table 5.1 shows how unemployment rates changed from 1960 to 1984. This is a good news–bad news story. The good news is that, between 1960 and 1984, there was virtually no change in the ratio of unemployment between blacks and whites. The bad news is that blacks continued to be more than twice as likely as whites to be unemployed.

This higher unemployment rate can be expressed in another way. Table 5.2 shows that overall employment ratios declined 8 times more for blacks than it did for whites from 1965 to 1984. *Employment-population ratio* is the ratio of the employed civilians to the total civilian population, excluding those who are institutionalized or in the armed forces. The larger the ratio, the more likely civilians in the population are to be employed.

For males from 18 to 24 years old, the average decline from 1965 to 1985 was 21 percent for blacks and other nonwhites, whereas for whites it was only 3 percent. So, by any yardstick you choose, having a job became more difficult for inner-city blacks from 1960 to 1985. What effect might that have on other domains of social life?

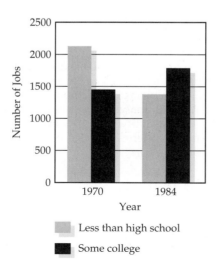

Less than high school

Some college

FIGURE 5.2

Central City Jobs by Mean Educational Level of Employees, 1970–1984 (in thousands)

TABLE 5.1 UNEMPLOYMENT RATES FOR BLACKS AND WHITES, 1960–1984

Year	Blacks and Other Races	Whites	Black-White Unemployment Ratio
1960	10.2%	4.9%	2.1%
1972	10.0%	5.1%	2.0%
1984	14.4%	6.5%	2.2%

SOURCE: From Wilson (1987). *The Truly Disadvantaged: The Inner City, The Underclass, and Public Policy.* Chicago: University of Chicago Press. Adapted from Table 2.4 (p. 31).

Joblessness and Marriage

One consequence of widespread unemployment is that it is harder for women to find eligible men to marry. The data in Table 5.3 are especially important if you assume that a marriageable man is, at minimum, one who is employed and of the same race. With this standard, we see that among 18 to 19 year olds, marriageable men for white women increased by 11 percent, but declined by 13 percent for black women. This is a net divergence of nearly 25 percent, increasing the black-white discrepancy to 28 percent. In the 25 to 34 age category, white women already enjoyed a great advantage over black women, with 86 marriageable men per 100 women, compared to only 69 marriageable black men per 100 black women. This advantage was increased over the two decades, as the marriageably white men remained constant at 86 percent, whereas marriageable black men declined to 62 percent.

In fact, this assertion is implicated directly in Table 5.4, where we can see that the disparity between blacks and whites in the percentage of female-headed households (with no husbands present) nearly doubled for blacks between 1960 and

TABLE 5.2 EMPLOYMENT-POPULATION RATIOS FOR CIVILIAN MALES AGED 16 TO 34, 1965–1984

Race and Age	1965	1975	1984
Black and Other Nonwhite			
16–17	28.8	18.4	16.2
18–19	53.4	38.5	34.0
20–24	81.6	60.3	58.3
25–34	90.0	80.4	76.3
White			
16–17	42.2	38.0	37.8
18–19	64.2	58.3	60.1
20–24	80.4	80.2	78.0
25–34	95.2	94.9	89.5

SOURCE: From Wilson (1987). *The Truly Disadvantaged: The Inner city, The Underclass, and Public Policy.* Chicago: University of Chicago Press. Adapted from Table 2.8 (p. 43).

TABLE 5.3 EMPLOYED MEN PER 100 WOMEN OF SAME AGE AND RACE

Race and Age	1960	1970	1980
White			
18–19	51	53	62
25–34	86	88	86
Nonwhite			
18–19	47	45	34
25–34	69	69	62

SOURCE: From Wilson (1987). *The Truly Disadvantaged: The Inner City, The Underclass, and Public Policy.* Chicago: University of Chicago Press. Adapted from Figures 3.2 and 3.4 (pp. 85, 87).

1984, while holding virtually constant for whites. Therefore, joblessness has a direct impact on the family, and you can project a variety of additional consequences onto that.[3]

The Social Isolation of Poverty

The final argument in Wilson's analysis concerns social isolation. To illustrate this phenomenon, he looks at the concentration of poverty in neighborhoods where poor people live. Figure 5.3 shows that being poor is a different experience for whites, blacks, and Hispanics. Specifically, poor whites live in areas that are economically and ecologically very different from those areas where poor blacks and Hispanics live.[4] That is, nearly 70 percent of poor whites live in non-poverty areas, while only 12 percent of poor blacks, and 20% of poor Hispanics do. Conversely, 40 percent of poor blacks and 31 percent of poor Hispanics live with other poor people. Less than 20 percent of poor whites live among the poor. This means that poor blacks are much more socially isolated from the networks that, notwithstanding the discrimination middle-class blacks may feel (cf. Cose, 1993), provide opportunity

[3]Joblessness is one cause of lower marriage rates. There is also the possibility that both men and women are less inclined to choose to be married.

[4]*Nonpoverty areas* are those neighborhoods where fewer than 10 percent of the residents are poor. *High poverty* is defined by neighborhoods where over 40 percent of the residents are poor.

TABLE 5.4 PERCENTAGE OF FEMALE-HEADED FAMILIES WITH NO HUSBAND PRESENT, BY RACE AND SPANISH ORIGIN, 1960–1983

Year	White	Black	Spanish Origin	Total Families
1960	8.1%	21.7%	NA	10.0%
1973	9.6%	34.6%	16.7%	12.2%
1983	12.2%	41.9%	22.8%	15.4%

SOURCE: From Wilson (1987). *The Truly Disadvantaged: The Inner City, The Underclass, and Public Policy.* Chicago: University of Chicago Press. Adapted from Table 3.1 (p. 65).

FIGURE 5.3

Concentration of Poor in Poverty and Nonpoverty Areas by Race, 1980

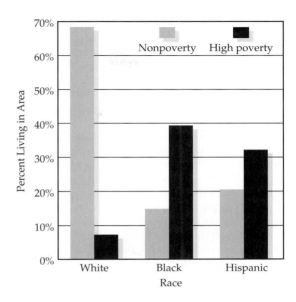

and access to economic resources. As we move more and more to an information-dependent, and education- and knowledge-driven economic order mediated by so-cial contacts, social isolation in poor nonwhite communities may be a prison that locks out hope for those trapped on the inside.

Public Policy and the Inner-City Poor
Following this analysis of joblessness and social isolation, Wilson makes his own public policy analysis. First, he argues, the civil rights protests of the 1950s and 1960s were aimed at providing opportunities to participate fully in society without discrimination (Wilson, 1987). Racial segregation was the legacy of *Plessy v. Fergu-son*, it consigned blacks and other ethnic minority groups to segregated and inferior status. Undoing that legacy involves changing laws so that artificial barriers, de-fined by race, no longer could thwart individual progress. However, Wilson notes that, by the end of the 1960s, racial segregation was now complicated by segrega-tion by economic class. For poor inner-city residents, changes in laws and pro-grams seemed to have little effect on their well-being. Open housing benefits only those who can afford to buy a home. Affirmative action benefits only those with sufficient training and education to be competitive for jobs. The inner-city poor be-came even more, not less, isolated from mainstream white society and a growing middle-class black (and other minority) society as well!

Importance of a Universal Approach to Social Policy

Wilson (1987) argues that, in a multiracial society such as the United States, where racial groups are interdependent, struggles for racial integration emerge when struggles against racial inequality appear hopeful (e.g., following the emancipation of the slaves, the New Deal, and civil rights gains of the 1950s and 1960s). However, when struggles against racial inequality appear hopeless, sentiments for racial segregation and racial solidarity become more prominent (e.g., Jim Crowism of the early nineteenth century, the law-and-order ideologies of the late 1960s and 1970s). Whether it is pro- or anti-racial integration, the issue is defined in terms of race— that is, "us" versus "them." Wilson (1987) argues that this focus on race blinded us to the real worsening of the plight of economically disadvantaged inner-city poor blacks and other minorities.

A second point Wilson makes is that attacks on poverty focused on the belief that joblessness among blacks was due to poverty and discrimination. Wilson (1987) argues that, although these were factors, the more important issue was the more general, unfavorable trends in U.S. economic organization (levels of technology, rates of economic growth, rates of unemployment). Economic organization, he argues, has an adverse impact on inner-city blacks that neither racial analysis nor poverty analysis addresses.

Simply put, then, blacks work in industries that are more susceptible to recession, to higher unemployment, to plant closings, and to layoffs, and, generally, are more subject to lower wages. These economic effects, played out over several decades, leave those who are most vulnerable to their influences in ever more socially isolated cultural contexts. There are consequences not just for the individuals who are unemployed, but for the entire community. Public policy that fails to recognize this dynamic process will ultimately fail to slow the erosion of the social and cultural capital of the inner-city poor.

For Wilson, public policy must be a comprehensive combination of economic and social-welfare policies that feature universal rather than race-specific strategies. Wilson suggests that, whereas historic racism may have separated blacks from whites, current racism is inadequate to explain the growing isolation of the inner-city black underclass, and race-specific policies will not be effective to ameliorate their plight. Specifically, Wilson suggests macroeconomic policies that would promote job creation and a tighter labor market, based on supply and demand, in which real wages generally rise. These policies cannot be implemented at the expense of rising unemployment, though, because history shows that in such a scenario blacks and Hispanics will suffer the most.

On-the-job training should be a key element and, as much as possible, should be located in the private sector. That is, any universal antipoverty policy must also feature training and retraining programs, at least a portion of which may be race-specific, because that is where the need is greatest. Finally, social policies should guarantee a level of support for children of single parents that insures their well-being. Moreover, to remove the stigma of race, he suggests social policies should be means-tested (i.e., based on demonstrated economic need) and therefore available to working-class and middle-class families, as well. Another important element of this overall universal package is child care. Although not advocating a federal child-care program, he does suggest that tax credits and subsidies go directly to working mothers as a means of enabling them to see that their children are well cared for.

In general, Wilson (1987) argues that fundamental macroeconomic forces most influence the economic plight of the inner-city poor. Policies that are not linked to these fundamental dynamics are doomed to fail, because they are tangential to the production of jobs, preparation for employment, and growth in wages. He also argues that race-specific policies tend to stigmatize the recipients, and in the worst case, demotivate them from active participation in the economy. This approach would use race-specific policies surgically as a means of insuring that the most egregious racial bias be counteracted. However, such programs would be secondary, not primary, approaches to social policy. Of course, the viability of this approach depends, in part, on the assessment of the role of racial discrimination in the worsening of the economic picture for poor inner-city residents. People may well disagree on the relative importance of racism in contemporary social affairs. It is easy to underestimate the role racial discrimination plays in maintaining the status of the inner-city poor.

E VIDENCE OF THE CONTINUING RACIAL DIVIDE

While the debate was growing about the causes of the deepening racial divide, the facts supporting the observation that Americans were growing apart along racial lines was accumulating. Three illustrations of these trends are shown by (1) increases in race-based violence, labeled generally "hate crimes," (2) growing racial differences in beliefs about the degree of racial inequality and the causes for existing differences, and (3) a more visible and vocal movement among African Americans toward self-segregation and group-centered standards in a variety of domains. We will consider each factor in turn.

Hate Crimes and Increasing Racial Violence

Beating slaves, lynching black people, and bombing churches, homes, and cars constitute part of a legacy of violence directed against African Americans (and other minorities) in this country. Such acts as defacing synagogues, attacking Jews, raping women, and beating homosexuals have all been prevalent in U.S. society for many years. So, why, in 1989, did President Bush sign into law the Hate Crimes Act?[5] What are *hate crimes*?

One way to think about the Hate Crimes Act is as a declaration that we, as a society, will no longer tolerate hatred directed at members of any racial, religious, ethnic, gender, or sexual-orientation groups. Of course, most of these acts are already illegal and punishable by law. But the hate-crime violence in the 1980s reached a height that threatened our post-civil rights era self-concept. If we had, indeed, created a society that no longer tolerated racial discrimination—and hoped to maintain this environment—then we must not tolerate egregious and violent transgressions of this declaration. However, the Hate Crimes Act was, like so many other developments, a good news–bad news story.

The good news is, of course, that the government went on record as saying "We are watching and want you to report any evidence that racial, religious, and other forms of aggressive intolerance still occur. The Justice Department is tracking these events and, somewhere down the road, there will be an accounting and an appropriate policy response." The bad news, of course, is that in the more than 20 years since the passage of the Civil Rights Act of 1964, we still find it necessary to document continued violence and animosity toward racial groups—that is, such actions still take

[5]President Bush signed into law The Hate Crimes Statistics Act of 1990 (Public Law 101-275) which established hate crimes as a reportable category in uniform crime statistics. Reportable bases of hate crimes include race, religion, ethnicity, and sexual orientation. By the end of 1989, 22 states had already enacted their own hate crimes statutes. North Dakota was first (1973), followed by Massachusetts (1979). By 1995, another 10 had signed such laws, making a total of 32 states having hate-crime statutes.

place. It is surely myopic to think that in a country of over 250 million people, no one would hold racially hostile attitudes and beliefs and act on them. Some might say that because we are focusing on prejudice and racism in this book, we may be guilty of making too much of the evil done by a few. Keep this in mind as we proceed.

Violence on College Campuses

The National Institute Against Prejudice and Violence (NIAPV) tracks incidents of violence and intolerance in U.S. society. In its first working paper (Pinkow, Ehrlich, and Davis, 1990, p. 1), the NIAPV defined *ethnoviolence* as ". . . an act motivated by prejudice with intent to do physical or psychological harm . . . [based on] . . . race, religion, ethnicity, national origin, or sexual orientation." In 1987, 47 college campuses reported incidents of ethnoviolence. In 1988, the number reporting such incidents more than doubled, to 105, and in 1989, that number increased to 109.

Pinkow et al. (1990) summarized such reports over several years. Their analysis of the data lead them to make the following points (Pinkow et al., 1990):

- Between 20 and 25 percent of minority students have been victimized by ethnoviolence during any given academic year. Levels of such victimization of gay men and lesbians are estimated to be even higher.
- It is estimated that between 800,000 and 1 million college students are victimized annually by ethnoviolence.
- The main forms of victimization are psychological; they include harassment and verbal forms of intimidation.
- Over 80 percent of victims do not report the incident.
- Twenty-five percent of victims had been harassed on more than one occasion.
- Thirty-three percent of victims reported that the experience had seriously affected their interpersonal relationships on campus, leading typically to withdrawal and isolation.

Table 5.5 shows selected incidents Pinkow et al (1990) classified as ethnoviolence.

These examples are not necessarily representative of either the overall nature or the scope of ethnoviolence. However, they do illustrate that people have a need or desire to express hostility, disrespect, or anger at members of groups. The psychological need involved in these acts must be explored. Is it a feeling of fear, jealousy, racial superiority, or gender superiority that prompts these acts of violence? Different people probably have different reasons for committing these acts. However, it is indisputable that a negative climate of distrust and dislike in our time further distances people from one another.

Hate Speech: A Special Case of Hate Crimes

As Pinkow et al. (1990) noted, campus ethnoviolence consisted primarily of some type of psychological attack, often in the form of verbal statements or symbolic acts (e.g., white fraternity men performing in blackface). If these acts are responsible for the serious emotional distress suffered, then indeed, hateful speech may be considered a violation of one's rights.

Whereas physical assault is easy to document—although even that is not always easy to lay directly to racial motivation—psychological assault is more difficult to pinpoint. For example, incidents at Brown University, University of Pennsyl-

TABLE 5.5 INCIDENTS OF ETHNOVIOLENCE ON COLLEGE CAMPUSES, 1989

College or University	Incident
University of Akron	The president of the gay and lesbian student group was pelted with eggs by a group of five men at the school's May Day festival. The men also allegedly harassed people at the gay and lesbian booth, made derogatory remarks about homosexuals, and then threw oranges at the booth.
Brooklyn College	Three Jewish students were attacked early Sunday morning when they emerged from a party at the Hillel House Jewish student center. They were beaten, kicked, and hit with beer bottles by approximately 20 young men. The attackers, white men in late teens and early twenties, shouted anti-Semitic slurs and left one student with a ruptured spleen, broken leg, and knee injuries, and another student suffered a skull fracture.
Brown University	Two white male students were attacked inside a doughnut store at about 2:00 A.M. The attackers, who were black, shouted, "You can't look at me like that" and "You white cheesecakes are going to pay." One student was struck and received a cut under his eye.
University of California, Davis	An Asian American professor found a swastika scratched onto his office door.
California Polytechnic University	A Japanese American student was walking to her car when she collided with a white male on a skateboard. The skateboarder then shouted, "You Asians are taking all the jobs away from Americans. Why don't you go back to Taiwan, Korea or Vietnam—wherever you came from—you nigger lover!"
University of Florida	Six black female students were chased and threatened by six whites with a pipe and sticks. One of the white men smashed the window of one student's car with his fist.
Michigan State University	"Die Nigger" was scrawled over a collage of personal photographs on the dormitory door of a female student.
University of Mississippi	Members of Beta Theta Pi painted "KKK" and "We hate niggers" on the chests of two white pledges and dumped them on the campus of the predominantly black Rust College.

SOURCE: Pinkow et al. (1990) (pp. 8–39).

vania, and Harvard University were highly publicized as harassing experiences based on race.

In January of 1990, Douglas Hann was celebrating his 21st birthday at Brown University and yelled anti-black racial epithets including "Nigger" at black students in a courtyard. When a student in the dormitory opened his window and shouted "keep it down," Hann replied with more racial and sexual obscenities. Mr. Hann was expelled from Brown University under the conduct code promulgated by its President, Vartan Gregorian, who made it clear that the policy seeks to punish behavior and not restrict speech:

The University's most compelling challenge is to achieve a balance between the right of its individual members to operate and speak freely, and the fostering respect for and adherence to community values and standards of conduct. (Gregorian, [1991] p. A25)

Eden Jacobowitz was studying in his dorm at the University of Pennsylvania when a group of African American women made enough noise outside to disturb him. He yelled out at them to quiet down, referring to them as "water buffalo," a loose translation of the Hebrew word, "beheyma," meaning "rude person." He contended that he meant nothing racial by it at all, but the African American students claimed he called them "black" water buffalo. A significant furor ensued, but eventually the women withdrew their complaint.

In a third case, a Harvard student, Brigit Kerrigan, draped a Confederate flag outside of her Kirkland hall dormitory. The flag provoked many students and angered many African Americans. Kerrigan claimed that the flag was not meant to reflect either the KKK or racism, but the South, where she was from. In response, an African American student, Jacinda Townsend, upped the ante by flying a swastika outside her window in a provocative act designed to threaten the free speech code. These are just some examples of how there is escalating anger and hostility over symbols and sensitivity to them is linked closely with speech and protection from fear of racial, gender, or religious crimes.

The increase in frequency and intensity of crimes driven by racial animosity, dislike, and intolerance was an important story of the 1980s. Just as important were the growing differences between those who increasingly expressed their outrage at any acts of or implications of intolerance and those who felt that the outraged reactions were extreme. The latter often argued that the reactions to intolerance were characterized by a moralistic self-indulgence and self-righteousness that was soon labeled *political correctness.* Again, wedges continued to be driven between factions of our society. Rather than marking a time when the people of the nation came together—regardless of race, ethnicity, religion, or gender—the 1980s seemed to draw groups of Americans farther apart.

Many college campuses and local communities developed "speech codes" that specifically prohibited hateful speech and prescribed punishments when it occurred. These codes have been challenged in court and, in the main, have been declared unconstitutional as violations of the First Amendment guarantees of freedom of speech. A second reason they have been rejected by the courts is that the basis for deciding which groups are protected by the codes and which not is considered arbitrary. Why should an illegal action, with specifiable punishments, be judged more harshly and with more severe punishment if the target is a member of a particular racial, ethnic, gender, or religious group? Policies protecting the sensitivities of some groups under the speech code umbrella and not protecting others indicated to the Court that the concept was not clear enough to be enforceable.

The point here is that the desire to ensure, and mechanisms instituted to increase, civility and tolerance at times seem to produce intolerance and incivility. Again, we seem to struggle with precisely how to realize a society in which prejudice and discrimination, racism, and sexism have no place. In fact, however, the basic principles of freedom give people room to be and do all of these things.

Beliefs about Inequality: Kluegel and Smith

It has been argued that Americans have an undying belief in what we might call "the American way," which is described as a belief in widespread opportunity (e.g.,

Horatio Alger), individual responsibility for achievement (e.g., "the *harder* I work, the *luckier* I get!"), and the acceptance of unequal distributions of rewards (e.g., the "equity principle," which argues that if rewards are proportional to inputs, equity exists and inequality of rewards is justified). This pattern of beliefs is referred to as the *dominant ideology* in the United States and is generally traced to conservative as opposed to liberal public policy perspectives (cf. Kluegel and Smith, 1986).

What Kluegel and Smith (1986) argue—and provide ample statistics to support—is that whites believe in this dominant ideology more than minority groups do. As a result, each group perceives a difference in the locus of problems of inequality. Therefore, each group diverges further in its endorsement of remedies for inequality. Let's look briefly at illustrative examples of beliefs about inequality.

Opportunity

The dominant ideology holds that the United States is a land of opportunity. Kluegel and Smith (1986) argue that, in spite of the civil rights movement, Americans largely believe opportunity is widely available. In 1952, 88 percent of Americans agreed that "there's plenty of opportunity in America today . . . anyone who works hard can go as far as he wants." In 1966, this percentage had declined somewhat, to 78 percent. Comparing the opinions of blacks with those of whites, we find that blacks felt they had less overall opportunity, and less personal and educational opportunity. They were more likely to be held back by outside forces than whites did. Moreover, blacks more than whites felt opportunity was enhanced by coming from either a rich or middle-class background, but diminished if you were black or a woman. In comparing women's attitudes on this issue to men's attitudes, Kluegel and Smith (1986) found that women differed from men in that they had a lower perception of general opportunity and personal opportunity. Women also had a higher perception of being held back. Therefore, those whose outcomes are lower perceive barriers to be higher. Is it sour grapes, scapegoating society, or some overall unwillingness to face the truth? Or is it something more? Let's look further.

Explanations for Economic Outcomes

Why are people economically successful in this society? Is it something about them (e.g., motivation, ability, character) or their circumstances (e.g., luck, social discrimination, birthright)? For the most part, Americans believe that both wealth and poverty result from individual characteristics. Americans typically believe wealth is determined primarily by personal drive and risk taking, hard work and initiative, and inheritance. Poverty, according to most Americans, is the result of a lack of thrift, effort, and ability; loose morals; and sickness or physical handicaps. Between 1973 and 1982, data showed that Americans believed that "hard work and ability" explained about 65 percent of one's economic position in life, compared to a steady 10 percent who believed it to be explained by "luck or other factors."

For blacks and women, the patterns are quite different from those of the nation at large. Kluegel and Smith looked at the extent to which respondents endorsed the belief that individual influences (i.e., character, motivation, ability) affected the likelihood of one's achieving wealth or suffering poverty, or the opposing belief that structural influences (i.e., social policies, poor schools, discrimination) did so. Figure 5.4 shows that women and blacks were *more* likely to believe there were structural explanations for both wealth and poverty, and *less* likely to believe there were individual explanations for wealth, than men or whites were, respectively.

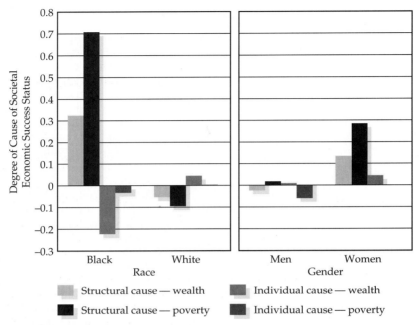

FIGURE 5.4
Explaining Causes of Poverty and Wealth

Most Americans feel that economic outcomes are explained by individual qualities. Furthermore, they feel that their own outcomes can be explained that way. These beliefs are stable and, according to Kluegel and Smith (1986), reflect the powerful influence of the dominant ideology on our judgments and perceptions.[6]

Belief in the Justice of Economic Inequality

Recall the Eastland and Bennett (1979) analysis in Chapter 4 that called numerical-equality goals "immoral" because they violate the principle of individual responsibility and opportunity. The final plank of the dominant U.S. ideology is a belief in equity—that is, economic rewards (salary and social and economic well-being) *should* be proportional to individuals' inputs to society (e.g., ability, hard work, and sacrifice). According to this theory, if economic rewards are proportional to individual contributions, then the unequal outcomes are justified by the unequal inputs or contributions.

The poles of this debate are generally framed in marxist (equality of outcomes) and capitalist (equity of outcomes relative to contributions) terms. The following critical questions reflect the divide here:

[6]More recently, Weiner (1995) has shown how far this perception of individual responsibility goes. He shows how moral judgments are attached to personal responsibility so that failure or bad actions are attributed to the character of the person who is labeled "sinful," to signify his transgression of moral standards of conduct. When bad things happen to "good" people or when people behave badly but are *not* responsible, then a "sickness" model is applied for which there are no moral or character repercussions. Needless to say, this lack of sympathy with those conspicuously unsuccessful people in our society has implications for social policy.

Marxist beliefs

1 More equality of income would allow my family to live better.
2 More equality in income would avoid conflicts between people at different levels.
3 Incomes *should* be equal, because every family's needs for food, housing, and so on are equal.

Capitalist beliefs

1 Making incomes more equal constitutes socialism, and socialism deprives people of individual freedoms.
2 Incomes should *not* be made more equal, because that would keep people from daydreaming of (and working hard toward) someday becoming a real success.
3 Incomes *cannot* be made more equal, because it is human nature to always want more than others have, and people would still be dissatisfied.

For the most part, Americans believe we have just about the right amount of income equality (52%) and that skills (not family needs) should determine income (81%). Most Americans disagree that people should receive the same income regardless of their job (64%) and disagree that people should be paid based on what they need to survive rather than based on what they do (45%). Simply put, the average American endorses capitalist beliefs. Big surprise!

In general, then, we believe that income inequality is just. But, as you might expect, this belief is not uniformly held across segments of the population. Specifically, as we have seen previously, blacks and women typically have slightly different views. As we can see in Figure 5.5, fewer blacks than whites believe that income should be based on the primacy of skills over family needs (61% vs. 81%) and that their personal incomes are *fair* (25% vs. 57%), and more believe that there should be more income equality than there is now (65% vs. 38%). Women join men in believing that one's skills more than one's family need should determine income. But they diverge from men in that they tend to judge their own personal incomes to be less than fair and to desire more income equality.

The dominant ideology implies that social policies that seek to redistribute resources to the poor are in direct conflict with what *should* be true and just. Further, the dominant ideology is in direct conflict with the beliefs held by most blacks and women. As we approach the twenty-first century and become increasingly multicultural, multiethnic, and multiracial, and as membership in out-groups is linked to poorer economic outcomes, these findings suggest polarizing, divergent perspectives on both causes and consequences of inequality. Public policy, as Wilson stated earlier, will have to accommodate these different perceptions and experiences. The 1990s, as we are seeing, continue to play out these conflicts as social-policy makers try to manage the diversity of people in an economically singular society.

The divergence of beliefs about fairness and equality have take on more group-specific meanings in the 1980s. The dominant ideology where white advantage is judged to be fair, is now contrasted with an Afrocentric ideology in which African-centered ideas provide new models of fairness and worth.

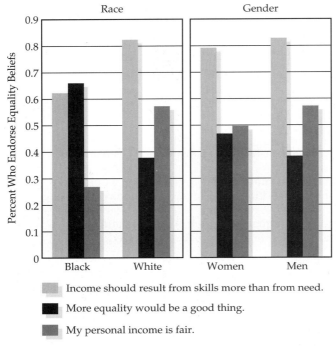

FIGURE 5.5
Race and Gender Differences in Perceptions of Equality

Afrocentrism

For African Americans, the 1960s ended with "Black is beautiful" as a new cultural attitude of self-worth, and black studies programs on college campuses as the intellectual and political energy that gave it meaning and utility. (We saw evidence of this in Chapter 4.) In the 1980s, Afrocentrism became a more formalized approach to African American life.

The symbolic attitude of Black is beautiful, dashikis, and afros, gave way to a more structured and serious attempt to provide a depth of cultural meaning that would lay a foundation for a changed African American ethos. The sloganeering of James Brown ("Say it loud, I'm black and I'm proud") and Jesse Jackson ("I am somebody") did not constitute a campaign for change so much as reassuring self-talk. The invention of Kwanzaa in the 1960s set the tone for a substantive merging of African, white American, and Jewish influences in the elevation of black life to cultural integrity and meaning. As later formalized, *Afrocentrism* became simply ". . . placing African ideals at the center of any analysis that involves African culture and behavior . . . at the center of [our] approach to problem solving." (Asante, 1987, pp. 6, 198). It is this problem-solving approach, centered in a rediscovery and utilization of an African worldview, that defined the spirit of the 1980s.

The civil rights movement followed from the premise that racial differences were minimal and that there was a fundamental, shared dimension of human experience. It

Kwanzaa celebrates the harvest and the principles of unity and cooperation of African American people. (Kathy McLaughlin/The Image Works)

held that there was no legitimate basis for any differential judgment or treatment. Character was all that mattered, and race had no ultimate systematic bearing on character. By this analysis, though, the historical status quo was left intact, and blacks, Hispanics, and women, as groups, could claim equality only to the extent that they approximated the set of attributes historically associated with whites and with men.

Afrocentrism gave voice to the view that there was something meaningful about African culture that informed the collective experiences of people of African descent. It further articulated the point that it is the systematic denigration of that African cultural legacy that has deprived African Americans of a basis for deriving positive esteem from their historical past. Afrocentrism, in short, became an intellectual strategy for repairing damaged collective esteem and for placing black life in a positive cultural context. At one level, it served as a protective defense against the chauvinism of Eurocentric cultural claims and, at another, as a staging ground for aggressive assaults on the excesses of European cultural superiority. It gave voice to individuals who were seeking a basis for personal meaning in a society that so easily stigmatized people. (We will review Afrocentrism again in Chapter 16 when we consider the "culture wars," occasioned by diversity and competing claims for cultural difference and authenticity within the United States.)

MICROLEVEL MANIFESTATIONS OF RACIAL BIAS

The racial divide grew broader and deeper in the 1980s. In spite of this, the popular belief that race relations and racial attitudes were no longer a problem persisted.

That was a belief held by whites, primarily. It was illustrated in their responses to questions about the degree of bias in U.S. society and the consequences of bias for blacks and other minority groups. This belief was not widely shared by blacks and, to a lesser extent, Hispanics. This comfortableness with race relations was somewhat illusory, as events of the 1990s would point out.

Afrocentrism increased the ideological differences between blacks and whites because it emphasized an experience that was largely outside the purview of whites. To a large degree, white acceptance was predicated on the notion that, except for skin color, blacks and whites were alike—both were American and both were searching for that American dream: "Eliminate racial discrimination and we can all be one happy family." Race runs deeper than that as we will see in our discussion of racism in Part 3. However, even in the 1980s there was ample sociopsychological evidence that whites not only held deep-seated racial attitudes and beliefs, but also reacted with emotion and affect to blacks in ways that contradicted what they purported to feel.

In the remainder of this chapter, we will take a brief look at three of these ideas: symbolic racism (Sears, 1988), modern racism (McConahay, 1986), and aversive racism (Gaertner and Dovidio, 1986). Each of these ideas propose, in different ways, that deep-seated (perhaps unconscious), negative attitudes persist in people who may believe themselves to be purely nonprejudiced. They also share the view that this deep-seated negativity derives from a conflict between important values of the Protestant work ethic (e.g., the dominant ideology described by Kluegel and Smith, 1986) and humanitarian-egalitarianism beliefs (cf. Katz and Haas, 1988) and concur that these semiconscious or unconscious processes can influence thoughts and behavior of people who might think of themselves as nonprejudiced.

Symbolic Racism

Sears (1988) suggests that traditional forms of racial bias are reflected in hostility, antagonism, and derogation of blacks as a group, as a people, and as a culture. This negativity was further indicated by endorsement of formal inequality based on the fundamental antiblack sentiment and beliefs (Sears and Kinder, 1970). However, with the gains of the civil rights movement of the 1960s and the growing role of the government in advancing black rights and enforcing their legitimate expression, those traditional antagonisms lost public acceptance and "went underground," persisting in the form of symbolic racism (Sears, 1988).

Symbolic racism was defined as the intersection of antiblack sentiment and feeling and a strong endorsement of the traditional U.S. values of individualism reflected in the Protestant work ethic. Explicitly stated, symbolic racism was a new form of racial attitude, consisting of

> a blend of anti-Black affect and the kind of traditional American moral values embodied in the Protestant Ethic . . . a form of resistance to change in the racial status quo based on moral feelings that Blacks violate such traditional American values as individualism and self-reliance, the work ethic, obedience, and discipline. (Sears, 1988, p. 56).

Symbolic racism is an attitude that is expressed in three domains, as follows:

1 Antagonism toward blacks' demands
   a. "Blacks are getting too demanding in their push for equal rights."

    b. "Blacks shouldn't push themselves where they're not wanted."
    c. "It is not easy to understand the anger of black people today."
2   Resentment over special favors for blacks
    a. "Over the past few years, blacks have got more economically than they deserve."
    b. "The government should *not* help blacks and other racial minorities—they should help themselves."
3   Denial of continuing discrimination
    "Blacks have it better than they ever have before."

The more respondents agree with each of these comments, the more they can be characterized as holding symbolic racist attitudes. Such respondents (symbolic racists) share a basic antiblack sentiment and endorsement of traditional U.S. values.

Underlying the symbolic racism category concept is the proposition that these attitudes result from preadult socialization of normative values and beliefs. The traditional values are embraced without question, the target group is disliked, and a reason for the dislike is rationalized as a failure of the group's members to uphold core values.

Later, as adults, one can embrace the core values, reject anyone who fails to reflect them (in one's own view), and thus, without declaring oneself to be racially motivated, oppose issues that are favorable to blacks—or whatever target group is in question.

Using responses to questions such as those presented above, research has shown that symbolic-racism attitudes of whites could reliably predict opposition to busing, affirmative action, and bilingual education, and voting against Tom Bradley (mayor of Los Angeles) and Jesse Jackson (in his 1984 bid for the presidency), as well as positions on marginally racial issues, such as tax reduction.

Sears argues that symbolic racism has a far greater effect on white attitudes and behavior than does the old-fashioned, hostility-antagonism racial hatred. Symbolic racism is highly correlated with traditional racism in that both have a strong antiblack component. However, it is different in that it incorporates a focus on traditional values, whereas traditional racism does not. Research showed that the frequency of old-fashioned racism among subjects was much lower, in general, than that of symbolic racism (Kinder and Sears, 1981) and that, for the most part, symbolic racism scores predicted whites' behavior more reliably than measures of old-fashioned racism did.

In addition, symbolic racism distinguishes itself from other types of negative racial attitudes—specifically, those based on perceived realistic threat. So, for example, opposing busing as a means of achieving racial balance might reflect a symbolic-racism influence, but only to the degree that self-interested concern is not involved (e.g., if one has no children in the school system). Many data support the observation that symbolic-racism attitudes predict opposition to busing but that perceived personal racial threat does not (e.g., Kinder and Sears, 1981).

There are several criticisms of the symbolic-racism view (cf. Bobo, 1988; Sinderman and Piazza, 1993), which we will entertain in Chapter 6. For now, let's simply note that the symbolic-racism approach argues that looking for racism under the same old rocks and in the same old utterances will result in misleading data. These theorists propose that racism has taken on a new mantle, cloaked to some extent in patriotism and a conservative return to good, old-fashioned values. This view is supported by the Kluegel and Smith (1986) findings and provides another way of understanding the status of race relations as they unfolded in the 1980s.

Modern Racism

McConahay (1986) offers four principles of *modern racism*:

1   Discrimination is a thing of the past, because blacks now have the freedom to compete in the marketplace and enjoy those things they can afford.
2   Blacks are pushing too hard, too fast, and into places where they are not wanted.
3   These tactics and demands are unfair.
4   Therefore, recent gains are undeserved, and the institutions are giving blacks more attention and status than they deserve.

If these ideas reflect modern racism, McConahay (1986) shows us why people who hold these beliefs do *not* consider themselves to be racists. First, people accept the idea that racism is *bad*; however, they claim they are not racists, because these traditional values are not racially inspired beliefs but *empirical facts*. Second, racism, in their view, is only what can be classified as "old-fashioned racism"—that is, holding negative black stereotypes such as believing them to be characterized by ignorance, laziness, and dishonesty, and supporting racial segregation and open acts of discrimination. Modern racists, according to McConahay, do not identify themselves as racists, because (1) they see their beliefs as factual and (2) they do *not* hold old-fashioned racist views.

The net effect of this thinking is that whites can embrace attitudes that reflect the above reasoning while rejecting beliefs associated with old-fashioned racism. However, negative racial affect, according to McConahay (1986), lingers on and influences how relevant information is interpreted and how such information affects "modern racists" when they are called on to interpret new events or to engage in activities such as voting, giving opinions, serving on juries, or interacting with blacks on a day-to-day basis. Is this really racism? McConahay and colleagues set out, first of all, to measure modern racism, then to show that it reliably predicts whites' attitudes and/or behavior in just such situations.

Measuring Modern Racism
After several years of testing numerous items that tap white attitudes toward blacks, a six-item Modern Racism Scale (MRS) was developed. These six items, answered on a five-point scale that indicated strong disagreement to strong agreement, follow:

1   Over the past few years, the government and news media have shown more respect to blacks than they deserve to be shown. (Strongly agree = 5)
2   It is easy to understand the anger of black people in the United States. (Strongly disagree = 5)
3   Discrimination against blacks is no longer a problem in the United States. (Strongly agree = 5)
4   Over the past few years, blacks have received more economically than they deserve. (Strongly agree = 5)

5 Blacks are getting too demanding in their push for equal rights. (Strongly agree
   = 5)
6 Blacks should not push themselves where they are not wanted. (Strongly agree
   = 5)

Old-fashioned-racism items consisted of blatant forms of discrimination—such as opposition to open housing, opposition to racial intermarriage, opposition to the 1954
Supreme Court desegregation ruling, opposition to having black neighbors even of
equal income and education, and opposition to full racial integration. One of the important distinguishing principles of the modern and old-fashioned forms of racism is
that the latter is *reactive* (i.e., people do *not* consider themselves racist, because they reject these blatant attitudes), whereas the former is *nonreactive* (i.e., respondents do not
consider them to reflect racism, and, therefore, endorse them willingly and openly.)
     To test this reactivity assumption, McConahay, Hardee, and Batts (1981) had
white male undergraduates fill out a "student opinion" survey that consisted of
items that reflect both the modern and the old-fashioned racism. The questionnaires were administered by either a black or white female experimenter. The experimenter left subjects alone to fill out the scales and had them place the completed surveys anonymously in a folder before her return. It was expected that, for
the old-fashioned items, subjects would be more conscious of the racial content
when there was a black, as opposed to a white, experimenter and would possibly
moderate their answers to be more positive, even though the surveys were anonymous. It was also expected that this would not happen for the modern racism
items, because, it was argued, they were not perceived to be racist! The results confirmed these predictions. There was a significant difference in answers between the
black and white experimenter conditions for the old-fashioned items such that the
racial attitudes were more positive when the experimenter was black. There was no
experimenter difference for the modern racism items. The authors interpret this
finding as support for the nonreactivity of the MRS.[7]
     There is substantial similarity between the symbolic and modern racism con-
cepts. Both argue that negative affect (expressed emotion) is attached to black people early in life. This negative affect lurks in the hearts and minds of whites and influences judgments and perceptions in their adulthood. Modern racism, more than
symbolic racism, emphasizes the cognitive aspect of the attitude and suggests that
the splitting apart of old-fashioned and modern racial beliefs is a more conscious
cognitive process. The MRS has become a standard for measuring racial prejudice.
It is short, has been extensively validated, and has proved to be reliable.

Aversive Racism

Gaertner and Dovidio (1986, p. 62) define *aversive racism* as ". . . a particular type of
ambivalence in which there is conflict between feelings and beliefs associated with
a sincerely egalitarian value system and unacknowledged negative feelings and beliefs about Blacks." This ambivalence arises from the assimilation of both an egalitarian value system and the opposing feelings and beliefs derived from the historical, as well as contemporary, cultural context of racism. That is, as children, people
become socialized to the dominant racial biases of this society. Second, these biases

[7]We will return to this question of nonreactivity in Chapter 6. There is new evidence that both challenges
this assumption and supports it, using increasingly sophisticated and sensitive measurement techniques.

are further ingrained via mechanisms of human cognitive processes that facilitate the formation of stereotypes and the production of prejudicial judgments.

As with symbolic and modern racism before, the foundation of aversive racism is laid by a cultural context of racist attitudes, values, and beliefs. The resultant prejudices, stereotypes, and negative feelings then become attached to members of racial groups as judged by society. This negative affect, though, is not hostility or hate (rather like what we have called "old-fashioned racists," and what Gaertner and Dovidio call "*dominative* racists," after Kovel [1970]). Instead, the aversive racist feels discomfort, uneasiness, disgust, and sometimes fear in the presence of blacks or of race issues. These feelings tend to motivate avoidance rather than intentionally aggressive, destructive, and hostile behaviors directed at blacks.

When is aversive racism most easily and accurately detected? Gaertner and Dovidio (1986) argue that aversive racists are strongly motivated by egalitarian values, as well as antiblack feelings. Therefore, they should be most vulnerable to behaving in a racist fashion when normative structures that clearly define acceptable egalitarian behavior are weak, ambiguous, or conflicting. To test this proposition, Frey and Gaertner (1986) had white female college students work on a task with either a black or white female partner (the experimental confederate). The subject was asked for help by her partner for reasons that were either self-induced (*internal locus*—the partner had not worked on the task very hard) or beyond the person's control (*external locus*—the task was unusually difficult). The subject was able to help by giving the partner Scrabble letters and bonus points to help them win a prize. Frey and Gaertner (1986) reasoned that the race of the partner would not matter when norms were clearly in support of helping (external locus). When the norms were not supportive of helping—that is, when the partner had been lazy (internal locus) and still asked for help—they expected that the partner's race would matter, with blacks receiving less help than whites received. The results, shown in Figure 5.6, strongly support these predictions.

These findings show that when conditions are favorable for positive interactions and "obvious" choices, people will "do the right thing." But when there is "wiggle room," the possibility of negative attitudes giving rise to racially biased behavior becomes more likely.

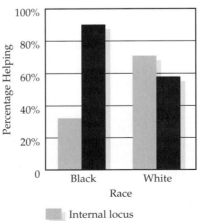

FIGURE 5.6

Helping Blacks and Whites as a Function of Locus of Need

Additionally, Gaertner and Dovidio (1986) argue that, even when egalitarian norms are clear, aversive racists may well search for nonracial factors in order to explain or rationalize their unfavorable behavior toward blacks. In this regard, they believe, the aversive racist is more similar to the modern racist than to the old-fashioned racist. Dovidio and Gaertner (1981) conducted an ingenious study to test this proposition. Subjects who scored high or low on the MRS were introduced to either a black or a white confederate who was either their supervisor or their subordinate, and who had either higher or lower task-relevant intellectual ability. Before any real interaction, but after the above information was made known, the confederate knocked a container of pencils to the floor. Under which conditions would the subject offer their confederate the most help?

Putting the issue in an affirmative-action context, Dovidio and Gaertner (1981) argue that if it is a fear of unqualified blacks getting jobs, then subjects should be more positive to the *more* qualified confederate and help him most. If, on the other hand, the opposition to affirmative action really reflects the fear of a status reversal—that is, of blacks' achieving superior positions over them—then they should help the supervisor less, regardless of his ability. Gaertner and Dovidio present the results as supportive of these expectations, noting that black supervisors were helped *less* often than were black subordinates (58% vs. 83%), whereas white supervisors were helped somewhat *more* often than white subordinates were (54% vs. 41%). Ability did not matter, because blacks of both high and low ability were helped about as frequently (70% of the time). But, for whites, high-ability confederates were helped much more often than were low-ability subjects (67% vs. 29%).

Although these data are consistent with the predictions, Figure 5.7 offers another interpretation. When you compare helping supervisors and helping high-ability confederates, there appear to be virtually no racial differences. However, when the confederates are lacking in status (subordinate) or intelligence (of low

FIGURE 5.7

Helping Blacks and Whites as a Function of Relative Status and Ability

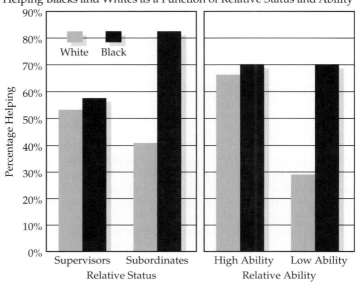

ability), then subjects are *more* helpful to blacks. So the question that arises is, Do these data support an aversive racism suggestion of subtle bias *against* blacks, or do they suggest subtle bias *for* blacks, *as long as they remain in their place* (i.e., subordinate and "dumb"). This, too, could be easily interpreted as a form of aversive racism, but rather than emphasizing discomfort, uneasiness, or disgust in the presence of blacks, they suggest the flip side of comfort and ease *as long as blacks remain in their place.*

One interesting finding came out in postexperimental questioning. Subjects accepted white high-ability confederates as somewhat more intelligent than themselves, but black high-ability confederates were rated as significantly lower in intelligence. This finding may be one of the most compelling examples of subtle bias. As we will see in Part 3, racism is more about in-group bias than out-group derogation, it is more about feelings of personal or group superiority than it is about other-group inferiority. This result certainly suggests that white subjects felt superior to blacks, even when they were instructed that they were, in fact, not superior by a presumably authoritative source. The degree of prejudice shown on the MRS bore no relationship to these effects.

The symbolic, modern, and aversive racism analyses show a variety of ways in which racial bias persisted in a time when it was believed to have substantially subsided. This is not to accept the view that nothing had changed, but it does make a compelling case for the persistent effects of cultural socialization, lingering affective reactions, and the subtle influences of these processes on attitudes and behavior. The effects are not always obvious, and one may easily mistake his or her feelings of openness and nonhostile attitudes as evidence of a lack of prejudice.

The important similarities in these lines of argument include the following:

1   Negative affective associations to black people
2   Ambivalence between feelings of nonprejudice or egalitarianism and those negative feelings
3   A tendency for people who aspire to a positive, egalitarian self-image to nevertheless show racial biases when they are unaware of how to appear nonbiased

The net effect of these studies is to suggest that there is a profound undercurrent of racial animosity not only in those overt bigots who got so much attention in the 1960s, but among more overtly friendly and reassuring people. The latter are, perhaps, the very ones whom Kluegel and Smith (1986) found believed in the dominant ideology of opportunity, personal responsibility, and the fairness of inequality.

*S*UMMARY

The lesson of the 1980s, perhaps, has to do with a collision of reasonable, important, and correct ideas. For any issue that we have reviewed in this section, there are two views. Each rests on somewhat different assumptions and interpretations and leads to different expectations and actions. It is not so much a question of *which* view is true or correct, but *under what conditions* it is true or correct. These debates are not winnable in any conventional sense. The balance, equilibrium, or "solution" plays out not at a moment in time, but over time. Are comprehensive exams better than proseminar for teaching the content of psychology? The "correct" answer to this question varies over time, being Yes in one decade and No in another within the same department with substantially the same faculty making the call.

Consider the hate-speech debate. Those who support it argue that hate speech creates a hostile environment in which learning cannot be fully achieved. It therefore violates the Fourteenth Amendment promise of equal protection. The counterargument is that the very first thing our founding fathers set forth was freedom of expression in the First Amendment. However offensive the speech, once we begin curtailing that freedom, we take a giant step toward becoming a society that is no longer free. We cannot *choose* between the First and Fourteenth Amendment and *win* as a society. We must balance the two and try to make each as broadly applicable and enforced as possible.

Of course, there are both individual and structural contributions to poverty and to wealth. People will assess the relative importance of these contributions differently, but both are true. We have a basis for compromise and common ground, but we often see the differences as paramount. The 1980s perhaps should be known for drawing out the distinctions, the differences among us. The 1960s called for harmony, coming together—we shall overcome, integrate. In the 1980s we seemed to be moving further apart. Racial, ethnic, and gender solidarity defines an in-group and distances us from those outside the group. We will look more closely at these processes in Part 2. Suffice it to say that the strength of common ties and experience must be weighed against the negative consequences of reduced contact with, understanding of, and appreciation of others.

PART TWO

---　❖　---

The Psychology of Prejudice

I am colored and
America's colorblind.
So, do you see me?

J. M. J.

6

*P*erspectives on *P*rejudice

❖

*I*NTRODUCTION

A little over a year ago, I received a letter from a white woman who lived in New York City. She identified herself as "someone who worked closely with black colleagues in an electronics laboratory and later as a teacher of black high school students." She detailed the following experience:

> I was store shopping and fiddled with the catch on my pocketbook, when I heard a voice address me: "You don't have to worry. I belong to the store." I looked to where the voice was coming from and for the first time saw a young black man smiling at me. I was so shocked that he thought I was fiddling with my pocketbook to protect it from him, that all I could do was smile back.

The remarkable thing about this incident is the multiple layers and perspectives of the problem. The black man was responding to what he believed to be the stereotype that whites in general may have of blacks, "prone to violence!" In responding to this suspicion, and his own feelings of vulnerability, he used his own stereotype of whites (i.e., that they automatically assume a black man has dubious intentions) to frame his response. The woman was very upset by being stereotyped. She wished she had answered, "You insult me with your racism. So you think all white people are the same, suspicious of black people." The encounter, though, took place amidst great civility and courtesy. The man calmed her of any suspicions and, presumably, through his smile, put her at ease. She smiled in response, thereby "thanking" him for his concern and/or assuring him of her open-mindedness.

This example illustrates a couple of things. First, expressed prejudice is always characterized by one's responding to a person on the basis of that person's group membership, irrespective of the social or behavioral "facts" the specific person incorporates. What should be an inter*personal* interaction transpires as an inter*group* encounter. The course of the interaction is determined more by the expectations, assumptions, and beliefs about the group to which the person belongs, than it is by the qualities of the given individual. Second, prejudice involves the assumption that somehow all members of the group are alike in some specific way. In the example, the young man seemed to assume that the woman's behavior could only be explained by racial fear or suspicion. The young woman felt she was not being treated as who she was—a person who respected racial differences, participated in a constructive way in the education of black students, and whose behavior was unrelated to the presence, much less the color of the young man. This perception of group characteristics (blacks are violence-prone; whites are racism-prone) colored the interaction and tainted a simple situation. This is one legacy of prejudice and racism in the United States.

Why is prejudice a problem? Prejudice is a problem because it is intimately linked to negative feelings about people. These people about whom we hold negative feelings are usually different from us in a variety of ways. But prejudice is more than simply not liking someone based on the group that person belongs to. It seems that, at its core, prejudice involves not understanding someone, thinking someone is something he or she is not, and reacting to those thoughts and feelings in ways that increase antagonism and conflict. Prejudice breeds bias, discrimination, detachment, and possibly fear. It may also be a response to fear, uncertainty, and insecurity. People often resist the unknown, changes, and things and people that are different. People feel more comfortable with the old and familiar, the usual. People like—and usually feel more comfortable with—people that are known, people whose behavior can be predicted and understood by comparison with oneself. People grow uncomfortable with people they don't know or whom they think they know but feel negative toward.

But is there another level at which we may find the answer to the question. (This answer is treated in more detail in Part 3.) We have inherited in our society a complex set of beliefs about race. These beliefs strongly state or unmistakeably imply that non-white racial groups generally, and blacks in particular, are inferior to whites, lack the values systems whites hold, and may be either threatening to society (in the strong form) or undeserving of full status and participation in U.S. society. Against this backdrop of cultural signification and beliefs, it is easy to formulate biased judgments against the group and to employ these group-based beliefs in the assessment of individual group members. Prejudice engenders or results from such a system of thinking.

For whom is prejudice a problem? Prejudice is a problem for the United States and all its citizens. It is a problem for the targets of prejudice, because they suffer negative and discriminatory treatment that is unwarranted by their behavior or circumstances. It is a problem for the prejudiced person, because he or she is engaging in a level of incivility or inhumanity that lowers his or her stature as a person. It is a problem for our society in general, because prejudice denies people equal opportunity, in violation of our U.S. "creed"; it thereby reduces the overall talent pool from which we can draw as we build a stronger and better nation.

Studies of the nature of the problem typically focus on the prejudiced individual. Gaines and Reed (1995) argue that our ability to gain an understanding of prejudice is limited by this almost exclusive focus on the majority individual relative to the minority, on the white persons relative to the black, and most generally on the perpetrators of prejudice relative to the targets. They suggest that reactions of targets is a missing element in our understanding of prejudice. This deficiency in analyses of prejudice is related to the distinctions one may draw from the approach taken by DuBois (1903), which emphasized the consequences of prejudice for black targets, and by Allport (1954), whose analysis, albeit broad in scope, primarily focused on those individualistic concepts that were more amenable to laboratory research and an individual, unit-of-analysis explanation. [This issue will be addressed, in part, in the later analysis of target reactions (Chapter 10) and the cultural analysis of racism (Chapters 12, 13, and 16).] Also rounding out our understanding of prejudice is the fact that blacks and other minorities can also be prejudiced against whites and each other. Although individual prejudices can be problematic, they do not reach their ultimate impact until they join with institutional and societal power. When that occurs, prejudice plays a big role in the maintenance and expression of racism.

In this chapter, we will explore the nature of prejudice as a concept and as a matter of interpersonal behavior. We will first focus our attention on what prejudice is, by reviewing *definitions* and adopting a working definition that will guide the remainder of our analysis. We will next describe and assess *theories* of prejudice that have been offered to explain its nature and processes. How we *study* prejudice—that is, what experiments are conducted in the laboratory or in field settings that illustrate the operation of prejudice—will be the focus of the next section. Next, we will consider a main dimension of prejudice, *attitudes*. It has long been argued that racial attitudes form the basis for racial judgments that lead to the biased or discriminatory behaviors that we identify as prejudice. Measuring racial attitudes and their consequences in behavior are critical to any understanding of prejudice. Finally, we will discuss the distinction between prejudice and *discrimination*.

*D*EFINING PREJUDICE

For social psychologists, the essential nature of prejudice has to do with interpersonal relationships, with how individuals behave toward others. Prejudice is suggested when a person treats a target other person more negatively than can be explained by chance or by the facts of the target's demeanor or behavior. The explanation for this more-negative-than-expected treatment is given by aspects of the target person that do not provide a *legitimate* basis for judgment, such as the color of her shoes, the size of his wallet, the texture of her hair, the color of his skin, the size of his eyes, the width of her nose, or his name.[1]

---

[1] There may be some disagreement about what constitute *legitimate* reasons for prejudice. D'Souza (1995) argues that much racial discrimination can be understood as "rational," based on statistical averages that suggest negative behavior or evasive or discriminatory behavior based on race is justified. This is so, according to D'Souza, whether the statistical expectation is false in the individual case or not. We will discuss the implications of this approach further when we take up individual racism in Chapter 14.

THE ALUMNAE

"I'm not prejudiced against all policemen in general, I just dislike each and every one of you individually."

(Reproduced by permission of the Register and Tribune Syndicate, Inc. © 1970)

Prejudice as Rejection of a Person Based on Category Membership

To further our development of a working definition of prejudice, we will consider an example taken from the classic G. W. Allport (1954) book. A Canadian social scientist by the name of Wax (1948) sent *two* letters requesting room accommodations to over 100 different holiday resorts that had advertised their facilities. Mr. Wax signed one letter "Mr. Greenberg" (presumably, a Jewish man) and the second letter "Mr. Lockwood" (presumably, a non-Jewish man). The results follow:

	Percent Who Replied	*Percent of Responders Who Offered Accommodations*
Mr. Greenberg	52%	36%
Mr. Lockwood	95%	93%

The result of this little survey revealed what Allport considered were two basic ingredients of prejudice: (1) There is definite *hostility* and *rejection*, and (2) the basis for rejection is *categorical*. " 'Mr. Greenberg' was not evaluated as an individual. Rather, he was condemned on the basis of his presumed group membership" (Allport, 1954, p. 5).

The *Alumnae* cartoon offers an illustration of how to "beat the prejudice rap." You simply avoid judging individuals on the basis of characteristics of the group. There is nothing wrong with disliking someone, just do it invariably and inflexibly on the individual "merits" of the case!

In the first edition of *Prejudice and Racism* (Jones, p. 51), *prejudice* was defined as follows:

> The prior negative judgment of the members of a race or religion or the occupants of any other significant social role, held in disregard of facts that contradict it.

According to this definition, the generalizations on which prejudice is based not only are faulty, they are also inflexible. That is, information that renders the judgment inappropriate should lead to its abandonment. When it does not, prejudice is operating. It is this cognitive inflexibility that gives prejudice its irrational dimension.

Prejudice as Cognitive Rigidity

The following dialogue from G. W. Allport (1954) illustrates this cognitive rigidity:

Mr. X: The trouble with the Jews is that they only take care of their own group.

Mr. Y: But the record of the Community Chest campaign shows that they give more generously, in proportion to their numbers, to the general charities of the community, than do non-Jews.

Mr. X: That shows they are always trying to buy favor and intrude into Christian affairs. They think of nothing but money; that is why there are so many Jewish bankers.

Mr. Y: But a recent study shows that the percentage of Jews in the banking business is negligible, and smaller than the percentage of non-Jews.

Mr. X: That's just it; they don't go in for respectable business; they are only in the movie business or run night clubs.

Mr. X does not think highly of Jews, and makes wide-ranging judgments about them in order to support this belief. When challenged with facts, he does not alter his judgments, he simply shifts the conversation to another negative aspect that he finds supportive of his generally negative attitude toward Jews. This *inflexibility of generalizations* is a critical component in the concept of prejudice.

Prejudice as Negative Judgment of or Feelings About a Person

Prejudice can be based on favorable *or* unfavorable judgments, but most scientific approaches emphasize the antipathy, the negative judgment—that is, the *unfavor-ableness*. For example, Aboud (1988, p. 4) writes: "The most salient characteristic of prejudice is its negative, hateful quality. This negativity defines prejudice." Why is this so? The reason is pretty simple—negative events are more distinctive than positive ones. A man who goes down to the post office with seven different automatic weapons and kills 25 people gets much attention. A man who goes to the office and takes flowers to 25 coworkers does not make the newspaper, not even the Metro section. So, negative attitudes and actions are salient, positive attitudes and actions are not. But this really has created a problem for our study of prejudice (cf. Gardner, 1994).

Wilbanks (1987, p. 27) makes negativity a centerpiece of his definition of what he calls *racism*: "Racial prejudice is defined as the attribution of negative traits and motives to other ethnic or racial groups."[2] However, unlike the approach in this text, and that of most people who study prejudice, he feels that there is a "double standard of racism" because "the terms *racism, prejudice,* and *discrimination* have generally been used only to refer to the attitudes and behavior of whites." His defi-

---

[2] Note that Wilbanks (1987) seems to use *prejudice, racism,* and *discrimination* interchangeably, sometimes defining one in terms of the other. We believe strongly that there are important differences among all of these terms and will try to clarify them as we go along.

nition, then, is meant to eliminate the double standard by leaving unspecified the groups in question, thereby enabling consideration of any group as either targets or purveyors of prejudice. He concludes:

> Thus a particular racial group is racially prejudiced to the extent that other ethnic groups are viewed as "them" and assigned negative traits and motives and "we" are assigned positive traits and motives. By this definition blacks are more racially prejudiced than whites. (Wilbanks, 1987, p. 27)

This definition and explication of what it means suggest why attempts to define prejudice can be problematic. One's definition constructs the terms under which the phenomenon is said to exist. If a given event *does not* meet the criteria of the definition, then it cannot be classified as an instance of it. And conversely, if it does meet the definition, it is an instance of the phenomenon. Those aspects that one chooses to include in the definition, then, determine the context and content—and, perhaps, conclusions—of the discussion. One must try, therefore, to be broad and encompassing in defining the term *prejudice* so as to permit the widest examination of the phenomenon.

The tendency to assign traits, whether positive or negative, to a whole group of people is an aspect of stereotyping, which we discuss in Chapter 7. Do blacks hold prejudices against whites? Surely they do. Do women hold prejudices against men? Surely they do. Intergroup conflict is a subject that we consider in depth in Chapters 8 and 9. The fact that one group holds significant power and influence over the life outcomes of another group means that the existence and operation of prejudices of the first group toward the second group have far greater impact on society than the reverse scenario would have.

Prejudice as Positive Feelings for the In-Group

One thing we have learned in social psychology over the past 25 years is that *intergroup bias*—the tendency to treat members of other groups differently and more negatively than we treat members of our own group—is precipitated more by *in-group favoritism* than it is by *out-group antipathy* (cf. Brewer, 1979). That is, we do not so much treat people from other groups worse, we treat members of our own group better! By any definition, in-group favoritism is a prejudice. By all empirical accounts, it explains more of the variance of biases in intergroup relations than does negative out-group discrimination. So why are we attempting to fight prejudice with one hand tied behind our backs, as it were? It is important to recognize that a fully balanced understanding of prejudice requires that we look not only at the animosities that are associated with negative prejudgments about people and the groups to which they belong, but also at the expressions of attraction, cohesion, and liking we direct toward our intimates and like-minded associates.

Prejudice as Generalization from the Group to the Person

Perhaps the most critical aspect of prejudice is what G. W. Allport (1954) called *categorical judgment*—the tendency to judge individuals on the basis of their group membership. Whether the judgments we make are positive or are negative is not ultimately the criterion of prejudice. Making judgments about individuals on the basis of characteristics of the social group to which we assign them, this is the essential criterion of prejudice.

It also does not matter whether the group characteristics are accurate or not.

Every group consists of members who share certain characteristics or attributes and do not share others. For example, siblings share family membership and even substantial genetic commonality. However, it has been shown that 50 percent of the variance in personality and basic psychological functioning is based on *nonshared* environmental influences. (Plomin, 1988, 1990). That is, in studies of siblings reared in the same family, it is estimated that 40 percent of the variance in their cognitive abilities and personalities can be attributed to genetic factors. That leaves 60 percent explained by environmental factors, of which only 10 percent is explained by the environment the siblings share, and 50% is explained by their divergent experiences. These divergent experiences include their treatment of each other, their peer interactions, and perhaps different parental treatment. The critical question thus becomes "why are children in the same family so different from one another?" (Plomin, 1990, p. 129). The point is that variability *within* human groups is great, and any attempt to judge an individual group member on the basis of assumptions about the group is very likely to be flawed. African Americans are more likely to live in poverty than whites (33% vs. 12%), more likely to live in urban settings (65% vs. 48%), and more likely to be unmarried mothers or fathers (49% vs. 19%). If you meet Joseph, a 17-year-old African American, and you assume that he comes from a poor urban environment and has fathered at least one child, statistically, you are more probably correct than if you made the same assumptions about Heathcliff, a white 17-year-old. But, your assumptions may have nothing to do with who Joseph is. So statistical plausibility or even probability, is no excuse for categorical thinking and discriminatory behavior.

The process of faulty judgment was illustrated in the farcical movie *Amos and Andrew*. One of the title characters, Andrew Sterling, was just moving into his new summer home on Nantucket. Neighbors walked by as he was settling in and, unaware that he had bought the place, saw him trying to fix his stereo. They immediately panicked, assumed him to be a burglar, and called the police. When informed of their mistake, the neighbors attempted to justify their action by arguing that when a black man with a stereo in his hands appeared in their neighborhood, what else could it be but burglary? In fact, it turns out that Andrew was a Pulitzer prize–winner, had appeared on the cover of *Forbes* magazine, and was a celebrity of some note.

The point of the scene is that Andrew is a person. We are each individuals who share certain attributes, values, preferences, and goals with many other people. Any time we make assumptions about individuals on the basis of any one of the groups to which they belong or—to which we think they belong—we are guilty of a prejudice. When we persist in those beliefs about the individual, in spite of information to the contrary that is based on experience, then we may be said to *be* prejudiced! Even if our beliefs about the group are largely correct, assigning those beliefs to each individual may well be wrong.

Prejudice as Group Dominance in Historical Perspective

Duckitt (1992a; 1992b) suggests that our definition of prejudice will depend on the historical era under discussion. *Prejudice* was originally conceived by social scientists to describe racial antipathies based on white dominance and colonial expansionism. In this sense, prejudice was viewed as a *natural* expression of racial superiority, hence it was not considered a problem or an injustice, as it is today. But, as the legitimacy of white domination was challenged and racial discrimination persisted in a variety of forms, prejudice was seen increasingly as irrational, unconscious, and pathological, albeit normative, and as an inevitable consequence of categorizing people into social groups. Duckitt points out that all of these views of prejudice constitute the total definition of the phenomenon. It is only the specific problem or characteristics that vary, depending on the sociohistorical problem that is salient at the time. According to Duckitt (1992a; 1992b) the current notion of prejudice is "the universal cognitive processes that are the inevitable consequence of social categorization."

Prejudice Is Based on Experience, Too
In most models, prejudice is often reduced to a simple, negative attitude toward members of a group. Historically, the critical aspect of prejudice was seen as ignorance of or lack of experience with members of the target group. Although prejudicial attitudes may be developed based on erroneous facts associated with a group that are untested and contradicted by experience, those attitudes may also be based on experience with members of the group. The experience-based attitudes are, therefore, more grounded in reality than some of the ignorance-based definitions have assumed them to be. Experiences with an individual from a salient (racial) group may serve to establish beliefs about the group. These experiences may then provide a framework in which to organize perceptions and interpretations of behaviors of any specific group member. Therefore, the prejudicial treatment of a newly encountered member of the target group may be the end of a chain of reactions that began with an actual experience with another member of that group.

Working Definition of Prejudice

Let's review the discussion of prejudice:

1   Prejudice is an evaluative judgment or behavior directed at a person.
2   Although any given evaluation may be favorable or unfavorable, positive or negative, analyses of prejudice are usually concerned only with the negative evaluations.
3   The evaluation is based, to a significant degree, on real or imagined characteristics of a group to which the person belongs or is thought to belong.
4   The person may or may not possess the characteristics ascribed to him or her.
5   To the extent that the person does not possess the characteristics assigned, whether positive or negative, the evaluative judgment and corresponding behavior are prejudicial.
6   The persistence of this pattern of evaluation and inappropriate behavior when contradictory information is presented is an indication that prejudice exists.
7   Prejudicial attitudes and behavior may result from actual experiences with members of the target group.

With these basic points as guides, we can now offer a working definition of prejudice. It is on this definition that we will base our discussion when we refer to *prejudice* in the remaining chapters of this book.

> **Prejudice is a positive or negative attitude, judgment, or behavior generalized to a particular person that is based on attitudes or beliefs held about the group to which the person belongs.**

There are two important aspects of this definition to make note of. First, both positive and negative attitudes are important to prejudice. Although we frequently think of its negative aspects, research shows that in-group bias often plays a larger motivational role in the treatment of out-groups than out-group hostility does. Second, the principle of generalization from the group to the individual, a process known as *categorical judgment*, is at the heart of what we mean by *prejudice*. Let's now turn to the theories that describe the origins and processes of prejudice.

*T*HEORIES OF PREJUDICE

Theories of prejudice try to explain why it happens. Why are people prejudiced? Why, in other words, do people feel negatively about, unfairly evaluate, or behave negatively toward target people on the basis of how they themselves feel about their group? There are two issues expressed in this question: (1) Why do they feel negatively toward the target group, and (2) why do they generalize that feeling to apply it to individual group members?

Theories of prejudice will vary as a consequence of where the authors have chosen to assign responsibility—the level of casual explanation. G. W. Allport (1954, pp. 208–217) proposed six levels at which prejudice could be stimulated or caused, as follows:

- *Historical approach*—This approach suggests that only when the total background of social conflict is understood can its current expression be understood. According to this view, racial prejudice is a product of the historical forces set in motion by slavery, Jim Crow, and the unfolding of racial dynamics over the last century. Prejudice, then, has been and continues to be promoted in order to preserve the racial dominance that was established long ago.
- *Sociocultural approach*—The sociocultural approach is favored by sociologists and anthropologists. This view suggests that prejudice is a result of ethnocentric preferences for standards of progress and materialism. Beliefs and values associated with upward mobility, economic success, and the material representations of such success define *merit* and *goodness*. People who lack these symbols of success are looked down upon. According to this approach prejudice is directed at those who are situated at the bottom of the sociocultural, socioeconomic ladder.
- *Situational approach*—The situational view looks to contemporary patterns of social and economic forces for explanations of prejudice. According to this view, prejudice may arise from political correctness or from opposition to it, from preferential treatment or the lack of it. Here, contemporary situational sources of conflict are believed to sow the seeds of prejudice.
- *Psychodynamic approach*—The psychodynamic approach has three premises: (1) It assumes humans to be fundamentally prone to hostility and, therefore, seeks to explain prejudice as an inevitable result of this quarrelsome nature. Hostility arises from concerns with economic or material advantages (i.e., anyone who stands in my way is a threat and must be dealt with), fear and defensiveness (e.g., concern with one's own well-being and reaction to any perceived threats), and a need for prideful self-aggrandizement. (2) It assumes that humans, at birth, merely seek comfort, love, and nurturance. But, as they fail to receive these in sufficient degree, they become frustrated, and this frustration activates

the hostility assumed to lie latent in human nature. (3) This view also assumes that only some people, by virtue of their characters, become prejudiced. These "prejudice-prone" people are notable for being insecure and anxious, having a need for order and consistency, and being suspicious of change and difference. *The Authoritarian Personality* (Adorno et al., 1950) describes this character type.

- *Phenomenological approach*—The phenomenological view explains prejudice as arising from the immediate experiences in a situation—that is, how the target person is perceived or what expectations are aroused. This view assumes that historical, sociocultural, and character-based factors all converge to define and determine the immediate reaction in the situation and provide a causal explanation for the prejudiced person's behavior.

- *Stimulus-object approach*—In the stimulus-object view, the final and most proximal cause of the prejudice is sought in the target of prejudice himself or herself. This approach looks for real differences between groups that may provide a basis for intergroup antipathies that could explain the negative treatment in a given situation. A balance between what G. W. Allport (1954) calls *earned reputation* (real, true characteristics of the stimulus target) and considerations irrelevant to the target (i.e., characteristics of the perceiver or actor, including stereotyping, guilt projections, scapegoating, conformity to racial norms, etc.) reveal the extent to which a person is judged to be prejudiced. The greater the weight that is given to irrelevant considerations, the more prejudice is evidenced.

These broad theoretical approaches to the study of prejudice (Figure 6.1) illustrate how we move from macro to micro levels of analysis—from examination of the broad historical sweep of time to analysis of the immediate situation and the specific target persons involved. Social psychology has focused primarily on the individual level of analysis. Prejudice is fundamentally a social psychological issue in that it is manifested at the level of the individual—individuals are prejudiced. However, the biases indicative of prejudice may arise as a result of socialization to specific beliefs and values, or conformity to norms of behavior. Is an individual who is dutifully socialized to adhere to certain beliefs responsible for them? If not, who is? How do we apportion responsibility among individuals, groups, and society? To be sure, prejudice is a problem in the United States and in the world. But we must continue to ask "Whose problem is it"?

For the most part, prejudice has continued to be understood as an individual-level phenomenon; therefore, individuals are held responsible for its occurrence. But the degree of an individual's responsibility is determined, in part, by the degree of intentionality. Consider a child, Eric, who pulls a chair up to the counter and reaches up to take a cookie from the cookie jar on the shelf, even though he has been told not to do so. In the process, he knocks the cookie jar over and it breaks. He is responsible for breaking it, although his doing so was certainly not intentional. Now, consider another scenario featuring the same child. Eric wants to fix breakfast for his ailing mother. He climbs up onto the chair to get a cup from the cupboard in order to make his mother some hot chocolate. While getting the cup, he accidentally knocks the cookie jar over and it breaks. Here, again, he is responsible for breaking the cookie jar. In a third situation, our young accident-prone subject is angry with his mother for forbidding him to eat any cookies. Eric angrily goes outside after being told he cannot have a cookie. Still angry, he picks up a stick, reenters the kitchen, and smashes the cookie jar into bits. He is responsible for breaking the jar in this situation, as well.

In which of these scenarios is Eric judged to be most responsible for breaking

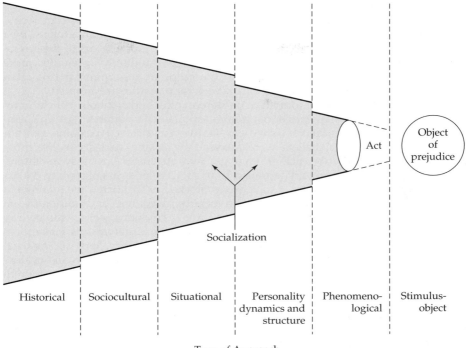

FIGURE 6.1

Theoretical approach to the study of prejudice. (Adapted from G. W. Allport, *The Nature of Prejudice* (pages 13, 14, 206–218, 281, 469, and 570) ©1979 Addison-Wesley Publishing Company, Inc. Reprinted by permission of Addison-Wesley Longman Publishing Company, Inc.)

the jar? Most people would say he bears most responsibility in scenario 3, followed by scenario 1, and least in scenario 2. Two variables explain this ordering—intentionality and validity of purpose. Eric is most responsible when his intention matches the outcome. His responsibility is lessened when it does not match, as in the first two cases. However, the degree of responsibility reduction is less when his purposes are considered invalid, as when he is stealing cookies. The determination of his degree of responsibility reflects what we as a society think about him—whether he is flawed by a character defect or a basically good child to be forgiven because he is merely a victim of fate (Weiner, 1994).

Contemporary theories of prejudice in social psychology emphasize factors close to the interaction situation and residing in the individual. These factors will be examined in more detail in the remaining chapters of Part 2. For now, we will briefly discuss how several components come together to provide explanations for prejudice.

Prejudice Arises from Beliefs, Emotions, and Values
Zanna (1994) has proposed four sources of influence on the development and occurrence of prejudice. The four sources are *stereotypical beliefs* (i.e., the notion that

typical members of the group possess certain characteristics or traits), *symbolic beliefs* (i.e., the notion that typical target group members violate cherished majority- or dominant-group traditions, customs, and values), *emotions* that are aroused by a member or members of the group, and *past experiences* with members of the group. This multiplicity of factors makes gaining an understanding of prejudice more complicated but helps to capture some of the scope of description that is often missed when simple and sovereign explanations for prejudice are adopted.

Zanna (1994) collected information on stereotypical and symbolic beliefs, emotional reactions, and past experiences from a sample of 71 dominant-group Canadian students regarding French Canadians, Native Americans, Pakistanis, and homosexuals. Stereotypical beliefs were assessed by asking subjects to list those characteristics that describe each group (e.g., "they are cheap," or "they are intelligent"). Symbolic beliefs were determined from subjects' answers regarding the extent to which typical members of each group blocked or facilitated the attainment of certain values (freedom, world peace, beauty), customs, or traditions (e.g., Canadian work ethnic, respect for law and order). Emotions were evaluated by asking subjects to indicate how typical members of the target groups make them feel when they think about them (e.g., proud, disgusted, angry, happy). The measure of prejudice was provided by having subjects rate each group on an "evaluation thermometer" ranging from 100° (extremely favorable) to 0° (extremely unfavorable).

Results showed that subjects were most favorable toward English Canadians (their in-group) and least favorable to homosexuals. Attitudes toward French Canadians, Native Americans, and Pakistanis were intermediate, in descending order of favorability. Correlations between the prejudice score and stereotypes were positive for each group, which shows the stereotype-prejudice connection. There was also a positive relationship between symbolic beliefs and prejudice, even after the effects of stereotypic beliefs were statistically removed. Similarly, there was a relationship between affect and prejudice after controlling for stereotypical beliefs. What these findings show is that prejudice can be explained by several different factors. Each of those factors contributes unique variance to the explanation.

In addition, the data in Figure 6.2 suggest that the patterns of prejudice vary with the target group. There is only a weak relationship between stereotypes, symbolic beliefs, and affect for English Canadians, but a strong relationship between prejudice and all three for French Canadians and homosexuals. Symbolic beliefs play a larger role in prejudice toward Native Indians and French Canadians, and affect plays a greater role in prejudice toward Pakistanis.

The advantage of this multiple-factored view of prejudice was demonstrated further. Data showed that respondents who scored high in right wing authoritarianism were more prejudiced than those who were low scorers; also, the degree of prejudice was predicted better by the presence of *symbolic beliefs* than by stereotypical beliefs. Therefore, this view of prejudice, as well as the research based upon it, indicates that conventional ideas of racial stereotypes explain some, but not all, of the phenomenon. Emotions play a big role, as does the extent to which a group is seen as "like us," enhancing "our way of life," or supporting our "sense of values." When "family values" are cited in contemporary political discourse, it seems to be a code term used to indicate whether a person or group is thought to enhance traditional U.S. values, or to undermine them. Identification of racism as symbolic or as modern, as discussed in the previous chapter, brings out this same set of issues in trying to explain race-related political behavior and policy support.

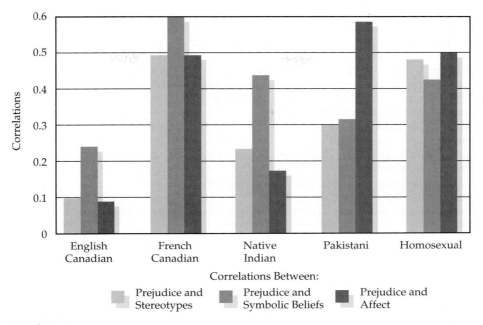

FIGURE 6.2

Correlations of Stereotypes, Symbolic Beliefs and Affect with Prejudice. (Adapted from Zanna [1994] Table 4, p. 16.)

Terror Management Theory

Implicit in the Zanna (1992) analysis is that symbolic beliefs represent core cultural values to which a person may be socialized. The degree of loyalty to those values may differ across populations (e.g., right wing authoritarians may adhere to such values more closely). An intriguing theory of how core values and beliefs may influence prejudice reactions is provided by *terror management theory* or TMT (cf. Solomon, Greenberg, and Pyszczynski, 1991; Greenberg, Pyszczynski, et al., 1990). TMT suggests simply that people are in terror of death and all of the aversive experiences associated with it. People's cognitive abilities enable them to contemplate the inevitability of their own demise. The resultant anxiety pushes them to ever greater cognitive and emotional lengths in order to develop a buffer against this anxiety. They therefore must develop a *cultural anxiety-buffer*, which consists of two components: (1) a faith in the validity of a cultural conception of reality that provides meaning, standards of value, and the promise of immortality, and (2) the belief that one is meeting those cultural standards of value. Processes of consensual validation through social comparison (cf. Festinger, 1954) help people to determine how well they are upholding important cultural worldviews.

The importance of this cultural anxiety buffer increases as thoughts of one's mortality increase. According to the theory, when one is confronted with death anxiety, the social-comparison, cognitive, and emotional processes enable one to bolster the commitment to a cultural worldview by embracing those who share it, and by rejecting those who threaten it. Prejudice, then, may be seen as a terror management reaction to perceived threat and heightened awareness of one's mortality.

Greenberg, Pyszczynski, et al. (1990) tested these propositions in a series of studies. Death-anxiety levels were manipulated by making subjects' mortality salient. This was done by asking them "to write about what will happen to them as they physically die and the emotions that the thoughts of their own death aroused in them" (Greenberg, Pyszczynski et al., 1990, p. 310). Half the subjects were given this instruction, and the other half either were not given any further instructions or were assigned a different writing task (e.g., "describe the emotion that the thought of food arouses in you"). In the first study, Christian subjects rated Jews and Christian targets equally when mortality was not salient. However, when it was made salient, Christian subjects rated Christian targets significantly more positively and Jewish targets significantly more negatively. A second study showed that a measure of authoritarianism distinguished responses to death salience. Specifically, *low authoritarians* were not influenced by death salience in evaluating other subjects who were similar to themselves (based on degree of similarity in responses to an attitude questionnaire). However, *high authoritarians* evaluated similar others *more* favorably when death was salient. This shows that in-group preference or liking for like-minded people is affected by death anxiety, but only for high authoritarians. Another finding concerning how authoritarians responded to dissimilar others was even more intriguing. Although all subjects in this particular study rated dissimilar others less positively, low authoritarians rated dissimilar others *more* positively when death was salient, but high authoritarians rated dissimilar others *less* positively when death was salient. Putting these findings together, we see a very troubling pattern in which perceived threats to personal well-being lead people to close ranks and value in-group members even more, and to correspondingly devalue out-group members. Therefore, any threat to personal well-being would be expected to heighten the likelihood of evoking prejudiced reactions to people who are different. Moreover, these effects are more pronounced in certain personality types—namely, in authoritarians.

Although the threats in the studies discussed above were only indirect or implied (e.g., difference in religion or attitudes), a third study showed that the same effects were obtained when cultural values were attacked directly. In this study, subjects read a one-page transcript of one of two interviews. One interview was highly critical of the U.S. political system, the other, highly laudatory. The interviewee making the remarks was the president of the American Communist Party or a Nobel laureate in political science from Harvard, respectively. The same effects of mortality salience were obtained here. There was more negative judgment of the critical interviewee, *regardless* of his credentials. This finding implies that the threat itself was sufficient to arouse the culture anxiety buffer that mediated subjects' responses to the threat, independent of the credibility of the analyst.

Therefore, TMT can be seen as a provocatively powerful instigator to prejudiced thoughts, feelings, and actions. But, there is some good news here as well. Although death salience usually increases intolerance, Greenberg, Simon, et al. (1992) found that death salience increases commitment to the dominant cultural worldview, regardless of its content. Therefore, if the cultural worldview is inclusive and democratic, then death salience makes a person *more* likely to become *tolerant*. (We will return to TMT in the discussion of some of the implications of racism in Chapter 16.)

Prejudice Is Influenced by Personality
Ego-defensiveness (i.e., blaming others for one's own misfortune, or scapegoating; cf. Dollard and Miller, 1941) or a flawed personality, as suggested by authoritarianism

(Adorno et al., 1951), have been dominant theories for explaining race prejudice. For the most part, prejudice enters into our analysis as an explanation for negative antipathies toward out-groups. The most famous personality explanation centered on the *authoritarian personality*. The authoritarian personality type (Adorno et al., 1951) could be considered a syndrome of characteristics, including a tendency toward ethnocentrism; hostility toward out-groups; emphasis on obedience, discipline, and respect for authority; and dogmatic or rigid thought beliefs.

The personality of the authoritarian is a repressed personality. Shrinking from the harsh discipline he or she has experienced, the subject internalizes obedience. Simultaneously, the subjects with hostility against the harsh discipline; they project their own anger onto others who are different. The connection between the authoritarian personality and prejudice, then, is via ego-defensiveness, rationalization, and fear of any threats to the carefully constructed basis for psychological well-being.

The *right wing authoritarian* or RWA (Altemeyer, 1993) has been described as a person who projects his or her harsh disciplinary socialization onto the society and therefore is heavily influenced by established sources and embodiments of authority. These RWAs submit to authority, condone their own aggressiveness and hostility (if they perceive it at all) as sanctioned by authority, and claim traditional or conventional loyalty to established norms as a moral obligation. Altemeyer developed a measure of RWA and found that it correlated significantly with conventional measures of prejudice, such as ethnocentrism, hostility toward homosexuals, antiblack attitudes of white South African students, and support for the Communist party in its opposition to democratization.

We have examined various theories about the psychological basis of personality development. What is clear is that, in adults, the characteristics of authoritarianism are a reliable and persistent indication of the likelihood of prejudice. The personality approach to prejudice emphasizes psychological needs that will not easily be changed by simple information or subtle reconfigurations of work or other societal groups. For the most part, research in social psychology has tended to move away from these hard-to-change explanations for prejudice. Instead, it has begun to concentrate more on the middle ground, that of cognitive processes and social stimulus properties. Nonetheless, there may be significant aspects of prejudice that personality approaches serve to illuminate. For example, the pro white or in-group perspective raises the possibility of a "*superiority personality*." This, in fact, is the nature of the *social dominance orientation* approach (Sidanius, 1993). Sidanius and colleagues have shown remarkable insight in their accounting of traditional race- and gender-related prejudice effects. We will discuss this issue more in Chapter 8.

Prejudice Results from Cognitive Processes

Over the past 25 years, social psychological ideas about prejudice have expanded from the earliest, a firm belief in the intentional, self-serving nature of prejudice, to the view that prejudice may well be unintentional and even unconscious. Whereas educating people and changing their attitudes was seen as the antidote to prejudice in the 1950s and 1960s, more recent assessments of prejudice suggest this ameliorative prescription may need to be rethought.

Work by Banaji and Greenwald (1993; Greenwald and Banaji, 1995), for example, suggests that implicit stereotyping occurs as individuals internalize social structures in their cognitive representation of them. For example, men are assumed to be more famous than women, and this leads subjects to make memory mistakes when simply trying to recall the names of people who may or may not be famous. No conscious motivational bias is supposed. Rather, cognitive processes that respond to stimulus salience, accessibility, and vividness (cf. Fiske and Taylor, 1992) can produce biasing results when the social world is structured that way.

Similarly, as noted earlier, Devine (1989) shows that social perceptions and impression formation are influenced by exposure to stereotypical information, even when that information is not available to conscious manipulation. Other cognitive mechanisms, such as illusory correlation (Hamilton and Gifford, 1976), explain the formation of stereotypes as the result of the co-occurrence of infrequent negative behaviors (e.g., violent acts) and of minority status.

This shift away from individual motivation toward unconscious cognitive processing of biasing social information tacitly acknowledges that prejudice may have origins outside the individual prejudiced person, even if its expression is directly reflected in individual behavior. That is, prejudice is rooted in U.S. society, and individuals who are socialized within its institutions toward the goal of maintaining the overall culture will be susceptible to thinking and behaving in prejudiced ways.

MEASURING RACIAL ATTITUDES AND LINKING THEM TO PREJUDICE

Attitudes are a central concept in social psychology. In fact, Allport (1935, p. 4) defined social psychology as "the scientific study of attitudes." Attitudes are similarly a central feature of any analysis of prejudice. Attitudes are typically conceived as evaluations of an attitude object.

> . . . an overall categorization of an attitude object along an evaluative dimension (e.g., favorable-unfavorable, positive-negative). (Haddock, Zanna, and Esses, 1993, p. 1106)

For our purposes, one's racial attitude consists of how one categorizes a racial group or a member of a racial group along an evaluative dimension of positivity-negativity. Our working definition of prejudice follows this attitudinal approach in that it concerns one's linking a negative attitude toward a target group to a specific member of the group.

Over the years, racial attitudes have been measured in a variety of ways—typically, in order to demonstrate the extent to which whites have negative attitudes toward blacks. The importance of this information resides in the basic belief that attitudes can be used to *predict* behavior. Therefore, knowing that a person has a negative attitude toward a racial group, one can infer, with reasonable assurance, that the person is likely to behave negatively toward individual members of that group. The link between attitudes and behaviors, however, is more complex than this simple idea suggests.

In Chapter 3 we reviewed the LaPiere (1994) study, which showed that attitudes toward an Asian couple, as indicated by responses to a questionnaire, were not consistent with actual behaviors to the Asian couple. The attitudes were more negative than the behavior was. Over the years, more sophisticated measures of attitudes and more theoretically detailed accounts of their relationships to behaviors has given us a better understanding of the issues of prejudice.

One important idea about attitudes is that they are not "computed" each time an object is presented for evaluation. That is, your attitude toward homosexuals, for example, is not computed anew when you are asked a question about homosexuals or see a gay man or a lesbian. Rather, your attitude can be viewed as ". . . an association in memory between a given object and a given summary evaluation of the object (Fazio, 1995, p. 247)." This approach to attitudes makes the important assumption that attitudes hang around in your head with their evaluative labels intact. This means that when you are asked a question, say, about blacks, your associations between blacks and a predominately positive or negative summary evaluation are activated, called into consciousness. Your responses or your behavior, then, will be influenced by the nature of these associations in memory—this racial attitude. One implication of this view is that attitudes can be "activated" by a question, an image, or a person.

In order to understand prejudice, then, one must be able to measure these associations between category labels of social groups (Chicanos, lesbians, Jews, American Indians, African Americans, etc.) and the summary evaluative judgments that are connected to them in memory. These connections can result from direct experience with a member or members of the target group; indirect experience, as when parents or other personally significant people talk about them in evaluative terms; or indirectly or second hand, as from observations of television, movies, and the like.

Although attitudes are most commonly associated with evaluative summaries, they are derived from *cognitive information* (beliefs about the group), *affective information* (how we feel about the group), and *past information* (how we have previously behaved toward the group) (cf. Zanna and Hempel, 1988). Therefore, beliefs (cognitions), feelings (affect), and experiences (behavior) all contribute to the formation and expression of attitudes. These conceptions stake out a broad and important territory for the study of prejudice.

One of the important issues in studying prejudice concerns the changes over time of racial attitudes. The primary arguments in this book have been historical; that is, we have noted that race relations have unfolded over the years as expressions of sociocultural attitudes, beliefs, and practices. The connection between public expression of racial issues, (i.e., what we say) and privately held attitudes (i.e., what we feel and believe) has become a major concern in social psychology, and has great relevance to the study of prejudice. In the following pages, we will take a brief look at the advances in the measurement of racial attitudes. The evidence obtained from them will be important to assessing our current understanding of prejudice.

Unobtrusive Measures of Racial Attitudes

In the early 1970s, social psychological research demonstrated that what people said about racial groups may not correspond to what they felt. If this were so, then methods for getting at what people felt were needed in order to gain a more accurate measure of racial attitudes. Weitz (1972), for example, showed that a measure of affective reaction to a black person detected negative feelings that belied previously expressed statements that showed no racial biases. Sigall and Page (1971) showed that when subjects were asked questions about their racial attitudes under conditions that allegedly revealed their "true" attitudes (e.g., the "bogus pipeline"), they gave more negative racial attitudes than when they were not under this covert surveillance.[3] For example, subjects rated African Americans as *more* sensitive than other Americans on a paper-and-pencil measure. However, when subjects were hooked up to the "bogus pipeline," they rated African Americans as less sensitive! Finally, Gaertner (1973) had black- and white-sounding confederates make phone calls asking for emergency help because the caller was stranded on the expressway and needed a tow truck. The caller pretended to have dialed a wrong number from a pay phone with his or her last dime. The confederates called members of the Conservative and Liberal parties in New York City. As expected, Conservative party members helped the black caller less often than they helped the white caller (65% vs. 92%), and Liberals showed no significant difference in responses to the black and white callers (75% vs. 85%). However, Liberals hung up *prematurely* (before they could learn of the motorist's problem) more often when the caller was black (19%) than when he or she was white (3%). Thus, Gaertner (1973) was able to show both direct racial bias (for Conservative party members) and indirect, or "aversive," racial bias (for Liberal party members).

Speed of Response Indicates Racial Biases
Even in the early 1970s, the unobtrusive measures of racial attitudes described above revealed racial biases in feelings and reactions to racial groups. This sophisticated measurement approach was further advanced by the idea that reaction time to stimuli could be a signal of the true nature of an attitude. This follows from the Fazio (1995) notion that an attitude is an association in memory of an object with an evaluation. The stronger the association, the stronger the attitude, and the more quickly it can energize a behavioral response. Several studies illustrate this reasoning and its affect on behavior.

Gaertner and McLaughlin (1983) paired *black* and *white* with negative words (e.g., *lazy, stupid,* and *welfare*) and with positive words (e.g., *smart, ambitious,* and *clean*) in a lexical-decision task in which subjects are required to judge whether two strings of letters are both words. Sometimes they are words, as indicated above; sometimes, they are nonword strings, such as *chrtp.* As expected, subjects made these judgments more quickly when *white* was paired with positive words *and* when *black* was paired with negative words. This finding suggests that racial attitudes include both a positivity bias for whites and a negativity bias against blacks. This result was replicated by Dovidio, Evans, and Tyler (1986) using a slightly different lexical-decision task—could a presented word, say, *ambitious* ever be true of the word that preceded it, say *black*? These studies begin to show that racial attitudes form systematic cognitive structures that influence basic processing of social information.

Automatic reactions to racial stereotypes affect perception. Devine (1989) argued that racial biases may be an automatic response to the prevalence of cultural stereotypes. Therefore, the racial attitude associated in memory with blacks is a negative representation of blacks as derived from biasing cultural stereotypes. She illustrated the plausibility of this idea by "activating" or "priming" a racial atti-

---

[3] The *bogus pipeline* is a machine equipped with bells and whistles that contains a locked wheel that subjects hold on to. Through electrodes attached to the subject's arm, the bogus pipeline allegedly is able to detect small muscular movements and to identify them as tending toward either the right or the left. A leftward movement is associated with a tendency to disagree, and a rightward movement, a tendency to agree with a statement. Subjects are asked questions, and the machine whirls and pings and finally spits out their "true" responses.

tude with culturally stereotypic words (e.g., *nigger, lazy, welfare,* and *Africa*). The activation of the racial stereotypes was done subliminally by presenting the words via tachistoscope for only 0.8 milliseconds. Subjects were instructed to watch a dot in the center of the visual field and to simply report in which of four quadrants a symbol appeared. They were unable to report with accuracy above a statistical chance result the words that they had, in fact, seen. To vary the degree of activation, Devine presented 100 trials on which either 80 were race-relevant, stereotypical words (high prime) or only 20 words were race-relevant (low prime). In order to assess whether priming the attitude or stereotype in this way had any effect on behavior or judgment, she had subjects read a scenario. The scenario depicted a day in the life of a fictional character named Donald. Donald gets into a variety of contentious situations such as deciding he does not want something he has just bought and demanding his money back, refusing to pay his rent until his landlord paints his apartment, and sending a dirty glass back to the kitchen at a restaurant. Subjects form impressions of Donald, which include indications of his aggressive or hostile nature. Devine reasoned that aggressiveness was part of the African American stereotype; therefore, by activating the stereotype, the association of aggression with it will make it more accessible in memory and will affect subjects' judgments of Donald. That is what she found. Subjects with 80 percent primes judged Donald to be more aggressive and hostile than those with only 20 percent racial primes. This effect of the magnitude of the racial primes had no differential influence on judgments of Donald on traits unrelated to hostility. Moreover, the effect was the same for subjects whether they scored high or low on a measure of modern racism (cf. McConahay, 1986). Devine (1989) concluded from this that racial attitudes or stereotypes are connected in memory in the cognitive structures of people socialized within this society. They can be activated by appropriate environmental cues and, once activated, influence the social perceptions and judgments people make. Therefore, to some extent, prejudice may be an automatic response to living in a racialized society. (We will explore the implication of this possibility in more detail in Part 3 "Racism.")

The racial environment directly and unconsciously influences behavior. A similar finding relating to the automatic activation of racial attitudes has been labeled the *chameleon effect* by Bargh and Chen (1996). Bargh and Chen argue that if activation of an African American stereotype can influence a person's perception of a target's hostility, then it ought to also increase the likelihood the person will behave in a hostile manner.

To test this proposition, subjects participated in a computerized visual task. They were required to judge whether a visual field containing a number of circles (ranging from 4 to 25) contained an even or an odd number of circles. This exceedingly boring and tedious task was preceded on each trial by a subliminally presented photograph of a young African American or Caucasian male face. At the end of the 130th trial, an error message appeared ("F11 error: failure saving data"). Later, subjects were notified of the consequences of the error by means of an on-screen message: "You must start the program over." Needless to say, the subjects were very upset at having to do this boring task over again, and they showed it. The experimenter then came into the room, fiddled with the machine, and said, "I'm sorry but you'll have to do the experiment over again." He fiddled some more and then announced that he had found the data and that the subject wouldn't have to repeat the experiment after all. The critical measures were (1) the subject's initial response to the computer message, which was videotaped; and (2) the experimenter's rating of the degree of hostility subjects showed.

The results showed that both the experimenter's ratings and judges' blind ratings showed more hostility for subjects who had been subliminally primed with images of African American male faces than those who had been primed with images of white male faces. Moreover, as Devine (1989) found, these effects were unrelated to subjects' scores on modern racism. Therefore, the chameleon effect suggests that attitudes or perceptual processes can be directly affected by the environment. What people feel, perceive, and even think can be directly influenced by what is around them—that is, the images, pictures, and words. Although precisely what gives images, pictures, or words their meanings was not studied here, evidence of the ability of these images to influence behavior directly "without conscious involvement" is an illuminating new piece of the prejudice puzzle.

Automatic activation of racial attitudes—a bona fide pipeline. The studies by Devine (1989) and Bargh and Chen (1996) were directed at the effects of racial stereotypes on perceptions of hostility and of hostile behavior, respectively. Fazio, Jackson, Dunton, and Williams (1995) were interested in attitude measurement itself. They were interested in demonstrating the idea that attitudes are stored in memory as evaluative summaries of attitude objects. Whereas Sigall and Page (1971) tricked subjects into revealing their true attitudes by means of the bogus pipeline, Fazio et al. (1995) wanted to show that one could measure "true" attitudes directly—hence, the measurement's name, the *bona fide pipeline*.

Subjects were presented with a series of twelve adjectives that were predominately positive (e.g., *attractive, likable,* and *wonderful*) and twelve that were negative (e.g., *annoying, offensive, disgusting*). They were instructed to press one of two buttons as quickly as possible. Pressing one button indicated that the word was predominately positive (button labeled "good"), whereas pressing the other indicated that the word was mostly negative (button labeled "bad"). Preceding each trial, subjects were shown a photograph of either a black or a white person for 315ms in the context of a "detection task" learning the faces while indicating as quickly as possible the connotation of the adjective that immediately followed the face. The critical score was the extent to which reaction times changed during these experimental trials from a pretest baseline measure that was taken without any pretrial photos. Facilitation was defined by the speed of response to the experimental trials with faces compared to the pretest trials without faces. A response was considered to be facilitated when the trial responses were faster than the pretrial responses to the same words had been. Facilitation scores were taken as a measure of racial attitudes. The greater the facilitation score, the stronger the attitude. Figure 6.3 shows that, for white subjects, facilitation was greater for *positive* words preceded by white compared to black faces, and for *negative* words preceded by black as compared to white faces. That is to say, whites showed positive attitudes toward whites and negative attitudes (or possibly simply less positive attitudes) toward blacks.

Results for black subjects showed the reverse effect. Facilitation scores were greater for images of black faces as compared to those of white faces when words were *positive,* and for white faces as compared to black faces when words were *negative.* Fazio et al. (1995) take these results to be a clear indication that racial attitudes can be automatically activated as evaluative associations to an individual member of the racial group.

Moreover, they were able to detect in-group biases in racial attitudes. The pattern of in-group bias was reflected by subjects' higher facilitation scores on positive adjectives and lower scores on negative adjectives when the trials were preceded by the image of a same-race face. This pattern was found for both black and white subjects, as Figure 6.3 shows.

To further confirm the utility of this measure of attitude and its relation to behavior, a black female experimenter evaluated the degree of friendliness and interest in psychology for all white subjects. She was blind to the subject's racial attitude. This measure correlated significantly with the attitude measure, based on facilitation scores (.31). In addition, subjects had been asked to give their assessment of the verdict in the Rodney King trial in Los Angeles. They were asked whether or not they thought (1) the verdict was just, (2) the angry response of the black community was just, and (3) how much responsibility for the ensuing riots each of a number of groups (blacks, Koreans, the media, and the Los Angeles Police Department) deserved. The *more* favorable subjects were on the unobtrusive measure of racial attitudes, the *less* responsibility they felt blacks deserved for the riots (i.e., they held a more positive view of blacks). Therefore, this measure of racial attitude is derived from individual reactions of subjects to photographs of black individuals. Although subjects were aware of the race of the faces they saw, the evaluation task was exceedingly complex and involved over 50 trials, so their ability to control the influence of the faces on their reaction to the words was minimal. Therefore, this measure, as Fazio et al. (1995) claim, can indeed be seen as a bona fide measure of racial attitudes.

The Modern Racism Scale—A nonreactive measure of racial attitude?
We discussed at some length the modern racism concept and the scale designed to measure it. We also compared modern, symbolic, and aversive racism, all of which

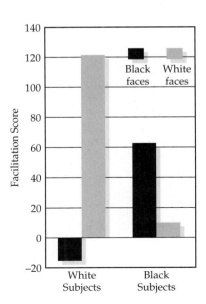

FIGURE 6.3

Facilitation Scores for Black and White Subjects as a Function of Viewing White or Black Faces. (Adapted from Fazio et al, 1995.)

were shown to be new representations of racial judgments that were not meant to be detected as such. The norms of our society have evolved to the point that it is no longer generally appropriate or desirable to say things that might be construed as offensive or that imply racial superiority. It is a short step from holding a negative thought about a person from a stigmatized group and being labeled a "prejudiced person."

Our final consideration of the measurement of prejudice will explore the extent to which the modern racism scale (MRS), which is widely used as a measure of racial attitudes, is sufficiently nonreactive to provide a "true" measure—that is, one that can be taken for what it represents. The results of using the MRS are mixed. Devine (1989) demonstrated that all subjects, regardless of MRS scores, showed the automatic reaction to the African American stereotype activation by judging Donald to be more hostile. Bargh and Chen (1996) showed that, regardless of their MRS scores, white subjects were more angry when made to redo the tedious and boring task when they had been subliminally primed with images of black faces than they were when they had been primed with images of white faces. Finally, Fazio et al. (1995) showed that their unobtrusive measure of racial attitude predicted behavior and judgments of responsibility for rioting in Los Angeles following the Rodney King verdict, but *not* scores on the MRS. These findings raise questions about the validity of the MRS as a measure of racial attitudes. In addition, Fazio et al. (1995) showed that when subjects were reassessed on the MRS two to three months (time 2) after an initial administration (time 1), their second scores were significantly influenced by the race of experimenter who administered the MRS. Scores at the second administration were significantly higher on racism when the measure was taken by a white experimenter than they were when administered by a black experimenter. The correlation between time 1 and time 2 was .68 when the experimenter was white and .29 when the experimenter was black. This suggests that subjects most likely altered their responses in the presence of the black experimenter.

However, there is evidence on the other side, as well. For example, Devine (1989; Devine, Monteith, Zuwerink, and Elliot, 1991) has shown that reliable and important distinctions can be found between subjects who score high on the MRS and those who score low.

High Modern Racism scorers, unlike low scoring subjects, did not suppress the effects of stereotypes on their judgments when given a chance to do so. Moreover, when they receive feedback suggesting they are biased toward either black males or gay men, those with negative attitudes (as measured by the MRS for blacks or the Heterosexual Attitude Toward Homosexuals [HATH] [Larsen et al., 1980] for gay men) felt no *compunction* about their biases, but those low in modern racism or anti-gay attitudes felt emotional distress when made aware of their biases. Although the HATH is different from the MRS, it is similar enough to support the idea that paper and pencil measures of social attitudes can be useful in explaining differences in prejudicial attitudes and behaviors.

Fazio et al. (1995) also found that the subjects who scored high on the MRS also were more likely to believe that the Rodney King verdict was just, that blacks were more responsible for the riots, and to rate the photographs of black people used in the study (when presented in a normal manner) as less attractive. Therefore, although the MRS did not correlate with the unobtrusive measure of racial attitude and showed itself to be affected by the race of the experimenter, it nevertheless showed a correlation with racial judgments that made sense as a product of higher antiblack attitudes.

However, Fazio et al. (1995) do not interpret these correlations as evidence that the MRS provides an accurate measure of racial attitudes. Instead, they suggest that the MRS will be predictive of any racial attitude that involves a willingness to express prejudice and/or political conservatism.[4]

Finally, Wittenbrink, Judd, and Park (in press) have made a strong claim for the utility of the MRS. In their experiment, white college students performed the lexical-decision task developed by Dovidio, Evans, and Tyler (1986), in which subjects make a judgment about whether a given attribute adjective (say, *smart*) "could ever be true of" a particular noun (say *house*). In this study, the nouns used were three— *white, black,* and *house.* The 24 attributes used included 8 words that described houses but not people, and 16 that described people, 8 of which were stereotypic of African Americans and 8 of which were stereotypic of white Americans. For each set of stereotypic words, half were basically positive (for blacks, *humorous, athletic, musical, streetwise;* for whites, *intelligent, independent, successful, wealthy*) and half were negative (for blacks, *ignorant, poor, dishonest, violent;* for whites, *boastful, stubborn, materialistic, exploitative*). Prior to each lexical-decision trial, one of four types of subliminal prime words was flashed on the computer screen (*white; black;* a nonword letter string; or a nonperson filler, such as *lemon, table,* etc.). Response facilitation was measured as the latency of response to the race prime (black or white) compared to the neutral prime (house). The faster the response to the lexical task following *white* or *black* compared to *house,* the more facilitation.

Figure 6.4 shows the pattern of prejudice indicated by Wittenbrink et al. (in press) to be similar to the findings of Fazio et al. (1995). That is, positive white stereotypes and negative black stereotypes produced the greatest response facilitation. This pattern corresponds to in-group prowhite bias, and out-group antiblack bias. However, whereas Fazio et al. (1995) found no correlation between this "implicit prejudice" measure and scores on traditional paper-and-pencil measures of racism, Wittenbrink, Judd, and Park (in press) did. In this study, implicit prejudice correlated significantly with high scores on the MRS (McConahay, 1986), antiblack attitudes (Katz and Haas, 1988), aversive racism (Gaertner and Dovidio, 1986), and attitudes about reverse discrimination.

It is significant to note that these microlevel measures of racial attitude seem to reliably assess racial sentiment. Furthermore, these racial sentiments reveal themselves in behavior, as shown by Fazio et al. (1995) and in expressions of out-group antipathies, and, perhaps, in-group preferences, as shown by Wittenbrink, Judd, and Park (in press).

How Is Prejudice Studied?

Societies aren't prejudiced, groups aren't prejudiced, people are! This focus on people or individuals is quite compatible with the experimental approach in social psychology, where the individual is the unit of analysis. The individual-level analysis asks some basic questions about prejudice, such as (1) how people become prejudiced; (2) what the psychological mechanisms that typify and sustain prejudicial thought and behavior consist of; and (3) how the incidence of prejudice can be reduced. Most social psychological research on prejudice is aimed at answering one of these questions.

---

[4] The symbolic and modern racism view has been criticized because of its close connection to political conservatism. The question arises as to how one can, *in principle,* hold politically conservative views or accept the truth of negative social stereotypes and not be branded as a racist? Sniderman and Piazza (1993) argue convincingly with empirical support that attitudes may be more complex than the MRS presumes. Issues of education level and political ideology affect the conclusions we can draw about the meaning of racial attitudes.

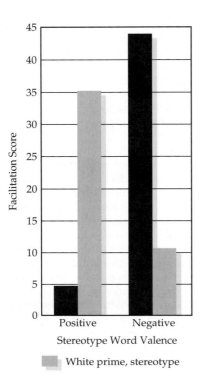

FIGURE 6.4

Facilitation Scores on Positive and Negative Race Stereotypic Words as a Function of White and Black Primes. (Adapted from Wittenbrink, Judd & Park [in press].)

For the most part, prejudice is indicated by negative attitudes or behaviors directed at a person who differs from an actor on some salient social dimension. Sometimes, this differential treatment is inferred from group data. That is, a number of subjects are assigned to different conditions wherein—the target of their evaluations or behaviors are either white or black, male or female, gay or straight, in general, "stigmatized" or not. The group means are then compared, and when the behavior is more negative toward the stigmatized target than toward the nonstigmatized target, prejudice is inferred. Consider the following study by Rogers and Prentice-Dunn (1981).

White subjects arrive for a study on the effects of biofeedback and behavior modification. Subjects arrived at the experiment in pairs. One (the real subject) is there for the behavior modification, and the other (the confederate) is there for a biofeedback study. The experiment was designed so that the behavior-modifier subjects were to shock the biofeedback confederates whenever their heart rate fell below some predetermined level. Subjects were randomly assigned to one of four conditions—(1) biofeedback confederate insults them, (2) confederate does not insult them, (3) confederate is black or (4) confederate is white. When the subject is insulted, he overhears the biofeedback confederate talking with the experimenter. When asked if he minded the subject's shocking him, he comments that the equipment looks pretty complicated and then wonders whether a subject as "dumb" looking as this one could follow directions properly. When asked if they want to withdraw, the biofeedback subjects respond that they hope the behavior-modifier subject is not as stupid as he looks. Finally, when asked if he knew the behavior-modifier subject, the biofeedback subject responds, no, he didn't know them personally, but he "knew their type," he could tell they thought they were "hot stuff."

The research question here is, Does the subject treat the biofeedback confederate differently as a function of his race? The behavior in question is aggression. Aggression was measured as a function of the intensity and duration of shocks delivered to the biofeedback confederate when his heart rate fell below the predetermined level. Figure 6.5 shows that, for whites, the level of shock administered to the biofeedback confederate when his heart rate fell below the appropriate level was unaffected by whether or not he had insulted the behavior-modifier subject. However, for black biofeedback confederates, shock levels are lower than they are for whites in the no-insult condition, but *much greater* than they are for whites when the behavior-modifier subject had been insulted. This differential pattern of behavior by the white subjects toward the black confederates compared to white confederates is an indication of prejudice. There is nothing specific about the black confederate that explains differential treatment by the subject, except his skin color. It is assumed that his skin color activates his racial group membership and, along with it, attitudes toward blacks. Being insulted by a black person, apparently, arouses greater anger in white subjects than being insulted by a white person does. This differential negative treatment of a black person on the basis of his group membership implies that a prejudicial judgment has been made and has led to prejudicial or discriminatory behavior.

But we should note here that no individual subject is asked to make a comparative judgment between a black and white person. He does not set the shock machine at one level for a black person and at a different level for a white person. This sort of experiment is called a *between-subjects* design, because the variables of interest (the race of the biofeedback confederate and whether he insulted the subject or not) had different subjects in each condition. Because subjects were randomly assigned to the four experimental conditions, it can be concluded that nothing about them personally explains the differences in results. The best explanation for these results is that there is a differential response to the stimulus conditions.

FIGURE 6.5

Aggression as a Function of Insult and Race of Victim. (Adapted from Rogers & Prentice-Dunn [1981, p. 68].)

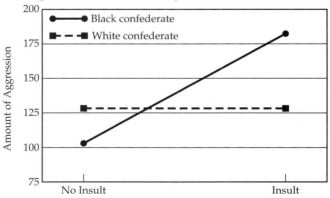

Because of the high regard in which experimental investigations of individual-level variables are held in social psychology, studies of this sort are highly characteristic of the data upon which knowledge of prejudice is based. There are also available studies that make comparative judgments. That is, there are studies in which individual subjects make judgments of in-group targets and out-group targets. Differences between the types of targets can be deduced *within the same subject*. In these cases, an assessment can be made regarding whether or not a given subject treats a given black person differently from a white person.

Recall the Word, Zanna, and Cooper study (1974) in which Princeton undergraduates interviewed black *and* white high school students. In that study, each real subject interviewed three people, two white and one black. The first interviewee was always white, the next two were counterbalanced between white and black. The behavior in question was whether or not the white interviewers treated the black person or the second white person differently. In making this comparison, each subject's response for each race of interviewee was calculated. Differences found could then be shown to reflect comparative differential treatment by race. In this case, it could be concluded that the white subjects treated the black interviewees differently than they treated the whites. This is direct evidence of prejudice, because the confederates were matched on relevant characteristics and trained to behave in comparable ways. Therefore, any differential treatment was a reflection of the subject's more negative treatment of the black interviewee relative to treatment of the white interviewee.

It is not easy to study prejudice directly in the research laboratory. We most frequently study the formation of expressions of stereotypes or measure racial attitudes. Based on the presumed connection between racial attitudes and behavior, we make the assumption that holding negative stereotypes or racial attitudes predisposes a person to behave in a prejudiced way. Even more difficult is the study of positive instances of prejudice. As we noted earlier, prejudice is exemplified by a too-positive assessment of a person based on in-group status (e.g., Greenberg et al., 1992). Gaertner and colleagues (in press) have attempted to distinguish out-group antipathy (negative prejudice) from in-group preference (positive prejudice).

Gaertner and colleagues (in press) evaluated the proposition that racial bias may reflect prowhite attitudes as much or more than antiblack ones. Recall the Frey and Gaertner (1986) study (Chapter 5). In that study, the subject's partner needed help because he had a more difficult anagram task than the subject had (hence, he was deserving of help) or had an easy task but played around and did not try very hard (hence, he was undeserving). When the partners were deserving of help, they were helped equally—whether they were black or white (95% and 100%, respectively). However, when they were undeserving, whites were still helped a lot (93%), but blacks were not helped much at all (30%). This finding is typically discussed as reflecting antiblack bias (30% vs. 93% helping). However, it could also be perceived as prowhite bias—that is, whites were helped all the time, whether they deserved it or not!

Gaertner and colleagues (in press) describe several studies of aversive racism that could be interpreted from either a prowhite or an antiblack perspective. The critical issue here is that by defining prejudice solely as a negative or unfavorable attitude and seeking to measure it accordingly, we may be missing a very important component of prejudice—its pro–in-group quality. Our working definition acknowledges this perspective. The unobtrusive measure of Fazio et al. (1995) also detects this in-group bias. Therefore, when experimenting and measuring, it is crucial that both pro–in-group biases and negative out-group biases be examined.

How Does Prejudice Relate to Discrimination?

The problem of prejudice rests primarily in the biased behavior that follows from prejudiced thinking and judging. Documenting this biased behavior, which we call *discrimination,* is one of the central aspects of the study of prejudice. Demonstrations that discrimination takes place have been intimately linked with the *minimal-group paradigm* (described briefly in Chapter 4 and examined in more detail in Chapter 8). Associated with the work of Tajfel (1978), this experimental approach arbitrarily divides subjects into two groups (hence, they are members of groups in only the most *minimal* way) and creates a pretext for distributing some valued resource, (e.g., points, money, praise) to others who "belong" to one of these minimally constructed groups. In Chapter 4, we referred to the preference for abstract art of Paul Klee or Wassily Kandinsky. Given the opportunity to distribute some valued resource to Kandinsky or Klee lovers, Klee lovers give more of it to fellow Klee lovers and less of it to Kandinsky lovers. They can therefore be said to *discriminate* between the two. One of the important questions to which we will return later is whether they discriminate *against* the Kandinsky-ites, or *for* the Klee-ites?

This may appear to be somewhat trivial, but the wealth of research using the minimal-group paradigm has proven how powerfully even this most minimal representation of a group can affect one's behavior toward group members. When we talk about discrimination in common contexts, it becomes a far more serious matter. For example, when we look at who gets loans to buy a house, we find that members of certain ethnic or racial groups are less likely to be approved, even when we control for their financial status.

In 1993, for example, ABC television's hidden-camera episode of *Prime Time Live* followed two male "testers" who had been matched, as much as possible, on appearance, education, and style, with the critical exception of race—one was black and one was white. The video showed them trying to rent an apartment, buy a car, browse in a stereo store, and so forth. The camera documented the differential treatment of the two men. The black man went to rent an apartment and was told there are none available, the last one was rented that morning. The white man followed him by a few minutes and was not only told an apartment was available, but was given a key and told to take a look. When Diane Sawyer came back to point out the discrepancy, the proprietor denied any discrimination. The fact is that the black man was treated differently from the white man. As far as one can tell, the only difference was the color of his skin *and* the set of beliefs about what might happen as a result of renting an apartment to him.

Therefore, discrimination is the behavioral manifestation of prejudice. Discriminatory behavior follows from some degree of preference for one person over another, and that preference is derived from a judgment about the group to which the person belongs or is thought to belong. There is an old saying, "Sticks and stones may break my bones, but names will never hurt me." Well, discrimination may be thought of as the "sticks and stones of prejudice"!

*S*UMMARY

This concludes our general discussion of prejudice. This chapter introduces prejudice as a problem by which individuals are judged in terms of their group membership. Prejudice is a social problem because the group is ascribed negative and undesirable characteristics, then individual members of the group are presumed to possess those traits, and are treated as if they did. Although we usually focus on this negative group evaluation aspect, prejudice also involves positive group judgments, usually of our own group. Therefore, *in-group bias*, fostered by positive prejudices for people like us, is also an important aspect of the problem.

We discussed how prejudice comprises not only these generalizing tendencies from the group to the individual, but also involves personality and cognitive characteristics of the perceiver, cognitive rigidity, authoritarian personality, and a belief in the *naturalness* of social dominance. That is, people who demonstrate the most prejudice generally feel that it is natural for groups to be arranged in hierarchical fashion and that inequalities of group outcomes which reflect that hierarchy are normal and *should* be maintained.

Prejudice is typically related to stereotypes of the group, usually framed in terms of individual characteristics (blacks are lazy, Jews are cunning, Americans are ambitious, etc.). But we have seen evidence that prejudice is related also to attitudes about the beliefs different groups hold that may symbolize an absence of traditional values. Believing in a spirit world, same-sex marriages, and government responsibility for racial equality may reflect group differences that become a target for prejudicial attitudes and behaviors. Moreover, simple feelings of discomfort around members of certain groups may contribute to prejudicial practices. The implication of that is that prejudice is not a simple link between false stereotypes of a group and discriminatory treatment of its members, but a complex patterning of stereotypes, beliefs, and feelings that trigger attitudes and behaviors toward people.

Prejudice rests primarily on attitudes. Social psychologists have become increasingly sophisticated in their measurement of attitudes and thus in their ability to detect prejudice or the potential for it. We reviewed theory and research which suggests that racial attitudes have strong automatic components that may exist and operate outside of conscious awareness. Our perceptions of others, our speed of making evaluative judgments, and our emotional reaction to situations and people who are associated with racial groups are all influenced in subconscious ways by our racial attitudes and feelings. This suggests that acting as though race doesn't matter may be easier to say than to do.

An important concern is raised about how racial attitudes, and hence the potential for prejudice, have changed over the years. Some theorists argue that overt expressions of racial bigotry and bias have changed not so much in feeling but in expression. The expression of racial biases can be found in symbolic terms related to social policies and political activities. The antiracial sentiments, in this way of thinking, attach to social policies that are presumed to benefit the racial group and lead to opposition to the policy. This modern, symbolic, or aversive racism is strengthened by some of the findings reviewed in this chapter.

Other theorists believe that equating opposition to social policies presumed to benefit a particular group is too broad a brush with which to paint prejudice. One cannot thus distinguish principled support of social policies with irrational opposition to racial and other groups. The question of when prejudice arises, to what is it responsive, how is it manifested, and what role society plays in it are explored in greater detail in the remaining chapters of Part Two and in Part Three.

The remaining chapters of Part 2 will draw out the social psychological research on stereotypes and their role in the perpetuation of prejudice (Chapter 7); the problems of intergroup relations (Chapter 8), and specific factors that maintain conflict and that may hold promise for their attenuation. Chapter 9 describes conflict in three major areas in the world: Rwanda, between Hutus and Tutsis; the former Yugoslavia, among Bosnian Serbs, Bosnian Muslims, and Croats; and Northern Ireland between Protestants and Catholics. These three sources of intergroup conflict, features of our social psychological analysis of intergroup relations, and mechanisms of prejudice will be compared. Chapter 10 proposes that the target of prejudice may have some critical say both in determining whether a given behavior will be experienced as prejudice and how perpetual stereotyping and stigmatization may affect a stigmatized target's behavior. Finally, Chapter 11 tries to pull all of these studies and analyses together by summarizing what we know about prejudice and how this knowledge will inform our strategies for reducing its prevalence in society.

7

Psychological Mechanisms of Prejudice: Stereotypes

---------- ❖ ----------

Introduction ◆ What are stereotypes? ◆ *Stereotypes as inaccurate prejudgments or accurate overgeneralizations?* ◆ *Stereotypes as individual or consensual beliefs* ◆ *A working definition of* stereotype ◆ How are stereotypes measured? ◆ Where do stereotypes come from? ◆ *Categorization* ◆ *Illusory correlation* ◆ *Perceiving social groups* ◆ How are stereotypes structured and how do they function? ◆ *Stereotypes as cognitive structures* ◆ Stereotypes influence perception and behavior ◆ *Stereotypes affect what information is attended to and encoded* ◆ *Stereotypes can influence how information is construed or interpreted* ◆ *Stereotypes can influence how information is processed* ◆ Why are stereotypes so important to prejudice? ◆ *Our reaction to social groups depends on what we think or how we feel about the groups* ◆ *Unconscious processes link stereotypes to prejudice* ◆ Summary

> *"To believe that a person's race controls his point of view is to stereotype him."*
> Fifth Circuit Court of Appeals, *Hopwood v. Texas*, March 18, 1996

INTRODUCTION

Stereotypes connect people together who may not go together. The Supreme Court in *Hopwood v. Texas* rejected race-based admissions policies because, the justices argued, knowing only a person's race does not tell you what he or she thinks, feels, believes, likes, or dislikes, what talents or abilities he or she has, or what values he or she possesses. What matters about people, the Court implied, is not signified by the color of their skin or the racial designation checked on their applications. Because what we learn by knowing a person's racial status is, in the Court's view, not meaningful, using it as a determinant of an important decision, such as admission to law school, is unacceptable. In the Court's view, the substantial variability among people within racial, ethnic, or gender groupings is so great that the category label itself has no intrinsic meaning. Therefore, treating people solely on the basis of their ethnic, racial, or gender category is, in the Court's words, "to stereotype them," and the Court deemed that unacceptable.

Stereotypes are a problem in our society. The underlying principles of a society that is based on the supreme importance of individuality are violated by the institutional reliance on or promotion of stereotypes. Not only does a stereotype put people together who may not go together, it frames an expectation that may not fit a given individual. What do we "know" about someone when we know that he or she is African American, a woman, a gay man, a lesbian, a Hindu, a Jew, or poor? We don't *know* anything, but we may *suspect* some things. We may suspect that the Jew is concerned with money or is smart. We might believe the gay man to be artistic, or unassertive, or morally perverse. We may expect the woman to be emotional, conformist, and nurturant. We may expect the African American to be athletic, musical, aggressive, unintelligent, and so on. We know that these suspicions, or to put it more neutrally, *expectancies*, shape what we perceive—and subsequently influence our judgment of and behavior toward a person.

Yes, stereotypes are a problem in our society. Lee, Jussim, and McCauley (1995) tackle the common assumption about stereotypes being bad and inaccurate. Jussim, McCauley, and Lee (1995) propose that stereotypes may be conceived along two independent dimensions; accuracy (accurate vs. inaccurate) and valence (positive vs. negative). Social psychologists, by their analysis, have focused almost exclusively on only one of the resulting quadrants (inaccurate-negative stereotypes). They suggest that negative stereotypes can be accurate (blacks *are* poorer than whites) and that positive stereotypes can be inaccurate (beautiful people are *not* better) and they can be accurate (people who make more money tend to have higher IQs). But by focusing on the negative and inaccurate stereotypes, a biased picture emerges. Jussim, McCauley, and Lee (1995) catalog the many problems of bias that stereotyping causes in social perception and judgment. Following is a list of possible reasons that stereotyping is a problem:

1   *Stereotypes are factually incorrect.* It cannot be true that all members of a group possess specific traits. Even the most salient race characteristic, darker skin color, is not possessed uniformly, or at all, by all African Americans. Not all Hispanics speak Spanish. Not all American Indians are spiritual nor do they all live on reservations. So, a stereotype, as an all-or-none characterization of a group, is bound to be wrong. But maybe this is not what we mean by *stereotype*. Let's dig deeper.

2   *Stereotypes are illogical in origin.* Stereotypes do not arise from personal experience, but from hearsay or second-hand information. Maybe our parents tell us something about a group, either directly or indirectly. Maybe we draw inferences about a group based on certain information—for example, the Turks massacred millions of Armenians, or Bosnian Serbs massacred thousands of

Bosnian Muslims. So, it may be inaccurate or it may not be. It may be illogical or it may have some basis in fact.

3   *Stereotypes are based on prejudice.* According to this view, stereotypes simply reinforce already held beliefs and rationalize them. For example, the belief that women are nurturing and not able to make "tough decisions" may be a rationalization for keeping them out of the workplace or top decision-making positions. According to this view, stereotypes don't *cause* prejudice, they *reflect* it.

4   *Those who hold stereotypes are irrationally resistant to new information* that contradicts the stereotypes. We have already seen how difficult it is to change or rebut stereotypes. How many disconfirming examples do we need in order to change our mind? Stereotypes are problems because those who adhere to them tend not to change these beliefs easily, so that if the ideas are shown to be inaccurate or illogical, these peoples' resistance to change becomes a problem.

5   *Stereotypes exaggerate group differences.* Exaggeration is a part of being inaccurate, but the principal adverse effect is that it facilitates group categorization and all the processes that follow from that. People thereby believe they have less in common than they do, and this does not aid in interpersonal or intergroup relations.

6   *Stereotypes are ethnocentric.* That is, we tend to assign and evaluate the traits of others on the basis of our own preferences. A negative stereotype may not only be inaccurate *because* it is a stereotype, but its specific negativity—which does the major damage—is determined by in-group standards. For example, being loud is negative if we, as a group, prefer quiet. Being materialistic (a trait frequently associated with Americans) is negative if we prefer a contemplative life. However, this trait is often highly valued in a capitalist and individualistic society. Therefore, the ethnocentric bias inherent in stereotypes adds an evaluative dimension to the perception of group differences.

7   *Stereotypes imply genetic origins of group differences.* This aspect of stereotypes relates to the idea of *biological essentialism*—that is, the theory that differences between groups are based on biological qualities that distinguish them from others. Thereby not only are group differences exaggerated, but they are also immutable and, hence, irreconcilable.

8   *Stereotypes underestimate out-group variability.* The idea that "they all look alike," captures the exaggerated idea of out-group homogeneity. This flaw in the concept of stereotypes contributes also to the faulty connection of group members who may not go together.

9   *Stereotypes lead people to ignore individual differences.* As we saw at the end of Chapter 6, reducing prejudice, in part, involves perceiving and valuing individuality. Reliance on stereotypes works directly against that possibility; hence, adherence to stereotypes stymies efforts to reduce prejudice.

10 *Stereotypes lead to biased perceptions of individuals.* This aspect of stereotypes is a variant of the previous problem in that our judgments of an individual may be heavily influenced by what we think about the group to which he or she belongs or to which we assign him or her. This connection can happen explicitly or implicitly, consciously or unconsciously.

11 *Stereotypes create self-fulfilling prophesies.* We have already seen how the process of self-fulfilling prophesies works in the Word, Zanna, and Cooper (1974) study documenting this phenomena. If we use stereotypes to guide our expectations or suspicions, we may *see* in reality what we expected to see before the fact. Even worse, Steele and Aronson (1995) have shown that the targets of

stereotypical expectations may behave in ways that fulfill them, even as they are trying mightily to disconfirm the expectations.

Stereotypes are not solely at the root of all of the problems associated with them. But the above summary does describe the range of problems that makes this difficult and troublesome phenomenon such an important contributor to many social problems. In the analyses that follow, we will not try to prove what a stereotype really is or is not. Instead, we will review the variety of ways in which stereotypes and stereotyping have been studied and what we think we know about stereotypes and the process of stereotyping. We will also try, where possible, to identify the implications of this understanding in terms of the real problems of prejudice and racism in our society.

The topic of stereotypes has been widely studied in social psychology. Although there have been important historical studies, most of what we know about stereotypes has been learned through conceptual developments and vigorous research in the past 20 or so years—all since the first edition of this book appeared. Because many excellent summaries of the work on stereotypes are already available (cf. Hamilton and Sherman, 1994; Mackie and Hamilton, 1993; Stangor, et al., 1994), we will resist doing a comprehensive review of this voluminous literature. The pages that follow summarize what we know about stereotyping in relationship to broad and significant questions. Specifically, we discuss:

1   What stereotypes are and a working definition of the term.
2   How stereotypes are measured, which tells us both what we think they are, by virtue of how we measure them, and how they may evolve over the years.
3   Where stereotypes come from, including an examination of the origins of the content of stereotypes as well as the mental processes that make them more likely to develop.
4   How stereotypes and stereotyping lead to prejudicial attitudes and behaviors.
5   Some specific consequences of using stereotypes for making social judgments and the implications for social behavior.
6   Ways in which stereotypes specifically contribute to the occurrence of prejudice and possible ways to counteract this process.

WHAT ARE STEREOTYPES?

Literally, a *stereotype* is a metal plate that is used to make duplicate pages of the same type. Social commentator Walter Lippman borrowed this term back in 1922 to describe what he considered to be a biased perception. The bias was evidenced by comparing those "pictures" we had in our heads of someone and the reality the person presented to us. The bias resulted from preconceptions that were the result of the stereotyping process, whereby we "stamped" every member of the group as a duplicate of every other member—in other words, we created a stereotype. When we encountered a member of the group, we did not see him or her realistically. Instead, we saw the image of him or her filtered through this mental picture of the group we had stereotyped.

Stereotypes as Inaccurate Prejudgments, or Accurate Overgeneralizations?

When we formulate a stereotype, we make generalizations about members of a group. These generalizations assume a high degree of homogeneity, a degree that is never reached in reality. Not only is the degree of homogeneity among group members far lower than stereotypes postulate, the traits that form the content of stereotypes may not actually exist, or may not exist to the extent assumed. In short, stereotypes are fuzzy and unreliable. Most likely, they are not an efficient or accurate way to make judgments about our social world. When we apply this mental picture of a modal or exemplar group member to a specific person with the expectation that the person will actually match it, we are making a prejudgment. We thereby impose our own categorical thinking on the individual and fail to appreciate the person's own unique character. This is the fundamental flaw in reliance on stereotypes.

On the other hand, stereotypes are not based on thin air; there is usually a "kernel of truth" (Klineberg, 1935) to them. Therefore, they are often not wholly inaccurate. They may, indeed, capture the base rate with which given traits or characteristics exist among the members of a particular group. For example, it is a stereotype to

Giants come in different sizes! Mugsy Bogues at 5' 3" and Kareem Abdul Jabbar at 7' 3" define the polarities of height but share awards at the Jim Thorpe Pro Sports Awards ceremony on July 8, 1995, in Los Angeles. Mugsy was awarded for inspiration and Kareem for lifetime achievement. (AP/Wide World Photos)

say that basketball players are tall. On average, however, they are. That is, the height base rate for basketball players is an average height that far exceeds that of the public at large. Kareem Abdul Jabbar is a recently retired professional basketball player who scored more points than any other player in the history of the National Basketball Association. He is 7 ft. 3 in. tall and is a good exemplar of basketball players and fits the stereotype well. Mugsy Bogues, who plays for the Charlotte Hornets (at this writing), is 5 ft 3 in tall. Although he is a basketball player, he is *not* a good exemplar of basketball players, as he does not fit the stereotype. The point is that even when a stereotype is largely true, it reflects no more than a probability that a member of the group will possess the trait on which the group is being stereotyped. For example, Bogues has many other qualities vital to basketball players—such as excellent hand-eye coordination, speed and quickness, the ability to dribble a basketball, keen vision, and so forth. This teaches us a lesson. A stereotype is not a basis for judging any specific individual member of a group. Why? Because each person is unique by virtue of the fact that he or she may possess many different attributes. Some of these qualities may be associated with one group to which the person belongs, and others may be associated with another group. To base our judgment of a person solely on one attribute—however accurate or representative it may be of a group to which the person belongs—may cause us to misjudge that person. Moreover, when the attribute in question is negatively valued, the problem is compounded.

Reliance on stereotypes is bad because if often leads to such misjudgments and the consequences of such negative valuations. Nonetheless, stereotyping is done all the time by most people. Fiske and Taylor (1991) describe this tendency to simplify the complexity and heterogeneity in the human social world by exaggerating homogeneity among people as a kind of "cognitive miserliness" (p. 13). That is, we save ourselves from the effort of analyzing and judging each unique event, object, idea, or person anew by relying on stereotypes. We may rely on past experiences, guesses, hunches, assumptions, and whims. We package it all under relatively stable decision-making and concept-formation processes and thereby perceive order in the external world. However, this orderliness may only exist in our psyches. This does not deter us, necessarily. Neither are we deterred by the possibility of error. Quite the contrary, we often actively recruit information because it sustains the correctness of our judgments, not because it is an accurate reflection of reality.

Stereotypes as Individual or Consensual Beliefs

Ashmore and Del Boca (1981) describe three approaches to studying and understanding stereotypes:

1 *Cognitive approach.* In the cognitive approach, a stereotype is simply viewed as a cognitive representation of social information about people and groups of people. As such, a stereotype is "a cognitive structure that contains the perceiver's knowledge, beliefs, and expectations about a human group" (Hamilton and Trolier, 1986, p. 133).
2 *Psychodynamic approach.* In the psychodynamic approach, a stereotype is seen as a mechanism that serves ego-defense purposes. That is, stereotypes "protect" the ego from perceived threats from others and bolsters the self. Stereotypes may also serve to derogate others and, by implication, to elevate the self or the group to which one belongs.
3 *Sociocultural approach.* In the sociocultural approach, a stereotype is held to em-

anate from the sociocultural context in which we live. Stereotypes help us to define the norms of our own groups—in part, by distinguishing those characteristics of different others. Our sociocultural environment teaches us what others who are important to us think.

These three approaches identify different levels of analysis that are applied to the stereotype idea. Stereotypes may be described at the individual level (e.g., as a picture in someone's head) or at the group level (e.g., as a summary of what a group of people feel about themselves or about another group). It is agreed that stereotypes are beliefs—but whose beliefs are they, anyway? As the individual-level view places the beliefs in the head of an individual under this approach, these beliefs belong to him or her. The group-level implies that particular beliefs are shared by a social group and reflect community-wide patterns. The former is what we conventionally think of as a stereotype, and the latter is what Gardner (1994) and others call *consensual stereotypes*. We will learn of the differences between the two in the next section. For now, we make note that our definition must accommodate both of these viewpoints.

A Working Definition of Stereotype

Taking these issues into account, we must accept that a stereotype will involve both positive and negative beliefs about the characteristics of a group of people. These beliefs might be relatively accurate or inaccurate in representing the group. A stereotype may reflect the beliefs of a single person or it may be a set of beliefs shared by a group about another group. These considerations of stereotypes lead us to the following working definition:

> A *stereotype* is a positive or negative set of beliefs held by an individual about the characteristics of a group of people. It varies in its accuracy, the extent to which it captures the degree to which the stereotyped group members possess these traits, and the extent to which the set of beliefs is shared by others.

Simply holding a stereotype is not necessarily problematic. A stereotype, even if evaluatively laden and negative, only becomes problematic when it is actively used to affect how we treat a specific other person. We can therefore distinguish between existence of a stereotype (and all the characteristics that it entails) and the process of *stereotyping*, which we define below:

> *Stereotyping* is the process by which an individual employs a stereotypical belief in the evaluation of or behavior toward a member of the stereotyped group.

With these definitions of stereotype and stereotyping for guidance, let's proceed with our discussion.

HOW ARE STEREOTYPES MEASURED?

The Katz and Braly (1933) classic study, the first attempt to actually measure stereotypes, was discussed in Chapter 3. As noted earlier, this work was replicated in succeeding decades (e.g., Gilbert, 1951; Karlins, Coffman, and Walters, 1969). These studies of stereotypes share a common goal, to determine the content of stereotypes about different national or social groups.

Checklist Approach

For Katz and Braly (1933) a stereotype was a set of traits that were thought to characterize some groups more than they characterized others. By this criterion, American blacks were lazy, musical, and superstitious; white Americans were ambitious, materialistic, and intelligent; and American Jews were stingy, clannish, and so forth. Subjects were given a set of 84 trait adjectives and asked to check the 10 traits they thought best applied to each of several defined groups. They then went back and selected the five attributes that best described each group. A stereotype was identified and formulated simply by listing those trait-adjectives most frequently checked by the subject group (white Princeton men).

The results of attempt to assess the content of stereotypes were obviously limited by several factors.

1   What would a different group of subjects check? Are these traits general stereotypes or specific to each subject group? The Katz and Braly (1933) method implies that a stereotype is only defined on the basis of consensual beliefs of the respondents. By implication, then, a stereotype cannot exist apart from the particular group that believes in it.
2   The researchers chose the traits. However, are these traits the ones these subjects would have chosen?
3   What did a checkmark mean? Did it signify that all members of the group possessed this trait, that a good proportion of the group possessed it, or that certain members of the group possessed it?
4   Did the subjects agree with the stereotype, or were they simply aware of its existence?
5   On what basis did the subjects arrive at their judgment—personal experience, the newspaper, word of mouth?
6   Finally, to what extent were the characteristics of a group compared to those of other groups? White Americans are ambitious compared to whom? Is this a relative or an absolute judgment?

In spite of these questions about its true validity in measuring stereotypes, use of the Katz-Braly method persisted for at least 3 $\frac{1}{2}$ decades.

Percentage-of-the-Group Approach

In the 1970s, several researchers attempted to get past the idea that a stereotype only existed as a consensually validated belief held by a particular group of people. Brigham (1971a) asked subjects to judge not simply whether a group possessed a trait or not, but what percentage of its members possessed the trait. Using this procedure, Brigham found that, in many instances, all five of the "most characteristic" traits for a given ethnic group were thought to be possessed by less than half of its members. Moreover, Brigham (1971a) found that, in many cases, the average percentage of the group thought to possess a trait was unrelated to the way subjects felt about the group.

McCauley and Stitt (1978) used research in the psychology of prediction to improve upon the within-group percentage measure of Brigham (1971). They developed what they called a *diagnostic ratio (DR)*. Consider the stereotype of Germans, who are often considered to be "extremely nationalistic." Is that a stereotype? How would it be measured? The first question McCauley and Stitt asked was, What percentage of people in the world do we judge to be extremely nationalistic? (This provides us with base-rate information.) The next question was, What is the probability that, upon learning that someone is German, you would expect them to be extremely nationalistic? (This informs us regarding the stereotype's representatives. That is, how similar is extremely nationalistic to being German?) The question addressed by the diagnostic ratio is this: To what extent is the probability of being extremely nationalistic *if one is German* greater than the probability of being extremely nationalistic among other peoples of the world? It can be expressed in the following formula:

$$DR = \frac{P \text{ (trait/ethnic group)}}{P \text{ (trait/all people)}}$$

In the example, if the probability of being nationalistic is higher for a German than it is for a person of any other nationality, then the diagnostic ratio is greater than 1.0. If it is lower, the diagnostic ratio is less than 1.0.

Table 7.1 shows the results of calculating the diagnostic ratio for several traits found by Karlins, Coffman, and Walters (1969) to be stereotypical of Germans (efficient, extremely nationalistic, industrious, and scientifically minded), along with five traits not shown to be part of the German stereotype (ignorant, impulsive, pleasure-loving, superstitious, and tradition-loving). If this ratio is successful in identifying stereotypes, then the DRs should be greater than 1.0 for those traits identified to be part of the German stereotype, but less than 1.0 for the other traits.[1]

[1] We should also acknowledge that a group may be *less* typical in possessing a trait than others, to the point that this becomes part of a stereotype. For example, Asians may be perceived as highly intelligent but not assertive. Therefore, being unassertive may lead to a DR of less than 1.0 for Asians on assertiveness, which could be an important part of the Asian stereotype.

TABLE 7.1. THE DIAGNOSTIC RATIO MEASURE OF STEREOTYPES

Description	All people who possess the trait, % (1)	People who possess the trait and who are German, % (2)	Diagnostic ratio (2)/(1)
Efficient	49.8	63.4	1.27
Extremely nationalistic	35.4	56.3	1.59
Ignorant	34.0	29.2	.66
Impulsive	51.7	41.1	.79
Industrious	59.8	68.2	1.14
Pleasure-loving	82.2	72.8	.89
Scientifically minded	32.6	43.1	1.32
Superstitious	42.1	30.4	.72
Tradition-loving	62.4	57.2	.91

SOURCE: McCauley, C. R. & Stitt, C. L. (1978). An individual and quantitative measure of stereotypes. *Journal of Personality and Social Psychology, 36,* 929–940. Adapted for Table 1, p. 932.

The utility of this measure of stereotypes is shown by considering which traits are most highly endorsed regarding Germans. The probability that a German is pleasure-loving is 72.8, the highest probability among all the traits. However, the diagnostic ratio is only .89! That is because an even higher percentage of the world's people are thought to be pleasure-loving. Conversely, only 43.1 percent of Germans are thought to be scientifically minded. However, the DR for that trait is 1.32! Conversely, the DR for "ignorant" is only .66, which suggests that ignorance is definitely *not* part of the stereotype. Therefore, significant departures from the theoretical neutral point can be meaningful. The DR, then, tells us the degree to which a given trait is thought to be typical of a particular group, *relative* to people in general. This measure of stereotypes has some extremely positive features that make it very useful.

There are several advantages to using this measure. But the chief advantage is that we are no longer required to obtain group consensus in order to determine whether or not an individual possesses a stereotype of a particular group. Stereotype measurement has, with the DR, become an individual measure of social perception.

Finally, McCauley and Stitt (1978) sought to test the validity of the DR in a diverse sample of subjects. Sixty-five subjects, from six different subject groups—high school students, college students, union members, choir members, social work students, and caseworkers—rated the percentage of all Americans and the percentage of black Americans who (1) completed high school, (2) had illegitimate children, (3) were unemployed, (4) were victims of violent crimes, (5) were on welfare, (6) had four or more children, and (7) were female heads of family. The DR was calculated by dividing the percentage of black Americans by the percentage of all Americans who could be characterized by these attributes. These DRs were compared to a theoretically neutral value of 1.0, which would be found if black Americans and all Americans were equal in their representation on these attributes. There were six different subject groups and seven different characteristics, so that there were 42 different DR measures. Thirty-seven of them were significantly different from the neutral value of 1.0. McCauley and Stitt (1978) concluded that indeed the DR can serve as a measure of stereotype perceptions.

However, the authors also calculated the *true DRs*, on the basis of census information. For example, the high school dropout rate is 8.9 percent for whites, 13.6 percent for blacks, and 35.3 percent for Hispanics. The overall rate is 12.5 percent. Therefore, the DR for blacks is 1.08, for whites it is .71, and for Hispanics is 2.83. If the subject estimates produced a DR significantly above 1.0 for blacks, the DR would be incorrect. If they produced a DR significantly greater than 1.0 for Hispanics, the DR would be statistically correct.

In the study described above, although 37 of the DRs differed from 1.0 theoretically (the neutral value), none of them were more extreme than the true DRs based on the census. That is, although subjects did produce results that suggested significant stereotyping, their results were not at great variance with the results produced by analyzing actual census data. What can we make of this? Well, analysis of the data suggest that the validity of a given standard for measuring a stereotype will depend on the method and data we use to assess the standard. For example, if we had stopped with the DR, and had not looked at the statistical data from the census, we would have concluded that the subjects made more extreme ratings of black Americans in the seven characteristics than they made of Americans in general, and that this was indicative of stereotyping.

In the DR method, we have an intuitively appealing ratio measure of stereotyping, but we still must ask the question, have we truly identified a stereotype? That we can distinguish one group from another does not, by itself, establish that a stereotype exists. And, to reiterate, even if the stereotype is reasonably accurate, applying it in a preconceived way to an individual member of a group based on that person's group membership alone is still indicative of a prejudice!

Free-Response Approach

Devine (1989) was interested in the relationships of stereotypes to prejudice. (We will review her research in more detail later, but for now, we will concern ourselves with how she measured stereotypes.) Devine was especially interested in the *content* of stereotypes. She wanted to eliminate cues that suggested to subjects what the experimenter or others in society may have thought about the stereotypes. That is, she wanted to study subjects' knowledge of stereotypes, not what their opinions or beliefs about stereotypes were. She used a "thought-listing" procedure in which she simply asked subjects' to write down what they considered to be the cultural stereotypes of blacks, resulting in a group of categories. Because subjects were asked to report their knowledge of stereotypes, these categories are, by definition, indicative of subjects' *beliefs* about stereotypes of blacks in U.S. society. These free responses were coded into 15 categories, as shown in Table 7.2. The salience of each stereotype category is suggested by the proportion of thoughts assigned to each. According to the judgments of this college sample of white psychology majors categories, blacks are poor, athletic, criminal, aggressive or tough, sexually perverse, low in intelligence, and lazy.

That these estimates reflect general "knowledge" is demonstrated by comparing subjects who scored high on a measure of prejudice with those who scored low. Table 7.2 shows that subject's scores on a prejudice measure bore no relationship to that person's knowledge of the stereotype content. None of the differences between high- and low-prejudice subjects were statistically significant. This finding confirms Devine's idea that stereotypes are "part of the social heritage of a society and no one can escape learning the prevailing attitudes and stereotypes assigned to major ethnic groups" (Devine, 1989, p. 5).

Esses, Haddock, and Zanna (1993) suggested that the consensual approach, which relied on group comparisons, was inadequate to get at what an individual person believed and how *that* belief related to behavior. They went beyond the thought-listing procedure of Devine (1989) by also asking the subjects what the particular thoughts *meant* to them. Therefore, the specific content—say, hostile—might mean different things to different people, or even different things to the same person at different times. Moreover, how generally a trait is perceived to characterize a given group is also critical. Therefore, assessing a subject's association of the idea of hostility with blacks may not tell the whole story. The significance of a subject's association of a trait with a group will depend on whether it is evaluated negatively or positively, and whether the subject thinks the trait is *highly typical* (i.e., characteristic of a large number of group members) or only a *selective* trait (i.e., characterizing, perhaps, those who fit a hostility subtype).

The Esses, Haddock, and Zanna (1993) procedure requires subjects perform three activities, as follows:

1   List characteristics, using simple adjectives or short phrases, that they would use to describe *typical* members of the group, using as many characteristics as they think necessary in order to convey their impressions.

TABLE 7.2 THE PERCENTAGE OF HIGH- AND LOW-PREJUDICED SUBJECTS WHO IDENTIFY CULTURALLY STEREOTYPIC CHARACTERISTICS OF AFRICAN AMERICANS

Category	High Prejudice	Low Prejudice
Poor	.80	.75
Athletic	.75	.50
Criminal	.65	.80
Aggressive or tough	.60	.60
Lazy	.55	.75
Descriptive terms*	.55	.50
Low in intelligence	.50	.65
Uneducated	.50	.50
Sexually perverse	.50	.70
Rhythmic	.50	.40
Ostentatious	.50	.40
Food preferences	.25	.35
Family characteristics*	.25	.30
Inferior	.20	.30
Dirty or smelly	.20	.30

*Descriptive terms were things like "afro" or "brown eyes." Family characteristics included "many children," "single-parent homes."

SOURCE: Devine P. G. (1989). Stereotypes and prejudice. Then automatic and controlled components. *Journal of Personality and Social Psychology, 56,* 5–18. Adapted from Table 1, p. 8.

2 Examine the characteristics they have listed and rate the valence of each along a dimension from negative to positive (– –, –, 0, +, ++)
3 Once more examine the characteristics and indicate the percentage of the group to which each characteristics applies (from 0% to 100%).

To compute a stereotype score, the subject's valences are coded from -2 to +2, and percentages are divided by 100 so that they vary from 0 to 1. [The stereotype score is the product of the percentage times the valence, summed, across all characteristics that were listed and divided by the total number of characteristics.]

Esses, Haddock, and Zanna (1993) tested the utility of this measure, in a study of adult Canadians at the Ontario Science Center. They asked the subjects to evaluate six Canadian ethnic groups using this procedure. They also obtained the subjects' global ratings of overall favorability of each group. The mean attitude ratings placed English Canadians as the most highly regarded (78), followed by Chinese (69), Jews (67), Native Indians (66), Pakistanis (54), and Arabs (46). What was significant is that the stereotype measure correlated significantly with each of these ratings. Using a similar procedure, Eagly and Mladinic (1989) found that a stereotype measure predicted attitudes toward men and women, as well as toward Republicans and Democrats.

The measurement of stereotypes has come a long way since the original checklist approach of Katz and Braly (1933). The basic idea that stereotypes were simply associations, held by a community of like-minded people, between certain traits or characteristics and membership in an ethnic or a racial group has been updated and refined. We no longer have to assess the consensual beliefs of group members. We now are able to evaluate the beliefs and knowledge about stereotypes held by individuals and the extent of such stereotypes. The next task is to determine how individuals acquire these stereotypes.

WHERE DO STEREOTYPES COME FROM?

For the most part, a large majority of social psychologists utilize the cognitive definition of stereotypes. That is, they believe that a stereotype is a belief about the extent to which members of a group share certain attributes to a degree not typical of other groups or of people in general. These beliefs function according to the principles of basic cognitive structures. Therefore, understanding their operation at the individual level can be accomplished by employing the research methodologies of social cognition.

From this perspective, the question of where stereotypes come from is basically the question of how beliefs or concepts are formed. Without doubt, the first place we would turn in seeking the answer to this question is to an individual's social environment, parents, siblings, peers, and "significant others." Taken together, these people provide a context, a subculture whose values and beliefs are the most likely determinants of how a young person is socialized to the community of people and thereby develops certain beliefs about ethnic or racial groups.

In addition to these socializing influences, we also know that the influence of television and other broadcast and visual media has grown enormously in the past 25 years. These media are regularly cited for their influence on attitudes, beliefs, and behaviors of those who watch and listen. The younger the individual is, and the less formed his or her beliefs are, the more likely it is that the person will be affected by the messages that come across the airwaves. Who could doubt that the stereotype of blacks as poor, criminal, lazy, and athletic identified in the Devine (1989) study is not derived, in part, from the portrayals of blacks on television, in the movies, and in broadcast and print news coverage. Why would we suppose that blacks are believed to be heavier users of illegal drugs when the data show that this is not the case. Lippman (1922) described stereotypes as "pictures in the head," as noted earlier. Whose head or heads hold these pictures? Pictures in an individual's head are fairly simple to reconstruct, through surveys and interviews, and often can even be inferred from certain behaviors. But what about "pictures in society's collective head (cf. Stangor and Schaller, 1994)." The language, pictures, beliefs, and social structures of society do strongly suggest or convey certain pictures, which society absorbs. How is this done? When we ask how stereotypes develop, we must ask two questions: (1) How does an individual come to believe certain things about different social groups and their members? and (2) how do social groups come to be portrayed or talked about in certain ways that distinguish them from others?

The pictures in society's head define the *content* of what we collectively believe about social groups. The checklist approach seeks to define that content by demonstrating a consensus among people about what traits or characteristics exist for what groups. Stangor and Schaller (1994) believe that this content is consensually shared across members of the cultural group and thereby becomes a common ground for consensual behavior. The images that endure are those that (1) are consistent with what we expect and (2) are salient and distinctive (Fiske and Taylor, 1992). Social psychologists have focused attention on basic elements of cognitive processes and structure that support the formation of stereotypes. Hamilton and Sherman (1994) suggest two cognitive processes that aid and abet the formation of stereotypes—*categorization of people into groups* and *illusory correlation*. Let's consider how each of these might lead to the formation of stereotypes.

Categorization

As noted earlier, a *stereotype* is a generalization about the characteristics of members of a group. To form a stereotype, one must be able to define who is in and who is not in the group one is stereotyping. The easier it is to define the group, the easier it is to stereotype the members. The easy-to-define characteristics common to stereotypes are called *primitive* categories because they operate so basically, so automatically (Brewer, 1988; Fiske and Neuberg, 1990). Among the most obvious ones are race, gender, age, and height. Simply seeing some particular type of people may be sufficient to form group definitions when primitive categories are salient.

Seeing a group of people as distinguishable from others is only a first step. In order to stereotype the group, those members must be ajudged to possess certain traits or attributes that are, to some degree, distinctive to them as a group. Once we have a categorized group, what determines which traits or attributes are assigned to them?

One explanation for the assignment of stereotypic traits is provided by the "kernel-of-truth" hypothesis (Klineberg, 1935). This hypothesis suggests that stereotypes are overgeneralizations of traits that happen to exist in some measure in the given group. How are such "real" differences between groups determined? In the McCauley and Stitt (1978) study, the actual differences between black Americans and the overall U.S. population were in fact *greater* than the differences perceived by the study subjects. Application of the kernel-of-truth hypothesis suggests the possibility that people project or generalize from their own experience to the group as a whole. There are now a number of issues to be examined: How much experience is required in order to formulate a generalization? What experiences are most likely to produce such generalizations? Is it any old trait that gets projected onto a group, or are some more likely to be projected onto the group than are others?

Remember, the psychodynamic view of stereotypes suggests that they serve an ego-protective function. If that is so, then we might expect that the content of stereotypes would bear some relationship to personal ego needs. Perju-Liiceanu (1992) assessed the three most positive and the three most negative stereotypes that Rumanians held about Gypsies, along with the subjects' personal and in-group values. On the positive side, she found that Gypsies were thought to have high solidarity, to maintain traditionalism in their relationships, and to be highly talented. On the negative side, they found that Gypsies were considered to be dishonest, lazy, and uncivilized. Results showed that the attributes assigned to Gypsies depended in large measure on the salience of both personal and in-group values. That is, the more subjects valued honesty, intelligence, and cleanliness and the more important were in-group values of hospitality, love of country, and humanness, the more likely they were to emphasize the negative stereotypes of Gypsies—those traits that differed most from their in-group values. This finding suggests that stereotypes do not arise simply from judging another group, but are influenced by the salience of one's personal and group identification and values. Thus, to understand the content of stereotypes and the tendency to form them, we need to carefully consider how people feel about themselves and their own group. The more salient personal and in-group values, the more salient are the boundaries between self and other and the easier it is for stereotypes to form.

Examination of this approach takes us to the underlying motivational system of individuals and collections of individuals. That is, stereotypes evolve from ethnocentric beliefs or values and aid in the evaluation of the characteristics of people outside our own group. We feel better about our group—and, hence, about ourselves—when these distinctions are made. The cognitive approach suggests that understanding motivation is not necessary in order to understand stereotyping. The cognitive view suggests that we simply categorize people into groups because it is efficient to do so and because categorization helps us to order our social world and to predict and anticipate social outcomes. However, there is room in the categorization approach for examination of the motivational bases of stereotyping, because it proposes that people have a need to evaluate themselves positively. As a person's self-definition is, in part, socially constructed from available environmental inputs, it is easier to have a positive view of one's self if the social world corroborates it. Thus we may cling to social categories not only because of its utility in organizing our social world, but because it helps us to define who we are.

Do we categorize people into groups in order to make sense of our social world, or do we categorize people into groups in order to evaluate them against the positive qualities of our own group (the frame of reference) thereby assuring ourselves of a positive social identity (Tajfel, 1978). The categorization approach posits that how we categorize our social world is connected to how we categorize ourselves. Therefore, the motivational tendencies toward self-enhancement are related to our social values, judgments, and beliefs. The cognitive processes may be mechanisms by which we create a social world that sustains our personal needs and nurtures our desires for positive self-regard. Luhtanen and Crocker (1992) developed a measure of collective self-esteem that assesses the extent to which people base their personal well-being on their social attachments and affiliations. Luhtanan and Crocker (1992) propose that *collective identity* be used to reflect the extent to which a person identifies with his or her social group, and *collective self-esteem* (CSE) be used to denote the value a person places on his or her group membership. They developed the Collective Self-Esteem Scale (CSES) to assess four aspects of CSE:

Membership—How good a member of your group are you?
"I am a worthy member of the social groups I belong to."
Private—How good are the social groups to which you belong?
"I feel good about the social groups I belong to."
Public—How good do others think your group is?
"In general, others respect the social groups that I am a member of."
Identity—How important are your social groups to your self-concept?
"The social groups I belong to are an important reflection of who I am."

Studies using the CSES have shown that CSE scores predict subject's responses to a group threat, with those high in private CSE reacting to a threat to the group in ways that were in-group enhancing. Subjects low in private CSE did not. This suggests that if your group is important to your well-being, you will behave in positive ways toward individual members and to the standing of the group. Ethier and Deaux (1990) found that in a Hispanic sample, women identified with the group more than men did, but cultural background made more of a difference in CSE for men than for women. Arroyo and Zigler (1995), more recently, have shown that African American adolescents low in CSE have higher scores on a measure of race-lessness than those high in CSE.

How we feel about or evaluate others is intimately connected to how we feel and evaluate ourselves. Therefore, categorizing and judging others is closely associated with feeling good about ourselves. The traits we ascribe to others depend on personal motivational goals served by group status and whether it contributes in a positive or negative way to our psychological well-being.

Illusory Correlation

Just as the term implies, an *illusory correlation* is the perception that two things are correlated or associated when, in fact, they are not. "Blondes have more fun" correlates having fun with being blonde. A fairly recent article in the *Washington Post* (1994) described how a mother dyed her daughter's hair from brunette to blonde because she was afraid her young daughter would not be socially popular as a brunette. The change "worked," and the girl received more attention than she had in the past. By the time she was an adult, she had been a blonde for many years. She noticed, however, that although she was good at what she did—and even successful, by most standards—she was not really having fun. Men were not taking her seriously. So, she reversed the experiment and again became a brunette. She was treated with more respect, had more substantive encounters with men, and found that she was enjoying herself more. Is it possible to conclude, on the basis of cases such as this one, that believing blondes have more fun is an illusory correlation, an association that does not exist in fact?

In the illusory-correlation explanation for the formation of stereotypes, it is claimed that illusions of association between two variables are heightened when they share *distinctiveness* and *infrequency*. Somehow, our mental processes attach a greater degree of association to those things that stand out but are not statistically more likely to occur. According to this view, this association is not motivated by self-enhancement tendencies or by a need to belong to highly regarded social groups. It is a fault of how we process social information.

Hamilton and Gifford (1976) tested the illusory-correlation idea in the following way. Subjects read a series of statements about behaviors (desirable or undesirable) that members of two groups exhibited (group A and group B). For example, "John, who is a member of group A, visited his sick mother in the hospital." The 39 sentences were constructed so that group A members outnumbered group B members 26 to 13; desirable behaviors outnumbered undesirable behaviors 27 to 12. Notice that group A and group B *do not differ* in the percentage of desirable and undesirable behaviors associated with them. For both groups, 33 percent of the described behaviors are undesirable (9 out of 27 for group A; 4 out of 12 for group B); and 67 percent are desirable (18 out of 27 for group A, and 8 out of 12 for group B). Therefore, Hamilton and Gifford (1976) verified that there was no correlation between the type of behaviors and group membership. Therefore, any perception that there was a correlation would be *illusory*.

According to the illusory-correlation theory, the association of infrequent undesirable behaviors with infrequent group B members should heighten subjects' perception of their co-occurrence. That is exactly what Hamilton and Gifford (1976) found. Subjects were shown the 39 behaviors and asked to identify whether a member of group A or group B had performed the behavior. The average numbers of group A and group B members who were associated with the desirable behaviors and with undesirable behaviors are given in parentheses in Table 7.3. The averages for desirable behaviors were pretty close to the real occurrences—17.52 for group A members and 9.48 for group B members. However, for undesirable behaviors, biases occurred in two directions: (1) Group A members were perceived to have carried out fewer undesirable behaviors than they actually did (5.79 instead of 8) and (2) group B members were perceived as carrying out more undesirable behaviors (6.51 instead of 4). This result supports the illusory-correlation effect, because shared infrequency did produce a heightened association of people with behaviors.

However, this result also showed that the perception of undesirable activities being performed by the majority was suppressed. This raises the possibility that the illusory-correlation effect may have two components: (1) an *increased* correlation of a minority group with infrequent behaviors and (2) a *decreased* correlation of majority-group members with infrequent behaviors.

To show that this effect was fundamental to the shared infrequency pattern, Hamilton and Gifford (1976) reversed the frequency of desirable and undesirable behaviors in a second experiment. When this reversal was effected, subjects in group B (the minority) were perceived to have performed more *desirable* behaviors, and members of group A (the majority) were perceived to have performed fewer desirable behaviors.

In addition, subjects were asked to evaluate the members of groups A and B on positive and negative trait adjectives (e.g., *popular, sociable, industrious,* and *intelligent; irritable, unhappy, lazy,* and *foolish*). It was expected that, on the basis of the selective memory and disproportionate association of undesirable behaviors with group B, members of group B should correspondingly be judged less favorably. And, indeed, they were: Group A members were rated 6.91 on positive traits and 4.39 on negative ones. By comparison, group B members were rated 6.15 on positive traits and 5.31 on negative ones. So, by pairing members of a minority group with undesirable and distinctive behaviors, Hamilton and Gifford (1976) demonstrated that these undesirable behaviors would be more easily remembered *and* that, because the behaviors were undesirable and associated with the less frequent group, the evaluation of those group members would be more negative. All of this occurs in judgments of hypothetical, no-name people, from data that provides no statistical support whatsoever for the association. Does this then provide an explanation for the formation of stereotypes that is not based on motivational properties of ego-defense or sociocultural learning?

TABLE 7.3 ILLUSORY-CORRELATION PATTERNS IN THE FORMATION OF STEREOTYPES

	Desirable Behaviors	Undesirable Behaviors	Total
Group A	18 (17.52)	9 (9.48)	27
Group B	8 (5.79)	4 (6.41)	12
Total	26 (23.31)	13 (15.69)	39

SOURCE: Adapted from Hamilton and Gifford (1976). Table 1, p. 397.

McArthur and Friedman (1980) sought to answer that question. They conducted a replication of the Hamilton and Gifford (1976) studies; however, they used real demographic group pairings (old and young people; black and white people; men and women) instead of the abstract groupings used by Hamilton and Gifford (members of group A and group B). Subjects were presented with eight 4- by 6-in index cards that provided "case histories" describing desirable or undesirable behaviors. Each card included a photograph of a patient that had been evaluated by a psychiatric social worker. The infrequency of each demographic group was created by using only two of the particular demographic category (e.g., for race, half the subjects saw two black and six white patients; the other half saw two white and six black patients). In each case history, undesirable behaviors were less frequent than desirable behaviors were.

McArthur and Friedman (1980) found that illusory-correlation effects occurred when infrequency distinctiveness and associative distinctiveness combined. That is, when low-frequency stimulus groups (i.e., black people, old people, and women) were associatively linked with the undesirable behaviors, illusory correlations were found. When whites, young people, or men were the infrequent group, the more infrequent *desirable* behaviors were more strongly linked to them. This finding suggests that shared infrequency may reflect a way in which minority groups who are associated with distinctive, negative, and infrequent behaviors *continue* to be stereotyped. It also suggests that, for majority people with positive associative links to behavior, a positive "halo" is perpetuated by the illusory-correlation processes.

It also suggests the existence of a stereotyping catch-22 for persons from minority groups that already have negative social stereotypes. Examples of positive behaviors by members of these groups do not influence judgments of the group as much as instances of negative behaviors influence such judgments. Conversely, negative behaviors by members of positively regarded majority groups do not influence judgments of their group to the same degree as instances of positive behaviors do. The implication here is that once a group has a positive association, it is much harder to deflate it. Once your group has a negative association, it is much easier to maintain it!

Perceiving Social Groups

The kernel-of-truth view of stereotyping suggests that stereotypes arise from some factually true and distinctive characteristic of a group, which is then overgeneralized to individual members of the group. Hoffman and Hurst (1990) suggest that gender stereotypes are typical of this kernel-of-truth idea. Specifically, they propose that the different social roles occupied by men and women explain the content of stereotypes about them. If men occupy different roles than women do in a given society (e.g., the work they do is regarded as important, they have leadership positions, they make more money and have more control than women do), are we to conclude that they occupy these roles *because of* the kind of people they are (i.e., because of their personalities)? Are we also to believe, given such a status for males, that women are consigned to social roles that have less control, make less money, and are less highly valued in the workplace? Remember that Myra Bradwell was denied entry to the bar in Illinois (back in 1879). It was believed that women should not be lawyers, because they did not possess the personalities to do legal work and that their being lawyers was not ordained by "natural law" of humankind. Therefore, the Illinois Supreme Court concluded, it would be wrong for the Illinois bar to accept Bradwell's petition to be admitted to that association. Appropriate roles—and hence, opportunities—were prescribed by a set of beliefs about men and women and about what activities were appropriate and inappropriate for each gender to do. This example leads to the question of whether stereotypes follow from *what people do* in society (i.e., their social roles) or whether they follow from *attempts to rationalize social roles* that are prescribed by social beliefs?

To test the possibility that gender stereotypes may result from rationalizations of imposed gender differences and not from observations of real differences, Hoffman and Hurst (1990) had subjects read make-believe vignettes that described a hypothetical people, composed of two groups, who live in the countryside near large cities. The two groups corresponded to two types of people, *child-raisers* and *city workers* (i.e., to social roles). The groups were described in either biological terms (as two different species) or in cultural terms (as two different subcultures). In some cases (about half), 20 percent were child-raisers and 80 percent were city workers; in the other half, these percentages were reversed. Subjects were asked to simply judge the personal qualities of the people described.

Results showed that the so-called city workers were judged to be more male-like, or "agentic" (competitive, self-confident, ambitious), and the child-rearers were judged to be more femalelike, or "communal" (affectionate, gentle, emotional, etc.). This was more pronounced when the groups were thought to be *biologically* different. That is, when the distinction was biological, child rearers were thought to be more communal, and city dwellers were thought to be more masculine. The effect was even more pronounced when subjects were asked to *explain* why people would occupy the roles they did. These findings suggest that the exaggerated link between occupational role and personality traits results not only from the extent to which members of a group occupy that role, but also from an attempt to explain the division of people into those roles. In other words, we do not simply infer trait differences from the different roles people occupy. These trait inferences, instead, are also *exaggerated* because we are forced to explain or rationalize their existence.[2]

Two things stand out from these results. First, the funneling of social groups, for whatever reason, into different occupational niches leads us to infer that such groups communally possess different personality attributes and that the possession of these traits makes this occupational segregation "natural." Second, when asked to explain this covariation, we readily come up with explanations that reinforce the existence of the stereotypes we have drawn.

It is generally believed and, often demonstrated, that biased memory for stereotype-consistent information serves to sustain stereotypes (Higgins, King, and Mavin, 1982). It certainly is plausible: Confirming a stereotype validates our social perception and renders our expectancies about people more secure. However, there is also reason to believe, and ample evidence to support, the idea that we are more likely to pay attention to stereotype *disconfirming* information. This information challenges our understanding of the world. That is, if we cannot make it conform to

---

[2] We should note that this effect was replicated using less-gender-linked groupings by social roles—namely, people who worked in the free enterprise sector versus those who worked in the research or educational sector. The former group was judged to be more agentic, and the latter more communal. The perception of the correspondence between occupational role and personality was again greater when an explanation or rationalization of this linkage was requested.

our expectations, we may have to change the way we think about people—a process that arouses our defenses.

Piaget (1952) showed that children acquire a stable view of the world and their place in it by forming schematic representations of that world that direct the perception and assimilation of new information. When the new information doesn't fit the emergent schema, they actively seek out reasons for this in the external world. They do not immediately challenge their emerging knowledge of how the world is supposed to work. In other words, kids are confident in their schemas and, when the world fails to conform, they blame the world. Therefore, it makes sense that, when we hold stereotypes that are only weakly formed, but strongly believed, disconfirming information is a challenge and becomes the focus of our attention. When this occurs, disconfirming information is more likely to be remembered than confirming information is, because the former arouses more active cognitive processes and may even arouse emotional defenses.

Stangor and Ruble (1989) tested this idea by asking college students to make overall impressions of two anonymous fraternities from a sample of 60 described behaviors. The behaviors were manipulated so that one group appeared to be extroverted and the other to be introverted. Stangor and Ruble (1989) manipulated the degree of experience subjects had by exposing one group to 30 additional sets of behaviors by fraternity members. As expected, subjects in the "experienced" group remembered more stereotype-congruent information than "inexperienced" subjects remembered. Moreover, this effect was obtained more strongly for the extroverted condition, which was a stronger stereotype of fraternity members in this college population.

Two implications of this study are that (1) it is harder to disconfirm a stereotype in actual behavior and (2) the stronger a stereotype is held, the more likely we are to remember confirming behaviors and to form impressions of people that are consistent with the stereotype. Therefore, there is an *automaintenance* quality to stereotypes. That is, we tend to confirm our expectations in interpersonal interactions, and this expectancy-confirmation process tends to sustain the expectations.

Neuberg (1994) proposes that the tendency toward automaintenance aided and abetted by the social goals that people bring to interactions. That is, if we *want* to confirm a negative stereotype, we will selectively perceive, evaluate, and interpret behavior in such a way that it is consistent with our expectations. Neuberg (1994) offers the following illustration of how a perceiver interested in confirming that a Hispanic job applicant is unqualified might behave:

1 *Ask biased questions:*
   "So, Mr. Gomez, tell me about a recent job of yours in which you didn't perform as well as you would have liked?"
2 *Pay close attention to expectancy-consistent behavior:*
   Take special note that Mr. Gomez got lost on his way to the personnel office.
3 *Interpret ambiguous or expectancy-inconsistent behavior as expectancy-consistent:*
   Interpret Mr. Gomez' being laid off from his previous job as having been fired.

These biased processes enable a person to confirm stereotypic expectations in spite of the disconfirming factual information revealed in an interaction. These confirmation tendencies are enhanced further if we are in a hurry or in need of making snap judgments.

Making more accurate judgments is enhanced when the perceiver is motivated to be accurate or when he or she wishes to present himself or herself in a positive light. More accurate judgments are also likely when the target is motivated to present herself or himself accurately, not necessarily as he or she concludes the perceiver thinks of him or her. In sum, automaintenance of stereotypes is associated with a range of self-fulfilling–prophesy dynamics that take both the perceiver and the target into account.

Considering the contemporary world, with its increasing visibility of diverse groups, we might expect that stereotypes of different groups would vary in the degree of clarity and certainty we believe that they provide us about the group. The stereotypes of the disabled, for example, are likely to be less systematic than the stereotypes of women; a stereotype of gays and/or lesbians is likely to be less systematic than a stereotype of Hispanic immigrants is, and so on. In addition, the greater the within-group variability, the less secure the stereotype of that group is likely to be. All of these factors diminish the confidence with which stereotypes are held. They may have the cumulative effect of minimizing the memory-bias for confirming information and thereby may reduce the *automaintenance* qualities of the stereotype. Moreover, the social goal of presenting ourselves as nonprejudiced may make the presentation of targets more positive. But targets may also have goals of disconfirming an expected stereotype and, in trying to do so, may confirm it, as noted earlier (cf. Steele and Aronson, 1995).

A final issue for the discussion of the formation of stereotypes is the question of when stereotypes are most likely to be formed. That is, what traits or qualities are most likely to be perceived as stereotypical of a group? One answer may be "those traits that are most salient and important in our own group." For example, if members of group A tend to wear brown shoes and members of group B tend to wear black shoes, it is not very likely that the group differences in shoe color would be a basis for drawing a stereotype. But if group A members are fastidious and concerned with punctuality and neatness, and group B members tend to be free-wheeling and indifferent to punctuality, these distinctions may loom large as a stereotypic difference. Therefore a characteristic that is central to a group's self-judgment, that shows a large between-group difference, and a low within-group variability (i.e., that they or we tend to be alike in this) is the most likely candidate for a stereotype (Ford and Stangor, 1992).

When we look at the content of stereotypes, we find that those stereotypes most salient and resistant to change meet the above criteria. Moreover, stereotypes of groups will differ in fundamental ways because they maximally distinguish themselves on *different* traits. That is, stereotypes of Jews are different from stereotypes of blacks, from stereotypes of women, from stereotypes of Hispanics, from stereotypes of gay men, from stereotypes of lesbians, and so on. Issues of intelligence, masculinity, morality, religion, language, and custom, all significant factors in our culture, are perhaps most contrasted by these groups. Therefore, stereotypes will be most easily developed and differentiated along these issues.

The Hoffman and Hurst (1992) study argued that stereotypes and their content were not neutral observations of observed data, but motivated rationalizations of cause-effect judgments. This issue is critical ultimately to our understanding of prejudice. Is stereotyping an "innocent" attempt to make sense of the social world, and the observed biases simply by-products of the way in which the mind works? Or, is stereotyping the result of a biased pattern of perception and cognitive judgment motivated by a need to secure a positive sense of self and a feeling of security and well-being? These questions cannot simply be answered by a yes or a no.

It is likely that both of these sources of stereotyping occur. At times, biases result from the way in which the mind works, compounded by the social patterns of society. At other times, personal needs and desires may drive us toward stereotypical judgments. Understanding the cognitive and motivational aspects of stereotypes and how they interact is a primary goal of society psychologists.

HOW ARE STEREOTYPES STRUCTURED AND HOW DO THEY FUNCTION?

We know something about what stereotypes are, how they are measured, of what they consist, and where they originate. What do these things have to do with prejudice? Simply put, stereotyping leads to prejudice, as noted earlier. The critical question then is, How do stereotypes foster the kind of biased perception or judgment that is directed at individual members of the stereotyped group? Social psychologists have spent several decades investigating this very question and we now know a lot about these mechanisms. In this section, we will consider how stereotypes are structured and how they work.

Stereotypes as Cognitive Structures

The early studies of stereotypes focused on their qualities as belief systems, which were often regarded as erroneous and based on faulty reasoning. The essence of a stereotype was believed to be the content: Blacks are lazy and musical; Jews are shrewd and clannish; white Americans are industrious and ambitious, and so on. But, with the rise of social cognition as a systematic approach to stereotypes came the idea that stereotypes are organized just as other cognitive structures are and that they function in a similar manner.

Stereotypes have content, structure, organization, and functions. Worchel and Rothgerber (in press) summarize these aspects of stereotypes in terms of their multidimensionality. Even today, we mostly consider the content of stereotypes (e.g., a given group is lazy, smart, tall, or hostile), the groups who are stereotyped (women, gay men, Jews, the elderly, etc.), or how homogeneous or heterogeneous the group members are. Nonetheless, Worchel and Rothgerber (in press) argue that all of these factors are part of what a stereotype is. All of these factors exist at both the individual level and the group or consensual level. Groups determine the content and interpretation of stereotypes (by means of ethnocentrism and through socialization processes), but the relative weighting of specific traits or the perception of what percentage of the group possess a trait can be subject to individual variation. Culture influences how central a group perception is to the perception of an individual. Therefore, it influences the relative importance that a given stereotype may have. So the distinction between the individual-level ("in-the-head" cognitive structures) and the group level (consensus among group members), stereotypes should be kept in mind. This section will focus primarily on the individual-level structure of stereotypes.

We have examined the content of stereotypes already, and an understanding of the structure is provided by attempts to determine how the specific contents are organized. Ashmore and Del Boca (1979) showed that there was hierarchization in stereotypes. That is, a broad-category stereotype—say, of black Americans—might consist of several subtypes (e.g., athletes, militants, criminals, and middle class).

Subtyping presents us with a more complex cognitive structure of stereotypes than simple single-category descriptions of traits do.

Ashmore and Del Boca (1979, p. 219) defined *stereotype* with respect to gender as "the structured set of beliefs about personal attributes of women and men." Ashmore and Tumia (1980) had college students sort a set of 66 traits as a way of distinguishing among people they knew. I might use *warm*, for example, to describe my friend Joey, but not my friend Alex. *Funny* may describe Alice, but not Jafar. *Sentimental* is Helene all the way, but not Winifred. Using a multidimensional scaling technique, the authors then sorted the traits into those that went together (i.e., often co-occurred in descriptions of the same people) and those that were "psychologically distant" (almost never co-occurred, such as *warm* and *unsociable*). Two dimensions accounted for how subjects evaluated people they knew—social desirability and potency. With respect to social desirability, people were either good or bad at social activities. With respect to potency, people were either "hard" (e.g., critical, scientific, aggressive) or "soft" (e.g., sentimental, naive). The gender stereotype was revealed by the systematic linking of certain traits to female friends or to male friends. Two findings were salient. First, social desirability did not distinguish men from women, so that it cannot properly be viewed as part of the stereotype. Second, and not surprisingly, males were much more likely to be described by trait adjectives derived from the "hard" end of the continuum, and women by those from the "soft" end.[3] However, these gender distinctions were much more likely to be made by men than by women. Therefore, the hard-soft distinction did describe gender stereotypes fairly, but apparently the structures were more accessible to men than they were to women.

Eagly and Mladinic (1989) showed that gender stereotypes were shared by both men and women, but there was a different configuration for each gender. They had men and women subjects evaluate four groups of eight traits. Each trait related to a gender stereotype, as shown in the following table.

	Masculine	Feminine
Positive	independent	helpful
	self-confident	aware of others' feelings
	competitive	warm to others
	feels superior	understanding
Negative	egotistical	spineless
	hostile	gullible
	arrogant	whiny
	greedy	complaining

Figure 7.1 shows that *overall positive ratings* (i.e., positive judgments minus negative judgments) were higher for women on women-stereotypical traits and were higher for men on men-stereotypical traits for *both* men and women raters. However, these gender-linked positivity ratings were greater for women than they were for men. That is, women tended to judge women more favorably on positive feminine-stereotypical traits, and men more favorably on positive masculine-stereotypical traits than men did. However, whereas women rated women as neutral on masculine traits, and men as neutral on feminine traits, men saw these associations

---

[3] More recent work on gender by Eagly (1991) confirms the breadth of this hard-soft dimension. According to Eagly, women are perceived to be more communal and men more instrumental. Put in popular terms, *Men are from Mars, Women are from Venus* (Gray, 1992).

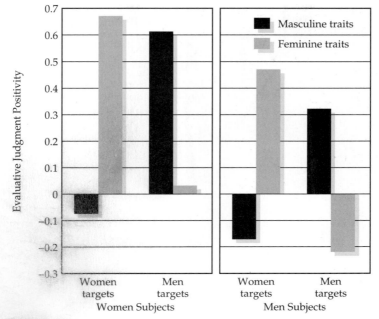

FIGURE 7.1

Positivity of Judgments of Men and Women Targets on Masculine and Feminine Traits by Men and Women Subjects.

more negatively. That is, men tended to rate women negatively on masculine traits and to rate men negatively on feminine traits.

These findings show that there is a consensually shared gender stereotype and that people who fit the stereotype are evaluated more positively. It also shows that stereotypes may lead to unfavorable outcomes, even when their content is primarily positive. Women are rated positively by men, but only on feminine stereotypical traits. They are viewed negatively on masculine stereotypic traits—that is, on those traits most likely to be associated with occupations or social roles that carry the highest prestige. And, finally, it suggests that the content of stereotypes is indeed attached to social roles, and that people are judged on the basis of their ability to fit these socially prescribed expectations.

An important observation in the Ashmore and Tumia (1980) study was that subjects made distinctions among women, so that some subjects saw women who were soft as "nurturant" (e.g., honest, sincere, and sentimental), whereas others saw soft women as "quiet, thoughtful" (e.g., meditative, modest, reserved). A person who perceives a "soft" woman as nurturant may make different judgments and hold quite different expectations than would a person who thinks a "soft" woman is quiet and thoughtful. Therefore, even when there is consensus about what stereotypes are and who possesses them, their *meaning* may vary from person to person. What happens when a woman does not fit a gender stereotype? In the everyday world of human interaction, stereotypes are not just games social psychologists play. They are profoundly significant determinants of how people are treated and, as such, can have a profound effect on a person's life. Consider the case of Ann Hopkins.

Ann Hopkins caught in a catch-22. Gender stereotypes discount her performance and productivity. Social psychology demonstrates the flawed reasoning of gender stereotypes, and Hopkins wins a settlement. (Cynthia Johnson/Time Magazine)

Sex-Stereotyping in the World of Work

Ann Hopkins worked at Price Waterhouse, where she was one of the most productive account associates. In 1990, she came up for review for possible promotion to partner. In spite of her outstanding performance record, which placed her in the top 5 percent of the associates both in sales volume and monies earned for the company, Ms. Hopkins was not promoted. Almost all of us have experienced outcomes we do not like and do not think are fair. However, Ms. Hopkins felt that she was put in a particularly untenable and unfair position because of the specific issues raised with regard to her promotion. Her performance did not seem to matter to the reviewers as much as her "style" mattered. In fact, her superiors offered the following unsolicited comments about Ms. Hopkins:

"She needs to go to charm school."

"She needs to wear more and better make-up."

In short, Ann Hopkins was not "soft"—she did not fit the female stereotype. That the people making the judgment were largely men (only 3 of the 560 partners were women) should not surprise us. And because we know that gender-discrepant behavior seems to matter more to men than to women (cf. Eagly and Mladinic, 1989), we should perhaps not be too surprised by this outcome. Ms. Hopkins sued Price Waterhouse. Judge Arnold Gesell ruled, in part, that Ms. Hopkins was put in a catch-22 situation. If she performs well using "masculine" traits, she is rejected for not being feminine; however, if she is nice and "soft" (i.e., stereotypically feminine), she will not be as productive and could be denied promotion on performance grounds.[4] The content of stereotypes matter in the real world.

Subtyping of Stereotypes: Not all "X's" Are Alike
There are approximately 31,212,000 African Americans in the United States, 150,000,000 women, 25,939,000 Hispanics, 1,902,000 American Indians, and 8,727,000 Americans of Asian ancestry (Russell, 1995). Does it make any sense to talk about these millions of people as Asians, blacks, women, American Indians, and Hispanics? Although they surely have some things in common, they just as surely have many differences.

The stereotype tries to encapsulate certain features or attributes of a salient social group, but this attempt is doomed to failure. As you will see later on, people are not so naive as to be unaware that it is not fair to make diagnostic judgments about individuals on the basis of their group membership. One of the ways we can and do reduce this enormous number of people into groups of a more manageable size is to create subtypes or subgroups. Subgroups have their own set of characteristics. This set of characteristics may include some of the traits attributed to the superordinate group, but it may also have unique elements.

Subtyping enables us to acknowledge the diversity in a group without having to change what we think about the group as a whole. Devine and Baker (1991) illustrated this functional utility of black subtypes. In their study, white undergraduates were given booklets that listed at the top of each page a specific black-referent label, and were asked to write down those characteristics that captured the cultural conception of the group. In addition to the global category "blacks," labels included several subtypes, such as "black athlete," "black businessman," "ghetto black," "streetwise black," and "welfare black." The results showed three clusters of stereotypes or subtypes, which could be described as follows:

1 *Evaluative*: positive (intelligent, ambitious, successful, upwardly mobile) or negative (hostile, poor, dirty, negative personality, oppressed, and lazy)
2 *Athletic* (athletic, physical characteristics, and ostentatious)
3 *Possessing unique characteristics* (musical, upwardly mobile, poor)

Table 7.4 shows how the global rating of blacks and each black subtype were evaluated in these three constellations.

These results suggest that the global black stereotype is negatively valued, as are the streetwise, ghetto, and welfare subtypes. Only the athlete and businessman subtypes are valued positively. We also note that not only the athlete subtype is valued on the athletic constellation, but the global category of blacks is valued along that constellation. This suggests the possibility that the athlete subtype may have a more generalizable influence on the superordinate group than other subtypes would. It further illustrates how subtyping processes can separate out positive exemplars from a group, leaving the global judgment of the group with predominantly negative characteristics.

Now that we have a methodology by which to classify subtypes of broader categories, we may specify what comes to mind when the given category label is in-

---

[4] Susan Fiske, a social psychologist, provided expert testimony regarding sex stereotypes. Her testimony and the work of several other social psychologists were organized in an *amicus curiae* brief in support of Ms. Hopkins. It was on the basis of this brief that Judge Gesell reached his catch-22 conclusion. For a complete account of this case, see Fiske et al. (1991).

TABLE 7.4 FAVORABLENESS RATINGS OF STEREOTYPES AND SUBTYPES OF BLACKS

Stereotype subtype	Constellation		
	Evaluative: positive or negative	Athletic	Possessing unique characteristics
Blacks (global category)	−1.636	1.964	1.677
Streetwise	−1.048	−1.022	−0.662
Ghetto	−1.656	−0.674	0.004
Welfare	−1.753	−1.442	−0.477
Athlete	1.739	2.418	−1.760
Business	4.554	−1.092	0.890

SOURCE: Data from Devine and Baker (1991). "Measurement of Racial Stereotype Subtyping." *Personality and Social Psychology Bulletin 17*, 44–50. Table 3.

voked. For example, when we say "Hispanic," who comes to mind, and what personal attributes do we attach to the individual? The structure and operation of stereotypes are much more complex than simply saying "blacks are musical," "women are emotional," or "the elderly are forgetful." The *meaning* of a social category or the stereotype that we attach to it will depend on the *exemplar* that comes to mind when the category is evoked (Smith and Zarate, 1992). Therefore, the more positive exemplars that are available, the more favorable will a group judgment be. A "bottom-up" approach to stereotyping suggests that, because we sometimes create group categories from individual experiences, the generalization from subtypes to the global category may be a possible tool for modifying social stereotypes.

STEREOTYPES INFLUENCE PERCEPTION AND BEHAVIOR

Historical interest in the content of stereotypes has given way to the processes of stereotyping. The question of primary interest now is, How do the cognitive structures affect the perception of people and the behaviors that follow from that perception? Hamilton, Stroesner, and Driscoll (1994) propose three ways in which stereotypes influence how we process social information, perceive our social world, and behave toward others. Stereotypes affect (1) the social information to which we pay attention, (2) how we interpret that information, and (3) how we process that information. The following section will examine each of these sources of influence.

Stereotypes Affect What Information Is Attended to and Encoded

A stereotype will affect what we attend to and therefore, what we later remember. Cohen (1981) had subjects watch a videotape of a man and woman (a married couple) first having dinner, then having an informal birthday celebration in their apartment. The couple was played by professional actors. The woman's character was designed to possess one of two sets of attributes that would be plausible for either a librarian (e.g., has artwork on the wall, is not affectionate toward husband, drinks wine, and plays the piano) or for a waitress (e.g., has a bowling ball, drinks beer, plays the guitar, and is affectionate toward husband). Subjects watched the videotape and formed an impression of a woman who (they were led to believe) was either a librarian or a waitress. Since the *objective information* (i.e., what was shown or said on the videotape) was fixed, any different impressions the subjects formed would depend on what they expected to be true of a librarian (or of a waitress).

Subjects were asked to indicate what they remembered from the tape in a forced-choice format. That is, one of the choices was always correct (it had appeared in the tape), and the other was not correct. It turned out that subjects remembered accurately more of the information that was consistent with the occupation they were told the woman pursued. For example, when the couple were shown drinking wine, the subjects were more likely to remember that fact when the woman was presented as a librarian. Or, as another example, subjects were more likely to remember the presence of a bowling ball in the apartment when the woman was a waitress, and so on. In short, what subjects "saw" (encoded)—or, at least, "remembered seeing"—was influenced by the expectancy established by the experimenter. Because the specific characters were determined by essentially asking subjects to generate the content of a librarian or a waitress stereotype, this study provides evidence that the content of a stereotype and its activation will affect the selective perception, encoding, and memory of social stimuli.

Another point is noteworthy here. If subjects were given information about the woman (i.e., given an expectation of what she *might* be like), they were more likely to correctly identify and remember *all* information—whether it was consistent with the stereotype or not! It might seem, therefore, that the stereotype serves an organizing function that allows us to quickly remember the information that is consistent with the stereotype and, perhaps, to interpret inconsistent information in such a way that it is rendered plausible *within the stereotype* we already hold. If this latter process is true, we can imagine how difficult it would be to change a stereotype.

Stereotypes are widely believed to increase our ability to perceive and remember stereotype-consistent information, but the opposite argument can also be made. That is, stereotype-inconsistent information may, in fact, be more startling and vivid. Therefore it may exert more influence on our perceptual and mnemonic processes than is exercised by stereotype-consistent data. How might this work? The stereotype of the overworked librarian is often used in romantic comedies to shake the audience up. For example, the stereotypical librarian suddenly lets her hair down, throws away her heavy glasses, and begins behaving as if she were well, a waitress! We are technically surprised by this behavior—except that it is now a cinematic cliché, so perhaps less so nowadays—and focus attention on explaining the departure from our expectation. Therefore, the new behaviors stand out and are likely to be watched more closely and remembered better. Social psychological research has supported this basic process in several studies (e.g., Hastie, 1984).

So in sum, stereotypic structures affect what we expect to happen in our social world when people who fit our stereotype appear. These expectations affect how we process social information, and what we remember about people. The "pictures in the head," described by Lippmann (1922), are not just photo album entries, they are virtual realities in that we see them as if they were the real things. The physical person who provides the stimulus for our perception and evaluation bears, at best, an uncertain similarity to the virtual reality in our head. Do we take the time to discern the points of divergence? When the "facts" are consistent with our virtual reality picture, we have no need to do so. However, when the facts diverge from our picture, we pay close attention. But we usually pay attention only for the purpose of reconstruing the behavior so that it will make sense in the context of our prior knowledge or expectation. Even this process of "explaining away" the inconsistency is attenuated when we have other things on our mind (cf. Stangor and Duan, 1991).

Stereotypes Can Influence How Information Is Construed or Interpreted

Ann Hopkins, in the case described earlier, was probably not more assertive than most men in the company were. However, her behavior was probably not judged against that of other men, but against the female sex-role stereotype. By that measure, her behavior was viewed as even more assertive than it probably was. By establishing an anchor for behavior, the stereotype creates an evaluative set of traits that can increase or decrease the extremity of a judgment of an individual. That is, behavior that is inconsistent with stereotypic expectations is judged more extremely than stereotype-conforming activity is. This extremity judgment can go in either a positive or negative direction. Ann Hopkins was judged *more* assertive, and Senator Edmund Muskie of Maine, who was thought to have cried during a public news conference while he was running for the Democratic nomination for President, was judged too "soft" for the office. This show of "softness" was cited as marking the end of any realistic hope he may have had for the nomination. By contrast, when Pat Shroeder, a Colorado representative, cried in a similar situation, it was duly noted. However, little of consequence happened because of her show of "softness." The point here is that the *meaning* of behavior will depend not just on what a person does, but what the perceiver expects that person to do. Stereotypes guide our expectations and thus play a major role in what specific behaviors *mean* to us. If an expectation is based on group-based properties (i.e., stereotypes) related to gender, ethnicity, or race, for example, that expectation plants a seed that often grows into prejudice.

But, as anyone who has ever tried to grow a garden knows, not all seeds sprout. And, of those that do sprout some fail to thrive. We might use this gardening metaphor to help us visualize a two-stage process that can be applied to stereotype-confirmation. The first stage consists of formulating a hypothesis about what a person is like or what a person might be expected to do in a situation, on the basis of the individual's group membership. This is how stereotypes work. The stronger the group-based expectation, the more strongly held is the stereotype. Going back to our metaphor, the seed of prejudice is placed in fertile soil. But there is a second stage, the *facts* of the person's behavior. These behavioral facts, unlike the stereotype itself, are rooted in objective reality and **should** provide a stronger basis for any judgment of the person than the stereotype can provide. Therefore, in theory, whatever expectation was established by the stereotype may be rejected when the behavior contradicts it.

This two-stage process was articulated by Darley and Gross (1983). The authors tested the process by having college-age subjects evaluate the academic performance of a fourth-grade child, Hannah. Hannah was described in one of two ways—as coming from high (positive-expectation) socioeconomic circumstances or from low (negative-expectation) socioeconomic circumstances. Subjects were asked to evaluate Hannah's ability based solely on her SES status, and/or a videotape that showed Hannah performing several academic problems. Darley and Gross (1983) argued that subjects will not necessarily judge a person on the basis of stereotypes held about the group to which the person belongs. They proposed that subjects often know that there is variability among group members and that they need to evaluate the specific person in order to be totally fair. The process does not seem to evidence any prejudice at all. In fact, subjects were given the option of checking off an item indicating that they had insufficient information from which to form a judgment about Hannah's ability instead of evaluating her. It was predicted and found that, when all the subjects knew of Hannah was her SES status, they were significantly more likely to check "insufficient information." Therefore, they knew that Hannah should not be judged solely on the basis of a stereotype they possessed about members of different SES levels.

The results further showed that simply knowing Hannah's SES background *did not* affect subject's judgments of her ability (Darley and Gross, 1983). For the most part, she was expected to perform at fourth-grade level, regardless of her SES. So far, so good. When possessing only stereotypic information, subjects were more likely to say they had insufficient information upon which to judge Hannah. And, when they did make a judgment, it did not differ as a function of Hannah's SES level.

However, when subjects actually watched Hannah perform the tasks, they felt they had a better basis for evaluating her (i.e., sufficient information). In these cases, those subjects with a positive expectation for her performances based on her SES level, *perceived* that she performed better. Specifically, they felt the test was harder, that Hannah had gotten more problems correct, and they reported more of Hannah's positive behaviors when she was presented as someone from a high, as opposed to a low, SES. "On every measure, positive-expectancy subjects made interpretations more favorable to the child than did negative expectancy subjects" (Darley and Gross, 1983, p. 26).

So there is good news and bad news here. The good news is that subjects were properly hesitant to make judgments of Hannah's ability when they knew nothing of her performance. They were unwilling to make inferences based on stereotypical information. But, the bad news is that, when they actually had behavior upon which to base an evaluation of Hannah, they thought they could make better (fair) judgments about her and they attempted to do so. Nonetheless, their judgments now became distorted by the SES information they had suppressed in the absence of more diagnostic-performance information. It is ironic that people seem better able to give others the benefit of the doubt when they have too little information than when they have enough. When they have enough, they often plunge into an evaluation process that is filled with error, distortion, and unconscious deceit. And the "kicker" is that they are more convinced than ever that their judgments are better informed, fair, and correct.

How might these findings apply to a situation in real life? Suppose we have Tarik, a black employee who is widely regarded as being a beneficiary of an affirmative action decision, and Wendell, a white employee hired at the same time. Do we immediately assume Tarik is less qualified than Wendell is? Much of the popular discourse on affirmative action would say yes. However, the Darley and Gross (1983) findings suggests that people might suspend judgment because the information of the affirmative action decision alone is an insufficient basis upon which to judge Tarik's ability and, therefore, they would *not* assume he is less capable than

Wendell is. But now let's assume that Tarik and Wendell show up to work and start doing their job. Now comes the rub. According to the Darley and Gross (1983) finding, coworkers, knowing or suspecting Tarik's affirmative action status, may evaluate his performance more negatively and evaluate Wendell's more positively, *even if the two performances are objectively indistinguishable.* Now coworkers become convinced that Tarik is less qualified, less capable, and doing a poorer job than Wendell. Affirmative action programs are again perceived to have elevated inferior minority beneficiaries over superior whites. And the coworkers now feel it is the policy that is wrong, not their biased judgments. As you can see, there is much work to be done.

There is another way of looking at these results. Rather than assuming that the subjects in the Darley and Gross (1983) study did not form biased expectations of Hannah's probable level of performance because they were so conscious of fairness, perhaps we should assume that they suppressed any biases in an effort to appear unprejudiced. When they had a "legitimate" reason for formulating a negative opinion of low-SES Hannah, they did so. This possibility is supported by the work on *thought-suppression* (Wegner, Erber, and Zanakos 1993). For example, if we are told not to think of a white bear, the image typically comes rushing to mind. Efforts to suppress it may be successful but, once the suppression is removed, we are *more* likely to think of it than if we had not tried to suppress these thoughts in the first place. This *hyperreactivity* to suppressed thoughts of the white bear is known as the *rebound effect*.

Therefore, to phrase it in everyday terms, our subjects may cut lower-class Hannah some slack initially but, once they are freed up from the suppression of their thoughts, they let her have it! This line of reasoning was, in fact, explored in an experiment by Macrae, Bodenhausen, Milne, and Jetten (1994). In this study, subjects were shown a color photograph of a male skinhead. They were then asked to compose a brief passage describing a typical day in the target's life (passage 1). Before performing the task, half of the subjects were told that psychological research has shown that impressions of individuals are often biased by the evaluator's stereotypic preconceptions. So, the subjects were asked not to think about the skinhead in any stereotypic way as they wrote their brief description. Control subjects were not given this suppression instruction. After all of the subjects finished this task, they were shown another photo of a male skinhead. Now they were asked to write a description of the target (passage 2). However, this time, no stereotype-suppression instruction was given to any of the subjects.

The experimenters rated the stereotypicality of each description. Macrae et al. (1994) found that, for control subjects, the two descriptions were equally stereotypical (6.95 for passage 1 and 7.08 for passage 2). Therefore, the suppression instruction had worked for the experimental subjects, because their stereotypic score for the first passage was only 5.54. This score was significantly lower than the score for the controls. However, when the experimental subjects were no longer required to suppress their stereotypic thoughts about skinheads, their ratings increased to 7.83. This rating was significantly higher than that of their first description, *and* higher than that of the controls. In a second experiment, two sets of subjects wrote passages—one group under suppression instructions, one group not. Following this, each subject was led to a second room where he or she was to meet the subject of the essay. When the subject arrived, the target's coat was there but the subject was told he had "just stepped out." The subject was instructed to take one of the eight chairs that were lined up in a row. The skinhead had already claimed seat 1. How close to the first seat did they sit? Stereotype-suppressed subjects seated themselves further away (mean seat of 5.25) from the skinhead than control subjects did (mean seat of 4.41).

The findings of these studies raise a very interesting possibility. If subjects, in fact, hold negative feelings or stereotypes about a group and suppress those feelings when they encounter a member of the group, their actual level of discomfort and hostility may increase. Further, when conditions arise that make it permissible to behave in a somewhat more negative manner toward the target, the previous suppression may now make things worse. This possibility makes it important that we not mistake superficial, social-driven public expressions of acceptance for deep-seated, positive attitude changes. When a person does genuinely desire such changes, then perhaps examining biased thoughts and seeking to control these thoughts will have positive effects (cf. Devine, 1989). However, trying to repress negative thoughts and their expression, as anti-hate speech codes do, could have an unintended negative effect on solving the problem.

Stereotypes Can Influence How Information Is Processed

Once a person is categorized into a group, the content of the stereotype about the group is activated. Once the stereotype is activated, it influences expectations about the kind of person the individual is and how he or she is likely to behave in specific situations. As we saw in the Darley and Gross (1983) study, information about the target can be processed in a biased manner that upholds or confirms the stereotypic expectations. An additional consequence of this biased processing is that the perceiver's biases may affect the behavior of the target! This is commonly known as the *self-fulfilling prophesy*. The Word, Zanna, and Cooper (1974) experiments demonstrated how this mechanism works and what some of its real-world consequences might be (discussed in Chapter 9). For now, we will merely note the powerful influence of biased social-information processing on behavior. The prejudiced person categorizes a target other person. The content of the activated stereotype provides a basis for social or behavioral expectation. It also evokes perhaps, some affective reaction to or feeling about the target. The stereotype and the feeling combine to create a pattern of subtle, nonverbal behavior that signals the low expectation and the negative feeling. The target senses this and may adjust his or her behavior in a negative fashion. Having unwittingly undermined the behavior of the target, the prejudiced person can now make an objective assessment of the target that *confirms* the original expectation. Thereby, the prejudiced person's world conforms to his or her expectations for it.

WHY ARE STEREOTYPES IMPORTANT TO PREJUDICE?

The pivotal reason that stereotypes are so important to the study and understanding of prejudice is that we treat people in biased ways because we treat them *as if* they possessed attributes associated with the group to which they belong (or in which we place them). We do so in spite of or prior to any knowledge of the individual's actual personal attributes. If there were no groups, there would be no prejudice!

But we have seen that stereotypes are complex and may be positive or negative, depending on whether we are typing the whole group or, perhaps, some sub-set of the group. For example, if you have a negative attitude toward blacks, it may be that *blacks* to you means poor, uneducated, urban-dwelling black males. How-ever, if *black* means to you hardworking, highly educated, talented black busi-nessperson, the stereotype would be decidedly different both in content and evalu-ation from the stereotype of the negative evaluation (cf. Devine and Baker, 1991). Moreover, simply possessing a stereotype—even one with negative implications or connotations—does not necessarily mean that you will evaluate a person nega-tively. As Darley and Gross (1983) showed, to the extent that one recognizes that the information upon which an evaluation is based is not diagnostic, the data will be suppressed as invalid to judgments about people. So when and how do stereo-types become a basis for evaluative judgments and for biased behavior? In short, how do we get from the possessing a stereotype to behaving in a prejudiced way because of the stereotype?

Our Reaction to Social Groups Depends on What We Think or How We Feel about the Groups

Much of the work we reviewed above follows from the traditions of social cogni-tion. That is, the preferred way of explaining behavior, even prejudice, is to argue that our thinking faculties are biased as a result of some tricks nature has played on us regarding the way we routinely process social information. In the minimal-group paradigm, for example, it is held that people show bias in favor of their own group members and against out-group members, even when the basis of group membership is as abstract as a preference for paintings of a particular artist. Com-bining people and traits—both of which are distinctive by virtue of their infre-quency—leads us to overinterpret their association. When the traits are negative and the group is an ethnic or racial minority, we have a fertile informational context for the formation of negative stereotypes.

But what about the passion, the fire, the drama of prejudice? How can we ex-plain the determination of Governor George Wallace as he stood at the gates of the University of Alabama forbidding entrance to Autherine Lucy, a young black woman? Why did over 10 men conspire to brutally murder three young civil rights workers—Andrew Goodman, James Chaney, and Arnold Schwerner—in Alabama? There 10 men felt passionately about the relationships of blacks and whites in the South. Could it be that the passions, the emotions are more than simple expressions of liking, of judgments of how many people in the group possess certain traits, or of the likelihood that a person will be good in math? Perhaps this isn't really preju-dice, but something far more sinister and deep—racism. Perhaps, but we are not at a point in our discussion at which we can answer this question. For now, let's con-sider some work on prejudice that seeks to identify and aid our understanding of the emotional responses of prejudiced people.

Stephan and Stephan and their colleagues have found that the simple assess-ment measurements of stereotypes do not correlate very well with prejudice of whites toward Asians (Stephan and Stephan, 1985) or toward Hispanics (Stephan and Stephan, 1989). In a recent study (Stephan, Ageyev, Coates-Shridor, Stephan, and Abakina, 1994), the relationship of stereotypes to prejudice was studied cross-culturally in samples of Americans and Russians. Each group was asked to indicate the percentage of Americans, Russians, and Iraqis who possessed certain traits that had been shown in previous studies to be highly stereotypical with respective to each group. Subjects were asked their emotional reaction to each of the three target countries, as well as to each of the traits that constituted the stereotype of each group.

In general, the authors found that subjects' emotional reactions to these national groups was best predicted by their evaluation of the traits that constituted the stereotypes of the groups. For example, Americans tended to think that Iraqis were cold, defensive, fatalistic, hostile, ignorant, insecure, obedient, and untrustworthy. Russians, however, held Iraqis to be religious, fanatic, patriotic, aggressive, proud, enduring, reserved, and patient. A stereotype-evaluation index was computed in which the mean evaluation of each trait associated with each group was multiplied by the percentage of members of the group thought to possess the given trait. Consequently, the more positively a trait is valued and the more characteristic of the group it is perceived to be, the more positively should be the emotional reaction to the group. For Americans, the emotional reaction to Iraqis was most extreme, a finding that was very well predicted by this index. For Russians, the emotional responses to all three groups were accurately predicted by this evaluation-stereotype index.

We may conclude from this that simply possessing a stereotype is not enough to explain prejudiced behavior. In order to explain prejudiced behavior, we must know how to evaluate the specific traits that constitute a given stereotype. If either the traits are not strongly associated with the stereotype or they are not highly evaluated (i.e., either high positive or high negative), the results will show only a weak relationship with how subjects feel about a target racial, ethnic, or national group.

Stangor, Sullivan, and Ford (1991) were also concerned with feelings people have about other groups. In an experiment, subjects' stereotypes of nine social groups were first assessed using a free-response format. Second, an independent group of subjects listed the stereotypes associated with each group. The most-frequent positive and negative traits were then shown for each group, and subjects were asked the percentage of the group that possessed positive and negative traits independently associated with each group, as well as the percentage of people in the world that possessed these traits. Third, they were asked to state whether any member of the target group because of something they have done or something you know about them ever made you feel *positive* (e.g., hopeful, inspired, proud, respectful, or sympathetic) or *negative* (e.g., afraid, angry, disgusted, frustrated, or uneasy). Finally, all subjects were asked to rate each target group on a 10-point scale with labels ranging from "extremely unfavorable" to "extremely favorable." The results showed that the best predictor of overall attitudes toward the groups was the subject's emotional reactions to the groups. For example, the more they had interacted with Arabs in ways that had made them feel positive (e.g., hopeful, inspired), the more positively they rated Arabs. The more interactions with the target group had made subjects react negatively (e.g., afraid, angry, disgusted), the less positively they rated the group. The effect of affect was greater than both individual stereotypes and group stereotypes were in accounting for these attitudes.

What is important about the Stephan et al. (1994) and Stangor et al. (1991) studies should be obvious—feelings count! In fact, they may count for more than the content of stereotypes does. A great deal of additional research supports this conclusion (cf. Zanna, 1994). For example, Esses and Zanna (1995) showed that negative stereotypes were more likely to be attributed to various target groups (Native Indians, Pakistanis) when people were in negative moods. That is, how we feel about other people and how they make us feel has a strong influence on what we say about them and perhaps, although it was not studied in these experiences, how we behave toward members of the group. Whereas the social-cognition analysis suggests that the negative stereotype activates biases that undermine the likelihood of positive interactions, these studies suggest that our behavior toward target others may well depend on the actual encounters we have with members of the group or on how we evaluate the characteristics associated with the group. These factors change over time and are different from person to person. Therefore, we may conclude that stereotypes are extremely powerful in both direct and indirect ways. But there is still room for people to make adjustments to their thoughts and behaviors in an effort to reduce tendencies for prejudiced thought and behavior.

Unconscious Processes Link Stereotypes to Prejudice

The final issue we wish to consider in this chapter is a powerful one. How many times have you heard someone claim not to be prejudiced and that they believe that every person should be judged on his or her merit. We are all human beings, and each enjoys individual rights. As a society, we endorse the idea that we should aspire to become a color blind society and, if that were achieved, we would have put the problems of prejudice behind us. These are certainly reasonable ideas and ones that are difficult to argue against. However, many social psychologists are coming to the view that some very powerful dynamics of how we think, process social information, and subsequently behave are critically influenced by processes of which we are largely unaware.

Banaji and Greenwald (1994) argue that there is much to gain from considering the operation of unconscious processes in prejudice. They suggest that by frequently relying on explicit references to target groups, as we do in most measurements of stereotypes, we miss the operation of subtle biases that influence everyday behavior. That is, people may form "implicit" stereotypes of which they are unaware. Analysis of the selective and systematic biases in memory reveal that people hold stereotypical views of particular groups (e.g., gender and race groups) and that their implicit assumptions about these groups are affected and revealed by what they remember.

Banaji and Greenwald (1994) demonstrate how this process may work in a creative study they call "becoming famous overnight." On the first day of the experiment they provided subjects with a list of famous names (e.g., actors, musicians, and writers such as Gladys Knight, Dave Brubeck, Doris Lessing, Thornton Wilder, Jane Wyman, and Rod Steiger) and nonfamous names. All of the names were equally divided in terms of gender. Subjects were instructed to read the list of 72 names (36 were famous and 36 were nonfamous; 36 were males and 36 were females) for the ostensible purpose of judging the ease of pronunciation. On the second day, 48 hours later, the subjects were shown a new list of 144 names. This second list consisting of the original 72 names, plus 72 new names configured exactly as the first set had been and randomly interposed among the old ones. For each name, subjects were asked "Is this person famous or not?"

The results of the study replicate the finding that we "remember" original, nonfamous names as famous more frequently than we remember *new*, nonfamous names. The former, by virtue of having been seen before, are more salient in memory. This salience makes us more likely to remember them inaccurately as being famous. The really interesting finding, though, is that this misremembering tendency was different for male and female names. That is, both male and female subjects tended to remember previously seen nonfamous *men* as famous more frequently than they remembered previously seen nonfamous *women* as famous. The authors conclude that "familiarity is more likely to be interpreted as fame when the name is male than when female (Banaji and Greenwald, 1994, p. 63)."

This study shows how basic memory is structured in such a way as to reflect assumptions about people. If we were to ask 100 people the question, "Who are more numerous among famous people, men or women," the answer would likely be "men." But, when we present people with a simple task with the names of equally famous men and women, in equal numbers we might suppose that the subjects' wish to be accurate in a simple lab experiment would override this assumption of societal recognition? Apparently this is not the case. As with the illusory-correlation work (Hamilton and Gifford, 1976) and the hypothesis-confirmation study of Darley and Gross (1983), this study shows how fundamental are the mental processes that serve to create and sustain biased judgments of people.

Women are dependent and men are aggressive. These assumptions about characteristically different traits of men and women have been alluded to earlier. To demonstrate the idea of implicit stereotyping, Banaji et al. (1993) had subjects participate in two "different" experiments. In the first, subjects were asked to unscramble 45 four-word sentences that were either neutral in meaning or suggested either a trait of dependence (e.g., "conforms to others," "takes verbal abuse") or a trait of aggressiveness (e.g., "threatens other people," "abuses animals"). After subjects had completed these tasks, the experimenters assumed that subjects were primed to think about either dependence or aggression. That is, because the subjects had just created sentences that suggested either submission and compliance or aggressiveness, these traits would be more salient in their minds. In the next experiment, subjects read a paragraph that described either a male target (Donald) or female target (Donna) engaging in a series of behaviors that were quite weakly linked to either dependence behaviors (". . . but wanted to check with his or her girlfriend or boyfriend first") or aggressive behaviors (". . . noticed her or his mug was dirty and asked the waitress for a new one"). How did subjects judge Donald or Donna regarding the traits of dependence and aggressiveness?

The results showed that, when subjects had been primed for dependence in the first experiment, they judged Donna as *more* dependent and Donald as *less* dependent than did those primed with all neutral traits. Conversely, priming subjects with aggressiveness made them see Donald as more aggressive, but it had no effect on their perceptions of Donna. These studies show implicit stereotyping, because they demonstrate that a previous experience (exposure to names or trait activation) affects social perception in ways that reveal the underlying stereotypical structure and expectations—*even though subjects are not conscious of the influence*. These effects reveal gender stereotyping, because they occur selectively, in accordance with the content of gender stereotypes. Men are famous and aggressive, women are nonfamous and dependent. Our memory and perceptions operate as if these statements were actually true—even when the objective reality of these experiments indicate that they are not true at all.

We have reviewed much evidence that suggests that people often behave in prejudicial ways without being aware of it. The automatic components of prejudice create an insidious problem in devising any strategy to reduce its occurrence (Greenwald and Banaji, 1995). Traces of past experiences (e.g., a scene in a television show, an admonition from a parent to avoid strangers, expressions of homophobic attitudes by parents, hostile racial jokes told by close friends) that we may be unaware of influence our behavior. In the Banaji and Greenwald (1994) study discussed earlier, subjects "remembered" seeing more nonfamous male names as famous than they remembered seeing nonfamous females names—in spite of the fact that there was no objective basis for that "perception." Why did subjects so consistently see this gender-related "fact"? Because, in our society, men are given more prominent coverage for their accomplishments than women are, and they more frequently are assumed to do "important" things. For example, it has been shown that, in newspaper photographs, the size of the face relative to the rest of the body is a sign of perceived social importance or power (Archer, Tritani, Kimesa, and Barrios, 1983). Systematically, both in newspapers and in other public representations of men and women, men are portrayed in higher face-size profiles than women are. This is one possible trace experience of people (men and women) that could explain the tendency to "remember" more men as being famous than women as being so.

Gilbert and Hixon (1991) asked what conditions are required for the activation of a racial stereotype as proposed by G. W. Allport when he claimed that "A person with a dark brown skin will activate whatever concept of Negro is dominant in our mind" (G. W. Allport, 1954, p. 12). They argued that we must have the capacity to process the "brown skin" and link it to the dominant concept of *Negro*. Gilbert and Hixon (1991) reasoned that, if they occupied the person with other mental activity, they should be less likely to activate this race-based concept in the subjects. To test this hypothesis, they had subjects watch a video in which a female assistant turned over 19 cards that contained word fragments, such as P__ST, RI__E and so on. Subjects were required to complete the word fragments in as many different ways as possible (e.g., P__ST—POST, PAST, and PEST). While watching the video and completing the fragments, subjects in the experimental condition ("cognitive busyness") were asked to remember an eight-digit number, while a control group was not asked to do this. Moreover, one-half of the subjects saw the cards being turned over by a Caucasian assistant, the other half, by an Asian assistant. There were five stereotypical words: SHY (S__Y), SHORT (S__ORT), RICE (RI__E), POLITE (POLI__E), and NIP (N__P). Each of these fragments could have been completed in a way other than the stereotypical way. The number of times a fragment was completed with a stereotypical word was a measure of the tendency to link the stereotype to the Asian assistant.

The condition that produced the most stereotypical completions of the word fragments was when the assistant was Asian and the subjects were NOT cognitively busy. Therefore, the activation of an Asian stereotype required the presence of an Asian target and the cognitive capacity to bring forward the characteristics associated with the stereotype. In a second experiment, the subjects' Asian stereotypes were also activated. The subjects were shown an Asian assistant while they were either under cognitive busy conditions or not-busy conditions. Again, cognitive busyness inhibited activation of an Asian stereotype. Subjects next listened to an audiotape of a typical day in the life of the assistant, from which they were to form an impression of her. They listened to this tape under busy conditions (they had to detect whether a given letter appeared on a screen) or not-busy conditions. They rated the assistant on nine traits that were synonyms or antonyms of the stereotypical traits from the first study. When subjects' stereotypes had been activated (e.g., when they saw an Asian assistant under the not-busy conditions), they were *more* likely to make stereotypic impressions of the target when they had listened to the audiotape under cognitive busy conditions. These findings suggest that cognitive busyness will decrease the likelihood that a stereotype will be activated. However once a stereotype is activated, busyness will *increase* the likelihood of its being applied. The main point of this research is that merely being exposed to a person does not automatically activate a stereotype, the cognitive resources for doing so must be available. But, once the stereotype is activated, mindless processing makes it easier to use the stereotypes in forming social judgments.

*S*UMMARY

Stereotypes are thought by many to be the engine that drives prejudice. Pictures we hold in our heads influence, in subtle and powerful ways, our perception and judgment of a specific other person. This hypothetical other may be an image of a "prototype" of the group or an "exemplar" who represents the entire group to us. Stereotypes are prejudicial because they involve generalizations. These generalizations may range from specific individual exemplars to the group as a whole (Roger, a popular member of I Eta Pi fraternity, got drunk and "hurled" on people waiting in line to see the concert, thus reinforcing the idea that fraternity men are drunken Neanderthals) or from prototypical group members to specific individuals (when I learned that Roger was a member of I Eta Pi, I expected him to behave in a boorish and uncivilized fashion).

Stereotypes exist in the heads of individual people as beliefs or expectations, or they may be a composite of what a group of similar people believe. The former we can understand by observing how people behave differently toward people whom they classify in, or are led to believe fall into, different social groups. However, when we learn what to expect from others, in part by learning what others in our group expect, we are operating in a stereotypical fashion on consensual beliefs. Consensual stereotypes tell us as much about a cultural milieu as they do about individuals within it. In our society, consensual stereotypes play an important role as a result of strong socialization pressures and the effects of media portrayals of different groups.

How we measure stereotypes depends in part on whether we think of them as based in the heads of individuals or across the members of specific groups. Early measures like those of Katz and Braly (1934) tended to assess stereotypes as consensual beliefs. More recently, the individual level of analysis has enabled us to look at how individuals structure their perceptions of members of a group. This perception is revealed through procedures that allow subjects to tell us what they think people in a group are like. Their reports of specific traits or characteristics reveal individual level stereotypes, as well as their perception of consensual stereotypes.

Moreover, we also can distinguish between inaccurate judgments about the characteristics of a group that might be self-serving and accurate descriptions of modal characteristics possessed by a group. The question of whether a stereotype is accurate or inaccurate, positive or negative raises some additional points of complexity about the stereotype concept.

Stereotypes exist in part because information about people is selective and often distinctive. When information is distinctive and the groups to which it is attached are also distinctive, there is a tendency to overgeneralize from individual to group characteristics. This is known as *illusory correlation*. There are also tendencies to perceive groups as having definable characteristics when those characteristics are different from our own along dimensions that are important to us. The more important a characteristic is to us personally or to our group, the more likely a group that is different from us on that dimension will be perceived stereotypically. These observations tell us that stereotypes occur in a fairly natural way as a result of factors that make group differences salient.

Because stereotypes are formed so naturally, they are not easily changed. Because they may serve to bolster self-esteem, they are also resistant to change. One way in which stereotypes resist falsifying information is from processes of subtyping, by which a person who contradicts a global expectation is put into a separate subcategory that has no influence on the stereotype of the general group. Mae Jemison may be a Ph.D. nuclear physicist, an astronaut, and a woman, but in that atypicality, she does not influence what one generally thinks of African Americans or women.

Stereotypes play a vital role in our everyday life because they have been shown to affect what information we pay attention to and remember, how we interpret that information, and how we use it to form judgments. Finally, stereotypes can operate at an unconscious level and thus influence our thoughts, feelings, and behaviors without our awareness that this is happening. Because stereotypes play such a critical role in prejudice and can have subtle but powerful influences on our every thought and action, they are one of the most crucial elements in understanding the continuing power of prejudice.

8

Psychological Mechanisms of Prejudice—Intergroup Relations I: Theory and Research

❖

Introduction ◆ Two models of intergroup processes ◆ *Social competition—The common-predicament model of Muzafer Sherif* ◆ *Social categorization—The minimal-group paradigm of Henri Tajfel* ◆ Social processes that influence intergroup relations ◆ *Social identity theory (SIT)* ◆ *Optimal-distinctiveness theory* ◆ *Belonging to a stigmatized group* ◆ Cognitive processes that guide intergroup relations ◆ *Us and them—Groups as entities and actors* ◆ *Out-group homogeneity* ◆ *Complexity and extremity* ◆ *Categorical generalization—Exemplar versus prototype* ◆ The Dynamics of intergroup conflict ◆ *Social dominance theory* ◆ *Intergroup anxiety* ◆ Summary

"The rich are different from us."
—F. Scott Fitzgerald
"Yes, they have more money."
—H. L. Mencken

*I*NTRODUCTION

*I*n order for us to understand prejudice, we must have a clear understanding of what a group is. A *human group* is a social category of people who, in varying combinations, interact and mutually affect each other and who share goals, experience, traits, or characteristics. There is a strong tendency on the part of most people, to look for those things people have in common in order to determine whether or not they constitute a group, or to put people who share salient qualities (e.g., skin color) into the same group. The rich have more money, the poor have less. And so it goes.

Our tendency to categorize people arises, it is believed, from an evolutionary pressure to distinguish friend from foe. In this context, *friends* can be defined as those people who extend our own genetic viability. Put simply, they are people who enhance and protect our lives, encourage us, and facilitate and advance our goals, and extend the same aid to our genetic offspring. Foes, by contrast, are those people who would undermine, endanger, inhibit, or attack our well-being and the well-being of those genetically connected to us. Therefore, there is good reason for us to distinguish people on the basis of whether they are with us or against us, in our group or in another group, friends or foes. Self-interest and self-protection motivates us to place people into categories, because use of human categories helps us to make efficient judgments that enhance and protect us.

We also categorize, in part, in order to make it easier to transact the business of our lives with the rest of the world in a reasonable way. There are about six billion people on the planet. There is no way we can process relevant social information about each person we meet and still maintain reasonable patterns of interaction. We do and must take shortcuts; we must make judgments that significantly reduce those billions of people to a much smaller number of categories. For example, categorizing people by gender allows us to divide the population into only two groups about which we can generalize. It is easier for us to think about the large number of people in the categories into which we place them and it is much easier to formulate feelings about the category in lieu of making a great many individual judgments.

The available social psychology work on intergroup relations falls into two camps. The first can be called the "competitive self-interest" camp. In this approach, we divide people into categories that help us determine how best to maintain our physical and psychological well-being. In our society, physical and psychological well-being are associated with competitive advantage. The social-competition approach suggests that competition leads to conflict, which, in turn, produces *both* in-group preference and out-group hostility, as diagrammed below:

Social competition→group conflict→in-group preference and out-group hostility

The second is the "social-categorization" camp. In this approach, we categorize people in order to make our cognitive and behavioral tasks of living easier. Categorization reduces the relevant social information about people to simpler, neater, and fewer units. The aim of this process is not, presumably, to secure self-interest or self-enhancement, but greater efficiency and practicality in our daily lives. But, as we shall see, once we make the categories, other basic instincts take over, and we treat those people *within* our group differently, and better, than we treat other people—those outside our group. Therefore, the mechanism of perceiving people as members of particular social categories allows us to define who is in and who is out, and to treat those in our group differently and more favorably, as represented below:

Social categorization→in-group preference

The objective of this chapter is to explore the nature of intergroup relations as they are framed by the social-competition and social-categorization perspectives, respectively. The factors that generate intergroup conflict and the social-psychological processes that sustain, increase, or diminish it will be described and discussed. This chapter begins with a presentation of the two major perspectives. These views are represented here by discussion of the work of Muzafer Sherif on social competition and Henri Tajfel on social categorization. These approaches emphasize, respectively, the affective, emotional, and self-interested perceptual processes and the cognitively mediated perceptual processes that guide intergroup relations. The second section explores those social processes that influence intergroup relations. The issues explored include how being situated in the social world affects relationships with people who belong to different groups, and how we balance the desire to enhance our standing by belonging to valued groups and the desire to differentiate ourselves from others to assert our individuality. The section also examines just how important belonging to a dominant group is to our personal well-being. The third section reviews what we know about the cognitive processes that underlie social categorization and mediate its effects. The final section reviews the implications of these data for real-world conflict. How much of conflict can be explained by simply dividing people into groups and favoring our own? How important are the enduring personal histories, animosities, and real conflicts over tangible outcomes?

TWO MODELS OF INTERGROUP PROCESSES

Intergroup processes concern how individuals of different groups interact with each other when one or both of their group memberships are highly salient and influence the course of the interaction. Two approaches that have dominated social psychological research and theory, as noted earlier—social competition and social categorization. The former, associated with Muzafer Sherif, is typified by the "hard" conflict situation wherein animosities are built up over competitive dynamics that create realistic win-loss consequences of intergroup relations. The second is "soft"; that is, there is no competitive gain at stake, at least formally, yet the distinctions are somehow psychologically real, and exert influence on the course of interactions between members of different groups.

Social Competition—The Common-Predicament Model of Muzafer Sherif

Sherif and Sherif (1953) were interested in the relations between and among groups involved in different levels and types of conflict situations, including war and peace, harmony and conflict, domination and slavery, business and thievery, and so on. Sherif and Sherif (1953) argued that the future of the human species depends, in part, on our ability to solve problems of intergroup conflict. Racism is a specific form of intergroup conflict. Prejudice is a process that sustains and reinforces intergroup conflict or the potential for such conflict. The Sherifs' basic goal was to figure out how to make intergroup relations more positive and more harmonious, and less negative and acrimonious. Although they were writing over 40 years ago, these goals—more harmonious and less conflicted intergroup relations—continue to be of primary concern to social psychological research.

Working Definitions of Group Relations
Certain basic concepts are important to Sherif's analysis. Here are some of the basic definitions he used:

> **Group: A social unit consisting of individual members who are interdependent and possess values that regulate their behavior in ways that matter to the group.**

> **Ingroup: Those fellow members of a group to which a given person belongs physically or psychologically.**

> **Out-group: Those social units of which a person feels he or she is not physically or psychologically a part.**

> **Intergroup relations: Those relations that occur "whenever individuals belonging to one group interact, collectively or individually, with another group or its members in terms of their group identification." (Sherif, 1966, p. 12.)**

These definitions emphasize the interdependence of group members and the dual nature of their closeness—physical and psychological. Sherif (1966) sought to demonstrate a dynamic process by which real social conflict was created, maintained, and then reduced under controlled research conditions. He felt that, in order to understand how the passions of group identification in a competitive context worked, it is necessary to create a *maximal group,* that is, a group filled with a sense of history, passion, and a desire for advantage in face-to-face competition with other groups. After successfully producing this sort of real-world competitive, conflicted context, Sherif (1966) hoped to study those variables that would restore order, harmony, and positive intergroup relations. Let's see how he did this.

Robbers' Cave
In one study, Sherif and colleagues (Sherif, Harvey, White, Hood and Sherif, 1961) selected 11- and 12-year-old boys to participate in three separate experiments conducted in different campsites in Oklahoma. Each of these maximal-group experiments lasted about three weeks. The boys were selected from different neighborhoods and locations; they did not know each other prior to coming to the camps.

Stage 1—group formation. The boys were initially housed in one large bunkhouse. All activities were campwide. The youths had free choice of buddies, eating companions, and so on. After friendships had been formed, boys were asked to name their best friends. Based on their responses, two groups were formed so that each boy was in a group where one-third of his new groupmates were "old" friends, and two-thirds of his groupmates were *not*. Therefore, ties among the groupmates were based largely on *newly* formed friendships. To further solidify the group formation, each group engaged in separate activities designed to encourage interdependent interactions, and strong in-group cohesion, attraction, and coopera-tion. Each group of boys had cookouts, did chores, divided up work and play tasks, and so on. Following a one-week period, the boys were again asked to name their best friends. Friendship ratings showed that, after this period of group formation, boys had switched virtually all of their friendships to those boys within their new group. Figure 8.1 shows who they chose before they were separated into groups, and who they chose after.

Boys from group A had chosen *current* group A members an average of 35.1 percent of the time prior to group formation. However, they chose such members 95.0 percent of the time after group formation. Similarly, boys from group B had chosen an average of 35 percent of their friends from *current* group B before group formation but 87.7 percent after. So, Sherif et. al. (1961) had successfully created two groups whose friendships were almost entirely based on interactions that oc-curred after the groups had been formed. In preparation for the next experiment (stage 2) the new groups were given social identities by being named—group A was known as the "Eagles," and group B as the "Rattlers."

Stage 2—intergroup conflict. The staff arranged a tournament of games be-tween the Eagles and the Rattlers—baseball, touch football, tug-of-war, a treasure hunt, and so on. What began as a good-spirited and sporting competition degener-

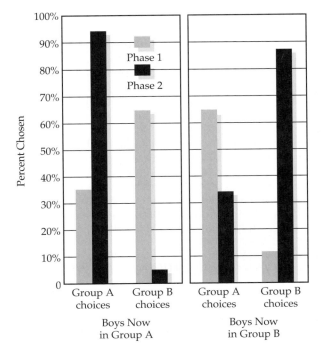

FIGURE 8.1

Percentage of Boys Choosing Friends from Current Group During Phase 1 and Phase 2 of Group Formation.

ated into hateful, mean-spirited competition. The boys called their rivals sneaks, cheats, and stinkers; they stole their rivals' flag; and fights became commonplace between members of rival teams. Just as much as conflict and competition increased *between* groups, cohesion and solidarity increased *within* each group.

During the tournament, a game of bean toss was introduced. Team members had to pick up as many beans as possible from the ground in a specified period of time. A narrow opening in the collection receptacle precluded the boys' counting precisely how many beans they had collected. The pile of beans collected by each player was projected onto a screen, and each player was asked to estimate the number of beans. Examination of these estimations showed that the winning-team members not only overestimated the number of beans for everyone, but especially for their own team members (an average of 47, compared to 40 for the opponents). Members of losing teams also overestimated their own team members' beans (about 38), but underestimated their opponents' beans (34).

The biases favoring the in-group and demeaning the out-group were even more dramatic in an earlier field experiment (Sherif and Sherif, 1953). This same paradigm produced not only the changes in friendship and biased perceptions, but the interactions of the two groups in this experiment (Red Devils and Bull Dogs) deteriorated into physical fights, food fights, and other disruptive acts. For example, one group left food out in the mess hall so that, when the other team had to clean up, it had become infested with bees and other flying insects.

Sherif's research (Sherif and Sherif, 1953; Sherif, Harvey, White, Hood, and Sherif, 1961; Sherif, 1966) here shows that we like people in our group more than we like people outside our group and that this tendency increases when we are in competition with other groups. Biases in liking are further reinforced by biases in perception. We actually *see* the behavior and performance of our friends as different (and, more positive) compared to the behavior of other groups' members. Eventually, these differences in group membership, energized by group competition, escalate into dramatic, and emotion-laden conflict. In the study cases, conflict was intense and persistent. Its manifestation included verbal and physical assault, and both symbolic and literal derogation.

Let's return to the progression of the robbers' cave experiments. Having created this intensely competitive and hostile intergroup situation, Sherif et. al. (1961) attempted to change the intergroup relationship from conflict to harmony. Despite efforts to get the combatants to do things together harmoniously, intergroup activities continued to erupt in competitive hostilities. Only when the setting produced a goal that could not be reached by one group alone were hostilities reduced and did cooperation ensue. Such settings involved creating what Sherif (1966) called *superordinate* goals (goals that, by their nature, cannot be reached by any one group acting alone). Cooperation was thus insured. As a result of this study, social psychologists believe that creating superordinate settings is a promising strategy in reducing intergroup-competition-based conflicts. (We will look at this again when we consider ways to reduce prejudice, in Chapter 11.)

Social Categorization—The Minimal-Group Paradigm of Henri Tajfel

Tajfel (1969) posed a different question and developed a different research approach than that used by Sherif (1969): Must intergroup conflict *necessarily* arise from competitive or conflicted relationships borne of interaction *or* can intergroup conflict result from the simple fact of categorizing ourselves and others into groups? Tajfel and his colleagues (1969) believed that, when you eliminate all of the basic competitive processes, people will *still* behave in a competitive self-interested way as long as they are allowed or encouraged to categorize themselves and others into groups.

Tajfel's aim in creating this minimal-group paradigm was to eliminate all of those processes associated with group competition—namely, face-to-face interaction, conflict of interest, previous hostility between the groups, and any link between group behavior and self-interest. This *minimal* group, then, is all in the head of the perceiver. In this approach, there is no real basis for interaction, the subjects know virtually nothing about the other person except the distinction created in the laboratory that places him or her in one group and the subject in another.

In the classic experiment, subjects performed trivial tasks, such as guessing the number of dots in rapidly projected clusters of dots or expressing their preference for one of two abstract paintings—one by the artist Paul Klee, the other by Wassily Kandinsky. Subjects were then ushered into separate cubicles and asked to make some judgments about how to allocate points worth real money between two *other* people, one of whom is like the subject (say, prefers Klee) and the other of whom is different from the subject (say, prefers Kandinsky). Subjects allocated more money to the member of the pair who was similar to him or her. Why did the subject seem to favor the person who, for example, preferred Klee, as the subject did?

Because the only information or knowledge subjects had of the other people was trivial, Tajfel (1969) argued that the preferential treatment mechanism served to *depersonalize* both parties. In a depersonalized situation, all that mattered was "whose side one was on," in a manner of speaking. Therefore, part of the explanation of the differential treatment is that, if all you know is that someone is like you in some (minor) way and another person is different from you, then you depersonalize both and favor the like-minded person! Tajfel goes on to argue that once you can depersonalize someone (i.e., completely ignore their individual characteristics and experiences), it is possible to *dehumanize* them. Therefore, the powerful effect of the minimal situation on in-group preference has strong implications for situations in which there are much more salient differences and sources of group conflict.

This approach, then, establishes a continuum where at one extreme interaction is completely *interpersonal*—that is, two people relate to each other completely, exclusively, and totally in terms of what each apparently brings to the interaction. In other words, factors such as, how one looks, what one says, how one says it, what one does, how one does it, and so forth form the complete basis of the encounter. At the opposite extreme is the completely *intergroup* interaction. In this case, the individual is completely depersonalized (as in the minimal paradigm) and his or her only significance lies in the particular group membership.

In reality, the interactions in most encounters fall somewhere in between. What matters is how the individual perceives the encounter. If it is perceived as lying closer to the interpersonal end, then the given individual will pay more attention to the particular characteristics of the other person. If it is seen as lying closer to the intergroup end, then what will matter most are the characteristics of the group. In the latter case, the situation involves great reliance on stereotypes; in the former, the reliance on stereotyping should be much lower.

(a) You make the call—Do you like this Kandinsky painting? (*Small Worlds,* 1922, Art Resource, NY)

Tajfel (1969) was able, with his minimal paradigm, to create a situation in which the subjects were depersonalized and the encounters were almost entirely *intergroup*. He thereby provided a "pure" context for studying basic processes in intergroup relations. The basic premise of Tajfel's approach is that the mere fact of categorization leads to the dynamic processes of intergroup behavior that fosters preferential treatment of others like oneself. Tajfel (1969) therefore, proposes a basic social psychological mechanism whereby perceiving the existence of human categories leads to self-interested behavior that favors one's self and members of the categories the self belongs to and that disfavors others who belong to different human groups.

Why Should Mere Categorization Produce In-Group Bias?
We have, for a long time, associated intergroup conflict with dramatic, emotional encounters: Lester Maddox standing at the door of a restaurant in Georgia in 1962, proclaiming that blacks would not be integrated into the social, educational, and cultural life of the South if he had anything to say about it; the murders of three civil rights workers in Mississippi in 1964; and Louise Day Hicks taking to the streets of South Boston in dramatic opposition to forced busing in that city in 1974. In fact, when we think about prejudice, the images that come to mind are emotionally and physically dramatic examples of intergroup conflict.

The mere categorization approach argues that categorizing people into distinct human groups can produce many of the underlying features of group conflict with-

(b) Or this Klee painting? Out of small differences mighty conflicts can grow! (*Destruction and Hope*, 1916, Art Resource, NY)

out the commonly associated tension, emotion, and various sources of major real differences. The work of Tajfel (1969, p. 80) signaled the rise of a cognitive, anti-motivational explanation of prejudice with the following defensive account of social relations:

> [While] we have the rational model for natural phenomena; we seem to have nothing but a blood-and-guts model for social phenomena. In this new blood-and-guts romanticism . . . man's attitudes and beliefs concerning the social environment are seen mainly as a byproduct of tendencies that are buried deeply in his evolutionary past or just as deeply in his unconscious.

Tajfel claims that analysis of social relations between and among groups has been totally focused on the blood-and-guts assumptions of motivation and evolution whereby all human conflict serves some basic Darwinian instinct of survival. He argues, though, that this view needs to be balanced by the extension of rational models of human thought and judgment in the physical domain to the dynamic interactions of social life. To achieve this goal, Tajfel (1969) offers three principles:

1 *Categorization*—Categorization enables us to reduce complex, large, and continuous human dimensions (e.g., individual variations in height, sex, skin color, language, dress, attitudes, beliefs, and religion) to smaller classifications that are discontinuous (e.g., race or gender may, for some people, be reducible to two categories each). We sometimes act as if the 280 million Americans can be reduced to *four* race and gender categories (whites, people of color, men, and women).

2   *Assimilation*—The process of assimilation is one of social learning—it comprises the ways in which children *learn* the content of human categories (e.g., stereotypes). In Tajfel's analysis, children learn evaluative judgments (good-bad, right-wrong), as well as preferential judgments (beautiful-ugly, rich-poor). Although these evaluations are theoretically continuous (ranging from 0 to 100), they are learned as *categories* of judgment and become attached to human groups. Through socialization, we learn to assign the negative aspect of the classification to groups other than our own and to assign the positive aspects to ourselves and our own group.

3   *Search for Coherence*—The search for coherence is the motivational force that determines how we react to specific intergroup situations and how we try to make sense of the flux and change of daily events. By this reasoning, in order to simplify the social world and to render it more predictable, we prefer to see people as behaving in a manner consistent with our categorization of them. That is, we like mean people to behave badly and good people to behave well. What happens when they behave out of character? The search-for-coherence principle assumes that, when the self-image is implicated, this process will render judgments that preserve the integrity of the self (see also Steele, 1988). For example, we might rationalize that bad people really don't behave well, and when they appear to, maybe their intentions were misunderstood, or they were trying to gain a positive image so that they could more easily do a bad thing. Soap opera characters do this all the time. Or, if a "good" person behaves badly, we are likely to conclude that the behavior is the result of some situational influence and not the result of the individual's true personal disposition, which would contradict our judgment that the individual is good.

When these three processes are put together, we have the basis for categorizing people into human groups, reducing large and continuous personal characteristics to simple classifications, assimilating a set of culturally shared values and norms to these categories, and, finally, perceiving the social world of actual interactions in ways that preserve the hierarchy of own-group preference and superiority.

According to the social categorization view, then, prejudice underlies the processes of intergroup conflict, in large part, because of these cognitive processes that emanate from cultural socialization, human cognitive development, and social perception. Although the consequences of these sequential judgments are fundamentally what we term *prejudice*, Tajfel (1969) argues that a blood-and-guts analysis of evolutionary necessity is not required to explain prejudice. In this view, prejudice results from the diversity among human beings and the tendency to try to *reduce* this diversity. However, the simplicity we seek is not random; it is very specific, we want a simple world in which we and our group are the best. Our culture tells us that it is possible and desirable to evaluate people. It also informs us along what dimensions of human character that such assessments should be made. We further learn that our group possesses more of the best characteristics and that other groups possess fewer of them. It seems, therefore, that prejudice is an inevitable consequence of growing up in the world of human beings. Tutsis are presumably prejudiced toward Hutus, Irish Catholics toward Irish Protestants, Bosnians toward Serbs, Quebecois towards English Canadians, and so on. If prejudice is the more or less automatic result of diversity, evaluation, and social cognition in society, then it should generally be found around the world in roughly the same form and probably similar frequency.[1]

The Klee and Kandinsky groups in the Tajfel (1969) experiments acted similar to the Eagles and Rattlers groups of the Sherif (1966) studies, at least with regard to the judgments of value that favored own-group members over other-group members. But, unlike the groups in Sherif's studies, the two groups in the Tajfel experiments had not built up really significant interactions that facilitated conflict and competition.

So, we ask, Is competition and conflict necessary to spark in-group bias or is mere categorization enough? Can we understand conflict and the favorable treatment of similar others as a function of intrapersonal processes that operate within the heads of people, or do we require a more detailed contextual analysis of intergroup processes that follow from real interaction among people?

Prejudice and racism have a deep and intense history in the United States and around the world. Can we reduce these intense dynamics to the simple process of and need for categorizing differences? Is real conflict necessary or inherent in real-world examples such that it cannot be reduced to simple categorical processes? What forms will bias take? In the lab, we have had subjects allocate small sums of money to people of their own group and of outgroups. We then show that they favor members of their group in doing so.

In the real world, men may rape women of the other group or may lynch or castrate men of the other group. Do they do this simply because they are of different gender, ethnicity, religion, or skin color? In the Sherif (1966) experiments, boys of different groups fought, called each other names, and violated the property of members of other groups. These behaviors are manifestly different and, arguably, more intense than the allocation of rewards or perceptions of performance, fitness, or ability. This does not necessarily mean that the theory of realistic group conflict, to the exclusion of the social-categorization effects, offers the only explanation for real-world conflict. It is possible—and perhaps likely—that the processes illustrated by the mere categorization approach underlie and sustain the biased perceptions that motivate the intense biased behaviors we observe in the real world. That is, the mere categorization approach illustrates the biased cognitive processes that become attached to the distinctions we make among people in forming human groups. The intensity of these biases will vary with the others' perceived threat to self-image, well-being, and own-group superiority. In order to get a complete picture of the intergroup-relations' effects on prejudice, then, we need to understand *both* the mere categorization processes *and* the nature and consequences of competition and conflict.

---

[1] It is, however, my belief that each instance of intergroup conflict may have determining properties that distinguish it from other, apparently similar situations. These distinguishing properties, in the case of race, will determine what specific features of people become the basis of categories (e.g., we talk about race in terms of skin color, but a drop of African blood was once sufficient to categorize one, regardless of behavior, phenotypical appearance, and so on, as black). This goes well beyond the simple categorization, assimilation, and search for coherence that the cognitive model of prejudice proposes. We will explore this idea in more detail in Chapter 11. The conflict between Tutsi and Hutu in Rwanda, which illustrates this issue, will be discussed in the next chapter.

SOCIAL PROCESSES THAT INFLUENCE INTERGROUP RELATIONS

What do we gain by joining groups? What determines what groups we join? Why are some groups "natural enemies"? (e.g., Democrats and Republicans). This section examines why we join groups and what processes are evoked by belonging to groups. We belong to some groups by birth (race, gender); we belong to others, to a large degree, by choice (e.g., political parties, occupations, neighborhoods), and we belong to some as a result of both choice and birth (e.g., ethnicity).[1] Because humans live in a social world, and because the permeability of boundaries between self and others varies in degree—from rigid and firm in strong individualistic cultures such as ours, to semipermeable and fluid in more collectivistic cultures, such as Japan, South American countries, and African countries (cf. Markus and Kitayama, 1991; Nobles, 1991; and Triandis, 1994)—understanding the social aspects of intergroup relations involves understanding the relationship between the self and the group.

Social Identity Theory (SIT)

"Sisterhood is powerful." "Black is beautiful." Both of these slogans express a positive social identity. *Social identity* is that part of an individual's self-concept that is based upon the value and emotional significance of belonging to a social group (cf. Tajfel, 1978; Taylor and Moghaddam, 1994). Social identity is a way to "feel good" about oneself in a social world. In order to feel the best, according to SIT, we should accord the most *positive* attributes to the group to which we belong. Further, we should see these groups to which we belong as *distinctive* from other groups—those to which we do not belong. The positive and distinctive nature of our in-groups is determined through four social psychological processes, as follows:

1   *Social categorization.* The process by which we categorize the social elements of our environment—namely, other people—is called *social categorization*. In this process, we order people into sets that either include or exclude ourselves. The sets that include us—for example, friends, family, fellow Greeks, teammembers, and classmates—we see in a different way, evaluate in a different way, and feel differently about.
2   *Social identity.* In addition to being the name of the theory, *social identity* is also one of the processes. By identifying positively with a group that we and others value, our self-concept is enhanced. The social identity process, as conceived, assumes that people have a fundamental need or desire to be positively evaluated themselves and that they satisfy this need or desire, in part, by belonging to positively evaluated groups.
3   *Social comparison.* How do we know that our group is either distinctive from other groups or positively evaluated relative to other groups? According to SIT,

[1]Mary Waters studied predominately white members of different ethnic groups and concluded that "Census data and my interviews suggest that ethnicity is increasingly a personal *choice* of whether to be ethnic at all, and for an increasing majority of people, of which ethnicity to be" (p. 147). She labeled *symbolic ethnicity* as clinging to an ethnic identity when it does not affect much in everyday life, and distinguished from racial minority status, in part, by the fact that choice of ethnic identification was possible, whereas racial identification was not.

we make *social comparisons*. To make a comparison, we must have some basis for comparison—that is, compared to what? Maquet (1961) shows that the Tutsi tribe in Rwanda was physically much taller than their rival tribe, the Hutus, and that this height differential was a positive aspect of social identity. Maquet argues that this distinguishing aspect of social identity was achieved, in part, via social comparison. It is no surprise that, in order for a social comparison to give us the results we seek (i.e., positive advantage relative to the out-group), we need to make comparisons on dimensions that we feel will favor ourselves and our group. Generally, we make comparisons in terms of dimensions in which we feel ourselves to be most capable. However, there are times when we will choose dimensions on which others are thought to be worse. This is called *downward* social comparison (Wills, 1981); it has been shown to help us feel better about ourselves when we face an ego-threatening situation (cf. Taylor, 1983). Social identity processes are enhanced when we compare our own group with other groups—groups that are stigmatized. Even if our own groups are not great, if we think we are better than others, we can derive psychological benefits from downward social comparison.

4   *Psychological group distinctiveness.* Social identity theory asserts that human beings have as much need for distinctiveness as for positive self-concept. That is, if we are positively evaluated, that positivity becomes even greater if we are uniquely so! According to SIT, these tendencies lead to the *false uniqueness effect*, by which people perceive their positive traits to be more unique than they really are (Marks, 1984). However, being distinctive is not always a good thing. We do not want to be distinctive on characteristics that allow others to draw a negative inference about us. When comparing ourselves to others on these attributes, we tend to see ourselves and our group as *less* distinctive. This effect, known as the *false consensus effect*, describes how we too gladly share our negative qualities with others. For example, people who cheat believe cheating is more widespread than it really is (Ross, Greene, and House, 1977). Social identity theory tells us we *need* to have such distinctiveness, but only when it suits us! When distinctiveness implies something negative about ourselves or our group, we wish to mingle with the crowd, and thereby to deflect attention from our negative qualities.

So what does all of this have to do with intergroup relations? Simply put, the processes of social identity are such that, in making comparisons, we tend to selectively focus on certain characteristics. We are apt to select traits for which we can expect a favorable social comparison with others who are different from us. Moreover, in the process of the assessment, we exaggerate those differences as a way of making our positive qualities more distinctive, more special, and, hence, a basis of even more positive self-regard. These dynamics, according to social identity theory, lead people to project negative qualities onto others and embrace positive qualities for their own group—in each case, exaggerating the truth. If realistic group conflict also occurs, then, as you may imagine, the perception of differences is not only negative but threatening. It becomes easier, therefore, for people to justify negative behavior toward the threatening out-group.

Optimal-Distinctiveness Theory

Social identity theory describes ways in which the self merges with the member group from which a person derives positive esteem. However, according to SIT, we also draw positive esteem from our own personally claimed character, achieve-ment, and accomplishment. These two approaches to self-esteem locate the source of esteem either in social relations or in individually identified characteristics.

These twin tendencies toward social identity (depersonalization) and personal identity (individuation) create a tug-of-war within the self. We might expect that depersonalization pressures reinforce group identification and, thereby, make in-tergroup relations more salient. When the social identity is salient, opportunities to either exaggerate or reduce intergroup conflict will be plentiful. As we saw with the stereotype research, we need to have the group in mind in order to affect the way we think about it. At the same time, if individuation pressures are great, we tend to diminish our own group-based identification. We are, thereby, perhaps, less in-clined to judge others whom we meet on the basis of their group membership. We will see, in Chapter 11, that both group-based and individual-based strategies for reducing prejudice have been proposed, and both have merit.

Brewer (1991) has proposed a model, *optimal-distinctiveness theory*, that specifies those conditions that determine when we are more likely or less likely to be group- or individual-identified. Shown in Figure 8.2, the model suggests that each of us has opposing processes, reflecting "a fundamental tension between human needs for validation and similarity to others . . . and a countervailing need for uniqueness and individuation (Brewer, 1991, p. 477)." That is, we want very much to be our own person, to be known by our unique qualities or style, but we also need to fit in, to belong, to derive support and encouragement from fellow and generally like-minded human beings. If either of these tendencies becomes too strong, Brewer ar-gues, the countervailing forces kick in, and we move in the opposite direction. If we get too wrapped up in our group identification, we may seek greater differentiation or self-expression. If we are too isolated in our uniqueness, we may seek member-ship in groups and emphasize our social connectivity. The maximum satisfaction occurs when the need for distinctiveness and the need for belonging are balanced. To the left of this optimal point, our assimilation needs are higher than our level of social categorization permits, so we feel relatively lonely or left out. To the right of

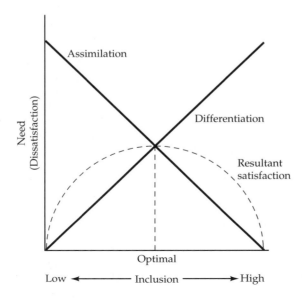

FIGURE 8.2

The Optimal Distinctiveness Model. SOURCE: Taken from M. B. Brewer (1991). "The Social Self: On Being the Same and Different at the Same Time. *Personality and Social Psychology Bulletin* 17, p. 477 (Fig. 2).

this point, our needs for differentiation are higher than the high level of inclusion in social groups allows, so that we feel *constrained* by our social identity. Our commitment to the group and satisfaction with our own individuality will be maximum where the two tendencies intersect.

The implication of this model is that ". . . distinctiveness *per se* is an extremely important characteristic of groups, independent of the status or evaluation attached to group memberships (Brewer, 1991, p. 478)." Therefore, groups maintain their attractiveness to their members, in part, by distinguishing themselves from other groups. Groups must provide positive rewards for being in the group. They must also reward group members by demarcating the boundaries with other groups, thereby conferring privileged distinctiveness on members of the in-group.

In a way, this dynamic is implicated in the diversity movement. That is, individuals seek to distinguish themselves from others because the positive rewards of membership in the society at large are limited by negative stereotyping and stigmatization. These stereotyping processes *also* deprive individuals of uniqueness. Therefore, they make it difficult for members of stereotyped groups to enhance self-esteem through social identity processes.

Individuals from stigmatized groups may enhance self-esteem, then, by identifying more strongly with their ethnic, racial, or gender group—that is, by sharpening the boundaries with majority groups—and thereby getting closer to the optimal level hypothesized by Brewer. Because society at large has differential capacity to provide social identity bases for self-esteem, subgroups seek identity enhancing contexts that often put them in conflict with other groups. Optimal distinctiveness theory may be very useful in enabling us to understand the shifting boundaries of intergroup relations and may aid us in determining when these boundaries are likely to take on competitive or comparative characteristics.

Belonging to a Stigmatized Group

We must note, however, that creating a positive social identity is certainly easier if one can choose to belong to social groups that are themselves positively valued in society, or that possess characteristics that are positively valued. For example, it is easy to see that belonging to the Mensa Society (members must have IQ scores higher than 160) in a society that values standardized abstract measures of intelligence is a basis of positive social identity. It is also easy to see that belonging to the most popular sorority on campus, for example, is a social identity enhancer. But what happens if you belong to a group that is stigmatized (e.g., by skin color, language, age, gender, or sexual orientation). How do you utilize social identity processes to create and maintain a positive self-concept? Social identity theory proposes several ways by which self-enhancing social identity processes occur for members of stigmatized groups (Crocker and Major, 1989):

1 *Social integration.* A group may seek to become absorbed into a more positively valued group. This is obviously more easily done when the basis for group membership is more abstract and subjectively determined (an athlete can go to law school and become a lawyer), or if the criteria can be otherwise manipulated (e.g., by a change of name, skin color, or physical features).
2 *Redefining the value of group qualities.* Members of a group may enhance their self-concept by redefining previously viewed negative qualities in more positive terms. "Black is beautiful" illustrates this strategy for African Americans.

But it can extend to less obvious qualities. For example, "musical" was one of the "Negro" stereotypes revealed in the Katz and Braly (1935) studies. Rather than rejecting musicality as a stereotypical group characteristic, one can embrace it as an example of uninhibited openness to one's feelings, a connection and awareness of one's body, and an example of a fundamental humanity. This is not a cognitive hocus pocus that merely calls *up* "down" and *black* "white." Rather, it represents a different way of viewing the world and of valuing human preferences, tendencies, desires, and capabilities.

3 *Developing new dimensions for comparison and evaluation.* A group may also create a positive self-concept by developing new categories for comparison and evaluation. This involves rejecting those traditional dimensions that typically have been chosen by the dominant group as a way to maintain its advantage. This strategy suggests looking anew at dimensions of merit and value. For example, being a good manager would no longer be defined as wielding unconditional control over supervisees, but as maximizing productivity, morale, and intergroup harmony among coworkers. When new criteria are introduced, old disadvantages dissolve and there is greater opportunity for successfully meeting new criteria.

4 *Competing directly with the dominant group.* This strategy, realistic group conflict, is seen around the world. In this approach, one group confronts another, with the ultimate aim of gaining positive identity through physical control and ascendance.

Social identity processes describe how people enhance their personal esteem through group affiliations and identifications. To the extent that one has a choice of groups to join, this strategy can be fairly simple: For example, you choose to join the popular Greek organization, develop your athletic skills, watch your diet and exercise, study hard, look for high-paying jobs, and so forth. You find the characteristics valued in your society and join groups that are associated with them. If by birth, or by accident (say a disfiguring disability caused by an accident) you belong to groups that are not positively valued, you have fewer options. In matters of race and ethnicity, intergroup conflict is exacerbated by the goals of social identity. Belonging to a dominant group (e.g., whites, men) provides social identity advantages that stand in opposition to the disadvantages of stigmatized-group membership.

The situation where a subdominant or stigmatized group seeks to gain some measure of control or social esteem, or where members of those groups seek to do so, is the focal point of intergroup conflict. There is conflict mainly because the dominant group or its members perpetuate the stigmatizing or controlling behavior. Therefore, the social goals or motives are different for dominant groups and for subdominant groups. For example, when black students seek to have a separate prom or their own student center, they are at once seeking a nonstigmatizing environment (i.e., one in which the threat that they will be treated with disrespect, assumed to be less capable, or subjected to social styles that are unwanted is reduced) and a degree of control (e.g., ability to choose styles of music, social and cultural events, and modes of interaction).

Except for the social integration strategy, all avenues for obtaining positive social identity while belonging to stigmatized or subdominant groups tend toward social segregation and/or social conflict. One consequence of this dynamic process is that reducing stigmatization and power or control inequalities may be a prerequisite for, not a consequence of, improving intergroup relations.

COGNITIVE PROCESSES THAT GUIDE INTERGROUP RELATIONS

This section considers some cognitive processes that result from or perpetuate social categorization. One of the processes, illustrated in the Sherif (1966) studies, is *biased social perception*. The cartoon below illustrates how categorization processes can affect the way we perceive and judge our social world. This perception of our social world is colored by the extent to which we categorize people into groups, the expectations that this categorization leads to, and the values or feelings that these social distinctions cause in us. To what extent does the act of categorizing people lead us to expect that the targets actually have similar characteristics or tendencies to act in similar fashion? When we think about a social category, what do we think about? What image comes to mind when we think about Latinos, is it the local television news anchor with no discernible accent who is only classifiable as Latino by her name, or is it the heavily accented woman who provides maid service in a hotel? Group-based judgments will depend on what image comes to mind to exemplify the group.

Us and Them—Groups as Entities and Actors

I recall vividly an occasion during my high school football years when we got together for team pictures. We had an offensive tackle, Gary, who weighed what was

"It's a cat calendar, so it may not be all that accurate."

Suspicions of difference. (Drawing by Ziegler; © 1995.) From *The New Yorker,* January 30, 1995, p. 60.

then an enormous 320 pounds. Our offensive backfield coach called out to Gary, "Come here, Gary. I want to take a team picture of you." Apart from the rag on his weight, the humor came in the preposterous idea that a single person could be a *group!* Well, what about the opposite idea, that a group could be a "person"? Well, not exactly a real person, but could a group be thought of in the same way an individual is thought of, as possessing specific characteristics just as individuals do (e.g., honesty, height, skin color, and intelligence) *including* the ability to act (e.g., to run, jump, hit, go)? Donald Campbell (1958) raised the question first by asking why some aggregates of people can be considered entities and others cannot? Why, for example, are "women" an entity and "brunettes" not? Campbell (1958) argues that an entity can be defined by four properties, as follows:

1 *Proximity* — People close together are more likely to be perceived as part of the same grouping.
2 *Similarity* — Similar people are more likely to be perceived as belonging to the same group.
3 *Common fate* — People who move together—that is, in the same direction—as we perceive them at different times are thought to belong to the same group.
4 *Pregnance* — People who form a pattern or spatial organization are perceived to be part of the same group.

When an aggregate of individuals meets these entity criteria, it is said to possess *entitativity* — the degree of having the nature of an entity, of having *real* existence (Campbell, 1958, p. 17).[2] Let's consider, for a moment, African Americans. They have, over their history, shared proximity through racial segregation; similarity in skin color; common fate via the slave trade, slavery, discrimination, and oppression; and have formed social psychological patterns through social stereotypes and contrasts with Americans of European descent and have formed a spatial pattern through residential segregation processes. Some may conclude that, to the extent that a group meets these four criteria of entivity, it will be seen as having a real existence that transcends the facts and characteristics of individual members.

Is it a good or a bad thing to possess entitivity? First of all, it is a feature of the *perceiver*. So, to coin a phrase, "Entitivity is in the eye of the beholder!" We may think of this as a logical extension or description of what we have discussed at length as a "stereotype," but it is different. Whereas a stereotype is a relatively fixed set of attributes that is thought to characterize a group of people to some nonspecific degree (e.g., as few as 20% of a group's members may be thought to possess a characteristic judged to be stereotypical), when we say a group has entitivity, we mean that it has the real capacity for thought, feeling, and behavior.

Ross Perot was speaking to the annual convention of the NAACP in Texas during his 1992 campaign for the presidency. He created an uproar when he referred to his audience of conventioneers as "you people." What did he mean, and why was everyone so upset? When a group is perceived as an entity, then the criteria are assumed to be met! That is, if we are a group, then we are similar, we share proximity and a common fate, and together we create a "good form." In effect, this entitivity view strips members of the group of their individuality. Moreover, in our society, the group is also stigmatized. If there is anything valued in the United States, it is

---

[2] We will use a shortened form, *entitivity*, in all further discussions.

individuality—of expression, rights, and freedom. Race and common history give African Americans, in the eyes of most whites, entitivity. In being accorded entitivity, individuals lose their individuality. The group is treated as if it were real—to the exclusion of individual distinctions—and patterns of bias persist because similarity across people is exaggerated.

More recently, Abelson (1994) has offered another take on entitivity. Specifically, he raises the question of the ability of entities to *act* in a relatively organized and coherent fashion. Abelson terms this capacity to act *actitativity*, the perception of groups as ". . . purposive organizers of self-interested activities."[3] Whereas entitivity gives a group *thing-ness* qualities that exist in a relatively immobile, unchanging fashion, actitivity gives groups *doing-ness* (*people* are accustomed to being verb-like; cf. Fuller, Agel, and Fiore, *I Seem to Be a Verb*, 1970), which is the capacity to act with intention, purpose, and motivation. A group that is only characterized by the qualities that make it a thing is passive, an object of perception. However, a group characterized by doing-ness has the capacity to affect others in an organized and motivated way. In short, an actitive group has to be reckoned with in a way an entitive group does not. For example, if an entitive group possess qualities I do not like or value, I may not like members of the group, or the group as a whole. But, if an active group possesses intentions that I do not like, I may not only dislike its members and the group, I may fear them.

In the United States, we have long held African Americans to thing-like qualities, or stereotypes. We have, as a society, made judgments about the group and treated it and its members in various ways—almost always bad. We can behave toward a group as if it were an object, and that is what we have generally done. But, in the 1960s, something changed. The black power movement, perhaps, combined with the "black is beautiful" self-expression trend changed the black stereotype from entitive and thing-like to actitive and verb-like. The civil rights movement was just that—a movement that people joined, whether they were black, white, old, young, blue, or green. But, once blacks became collective actors, the action was linked to the group itself. Black interests were no longer easily linked to white interests or to U.S. interests. In part, intergroup conflict escalated, I would argue, as a result of this new perception.

Whereas entitivity is characterized by similarity, proximity, and common fate, actitivity is associated with statements of intent, mass participation in events, achievement of purposes, and unanimity of justifications. When a group acquires actitivity status, then one member of the group is not merely an exemplar of a stereotype (a bundle of traits and characteristics) but a precursor of action. For example, a black person who moves into an all-white neighborhood may be perfectly matched with the neighbors on every dimension that matters (education, economic status, values, respect for law and order, etc.) But, as a symbol of group-actitivity, that individual viewed as representing merely the opening wave of a tide or group action, of a larger number of black people who will move in and "take over" the neighborhood.

"Sticks and stones may break my bones, but names will never hurt me" is a well-known adage. But sticks and stones only break bones when hurled or otherwise wielded! Actions matter and, when groups act in such a manner purposively and intentionally, the level of conflict escalates.

---

[3] Again, for simplicity, we will use the term *actitivity* in all further discussions.

Out-Group Homogeneity

We have already acknowledged that forming social classifications facilitates inter-group conflict via the mechanism of in-group bias. Tajfel (1969) has suggested the principle that helps to explain how this works. Recall his claim that

> . . . when a classification (e.g., race) is correlated with a continuous variable (e.g., aggres-siveness), there will be a tendency to exaggerate differences on that dimension *between* people who fall into distinct classes, and to minimize differences between people *within* each of those classes.

This process of sharpening the boundaries between groups involves heightening the similarities of people within out-groups on dimensions of judgments for which there exist real group differences. For example, if group A is (or is thought to be) more aggressive than group B is, then Freddy (who is an "A") will be more likely to be judged aggressive than Joey (who is a "B"). Sagar and Schofield (1980) showed this to be true when junior high school judges rated ambiguously aggressive events (bumping into someone in the hall, poking someone with a pencil, asking someone for their piece of cake in the lunchroom) more hostile when associated with a black than with a white actor. Moreover, other members of group A will be more likely to be judged on aggressiveness similarly to Freddy, and differently from Joey. There-fore, members of group A become more alike as real differences among them are re-duced, and they become collectively more different from group B.

In simpler words, if we as a species made no distinctions among us in social categories or classifications, then we would better see how *different* individual peo-ple are from each other. But, once we classify people, we tend to become quite taken with the idea that, because they are classified as a group, the members of the group must be alike (i.e., they must have essential characteristics that conceptually or perceptually bind them together; cf. Medin, 1989). The characteristic that makes them a group may be shared by members, but we come to believe that other char-acteristics, which are not part of the group identification, are also shared. If there is no classification, then there is no advantage to drawing distinctions. But, as Tajfel and Sherif have shown and history has amply recorded, we do draw human dis-tinctions. The result of those distinctions is the linkage of traits to classes or groups.

This *out-group homogeneity effect* (increased perception of out-group members as similar) has been demonstrated many times in laboratory research (e.g., Judd and Park, 1988; Park and Judd, 1990; Park and Rothbart, 1982; and Quattrone and Jones, 1980). For example, Judd, Ryan, and Park (1991) had business and engineer-ing majors make judgments about either business majors as a group or engineering majors as a group (in- or out-group, depending on the subject's major). Subjects were asked to consider the group as a whole and to judge how many of its mem-bers were likely to fall at different places along a dimension of extroversion. They were also asked to estimate the percentage of the group (from 0 to 100%) who pos-sessed the trait of extroversion. Third, they were asked to show the mean and range of scores members of the group would have on a test that measured extroversion. From tasks such as these, Judd, Ryan, and Park (1991) were able to show that the business majors saw the engineering majors as more homogeneous and that the en-gineering majors saw the business majors as more homogeneous (lower standard deviations). These authors also compared judgments of out-group members by in-group members with out-group members' own judgments. They could thereby determine how sensitive subjects judgments of out-groups were to the actual variations in the group. In general, subjects showed much greater sensitivity to the actual range and mean judgments of other members of their in-group than they did to those of members of the out-group.

Members of out-groups are perceived as less variable and more stereotypic than in-group members. It is also important to note that those subjects who perceived this to the greatest degree were more sensitive to the actual variability of in-group members than they were to that of out-group members. That is, the more likely business majors were to perceive fellow business majors as variable, the more likely they were able to perceive engineering majors as homogeneous. Therefore, it seems that there is a degree of sensitivity to the real attributes of people in our own group that disappears when we judge members of other groups. What is this sensitivity due to, and why does it go away when we judge out-groups?

One explanation is that we are simply more *familiar* with members of our own group. If we have little contact with members of other groups, they subsequently will be less differentiated in our minds—they are perceived to act and look alike! Park and Rothbart (1982) showed that this effect could be a result of actually deriving different information from encounters with in-group and with out-group members. They found that information that is not well-differentiated between group members (e.g., women and men) will be remembered equally well by men and women. However, when the information is differentiated along gender lines, men will remember information about men better and women will remember information about women better.

Linville, Fischer, and Salovey (1989) argued that familiarity increases the range of contacts one has with in-group members, and that, therefore, a broader range of experiences is actually associated with in-group members. Let's recall a bit of statistics. The larger a sample is relative to the population from which it was drawn, the more reliable the estimate that can be made about the true population characteristics. Linville et al. (1989) argue that the samples of familiar in-group people are larger—hence, more reliably variable—than they are for out-groups, for whom samples are small relative to the populations. This seems neat and makes a lot of sense.

However, along come Judd and Park (1988), who used a minimal-group paradigm to create in- and out-groups. Although in this study, subjects had no familiarity at all with the groups, the same tendency toward out-group homogenization was evidenced. So, although the familiarity basis for out-group homogeneity may be inadequate to explain it, the phenomenon does exist. Perhaps the process of categorizing people implies a salient commonality among people in the group that has the power to assimilate other characteristics to the primary organizing principle. This would probably be most true when the characteristics are affectively similar to, or *representative* of, the predominant feeling one has for the group.

Taylor, Fiske, et al. (1977) demonstrated that out-group homogeneity efforts could actually alter our perception of what we saw or heard. They had subjects view a group interaction where the groups were mixed (half and half male and female or black and white) or in which there was a *solo* female or black member of the group. In each case, subjects were asked about a specific female or black member's behavior. In the case of mixed groups, subjects became confused about *which* black or female member had contributed particular ideas to the group. They knew whether a black or white person had said something, but not which one! When there was a sole black or female group member, however, subjects were more likely to perceive him or her as talking more and being more influential than they were when the same person said the same things, in a racially mixed or mixed-gender group, or in a racially or gender-homogeneous group. Solo status heightened memory even to a point of distortion. Group-based perception dulled memory, making out-group members homogeneous and, therefore, interchangeable.

Complexity and Extremity

Out-groups are more homogeneous and in-groups are more heterogeneous, according to Linville and her colleagues (1989), because category familiarity leads to *category differentiation* (Linville and Jones, 1980; Linville, 1982; and Linville, Salovey, and Fisher, 1986). In this process we make *more* distinctions among people in groups with which we are familiar, and *fewer* distinctions among people who are out-group members.

The negative side of this tendency is that we perceive out-group members as homogeneous, undifferentiated, and stereotypical. However, Linville and Jones (1980) showed what they called the *complexity-extremity* effect. They reasoned that the *less* complex a group is perceived to be, the more extremely people from those groups will be judged. To test this idea, they had white college students evaluate several law school applications. The applications varied in strength or quality and contained information that allowed the race of the applicant to be determined. The same level of qualifications were paired for black and white applicants, and all subjects were white. What Linville and Jones (1980) found supported their predictions. *Strong* applicants who were black (out-group, less differentiated) were rated *higher* than comparable white applicants (in-group, more differentiated). *Weak* black applicants, however, were rated *lower* than weak white applicants were. Therefore, black applicants were polarized toward the extremes—good ones were made better and poor ones made worse. These same complexity-extremity effects were found using gender and age as group-level categories.

In these studies, complexity was manipulated by simply having subjects rate others who were in or outside their group (complexity was assumed to be greater for in-group members). The authors also suggest that individuals may vary in the extent to which they perceive a given group as more or less differentiated. Linville and Jones (1980) argued that a person who perceives another group as less differentiated should be more inclined to make extreme judgments of a number of that group. Conversely, a person who perceives that same group as more complex will perceive members of that group more moderately. Linville (1982, study 2) had male college subjects sort 33 traits into clusters of traits that they thought "went together." Subjects could use traits more than once and could create as many clusters as they thought were important or made sense. Half the subjects were told to think about college-age men, while the other half were told to think about men in their sixties and seventies as they completed this trait-sorting task. The number of clusters created was used as an index of the degree of complexity or differentiation these male subjects saw when judging the traits of men their own age or much older. Subjects were then asked to read two short vignettes depicting a man in either a very favorable or a very unfavorable light, who was either college age or much older. Subjects were asked to evaluate the target persons in the vignette (e.g., "What is your overall reaction to the person?" and to rate him on 10 traits (e.g., friendly, active, happy, and mentally healthy).

Results showed two things. First, ratings of old-age targets were more extreme than ratings of younger targets were—old men were liked *more* in the favorable and *less* in the unfavorable condition than were college-age males. Second, for the older targets, the evaluative ratings were more extreme for subjects who perceived older men in less-complex or less-differentiated ways. Therefore, the hypothesis of individual variation in perception of out-groups as more or less differentiated is not only true about in-group–out-group differences, it is also true about people who themselves show a high or low degree of complexity when thinking about other groups.

What we find is that familiarity perhaps linked to greater real-world complexity in our perceptions of others, will be related to (1) a reduction in how similarly we see others, (2) a likely reduction in the tendency to stereotype them, and (3) in the end, behavior that is less extreme and more sensitive to contextual nuance and individual variability. This approach to perceiving others would certainly be a step in the right direction for reducing prejudice. Conversely, situations that cause us to take cognitive short-cuts, that put added pressure on our cognitive capacity, or that speed up our need or desire to reach goals and achieve desired outcomes, will likely perpetuate these tendencies to see others in undifferentiated ways, and to make extreme judgments. Although sometimes the subjects' reactions to such situations will work to the advantage of the target, the types of negative biases we have already described suggest that the negative effects will probably be more common.

Categorical Generalization — Exemplar versus Prototype

One of the recurring questions about groups concerns how we define their salient characteristics. That is, when someone mentions Hispanics, who is it that comes to mind? Who *exemplifies* the category? Patrick Buchanan referred to illegal immigrants by a generic *José*, thus calling to mind illegal immigrants who were probably poor, non-English-speaking, and so forth. This image of Hispanics would trigger one set of ideas, beliefs, or attitudes about Hispanics and lead to one picture of the group. Alternatively, in the Clinton Administration, Henry Cisneros, secretary of the Housing and Urban Development department, is a tall, handsome, and eloquent man. He is a Mexican American. Is it he who comes to mind when *Hispanic* is invoked as a category? Or, is *Hispanic* a generic, or *prototypical*, term that is defined by some average or probabilistic set of attributes and qualities—for example, "José" is an immigrant; speaks with a Spanish accent; has dark black hair; is emotional; is of average or lower-than-average intelligence; lives in California, Florida, or Texas; and is likely to work in blue-collar or farm industry jobs.

Social psychological theory and research tries to determine which of these approaches best captures the way in which we typically think about groups and their members. The *prototype*, or top-down, view conceptualizes the group as a generic category. According to this view, the idea of the group brings to mind a standard set of traits and characteristics or stereotypes whenever it is invoked. The *exemplar*, or bottom-up, approach suggests that the group is defined by the set of traits and characteristics of specific people we encounter, averaged over all encounters. So, for example, if you mostly interact with migrant Hispanic farmworkers, then your view of the group will be heavily influenced by your perceptions of these people. However, if you grow up in a political household in Washington, D.C., you may think that Congresspeople and cabinet-level administrators are not uncommon among Hispanics.

Intergroup relations concern how two individuals interact when their group membership is highly salient. For example, how a person interacts with a person categorized as Hispanic will depend, in part, on what that categorization *means*. The meaning will be determined in part by abstractions of qualities ascribed to Hispanics and in part by the person's actual experiences with Hispanic people and how those are remembered. Smith and Zarate (1992) argue that exemplars are real people who are perceived to belong to a social group and about whom a person has ideas either based on first-hand experiences or formulated through media or other second-hand accounts. When a perceiver encounters someone whom he or she believes is in the target category (say, Hispanic), the information the subject associates with other exemplars will be retrieved from memory and will guide the perception—and, hence, the interaction—that ensues. Exemplars influence categorization (e.g., George is like that guy José I met in the airport last week) and can affect social judgment (e.g., José was a funny guy, so I may expect George to be funny and will probably be more attentive to his humor).

We can classify others more easily to the extent that they are more or less similar to the exemplars we have in mind. These exemplars are categorized in terms of their attributes. The attributes that are most salient to us are those that have the greatest personal relevance. Therefore, our evaluation of a person we meet will depend on our own social motivations and how closely the person approximates others with whom we have interacted or others whom we have conceived of as members of the group. The more salient a given attribute is in a person, the more likely it will be a basis for evaluation. Attributes that are more accessible (e.g., gender-based role expectations) or are more salient (i.e., any attribute that deviates from culture-based expectations) are more likely to influence social judgments and, hence, intergroup interaction.

Smith and Zarate (1992) argue that cultural expectations are "automatic" in our heads and provide "default" options against which departures are judged. These default values are associated with a given someone when specific information is not available. Therefore, personal qualities that deviate from those of white, male, able-bodied, heterosexual people are most likely to be salient. And, being more salient, they play a large role in the categorization and social judgment processes. Zarate and Smith (1990) demonstrated this idea by having subjects classify photographs of men and women who were black or white. Photographs that departed from a white male cultural default were classified according to the divergent category. That is, black males were more quickly categorized as black than as male; white women were more quickly categorized as women than as white.

The implication of these ideas concerns the processes by which we come to expect particular behavior, attitudes, or beliefs when we encounter a person. How quickly we categorize the person and into what group we place the individual will depend on the factors outlined above. The important implication of exemplar analysis is that it is very heavily influenced by specific experiences and memories and the cues that they arouse in a given social context. Exemplar analysis introduces far greater complexity into intergroup interactions. It makes them less automatic or prototypical and more nuanced in terms of both the perceiver and the target characteristics. It emphasizes that human interaction can influence the content of ideas about human groups and expectations for the course of interaction with out-group members.

The importance of these distinctions between the two approaches is that the prototype view seems to first establish an abstract representation of a group, and then filter all perceptions through it. It is difficult, from the prototype perspective, to see how to change what people think about social groups. According to this view, their perceptions are already biased by their expectations. By contrast, the exemplar view suggests that providing people with opportunities to interact with members of different groups will have the broad effect of changing who comes to mind when the group is invoked. For advocates of this view, for example, an advantage of diversity programs is that they bring people into contact with a wider range of persons in different groups. This potentially, will expand the range of people who come to mind and should have the effect of reducing perceptions of out-group homogeneity and the adverse consequences of our extreme judgments.

THE DYNAMICS OF INTERGROUP CONFLICT

The problem in intergroup conflict has been conceptualized as either competitive interest in and desire for scarce resources, or an evolutionary in-group bias favoring one's own group or "kind" over others. Fear that others' self-interest will compete with and undermine our own leads to selective biases that favor our own kind of people. But, overlying this basis of intergroup conflict is the broader societal context in which some groups are favored over others by virtue of their power, prestige, and hierarchical position. Some groups find themselves at the top persistently over time, and other groups consistently find themselves lower down in the hierarchy. *Top* and *bottom* are typically defined by material values (i.e., money and possessions such as homes, cars, and jewelry); social values (i.e., networks of friends and relations, who are themselves at the top of the material hierarchy); political values (e.g., control over resources, decision making, and power to define what is valued); and the demographic characteristics associated with each of these (e.g., race, gender, and age). Hierarchies are vertical in character; that is, they define things from top to bottom, high to low, lots to a little. In general, intergroup conflict occurs when groups jockey for position on a hierarchical continuum. Groups higher up strive to maintain their position or move higher, and groups lower down try to improve their position.

There are many ways in which hierarchies function in the maintenance and expression of intergroup conflict. We cannot consider all of the ways in which this works. However, in this next section we will look at how people view hierarchies (as a reasonable form of social organization), how they justify them as a means of preserving an orderly understanding of their social world, and how anxiety arises at the intersection of relationships between people who belong to different groups that occupy different places in social hierarchies.

Social Dominance Theory

The social dominance theory, or SDT (Sidanius, 1993), proposes that all societies are characterized by the following three attributes:

1   One finds group-based hierarchies in which at least one group is dominant over all others and in which that group enjoys a disproportionate share of the positive assets (e.g., wealth, prestige, education, health). In such hierarchies, also, at least one group is subordinate and enjoys a disproportionate share of negative

liabilities (e.g., poor health, poverty, low status, social stigma, low levels of education, and high levels of criminal punishment).

2   Groups compete over scarce material and symbolic resources as they seek to enhance their own relative positions on valued assets.

3   In this competitive relationship, groups use *ideological* strategies, such as gender- or race-based "natural" rights; concepts of national, racial, or ethnic superiority; or particular political ideologies, such as opposition to policies that advance the standing of groups with whom one is in competition.

By implication a group will seek to control both materially and symbolically those instruments of society that serve to maintain their group's dominance, and it will espouse policies, beliefs, and myths that legitimate and perpetuate its dominance. These policies or beliefs are promulgated by those at the top of the hierarchy and define a general theory of society. All members of society—and all groups—are subject to them and, therefore, tend to believe in or support them, in varying degrees. By this analysis, groups that are at the bottom of the hierarchy may even endorse policies that perpetuate their lower-level status.

Social Dominance Orientation

SDT describes the structure and functions of societies based on an evolutionary view of human social organization. A derivative of SDT is the *social dominance orientation* (SDO) theory, which asserts that people differ in the degrees to which they subscribe to the tenets of SDT. SDO reflects the extent to which individuals desire their in-group to dominate and be superior to out-groups (Pratto, Sidanius, Stallworth, and Malle, 1994). SDO is an attitude toward intergroup relations; it reflects whether one generally prefers such relations to be equal or hierarchical; one's group to be advantaged or superior. People who rate "high" on SDO are expected to favor hierarchy-enhancing ideologies and policies; people who rate lower on SDO tend to favor hierarchy-attenuating ideologies and policies.

This theory proposes that endorsement of social policies that have implications for group-based hierarchies (e.g., immigration, affirmative action, and busing to achieve racial integration) will vary as a function of a person's SDO. A person with a high SDO rating would be more likely to oppose immigration, affirmative action, and busing, because each of these policies would attenuate hierarchical advantage. That is, immigration, affirmative action, and busing all either insert persons lower in the socioeconomic hierarchy into higher positions (better jobs) or absorb resources that may have been used to support those more advanced in the social hierarchy. California's proposition 187 is an example of a hierarchy-enhancing policy. Moreover, the model proposes that the SDO levels may influence individual choice of social roles in that those with a high degree of SDO will tend to prefer roles that enhance or sustain the hierarchy (e.g., police, prosecutor) and those with lower degrees of SDO will more likely choose hierarchy-attenuating roles (e.g., social worker, teacher). Sidanius, Liu, Shaw, and Pratto (1994) have shown that these expectations can be empirically demonstrated.

Hierarchical arrangements in societies are sustained, in part, by *legitimizing myths*. Legitimizing myths present values, beliefs, and policies that have the practical consequence of creating, maintaining, or enhancing inequality among social groups. In the Sidanius (1993) analysis, these myths include *ethnic prejudice*, the hierarchy of ethnic groups and discriminatory treatment of those lower in the hierarchy; *nationalism*, the preference for one's own and denial of equality and opportunity to "foreigners"; *cultural elitism*, the belief that some members of society are better than others because the former embody the most positive virtues endorsed by societal members; *sexism*, maintenance of sexual inequality; *political-economic conservatism*, the belief in capitalism and its support of hierarchies based on business success; and *meritocracy*, the belief that status differences among people and groups are justified on the basis of merit—that is, those who have more must *deserve* it.

An SDO scale that tests the relationship of SDO to endorsement of these legitimizing myths has been developed (Pratto et al., 1994). It consists of 14 items that people are asked to rate in terms of their own positive or negative feelings about them. For example:

1   "Some groups of people are simply not the equal of others."
2   "It is not a problem if some people have more of a chance in life than others."
3   "To get ahead in life, it is sometimes necessary to step on others."
4   "In an ideal world, all nations would be equal." [reverse scored]

Response to these 14 items were scored on a 5-point scale from strongly disagree (1) to strongly agree (5) so that the higher the score, the greater a person's SDO.

As was predicted by the SDO model, SDO scores were positively correlated with measures of political-economic conservatism, belief in a just world, patriotism, antiblack racism, sexist attitudes toward women, belief in rape myths, belief in "law and order," and a preference for the Republican party. SDO scores were negatively correlated with endorsement of women's rights, social programs, gay and lesbian rights, and environmental policies. In sum, higher SDO scores were correlated with hierarchy-enhancing ideologies or beliefs across the board from specific groups to general policies both in this country and around the world.

A person's tendency to believe that social hierarchies are appropriate and, therefore, social inequality is okay is an important aspect of intergroup conflict. As SDO measures suggest, perpetuation of intergroup conflict is encouraged by a belief that somebody *needs* to be on top, and that privilege and advantage to such people or groups is *natural*, and, well, if it has to be, it might as well be me! Social dominance orientation has proved a provocative thesis and has directed the illustration of some quite interesting tendencies. For example, Sidanius, Pratto and Bobo (in press) showed that although opposition to affirmative action was correlated with *"principled conservatism"* (i.e., belief in core values of individual rights and a color-blind approach to fairness), it was nevertheless also correlated with racism (belief in white superiority and the acceptance of racial inequality) and a belief in social dominance. Therefore, the idea that people who oppose social policies that are perceived to benefit minority groups do so on the basis of *principle* and *not* on the basis of race or ethnicity (as argued by Sniderman & Piazza, 1993) is called into question, at the very least, by these findings.

SDO studies, then, suggest an individual-difference dimension to intergroup conflict. It may be that not all members of groups simply strive to achieve superiority and higher status, but that people differ in the extent to which they seek to be on top. Because everyone cannot be on top, it is also important to note that some people believe such a situation is okay. These people are more likely to endorse social arrangements that are disadvantageous to some segments of society. The problems of prejudice and racism themselves contribute to racial and ethnic inequality. SDO theory suggests at least one human tendency that may aid and abet divisiveness between and among groups, and escalate the conflict that occurs among them, *system justification*.

System Justification

Jost and Banaji (1994) argue, in general, that individual beliefs about others are properly thought of as justification systems that validate positive feelings about the self (ego-justifications) or one's group (group justification). Justification is "an idea being used to provide legitimacy or support for another idea or for some form of behaviour," according to Jost and Banaji (1994, p. 1). The great tendency to conceive all forms of social thought—and justifications for it—in terms of self- or group enhancement, preference, and favoritism is countered by data suggesting that, in many cases, people who are targets justify particular patterns of social relationships in which they are disfavored by the status quo. "Buying into the system" may be a way to legitimate personal gains at the expense of the perception of overall group status.

"*System justification* refers to the psychological process whereby an individual perceives, understands, and explains an existing situation or arrangement with the result that the situation or arrangement is maintained . . . in spite of the obvious psychological and material harm they entail for disadvantaged individuals and groups." (Jost and Banaji, 1994, p. 10; italics added). In this view, people may justify social-class differences by resorting to the stereotypes associated with those differences. They might thus explain the plight of the poor by referring to attributes that make such people poor. By using social stereotypes to justify social position, they intentionally or unintentionally hold the system harmless as far as its role in observed inequalities. This biased assessment is treated as if it were a true justification for the social arrangements. In fact, it is more likely a tautological derivation of cause from effect. The result of this flawed thinking is termed *false consciousness*, because it fails to properly consider the realistic dynamics of cause and effect in social arrangements and outcomes.

False consciousness offers a kind of sustaining mechanism, or legitimizing myth (cf. Sidanius, 1993), for social hierarchies that persistently place certain groups at the top and other groups lower down. If dominant and subordinate group members both accept the status quo and believe it to be not just fair but natural, then maintaining group dominance is easy. However, opposition to perpetual dominance of whites, for example, reveals itself in opposition to false consciousness, rejection of the status quo, and the systematic deconstruction of legitimizing myths and system justifications.

Intergroup conflict emerges also from the struggle over interpretations of system effects and the claim for legitimacy in justifying these outcomes. The interesting aspect of system-justification theory is not so much that it can happen and does happen (e.g., through negative self-stereotyping, belief in a just world, and fundamental attribution error), but what factors lead members of both dominant and subordinate groups to reject those justifications of the status quo that attempt to legitimate the natural and fair interpretation of social systems. Arguments over multiculturalism, diversity, social policy, and political correctness basically concern how our society functions and the legitimacy of both the processes and outcomes of the social system. This issue recurs when we discuss racism in Part 3.

Intergroup Anxiety

We have so far described intergroup relations primarily in terms of conflict. We have identified the sources of such conflict to be the realistic, competition-based desire for scarce material for psychological resources, a desire for personal and collective advantages, and the psychological and perceptual processes that accompany social categorization. However, another possible source of intergroup conflict may simply be our discomfort with members of out-groups with whom we are less familiar or about whom we may have negative expectations. For example, concern with not being prejudiced (cf. Dunton and Fazio, 1996), may arouse anxiety if we fear either that we are prejudiced or that another person may believe us to be so, even if we try not to be or don't think we are (see also Devine, Evett, et al., in press).

This section explores selective approaches to the role of anxiety as a mediator of intergroup interaction. According to these approaches, anxiety about interacting with a person from another group may influence some of the negative characteristics of intergroup relations.

Interpersonal, Interracial Interaction

Let's suppose that you have volunteered to participate in a psychology department experiment. When you arrive at the experimental site, you are ushered into a waiting room with one other subject who is of the same sex as you, but of a different race. The study requires that you fill out a questionnaire; however, the experimenter informs you that he has just run out and must go make some additional copies. Explaining that he will be back in a minute or two, he leaves the two of you alone. How do you feel? What will you say? Will you strike up a conversation and become friends? Will you nervously look at your watch, the ceiling, your shoes, wondering what you should say? Should you say anything? What you should talk about? What is the other person thinking?

William Ickes (1984) designed an experiment in which the above situation was created. The subjects were same-sex males or females and either black or white. The experimenter left them alone for five minutes. During that time, a videotape of their interaction was made. What do you suppose happened? Well, white subjects talked to, smiled at, and looked at their black partners more often and longer than black subjects did to whites. You might expect, then, that the white subjects were more comfortable in the interaction and they generally found such interactions to be more positive. However, if you thought that, you'd be wrong. In fact, white subjects reported the interactions were more uncomfortable, awkward, forced, and strained than their black counterparts did.

So, if they were so uncomfortable, why did they apparently work so hard? Conversely, why did blacks resist involvement with their white partners, *but* report less anxiety and a higher comfort level? Ickes (1984) suggests that maybe blacks are more accustomed to interacting with whites (a statistically likely scenario when, for example, blacks are a large minority on white campuses) and thus have managed to develop coping strategies to create maximum comfort in these interracial encounters. Most whites, not having mastered the art of interracial comfort, feel unsure of themselves and take on the burden of "making the interaction work." Perhaps this perceived burden results from the desire to show that they are not personally prejudiced or racist!

Ickes (1984) further showed that the pattern of interaction varied, depending on whether the white partner described himself or herself as an "initiator" of racial interaction (i.e., he or she agreed that "because of my feelings about the relationship between blacks and whites, I actively initiate social contacts with individuals who are not of my race.") or an "avoider" of racial interaction (i.e., he or she agreed that "because of my feelings about the relationship between blacks and whites, I tend to avoid individuals who are not of my race"). When Ickes compared dyads that involved white initiators, to dyads with white avoiders, the average of both members showed that partners tried not to offend each other, felt less nervous, or self-conscious, and were less influenced by the other. Overall, then, the partners in the initiator dyads seem to have had more positive interactions. In these same dyads, the white member directed the interaction more, felt a greater need to communicate with, and a need to compensate for the lack of responsiveness of the black partner.

By contrast, the dyads where the white partner was an avoider reported generally less effort to avoid offending the partner, greater nervousness, and greater reaction to the other. Further, in such dyads, the black member was as directive as the white member, felt a *greater* need to communicate than the white member did, and compensated more for the lack of responsiveness of the white partner. It seems, then, that the black member took a more active role when faced with a white partner who was disinclined to interact with him or her, but the white partner undertook this role when he or she was a self-reported initiator of racial interaction.

Racial interactions in such situations may involve significant feelings of anxiety, because each partner is reacting to the other and, depending on the situation, each may feel heightened self-consciousness that can actually increase the feeling of anxiety.[4] In the Ickes (1984) experiment, for example, the resulting anxiety of one member of the dyad is picked up by the other and affects his or her response. This suggests that the more racial groups go their separate ways, the less they know or understand about each other, the less they trust each other, and the greater the likelihood that this spiral of effects can poison interracial interactions.

Intergroup Anxiety Affects Social Attitudes
Stephan and Stephan (1985; C. Stephan, 1992; and W. Stephan, 1994) have proposed a theory of intergroup anxiety to explain the troubled course of intergroup relations. To begin, *anxiety* is defined as stress that is experienced as tension, apprehension, nervousness, and worry, and that is accompanied by heightened autonomic nervous system activity. When these feelings arise in situations that are perceived as personally threatening, anxiety is the result. Anxiety is to be distinguished from *fear*. The former either exists without objective basis or, when there *is* an objective basis, produces negative feelings that are disproportionate to the objective reality (C. Stephan, 1992).

The Ickes (1984) study suggested that the interracial interaction tended to spawn anxiety on the part of white partners, particularly those who were normally inclined to avoid interracial contact. Stephan and Stephan (1985) have suggested a more general model of anxiety as a mediator of intergroup relations. This model proposes that intergroup anxiety results from expected or actual contact with a person from another racial group. The potential sources of this anxiety are identified as follows:

---

[4] This sort of explanation of the effect of self-consciousness on anxiety and behavior was posed in a creative analysis by Baumeister (1984), who sought to explain the paradoxical negative effect of home field advantage in professional baseball and basketball. The data showed that the winning percentage for crucial sixth or seventh games in final play-offs were significantly lower for teams playing at home. Baumeister (1985) explained this in terms of self-awareness and showed additionally that the losing streaks were often the result of inferior play (more errors, lower shooting percentages and batting averages) than of the superior level of play of the visiting opponents. If this anxiety-based self-focus can cause deterioration of the performance of highly skilled and trained professional athletes, imagine what can happen to a "regular" person who is unskilled and anxious about interracial interaction!

- Negative psychological consequences for the self (e.g., incompetence, frustration, confusion, and embarrassment)
- Negative behavioral consequences for the self (e.g., verbal derogation, physical harm, and domination)
- Negative evaluations by other race-group members (e.g., disapproval, scorn, negative stereotyping, and judgments of inferiority)
- Negative evaluations by in-group members (e.g., rejection for having contact with out-group)

Any or all of these four antecedents of intergroup anxiety may play a role in the arousal of anxiety. Stephan and Stephan (1985) argue that intergroup anxiety plays a mediator role between these four conditions and a variety of responses:

Behavioral responses—Anxiety increases drive or motivated responding. Because anxiety is a negative psychological state, the most likely behavioral response is avoidance. If this is not possible, then the target will be treated as if he or she were a stranger (e.g., with rejection, aloofness, or suspicion).

Cognitive responses—Under feelings of intergroup anxiety, people are expected to use the simplest cognitive mechanisms possible in order to process information about the other person. This means that categorization, stereotyping, and schematic, simplified judgments will be more likely.

Affective responses—Emotional and evaluative responses are also expected to become amplified by intergroup anxiety. Intergroup anxiety elevates arousal, which may be transferred to other emotions or experiences. Therefore, if the interaction has some generally positive features, an individual may actually feel more positive because of the intergroup anxiety. Conversely, if the negative aspects dominate, they will be magnified out of proportion to the actual interaction.

The extent to which intergroup anxiety is aroused by the real or anticipated interaction with a member or members of another racial group will have the potential negative consequences of avoidance, stereotyping, or heightened arousal. Any such consequences should, in the long run, exacerbate rather than ameliorate intergroup relations. However, the likelihood of these adverse anxiety reactions is directly affected by (1) the extent of prior contact with members of the group (i.e., more contact leads to less anxiety), (2) cognitive representations of the group (i.e., when there is greater knowledge of the subjective culture, and there are lower levels of stereotypes, ethnocentrism, and expected group differences), and (3) situational factors, such as degree of interdependence (when there is more of it, there is less anxiety), and relative status (when groups are more equal there is less anxiety), etc.

The intergroup-anxiety model has been tested in several studies. It has made important contributions to our understanding of the patterns of intergroup relations. For example, Ybarra and Stephan (1994) assessed several factors that might be related to Americans' attitudes toward Mexican immigrants, including measures of symbolic threat, realistic conflict, intergroup anxiety, and stereotypes. These variables all predicted negative attitudes toward Mexican immigrants that accounted for 86 percent of the variance in these attitudes. In other studies (W. Stephan, 1994) intergroup anxiety alone accounted for 51 percent of the variance in negative attitudes toward the elderly and 77 percent of the variance in negative attitudes toward gay men.

Because anxiety involves feelings of tension—without the appropriate objective source for the tension—study of the phenomenon may provide the most useful accounts of interaction patterns in those fairly benign contact situations where we basically just don't know exactly what to do or what to expect. Feelings of anxiety may cause us to behave in ways that are indistinguishable from patterns of behavior associated with people who are simply responding to negative, hostile, or rejecting feelings about another person or group. It should be possible to distinguish between feelings of incompetence or insecurity and feelings of hostility. However, we should recognize that this distinction is not always easy to make.

As we will see later, when we encounter a person whom we really do not like or one whom we perhaps fear, then intergroup anxiety may not be the right way to explain the intergroup relations effect. It may well be more than intergroup anxiety that explains the Irish Catholic's relation to Irish Protestants, or the Bosnian Muslim's to the Bosnian Serb, or the Rwandan Hutu's to the Rwandan Tutsi. For now, we note that much inter*personal* interaction may be affected by inter*group* anxiety. Clearly the effect of anxiety is in the head of the perceiver more than it is in the behavior of the other. But, to the extent that behavior of one interacting partner is influenced by the behavior of the other, one's own thoughts, insecurities, and emotions can influence the behavior of the person who stimulates these feelings. His or her behavior, in turn, may reinforce one's own discomfort, confirm one's worst fears. The two may drift further apart interpersonally as a result—*not* because of anything either of them wanted or intended, but because of subtle influence of intergroup perception and intergroup anxiety on this interpersonal interaction (Devine, Evett, and Vasquez-Suson, in press).

SUMMARY

The issues in this chapter were presented in terms of social competition and social categorization. Hard conflict is violent, passionate, intense, and high-stakes competition. The representation of the out-group in these situations is selectively designed to maximize the distinctiveness on those dimensions most central to the contention. Soft-conflict situations, on the other hand, have most often been demonstrated in laboratory settings, where the basis of group differences typically consists of small, almost trivial distinctions in preferences, attitudes, or beliefs.

Too often we frame our analyses in either/or frameworks. Reliance on such frameworks suggests that either one or another approach is *the* correct way to look at things. Intergroup conflict, however, depends in part on the personalities of individual group members (e.g., high-SDO people may be more inclined to competitive relationships), whether social processes are based on prototypical or exemplar images of out-groups, whether we see others in simple descriptive terms (as entities) or doing terms (activities), the extent to which we are familiar with other groups, the extent to which other groups, arouse anxiety in us, and the extent of our need for belonging with others or differentiation from others. All influence the course of intergroup relations and intergroup conflict.

The individual processes that facilitate categorization determine which attributes are salient, dictate the ease of interaction, and sustain conflicts that are already in place. The group categorization of Eagles and Rattlers was created by Sherif and his colleagues (1961), but the perceptual and judgmental consequences of group categorization had a life of their own. These biasing processes had the same characteristics as those of the more benign, or soft, categorical situations wherein competition was not a central feature of the relationship. It makes sense, then, to suggest that categorization processes sustain, support, and perhaps compound the intensity of realistic group conflict. Our problem in reducing such conflict is thereby made much more difficult, because these fairly automatic cognitive and social tendencies lie in wait for real group differences in areas of real conflict over resources. Sidanius and colleagues (1993) believe such conflict is inevitable and has occurred around the world for as long as we have recorded history. It is hard to argue with this observation. However, concluding that, therefore, we can have no impact on the course of intergroup relations would be an error of significant proportions.

In the next chapter, the realistic group conflicts discussed are not manufactured by experimenters but evolve from real human social interactions. By studying such conflicts, we may be able to determine the degree to which the accounts of intergroup relations can be applied to real-world conflicts.

9

Psychological Mechanisms of Prejudice—Intergroup Relations II: Case Examples

❖

INTRODUCTION

War is a fact of human society. When I was young and living in the projects in a small town in northern Ohio, we used to get into rock-throwing fights with others who did not live in the projects. We were black, and they were black. Richard Wright, the author of *Native Son*, among other important novels, told in his autobiography of rock-throwing fights he got into with young white boys in the early 1930s in St. Louis (Gates, 1991). He complained of the whites having trees and landscaping to hide behind, whereas he and his friends had no cover. Warfare among ethnic tribes in Africa, among American Indian nations, among countries of Europe, and indeed, the great wars of this century all suggest that conflict among groups is fundamental.

It is also clear that these conflicts are not limited to racial differences, such as the black-white conflict that is the primary subject of this book. Blacks fight blacks, whites fight whites. Nor does having red, yellow, or brown skin color free people of the tendency to settle disputes by violence and aggression.

We sometimes become so preoccupied with the particular aspects of black-white conflict in the United States that we assume the conflict is attributable to the particular institution of slavery, the historic relations between Europe and Africa, and the particular history that is American. There are features of this history that are indeed unique and do not appear in precisely this form in other epochs and in other countries of the world. But to what extent is the conflict that we discuss under the topics of prejudice and racism a more general phenomenon of human society? To what extent is something such as the social dominance orientation, proposed by Sidanius and his colleagues (see Chapter 8, p. 228) as an individual difference attribute, represented as a universal attribute in human societies around the world and for all time? Are the principles of intergroup conflict, stereotypes and stereotyping, cognitive processes, and affectivity that we have described in preceding chapters applicable to all human societies?

We cannot answer these questions definitively here. But in the pages that follow we will selectively review major conflicts that have captured the world's attention in the early 1990s. Although the focus in the examples is on the conflicts as they stand in the late twentieth century, in each case we will see that the conflicts are borne of seeds sown centuries earlier. Just as is true of the problems between blacks and whites in the United States, the sources of the conflicts in Yugoslavia, Ireland, Rwanda, or elsewhere cannot be isolated from the contemporary dynamics of intergroup relations. The first edition of *Prejudice and Racism* made this point obliquely by its organization around historical themes. This second edition is similarly organized, as the cumulative, historic experience of citizens of the United States continues to affect the course that race relations take. Moreover, when we see this same sort of historical process unfolding in other societies—with rather obvious consequences—perhaps we will better see why an evolutionary viewpoint is needed if we are to understand—and, possibly, find solutions to—current conflicts.

In this chapter we will look in some detail at major ethnic conflicts in other parts of the world—conflicts where skin color and race *per se* are not fundamental to the hostilities. We will present these conflicts in their historical and contemporary context in order to gain a basic understanding of them, and then show ways in which the principles of the social psychology of prejudice may be applied.

The first section introduces a model of interethnic conflict that will serve as the basis for comparing each of the case examples. This model was extracted by Boucher, Landis, and Clark (1987) from analyses of several cases of ethnic conflict around the world. The second section discusses the three case examples of intergroup conflict: (1) in Rwanda between Hutus and Tutsi, (2) in Bosnia between Muslims, Serbs, and Croats, and (3) in Northern Ireland between Catholics and Protestants. Each case is analyzed from the perspective of the interethnic conflict model. The third section discusses the implications of these conflicts and our analysis of them from the perspective of social psychology. It further compares these conflicts to the basic character of black-white conflict in the United States.

*T*HEMES OF INTERETHNIC CONFLICT

Boucher, Landis, and Clark (1987) have developed a model for analyzing interethnic conflict in societies around the world. The Boucher, Landis, and Clark (1987) text describes and analyzes conflicts as varied as that between blacks and whites in Mississippi; between the Sinhala and Tamil in Sri Lanka; between the indigenous Maori and the immigrant European Pakehas of New Zealand; the conflict among the Chinese of Singapore, the Malays of Malaysia, and the Thais of Thailand on the Malaysian peninsula; between Puerto Ricans from Puerto Rico and people from the U.S. mainland; and between American Indians and whites. The discussion of these interethnic conflicts is organized around several models and themes of intergroup conflict. These themes, taken as a whole, suggest some commonalities. Analysis of these commonalities might help us formulate general principles of intergroup conflict.

Perceived Group Differences

People are different, and the differences matter. Any conflict between groups is aided by the perception that members of one's own group are different in important ways from members of the other group. We saw clearly in Chapters 7 and 8 that the persistence of group conflict is a function, in part, of maintaining the perception that the others are different in ways that somehow *justify* the conflict. The perceived differences may be erroneous (e.g., as in the information of stereotypes and their application to individuals) or insufficient to justify the conclusions we draw about the motivation or intention of others. The perceived differences may be physical (e.g., skin color or height), cultural (e.g., as reflected in dress, customs or beliefs), or psychological (e.g., that a given group is prone to laziness, dishonesty, intelligence, or high aspirations). Usually, the dimensions on which difference is perceived are central to the self-definition of the perceiving group, and its standing on those dimensions is considered better than the standing of the other group on the same measures.

Sovereignty of Land, Ethnicity, Culture, and Psyche

Group identity is central to most conflicts in that one's identity—expressed in terms of heritage, geographical boundaries, values or way of life—is usually challenged in conflict situations. In 1992, Pat Buchanan, an ultraconservative syndicated columnist and former speechwriter for President Ronald Reagan, was a candidate for the Presidency of the United States. In his view of U.S. society, diversity of people, beliefs, values, and lifestyles constituted a threat to the dominant white, Anglo-European society. He declared that defense of these white Anglo traditions amounted to a "cultural war." He sought to divide people into groups, *us* and *them*. According to Buchanan, *our* (white America) values, beliefs, and way of life are good and morally correct; *theirs* are bad and morally incorrect. More frequently, as in three case examples that follow show, land, sovereignty over land, and the power to control and define it are at the core of intergroup conflicts. For example, disputes over burial grounds and how they should be treated have arisen with American Indians and, more recently, with African Americans in New York City.

Third-Party Dominance and Interference

Much of the intergroup conflict around the world is exacerbated by the intrusion of outside groups. These intrusions most frequently occur as the imposition of colonial or hegemonic rule over native peoples. Very often this interference by outsiders creates advantages for one group over another within the society. The legacy of colonial expansion of European countries into Africa and Asia in the nineteenth century is a prime example. This intervention usually exaggerated existing tensions associated with group differences by aiding and abetting the ascendance of one group over another. The result was a vested interest in the new status quo by the favored group, and growing resentment and animosity by the disfavored group. The original situation has been rendered even more volatile, and when the outsiders departed, tensions erupted with ever greater energy and hostility.

Disparate Allocation of and Access to Power and Resources

The differential allocation of and access to power and resources may be a result of outside intervention, or it may be the legacy of the favorable status of one group compared to another. Whatever its source, unequal distribution of valued societal assets is a basis for conflict. The power and ability to control resources is directly linked to the actual or perceived well-being of groups and their members. It follows, then, that the more scarce resources are, the greater the potential that conflict will arise when one group has more power to control the resources and/or greater access to them. For example, in the 1960s the United States was rather prosperous, and economic growth occurred at a rapid rate. As the economy slowed down in the 1970s and stagnated toward the end of the seventies through the early eighties, people began taking a second look at the practical consequences of the egalitarian spirit that seemingly marked the civil rights gains of the 1960s and the implementation of remedies. Diminution of resources, coupled with a growing number of competing interests in how resources can or should be allocated, heightens both the sense of conflict and self-interested behavior.

Language and Language Policy

Language differences are intimately linked to ethnic and cultural differences. In the United States, this is true whether one speaks a fundamentally different language—such as Korean, Spanish, Japanese, or variation of the common language, such as black *nonstandard* English. In the United States, black parents have sued for the right of their children to be taught in black nonstandard English in the schools of Ann Arbor, Michigan (Smitherman, 1991). Several states have adopted "English Only" legislation that mandates that all official state business (e.g., driving license examinations, tax forms, voting ballots) be conducted in English only. Under such laws, those who do not speak English are required either to learn English or to do without the rights of citizenship. Even in countries where basically only one language is spoken (e.g., the former Yugoslavia) efforts are made to use language as a basis for joining together, as when Yugoslavia was formed in 1918, or for signaling important ethnic distinctions, as was the case during the conflicts in Bosnia. As another example, controversy over bilingual education in the United States is basically contested over issues of culture and identity (Hakuta, 1994; Padilla, Lindholm, Chen, and Duran, 1991; Huddy and Sears, 1995). Language differences not only contribute to the perception of group differences, they create communication barriers that exaggerate those differences through noncommunication, often characterized by lack of contact.

Processes of Conflict Resolution

Once conflict is created, how it is resolved is critical. (Modes of resolution of intergroup conflict will be discussed in greater detail in Chapter 11.) At this point in our analysis, we will merely note that Sherif (1966) found it very difficult to reduce the conflict between his Eagles and Rattlers through joint activities. (Refer to Chapter 8 for a discussion of these experiments.) The only way he found to do so was to create situations in which superordinate goals desired by both parties were unreachable by either without the help of the other group. History is replete with examples of joint activities undertaken to accomplish superordinate goals—treaties, declarations of cease-fires, peace accords, and so on. However, in some societies, the only acceptable means of "negotiating" disputes is war! Therefore, in any given case, the potential for resolving intergroup conflict will depend on what modes of conflict resolution are available, have currency, and can be practically implemented for that society. It is also clear that the potential for conflict resolution goes through periods of "varying possibility." Ideal, or "ripe," conditions (cf. Zartman and Aurik, 1991) occur when disputants have more to gain by a settlement than they do by continued hostilities. Each of the conflicts we will describe have reached a degree of "peace" as the result of ripe conditions for conflict resolutions. Whether the peace will hold may be built into the foundations of the given conflict—the factors that have sustained each for so long.

Religion

Finally, religion has consistently been an ingredient in intergroup conflict over the centuries. Religious differences can be a primary source of conflict (e.g., as with the Irish Protestants and the Irish Catholics) or they can exacerbate a conflict that arises from other conditions (e.g., as in Sri Lanka, between the Hindu Tamils and the Buddhist Sinhalese). Religion, like language, may serve as a basis for defining a group and making the differences between groups clearer and sharper. In terms of intergroup conflict, probably the more important aspect of religious differences—quite apart from real differences in values—is the cumulative effect of the perception of group differences. This is quite evident in the case of the conflict in Yugoslavia.

CASE EXAMPLES OF ETHNIC CONFLICT

There are certainly many examples of intergroup conflict that we could review. The three case examples—Tutsi versus Hutu in Rwanda; Catholic versus Protestant in Ireland; and Serbs, Muslims, and Croats in the former Yugoslavia—have been chosen because they are characterized by eruptions of great violence in the early 1990s and thereby drew worldwide attention to the sources of conflict. Further, they represent examples of conflicts that vary in the ways in which the various themes of interethnic conflict cited above are involved, yet nonetheless illustrate common threads. All of the conflicts share factors such as the influence of outside parties, religious and ethnic differences, acts of violence, differential access to resources, and repeated attempts to achieve a resolution of the conflict.

Life hangs in the balance. A lost Rwandan child searches among dead bodies for his parents in a camp outside Goma, Zaire, July 25, 1994. (AP/Wide World Photos)

In Chapter 8, we discussed two contrasting theories of intergroup conflict: Mere categorization, in which the simple act of categorizing people into groups unleashes a whole set of biased perceptions and self-interested behaviors, and realistic-group conflict, which is triggered by competition for mutually desired, but not mutually attainable goals. Because of the level of violence and the acts of genocide represented in these examples, these cases provide a useful, practical content within which to assess the power of the two models of intergroup conflict to account for these conflicts and the direction they may take. Can either model alone explain the facts of these conflict situations? Can they do so together? Or, do we need some new concepts to help us understand the level of intergroup conflict that exists in the world? Let's keep these questions in mind as we read the following examples of intergroup conflicts.

Rwanda—Hutu (Majority) versus Tutsi (Minority)

On April 6, 1994, Presidents Juvenal Habyarimana of Rwanda and Cyprien Ntaryamira of Burundi were killed when their plane was shelled by rocket fire as it attempted to land at the airport in Kigali, Rwanda.[1] The two were returning from

[1] Rwanda is known in the West for murder. It is also known for its gorillas and the work of Dian Fossey, the American naturalist who was murdered there in 1985. The movie *Gorillas in the Mist* gave us one version of Rwanda that, though filled with the intrigue of Ms. Fossey's murder and hinting at the potential for violence, did not prepare the world for the carnage seen in video footage of the Hutu-Tutsi civil wars.

Dar es Salaam, Tanzania, where they had met with other African leaders in an attempt to end the ethnic warfare that had been devastating their nations. Fighting between the Hutu and Tutsi tribes in both countries had left thousands dead and a much larger number of each group homeless refugees.

Both presidents were members of the Hutu tribe, which had maintained political power in Rwanda since that country was granted independence from Belgium in 1962. President Habyarimana had ascended to power in 1973 in a bloodless coup. President Ntaryamira had only become president in October 1993, when the previous president, Melchior Ndadaye, was assassinated during a military coup. Ndadaye, elected in 1993, was the nation's first Hutu leader, breaking the long Tutsi domination in Burundi. The Hutus constitute the vast majority of the inhabitants of both Rwanda and Burundi, accounting for about 85 percent of the combined total population.

The two nations' immediate response to the death of the two presidents was violence on a scale that exceeded even that of the bloody conflicts that the African leaders had been trying to end. The Hutus had no doubt that the rocket fire came from the Tutsi rebels. They proceeded to attack not only the rebel Tutsi guerrillas, but all Tutsi people. Hundreds of thousands of Tutsis were massacred and many of their bloodied corpses were thrown into the Akanyaru River. The Tutsi rebels retaliated, seeking out Hutu villages to destroy and Hutu people to kill.

So strong was the hatred, and so systematic the retaliation, that the mayor of one principality, for example, ordered Hutu followers to slay all Tutsis in the village. Reports the *New York Times* (Smerdon, 1994), one Rwandan Hutu farmer killed three Tutsi friends: "I killed three, a man and two women, with a big club . . . they were my neighbors. I knew them well . . . we had to do it or be killed ourselves as traitors or sympathizers" (Smerdon, 1994, p. 8). Another Hutu reported, in the following words, that he had killed an old man: "He was 74 . . . His name was Isaac Kimonyo. I saw him every day but I had to kill him on April 17. I hit him many times with a stick until he fell down dead" (Smerdon, 1994, p. 8).

Now, we must ask, does this pattern of behavior resemble that reported in the minimal-group paradigm? Can this in-group bias be distinguished from out-group hostility? Does the process of favoring those like-minded comrades who prefer Klee in any way resemble the intergroup dynamics that led to the slaughter of hundreds of thousands of people based largely, if not exclusively, on their ethnic group membership? Can we imagine—in an admittedly extreme scenario—the Rattlers killing the Eagles, or vice versa? It certainly does seem that the robbers' cave model bears greater resemblance to the Hutu-Tutsi conflict than does the Klee-Kandinsky model.

So why, we may ask, is this ethnic conflict so intense? What principles are operating here? First, we have to note some historically important facts in the case. The Tutsis are a tall, Nilotic people (also known as the *Watusi*) who migrated from Ethiopia in the fifteenth century and imposed feudal rule over the Hutus. The Hutus are a Bantu people. They are short and stocky and lived in the hills of the forest before the Tutsis arrived in the land (what is now Rwanda and Burundi). From 1899 until the end of World War I, the Germans colonized the Tutsi and Hutus in these lands (known then as *Ruanda* and *Urundi*). Belgium was given trusteeship over the territories from 1917 until their independence in 1962. The Belgians allied themselves with the Tutsi during the trusteeship period as a strategy for controlling the Hutu majority. This alliance resulted in political, educational, economic, and military advantage for the Tutsi. As Langston Hughes asked in his poem *Harlem*, "What happens to a dream deferred? Does it dry up in the sun, does it rot, or does it explode?" (Hughes, 1958, p. 123). Perhaps the question was answered by the events in Rwanda. When independence came to Rwanda and Burundi in 1962, the Hutus, by dint of their greater numbers, assumed power in Rwanda. However, in Burundi, the Tutsis managed to hold on to power. Burundi became a Tutsi stronghold, and Rwandan Tutsi rebels made Burundi a staging ground for their forays into Rwanda, where they maintained guerrilla action against the Hutu government.

The Tutsi and Hutu are physically different. Therefore, it is relatively easy for each to categorize the other as an out-group. This may, in fact, make it easier for each group member to justify hostility toward out-group members. But does awareness of differences in group physical appearance and the resulting group categorizations explain the degree of violence that consents to bludgeoning old friends to death because of their ethnic group membership? Let's see now how well the themes of interethnic conflict apply to the Tutsi-Hutu situation.

Perceived Group Differences. Clearly, in this conflict there are group differences that are physical, historical, and cultural. Tutsi tend to be lighter-skinned, look more European, and had been accorded a status of racial superiority by the Belgian colonists.

Sovereignty of land, ethnicity, culture, and psyche. Sovereignty of land and ethnicity is a constant challenge in Rwanda, because the ethnic group in power (the Tutsis) has systematically oppressed the group not in power (the Hutu) and reserved advantages for its own members. In a land of 5.8 million people, with poor soil and growing poverty, control of the land is virtually tantamount to control of life and death.

Third-party dominance and interference. The Germans—and, later, the Belgians—exacerbated the preexisting ethnic conflict by imposing an even more rigid socioeconomic structure that expanded the ethnic cleavage. The third parties, seeing the Tutsis as racially and culturally superior, created advantages for the latter. In short, they implemented a system that amounted to a *self-fulfilling prophesy*. That is, the Belgian interference capitalized on the Tutsi belief in their superiority and established it as a sociopolitical fact. Within the colonizing relationship, then, the Tutsis confirmed their cultural beliefs, adding strength to them that would be increasingly hard to overcome. Needless to say, once colonial rule ended, Hutus had plenty of resentment of the spuriously justified dominance of the Tutsi. Once the Hutus gained control, they made it inhospitable for Tutsi in Rwanda. Similarly, when the Tutsi were able to maintain control in Burundi, they did everything to consolidate their power. They systematically massacred Hutus that had managed to achieve a level of education or accomplishment that made them something of a threat to Tutsi domination. Thus, through systematic genocide, the Tutsi in Burundi enforced their own brand of a self-fulfilling prophesy by demonstrating the superiority they felt.

Disparate allocation of and access to power and resources. The disparate allocation of resources follows directly from the conditions described above. With superior resources of every kind, over hundreds of years, the Tutsi were able to dominate the Hutu.

Language and language policy. It does seem that the Bantu language has dominated the entire region, notwithstanding the sociopolitical situation. However, this has not served as a basis for advantage to either group.

Processes of conflict resolution. Although efforts at conflict resolution were tried in the form of treaties, cease-fires, and democratic elections, it seems clear that the legacy of violence ("tribes and cultures whose only common heritage, unless held in check by a brutal dictatorship, is warfare against one another," [Wharton, 1994, *NYT*]) has been the prevailing *modus operandi* for conflict resolution. Is this reliance on violent struggle a peculiar characteristic of the Hutu-Tutsi case?

Religion. Religion is not a key element to the ethnic conflict in Rwanda (and Burundi).

Ireland—Catholics (Majority) versus Protestant (Minority)

Recognizing the potential of the current situation and in order to enhance the democratic peace process and underline our definitive commitment to its success, the leadership of *Oglaigh na-h-Eirann*[2] have decided that as of midnight Wednesday, Aug. 31 [1994] there will be a complete cessation of military operations. All our units have been instructed accordingly. (Schmidt, 1994, p. A12)

After having received confirmation and guarantees in relation to Northern Ireland's constitutional position within the United Kingdom . . . . The Combined Loyalist Military Command will universally cease all operational hostilities from midnight on Thursday 13 October 1994. (Darnton, 1994, p. A1)

With these statements, 25 years of fighting between sections of the Irish Nationalist (primarily Catholic) community—represented by the IRA—and sections of the Northern Irish Unionist (primarily Protestant) community—represented by the Loyalist paramilitaries—was declared over.

What, you might ask, is the source of conflict in Ireland—after all aren't they all white, don't they all live within the democracy of Northern Ireland, haven't they never suffered colonization, enslavement, racism and other forms of domination that characterize the colonial oppression in Rwanda? Or have they? The fact is that oppression and conflict in Ireland are about as old as the conflict between Tutsi and Hutu in Rwanda and Burundi, dating to the mid-fifteenth century. Black-on-black and white-on-white conflict does occur between groups that are in many respects quite similar, in others quite different, but relative to the racial conflict in the United States, the differences seem small, the similarities much larger. However, what appear as small differences to outsiders turn out—like racial conflicts in the United States—to be tied to a long history of cultural, political, and economic conflict. Perhaps by looking at these contrasts, we will gain a broader insight into the generality of ethnic conflict.

Today's conflict in Northern Ireland is widely perceived as a sectarian struggle between the Catholic and Protestant communities within that state. Sporadic news reports available in the States seem to confirm this perception.

June 18, 1994—The Irish Protestant Ulster Volunteer Force shot to death six Catholics, including an 87-year-old man, as they watched Ireland defeat Italy in a World Cup soccer game in a pub just south of Belfast.

[2] *Oglaigh na h-Eirann* is the Gaelic name for the Irish Republican Army (IRA).

October 23, 1993—Nine Irish Protestants were killed by an IRA bomb attack in a fish shop in the heart of Protestant West Belfast.

In fact, by mid-June, 1994, after 25 years of the so-called "Irish Problem," 3,168 had been killed in this apparently sectarian struggle. That things are not quite so simple is suggested by yet another body count—the number of British killed in those 25 years: as many as 445 British soldiers, politicians, and civilians were killed both in Northern Ireland and on the mainland (*The British Independent*, September 1, 1994). Virtually all of them were killed by Irish Nationalist (primarily Catholic) paramilitaries.

In a country that is overwhelmingly Catholic, the Protestants are thought of as a minority. There is a tendency to cast the conflict in terms similar to those in Rwanda, where a minority (Tutsi) dominated a majority (Hutus) with the aid of a third party (Belgium). The story in Ireland has obvious similarities but diverges at important points and in important ways from the circumstances in Rwanda.

A tiny island (about twice the size of Massachusetts) sitting just miles off England's western coast, Ireland inevitably became a pawn in England's political and economic struggles over the centuries with the powers of Western Europe. From 1169 when Henry II established a settlement around the tiny port of what is now Dublin, thus becoming "Lord of Ireland," the English have had a foothold in Ireland. When the Tudors triumphed over the Yorks in the War of the Roses in 1485, the Irish–British conflict took on a religious tone. Henry VIII moved the English throne away from Catholicism in 1533 when he divorced Catharine of Aragon, but the Irish refused to convert to the Church of England. A ray of hope for Irish Catholics shone in 1685 when James II, an open Catholic, ascended to the English throne. His tolerance of Catholics was not tolerated by his peers and he was driven from England in 1688. When Protestants in Ulster heard that a Catholic King had been deposed in favor of a Protestant, they feared a massacre by Catholics was eminent. James II fled to Ireland where he laid seige to the Protestant stronghold of Londonderry. However, William of Orange (who became William III) sent a fleet of troops to liberate Londonderry and did so on July 12, 1690, at the Battle of the Boyne. Orange Lodges still mark the scene of celebrations of Protestant Ulstermen who gather on the July 12 anniversary of the Battle of the Boyne to repeat the oath of "no surrender" to the Catholics of Ireland.

With the coming of the Reformation and Counterreformation in the sixteenth and seventeenth centuries, this foothold became a stranglehold. Primarily to prevent Ireland from becoming a launching pad for attacks first from Spain and later from France, England inaugurated a policy of plantation (cf. Downing, 1981). A *plantation* was essentially a settlement of British citizens, British by culture and Protestant by religion, who were to be granted all favorable advantages. The most successful plantation was established in Ulster in Northern Ireland. The Irish chiefs had mounted an uprising against the British, and, to suppress this insurgency, the Ulster plantation was mounted with intense vigor since this region of Ireland was ". . . most Gaelic in character, most resistant to English rule, and most alien to the English . . . [in short] the stronghold of the Gaelic law, customs, and language" (Smith and Chambers, 1991, p. 2).

These British settlers were granted all of the best land and all of the most favorable circumstances *by law*. Their favored position was secured in 1690 when they supported William of Orange in his successful usurpation of the throne of England from James II. In return for their loyalty, the Protestants enjoyed the benefits of a set of "penal laws," which drove a deep and irreconcilable wedge between the native Irish Catholics and the pro-British settlers. Among other things, the Catholics had already been barred from serving in Parliament, but these laws now excluded

Catholics from the Armed Forces, the judiciary, and the legal profession. Catholic clergy were banished, and Catholic citizens were forbidden from holding long-term leases on land and, more, from purchasing it at all. They were forbidden to conduct schools, and the option of sending their children abroad for education was officially eliminated by law. In short, Irish Catholics were to England what African-descended Americans were to the United States—niggers!

Because of the success in Ulster, the Protestants came to be concentrated in Northern Ireland, and this small but powerful enclave became the focal point for the tensions between Ireland and England, Catholics and Protestants, Nationalists and Unionists.[3] With such conflicts between the natives and the settlers continuing across several centuries, it is not surprising that the Anglo-Irish Treaty that ended the Irish War of Independence (1919–1921), establishing the Free Irish State with formal authority over all of Ireland, allowed Northern Ireland to opt out of the Irish Free State. The pro-British section of Ulster was allowed to remain under British rule—in a state explicitly partitioned out of Ireland so as to preserve a substantial Protestant/Unionist majority of 66 percent. From the outset, this state (Northern Ireland) was overtly sectarian, with its first prime minister, Lord Craigavon, openly boasting of a "Protestant Parliament for a Protestant people." The state was characterized by decades of institutionalized discrimination against Catholics/Nationalists in everything from housing to jobs, from education to health services; a sectarian police force; and gerrymandered electoral constituencies (cf. Farrell, 1976).

Within Northern Ireland, the centuries-old racism, which the conquering English Protestants of the sixteenth and seventeenth centuries held toward the native Irish, surfaced in overt forms. The Protestants perceived themselves to be superior to the Irish, whom they stereotyped as uncivilized, primitive, and dumb. The powerful cartoons of the politically satiric magazine *Punch* perpetuated the Irish stereotype as long ago as the 1840s by drawing them to be ape-like, aggressive, destructive, and stupid (Downing, 1981). These negative stereotypes of the Irish continue today as they are portrayed as alcoholic, lazy, dirty, and undisciplined. One Protestant commentator observed that ". . . if a Roman Catholic is jobless and lives in the most ghastly hovel he will rear eighteen children and live on National Assistance" (Downing, 1981, p. 50). By contrast, a Protestant Loyalist song extols their virtue thus: "Proud and defiant—with folk self-reliant—A Loyalist giant—That's Ulster." In fact, while the distinctions between the Protestants and Catholics turn on religious differences ("We want no Popish tyrant priest to guide us on our way—We know not how to count the beads,—Such trash we throw away"), the differences are conceived in "racial" terms (de Paor, 1977).[4]

Thus it is that in Northern Ireland today, while there are no visible differences in skin color or language (use of Gaelic is not a big issue these days), discrimination is readily achieved through a multitude of demographic markers that easily differentiate the descendants of the natives and settlers to this day: surnames such as O'Neill versus Smyth, home address, school attended, sports club affiliation, and of course the pervasive religious distinction—Protestant and Catholic.

The struggle has been intense in part because of the selective intervention of the British (not unlike the Belgians in Rwanda), who controlled the political context in Ireland. First, in 1800, they abolished the parliament in Dublin, leaving the entire is-

---

[3] Unionists favored the joining of Ireland and England under common rule. Since they enjoyed advantages already as a result of the support of England, it was obviously in their best interest to do so.
[4] We should note that although the Catholic/Nationalist community of Belfast may well ". . . believe that all Protestants are bound to burn in purgatory," they do not seem to hold the same degree of bigotry as the Protestants do (cf. Bell, 1976). When they do resort to prejudiced bigotry, it is usually directed at the English.

land under the political control of England. Efforts at *Home Rule* (language applied to the attempt to create a unified Ireland) were mounted immediately. A Home Rule provision was passed by the British Parliament in 1911 and was made more explicit by the Anglo-Irish Treaty of 1921. But in both cases, Ulster was exempted from these rules. The struggle for a unified Ireland, needless to say, continues to this day. The Free Ireland movement, Sinn Fein, and the IRA escalated the struggle, and in response, England increased its support of Protestant Northern Ireland. With substantial aid from England, the Protestants of Northern Ireland upped the ante so that by the 1950s and 1960s, full-scale guerrilla warfare was common in the streets of Belfast, the capital of Northern Ireland, as well as the occasional terrorist attack in London.

Of great interest in this struggle is the transatlantic influence of the civil rights movement in the United States on the efforts of the Irish Catholics to gain equality. In 1967, the Northern Ireland Civil Rights Association (NICRA) was formed to promote the civil rights of Irish Catholics. The NICRA was founded on the principles of nonviolence and invited specific comparison with Martin Luther King. The perils of organized civil rights activities were soon apparent as Dr. Martin Luther King was assassinated only a year later. Ian Paisley took up a militant defense of the Protestant Irish from these civil rights incursions in an active way that escalated violence in the streets.

In 1976, the infringement of the civil rights of Irish Catholics came to an "official" end in Northern Ireland with the passage of the Fair Employment Act of 1976, which barred discrimination against Irish Catholics in the workplace and established the Fair Employment Agency to oversee implementation of the Act, to investigate complaints, and to mount a series of programs to ensure equal opportunity for Irish Catholics.

In Northern Ireland, as in the United States, differences in outcomes persist. Statistics amply show the second-class status of Catholics in Northern Ireland in income, political representation, and education (Smith and Chambers, 1991). Declarations of equality are challenged by continuing discrimination that is both intentional and perhaps unintentionally maintained by the legacy of historical discrimination and institutional and policy practices that maintain the biased status quo.

Perceived group differences

Although the Catholics and Protestants look alike, they are nevertheless perceived to be different. The Catholics originally were Gaelic and enjoyed a different cultural tradition. The Protestants were originally British and maintained that connection and identification over the years. Moreover, they enjoyed favored treatment under British rule, which created real differences that corresponded to the cultural differences that existed from the beginning. In addition, the Protestants perceived themselves to be superior and the Irish natives inferior. Stereotypes and perceptions of diminished values and beliefs buttressed these perceptions. The Protestants, in turn, were perceived to be pawns of the British, whose outside intervention was rejected by the Irish Catholics/Nationalists.

Sovereignty of land, ethnicity, culture, and psyche

Ireland is a Catholic nation and, except for Ulster in Northern Ireland, under the political control of the Irish Parliament in Dublin. However, at the core of the Protestant–Catholic dispute is the idea of political sovereignty. Ireland has not been willing to accept the presence of an autonomous political state in its midst. The geographical and political integrity of Ireland will not be compromised. Thus, Catholic Ireland seeks unification of its native land.

By contrast, the Protestants have enjoyed privileged status within Ireland and, with British support, political independence—at least from Ireland, if not from Britain. If Northern Ireland were to revert to the control of the Irish Parliament, similar to the case in Rwanda in 1962, the Protestants fear they would not only lose political autonomy and status, they would also be treated as badly as they have treated the Catholics over the years. In the end, it is land, sovereignty, and power that are inextricably tied to cultural identity.

Third party dominance and interference

Once again, a third party, in this case Great Britain, imposes self-interested control in such a way that one group ascends to a dominant position relative to another. In the case of Northern Ireland, it is the British third party that continues to play an active role in negotiating a settlement. Yet, self-interest makes it very difficult to imagine a way in which trust can be very high. The critical point is that, given real differences in the first place and an "artificial "status quo established and reinforced by a third party, instability in Northern Ireland results in part because a victimized minority is pitted against a privileged majority. As de Paor (1977) sees it, ". . . it is British attempts to govern in Ireland through a colonial regime [that] have given rise to most of the difficulties. . . ." (p. xix).

Disparate allocation of and access to power and resources

The penal laws established a clear disparity in power and allocation of resources that disadvantaged the Irish Catholics in relation to the Irish Protestants. Although enacted in the early 1700s, the legacy of this statutory disadvantage persists today. As in the United States with the passage of the civil rights legislation of the 1960s, passage of the Fair Employment Act of 1976 in Ireland has not eradicated discrimination against Irish Catholics in employment and has not eliminated the consequence of this disadvantage in income, employment, and economic opportunity.

Language and language policy

Although Irish is the official language of Ireland, very few of its people actually speak it. However, it has recently taken on a political significance among Northern Irish Nationalists as a way of asserting identity, pride, and solidarity, as we saw with the IRA proclamation of the cease fire. In the United States, the "English only" movement, policy on bilingual education, and legal skirmishes over "black English," all attest to the pivotal role language and language policy can play in interethnic struggles for power and control. Language can still play an important role in ethnic identification and political cohesion and thus energize and sustain intergroup conflict.

Processes of conflict resolution

The dispute between Irish Catholics and Protestants has gone on for over 400 years. The cease fire announced by the IRA in August 1994 was not the first. A 1972 cease fire had been proposed by the IRA, but it collapsed in 1975. It was the Catholics who elected to use a "civil rights" nonviolence approach after Martin Luther King's movement in the United States. This approach, far from successfully instituting nonviolent means of social change, spawned a backlash from the Protestant Loyalists that erupted in violent conflicts that led to direct rule of Northern Ireland by Britain. Thus, guerrilla war, mixed with political negotiation by two primary forces and a third party, meant that resolving the conflict would necessarily be circuitous, bloody, and slow in coming.

Religion

Although religion was not a significant factor in the conflict in Rwanda, it is at the core of the struggle in Ireland. Although religion defined the battle lines initially, it is not now a battle over religion. However, the confict is summarized and escalated by differences in religion between the Northern Ireland Protestants and Catholics. Thus, it seems fair to say that religion in Ireland, like ethnicity in Rwanda and race in America, provides a means of categorizing people into groups. Categorization makes it easier, then, to draw battle lines, to activate processes of group differences, and to rally behind group identification. We will see that religion plays a similar role in the conflict in the former Yugoslavia.

Bosnia—Muslims (Majority) versus Serbs (Minority)[4]

Yugoslavia (South Slavia) was formed in 1918 at the end of the World War I as a federation of republics (Bosnia; Croatia; Serbia; Macedonia; Montenegro, Dalmatia, Slovenia, Herzegovina, and Vojvodina). The federation was loose and, as with Ireland and Rwanda, popular unity was doomed by the existence of ethnic and religious differences. These republics contained Serbian, Croatian, and Slovenian ethnic groups. The mix was further complicated by the diversity of religious beliefs—Eastern Orthodoxy, Turkish Islam, and Roman Catholicism. We have seen how the affairs of one small country, aggravated by religious differences superimposed by third-country intervention and influences, can take several hundred years to sort out. We have also seen how a country with only two major ethnic groups and no major religious differences has struggled for hundreds of years and produced massacres and killings of hundreds of thousands. The conflict in Yugoslavia, in many respects, combines the dynamics of both the conflict in Ireland and that in Rwanda.

The Serbs in Serbia were mainly Orthodox, the Croats and Slovenes mainly Roman Catholic, and the majority of Bosnians, as well as some Croatians, were mainly Muslim. These Muslims had converted to Islam during the several hundred years of occupation and rule by the Ottoman Empire. The formation of Yugoslavia attempted to pull together several republics that had strong national identities—identities determined by not only geographical borders, but by religious boundaries.

Not only did the peoples of this Balkan country differ in religion, they were socially different. Serbian society has been described as peasant, patriarchal, and relatively homogeneous (Dragnich, 1983). This contrasted with the culture of the Croats, who were organized more along class lines, more urban-focused, and felt intellectual ties to Hungary. Slovenian society was also organized around class, but was more industrial than that of either Serbia or Croatia; it looked for inspiration to Germany. Both Croatia and Slovenia were dominated by the Austro-Hungarian empire and, under their domination, showed remarkable loyalty to the Hapsburg crown. Moreover—and this is surely a critical feature—throughout their educational life, the Croats and Slovenes were politically indoctrinated by the espousal of attitudes suggesting their superiority racially and culturally to the peasant Serbs.

Moreover, there was a minority of 15 percent in Yugoslavia who comprised Germans, Albanians, Hungarians, Rumanians, Slovaks, Gypsies (Romanian), and

---

[4] The majority-minority status needs clarification. Within Bosnia-Herzegovina, a federated state of the former Yugoslavia, Bosnian Muslims are the majority and Bosnian Serbs and the minority. In the totality of the former Yugoslavia, Serbs constitute the largest single group (about 44%). The focal point of the conflict is between Bosnian Muslims and Bosnian Serbs. The National Army is largely Serbian and has generally aided and abetted its ethnic allies in Bosnia.

others. Obviously the religious, ethnic, and political differences did not bode well for a unified republic of Balkan nations.[5]

One commonality that seemed to sew the seams of the federation was language—Serbo-Croatian. The language of the peoples, albeit similar in common discourse, showed the friction among the societies of Croatia, Slovenia, and Serbia. The Croats felt language was classical and that reciting Virgil was a sign of culture. The Serbs felt that the more important role of language was the recitation of popular local proverbs and as a means of strengthening of folk culture.

The Serbs had fought for their independence and, as a result of their struggle (primarily with the Turks), had established independence. This independent state was based on democratic principles and maintained through a parliamentary system of government. The Croats and Slovenes, by contrast, had lived under the domination of the Austro-Hungarian empire and, until now, had not formed an independent political state. The Serbs felt it logical that the political center of Yugoslavia should be in their capital, Belgrade. The Croats did not trust the Serbs and felt their capital, Zagreb, was the natural center of Yugoslavia. The Croats and Slovenes, having lived as exemplary subjects under Hapsburg rule for so long, respected authority and governmental functionaries. The Serbs, having fought off outside domination, were generally distrustful of authority.

Serbs lived not only in Serbia but in other areas, such as Croatia and Bosnia-Herzegovina. However, the commonality of Serbian thought and culture persisted even among Serbs living outside of these areas, despite their different political and geographical contexts. Because of their courageous and dedicated battle to remain independent, the Serbs had the most stake in the success of the federation, and have consistently done the most to maintain it. In fact, it was the Serbs, under Prime Minister Nikola Pasic, who declared Serbia's interest in World War I was the liberation and unification of all Serbs, Croats, and Slovenes. Thus, it was the Serbs who fought the Austro-Hungarian Empire and the Ottoman Empire and secured the independence of the Balkan states.

The new state of Yugoslavia (named the *Kingdom of Yugoslavia* in 1929) was seen by Serbs as an extension of Serbia. After all, hadn't the Serbs led the fight for independence? However, the other parties (Croatia, Slovenia, and Bosnia-Herzegovina) saw the arrangement as a voluntary federation of equal peoples who would, together, construct a new state with a new constitution (Denitch, 1994).

The Serbs held the Croats in low esteem, because the latter had not managed to throw off the yoke of domination by outside powers as the Serbs had. They held great enmity toward the Bosnians, who had converted to Islam under Turkish domination and had thus "sold out" their own religious and ethnic interests. For the Serbs, the Serbian defeat by the Turks at the Battle of Kosovo in 1389 was the symbol of Turkish treachery, and the pain would not go away. The continued presence of Bosnian Muslims continues to evoke that pain, and the Serbs have played upon these deep feelings in the current conflict. For example early in the fighting the Serbs unearthed the remains of King Lazar, a Serbian leader killed by the Turks at the Battle of Kosovo, as a way to arouse hostility toward the Bosnian Muslims.

Throughout its history, Yugoslavia has fought against very bad odds to remain together. This effort is attributed largely to the will of the Serbs, fostered first of all

[5] The last full census of Yugoslavia was conducted in 1981. It showed a population of some 23 million people, of whom 36.3 percent were Serbs, 19.8 percent Croats, 8.9 percent Muslims, 7.8 percent Slovenes, 7.7 percent Albanians, 6 percent Macedonians, and 10 percent divided among "Yugoslavs," Montenegrins, and Hungarians.

by Marshall Tito, who ruled with Communist support for nearly 30 years. But, recently, because of the desire of some of the republics for independence, (Macedonia, Croatia, Slovenia, and Bosnia-Herzegovina) the efforts of the central Yugoslav government became gridlocked, and the government was unable to rule within the confines of parliamentary law.

When the Bosnian people held an election in which they declared their independence from Yugoslavia, and Croatia supported that sentiment, the somewhat successful effects of the 75-year struggle to hold Yugoslavia's diverse peoples and republics together began unraveling beyond repair. When the Western powers "recognized" the sovereignty of Bosnia-Herzegovina, the Serbian effort to hold the federation together devolved into an effort to protect and support the Serbs who lived in the outlying provinces (mainly Croatia and Bosnia-Herzegovina). The Yugoslav National Army then was maintained by Serbs, and fought primarily in support of Serb minorities in Bosnia and Croatia against the Bosnian Muslims and Croatian Catholics.

Borislav Herak, 21 years old, remembers the day in late June 1992 when he and a companion shot down 10 members of a Bosnian Muslim family (Burns, 1992). Mr. Herak recounted his grisly tale first to Bosnian officials at the Viktor Buban military prison where he was being held on war crimes charges. He later retold his tale to Burns, during a seven-hour long interview. What he remembers most is the small girl, about 10 years old, who tried to hide behind her grandmother:

> We told them not to be afraid, we wouldn't do anything to them. . . . But it was taken for granted among us that they should be killed. So when somebody said 'shoot,' I swung around and pulled the trigger, three times, on automatic fire. I remember the little girl with the red dress hiding behind her granny (Burns, 1992, p. A1).

Mr. Herak described what we have come to know as "ethnic cleansing" (*ciscenje*):

> We were told that Ahatovici must be cleansed Serbian territory, that it was a strategic place . . . and that all the Muslims must be killed. . . . We were told that no one must escape, and that all houses must be burned, so that if anybody did survive, they would have nowhere left to return to. It was an order, and I simply did what I was told (Burns, 1992, p. A1).

Mr. Herak was charged by the Bosnian government with 29 murders and under Article 41 of the old Yugoslav criminal rule faced death by a firing squad. He reported not only killings he had done, but massacres carried out by others. He reported rapes followed by murders—of Emina, Sabina, Amela, and Fatima, among others—of women ranging in age from teens to 35 years old. The prison commander told him, "You can do with the women what you like. You can take them away from here—we don't have enough food for them anyway—don't bring them back. (Burns, 1992, p. A23).

Alija Izetbegovic, the president of Bosnia, updated the 1970 *Islamic Declaration* in 1990. This document now states, in part, that . . .

> . . . there can be neither peace nor coexistence between the Islamic religion and non-Islamic social and political institutions. . . . The Islamic government should and can start to take over power as soon as it is morally and numerically strong enough to be able to overturn not only the existing non-Islamic government, but also to build a new Islamic one (Mennard, *NYT*, 1992, p. A26).

Meanwhile by 1993, the Croats had successfully fought the Bosnian Muslims in order to gain control over the Herzegovina section of Bosnia, where a majority of Croats live. After achieving military victory, the Croats abandoned their support of Bosnian independence and smoothed over their conflict with the Serbs.

The story line paints a picture that we have seen in various forms and in varying degrees in the cases of Ireland and Rwanda. Cultural differences merge with ethnic and religious differences to exacerbate political struggles. Issues of cultural identity seem to magnify the "narcissism of small differences." For example, the Serbs have been unforgiving of the self-interest shown by the Bosnians, who accepted Islam as essentially a pay-off for loyalty (not, perhaps, unlike the Protestants in Ireland). They feel they are merely reclaiming their solidarity as an ethnic people, a solidarity that was stolen from them by the duplicity of Tito (a Croat-Slovene) and the complicity of the Western powers. The West's recognition of Bosnia was the proverbial last straw.

Perceived group differences. As Slavic peoples who speak the same language and have shared the same land for centuries, the parties make clear and not-so-subtle distinctions among them. Formerly Christian Slavs whose ancestors converted to Islam several hundred years ago are still called "Turks." Croats and Slovenes trace their culture to classical Rome and the high culture of the Austro-Hungarian Empire. Serbs are linked inexorably to the peasantry because of their mountain origins. Slovenes and Croats are disdained for "allowing" themselves to be ruled by outsiders. Serbs claim the right to govern on the basis of their courageous stand for autonomy and their fierce fighting to achieve it. It is common in contemporary U.S. society to liken the "cultural diversity" theme to *balkanization*— that is, the fracturing of people into small, distinctive, and self-contained cultural units as in the Balkan States of the former Yugoslavia, with self-interest as the primary *modus operandi* and *modus vivendi*. Having magnified the differences against a backdrop of similarity and commonality, any difference is exaggerated to the point of becoming a widening and unbridgeable gulf. These perceived differences can then serve to sustain and rationalize the acts of political defiance, military aggression, and human genocide. In fact, the relatively small differences are perceived as large, fundamental and a threat to one's way of life.

Sovereignty of land, ethnicity, culture, and psyche. Land is at the core of the Yugoslavia question, as is the case in the conflicts in Rwanda and in Ireland. It is not necessary to repeat the summary of issues presented in preceding pages. The critical theme spells out a saga of geographical boundaries (the Balkan states) coinciding with ethnic and cultural boundaries (Slovenes, Croats, and Serbians). The parties can be further subdivided along religious lines (Roman Catholic, Orthodox, and Muslim). Nationalism, defined at one level by political sovereignty, is completely confounded by ethnicity, religion, and psyche. As we have seen, these small differences have been expanded by the intervention of powerful outside forces. The Ottoman Empire left a destructive seed not only in the fact of perceived betrayal by conversion to Islam, but in the advantages that Islamic conversion accorded the Bosnians. These facts live in the Serbian psyche today. The Austro-Hungarian Empire played a role, as well. It reinforced, through the education system, the perceived superiority of the Croats and Slovenes, compared to the Serbs. Throw in the Nazi aggression and the Communist defense of World War II and we find reinforcement for the push to balkanize Yugoslavia, notwithstanding a desire on the part of Western countries and Serbians for a national political entity that would be a coherent nation-state. In the end, the fight for autonomy, fanned by outside intervention, has grown greatly beyond a constant struggle for cultural self-definition. The intense fighting in the former Yugoslavia is merely the perpetuation of the battle for independence of religious, ethnic, and cultural identities.

Disparate allocation of and access to power and resources. The use of special treatment accorded to selected groups by foreign powers plays a role in this conflict, as well. Bosnians who converted to Islam gained economic well-being. Croats and Slovenes who "went along" with the Austro-Hungarian occupation gained access to the largess and cultural developments of the empire. Under the Serbian-dominated Federation of Yugoslavia, the Serbs in Serbia to a great degree—and Serbs in Bosnia and Croatia to a lesser extent—enjoyed the advantages of ethnic in-group status. However, in this case, the allocation of resources does not seem to be as critical an issue as it is in Rwanda and Ireland.

Language and language policy. In Yugoslavia, language is more a consequence of conflict than a cause. That is, the disparate peoples of Yugoslavia spoke, for all practical purposes, the same language. In modern times, particularly in response to the current fighting, language has become a way to make small distinctions. Although Serbo-Croatian was widely recognized as the common language of all Yugoslavia, in the current battle the Serbs have sought to eliminate the "Croatian" from the language. The "new" language is to be simply *Serbian*. Linguists say that the commonality of Serbo-Croatian language across the Yugoslav republics and ethnic variations is greater than that shared by British and U.S. English. The Bosnian Muslims have begun adopting words from the time of Turkish domination of almost half a millennium ago. Bosnian Serbs have now adopted Serbian as their official language, despite the fact that their dialect is much more strongly tied to that of their Muslim and Croat neighbors. Therefore, the "weapon" of language—even if it is wielded in a clearly cosmetic, unapologetic ploy to create in-group cohesion—is a vital one in this battle among peoples.

Processes of conflict resolution. Until now, the conflicts among the Yugoslavian states have existed within a broader framework of outside domination. Conflict resolution has been limited by the requirements of the region's occupation by world empires and by the disruptions caused by World Wars I and II. The only successful conflict resolution has been the Serbian battle for independence from Turks, Fascists, and Nazis. In the context of the Yugoslav state, parliamentary voting was a means by which differing opinions were addressed. However, that was unsatisfactory, as it increasingly pitted all of the smaller republics against the Serbian-dominated national government. This produced voting marked by 4-4 ties and no resolution. Once Bosnia sought to break away and become independent, the Serbians resorted to the only historically successful means of conflict resolution in the region—military action.

Religion. It is quite obvious that religion plays a major role in the Yugoslavian conflict. However, as in Ireland, it is not a battle for conversion and religious imperialism. Rather, it is a battle for nationalism. Bogan Denitch (1994, p. 29), born of Serbian parents in Sophia, Bulgaria, notes that "Religion is the most commonly used *ethnic* identifier . . . ." Now a political scientist in the United States, Denitch was recently pretesting a questionnaire that included the question "What is your religion?" The Yugoslavian respondent immediately asked Mr. Denitch, "And what is yours?" Mr. Denitch replied that he was an atheist. The respondent shot back immediately, "I know all you damn intellectuals are atheists, but are you a Catholic, Orthodox, or Muslim atheist? I want to know your nationality" (Denitch, 1994, p. 29).

As with Northern Ireland, religion becomes a basis for categorization that transcends national boundaries, or even ethnic lineage. It is not enough to know that someone is Croat or Bosnian or even Serbian, because the group basis is the religious identification. Croats are distinguished by their Roman Catholicism, Bosnians by their Muslim beliefs and habits, and Serbs by their Orthodoxy. It is these religious ties that bind groups together across national boundaries and historical epochs.

DYNAMICS OF ETHNIC CONFLICT

In this chapter, we have surveyed three case examples of intergroup conflict. We will now seek to understand their shared dynamics. What do they have in common, in what ways are they different, and what can we learn from them about the general issues of intergroup conflict and its resolution? To what extent can the minimal-group conflict or the realistic-group conflict paradigms explain these conflict situations? How well do principles of social psychology help us to understand the dynamics of conflict at the individual level of perception, values and beliefs? Do these extreme and violent conflicts have real implications for understanding group conflict in the United States, or is the difference in violence indicative of a difference in the nature of the conflict? In other words, can we generalize from Bosnia, Ireland, and Rwanda to the black-white conflict in the United States? We will explore these issues next.

Minimal-Group versus Realistic-Group Conflict

First, it is quite clear that, in each example case, the disputing parties cleaved into groups that were perceived to be widely different physically, ethnically, morally, and culturally by each party. Whereas Tajfel (1978) created a minimal-group situation wherein distinctions between groups were trivial, these situations are maximal group situations wherein differences are believed to be vital and central to beliefs, values, and needs that define individual and ethnic identity. The Sherif (1966) field experiments created competition-driven animosity between the Rattlers and Eagles that reflects more easily the depth of hostility and protracted conflict seen in these current examples. Recall, for example, the Hutu man who killed his neighbors with a club *because they were Tutsi*! In Bosnia, a man's religious atheism was rejected as irrelevant because he had to be classified nationally in religious terms—Roman Catholic, Muslim, or Orthodox. Realistic-group conflict seems to be the stronger candidate for explaining extreme forms of intergroup hostility.

But we have gleaned quite a bit from the minimal-group paradigm. The ease with which in-group biases can be established helps us to understand how these tendencies could be so easily marshaled to support out-group perceptions that legitimate the hostility in which people engage. Von Hippel, Sekaquaptewa, and Vargas (1995) have shown, in a series of elegant experiments, how stereotyping affects, and is affected by, encoding processes. Subjects scoring high in prejudice and those scoring low in prejudice will read newspaper articles differently. Specifically, a high-prejudice person is more likely to selectively attend to information that differentiates members of his or her group from others by assimilating stereotype-congruent information and converting stereotype-incongruent information to congruent information. And when it is too incongruent, the person basically forgets it! These processes may be illustrative of dynamics that can be gleaned from basic research in the laboratory and extrapolated to conflict situations—even intense-conflict situations, such as those described here. In all cases, the disputants see or encode what they want to believe. In intense-conflict situations, everyone behaves *as if* a high-prejudiced person!

Intergroup Contact—The Problem or the Solution?

Which came first, the perception of group difference or the conflict? In the black-white situation in the United States, the way in which interracial hostility is thought best to be reduced is through interracial contact—this is known as the *contact hypothesis* (G. W. Allport, 1954).[6] But, considering the case example of Rwanda, is it not contact that created the conflict in the first place, when the Tutsi migrated to the Rwanda-Burundi area and gained ascendance over the Hutu? Was it not the insertion of Protestant British in the midst of Ireland that laid the seed for Catholic-Protestant conflict in Ireland? The fact is, group difference and conflict cannot be separated in these cases. It seems that group difference defines the nature and context of a given conflict. For example, the partial resolution of the extreme conflict situation in Bosnia has been achieved by segregating the conflicting groups by means of establishing geographical borders and nationalistic autonomy. Indeed, the situation in Bosnia is a little different from the cases of Rwanda and Ireland, in that the Muslim and Serbian groups were once the same, but *became* different. That is, it was not until a segment of the Bosnian population converted to Islam under Turkish domination that it became different from its Serbian brothers and sisters. This difference then created a basis for conflict—not over land, but over belief, value, and identity. It is similar to a white woman's marrying a black man in the United States and being rejected by her family, or the situation of a woman from a highly religious Roman Catholic family upon having an abortion. Violating certain central cultural or group principles can create differences that cannot be bridged. Haddock, Esses, and Zanna (1993) showed that *symbolic beliefs* (i.e., beliefs that are closely aligned with cultural values) shaped stereotyping judgments and prejudice behaviors as much—or more, in some cases—than did stereotypic beliefs based on trait ascriptions to different groups. Social psychological work on symbolic processes such as symbolic racism (Sears, 1988) and analyses of the new racism (cf. Barker, 1981, and Chapter 13) emphasize in-group preferences, cultural worldview, and ethnic identity as bases of intergroup conflict. Clearly, this cultural level of animosity dramatically fuels these extreme forms of conflict.

So, although in the lab we can create group differences and then observe how they affect individual judgments, these causal connections are not so easily observed in real-world situations. Nevertheless, it does seem pretty clear that the cognitive processes associated with both the mere categorization model and the realistic-group-conflict model operate in those conflicts. Whereas cognitive processes

---

[6] We will discuss this in more detail when we consider strategies for reducing prejudice in Chapter 11.

supply the perceptual wherewithal to make fine distinctions on the basis of group membership, it is the realistic conflict that supplies the emotional energy. For example, Muslims became different from Serbs, but they were still Slavic people with a common cultural history. Nevertheless, the Serbs called the Bosnian Muslims "Turks!" The display of the exhumed body of a former Serbian leader slain by the Turks served to fan the emotional flames of anti-Turkish—and, therefore, anti-Bosnian Muslim—hatred. Simply being different does not cause one to be raped, tortured, and murdered. But the calculated and selective perceptions of the nature and meaning of difference can create a belief system in which such behavior is justifiable to the actors.[7]

Relationship to Black-White Conflict in the United States

There are many similarities and as many differences between the black-white conflict in the United States and each of these examples. The perceived differences between blacks and whites are perhaps more dramatic and obvious than are those ethnic differences in each of the conflict situations above. However, these differences, over time, have diminished. One of the interesting potential parallels is that, as blacks and whites get closer to one another, the "narcissism of small differences" may become a more prominent factor in the conflict. That is, the perceived differences between the races may become the rallying point around which the racial and ethnic or cultural identity is forged. The stakes for difference then are higher, and the common ground is lessened. The concept of "rising expectations" was offered to explain the racial riots in the 1960s when, by all accounts, things were getting better, in terms of race relations in the United States, than they had ever been. Another way of looking at the heightened sense of racism in contemporary society is to see this reduced difference as a magnifying glass that exposes the smallest indication of difference as if it were no different from the more dramatic forms of racism prevalent in previous generations.

We can clearly see, though, that the nationalistic, separatist spirit has risen in recent years, not only in the United States, but around the world. This may be a natural consequence of a conflict defined in terms of core values. What makes it difficult in the United States is that the institutional and cultural context of the mainstream is pervasive, and nationalistic autonomy is extremely difficult to achieve. However, we may see the emergence of a kind of social nationalism in the United States (what some fear the diversity movement is becoming) as a reaction comparable to the emergence of political nationalism that characterizes the three case examples discussed in this chapter.

These comments are speculative. However, they do raise some interesting possibilities for analyses that might aid us in understanding contemporary racial conflict. The problem of the encompassing nature of the dominant culture (quite unlike the limited ability to dominate Yugoslavia by Serbia), exacerbated by the political, economic, and legal dominance of whites in the United States (begun during the era of slavery and maintained in varying degrees since), makes the black-white situation here different in important ways from all three of the examples discussed. However, we can see clearly that the perceptual processes and reactions are not altogether different. Moreover, it is compelling that the basic mechanisms and forms

[7] Paul Hill killed Dr. John Bayard Britton and his guard, Mr. James H. Barrett, outside an abortion clinic in Pensacola, Florida, on July 29, 1994. On December 6, 1994, Mr. Hill was sentenced to die in the electric chair for murdering Dr. Britton and Mr. Barrett.

of analysis of intergroup conflict spawned by conflicts in the United States have relevance to these situations.

SUMMARY

When I began writing about these case examples, I must confess that I wanted to show that realistic-group conflict was fundamentally different from, and not reducible to, the minimal-group theory—that is, that mere categorization could *not* explain intergroup conflict. As is almost always the case, the answers to complex questions are not rendered by simple either/or possibilities. The specific history and context of conflict creates the passion, intensity, and emotional energy that makes certain behaviors possible. Categorization into groups—as well as all of the perceptual biases of stereotyping and intergroup relations—come into play. For example, Serbs imagine that the Bosnian Muslims will act to make the Bosnian Serbs wear Islamic clothes and pray to Mohammed. The specter of a group that is not simply descriptively different (i.e., entitive), but capable of actions that adversely affect you (i.e., active), is a powerful force.

To conclude then, realistic conflict over resources, identity, and language may be the driving force behind intergroup conflict. However, this conflict is facilitated and sustained by the cognitive biases revealed by both the Tajfel and Sharif research. The degree to which the competing groups can be easily distinguished on dimensions that are central to one's own group definition will facilitate perception of differences and the maintenance of conflict. In the case of race in the United States, the maintenance of prejudice and racism was made possible, in part, by the supposition of large, defining race differences. Advances in race relations have seemed always to rest on demonstrating that those differences are, in fact, very small—if they exist at all. The only difference, this approach assumes is skin color. And that difference is meaningless. But, maybe there are differences that go beyond skin color. If there are such differences, what are they, and how do we proceed to resolve them?

Differences do seem to go with conflict. Can we have differences without conflict? The diversity movement seems to be the modern-day equivalent of the civil rights movement. The latter was framed in a simple binary context of black and white—although, in principle, it was not limited to categorization by skin color. We now have multiple arguments for inclusion, each predicated on difference. It is not incidental that diversity in the United States is linked to the idea of balkanization. We have seen how fragmentation in Yugoslavia has been a focal point for conflict for a very long time. Can difference be celebrated without conflict? The above case examples suggest that, probably it cannot. The final answer, of course, is not yet written.

POSTSCRIPT

Rwanda
The conflict in Rwanda continues, as refugees are still drifting in and out of Rwanda and Burundi. Violence flares up, and the government is anything but stable. The flames of ethnic animosity and cultural instability are fanned by the peoples' apparently short memories of the atrocities that afflicted both Hutu and Tutsi alike. We cannot predict where things will end up. However, just as racial and ethnic stereotypes have proven difficult to disconfirm or change, the suspicion, biased

encoding and perception, and, above all, the symbolic conflict over values—and the realistic conflict over life and death—suggest that this conflict will still be simmering for years to come.

Ireland
The cease-fire declared in the fall of 1994 was shattered on February 9, 1996, when a bomb exploded in a store in downtown London. Shortly thereafter, the IRA declared the cease-fire officially over, and hostilities were once again a daily threat. Although the conditions for a settlement may have been ripe in 1994, the conditions for a lasting peace may have moved away from ripeness. It is clear, once again, that the deep-seated conflict over values, sovereignty, and a way of life will not be settled easily. Cease-fires and negotiated agreements come and go, but the basic seeds of distrust continue to grow. On July 11, 1996, violence erupted in Drumcree, Northern Ireland, when a Protestant march through a Catholic neighborhood ignited old flames of passion smoldering since the battle of the Boyne in 1690 (Barbash, 1996). Fearing even worse violence in Londonderry, Protestants were forbidden to march there. However, the police reversed the ruling and, predictably, when members of the Protestant Orange Order marched through a Catholic neighborhood, violence erupted, shops were burned and looted, and skeletons of firebombed cars dotted the landscape of the municipal parking lot. July 12 comes every year, and it brings with it memory traces and emotional eruptions of centuries-old animosities.

Bosnia
In November 1995 in Dayton, Ohio, the United States brokered a peace settlement of the Bosnian conflict. The parties were clearly reluctant, but it appears again that the conditions were sufficiently "ripe" to close the deal. With the help of U.S. soldiers and the pressure of world opinion, a settlement was reached. It granted autonomy to the Bosnian Muslims and restored to them some of their land; it also granted autonomy to the Bosnian Serbs. The deal also made allies of Bosnian Muslims and Croats, but their ethnic differences seem likely to dissolve any close relationship in short order. Whether this deal will last—and the violence of ethnic cleansing laid to rest permanently—is for history to judge. It would not be surprising to see hostilities break out again.

10

$\mathcal{P}$sychological $\mathcal{M}$echanisms of $\mathcal{P}$rejudice: $\mathcal{A}$daptation and Coping of $\mathcal{T}$argets

❖

$\mathcal{I}$NTRODUCTION

James Garcia and Evaristo Vazquez were fortunate enough to be able to take a week's vacation in Jamaica. Both were born in Pennsylvania and neither had been out of the country before. Although they had a dream of a time in sunny Jamaica, they had a nightmare upon reentry. Here's what happened (as reported by Nat Hentoff, 1994). When they went to claim their luggage at Newark Airport, they were surrounded by customs agents, put into separate rooms and strip searched. These searches revealed nothing illegal and neither did a search of their luggage.

259

Agents decided to x-ray James and Evaristo. The two were therefore whisked away, in handcuffs, to St. Francis Hospital to be x-rayed. While the two were shackled at the ankles and handcuffed to the beds, x-rays were taken of them. Again, nothing illegal was found. Without so much as an apology, they were taken back to the airport and released. James Garcia asked the U.S. agents why they had been singled out. He was asked, in return, his nationality and age. He replied, "Hispanic and I'm 24 and my friend is 25." The agent replied, knowingly, "Well, there you go."

Is being Latino and male and in your early twenties a federal crime? Of course it isn't. Were James and Evaristo victims of stereotyping? Of course they were. Stereotyping, prejudice, and intergroup bias are not just topics that social psychologists study in the laboratory. They are facts of life that affect people everyday. This chapter is concerned with what these effects are—psychologically, behaviorally, and emotionally. In the United States, members of ethnic minorities and women are always under suspicion. They are under suspicion of being illegal immigrants, of being unable to speak or understand English, of harboring criminal intentions, of being unintelligent, of being likely to behave violently, or of being unable to lead or to make tough decisions.

In 1994, California voters passed proposition 187, which denies access to education and selected social services to illegal immigrants. Over 30 states have passed "English Only" laws, which require that all official transactions be conducted in English only. Those that cannot read or speak English fluently, may not gain access to services that they are entitled to as citizens or legal aliens.

Grady Garner is a student of mine who recounted the following story during a class in which we were discussing the issues of racial stigma. Grady was returning

Internment! Japanese Americans are gathered in San Francisco for a train trip to Santa Anita race track for assembly and transportation to internment camps, April 6, 1942. (AP/Wide World Photos)

home late at night from his job at Bennigan's in Chicago. He parked his car and walked the two blocks to his apartment. As he neared his complex, a white Chevrolet pulled up beside him and the man in the passenger side called out, "Get in the back." Grady looked at him incredulously and kept walking. Grady recalled what happened:

> "The driver darted out of the vehicle, and in a flash without a word, grabbed me by the throat and lifted me off the ground by my neck onto the tips of my toes and at the same time pinned me against the building with his free forearm pressed against my chest . . . with his nose one inch from mine started by shouting and spitting in my face. . . "What are you doing in this neighborhood? Where are you going? What's your name? Where do you live? What were you doing in that car? Whose car is it?"

Grady was scared to death. When he was able to catch his breath, he shouted, "I live in the f-ing building and that's my g'd car. Who the f- are you? What right have you to do this? Are you guys cops? What's your badge number? You have no right to do this."

When Grady asked to see his badge, and caught a glimpse of it, the driver released him, looked over to his partner, walked over to the car, and left. No apologies and no explanations.

The movie *Amos and Andrew* was Hollywood's way of making a few million dollars off the plight of young black men in the United States. But, as we saw with James and Evaristo and with Grady Garner, this is not a joke. Grady was suspected of something—it is not clear what—apparently for no reason other than he was a black man walking the streets late at night. What toll must it take to be continually under suspicion not for who you are or what's in your heart or what character you possess, but for fitting a profile, a stereotype that stigmatizes you and justifies capricious ill-will directed at you.

Americans of Japanese descent were under suspicion in the years following the bombing of Pearl Harbor. So great was the suspicion that, on February 19, 1942 (Nagata, 1994), President Franklin Roosevelt signed Executive Order 9066, giving authority to the secretary of defense to exclude all persons, citizens and aliens, from designated areas in order to provide security against sabotage or espionage. The U.S. Army implemented the order by removing all Japanese Americans from the West Coast and incarcerating them in concentrations camps in desolate areas of the United States.

The purpose of this chapter is to look at the reactions and coping processes of those who are targets of prejudice, stereotyping, and discrimination. How can or do they adjust, how do they buffer the stressful effects, how do they survive? Even if one has not been interned in a concentration camp, what effect does knowledge of the internment of one's ancestors have on self-esteem, self-image, and future expectations? What does the illegal and humiliating detainment, searches, and x-rays do to the psyche of James and Evaristo, to the many other Latinos who know that being Latino in many situations puts one under suspicion? What are the psychological consequences for black men who are under suspicion daily of potential violence, criminality, ignorance, or even of being uncivilized or just of being up to no good? How does it affect how you act, what you feel, what you think?

Social psychologists have spent most of their scientific careers focusing on the perpetrators of prejudice. Often what is missing from such discussions is an analysis of how the targets of prejudice react to and cope with it. If prejudice occurs in subtle and not-so-subtle forms on a daily basis, how do its targets adapt? The first

part of this chapter will consider the psychological predicaments caused by prejudice. For example, knowing that you may face prejudice in some form because of
your age, race, ethnicity, gender, or sexual orientation, you cannot take for granted
responses and outcomes that others may consider routine. Moreover, how you respond in one situation may affect your behavior in others, as well as how others respond to you. The predicament of knowing you are under suspicion and that your
reactions may affect you in adverse ways is a heavy burden to carry around. How
does society challenge targets of prejudice to make the adjustments necessary not
only to survive with their self-esteem intact, but to realize the American dream?
Given the challenges and corresponding barriers, how does one adjust? The second
section will explore specific mechanisms that may operate to facilitate adjustment
and coping. Current research in identity and identification, adaptation, and acculturation will be reviewed, and the important mechanisms that sustain the viability
and general mental health of the targets of prejudice will be highlighted.

PSYCHOLOGICAL PREDICAMENTS OF PREJUDICE

A *predicament* is a situation in which a person's psychological well-being is threatened. Prejudice or its potential is a threat to which a person must pay attention and
against which he or she must take corrective or evasive action. Our concern here is
with those situations that *cause* predicaments, and those *corrective and evasive actions*
one takes to fix them. Crocker, Major, and Steele (in press) suggest four conditions
that pose predicaments for people at risk for being targets of prejudice:

1 *Awareness of the devalued quality of one's social identity.* That is, one is aware that
   one's group is viewed negatively by others, particularly by those in positions of
   authority or who control valued and needed resources.
2 *Stereotype threat.* One is aware of negative stereotypes of one's group that operate in a specific domain (e.g., academic performance) and the potential that, as a
   group member, one may validate that stereotype by one's behavior.
3 *Experience with prejudice and discrimination.* Personal experience with racial, ethnic, or gender bias, or witnessing public examples of such bias raises an ever-
   present specter of prejudice that will threaten self-worth or, worse, real and important outcomes.
4 *Attributional ambiguity.* The threat of prejudice can be compared to objective
   evaluation or fair treatment, leaving ambiguity as to the motivation behind and,
   hence, the meaning of the evaluation. For example, is the clerk in bad temper
   today, or of a generally sour personality, or is he showing disdain for me because I am black?

Let's look briefly at some of the manifestations or experiences of these threatening
predicaments.

When I go to an ATM machine and a woman is making a transaction, I think
about whether she may fear I will rob her. Given that I have no such intention, how
do I put her at ease? Maybe I can't put her at ease, or maybe she has no such expectation. But, the thought goes through my mind. Stereotypes not only affect their
holder, but their target.

I am a person unique in the world. The total set of experiences, beliefs, abilities,
goals, and social relations I encompass are shared by no other person on the planet.
Each of us can say that. But I also belong to many groups—some chosen (profes-

sor), some inherited (male, African American). We all belong to different groups, as well. What distinguishes many of us, though, is that the groups to which we belong may play a greater role in determining our experiences.

If you are Latino or Latina, for example, you may run the risk of being mistaken for an illegal immigrant, especially if you have an accent. You may also face the stigma of being different and wish you could lose the accouterments of culture. A friend once confided in me that she dreaded it when her mother would make her tortilla-and-bean sandwiches when she went to school. She loved them but knew that they would link her to her Chicana roots. In those days (c. 1975), there was constant ambivalence about the melting pot as a cauldron of homogenization and assimilation. Losing one's culture—or, at least, evidence of it—appeared to be a prerequisite for success or, in some cases, even for opportunity.

For gay men and lesbians, the closet was where one's sexual orientation was housed. Bringing one's sexual orientation out into the open was surely an invitation to bigotry and prejudice. But with the emergence of the revolutionary trends toward self-definition (discussed in Chapter 4) came a more general willingness to publicly declare one's group affiliation and to do so with pride and honor. This was done in spite of the persistent tendencies in our society to stigmatize membership in certain groups, and to justify either negative treatment or the withholding of full citizenship rights.

So, as an individual, one is often faced with deciding whether to express one's personal character or to suppress it in the service of reaching desired goals or fitting in. Whether you view it as a predicament (unpleasant) or a *challenge* (i.e., the tension of making a wise choice that succeeds in moving one forward to one's goals), the choice is not simple, and its consequences are often negative or unpredictable. Although the choices may be challenging and the options not those that you prefer, *not choosing* is not a psychological option. Race, ethnicity, gender, or sexual orientation is a part of a person's identity and can be a basis for others' reactions to you or how you think about yourself, independent of whatever choices you make.

Psychologists have long been concerned with identity and self-esteem. Both factors reflect what a person thinks of himself or herself, and what value a person attaches to his or her identity. Moreover, we have questioned the effect of the value others attach not only to an individual as a person, but as a representative of the group of which one is a member. Social identity theory (SIT) made a positive connection between group membership and personal esteem. The research of the Clarks (1947), for example, made a negative connection between group membership and personal esteem for black children.

Racial, ethnic, or gender identity is a focal point for much of the psychological tension that arises from the predicament of prejudice. This tension is reflected in questions such as the following: Do I embrace the source of stigma to which my group is subjected and refuse to allow others to determine who we are and how we should be valued? Or, do I avoid thinking about the stigmatizing group characteristics, claim my individuality, and minimize group influences? These decisions can take on personal, political dimensions (cf. J. M. Jones, 1991), and making these real-world choices may involve compromise and adopting strategies for control of self-definition and self-worth. These issues may also lead us to question whether the powerful influences of circumstances and context offer much opportunity for individual choice at all.

The issue of racial identity is the place where much of the diversity discussion comes to rest. That is, group differences that have been judged nonrelevant by advocates of a melting-pot metaphor have been resurrected by others as a source of personal and group expression. Just as prejudice and racism result in positive in-group biases that parallel negative out-group judgments, so too does racial identity take on these properties. The stigmatizing agents of culture are morally suspect, and, besides, the argument goes, mainstream culture really isn't all that great. Racial identity can become a source of strength and pride, alas, and thereby, serve to promote psychological well-being.

But the predicament does not go away. In the name of *meritocracy*, America's house rules establish the ante and criteria for participation and rewards in the larger society. The chips reflect specific and characteristic traits, abilities, attitudes, values, and beliefs, without which one is forced out of the game. In many instances, these house rules conflict with those subcultural values on which racial and ethnic identity may be forged. Therefore, behaving in a way that allows one to feel good about oneself *and* that enables one to get a good job may be in conflict.

The late Ron Brown had a good job and felt good about himself. When he died tragically in a plane crash in the Balkan mountains of the former Yugoslavia on April 3, 1996, he was Secretary of Commerce of the United States. Brown, an African American who grew up in Harlem, had achieved a long list of "racial firsts." Not the least of these was his position as Secretary of Commerce. He ran the Presidential campaign of Jesse Jackson in 1988 and the successful campaign of President Bill Clinton in 1992. He chaired the Democratic National Committee and was widely believed to be responsible for the resurgence of the Democratic party in the late 1980s.

What was significant about Brown was his unyielding belief that being black and American were not oppositional—that one could, in fact, be a successful American *and* a strongly identified African American. He refused to be subjected to the "bifurcation of self" (cf. J. M. Jones, 1991) that Marvin Kalb had attempted to impose on Jesse Jackson in 1984. Interviewing Mr. Jackson (1984) on *Meet the Press*, Kalb (1984) asked:

Kalb:	"The question [is] are you a black man who happens to be an American running for the Presidency, or are you an American who happens to be a black man running for the Presidency?
Jackson:	Well, I'm both an American and a black at one and the same time. I'm both of these . . . .
Kalb:	What I'm trying to get at is something that addresses a question no one seems able to grasp and that is, are your priorities deep inside yourself, to the degree that anyone can look inside himself, those of a black man who happens to be an American or the reverse?
Jackson:	Well I was born black in America, I was not born American in black! You are asking a funny kind of catch-22 question. *My* interests are *national* interests.

Kalb seemed to want to bifurcate Jackson into mutually exclusive parts, one American and one black. Being a member of a stigmatized group tends to force this predicament on people. Either/or choices of who one is force an artificial reality on psychological make-up and behavior expression. Resisting this bifurcating tendency may be a matter of psychological self-defense. It may also be a crucial strategy for handling acculturative pressures that arise when one exists on the margin of multiple cultures. The psychology of this dynamic tension is important to all of us (*Sophie's Choice* and *Hamlet* are two dramatic choice dilemmas of psychological significance), but it seems to be a matter of greater moment for members of stigmatized groups, who face the prospects of having prejudice directed at them.

This introductory discussion sets the stage for consideration of some psychological processes of targets of prejudice. These processes, psychologically adaptive reactions to the predicaments caused by prejudice (and the source of the predicaments themselves) fall into several classes:

1   *Cognitive perceptual processes* serve to deflect or reduce the threat, or bolster or protect the self. Work on reactions to stereotype threats (Steele and Aronson, 1995; Spencer and Steele, in press) show some unintended negative consequences of these reactions. Assessment of attributional ambiguity processes illustrate ways in which both positive and negative outcomes can occur (Crocker and Major, 1994).

2   *Perceptual* and *attitudinal processes* are directed at bolstering the in-group and enabling its members to reject the stigmatizing out-group. African self-consciousness (Baldwin and Bell, 1985) proposes in-group bolstering processes, and cultural mistrust (Watkins and Terrell, 1988) describe behavioral consequences of distancing oneself from white out-groups.

3   *Dynamic processes* of intergroup interactions aid in transitions across the boundaries of the in-group and the out-group. Work on how people adjust to psychological marginalization (Frable, Blackstone, and Sherbaum, 1990) shows how marginalized individuals can enhance their capacity to manage interactions from a minority perspective. Living in two cultural worlds produce acculturative stress that can be relieved through a variety of strategies of bicultural adaptation (LaFromboise, Coleman, and Gerton, 1993).

4   The formulation of *personal social identities* that incorporate dimensions of group membership is an important way to bolster self-esteem while also distancing oneself from devalued attitudes imposed on one's group. For example, embracing ethnic (Phinney, 1994) and racial (Cross, 1995) identities will serve these self-protective roles.

PSYCHOLOGICAL MECHANISMS OF ADAPTATION AND COPING

Stigma is the identification of a trait, quality, or attribute as a "blemish" or a deficiency that separates the owner from others. Crocker, Major, and Steele (in press) propose that social stigma results when one possesses an attribute that conveys a devalued social identity in a particular context. One may, therefore, be stigmatized in one context (say, by being a woman in a physics class) but not in another (say, being a woman in an English literature class). Historically, though, being black in white America has provided a context of stigma that is broad enough to encompass most such experiences. To be sure, a stigma is in the eye of the beholder. However, when it is in the eyes of millions of people over decades and centuries, it becomes more than a perceptual illusion, it becomes a cultural fact! That is, if television, movies, books, newspapers, classroom teachers, bank officers, and store clerks all treat you as if you have a stigma, you may eventually come to act as if you do and experience life as if you do. One of the most enduring and unchanging sources of stigma is race.

One way of viewing progress toward tolerance in the United States is to suggest that the number of contexts in which being black, or a woman, or Latino, or old, for example, is stigmatizing has diminished. Although there may, in fact, be fewer stigmatizing contexts, our concern here is with the psychological and behavioral responses of stigma targets to those contexts. That is, how can or does a stigmatized person maintain a positive view of himself or herself in the face of a higher-than-average probability that prejudice may pose a predicament? One may instead discount the source of stigma, reflecting it back to the other, offending person. Or, the stigmatized person may deflect the stigma by focusing attention on other domains of self-regard.

One domain of self-regard that is important to participation in U.S. society—and subject to strong stigmatizing tendencies along racial, ethnic, and gender lines—is academic performance. Although the contexts may have differential stigmatizing potentials for members of different groups (e.g., math and science for women, English and literature for Latinos, and overall academic performance for African Americans), they may evoke common reactions to these prejudice-potentiating contexts.

Stereotype Threat—I Know I Can Do This, so Why Am I Not Doing Better?

One of the most prevalent domains of stigma for African Americans and Latinos is academic performance, which extends to women in the areas of math and science.[1] In the academic arena, black and Latino students are often under suspicion of an inherent tendency toward poor academic performance. C. Steele (Steele and Aronson, 1995; Spencer and Steele, in press) has proposed a theory of stereotype threat that may explain the tendency of African Americans and women to underperform academically in domains in which they face the predicament of stereotypical expectations of low performance. For example, evidence shows that blacks who are as well-prepared academically as whites (as indicated by Scholastic Assessment Test [SAT] performance) nevertheless obtain grade point averages about one-third of a point lower than those obtained by their white counterparts. Moreover, this disparity does not diminish as one goes from low to high levels of SAT preparation. It is as large for students whose SAT scores are two standard deviations *below* the mean as it is for those who score two standard deviations *above* the mean!

Steele suggests that reaction to a perceived stereotype threat may provide an explanation for this underperformance in the face of strong preparation. For Steele, the source of threat is the person's recognition that the majority group member suspects lesser ability on the part of the minority group member.

The experience of threat is based on (1) an individual's own poor performance in the past or (2) a widely perceived stereotype about the group of which the individual is a member. That is, the more poorly one has done in the past or the more widely and publicly a negative stereotype is held about one's group, the greater the threat one will experience.

Steele proposes that this threat arouses two basic reactions in one who is sub-

[1] I sat on the Faculty Council at Harvard University in 1972, when the decision to integrate Harvard and Radcliffe with regard to admissions procedures was made. The most vocal and passionate opposition to the merger came from representatives of the science and math departments, who declared that the merger would deliver a death blow to their viability and reputation as world-class departments. They expressed the view that women were not only uninterested in math and science but not good at it!

jected to it: (1) a disruptive apprehension based on the fear that one will verify or be judged by the stereotype; and (2) a rejection of the setting in which the threat of confirming or being judged by a negative stereotype is likely to occur—a process labeled *protective disidentification.* These two possible reactions have different implications for performance. The former leads to the ironic prospect that striving hard to disconfirm a negative expectation about performance may well produce the lower performance one is trying to avoid! This is a pernicious form of self-fulfilling prophesy. The consequences of the second reaction may actually be even worse—a reduction of the level of effort, or, more tragic, the rejection of academic performance altogether as an indication of self-worth. Disidentification with the academic domain may be a coping response to the stereotype threat that undermines the motivation to achieve. "When self-esteem is independent of outcomes in a domain, the *motive* to maintain self-esteem is lost. (C. Steele, 1996, p. 12).

What is central to recognize in this theory is that an individual need not internalize a societal stereotype, or need not believe he or she is incapable of performing at a high level in order for the phenomenon to work. The threat is posed by *group ability* stereotypes, and the performance disruption occurs because of anxiety about confirming them as an individual member of the group.

Steele and Aronson (1995) tested this idea by having white and black subjects perform a very difficult test comprising the most difficult items from the Graduate Record Exam (GRE). In the first study, the test was introduced as a study of those psychological factors involved in solving a verbal problem in one of three ways by telling them: (1) this test is "a genuine test of your verbal abilities and limitations (diagnostic condition); (2) to try hard "even though we're not going to evaluate your ability," (nondiagnostic); and (3) to "please take this challenge seriously even though we will not be evaluating your ability" (challenge condition) (Steele and Aronson, p. 799).

Performance on the test varied as a function of the subject's race and the perceived nature of the test. Figure 10.1 shows that blacks performed equal to whites

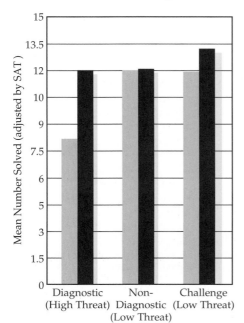

FIGURE 10.1

Test Performance as a Function of Racial Stereotype Threat. (Adapted from Steele, C.M. & Aronson, J. [1995] Stereotype threat and the intellectual test performance of African Americans. *Journal of Personality and Social Psychology, 69,* 797–811, Figure 1, p. 800.)

in the nondiagnostic and challenge conditions, but performed more poorly than whites did in the diagnostic condition. This finding supports the claim that it is the threat inherent in the situation that interfered with performance.

In a later study (Steele and Aronson, 1995; study 4), subjects were given the nondiagnostic instructions only. However, before taking the test, they were asked to indicate their age, year in school, major, number of siblings, and parents' education. Half of them were primed by being asked to write down their race. The other half were not required to indicate their race. The authors reasoned that if the stereotype threat was linked to the group, then linking the subject to his or her group would make the stereotype more salient and would effect performance, in a manner similar to the diagnostic condition of study 1.

Figure 10.2 shows no racial difference in performance when racial stereotype was not primed. This finding supports previous studies in which the test showed no racial differences were found when the test was not diagnostic of ability. However, when race was primed, black subjects now performed significantly more poorly than did whites. Therefore, making one's racial group affiliation salient had the same effect as making the diagnostic properties of the test salient. In both instances the stereotype threat increased (Steele and Aronson, 1995).

Finally, Steele and Aronson (1995) attempted to demonstrate the psychological mechanisms that accompany reactions to stereotype threat. Again, black and white subjects were given either the standard diagnostic or the nondiagnostic instruction. However, before taking the test (which they actually never did), they were to complete two tasks. The first was a measure of *stereotype activation* that required subjects to make complete words from word fragments by filling in missing letters. For example, ___ ___ CE might be *FACE* or *RACE*. Steele and Aronson (1995) expected that if the stereotype was activated by the diagnostic instruction, subjects would be more likely to complete these word fragments with stereotypical words. Other stereotypical words included *WELFARE, COLOR, TOKEN, POOR,* and *BLACK*. In

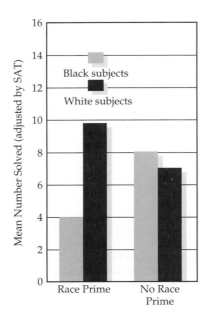

FIGURE 10.2

Test Performance as a Function of Priming Racial Stereotype. (Adapted from Steele, C.M. & Aronson, J. [1995] Stereotype threat and the intellectual test performance of African Americans. *Journal of Personality and Social Psychology, 69,* 797–811, Figure 4, p. 807.)

the second part of the task, a second set of words, such as *LOSER, DUMB, SHAME,* and *WEAK,* was used to determine whether the diagnostic interaction elicited *self-doubt* in those subjects. The subjects were instructed to perform the same word-fragment completion activity. The second task tested the possibility that subjects might react with *stereotype avoidance.* Students were asked to simply rate their preferences of a variety of activities and to indicate how self-descriptive various personality traits were. Both the activities and traits were stereotypically associated in varying degrees with African Americans (e.g., rap music, basketball, lazy, aggressive, or belligerent). There were no differences between white and black subjects in the activation of race-stereotypical or self-doubt words in either the nondiagnostic or control conditions, nor was there any racial differences in self-characterizations. However, in the diagnostic condition, blacks, compared to whites, made *more* race-stereotypical and self-doubting words, and showed *fewer* stereotypical self-characterizations.

Finally, in this same study, subjects were asked to indicate how prepared they were to take the test. Lack of preparedness was taken as a sign of *self-handicapping* (offering reasons why one's performance is not a true indication of one's ability). Black subjects, more than other subjects, in the diagnostic condition indicated they had had fewer hours of sleep the night before, had a reduced ability to focus, and thought the tests were more unfair. They also reported feeling more stress, in this they did not differ from whites in the diagnostic condition.

Spencer and Steele (in press) argued that stereotype vulnerability also applies to women in domains of science and math performance but not in English. Using a paradigm similar to that used in the study of racial stereotype threat, they studied the performance of women and men who were similarly qualified in their math and English ability (e.g., who had scored above the 85th percentile on both the math and English sections of the SAT or ACT tests and also indicated strong agreement to statements such as "I am good at math and I am good at English"). The subjects were tested on portions of the advanced GRE tests in mathematics and English literature. The paradigm predicted that women would perform equal to men on English where the women did *not* face stereotype threat, but would perform more poorly than men on math where they did face the stereotype threat. The results supported the hypothesis. Men and women performed equally well on the English test (29.3 for men, and 26.0 for women), but men performed significantly better on math than women did (21.3 for men, compared to 5.6 for women). This result mirrors the result of the racial study. Here, however, math ability expectation is the diagnostic condition, because of its tendency to arouse stereotype threat.

In a second study (Spencer and Steele, in press), men and women were given tests of varying degrees of difficulty. When the test was easy, there was no gender-based performance difference (men scored 57.1, and women scored 58.2). But when the test was difficult, men scored higher (24.8) than women did (10.0). In a third study, subjects were led to expect a gender difference in test performance (even though the nature of that difference was not explicitly stated) and were given only the difficult test. Men outperformed women by 26.7 to 5.8. But when subjects were explicitly told there was no gender difference in test performance, there was no difference in performance between men and women.

Interestingly, when subjects were told there was no gender-based performance difference in the test, men did more poorly than they did when they thought there was a difference. Conversely women did *better* when they thought there were no gender differences than when they thought there were. This finding suggests that removing the perception of gender differences may remove a psychological feeling of superiority or advantage for men. A presumption of gender differences seems to simultaneously *undermine* performance for women and *enhance* performance for men! The possibility that privileged status is a factor in higher levels of performance by members of advantaged groups merits further attention.

Let's tie this discussion up with one additional observation. Recall Steele's assertion: "When self-esteem is independent of outcomes in a domain, the motive to maintain self-esteem is lost as a source of motivation (1996, p. 12). Osborne (1995) sought to test the idea that a tendency to disidentify with the academic domain will be reflected by a reduced correlation between self-esteem and GPA. That is, if academic achievement is rejected as an important aspect of the self, then self-esteem will increasingly be *independent* of academic performance. Osborne (1995) evaluated data from the National Center for Educational Statistics (NCES) for 24,599 eighth-grade students from over 1,000 different schools in the United States. GPAs were correlated with self-esteem measures (Rosenberg, 1986) at the eighth grade and again at the tenth grade for black and white males and females. Figure 10.3 shows the changes in these correlations from eighth to tenth grades. We should note first that self-esteem was *higher* for black students than for white students in both the eighth and tenth grades. GPA and achievement test scores were higher for white students than for black students in the eighth and tenth grades. However, race-based GPA differences in the eighth grade were not statistically significant. As Figure 10.3 shows, the correlation between self-esteem and GPA is substantially the same across race and gender groups in the eighth grade. However, by the tenth grade, this relationship declines for all groups except white males. The most dramatic decline is for black males such that, by the tenth grade, there is virtually no relationship between self-esteem and GPA. Because self-esteem itself has not declined, we must conclude that the basis of self-esteem is typically found elsewhere for black males. The trend toward a lower correlation for women (black and white) and a small rising correlation for white males, may be an indication of the gender and racial advantage that converts to superior performance when gender and racial differences are suspected.

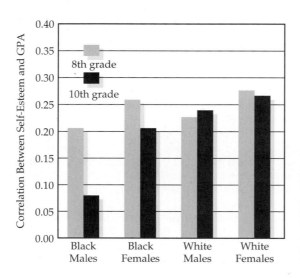

FIGURE 10.3

Changes in the Relationship Between Self-esteem and GPA for Black and White, Boys, and Girls. (Adapted from Osborne, J.W. [1995] Academics, self-esteem, and race: A look at the underlying assumptions of the disidentification hypothesis. *Personality and Social Psychology Bulletin, 21,* 449–455, Table 2, p. 454.

These studies, taken together, support the idea that psychological reactions to stereotypes may interfere with performance by members of stigmatized groups. It is important to understand how far this finding goes in explaining performance differences. But it is also important to figure out what mechanisms of adaptation accompany reactions to this stereotype threat that can sustain resilient coping outcomes. The threat of failure, prejudice, discrimination, or the imposition of a stereotypical evaluation can also lead one to work harder and more effectively to dispel or preempt the confirmation of the stereotype. That, too, is an important aspect of the reactions of stigma targets to their marginalized status.

It is also important to note that the disidentification process may have properties of the bifurcation of self, discussed earlier. That is, academic achievement is separated from self-identity. Academic success is therefore unrelated to psychological well-being. In the long run, this approach can, of course, be disastrous, as it imposes a significant limitation on life's chances for those who adopt it. Making the domain of academic performance less threatening and more nurturing is vital if students from stereotyped groups are to perform their best and if the disidentification process—that itself threatens psychological well-being in the long run—is to be short circuited.

The conclusion to be drawn from this research is that, in a societal context where intellectual inferiority is a basis of racial or gender stereotypes, when potentially stigmatized individuals are faced with situations in which the confirmation of those stereotypes is likely to occur, their levels of anxiety will be raised. This higher level of anxiety may then undermine performance so that these individuals perform at a level below their actual ability! The fact that racial and gender differences in performance disappeared when stereotype threat was removed supports this interpretation.

Attributional Ambiguity—Did I Do Badly or Are You a Racist?

The undergraduate students who take my "black psychology" course read autobiographical excerpts from African American writers of the twentieth century (Gates, 1991). The excerpts portray the difficulties of segregation, the fundamental unfairness of Jim Crow laws, and the strategies of coping. White students invariably conclude that, if they were in such situations, they would be angry and would have low self-esteem. Kardiner and Ovesy (1951, p. 81) themselves arrived at this conclusion, which they labeled the *"Mark of Oppression"* and described in these terms:

> The Negro, in contrast to the White, is a more unhappy person; he has a harder environment to live in, and the internal stress is greater. By "unhappy" we mean he enjoys less, he suffers more. There is not one personality trait of the Negro the source of which cannot be traced to his difficult living conditions. *There are no exceptions to this rule.* The final result is a wretched internal life.

Erik Erikson (1956) concluded that there is widespread support for the belief that feelings of inferiority and morbid self-hate exist in all minority groups. The widespread conclusion drawn from the famous doll studies of the Clarks (Clark and Clark, 1947, reviewed in Chapter 3) is that of African American self-hate. This theme is reflected in the studies finding that, although young African American children usually selected the brown doll when asked which one resembles them, well over half the time they selected the white dolls when choosing the one that was pretty, nice, or one that they would like to play with.

Crocker and Major (1989) draw our attention to the fact that although there is strong theoretical support for the assumption that belonging to a negatively stigmatized group will be causally linked to low self-esteem, there is scant empirical support for this stigma—self-esteem linkage.[2] They review data that suggests that blacks and Chicanos have self-esteem scores that equal or are higher than similar scores for whites. (Osborne, 1995, showed this also in his study on disidentification, discussed earlier.) Similarly, women do not show lower self-esteem than men do, nor are people who are physically unattractive, facially disfigured, learning disabled, homosexual, or juvenile delinquents lower in esteem than conventionally mainstream groups. Crocker and Major asked why?

Crocker and Major (1989) introduce the context of *attributional ambiguity* to explain why stigma may not lower self-esteem. Specifically, they suggest that when a stigmatized person receives negative evaluative feedback, or is insulted, or treated badly, the implication for self-worth may be ambiguous. It could be that the individual performed poorly and deserved the negative judgment, *or* it could be that the other person is simply letting personal prejudices color his or her judgments. If the *former* conclusion is reached by the target, then negative feedback may well lead to lowered self-esteem. If the *latter* is reached, however, the stigmatized person may *discount* the negative feedback by attributing it to the biases of the other person. In this case, self-esteem should be unaffected. In short, much of the analysis of the impact of oppression on black psychological well-being was not critical of the ability to separate out valid and invalid sources of judgment. Perceivable prejudice or racism renders evaluative judgments potentially invalid; hence, it reduces their relevance for assessment of the self.

One interesting implication of this analysis is that if the other's prejudice renders their evaluative judgment invalid, it should do so whether the judgment is positive or negative. Attributional ambiguity processes will thereby operate to the extent that either the other person is known to be prejudiced, or if it is suspected that he or she *may* be prejudiced, the extent to which prejudice *could* influence judgments or behaviors in a given context, either positively or negatively.

Attributional-ambiguity processes have been tested in three different studies using race and gender (Crocker, Voekl, Testa, and Major, 1991) and obesity (Crocker, Cornwell, and Major, 1993) as the stigma criteria. In a test of the race effect, black and white students were told that a white same-sex student thought he or she could or could not become friends with them. Each subject was led to believe that the other student either knew his or her race (the student was behind a one-way mirror and the blinds in front were up) or did not (the blinds were down). Crocker, Voekl, et al. (1994) reasoned that, when the blinds were up, subjects were in a state of attributional ambiguity. Therefore, any judgments made by the subject would potentially be affected by the other student's response to the subject's race. Results showed that, when the blinds were up, black students were more likely to attribute the other student's evaluations to race or prejudice. This tendency was greater when the evaluations were negative than when they were positive. Moreover, in general the subjects' measured self-esteem tended to decrease when there was negative feedback. However, this was not the case for black students when they could be seen by the evaluator.

---

[2] We should also note that Cross (1991) makes a similar point in his assessment of the literature on black self-hate theories. We will consider his alternatives in a later section of this chapter.

Crocker and Major (1989) argue that attributional ambiguity creates a predicament because it threatens one's self-esteem. This works in two ways: First, positive outcomes may be attributed to an evaluator's prejudice and not to personal merit. This ambiguity makes it difficult to "own" success! In the study just described (Crocker, Voekl, et al., 1991), self-esteem increased with positive feedback when the subject's race was *not* known (i.e., the blinds were down), but *decreased* when race was known. This result is not easy to explain. One possible explanation is that the ambiguity of positive feedback in such cases is disconcerting and that one cannot take it at face value may be frustrating.

Conversely, when negative judgments truly are biased, attributional ambiguity may nonetheless lead the target to accept the "possibility" that there is merit in the negative evaluation and, hence, put more credence in it than is warranted. This tendency was demonstrated by Ruggerio and Taylor (1995), who had women receive negative evaluations from a male whose perceived likelihood of being prejudiced was manipulated by the experimenters to be either very high (nearly 100%) or ambiguous (50%). Women attributed their evaluations to prejudice when it was very likely (nearly 100%). However, when the likelihood the evaluator was prejudiced was ambiguous, women tended to blame the negative evaluation more on the poor quality of their performance, and their self-esteem correspondingly declined. In short, striving for accurate self-appraisals is difficult under attributional-ambiguity conditions.

In a related finding, Ruggerio and Taylor (in press) showed that, when female subjects received negative evaluations from "sexist" men, their mood was unaffected. However, when they received negative evaluations from men whom they believed were "nonprejudiced", they showed more depressed affect. These two studies taken together support the idea that attributing negative judgments to characteristics of the evaluator does indeed serve a self-protective role for stigmatized people and could explain why the data do not strongly support the linkage of lowered self-appraisals and social stigma.

However, in a later study with overweight women, Crocker, Cornwell, and Major (1993) found that overweight women attributed rejection by attractive men to their weight and were correspondingly more depressed. Normal-weight women, by contrast, were more likely to attribute social rejection to characteristics of the rejecting male. Therefore, overweight women, unlike blacks (and women in general), do not attribute negative evaluations to external factors such as prejudice or discrimination. Rather, they internalize the blame for the negative judgment and suffer the emotional consequences. The differences have to do with two variables, *visibility* and *controllability*. All three groups—women, blacks, and the obese—have visible defining attributes. As a result, it is easy to attribute negative outcomes to the prejudice of the evaluator when the stigma condition is known. However, whereas gender and race are not controllable, most people believe that weight generally is. Therefore, one may well attribute the stigma to the self. The target may then feel responsible for the stigma and less easily project negative evaluations onto the other person (the evaluator). It seems, then, that the critical dimensions for producing the self-protective properties of attributional ambiguity are the two stigmatizing attributes of visibility and controllability.

But it may well be this self-protective function is successful when negative outcomes can be easily traced to biasing characteristics of the evaluator. When there is real ambiguity about the evaluator's motives or character, the threat or predicament may be greater, as we saw in the Ruggerio and Taylor (1995) study. The irony here is that, as we make progress in race, ethnic, and gender relations, the overt expressions of bias may lessen, but *ambiguity* about motivation and intention correspondingly increases. As a result, the self-protective processes of attributional ambiguity may be superseded by the negative consequences of such an ambiguous situation. That is, as has been said often in the black community, "I would rather know up front that someone is a bigot, than have to guess or infer it from subtle racist behavior." Maintaining a high level of mistrust can serve to unambiguously maintain one's awareness of the potential for biased judgments and, hence, maintain the self-protective properties of attributional ambiguity.

Just as members of dominant groups often suspect members of stigmatized groups of incompetence or wrong-doing, members of subordinate groups often suspect members of dominant groups of having a variety of biases, beginning with self-interest and behaviors geared to maintaining the in-group's cultural control. The next section of this chapter considers two models that emphasize psychological adaptations to white dominance and racial bias.

PSYCHOLOGICAL REACTIONS TO CULTURAL AND RACIAL DOMINANCE

When a person has suffered abuse over a long period of time, it is not surprising that he or she often becomes relatively untrusting of the abuser or abuser group. Victims of abuse become wary and vigilant. With vigilance comes a certain filter or screen that provides a ready interpretative system into which behaviors are fit. That is, a person whom you do not trust will validate one's mistrust by every untrustworthy act, and many acts of trustworthiness on his or her part will go unheeded. Every action that confirms a strongly held expectation is tallied as support for it, whereas acts that disconfirm it are quickly forgotten.[3]

This point can be illustrated with a joke: A turtle, a buzzard, and a pig were sitting around a campfire having a few beers and talking over old times. They discovered that they had left the basket with the food back at the house. So they drew straws to see who would go get it, and the turtle lost. He complained that he didn't want to go because, if he did, the other two would drink his beer. The other two gave him every assurance that they would not. He continued to protest until, finally, he agreed to go. After a few hours he was still not back, yet they waited, and no one touched his beer. They waited and waited until a few days, then weeks, had passed. Finally, after two months and no sign of the turtle, the pig finally said, "Well, it looks as if Turtle is not coming back," and he finally picked up the beer can and took a swig. At that moment, up popped the turtle, who proclaimed triumphantly, "See, I knew that if I went for the food you would drink my beer!"

Let's turn now to a formalization of this mistrusting tendency, the concept of cultural mistrust.

Cultural Mistrust

Terrell and Terrell (1981) reasoned that one of the persistent consequences of the cultural history of African Americans in the United States was mistrust of whites.

---

[3] There are, of course, always exceptions, as pointed out in Chapter 7. For example, stereotype disconfirming behavior may be quite salient or vivid and thus increase attention to and memory of it (cf. Stangor, Sullivan, and Ford, 1991). In general though, there is much evidence to support the salience-memory connection.

This *cultural mistrust* is pervasive. It applies to domains of work, economics, politics, education, and social relations. The level of distrust was captured in the Cultural Mistrust Inventory, CMI (Terrell and Terrell, 1981). The CMI, a 48-item scale, measures black respondents' trust for whites in four domains by asking them the degree to which they agree or disagree with statements related to each domain, as follows:

1   *Education and training*: "White teachers deliberately ask black students questions that are difficult so that the black students will fail."
2   *Interpersonal relations*: "It is best for blacks to be on their guard when among whites."
3   *Business and work*: "Whites who establish businesses in black communities do so only so that they can take advantage of blacks."
4   *Politics and law*: "Whites deliberately pass laws designed to block the progress of blacks."

Subjects respond to each of the items with a numerical value ranging from 0 (agree not in the least) to 9 (entirely agree). Items are scored so that the higher the composite score, the higher a subject's cultural mistrust level.

If a black person scores high on the CMI, what behaviors, on their part, are likely to be indicated? Nickerson, Helms, and Terrell (1994) examined the relationship among mistrust of whites, opinions about mental illness, and help-seeking attitudes among 105 black college students. Greater mistrust of whites was associated with more negative general attitudes about seeking help from clinics staffed primarily by whites and with an expectation that the services rendered by white counselors would be less satisfactory than those rendered by black counselors.

Terrell, Terrell, and Miller (1993) explored the relationship between black students' trust of whites and academic and occupational expectations. One hundred thirty-two black high school students (aged 12 to 15 years) were administered the Two-Factor Index of Social Position test and the CMI. Subjects were also asked to indicate which field they expected to enter and the educational level they expected to attain. No differences were found between educational expectations and level of mistrust. However, subjects with lower occupational expectations had higher levels of mistrust. This finding suggests that high levels of mistrust may have the net effect of reducing expectations for attainment as a result of disidentification processes.

Watkins, Terrell, Miller, and Terrell (1989) had college students rate the extent to which white and black college counselors could successfully advise students on a variety of student problems. In comparison to blacks who scored low on mistrust of whites, highly mistrustful blacks regarded the white counselors as less credible and less able to help them in four problem areas: general anxiety, shyness, inferiority feelings, and dating difficulties. This and earlier described findings strongly suggest that cultural mistrust of whites by blacks works to distance the latter physically, interpersonally, and emotionally from whites. Another finding illustrates how mistrust can lead to behaviors that may be self-defeating. Terrell, Terrell, and Taylor (1981) had 100 black college students who varied in their level of cultural mistrust take the Wechsler Adult Intelligence Scale (WAIS) from either a white or black male examiner. Figure 10.4 shows the results. Subjects who were high in cultural mistrust performed better when the examiner was black than when he was white. Conversely, subjects who scored low in cultural mistrust performed better when the examiner was white than when he was black. The latter finding may be

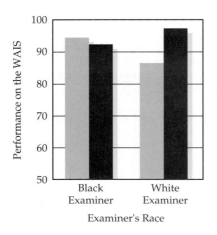

FIGURE 10.4

Test Performance as a Function of Cultural Mistrust and Race of the Examiner. (Adapted from Terrell, F., Terrell, S.L. & Taylor, J. [1981] Effects of race of examiner and cultural mistrust on the WAIS performance of black students. *Journal of Consulting and Clinical Psychology, 49*, 750–751.)

evidence for a disidentification effect. Perhaps the white tester signaled stereotype threat more to those high in cultural mistrust, and performance was undermined accordingly. Fordham and Ogbu (1986) have proposed that academic performance is associated with whites and performing well academically is therefore perceived by some as "acting white." This may be another aspect of disidentification and its relationship to poorer academic outcomes.

Therefore, the data seem to indicate that cultural mistrust is an individual difference with important implications for interracial, interpersonal interactions. To summarize, high levels of mistrust represent one source of adaptation to personal and collective experiences of discrimination, stereotyping, and disadvantage. It is important also to note that it is not necessary for an individual to have personal negative experiences with whites in order to develop high levels of mistrust. A high degree of mistrust could easily be an adaptation to the cultural portrayals and events seen regularly in the news, in movies and on television, or in neighborhood streets.

Crosby (1984) has shown that many individuals deny that they have ever personally been discriminated against. These same individuals will readily perceive that *other* members of their group have been discriminated against. Crosby showed that, in a sample of employees in the Boston area, matched on all relevant job characteristics (e.g., training, education, length of employment, attitudes, and job-prestige) they differed not at all in their perception of personal discrimination. Yet women, on average, earned $5,000 less per year than similarly situated men.

Crosby attributes this tendency not to perceive oneself as discriminated against when the evidence clearly shows that one's group is treated differently and more poorly than other groups to two processes: (1) *cognitive bias*—the difficulty of inferring bias from individual cases and (2) *avoiding villains*—the emotional discomfort experienced in confronting one's own victimization. With regard to the former, Crosby (1984) illustrates that when we look at the aggregate data, evidence of actual discrimination is abundantly clear. But, because individual cases can be "explained away," it is easy to sidestep in order to avoid blaming organizations for bias.

Taylor, Wright, Moghaddam, and Lalonde (1990) have labeled this tendency to perceive the discrimination toward others in one's group but to fail to perceive it against oneself as the *personal-group discrimination discrepancy* (PGDD). Studies have pointed out the general phenomenon by simply comparing subjects' responses to questions about the extent to which they have experienced discrimination in a given domain (say, housing, education, economics, or on the job) and the extent to which members of their group are likely to experience (or to have experienced) discrimination. The PGDD effect has been demonstrated in studies of women in Toronto who are South Asian or Haitian, black men in Miami, women undergraduates and nonuniversity women in Quebec, France, and immigrant women in Toronto from South Asia and Haiti, and Inuits in Arctic Quebec (cf. Taylor, Wright, and Porter, 1994). Based on some experimental evidence, Taylor, Wright, and Porter (1994) suggest that the PGDD effect is greatest for individuals who separate themselves from their group. That is, low social-group identity may be a mechanism that allows one to protect oneself from the perception of personal discrimination. When this is done, such individuals, although they may perceive widespread bias against others in their group, may tend to believe that their own efforts will be greeted with fair and honest appraisal. This may confer upon them a degree of control and psychological immunity from prejudice and discrimination. But, as Crosby showed, this "protection" may also blind them to the reality of the bias to be faced.

The cultural-mistrust mechanism serves to maintain a target's group-based identification. Therefore, the perception of group-related experiences will be personalized. The beating of Rodney King is a good example. Although many people, black and white, were outraged by the video footage of the beating, blacks were perhaps more likely to place this event in the context of a pattern of abuse, oppression, and discrimination, and were more likely to count it as evidence that whites cannot be trusted. Whites, on the other hand, were perhaps more likely to see it as an isolated, though outrageous, event. When such events occur, blacks and other stigmatized groups will more likely generalize such events to whites in general. Mistrust can be self-protective because it prepares a vulnerable person to make self-protective reactions or to avoid situations in which vulnerability is increased. The broader consequence of this adaptation strategy is that, as mistrust increases, chances of intergroup harmony or cooperation decrease.

African Self-Consciousness (ASC)

Whereas cultural mistrust of whites focuses blacks' attention on the negative expectancies regarding others who are not members of one's own group, another mechanism, *African self-consciousness*, or ASC (Baldwin and Bell, 1985, p. 62), ". . . affirms African American life and the authenticity of its African cultural heritage." African self-consciousness is described by attitudes and behaviors that comprise four attitude-behavior dimensions. A 42-item questionnaire has been designed that assesses a subject's standing on the ASC. Below are descriptions of the four dimensions and a sample item for each.

1   *Awareness-recognition*—Affirms black identity and African cultural heritage.

Sample: "Blacks born in the United States are black or African first, rather than American or just plain people."

2   *Establishment of survival priorities*—Recognizes survival of blacks as a priority and values the role institutions play in achieving that.
Sample: "Black people should have their own independent schools that consider their African heritage and values an important part of the curriculum."

3   *Self-knowledge–affirmation*—Supports active participation in behaviors that promote the survival and liberation of black people and active defense of their dignity and integrity.
Sample: "Racial consciousness and cultural awareness based on traditional African values are necessary to the development of Black marriages and families that can contribute to the liberation and enhancement of Black people in America."

4   *Resistance to oppression*—Recognizes racial oppression as an obstruction to meeting the action goals described above.
Sample: "White people, generally speaking, do not respect black life."

The critical constructs of the ASC rest on a cumulative perspective on racial oppression and prejudice in the United States. The ideas that black Americans and their African cultural heritage are devalued, that whites obstruct black progress and have, over time, obscured knowledge of African culture that would serve as a source of pride and a foundation for positive action for African Americans is a starting point for African self-consciousness. ASC shares with CMI the premise of the basic untrustworthiness of whites. But its most important role is as a mechanism that may enhance positive self-esteem. African Americans (and, by extension, members of other stigmatized groups) can gain personal esteem by attaching positive values to their group. The ASC describes one set of attitudes and beliefs that address simultaneously issues of prejudice, discrimination, and racism, *and* a mechanism of adaptation by which one can achieve personal feelings of control, value, and validity.

The ASC is believed to be responsive to affirming cultural experiences. That is, blacks from more African-affirming environments will have higher ASC scores. Correlational research shows connections between subjects' ASC scores and their parents' membership in black organizations (Baldwin, Brown, and Rackley, 1991), Afrocentric values in heterosexual relationships (Bell, Bouie, and Baldwin, 1990), and attendance at a historically black institution (Baldwin, Duncan, and Bell, 1987). Stokes, Murray, Peacock, and Kaiser (1994) found factor-analytic support for the four-dimensional structure of the ASC. The authors conclude that the ASC structure could be separated into four factors that roughly paralleled the four competency domains outlined above: (1) personal identification with the group, (2) self-reinforcement against racism, (3) racial and cultural awareness, and (4) value for African culture. ASC, then, serves to provide a self-protective world view that connects the self to the group, distances the individual from hostile out-groups, and promotes the in-group as a positive source of well-being.

High scores for these factors, combined with the overall lack of trust demonstrated by a high CMI, may somewhat explain the observation that blacks, more than whites, tend to believe in conspiracy theories as an explanation for unequal black status. Crocker, Broadnax, Luhtanen, and Blaine (1996) tested the hypothesis that belief in conspiracies could, in fact, result from a strengthening of group consciousness, rather than a heightened sense of powerlessness and external control ideology. They had 91 black and 96 white college students indicate their agreement with beliefs about a U.S. government conspiracy to hold blacks back. Sample items include the following

- Some people say the government deliberately singles out and investigates black elected officials in order to discredit them in a way that it doesn't do with white officials.
- Some people say black people are encouraged to use birth control in order to keep the number of black people small.
- Some people say doctors are deliberately infecting black babies with AIDS in order to kill off black people.
- Some people say the government deliberately makes sure that drugs are available in poor black neighborhoods in order to harm black people.

Responses to 13 conspiracy beliefs were summed to create a composite indication of belief in conspiracies against blacks. Measures of group consciousness were obtained from the Collective Self-Esteem Scale (Luhtanen and Crocker, 1992). Additionally, measures of powerlessness, externality attributions and psychological well-being (e.g., self-esteem, life satisfaction, depression, and hopelessness) were obtained.

Although belief in conspiracies against blacks was correlated with externality of attributions, group consciousness, for blacks, bore a stronger association to conspiracy beliefs than for whites. Moreover, belief in conspiracies was positively related to personal self-esteem and to racial group membership esteem for blacks, but negatively related to each of these measures for whites. In a somewhat surprising finding, belief in conspiracies was strongly related to racial identification for *both* black and white students. Because racial identification is high and self-esteem low in whites who believe in conspiracy theories, it is possible that greater identification with other whites, as well as belief in conspiracies, leads them to feel some degree of guilt, thereby lowering their personal esteem. For blacks, perhaps it is a kind of group defiance that confers positive esteem on those who believe in conspiracies and strongly identify with other blacks as a racial group. This linkage is precisely what the ASC pattern proposes as an indicator of positive mental health for African Americans.

One can see that both high ASC and CMI levels will increase the likelihood of attitudinal and behavioral withdrawal from interracial contexts. This withdrawal may be psychological or physical, rejecting or ignoring. In the past, sociopsychological models of prejudice did not pay much attention to the reactions of stigmatized targets. When they did, it was always from the assumption that the targets were harmed by prejudice in the form of feelings of diminished self-worth. Psychologists—and black psychologists, in particular—have begun to capture the spirit of the black revolution of the 1960s in the form of heightened self-worth and a corresponding reluctance to embrace generic cultural standards of acceptability that are biased toward white racial norms. Problems of prejudice—and ways of reducing its worst consequences—will have to be considered by examining both the adaptations of its targets, and the motives and beliefs of those who are its perpetrators. We will consider this dynamic further in chapter 11.

Let's turn now the generalized models of adaptation to being different in ways that place one at the margin between societies. Analysis of the resulting marginalization phenomenon provides another way of identifying the distinctions that may prompt bifurcation of self. The next section considers some models of such adaptation and some individual psychological consequences.

ADAPTING TO PSYCHOLOGICAL MARGINALIZATION

The discussions of the psychological mechanisms of, and adaptations to, prejudice and racism discussed so far all began with the premise of the predicament of prejudice and the *marginalization* of its targets. That is, when one is a target for prejudice, negative stereotyping, or stigma, one's position within the dominant society is marginalized, or lessened. How one adjusts to that marginalized status can be an important personal, as well as collective, decision. Moreover, the experiences one has as a marginalized person may well be quite different from those who can take their belongingness for granted. This section will look at two categories of marginalization processes—bicultural adaptation models (LaFromboise, Coleman, and Gerton, 1993) and master-status effects (Frable, Blackstone, and Sherbaum, 1990).

Bicultural Adaptation

We all belong to groups—often to many of them. We may play in the orchestra, serve on the student council, belong to a fraternity or sorority, be a member of a group such as Psi Chi, belong to a church, be a woman. A culture is more than a group. Cultures have definable values, beliefs, histories, and usually, physical or intellectual products (e.g., art, stories, language, symbols), and words, behavior, gestures, have meanings that may be unique to some configuration of these qualities in a given culture. (We will focus more specifically on culture in Chapter 15.)

Cultures may vary in scope, influence, size, and character; for example, they may be adjacent to another (e.g., those of the United States and of Mexico) or some may be embedded in others (e.g., American Indian cultures within the United States). When one or more cultures are embedded within another, it is very likely that members of the embedded cultures or *subcultures*, will have to function within the broader patterns of the surrounding cultures, or *superculture*. One belongs to two cultures and is thus *bicultural*.

Very often, the superculture controls important resources and opportunities. People must therefore function within specific rules in order to gain access to these benefits. The patterns of behavior, reward structures, values, and adaptational challenges that exist within a subculture may be different from those existing in the superculture. These differences can be a source of strain for people who live a bicultural life. One illustration of this strain is offered by the contrast of being a person of color in the white majority superculture of the United States and the reactions (often negative) it may elicit. Bicultural (or multicultural) people are frequently derisively labeled with the supercultural label of "white on the inside," and their indigenous or birth culture is referred to as the "outer shell." They may be termed, therefore, "black" on the outside and "white" on the inside ("Oreo cookie"); yellow on the outside makes one a "banana"; red on the outside makes one an "apple"; and brown on the outside makes one a "coconut." One's loyalty, commitment, and identity are challenged by this culturally perceived dualism.

Because prejudice and racism have created a cumulative mistrust of whites, and of white institutions, values, and beliefs on the part of nonwhites, a tension is created for people in marginalized groups. If one *embraces* the superculture, one may be suspected of "sleeping with the enemy," "acting white," or "going Anglo," for example. If one *rejects* the superculture, refusing to engage in meaningful interaction, one is at risk of limiting one's access to, possibilities within, and opportunities to achieve and advance in the broader society. The central challenge of bicultural adaptation is to maintain loyalty and connection to one's culture of origin, while also participating in a personally meaningful way in the broader society.

This situation, which I call the *duality dilemma* (cf, Jones, 1994), is addressed by LaFromboise, Coleman, and Gerton (1993) in terms of *cultural competence*—that is, the degree to which a person masters the important behaviors established by a culture or subculture to maintain communication, values and norms, attitudes, and beliefs that perpetuate the culture and enhance its organization and function. They suggest that in order for a person to be culturally competent, he or she must exhibit the following traits (LaFromboise, Coleman, and Gerton, 1993)

1   Possess a strong personal identity
2   Have knowledge of and facility with each culture's beliefs and values
3   Display sensitivity to the affective processes
4   Communicate clearly in the language of the given culture
5   Perform socially sanctioned behavior
6   Maintain active social relations within the group
7   Negotiate the institutional structures

If a person is bicultural, he or she would have to be competent in all of these ways in two different cultures that may be in conflict with regard to the competencies they require. For example, a person may speak fluent English but be unable to converse with elders who speak only Chinese. One may have a strong personal identity as a businesswoman that is at odds with one's other cultural identities or roles, say, as a wife and mother. A child of a subculture may be raised to be cooperative, deferent to adults, and collectivistic, only to find that, at school, activities reward competitiveness, assertiveness, and individualism (values of the superculture). One may find that social relations that aid one's professional life take one away from social contacts that keep one centered in one's other cultural life. There are many sources of conflict in this bicultural model.

LaFromboise, Coleman, and Gerton (1993) suggest five models by which a person may acquire competence in a second culture: (1) assimilation, (2) acculturation, (3) alternation, (4) multiculturalism, and (5) fusion. Each model has implications for the resulting relationships between the cultures. Following are brief descriptions of each model.

Assimilation
LaFromboise, Coleman, and Gerton (1993, p. 396) describe *assimilation* as ". . . an ongoing process of absorption into the culture that is perceived as dominant or more desirable." To be assimilated means to acquire the full range of competencies of the new culture, and to be accepted into that culture, and to be treated as if one belonged. Implicit in the assimilation model is the idea that one loses contact with the culture of origin and only thereby gains full acceptance into the new culture.

These requirements for assimilation create stress and anxiety as one loses support from the culture of origin and often fails, at least initially, to gain full access to and acceptance from the new culture. Some may question whether full acceptance is ever possible, arguing that adoption of the assimilation strategy for second-culture acquisition may doom a person to a life of anxiety and uncertainty. The person may find himself or herself caught in-between the two cultures. Marginalization has been associated with negative well-being among Ojibwa Indians by Kerchoff and McCormick (1955), for example, who found those Ojibwa with the strongest inclination to identify with the dominant group had the lowest self-esteem, fewer social relations, and more negative emotions when they faced rejection by that group.

Therefore, assimilation is stressful to the extent that it is incomplete or unattainable because of the marginalized persons ultimate rejection by the dominant culture—that is, it is stressful when it doesn't work. "Successful" assimilation, though, has been shown to have positive benefits by Miller (1990), who found that (in the context of racial relations) adopting an integration ideology, for example, that included commitment to the school, interracial friendships and attraction, and being a "model student," all improved the adaptation of black children who were being bused to predominately white schools. But, in the main, assimilation as a bicultural adaptation strategy has been shown to generate more stress and anxiety than it relieves.

Acculturation

As is often true of the assimilation model, the *acculturation* model assumes that the acculturated individual, ". . . while becoming a competent participant in the majority culture, will always be identified as a member of the minority culture (LaFromboise, Coleman, and Gerton, 1993, p. 397). Acculturation may be thought of as a prerequisite for participation in mainstream society. For example, the "melting pot" notion was basically an acculturation scheme that set out those standards of cultural competence one had to master in order to participate in society. These "competencies" were not about skills so much as attitudes, values, and images. Names, hairstyles, language habits, and dress were aspects of culture one had to master. The acculturation model's typical view of intercultural relationships as unindirectional and hierarchical often puts a bicultural person in an either/or situation, a cultural bifurcation dilemma.

A large body of research has shown that, the more completely one is acculturated, the less contact one maintains with and endorsement of one's culture of origin. For example, Goldlust and Richmond (1974), in a study of residents of Toronto, from a variety of ethnic groups, found that length of stay and level of education had the strongest influence on one's acculturation in the city, and had a negative influence on subjects' primary identification with the culture of origin. Although acculturation is usually seen as a zero-sum cultural conflict, most acculturation theorists propose multiple models of acculturation. Different models stress different domains of culture as those that acculturation can emphasize. For example, Szapocznik and his colleagues (e.g., Szapocznik, Scopetta, Kurtines, and Arandale, 1978; Szapocznik, Rio, Perez-Vidal, Kurtines, Hervis, and Santisteban, 1986) argue that acculturation proceeds in stages, with the acculturating person first acquiring the behaviors needed in order to survive, then adopting the supporting cultural values. Once one has successfully learned the approved behaviors, one can "get along" in the larger culture. Adopting the supercultures values may be the final step to fitting in. It is this last step that creates the biggest conflict in acculturative processes.

High levels of acculturation have also been associated with reduced levels of cultural mistrust. Atkinson and Gim (1989) used the Suinn-Lew Asian Self-Identity Acculturation Scale and the Attitudes toward Seeking Professional Psychological Help Scale to test acculturation and adaptation of 557 Asian-American students, including Chinese, Japanese, and Korean Americans. They found that the most highly acculturated students were those (1) most likely to recognize a personal need for professional psychological help, (2) most tolerant of the stigma associated with psychological help, and (3) most open to discussing their problems with a psychologist. This contrasts with the CMI result, which showed that high-CMI scorers were reluctant to go to white or Anglo therapists, and that, when they did so, they were likely to terminate treatment prematurely.

Acculturation models tend to explicitly pit acquisition of the values of, and competence in, the dominant culture against maintaining loyalty to the culture of origin (cf. Olmedo and Padilla, 1978). The greater the degree of acculturation, the greater the intergroup contact, the less the intergroup distance, and the ties to weaker the subcultural heritage and ethnic pride and identity. Acculturation, therefore, becomes a "political" issue to the extent that is viewed on a continuum ranging from *ours* to *theirs*, such that the closer one gets to "theirs," the farther one is from "ours"! This basic view is implicit in the Acculturation Scale of Landrine and Klonoff (1994; 1995), which consists of five dimensions of cultural knowledge and preference regarding African Americans. High scores on this scale demonstrate stronger ties to African American culture. Acculturation is implicated in individual racial or ethnic identity, as well. We will revisit some of these issues later in this chapter.

Alternation

The *alternation model* assumes ". . . that it is possible for an individual to know and understand two different cultures . . . [and] can alter his or her behavior to fit a particular social context" (LaFromboise, Coleman, and Gerton, 1993, p. 399). This model is most similar to the *bilingualism* model, in which one's success is predicated on the ability to speak two different languages fluently and the ability to converse competently in each as the situation or the mood demands. The great advantage of the alternation approach is that it breaks the negative relationship between two cultures by severing the either/or continuum. In this model, we have "orthogonal" cultural dimensions, the acquisitions of which are independent. In the alternation approach, one can maintain one's culture of origin, master a second culture (even a dominant one), and maintain them both over one's lifetime. Culture acquisition is therefore bidirectional and need not be hierarchical. It is this version of biculturalism that LaFromboise, Coleman, and Gerton (1993) endorse, and that offers the best opportunity to fulfill the twin demands of "belonging" and "uniqueness" (cf. Brewer, 1991) at the cultural level.

The alternation model is implicit in many approaches to schooling. Sunday schools, Hebrew schools, African Rites of Passage training programs, and modern reservation schools and Tribal Colleges all offer opportunities to obtain alternate, culture-specific training as a means of balancing the strongly acculturative tendencies of mainstream education.

Multiculturalism

The *multiculturalism* model emphasizes the distinctiveness of the two (or more) cultures and requires ". . . maintaining distinct identities while individuals from one culture work with those of other cultures to serve common national or economic needs (LaFromboise, Coleman, and Gerton, 1993, p. 401). Berry (1984) has argued persuasively for the multicultural model based on his view that four choices are available to individuals who live in pluralistic or diverse societies: assimilate, integrate, separate, or marginalize. Which of these choices one makes will depend on the relative importance of (1) maintaining one's culture of origin and (2) one's willingness to engage in intergroup contact. Berry argues that integration is the best approach to multiculturalism, because it allows individuals and groups to participate in common cause with others, and also to embrace and sustain their own cultural identities. The multiculturalism model is quite similar to the alternation model, but the former assumes a level of power sharing that gives different groups equal input to and control over societal processes. If power is unequal across groups, the conditions for mutual interaction may selectively favor members of one group over others.

The question of diversity is related to multiculturalism in ways that we are still trying to figure out. Some view multiculturalism as a "sneak attack" by marginal groups who seek to wrest resources from the dominant group. Achieving multiculturalism is not as simple as it sounds, and integration may be a theoretically desirable, but practically unattainable, goal.

Fusion

The *fusion model* ". . . represents the assumptions behind the melting pot theory . . . that cultures sharing an economic, political, or geographic space will fuse together until they are indistinguishable to form a new culture (LaFromboise, Coleman, and Gerton, 1993, p. 401). The ideal result of cultural pluralism is a new culture—a synthesis of the contributing elements to make a stronger, more representative whole. In this fused culture, group distinctions will have evaporated and the whole will take on many traits of those contributing the most influential and successful characteristics. In this view, a person should assimilate, knowing that the resultant culture will treat him or her as it treats every other person. For example, the colorblind concept is a fusion principle in which individuals, taken as whole, constitute the culture. In a colorblind society, whatever group distinctions one might make are subservient to the whole culture and the legitimate place each individual has in it.

These five models spell out some of the specific alternatives a person who comes from a marginalized subculture may consider in determining the best way to gain access to the resources and opportunities contained in the superculture. These alternatives may not be exhaustive and the degree of choice may be exaggerated. The important point to note, though, is that the American dream is not available for the mere taking. There are costs associated with participating in U.S. society and in setting goals that one hopes to meet. A change of social identity may be involved, and this potential source of strength and psychological well-being, as we have seen in previous chapters, is not always so easily embraced by marginalized groups.

To illustrate the complexity of adapting a successful strategy against marginalization Gurin, Hurtado, and Peng (1994) tested the idea that bicultural adaptation may follow either (1) a social mobility pathway that involves cognitive, affective, and behavioral processes that help a member exit from a disparaged group and identify with a more powerful group, perhaps even "passing" into it or (2) a social change pathway that, albeit involves cognitive, affective, and behavioral processes, is used primarily to shift the bases of comparison so that the disparaged group becomes superior, the meanings of attributes that have been disparaged become positive, and collective action for positive social change is valued. In this study, two distinctly different social identities were conceived and assessed in face-to-face structured interviews of two populations of adults of Mexican ancestry—those labeled "Mexicanos" (i.e., those born in Mexico and who chose Spanish for the interview) and Chicanos (i.e., those born in the United States and who chose English for the interview).

Mexicanos were more class conscious (e.g., middle-class is viewed as separate from working class) and were more attached to a broader sense of binational identity (i.e., both Mexican and Latin American), as well as a sense of Mexican American identity. Chicanos, by contrast, tended to have more complex identities, distinguishing farmworker from working class from middle class. Chicanos also tended to have a social change ideology, for example, as evidenced by embracing the "political *Raza*" concept as a means of endorsement of the pride of being Chicano and the political leverage that embracing the term entails. Latino attributes were transformed by Chicanos to positive ethnic labels and reflected unique experiences of political activity in the United States. Contact with Anglos was associated with middle-class status for Mexicanos, but with working-class status for Chicanos. Chicanos were also more likely to have contact with other ethnic groups—again, supporting the *political Raza* tendency of Chicanos in contrast to the pan *Raza* tendency of Mexicanos.

This study demonstrated how acculturative patterns, bicultural strategies for acquiring second cultures, and the politics of social identity all come into play in dealing with marginalization. We are only beginning to understand these dynamics in psychological terms. We will likely learn a great deal about the psychological processes of racial, ethnic, and cultural diversity by focusing our theoretical and empirical attention on problems of bicultural adaptation.

Psychological Marginalization

Targets of prejudice are very often marginalized in the United States. In a hypothetical, unbiased, colorblind society, we would treat people as if their color didn't matter, their race didn't matter, nor would other out-group membership matter. However, in our society as it exists, differences often do matter. If one is a homosexual teacher, one may not be allowed to teach. If one is a woman, one may not be allowed to tee off at a country club before noon. The marginalized live in two worlds—their lives are often arbitrarily restricted in one, but not in the other. What is the basis of the restriction? Usually, it is some *status* criterion. Skin color, gender, sightedness, ethnic or racial heritage, attractiveness, athletic skill, musical ability, and so forth. Marginalization is not limited to the disenfranchised.

A poignant example of marginalization was presented earlier in the exchange between Jesse Jackson and Marvin Kalb. People become marginalized when they live in two different worlds and their standing in one world is different from their standing in the other. For example, an American Indian living his whole life on a reservation lives in a single cultural context. But when he moves to the city, he now takes his cultural context with him, but enters a new world where he is no longer perceived in the way he once was on the reservation.

The characteristics that form the basis for marginality are termed *master statuses* by Frable, Blackstone, and Sherbaum (1990). According to Frable (1993b, p. 370) "By virtue of their physical appearance, behavior, or life circumstance, *master status* people are continually treated different. They belong to a social group that is *both statistically unusual and centrally defining.*" Because it is centrally defining, a master status cannot be ignored and often serves to define the essential character of

TABLE 10.1 MASTER-STATUS TYPES AS A FUNCTION OF VISIBILITY AND ACCEPTANCE OF STATUS DETERMINANTS

	Master-Status Acceptance	
Master Status Visibility	*Culturally Valued*	*Culturally Stigmatized*
Conspicuous	Physically attractive	Black Obese Facially scarred
Concealable	Intellectually gifted Wealthy	Gay or lesbian Rape or incest survivor

SOURCE: Frable, D.E.S. (1993a). Being and feeling unique: Statistical deviance and psychological marginality. *Journal of Personality, 61*, 85–110.

the person who is so classified. Master statuses typically vary in how they are evaluated (i.e., culturally valued versus culturally stigmatized) and the degree to which the status itself is visible (i.e., conspicuous or inconspicuous). Table 10.1 gives examples of groups to which people belong and whose acceptance levels vary along these visibility and evaluative dimensions.

Frable (1993a) argues that the effects of marginalization will vary, depending on the degree of visibility and the evaluation of the status. Specifically, she suggests that

1   Persons whose master status is concealable will be less inclined to share their status with others, will tend to underestimate the number of people who do share their status, and, therefore, will have an elevated sense of their own uniqueness. Consequently, they will be less likely to perceive others' opinions and values as similar to their own.
2   Persons whose master status is culturally valued will be sought out by others and rewarded for their status attributes. However, when a person's master status is both concealable and stigmatized, he or she will not be sought out and will not be rewarded.

Frable (1993a) argues that, as a result, persons with concealable and culturally stigmatized master statuses will tend to be socially isolated and to feel uniquely different from others. To test this idea, she had subjects from stigmatized, "invisible" groups (gay and hearing impaired) and stigmatized "visible" groups (black and obese), as well as nonmarginal student control subjects, fill out two questionnaires. The experimenters first asked the subjects to state their preference between two pairs of activities (e.g., watching gymnastics or track; eating ham or egg salad; naming a daughter Jennifer or Allison). Subjects indicated their personal preference and then estimated the percentage of university students of their age who would agree with their choice. The researchers next asked subjects to rate the degree of concern they felt over seven different issues (e.g., making new friends, finding a satisfactory romantic relationship, academic success, having enough money). Subjects then indicated their best guess of the percentage of undergraduates who would express the same degree of concern for each issue. The more similar subjects felt others would be to themselves, the less personal uniqueness they were assumed to feel and the greater the likelihood of consensus.

Results showed that the degree of consensus felt by subjects was as predicted by Frable, least for those having marginalized, concealable, and stigmatized master status (i.e., gays and hearing-impaired). Subjects from stigmatized visible groups (blacks and the obese) felt others' opinions would be much more similar to their own judgments. The results for the nonmarginal control subjects were most similar to those for the black and the obese subjects.

In a second study, subjects were divided into the four group status classifications shown in Table 10.1: positively valued and visible (physically attractive), positively valued and invisible (e.g., wealthy, intelligent, or athletic), stigmatized and visible (e.g., black, Hispanic, obese, or those with medically debilitating conditions), and stigmatized and invisible (e.g., gays, rape or incest survivors, juvenile delinquents, or those with unconcealable medical conditions such as diabetes and epilepsy). Subjects were shown 26 personal characteristics one at a time via a computer. The subjects had to make a judgment of the extent to which each of the 26 characteristics was more like themselves than a hypothetical average other student by pressing a button marked "me"; or more like the other student by pressing a button marked "not me." Results showed that subjects with invisible stigmas were more likely to pick the *me* button if the words themselves suggested uniqueness (e.g., rare, different, outsider) than when the words suggested similarity (e.g., normal, typical, commonplace). For subjects with a visible stigmatized status, and with all control subjects, the *me* button was pressed most frequently in response to the similarity words. This finding, then, suggests that invisible stigmatizing status is associated with heightened feelings of uniqueness and isolation, but visible stigmas are not. When one's stigma is visible, perhaps the heightened feeling of similarity helps to minimize the stigmatizing differences. When it is invisible, the fact that it is suppressed may add to the feeling of isolation. Either way, negative stigmas can lead to a psychological marginalization that does not promote positive feelings of self.

What do these findings mean? The good news is that, if you have a master status that is visible albeit stigmatizing, that visibility can serve to create a common ground that links you to others who are similar to you, and even to others who are not. This suggests that, in a society where difference is so often stigmatizing, identification of others who share one's status can be a source of social and emotional support. It can relieve feelings of aloneness and isolation. For example, on college campuses, belonging to a minority status group that is centrally defining can propel students to seek out similar others as a buffer or protection against potential negative feelings of isolation.

What about those with invisible stigmatizing status? These findings suggest that such a person would do well to seek out others who share his or her group status and, thereby, through public acknowledgment, make that status visible and enable it to serve as a basis for group cohesion. The bottom line of this work is that either marginality can be a source of isolation and negative experience, or it can be a basis for joining similar others in a positive expression of similarity. We must note, however, that the "politics of difference" (cf. S. Steele, 1990) concept suggests that group identification increases conflict on campuses. The work on marginality does not dispute that conclusion. However, it suggests, in addition, that group identification can also reduce feelings of marginality and produce a greater degree of psychological health for stigmatized groups.

*I*DENTITY STRUCTURES AND PROCESSES: COPING WITH STIGMA

One's racial and ethnic identity is shaped in part by one's adaptations to the predicaments of prejudice. This adaptation may be conscious—as in choosing a particular style of dress, one's cohorts or friends, one's attitudes toward schooling, career, values, and so forth. Or it may be reflected in the more or less automatic cumulative experiences of, say, being a person of color in the United States. One's racial or ethnic identity may dictate the relative closeness one feels toward other members of one's own group or the amount of contact one has with members of other groups. Racial, ethnic, and other group-based identity may also follow a *reactive* course of development (i.e., responsive to stigmatizing and marginalizing societal forces) or *evolutionary* dynamics by which cultural templates guide the formation of preferred patterns of behavior, thought, speech, values and attitudes, interpersonal style, and familial organization (cf. Jones, 1988; 1992).

Because the politics of prejudice and adaptations to it by targeted group members are a driving force in our psychological theorizing and research, the reactionary mode of racial identity development dominates our attention. Therefore, racial and ethnic identity are conceived in a problem context. How is it that one can and does develop positive personal identity structures that incorporate group position and affiliation when those group positions and affiliations are devalued by mainstream society? What are those structures, how do they work, and what evidence is there that they aid in the coping process?

Racial Identity

Racial identity describes a set of race-related adaptations to the sociopolitical and cultural constructions of race in our society (cf. Helms, 1995). All groups that can be described by racial labels, or as *socioracial groups*, can be characterized by their racialized adaptations and socializations. Simply put, who one is depends, in part, on what racial group one belongs to, what sociopolitical position that group has in society, and how one is socialized within that group and in relation to other groups. Adult identity is a cumulative consequence of cognitive, emotional, and behavioral processes throughout the lifespan. Racial identities diverge as a result of one's group experience and of the manner in which one internalizes aspects of one's own experience.

Most models of racial identity assume that ". . . overcoming internalized societal racial stereotypes and negative self- and own-group conceptions" (Helms, 1995, p. 189) is central to racial identity development. Racial identity models look at the adaptations of targets of prejudice and negative stereotyping, and beyond, to their status in society. They also look at the adaptations and sustaining properties of identity development of those who enjoy advantage and are typically the perpetrators of prejudice.[4]

Cross (1971) formulated a model of black racial identity development and internalization-commitment consisting of five stages: preencounter, encounter, immersion-emersion, and internalization (see Chapter 4 for a more complete discussion). The model was conceived to show a process of *nigresence,* or "becoming

---

[4] We will not be discussing white identity here. However a growing body of work has conceptualized the mental, emotional, and behavioral correlates of whiteness (cf. Fine, Weis, Powell, and Won [in press]; Jones and Carter [1996]; Rowe, Beherns, and Leach [1995]).

black," by which one evolved from a worldview that downplayed race and played up other aspects of experience (e.g., religion, work status, and social class) to one that encompassed one's race and made it central to one's sense of self and psychological well-being. In a refinement and update of his nigresence theory, Cross (1995) describes the stages in these terms:

1 *Preencounter*. The *preencounter stage* is characterized by the low salience of race, internalization of social stigma—and, possibly, of antiblack attitudes—miseducation about Western and African civilization, the acceptance of a Eurocentric worldview, and a tendency toward assimilationist strategies for personal development.

2 *Encounter*. The *encounter stage* consists of a series of events or encounters that "chip away" at the preencounter worldview. The encounters, or eye-opening events, are ultimately personalized and may lead to confusion, anomie, guilt, or anger. The person begins a metamorphosis, fueled by this personalized change in worldview, that propels him or her onward to the next stage.

3 *Immersion-emersion*. The *immersion-emersion* is a transition stage. In the beginning, the person is immersed in this new and wonderful world of blackness and all of its expressions in political, psychological, and cultural terms. Whereas race was avoided or downplayed in the encounter stage, it is the center of identity now. A degree of anxiety (what Cross calls *weusi* anxiety) accompanies this metamorphosis as a result of the purity with which blackness is embraced.[5] (Am I "black enough?") That anxiety eventually becomes too much, as the absolutist nature of the immersion is too confining and impossible to maintain over a long time period. The person thus emerges from this total immersion in blackness to seek more balance, more openness, a less confining strategy for internalizing blackness. The old and new identities are in conflict, and this transition stage may recycle itself until the person gains the clarity to move forward to the next stage.

4 *Internalization*. The preceding transitional stage is internalized in a new identity that is characterized by what Cross termed *weusi* pride (black pride) and self-acceptance (black self-acceptance). Public self-consciousness based on concerns about others' perceptions is replaced by inner self-confidence and personal standards of conduct and belief, in this *internalization* stage. Previous conflicts about racial identity are resolved, and the conflict over blackness and Americanness is settled in a bicultural adaptation characterized by (1) awareness that racism is part of U.S. society; (2) one may at any time be victimized by racism; (3) a developed set of ego-defenses to help one manage the occurrence of a racist episode; (4) a system-blame–personal-efficacy orientation that enables one to deflect hostile acts and judgments from the self; and (5) a religiousness that mutes anger, hostility, and the tendency to *demonize* whites.

5 *Internalization-commitment*. This fifth stage establishes a permanent commitment to blacks and the incorporation of this commitment in the lifelong activities and choices one makes. It is this final integration of the breadth of biculturalism with the primary identification with and commitment to one's racial group.

Helms (1995) has recently refined her racial identity development model (Helms, 1990), derived in part from the Cross model. It now describes *statuses* instead of

---

[5] *Weusi* means black in Swahili. Cross refers to weusi anxiety as the concern one has with whether an individual has adopted a black enough identity. This anxiety can be reduced through performance (acting in a manner that verifies one's blackness through dress, speech, attitude, etc.) and conformity (to norms established by the community of other blacks who exemplify a positive black identity).

stages. Thereby, Helms focuses attention on the interactive themes of different periods in one's life, one's ego-related development, and characteristic cognitive processes at each period. Helms's revised model consists of five statuses:

1 *Conformity (preencounter)*. *Conformity status* is evidenced by external self-definition that implies devaluing one's own group and accepting white standards of merit. In some cases, insisting on a multiracial identification or ethnic categorization may be seen as a subtle way to avoid racial group identification if the racial group is being stigmatized. There is often a tendency toward selective perception and "obliviousness" to socioracial concerns.

2 *Dissonance (encounter)*. The *dissonance (encounter)* state characterized by ambivalence and confusion concerning one's socioracial group, a loss of perspective and clarity, and marginalization between a failed assimilationist strategy and rejection of one's own group. There is also often a tendency to repress anxiety-provoking racial information.

3 *Immersion-emersion*. The *immersion-emersion* state is characterized by idealization of one's own racial group and denigration of whites and all that is associated with them. One's own group serves as a reference point for external definitions and as a basis for loyalty and commitment values. There is a tendency toward hypervigilance regarding racial information, as well as a tendency toward dichotomous thinking.

4 *Internalization*. The *internalization* state is characterized by positive commitment to one's socioracial group, internally defined and accepted racial attributes, and objective assessment of out-group members. There is often also a tendency toward flexible and analytic thinking.

5 *Integrative awareness*. The capacity to value one's own collective or group identity and to empathize with and collaborate with members of other oppressed groups, characterizes the *integrative awareness* state. A generally high level of humanistic self-expression is also typical and may be reflected in the tendency toward flexibility and complexity.

In addition to serving as a psychological guide to self-awareness and understanding, these statuses play a significant role in people's lives. They may serve to structure interpersonal reactions, as well as external events, and form the basis for harmonious or acrimonious interactions and relationships. The choice of bicultural adaptation, the preferred pattern of interpersonal interactions, and choices of sociopolitical action will be affected by one's racial identity.

Racial identity, then, is offered as a systematic way of accounting for ". . . the psychological or internalized consequences of being socialized in a racially oppressive environment . . . [whether] benefiting from or suffering under such oppression" (Helms, in press, p. 5). To understand prejudice and its consequences for targets, we need to understand, at basic psychological levels, how people internalize their racial status and develop and utilize psychological processes that reflect their level of racial identity. Helms (in press) has offered an excellent model for this process and has developed a scale for assessing where a person stands in this identity process.

Racial Identity Attitude Scale
The Racial Identity Attitude Scale, or RIAS, is a widely used measure of racial identity. It assesses the ego-statuses of subjects in a set of 50 items that represent the information processing strategies of people at the different status levels (Helms, 1990;

Helms and Parham, 1985). The five elements of the model structure are adaptations of the original Cross stages and incorporate aspects of the Atkinson et al. Racial-Cultural Identity Development (R/CID) approach (Atkinson, Thompson, and Grant, 1993). The status levels and representative black RIAS (BRIAS) items are listed below:

Status Level	BRIAS Item
Conformity	"I feel uncomfortable around black people."
Dissonance	"I feel guilty or anxious about some on the things I believe about black people."
Immersion-emersion	"I frequently confront the system and the (white) 'man'."
Internalization	"People, regardless of their race, have strengths and limitations."
Integrative awareness	"I involve myself in social action and political groups even if there are no other blacks involved."

Although the specific items of the example RIAS use content specific to African Americans—hence the actual scale is labeled "BRIAS"—Helms (in press) proposes that, conceptually, the theoretical model on which it is based may have generality to other ethnic minority groups. In fact, Helms has developed a RIAS scale for whites (WRIAS). It is based on a slightly different status structure, as follows:

Status	WRIAS Item
Contact—Acceptance of societal characterization of race; characterized by denial, naiveté.	"I wish I had a black friend."
Disintegration—Confusion about one's group commitment and ambivalent racial self-definition; characterized by disorientation, suppression.	"I do not feel that I have the social skills to racial interact with black people effectively."
Reintegration—Idealization of one's group and use of external standards to define oneself; selective perception, out-group distortion.	"I get angry when I think about how whites have been treated by blacks."
Pseudo-independence—Good-bad dichotomy of racial groups, and imposition of owngroup standards as a condition for acceptance; rationalization, selective perception.	"I feel as comfortable around blacks as around whites."
Immersion-Emersion—Questioning, analysis comparison of racial group status relative to other groups; hypervigilance, probing.	"I am making a special effort to understand the significance of being white."
Autonomy—Self-affirming commitment societally assigned racial group; flexible standards for perceiving others; integrating, intellectualizing.	"I involve myself in causes regardless of the race of the people involved in them."

As we will discuss in the next chapter, problems of prejudice are not amenable to one-sided analysis. Both the person alleged to be prejudiced and the target of prejudice are part of the interaction. Helms has attempted to incorporate both of these aspects in her measurement of the racial identity construct.

Our concern here is the extent to and ways in which racial identity is affected by one's experience and by the sociopolitical position of one's group in society. As the statuses of identity imply, interpersonal and intergroup interaction may take on quite a different character as a function of the status of interacting parties. Imagine an interaction between a black person at immersion and a white person at reintegration. One confronts the white man, and the other is angry at how blacks treat whites. These may be extreme cases, and we do not have epidemiological data on identity status across the populations. That is, we do not have a good sample distribution study of whites and blacks across these status. As a profile of where the United States is in terms of racial relations, it would be interesting to know where most people fall. Such a study would be a benchmark for those who wish to make changes in society, and perhaps, offer a preview of where race relations are headed.

Ethnic Identity

In general, one's ethnicity is contrasted with one's racial status on the basis of biological versus cultural considerations. *Identity* generally concerns how individual's experiences are internalized via cognitive processes, emotional reactions, and behavioral expressions. *Racial identity* was related to race-related adaptations to sociopolitical and cultural constructs of race. Ethnic identity is often viewed similarly, but is expressed more generally in terms of those dynamic forces that attach one to one's ethnic group. For example, Casas and Pytluk (1995, p. 159) describe ethnic identity as follows:

> . . . a set of self-ideas specifically related to one's ethnic group membership . . . [referring] directly to one's knowledge of personal ownership or membership in the ethnic group, and the correlated knowledge, understanding, values, behaviors, and proud feelings that are direct implications of that ownership."

Knight, Bernal, Garza, and Cota (1993) suggest that ethnic identity develops in children along five dimensions:

1   *Ethnic self-identification*—Identifying one's ethnic group and categorizing oneself in it.
2   *Ethnic constancy*—Recognizing that one's ethnic membership is constant across time, settings, and representations.
3   *Ethnic role behaviors*—Knowing the various ways in which members of one's ethnic group act that reflect the ethnic cultural values, styles, customs, traditions, and language.
4   *Ethnic Knowledge*—Knowing what values, styles, roles and so forth belong to or are characteristic of one's ethnic group.
5   *Ethnic feelings and preferences*—Describing how children feel about their group and the extent to which they prefer other members of the group and the set of values, style, and behaviors that are associated with them over other groups.

Latino identity explained. Police shooting of young Latino male triggers riots in the Mt. Pleasant section of Washington, D.C. Young Latinos stand up for their identity, culture, and respect. (Rick Reinhard/Impact Visuals)

Several variables are important to Hispanic ethnic identity, for example, including *familismo* (primary importance to one's immediate, as well as extended, family), a patriarchal family structure (sharply defined sex-role differentiation within the family structure), *respeto* (respect for the wisdom of age and experience), cultural fatalism ("take life as it comes"), religiosity (belief in God and the need for ritualized worship of the deity), and belief in folk-healing and the merging of physical and emotional well-being.

Sodowsky, Kwan, and Pannu (1995) suggest several characteristics of the many U.S. Asian groups, including personality traits such as silence, nonconfrontation, moderation in behavior, self-control, patience, humility, modesty, and simplicity. All of these traits are considered virtuous in the subculture. However, these ideals may run counter to traits commonly thought to predict success in the superculture (e.g., extroversion, self-confidence, competitiveness and assertiveness). Additionally, loyalty to others, collectivism, generosity, selflessness, and social harmony are valued characteristics. In fact Kitayama and Markus (1994) have shown that, among collectivistic students in Japan, for example, individual pride is most commonly experienced in the context of doing something positive for others. By contrast, for U.S. students, individual pride was most commonly associated with individualistic accomplishment, which usually implied triumph over others.

The tendency to view ethnic identity in terms of in-group knowledge and preference and self-categorization does not present the psychological challenges and conflicts that drive the racial identity model and place it squarely at the vortex of prejudice and racism dynamics. Ruiz (1990) introduced some of the dynamic influences that shape the likelihood of a young Hispanic child's developing a strong ethnic identity. He proposed five stages of ethnic identity processes, beginning with developmental influences from parents and family, and continuing on to acceptance by or rejection from other members of the group. Embracing one's group may be influenced by perceptions of whether the group is viewed positively or negatively in society and whether group membership is associated with negative outcomes such as poverty and prejudice. Conflicts among any or all of these aspects of ethnic affiliation may threaten ethnic identity, much as the conformity and dissonance statuses in the Helms model do. As with Helms, Ruiz proposes progress through effort in his "working-through" stage. In that stage, a person confronts his or her concerns and tries to reach an understanding that leaves positive ethnic affiliation and identity in tact. Finally, one's ethnic identity is secured in the "successful resolution" stage.

Phinney (1992) captured this active challenge–conflict-resolution process in her Multigroup Ethnic Identity Measure (MEIM). Phinney conceived ethnic identity as a social identity characterized by four attributes measured in subscales of the MEIM.

1   *Self-identification* of ethnicity—That is, how do you refer to yourself or use ethnic labels?
    Sample item:
    My ethnicity is
        (1) Asian, Asian American, Oriental
        (2) Black, African American
        (3) Hispanic, Latino
        (4) White, Caucasian, European (not Hispanic)
        (5) American Indian
        (6) Mixed—Parents from two or more different groups
        (7) Other (write in): _____
    "In terms of ethnic group, I consider myself to be _____."
2   *Ethnic behaviors and practices*—That is, what do you do that reflects your ethnic membership or with other ethnic group members?
    Sample item:
    "I am active in organizations or social groups that include mostly members of my own ethnic group."
3   *Affirmation and belonging*—That is, to what extent does one feel attachment to, pride in and affinity for one's group.
    Sample item:
    "I have a lot of pride in my ethnic group and its accomplishments."
4   *Ethnic identity achievement*—Indicating the extent to which one has worked at and explored the meaning of one's ethnicity and adopted it not simply as a legacy of socialization but as an internalized achievement of planful and focused personal development and commitment.
    Sample item:
    "I think a lot about how my life will be affected by my ethnic group membership."

The important contribution of the MEIM is that it proposed to measure ethnic identity as a generic psychological construct, independent of the specific content that might be relevant to particular ethnic groups. The overall ethnic identity score is simply the sum of the 23 items of the scale. Subscales allow one to assess the extent to which the overall ethnic identity may be or may not be reflective of specific aspects that influence a person's response.

Phinney (1992) reported that ethnic identity scores did not differ between a sample of Asian, black, Hispanic, and mixed-ethnic group high school and college students, but were higher for each group than they were for a sample of whites. No differences were found between high school and college samples, or, for the most part, between male and female samples. One important difference, though, was that, for high school students, higher ethnic identity scores were associated with higher grade point averages. There was no such relationship for the college sample.

Phinney, Devich-Navarro, DuPont, Estrada, and Onwughalu (1994) had 46 Mexican Americans and 52 African Americans fill out the MEIM. The subjects were then to answer an open-ended interview question that revealed the extent to which they characterized themselves as *ethnic* (i.e., more ethnic than American); *bicultural* (i.e., both American and ethnic), and *ethnocentric* (i.e., ethnic and separated from mainstream U.S. society and culture). The results showed that the majority of African Americans (54%) were bicultural, whereas, the majority of Mexican Americans (63%) were ethnic in their orientation. No Mexican Americans endorsed an ethnocentric orientation; 17 percent of African Americans did so. Results further showed that, for both Mexican and African Americans, the bicultural orientation was associated with more positive American identity scores. For Mexican Americans high in ethnic orientation, and for African Americans generally, less positive attitudes toward other groups were found. Finally, for African Americans, self-concept scores were most highly correlated with ethnic identity for students who adopted an ethnocentric orientation. For both Mexican and African Americans, self-concept was positively correlated with attitudes toward other groups, with the exception of ethnocentric African Americans.

These findings illustrate that ethnic identity scores do seem to work in similar fashion for different ethnic groups, although deviations are noteworthy. African American students seemed to have more positive self-conceptions and ethnic identification when they maintained greater distance from other Americans. This finding is consistent with the Crocker, Broadnax, et al. (1996) finding of higher self-esteem for subjects who endorsed government conspiracy theories against blacks. For blacks, at least, there is accumulating evidence that positive in-group affiliations and preferences are associated with distancing oneself from U.S. society and whites who are dominant in the mainstream.

We can conclude this discussion of ethnic and racial identity by simply noting that racial and ethnic groups share the tendency to be marginalized by virtue of their differences from white, mainstream Americans. These differences include different histories, patterns of behavior, values, beliefs, style, and language, among other things. Personality also reflects different values and, hence, presents the possibility of competitive disadvantage in certain institutional settings, or psychological conflict when the ethnic way of doing things in one's group is in conflict with what is perceived to be the preferred way in mainstream society.

SUMMARY

Prejudice poses a predicament for its targets that has psychological, emotional, and behavioral consequences. We have shown that prejudice, and its consequences, is not limited to treating another badly or discriminating against him or her. The simple threat of such adverse treatment can trigger reactions or adaptations that put one at a disadvantage, as in the stereotype threat processes proposed by Steele and colleagues. Moreover, progress in race relations may have an ironic downside in that evidence of persistent prejudice renders proclamations of progress ambiguous. Attributional ambiguity can have positive effects when we can gain clarity about others' motivations and thus discount their negative evaluations. But it can have adverse effects when there is truly ambiguity of intentions. People tend to opt for fairness over self-interest and, therefore, generally accept the worse until shown otherwise in ambiguous situations. Those who don't put themselves at this disadvantage may raise the stakes by putting potentially prejudiced people to a higher test. Finally, the possibility that prejudice explains negative evaluations can be applied to targets' successful efforts as well. Targets can't claim the psychological benefits of success if they have to discount a person's friendship or evaluative judgment because of that person's prejudicial leanings.

Being marginalized takes a psychic toll and often puts one in cultural and psychological conflict. The superculture tends to force people in marginalized ethnic or racial groups into either-or bifurcated situations that exacerbate the conflict already posed by marginality. Furthermore, by putting the carrot of opportunity and rewards behind the assimilationist option, the superculture forces a politicization of personal and group identity that may have the twin negative consequences of undermining performance and increasing intergroup conflict. The predicament of prejudice then is a problem not only for the target but for the society as a whole.

11

Reducing Prejudice

❖

Introduction ◆ Prejudice-reduction strategies vary among four approaches ◆ *The salvation approach—Focus on the perpetrators of prejudice* ◆ *The remediation approach—Focus on the targets of prejudice* ◆ *The colorblind approach—Treat every person as if his or her race does not matter* ◆ *The transactional approach—Consider the perspectives and purposes of all people* ◆ *Barriers to prejudice reduction* ◆ Reducing prejudice by modifying individual-level processes ◆ *Prejudice is a problem of categorization* ◆ *Prejudice is a problem of intergroup anxiety* ◆ Reducing prejudice through intergroup processes ◆ *Equal status contact* ◆ *Deprovincialization* ◆ *Social emotions* ◆ *Recategorization* ◆ Summary

*I*NTRODUCTION

Given the definitiveness of the work of Gordon Allport on the psychology of prejudice, we make its reduction the focus of the culminating chapter of Part 2. We have reviewed the facts of stereotyping, intergroup relations, and how targets of prejudice cope and adapt to bias. As with most complex social and psychological phenomena that create real societal problems, it is much easier to describe manifestations and even mechanisms that trigger or sustain the offending behavior than it is to get a firm handle on how to prevent or modify the behavior.

G. W. Allport (1954) closed his analysis of prejudice with a section titled "Reducing Group Tensions." The first chapter of this section was titled "Ought There to Be a Law?" Allport believed that improvement in intergroup relations required both public and private institutional and organizational support. Private support typically comes from organizations such as B'nai Brith, the Anti-Defamation League, the National Association for the Advancement of Colored People (NAACP), and *La Raza*. Within a community setting, such organizations can be more assertive and influential than public organizations can, according to Allport.

The public institutions involved are typically government agencies that are em-powered by laws. Laws contained in the Civil Rights and Voting Rights Acts, Fair Housing Laws, and so forth, which, when obeyed over a long period of time, estab-lish customs that direct conduct between and among members of different groups toward greater civility. Allport (1954) argues that, further, government executives such as the President of the United States can *decree* through Executive Order, for example, that certain conduct *shall* occur. President Roosevelt did so when he estab-lished the Fair Employment Practices Committee in 1941. So, too, did President Truman in 1948, when he forbade racial segregation in the military, and President Johnson in 1968, when he created the Office of Federal Contract Compliance Pro-grams (OFCCP) and the Equal Employment Opportunity Commission (EEOC).

We have civil rights organizations that work to improve intergroup relations, and we have laws and government orders that dictate the civil behavior of our citi-zens. The question posed by Allport in 1954 concerned whether laws could, in fact, reduce prejudice. William Graham Sumner answered in the negative when he de-clared, "Stateways *cannot* change folkways." (cited in Allport, 1954, p. 469). Those who hold this belief frown upon legislative activism as a remedy for social prob-lems of prejudice. Allport, however, argued that laws are not focused on prejudice itself, but on the conditions that perpetuate and sustain it. And he firmly believed that, when these conditions were changed, the undesirable prejudicial behavior would, in due time, change as well. G. W. Allport (1954, pp. 469–470) described this role in the following way:

> [the intent of laws is to] . . . equalize advantages and lessen discrimination. Only as a by-product of the improved conditions do people gain the benefits that come . . . from equal status contact . . . increasing the skills of minority groups, raising their standard of liv-ing, improving their health and education, have similar indirect effects . . . the establish-ment of a legal norm creates a public conscience and a standard for expected behavior that check *overt* signs of prejudice . . . legislation aims not at controlling prejudice but only its open expression . . . when expression changes, thoughts too, in the long run, are likely to fall into line.

The implication of this assertion is that attitudes *follow* behavior, as well as precede it. Just as a person may behave badly because of prejudicial attitudes, a person who refrains, for whatever reason, from negative behavior will come to have thoughts or attitudes consistent with the more restrained manner. However, Allport sounded a warning that, in light of current social policy beliefs and attitudes, and legislative and judicial directions, is highly relevant to contemporary strategies for remedying racial bias and discrimination:

> Prejudices are not likely to be reduced by laws which, in the manner of their passing, *arouse other prejudices.* (G. W. Allport, 1954, p. 473; *emphasis added*)

"In the manner of their passing" can be understood as the procedures by which laws come about. If those procedures are perceived to be flawed, then the outcomes will be discredited. In short, *procedural justice* (the manner in which decisions that affect what happens to people are made) is as important as *distributive justice* (the outcomes that people experience). In fact, research shows that the degree of per-ceived procedural justice is more influential in determining a person's support of affirmative action than concern with distributive justice is—even for those pre-sumed to be beneficiaries of the policies (Tyler, 1994). The debate over affirmative action procedures causes conflict because opponents see flaws in the procedure (affirmative action policies) as a justification for discrediting the outcomes (e.g., hiring more women and ethnic minorities). Supporters, on the other hand, believe that without these procedures the outcomes would be flawed, because ethnic minorities and women would not be chosen or would not be able to participate in proportion to their numbers or abilities.

In G. W. Allport's view, reducing prejudice could come about only if the leadership at the top articulated values that clearly rejected intolerance as an acceptable behavior and backed that position up with social policies that punished those who failed to abide by these precepts. Recently, the Supreme Court has sharply curtailed basic strategies of affirmative action as a remedy to racial and gender inequality. It has struck down local practices of drawing congressional districts in a manner that would increase the likelihood of the election of Latinos and African Americans to the U.S. Congress, for example. Affirmative action was regarded by many as the remedy to civil rights abuses against, primarily, African Americans and the strategy by which the principles of the Civil Rights Act of 1964 could best be implemented. Redrawing political districts in order to increase the probability of ethnic minorities' entering the Congress was similarly viewed as a good strategy for implementing the intent of the Voting Rights Act of 1965. However, today, it seems to many people that the leadership of the country has not only created a climate that is unsupportive of strategies to change the nature of race relations in the United States, but is actively opposed to those strategies that were worked out in the 1960s and 1970s.

Those who oppose social policies that evolved from the political and moral climate of the 1960s would not view themselves as racists, prejudiced, or anything of that kind. In fact, their opposition to affirmative action, for example, is often couched in the very terms of the Civil Rights Act itself. They maintain that policies of racial preferences for people of color violate the antidiscrimination plank of the law. The moral high ground of the 1960s was the right of a person not to be judged by the color of his or her skin, but by the merits of his or her character and performance. The logical end-point of this goal is a colorblind society. Whether it is or is not colorblind at the moment should not deter us from focusing on achieving this goal. As former Secretary of Education William Bennett noted:

> People of good will disagree about the means [but] I don't think anybody disagrees about the ends . . . I think the best means to achieve the ends of a colorblind society is to proceed as if we were a colorblind society . . . *I think the best way to treat people is as if their race did not make any difference.* (Sawyer, 1986, p. A8; *emphasis added*)

According to this view, the problems of racial prejudice cannot be solved by focusing on matters of race, but, it is argued, by ignoring them. The individual is what matters, not the group. Rights, we are reminded by many, belong to *individuals*, not groups. Therefore, any group-based decision is, by definition of Eastland and Bennett (1978) (cf. Chapter 4) for example, "immoral."

What does a colorblind society mean? we may ask. One definition comes from noted social critic and scholar Allan Bloom (1986). His view of the colorblind society comes through in his assessment of the failure to achieve racial harmony on college campuses. He notes that:

> . . . White and Black students do not in general become friends with one another . . . The forgetting of race in the university, which was so predicted and confidently expected

> when the barriers were let down, has not occurred. There is now a large Black presence in major universities . . . but they have, by and large, proved indigestible. . . . The programmatic brotherhood of the sixties did not culminate in integration but veered off toward Black separation. (Bloom, 1986, p. 91)

According to these analysts, the "forgetting of race" failed because blacks "proved indigestible." The goal of a colorblind society seems, by the analyses of both Bennett (see Sawyer, 1986) and Bloom (1986), to imply that blacks (or any other disadvantaged or discriminated-against group) should *themselves* act as if their race (or other group trait) did not matter and should minimize allegiance to and identification with their racial (or ethnic or gender) group in the service of individualism. But, if a person of color "forgets" his or her race, for example, and others do not, to what sorts of vulnerabilities is the person exposed? The French mathematician, René Pascal, wagered on the existence of God thus: If he were betting that God *did* exist and was wrong, what were his losses? Perhaps denial of a certain amount of pleasure and self-indulgence. But what if he bet that God did *not* exist and was wrong? Then, all his earthly pleasures would be the basis for a permanent assignment to Hell. Thus, on balance, Pascal reasoned that it was overall a better bet to believe in God than not to.

What if you act as if race doesn't matter, and you are wrong? If you are a white person, there are probably no immediate or even long-range negative consequences. If you are a person of color and are wrong, you make yourself vulnerable to limitations, obstacles, and barriers without assuring yourself of the ability to identify, confront, and remove them. That is, the results of forgetting that race has consequences may well differ for a white person compared to a black, red, yellow, or brown person. We come at these kinds of issues from different places. Solutions for one individual or group may constitute or entail problems for others.

Social psychology's approach to social problems is in theoretically grounded empirical science. Social psychologists cannot resolve, with certitude, matters of belief and principle, attitude, and differing perspectives on morality. However, by raising these points, it may be shown that any solution to the problems of prejudice must take into account the differing perspectives of all interactive parties, as well as the social fabric and context within which these prejudice-reduction strategies play out. For example, social psychologists know that unconscious and automatic processes affect social judgments (Devine, 1989; Bargh, 1992). It is also known that race is one of the most pervasive unconsciously motivating factors in our society. Therefore, if we act as if race doesn't matter, then we may leave ourselves open to automatic, unconscious biases that perpetuate discriminatory judgment and behavior. Social psychology can critique Bennett in ways that political activists may find difficult to do. Bringing science to the political and social discourse on race in our society is perhaps the most important contribution social psychologists can make.

Let's recall the working definition of prejudice:

Prejudice is a positive or negative attitude, judgment, or behavior generalized to a particular person that is based on attitudes or beliefs held about the group to which the person belongs.

The critical issues are that prejudice (1) can be positive *or* negative and (2) involves generalization from an attitude or belief concerning a group to a specific individual. The importance of the first point is that prejudice is not only a matter of antipathies people hold for out-groups, but affections they reserve for in-groups.

Therefore, reducing prejudices may involve loving ourselves less, as well as loving others more. The second point focuses on the generalization from the group to the individual. This involves two issues. First is the nature of the attitude, belief, or evaluation that one holds for the group (generally, we speak here of racial attitudes or group stereotypes). To reduce prejudice, then, is to reduce the tendency to form negative out-group attitudes and to believe in group-level stereotypes. The second concern is the generalization from the group to the individual. Changing prejudice will involve minimizing the tendency to make this generalization. The less we generalize from the group to the individual, the more we individuate a person's particular and unique qualities, and the more deliberative, methodical, and focused we are on them as individuals. It is also important to recognize that the formation of the racial attitude or stereotype in the first place results from generalization. For example, we conclude that the group possesses certain traits because we have observed those traits in some one or more people who are members of the group. Therefore, if we are to reduce prejudice, we also need to reduce the tendency to generalize from the individual to the group when such generalization is unwarranted. But we run up against a dilemma. One way to change the group attitude is to disconfirm it through individual examples. In this case, we want to generalize from an individual who contradicts our beliefs about the group, to the group itself. This contrary example should be evidence against the validity of the belief and, hence, should reduce the strength of the racial attitude. All of the other prejudice processes would correspondingly be diminished.

These issues must be kept in mind as we progress through this chapter. The material addressed here proposes various ways to modify attitudes, beliefs, and behaviors that reflect the processes of prejudice summarized above.

The aim of this chapter is to review what we know in social psychology that relates to possible strategies for reducing prejudice. The first section will look at the assumptions underlying the four approaches for producing change in prejudice in this society—the salvation, remediation, colorblind, and transaction strategies. The implications of these perspectives for prejudice reduction will be discussed. The second section will focus on individual-level processes. In general, these rely on strategies that reduce the development of stereotypes or lessen the likelihood that one will use stereotypes in making social judgments. For the most part, these approaches focus on the individual's thoughts, feelings, awareness, and commitment to fairness and equality. The third section will explore intergroup processes that aid in the reduction of conflict and antagonisms. This section concerns the ways in which people from different groups can be brought together in order to lessen hostility, change misconceptions, and provide a working environment in which new and more positive habits of interaction can be developed. This section, then, is more focused on intergroup dynamics. Implicit in these discussions is the idea that the strategy one chooses for reducing prejudice and its effects will depend largely on the views one has on the origin, maintenance, and manifestation of prejudice. Where possible, specific examples of attempts to moderate processes that contribute to prejudice will be provided and their effectiveness and implications assessed.

*P*REJUDICE-REDUCTION STRATEGIES VARY AMONG FOUR APPROACHES

There are several different approaches to how prejudice can be reduced, and each makes assumptions about the primary location of the problem. According to one view, the causes reside in the perpetrators, the prejudiced people, and the focus is on treating the problem by concentrating on such people. Other approaches suggest that although there may well be problems with people who are prejudiced (everyone is at least to a certain degree), improving the status or changing the behavior of the targets may be a viable strategy for reducing prejudice. A third approach asks that we forget race or any other stigmatized characteristic that can be shown to be an irrelevant basis for individual judgment. According to this view, simply treating people as individuals is the best way to eliminate prejudice. Finally, there are some who would argue that we must consider the entire context of interacting parties, the person designated as prejudiced, as well as his or her target.

The Salvation Approach—Focus on the Perpetrators of Prejudice

Prejudice has been associated with white Americans throughout this century. If prejudice is defined mainly as a problem of the thoughts, feelings, personality, and behavior of whites, remedies, by and large, must focus on the target groups. The contact hypothesis, for example, focused on bringing races and other groups together as a strategy to overcome prejudice because the outcome would be a change in the attitudes and behavior primarily of whites (as discussed in Chapter 3).

But what are the characteristics of the prejudiced individual? Prejudiced people are dogmatic and authoritarian (Rokeach, 1960; Adorno et al., 1950). They believe in hierarchies and in dominance of their group (cf. Chapter 8 of this text; Sidanius, 1993). They are resistant to efforts to change their ideas. In fact, efforts to change their beliefs may be interpreted as implying that the "natural" dominance order is under attack and thus cause them to become stronger in asserting their beliefs (cf. Greenberg et al., 1990).

Prejudiced people believe in negative stereotypes of racial groups and incorporate them in social judgments and behavior. They are inclined to categorize people into groups and to assign positive characteristics to their own group. Whatever the characteristics of the prejudiced person, the reduction of prejudice requires personal change in how one thinks, judges, perceives, feels, and behaves. All of those thoughts, judgments, perceptions, feelings, and behavior are *flawed* in the prejudiced person. Therefore, reduction efforts rely on conversion, redemption, or salvation processes.

The most common approach to reducing prejudice is through information and education—that is, the *salvation* of the prejudiced person. Much debate about how textbooks ought to be written, the appropriate content for general college education requirements, and the like suggests that if we only knew more about each other, we would be less inclined to react with fear, hostility, or bias toward people who are different. This general approach applies to majority and minority groups alike. College courses in African American studies, women's studies, Latino studies, and American Indian studies, as well as in world civilizations, all serve to reduce the ignorance people have about each other. Will this reduce prejudice? Perhaps. But it seems clear from earlier discussions that information alone may not be sufficient to counter the realistic appraisals and emotional reactions that interpersonal and intergroup encounters produce.

The *salvation approach* focuses on the perpetrators of prejudice—specifically, on converting them to nonprejudiced persons. To the extent that individuals believe in group dominance, are close-minded, have authoritarian personalities, or are social-ized to a racialistic in-group perspective, there is a significant limit to how effective targeting them for education-based change will be. Conversely, to the extent that biased individuals are influenced by biasing social information (e.g., media por-trayals of negative behavior, public discourse, and signification of inferiority or lower capabilities of minority groups), then *individual* salvation approaches are off target. What should be targeted is the nature of the social information from which biased attitudes and beliefs are derived.

The Remediation Approach—Focus on the Targets of Prejudice

The *remediation approach* assumes that, if the status of ethnic and racial minorities, women, and other groups that are frequently the target of prejudice improves, then tolerance and acceptance of members of these groups will grow, and animosity and bias will decline. This approach was at the center of the civil rights efforts of the 1960s. The strategy of expanding civil rights and liberties for minority groups and women took the explicit form of affirmative interventions. Integrating police and fire departments, college campuses, and small business access to federal spending, for example, all implicitly accepted the responsibility of undoing centuries of nega-tive bias. At its core, when the status of target stigmatized groups is improved, a basic similarity with majority groups is revealed, and, thereby, the basis for prejudi-cial thoughts, feelings, and behaviors is removed.

The remediation approach is a double-edged sword. On the one hand, it ac-knowledges, rightfully, that the effects of centuries of discrimination cannot be wiped out in a stroke of the legislative pen. On the other, it seems to accept the lower capabilities or performance of those it targets for remediation. That is, we as-sert racial bias as a cause in order to legitimate efforts to change the race-based out-comes that show inequality; then, we posit incapacity in the target groups in order to legitimate the remediation strategies.

The enduring legacy of prejudice and injustice belongs to all parties. Those who have been targets of the bias are disadvantaged in ways that can never be sat-isfactorily calculated. Some have argued that "40 acres and a mule" was a legiti-mate payoff to African Americans for the centuries of slavery. Japanese Americans were interned in camps during World War II; in 1992, Congress voted to pay each living survivor of the camps $10,000. Is there one specific act, or a dollar amount, that can make things right? No.

Those who enjoy the advantages of this historical pattern of bias also cannot easily calculate the extent of their good fortune. They must also recognize, as social psychology so amply shows, that the biases against minority groups reside at a subconscious level. When and how they surface—and with what consequences—is another calculation that is not easily made.

When we focus on the targets of prejudice, we assume that (1) the targets are disadvantaged cumulatively by bias and bigotry and need help if they are to com-pete successfully in an open society and (2) that the beneficiaries of bias may con-tinue consciously or unconsciously to preserve their advantages and the targets' disadvantages. Affirmative action is a remedy that seeks to address both of these beliefs. By implication, it suggests that in an open, competitive market, those tar-geted for affirmative action benefits would not fare well (1) because of their relative lack of experience and opportunity and (2) because the cards may be stacked against these same people through the subtle processes of prejudice. Affirmative action gives the targets an improved competitive edge (though still not as great as that enjoyed by the historical beneficiaries of bias) and reduces the latitude within which bias may operate.

So, the remediation approach puts great weight on moving ever-larger numbers of the target group into mainstream contexts. It acknowledges or assumes a level of inadequacy or even incapacity that *requires* remediation if the targets are to be successful. Recall Allport's view that equalizing advantages and lessening discrimination (what civil rights laws are meant to do) will improve the skills, raise the standard of living, and improve the health and education of minority groups. We will thereby diminish the overt signs of prejudice and over time the "thoughts too . . . are likely to fall into line (G. W. Allport, 1954, p. 470)

The remediation approach is inadequate because it assumes that simply bringing more minority group members into mainstream contexts (and establishing legal norms that support this) will change the overt expression of prejudice and that, over time, the covert thoughts will fall into line. In fact, the legal norms (affirmative action) are being challenged, attempts to control overt behavior (e.g., "hate speech" laws) have been ruled unconstitutional, and research shows that casting minority performance in remedial terms reduces it to below the actual capability (Steele, 1992; Steele and Aronson, 1995). If focusing on the perpetrator alone is flawed and focusing on the target alone is also flawed, maybe we should discard both strategies. That is the premise of the next approach.

Colorblind? (Drawing by M. Stevens; © 1996 The New Yorker Magazine, Inc.)

"Let's just forget for a moment that you're black."

The Colorblind Approach—Treat Every Person as if His or Her Race Does Not Matter

Under the colorblind approach, individual merit and character should be (and perhaps is) the primary determinant of a person's outcomes. This is seen as the only completely fair way to approach people. This strategy was articulated by William Bennett when he said the best way to achieve a colorblind society is to act *as if* color didn't matter. Martin Luther King's dream was that little black boys and girls (and all children) would one day be judged by the content of their character, not the color of their skin. Bloom (1986) believed the legacy of the 1960s was the "forgetting of race."

The colorblind view aspires to the creation of a race-neutral society, one in which race should not and does not matter. However, if we forget race (i.e., act as if it doesn't matter), will prejudice go away? Is this colorblind approach ultimately the only or best way to achieve equality in this society? There is a saying in Spanish that, loosely translated, means "If you will it to be, it can be so." Is the colorblind approach the only legitimate route to procedural justice in our society?

Belief in a colorblind society—and acting as if ours were one—results in decidedly different states of terrain for people from different racial, ethnic, and gender groups. As we saw in Chapter 6, subtle biases exist, often at subconscious levels. Acting as if race doesn't matter, when it does, leaves one vulnerable to the influence of race without prompting a conscious effort to prepare oneself for or minimize its adverse effects. That is, a colorblind approach may significantly underestimate bias in our society and leave both majority and minority alike unprepared to take action to ameliorate its negative effects.

There is another adverse impact of the colorblind approach. A person in a favored position may legitimately and honestly believe that acting as if one's race doesn't matter is the most fair, honest, and correct way to act. However, this assumption and strategy may be perceived or experienced by a member of a minority racial or ethnic group as offensive! Why offensive? Because of the double standard outlined above. "How can you, a white person, act as if race doesn't matter when you enjoy the privileges of race everyday. By so doing, you consign me to a status quo that incarcerates me in your privileged world as a welcome, but underprivileged, guest."

Apart from the asymmetry of power, there is the asymmetry of legal, cultural, and political standards. It is quite common for contemporary people labeled "political conservatives" to argue that the U.S. Constitution does not recognize the rights of groups, only the rights of individuals. This is a fundamental principle of a democracy that is ruled by the majority. In U.S. history, groups have long been singled out and passed over for inclusion in the fundamental rights of the nation by virtue of their group status. In the Constitution, for example, slaves, as a group, were divested of 40 percent of their humanity for purposes of taxation, without regard to their individual values, attitudes, work habits, or religious commitment. American Indians were herded onto reservations; Latinos were herded into the fields or urban barrios. Both groups were often limited to menial or low-paying jobs. Asians were herded into urban ghettoes (if not internment camps). All were rejected because the differences between their cultures and the dominant culture were deemed too prominent.

We are now, though, all Americans, and we all enjoy the same rights—to die and pay taxes. So why can't we emphasize the commonality and not the differences? Why isn't a colorblind approach the best way to make intergroup harmony a reality? The simple answer rests in the continuing significance of prejudice and racism. The victims are afraid to lose the leverage of knowing the enemy and working to mute its voice. The advantaged are often not even aware of their own privilege, and certainly not of the depth of feeling of the targets who are fighting, not for votes of approval, but for unqualified basic humanity.

So, the colorblind approach is flawed because its worldview does not conform to reality and because it puts many who would abide by its assumptions in danger of losing further ground. The next approach is one that, in principle, considers all aspects of the three approaches discussed above.

The Transactional Approach—Consider the Perspectives and Purposes of All People

Prejudice results from many different circumstances and tendencies. These circumstances include the facts of social differences in society. If social differences were completely uncorrelated with any meaningful set of values or social outcomes (e.g., academic performance, socioeconomic status, popularity, and physical attractiveness), then social differences would be meaningless. But, of course, they are not. The tendencies that prove so vexing and that give meaning to social differences have been summarized in previous chapters. They include the very human tendency to draw the social categories in the first place, to perceive individuals in terms of the social categories to which they belong or to which we assign them, and to make hierarchical judgments about the value each category holds within our society. The facts of social differences, in conjunction with the results of these basic human tendencies, create a status quo social order that makes prejudice a fundamental fact. The wonder is not why people are prejudiced, but how so many can avoid the most insidious manifestations of the prejudice disease (cf. Devine, 1996).

Prejudice is not something one can simply avoid, or ignore, or declare out-of-bounds. One cannot be fully aware either of one's own compelling human tendencies to categorize people and judge them on the basis of the categories that may, for the most part, reside in one's own head. It will take work. And it is not work that a person can do alone. One cannot end prejudice by oneself because the *acts that constitute bias depend, in part, on the target's reaction, as well as the actor's intention.*

Jack Kent Cooke is a wealthy man. He owns the Washington Redskins professional football team, among many other holdings (e.g., the Chrysler Building in New York City). In the mid-1990s, there was a growing reaction against the use of American Indian names, nicknames, and other designators for sports teams. Some teams changed their names as a result. For example, the Stanford Indians became the Stanford Cardinal; the St. John's Redmen became the St. John's Red Storm. When Cooke was approached about changing the name of his team, he responded that the term *Redskin* was synonymous with a fearless warrior, a brave and courageous young man. This sentiment is something he wanted to have associated with his football team. Many American Indians disagree. They argue that calling them the *Redskins* is like calling a team the *Blackies* or *Darkies*. The point is not whether you agree with this last point, but that Cooke defined the meaning of *Redskin* for *him* and rejected the American Indians' claim to define for themselves what *Redskin* denoted.

Is Cooke prejudiced? Should he not have the right, as an entrepreneur, a businessman who has taken financial risk to field a football team, to name his team and imbue the name with whatever symbolic meaning he wants?[1] It would be hard to argue that he should not have that right. Should the American Indians not have a right to define what images of their people are promoted and what terms used to designate them are derogatory in this society? Many of us would say yes to that, as well. If both of these views have merit, then how do we decide? Simply put, we have to negotiate! This brings us to the *transactional approach.*

> *Transact:* **To carry on or conduct (business, negotiations, activities, etc.) to a conclusion or settlement.** *Syn.* **exact, conclude, settle, manage, negotiate, conduct.**

Transactions require the participation of two or more sides, and they are not completed until there is a settlement, an agreement. The problems of prejudice, linked as they are to issues of race, ethnicity, culture, gender, and so on, cannot be settled by fiat, or simply by laws. They have to be negotiated. When two people become friends, for example, they must somehow come to an agreement that being friends is in their *mutual* best interest. When couples argue, it rarely ends well when one party is intent on "winning" the argument. There is always more than one side to the issue, and solutions do not last that take only one side into account.

Are the parties always equally culpable? No, to be sure. But part of the negotiation is to figure out what a reasonable representation of the situation is and what a reasonable course of action might be. As we have seen, what is deemed a reasonable representation of the situation will vary with the perspective of the perceiver. What is a reasonable or "fair" course of action will similarly vary. Obstacles to negotiated settlements include mistrust (Chapter 10), misperceptions (Chapter 7), and self interest (Chapters 8 and 9). There is much that may erode any confidence that prejudice reduction is possible in any meaningful way. Conflict between racial, ethnic, and gender groups seems to persist, in spite of many of our best efforts.

Neither the salvation nor remediation approach alone can work, because each treats only *one* of the elements of the problem. The colorblind approach seems to do worse—it *ignores* the problem altogether. The transactional approach offers the best hope for a final positive solution, but it poses many obstacles that must be overcome. It begins with a dialogue and a willingness to seek an understanding and to admit to being a contributor to the problem.

Building conceptual or theoretical models for a transactional analysis of prejudice requires combining some of the best work in social psychology. Elliot Aronson and colleagues (Aronson, Blaney, Sikes, Stephan, and Snapp, 1978; Aronson and Bridgeman, 1979) conceived of a basically transactional approach in the "jigsaw classroom" concept. This jigsaw experiment attempts to replace the competitive aspects of classrooms with a cooperative one (Slavin, 1990; Boykin, 1994). Instead of students' separating themselves from others in an independent fashion, or seeking to distinguish themselves from others by their superior performance, the jigsaw approach mandates student *interdependence* by placing them in six-person learning groups. Each member of the learning team holds only one-sixth of the total infor-

[1]Abe Pollin owns the professional basketball team in Washington, D.C. It was founded as the Baltimore Bullets, and became the Washington Bullets when Pollin purchased the team. By contrast, in 1995, Pollin decided that the nickname had taken on an inappropriate image, one associated with violence and killing. He conducted a public community campaign to change the name. Now the team is known as the "Washington Wizards."

mation needed to attain success. Each student thus has a unique and valuable piece of information that, like a jigsaw puzzle piece, is necessary to obtain the total correct solution to the problem. Children learn that the old competitive ways will not work and that they must now listen to others, ask appropriate questions of others, and regard each other as mutually valuable resources for the learning enterprise.

To test this idea, Aronson and colleagues (Blaney, Stephan, Rosenfield, Aronson, and Sikes, 1977) introduced the jigsaw classroom to 10 fifth-grade classes in seven different schools in the then recently desegregated public schools in Austin, Texas. The experimental classrooms were conducted three days a week for six weeks. It was found that children in the jigsaw group, compared to control students in the same schools, liked others more—both within and outside their own ethnic group (Anglos, blacks, and Chicanos)—showed significant increases in self-esteem, and, at least for Anglos and blacks, liked school more. Another study (Lucker, Rosenfield, Sikes, and Aronson, 1977) showed that the jigsaw classroom also improved academic performance for blacks and Chicanos, and did not alter the performance of Anglo students. Therefore, by putting students into an interdependent relationship and acknowledging the value of each students' contributions, Aronson and his colleagues were able to improve levels of liking and, it is hoped, friendship, self-esteem, and academic performance.

This research reflects the positive possibilities of a transactional approach. Through intervention, Aronson and colleagues created the necessity for a negotiated relationship in the learning environment. It was created structurally and procedurally. The changes in attitudes, values, beliefs, and performance that followed occurred on their own. What happened in these classrooms? Three mechanisms are offered in this approach:

1 *Increased participation*—The kids must interact with each other. (The marginalized Chicano could not remain "invisible," for example.) Greater participation was related to increased liking for school and increases in self-esteem.
2 *Increased empathic role-taking*—Interacting team members must listen to and try to understand each other, even if they have different communication styles. Paying more attention to one's classmates can improve one's own ability to understand how they think and what their gestures, phrases, and so forth mean.
3 *More similar attributions for success and failure*—The familiar model of high achievers shows they attribute both successes and failures to internal dispositions (skill and low effort, respectively). By contrast, low achievers make external attributions for success (easy task) and internal attributions for failure (lack of skill). In the interdependent jigsaw classes, students made the same kind of attributions for success and failure to fellow students that they made to themselves. This was not the case in competitive interactions. In short, it seems that students in the jigsaw classes came to see the other students as more similar to themselves.

True, the fifth-grade classroom and society at large are two quite different things. But a transactional strategy for reducing prejudice is clearly suggested by the jigsaw model. We need to create more independent, cooperative learning and achievement situations in society. Rather than pitting one against the other and rewarding the winner, we must create scenarios where the best performance will occur when the interacting parties share resources, abilities, knowledge, and friendship.

Barriers to Prejudice Reduction

The approaches to prejudice reduction summarized in the preceding pages are based on an interpersonal dynamic—that is, people from different groups are interacting with each other. The transactional model was offered as the best approach in the long run because it requires negotiated settlements and utilizes principles of bargaining, resource (power) sharing, and perspective taking that increase empathy and levels of interaction. Of course, these positive benefits don't just happen. In fact, there are many deep-seated and long-standing barriers to obtaining, in society at large, the kinds of transactions that are created in the jigsaw classroom. These barriers are not limited to ill-will or covert bias, although these are always possible elements. Rather, barriers often lie in the nature of dyadic interaction itself and in the social structures that frame them.

Differing Perspectives of Interacting Parties
First, we all know there are always at least two sides to every story. Each of us will naturally be inclined toward one side or another, but there at least two sides, and it is usually possible to understand the basis of each. But we know two things in social psychology: (1) We are more inclined to see the reasons for others' behaviors as *dispositional* (i.e., based on internal characteristics of the actor) and to grossly underestimate situational influences on others' behavior. (This is known as the *fundamental attribution error*, or FAE [Ross, 1977].) (2) Explanations for behaviors depend importantly on our perspective—that is, actors see, literally, a different context for their behavior (the external situation) than observers of their behavior do (the behavior itself). This is known as the *actor-observer effect* (Jones and Nisbett, 1971). Let's consider the implications of each of these in turn.

Fundamental attribution error. If I observe you behaving in a way that I disapprove of, the FAE theory suggests I am more likely to conclude that something about the kind of person you are, more than the situation you are in, is responsible for your behavior. From there, it is an easy step to conclude that behavior associated with a group is representative of the type of people the individual members of the group are, and not the situational constraints under which they may be operating. For example, Ross, Amabile, and Steinmetz (1977) set up a quiz game in which subjects were randomly assigned to play the role of quizmaster or contestant. Quizmasters were asked to make up difficult questions that would demonstrate their general wealth of knowledge—do you know where to find Bainbridge Island? the seventh book of the Old Testament? whether Europe or Africa has the longer coastline? These are some of the questions quizmasters came up with. Clearly, they had an advantage that was capriciously handed to them by the flip of the experimenters' coin. After the game was played for a while, observers were asked to evaluate the quizmaster and the contestants on a variety of attributes. Among other things, they concluded that the quizmasters were smarter than the contestants were! So, too, did contestants arrive at this conclusion. They were not, *by their own account*, as smart as the quizmasters.

In this experiment, the demonstration of knowledge was clearly under the control of the externally imposed social role to which subjects had been assigned. But the judgment of how knowledgeable subjects were did not accord this fact due recognition.

Over the years, being a member of a minority group—and, thereby, subject not only to prejudices of varying kinds but also, often, to clear and unmitigated discrimination—puts one at a disadvantage. It may even lead one to reactive behaviors. Slave revolts and slaves' running away from slavery are examples. Rather than seeing these as perfectly normal things to do, such behavior was once attributed to mental aberrations. Runaway slaves were considered to be suffering from "dypsocordoia," an *illness* that caused them to wander away from their slave masters (Guthrie, 1976).

Pettigrew (1979) proposed a modification of the FAE that he called the *ultimate attribution error* (UAE). UAE occurs when a racially biased or otherwise prejudiced person attributes the negative behavior of members of the target group to dispositional characteristics and the positive behaviors to external or environmental forces. This pattern of perceptions and evaluations does not simply fail to recognize the situational constraints on behavior generally, but selectively fails to recognize them in negative situations (e.g., poverty, and reduced levels of resources, training, and opportunity). Moreover, this judgment standard was readily employed in positive situations (e.g., academic or job success). We could call this UAE a "damned if you don't and discounted if you do" approach!

The FAE and UAE will be more pronounced when the target person is perceived as being more dissimilar to the perceiver. Therefore, any "cultural differences" that obscure underlying motivation; or that mask the symbolic or literal meaning of statements, gestures, and the like; or that result in contorted understanding of the intention or goal of a negotiation will reduce the likelihood of a transactional accomplishment. The good news is that the attributions of whites and minorities came closer together in the jigsaw classroom context of the transactional model. Therefore, reducing the perceived dissimilarity in society at large should also reduce the operation of perceptual biases.

Differences between actors and observers. It is said, "Don't judge me until you walk a mile in my shoes." This saying reflects the significance of the actor-observer effect. Although people perceive environmental factors as major influences on their own behavior, others are more likely to interpret such behavior in dispositional terms. Carry this to the intergroup context and we have an excellent example of a problem that often undermines intergroup relations.

What do we know about gay men and lesbians, African Americans, or Latinos? Many Americans only know what they see on the six o'clock news or in headlines that sensationalize already dramatic stories. Almost any poll of Americans will show a black-white difference in perceptions of the degree to which prejudice is responsible for the disadvantage blacks have compared to whites (e.g., Kluegel and Smith, 1986). If whites believe that prejudice is minimal and not a compelling explanation for the disadvantage of blacks, and blacks, by contrast, experience the bias (cf. Feagin and Sikes, 1995), then we have a classic actor-observer effect. Whites "observe" blacks from afar and conclude that, whatever their plight, it results from dispositional character (usually lack of effort, poor values, or lack of ability). Blacks look at experiences in their daily life and see external barriers to greater accomplishment. It is not surprising, then, that the perception of remedies to the disadvantaged status of black Americans would be different in the minds of blacks and of whites. The *problem* in need of remediation is different for members of the two groups.

An ingenious experiment by Storms (1973) showed how powerful this actor-observer effect is and how it can be modified—by literally changing the perspective. Storms used a video camera to tape an interaction. Observers watched through a one-way mirror. Actors made judgments that were typically more influenced by the situation, and observers made judgments that reflected a greater contribution of actor characteristics. Storms then played back the interaction for both actors and observers. However, Storms varied the camera vantage point so that the actor was now seeing himself or herself from the vantage of the observer and the observer now saw the interaction from the camera angle of the actor. When the two were then asked to evaluate the behaviors, they switched in their perception of the relevant influences. In fact, the video experiment enabled the observer to "walk a mile in the actor's shoes!"

One remedy to prejudice may be literally to come up with schemes that would enable a white observer of a black person's experience to walk in that person's shoes. The reverse would also be an important ingredient of this process. The net effect would be a convergence of perspectives and greater similarity in the inference of motives, intention, and so forth. However, we should also acknowledge that these differences in perspectives are based also on different histories for different groups in the United States.

Remnants of Centuries of Racial Bias Affect Perceptions and Judgments

The facts of slavery, Jim Crow, legal segregation, gender bias, hostility toward immigrants from non-European countries is all well known. Contemporary concerns with race relations are often divided into two camps: Those in the first camp (social liberals) argue that this history of bias has created an unfair and unlevel playing field. In order to even things out, according to this view, it is necessary to do more than simply acknowledge the historical bias and declare it finished. One must take aggressive action to stop the bias and to improve opportunities for its victims to compete fairly.

Those in the second camp (social conservatives) accept that things have not always been fair, but argue that laws were put in place during the civil rights era of the 1960s that make it illegal to discriminate. They further argue that the "preferences" accorded members of these disadvantaged groups do not, in the long run, make things better, for three reasons: (1) They violate the letter of the civil rights law; (2) they antagonize and alienate many whites, mostly men, who do not feel personally responsible for what may have happened decades and even centuries ago; (3) they "stigmatize" the beneficiaries and undermine their feelings of competence.

The first camp conceives strategies to accomplish its goal of a just society that include affirmative action programs, multicultural curricula, and prohibitions against hate speech. The second camp prefers a system of color and gender neutrality that is backstopped by vigorous enforcement of the laws against discrimination.

The second camp believes that the most important principles of the United States are free speech (First Amendment to the Constitution) and individual (not group) rights. It argues that *any person* who is discriminated against has recourse in the courts and that, in the long run, it is better to let fundamental U.S. political and legal institutions adjudicate the advancement of rights for every U.S. citizen. The first camp rejects this premise as "status quo-ism." It maintains that, in effect, the centuries of bias—with their now built-in institutional effects—have created special opportunities, privileges, and advantages for those who have been free to participate in and take advantage of the U.S. system for all these years. One cannot, it argues, remedy institutional bias against particular groups in society by adjudicating, one by one, egregious instances of bias. In fact, the subtlety and ubiquity of bias is often not obvious or evident.

For example, a young black man was made up to look white for a segment on the *Oprah Winfrey* television show (*Oprah Winfrey Show,* 1995). Among other things, the young man asked for directions of passing motorists as a white man and as a black man. He compared his experiences as a black and as a white man. They were dramatically different. He was treated cordially and given eager assistance when he was white. When he was black, he frequently was ignored. A segment of *Prime Time Live* with Diane Sawyer (1991) made a similar test. However, rather than pose the same person as either white or black, it used two different men, one white and one black. In one test situation, the white man was shown an apartment and told it was available only minutes after the black man had showed up and been told there were no vacancies. In another situation, each stood by his car, in which he had locked his keys. The video shows that there was a stream of would-be good Samaritans willing to help out the white man, whereas the black man is seen standing there by his car, frustrated, with no help in sight. What is crucial here is that if there were no white experience with which to compare the black experience, we might never know that blacks and whites have, on average, *different day-to-day experiences.* So, how do we protect the rights of people whose disadvantage is often not consciously promoted, not exposed, and not actionable in courts of law?

The First Amendment perhaps because it is first, seems to take precedence over all others. The Fourteenth Amendment mandates equal protection of the laws for all citizens, regardless of race, gender, or national origin. What happens when one person's right to free speech smacks up against another's right to equal protection? The Confederate flag, the white sheets of the Ku Klux Klan symbolize bias, hatred, and disadvantage of blacks, the swastika, the genocide of Jews. What are the emotional consequences of seeing these symbols of hatred and abuse? Are such emotional reactions reasonable? Does one have the right to be protected from these emotion-arousing symbols? Can one be? The First-versus-Fourteenth Amendment debate is another of the demarcations of varying perspectives. These variances are triggered by a view of U.S. history that is different for members of groups who have enjoyed privilege and for those who have been oppressed by the privilege of others.

The real problem is that these emotional feelings, the historical facts, these political and legal principles do not settle down neatly into a package that is easily balanced. The transactional model argues that conversation and dialogue are ingredients of any prejudice-reduction effort. For these conversations to take place, recognizing the legitimate basis of conflicting issues is a first step. There is no simple calculus of historical wrongs and privilege that tells us what to do. But, if we ignore the past, we will never understand why people from different circumstances see things so differently today.

REDUCING PREJUDICE BY MODIFYING INDIVIDUAL-LEVEL PROCESSES

In this section, we will consider ways in which individual processes contribute to prejudice and how modifying these processes, or the factors that influence them, will help reduce prejudice. This discussion begins with the assumption that prejudice is primarily a characteristic of individuals and of how they think, feel, and behave toward members of certain groups.

Strategies to reduce prejudice will necessarily depend on what we think its causes are and how we believe it to be expressed. If prejudice is evidenced simply by the untutored expressions of an ignorant person, then education may be the way to reduce it. If prejudice results from biases that affect the cognitive processing of social information (which may itself be biased), then we may alter those biases by restructuring that information. Prejudice is not a unidimensional, single-component concept, but a matrix of multiply determined beliefs, values, perceptions, and behaviors. There is no simple cure or "quick fix." Reduction of the overall levels will require the use of several different strategies that operate at different levels, ranging from the microlevel of individual perceptions, thoughts, and judgments, to interactive levels of interpersonal relations, to macrolevels that are influenced by social structures and historical meanings.

As we have seen, the human tendency to categorize people into groups results in biases that favor members of one's own group. Prejudice also results from anxiety about others who are different. This anxiety interferes with interpersonal relationships, often making them worse than they would otherwise be.

Prejudice is a Problem of Categorization

Once we categorize people into groups, we treat members of in-groups differently than we treat members of out-groups. These two tendencies—both to form social categories and to treat people differently on the basis of them—leaves us with what seems to be an insurmountable problem in terms of reducing prejudice and its consequences. Social psychological theory and research have produced three strategies for dealing with these tendencies as a means of reducing prejudice.

Decategorization
Given that categorizing people into groups is a problem, one approach suggests we promote the opposite tendency, *decategorization.* Research shows clearly that, when we are able to reduce the tendency to categorize, stereotype formation diminishes and resultant prejudicial attitudes and behaviors recede. For example, Brewer and Miller (1984) propose that the problem of category-based social interactions is at the heart of prejudice. People do not relate to one other as individuals, but rather as an African American and a European American, a gay man and heterosexual man, a Latino and an Asian American, and so on. With social categories as the basis of the interactions, biases in perceptions and behavior are likely to follow. The primary goal, then, according to Brewer and Miller (1984) is to find a way to decategorize perceptions and, subsequently, the basis of interactions. In order to decategorize others, we must do two things: (1) We must *differentiate* members of the out-groups, according them their individual identity that is distinctive to them as individual members of the out-group category (e.g., by emphasizing their roles as fireman, lover of opera, parent of a national merit scholar) and (2) we must *personalize* them by responding to them in terms of their individual relationship to ourselves (e.g, my neighbor, coworker, fellow jogger). The more information we have that is specific to individuals, the more easily we can differentiate them from other members of the out-group category.

Differentiation involves both seeing out-group members as distinctive from other "out-groupies" and seeing the self as increasingly divergent from other "in-groupies." This does not eliminate acknowledgment of the groups, but differentiates any two individual members when one of them is the self. This *personalization* comes about through contact and leads one to interact with an out-group member on the basis of individuating information about that person that is relevant to oneself. For example, Malik is a black adolescent male who loves to play chess and plays it well. This information may well differentiate him from others perceived to be in his out-group and may serve to personalize him as someone with whom one would like to play chess. The more opportunities for such differentiated and personalized interaction there are, the more likely the decategorization process will succeed. How does this happen?

Decategorization is most easily accomplished when intergroup contact meets the conditions of equal status, allows for disconfirmation of stereotypes, involves cooperative interdependence, ensures that egalitarian norms prevail, and promotes the establishment of intimacy. As we have seen, though, these conditions are hard to achieve. So, although decategorization is theoretically likely to reduce prejudice, it is impeded by the reality of societal conditions that inhibit the occurrence of the kind of contact that would allow these effects to happen.

Category Disconfirmation through Member Typicality

Prejudice is sustained by the stereotyping process. Conditions that weaken stereotypes ought to also reduce the occurrence of prejudice. But stereotypes are notably resistant to change (cf. Chapter 7). We may, for example, try to change stereotypes by pointing out that a person who is a member of a particular group does not possess the characteristics associated with that group. For example, Mae Jemison is an African American woman, a nuclear physicist, and an astronaut. She does not fit any stereotype of African Americans. Therefore, calling attention to her as an African American would, it is hoped, cause those holding a stereotype of African Americans to abandon or at least temper it.

Rothbart and John (1985) propose that stereotypes about a group can be disconfirmed in two ways: (1) through direct contact with members of the group and (2) through indirect "atmosphere" effects (e.g., laws, social norms, and parental and peer socialization). These contact situations may produce changes in a stereotype if two conditions are met: (1) the stereotype is susceptible to change (i.e., not tied to enduring personality processes and an individual's needs or strong countervailing influences) and (2) if the contact provides disconfirming information. Factors that influence a stereotype's susceptibility to change include how clear and easily documented the behavior is (i.e., the clearer the behavior, such as neatness and speech habits, the easier it is to disconfirm), the number of instances needed to disconfirm a trait (research shows that unfavorable traits require *fewer* observations to confirm, and *more* observations to disconfirm, than favorable traits require), and the number of instances in which it is possible to confirm or disconfirm a trait (e.g., friendliness is easy to confirm, bravery is not).

Therefore personal attributes that are unclear, unfavorable, and infrequently expressed will be most difficult to disconfirm. But there is another difficulty. The disconfirming information may be isolated from the prevailing stereotype. G. W. Allport (1954) described this process as *re-fencing,* during which beliefs are protected from disconfirming information by dividing a category into functionally isolated parts. For example, Dr. Jemison is no longer seen as a black American, but is now prototypical of an astrophysicist astronaut. Her ability to promote change in

Dr. Mae Jemison—African American, nuclear physicist, woman, astronaut, atypical exemplar! (NASA)

the stereotypical beliefs about black Americans depends, in part, on her ability to simultaneously reflect disconfirming information about the stereotype *and* to be prototypical of the stereotyped group.

You can see that reducing the tendency to stereotype is not easy. Rothbart and John (1985) argue that the best way to change a stereotype is to attach the group-category label (say, "black") to an instance of disconfirming information about the stereotype. Weber and Crocker (1983) showed that pairing a *prototypical member* of the social category with *disconfirming information* was shown to change the stereotypical judgment the most. They paired an atypical behavior (e.g., wearing ill-fitting clothes or having difficulty analyzing problems and reaching logical conclusions) with the social category "corporate lawyers." When the lawyers with whom this information was paired were otherwise prototypical of corporate lawyers (i.e., white, rich, married), this disconfirming information affected the judgments subjects made about lawyers. However, when this disconfirming information was paired with lawyers who were otherwise "poor fits" to the beliefs about lawyers (i.e., black, poor, and single), the disconfirming information had little impact.

The implication of this analysis is that when disconfirming information about a group stereotype is encountered and when the person is considered to be *atypical* of the group, people do no tend to change the stereotype about the group. Instead, they simply form *subtypes* of the group that are distinguished from (fenced off from) the group stereotype. One could argue that if new and disconfirming information is forced into people's consciousness, then a proliferation of subtypes may eventually make the superordinate category no longer effective in organizing attitudes about the group. But, in the short term, contact with disconfirming information may not affect stereotyped beliefs very much.

However, we also make note that it takes more instances to change beliefs about unfavorable and unclear traits, those that are most commonly associated with racial stereotypes, than it does to change those about favorable and unambiguous traits. Rothbart and John (1985) further note that repeated individual-level contact may not be effective because the individuals may be fenced off from the group and be considered atypical of others in the group. Furthermore, in order for disconfirming information to change the group stereotype, the group label must be salient. This is another argument against the colorblind approach. It is only when the group is salient that disconfirming information can have any impact on the stereotype of it.

Devine and Baker (1991) found that aggressiveness and hostility were traits associated with African Americans. The Rothbart and John (1985) analysis suggests that it is not through having friends who are black and peaceful or in seeing black nurses and priests pray for peace, for example, that this stereotype will change. Rather, it is most likely to change when a person thought to be typical of the group—say a "gangsta" rapper—is shown to be, say, nonhostile and unaggressive.

Maurer, Park, and Rothbart (1995) offer another view of these processes, *subgrouping*. Whereas in subtyping group members who disconfirm a stereotype are mentally clustered together and set aside as "exceptions to the rule," in subgrouping, clusters of individuals within a group are mentally linked together by virtue of their similarities (i.e., subgroups) and distinguished from remaining group members. However, unlike subtypes, subgroups may be perceived not just because they disconfirm a stereotype, but because they confirm it in a distinctive way. One of the consequences of this distinction between subtypes and subgroups is that subtypes leave the stereotype unchanged, even in the face of disconfirming examples, but subgroups lead the perceiver to appreciate the diverse ways in which group members may manifest the group stereotype.

Maurer, Park and Rothbart (1995) tested the subtype versus subgroup distinction by asking college students to sort information about 16 members of a group of volunteers in a Big Brother program (out of a total of 100 members), who were characterized stereotypically as helpful, politically liberal, and academically and socially competent, and as having come from relaxed family environments. Under subtyping instructions, subjects were simply asked to sort the people into two piles: one that confirmed and one that disconfirmed the prevailing stereotype. Under subgroup instructions, subjects were to sort the people into as many piles as they wished based on their similarities and differences. Information about the 16 individuals confirmed the stereotype in 13 cases and disconfirmed it in 3. In those confirming cases, four subgroups (of 4, 3, 3, and 3 people each) were created, each of which confirmed the stereotype in different ways. After completing these sorting tasks, subjects were asked to evaluate the overall stereotypicality of all 100 of the Big Brother volunteers, not just the 16 they had read about. Results confirmed their expectations that subjects who were led to using subtyping strategies perceived the group members to be more similar to each other overall, and disconfirming members to be more atypical of the group, than subgrouping subjects did. Thus subtyping processes by which one simply separates stereotype confirming from disconfirming members allows one to leave the stereotype intact by accentuating the homogeneity of the group and the distinctiveness of those disconfirming members.

Subgrouping leads one to perceive greater variability within the group even as the members are still perceived to fit the group stereotype. The importance of this finding is that even while maintaining the group stereotype, the perception of diversity within the group weakens the perceived homogeneity and thus the tendency to apply the stereotype to all members of the group.

Prejudice is a Problem of Intergroup Anxiety

If whites tend to think blacks are hostile or aggressive, and blacks tend not to trust whites, then interactions between them are likely to suffer from tensions and anxiety. S. Steele (1990) implied as much when he suggested that blacks fear the shame of discovering they may, in fact, be somehow inferior to whites and that whites fear they may be guilty of being racists as charged. The tensions of racial feelings, fears, and expectancies place a large burden on racial interactions. Members of different social groups may therefore avoid interaction because of anxiety. However, non-contact is sure to perpetuate the feelings that give rise to anxiety in the first place. What can be done to reduce anxiety in interpersonal, intergroup interactions?

Intergroup Contact May Reduce Anxiety

Stephan and Stephan (1995; Stephan, 1994) argue that the anxiety aroused by interpersonal experiences with members of racial or ethnic groups mediates the tendency to adopt positive or negative attitudes or evaluations of these interacting partners. They propose that most intergroup encounters are accompanied by anxiety. Therefore, the researchers were interested in the role of negative affect on social judgments. Anxiety consists of thought processes (worrying) and physiological reactions (a state of negative arousal). When we worry and feel negatively aroused, it will affect how we behave and what we feel in a situation. Stephan (1994) proposed that experiencing intergroup anxiety would have (1) behavioral consequences in that it would augment the dominant response in the situation, (2) affective consequences in the form of emotional reactions and polarized evaluations, and (3) cognitive consequences in that old patterns of stereotyping, expectations, and negative attitudes would be resorted to. To test this proposition, Stephan (1994) had white subjects perform a complex decision task about what to do about human survival after a nuclear holocaust. Each subject was paired with either a black or white confederate. Subjects were given feedback that the dyad's performance was disproportionately determined by the confederate. When the dyad did well, the subjects' emotional reactions were more positive toward the African American than toward the white partner. But when the dyad did poorly, the subject was more negative toward the black partner than toward the white partner. It was assumed that for white subjects, being paired with a black confederate would be more arousing than being paired with a white confederate. When the dyad was successful, this arousal energized a positive response, but when the dyad was unsuccessful, arousal moderated a negative reaction. The implication of this finding is that interracial interactions can heighten arousal and intensify the prevailing response tendencies. So a negative interracial interaction will be worsened and a positive one enhanced by the effects of arousal. They found similar effects when dyads with one white and one black partner performed tasks under cooperative (positive) or competitive (negative) conditions.

Stephan has repeatedly found that intergroup anxiety predicts attitudes and evaluations toward a variety of groups. Negative attitudes toward Mexican immigrants, the elderly, and gay men are all significantly related to the degree of intergroup anxiety they arouse in young white heterosexual subjects. Because Stephan and Stephan (1995) have found that the magnitude of these effects varies across social groups, they suggest that the frequency and conditions of contact will determine the magnitude and the nature of intergroup anxiety. Presumably, the more often intergroup contact occurs, the lower the degree of anxiety will be and the smaller the impact anxiety will have on attitudes.

Reducing prejudice, then, will depend in part on reducing the level of anxiety that is present in interaction situations. How can we do this? It seems clear, again, that contact is necessary. However, if the conditions are not "ripe," contact may worsen intergroup relations (cf. Zartman and Aurik [1991] for an analysis of "ripeness" that describes the conditions under which international conflict has the best chance of being reduced and a related discussion in Chapter 8).

Kicking the Prejudice Habit

Devine and colleagues (Devine, 1989; Devine, Monteith, Zuwerink, and Elliot, 1991; Devine, Evett, and Vasquez-Suson, in press) argue that widespread tendencies toward social categorization and stereotyping do not lead inexorably to prejudice. That is, in spite of the ease with which one can learn negative stereotypes about out-groups, and the profound impact these stereotypes can have when perceptions and interactions proceed automatically or mindlessly, one can bring these perceptual and judgmental processes under cognitive control and thereby reduce their adverse prejudicial influences. In essence, Devine and her colleagues suggest reducing prejudice is a lot like kicking a bad habit!

Devine and Monteith (1993) suggest that low-prejudice people may behave in prejudiced ways because of automatic consequences of socialization in a high-prejudice society. That is, a person's contact with a member of a negatively stereotyped target group automatically activates that stereotype and, if nothing intervenes, the person will react in a stereotype-consistent way (e.g., become fearful and clutch his or her wallet when an African American male enters the elevator). Now, if this person has established and internalized egalitarian standards as a central part of his or her identity, such behavior will be perceived to be discrepant with this identity. This discrepancy activates negative, self-directed affect (i.e., guilt, or even shame). This self-directed negative affect is associated with stereotype use and responses. Therefore, because these reactions are both aversive and inconsistent with the internalized, nonprejudiced identity, the person will attempt to regulate his or her behavior so as to remove the discrepancy and thereby reduce guilt and diminish the acceptance of stereotypes. Simply put, prejudice reduction may be a behavioral response to guilt!

This model somewhat resembles the joke about the psychologists and the lightbulb: "How many psychologists does it take to change a lightbulb? Only one, but the bulb has to really want to change!" (See also Dunton and Fazio, 1996.) Devine and colleagues focus their attention on low and moderately prejudiced people. The first important point about this model is that being white, heterosexual, or male is not *ipso facto* consignment to the purgatory of being prejudiced. Much of their research demonstrates that low-prejudiced people can, through controlled processes, evaluate their attitudes, beliefs, and reactions and reduce the expression of prejudice (Devine, 1989). Moreover, when they discover that they have behaved or reacted in a stereotypical way, they feel bad—they feel *compunction* (Devine et al., 1991). This bad feeling triggers specific efforts to eradicate these wrongful feelings and behaviors.

For example, Monteith (1991) made heterosexual subjects feel that their responses to a questionnaire revealed a level of antihomosexual attitude that was greater than their self-concepts would condone. Subjects then participated in a second study, supposedly unconnected to the first, in which their responses to various aspects of humor were assessed. Among the jokes that were rated were two that explicitly made fun of homosexuals. Monteith expected that, among low-prejudiced subjects, activating the prejudice-relevant discrepancy would reduce their reaction of amusement at the homosexual humor. She reasoned that they would regulate the humor behavior to guard against expressions of homosexual prejudice. Moreover, she did not expect this prejudice-relevant discrepancy to have any effect on high-prejudice subjects, because they would not find it necessary to regulate their behavior—to them, being prejudiced was not a problem.

Results show that the funniness of the jokes was rated lower overall by low- than by high-prejudice subjects, as shown in Table 11.1. In addition, as predicted, funniness ratings were lower in the prejudice-relevant condition than in the prejudice-irrelevant control condition for low-prejudice subjects, but the prejudice manipulation had no effect on funniness ratings for high-prejudice subjects. So, when not being prejudiced matters to us, and we detect that we may have failed to meet our own egalitarian standards, we will activate self-regulatory mechanisms that protect us from such behavior in the future. It feels bad, in other words, to be prejudiced and we try to do something about it.

But, *can* we do something about being prejudiced? Doing something about it is not entirely within our power. That is, what constitutes prejudicial behavior depends not only on what we do, but on how what we do is perceived! One may believe, for example, that treating people as individuals is the most unprejudiced thing one can do. That is, one should disregard race, gender, ethnicity, or sexual orientation, and treat everyone on their own terms as individuals. This is the color-blind approach, and it is a reasonable idea. However, it has two possible drawbacks: (1) It may be perceived as implying the person's race, gender, ethnicity, or sexual-orientation status is something to be overcome ("In spite of your race, Latifa, I will treat you as my co-worker"). Or (2) this egalitarian attitude may be perceived by the other person as condescending, at worst, or misguided, at best.

TABLE 11.1 FUNNINESS OF HOMOSEXUAL HUMOR AS A FUNCTION OF PREJUDICE LEVEL AND WHETHER AN ATTITUDE DISCREPANCY IS PREJUDICE-RELEVANT

Prejudice Level	Prejudice-Relevant Discrepancy	Prejudice-Irrelevant Discrepancy
Low prejudice	2.45	3.71
High prejudice	5.38	5.21

SOURCE: From Devine, P. G., Evett, S. R., and Vasquez-Suson, K. A., (in press). "Exploring the Interpersonal Dynamics of Intergroup Contact." In R. M. Sorrentino and E. T. Higgins (eds.), *Handbook of Motivation and Cognition: The Interpersonal Context* (Vol. 3.) New York: Guilford.

Knowing that one may not "know" how to behave so as to be perceived as nonprejudiced may be a source of anxiety in interracial interactions. Even worse, believing that there may be no way to behave that will not be construed as prejudiced in interpersonal relations involving members of other groups may arouse even more anxiety, leading eventually to avoidance of interracial situations.

Devine and colleagues (Devine and Monteith, 1993; Devine et al., in press) suggest that participants' merely being motivated to behave in a nonprejudicial fashion is not enough to create a smooth flow of interpersonal, intergroup interactions. Rather, they suggest that, in addition to such egalitarian motivation, one's success in intergroup interpersonal interactions will depend on one's self-perceived ability to respond consistently with one's nonprejudiced standards. This belief depends on one's expectation that one *can* behave in a nonprejudicial fashion (i.e., self-efficacy expectancy) *and* that the other person will accept the behavior as it was intended (i.e., expectancy outcomes). Under these terms, it is easier to *want* to do the right thing than to do it!

Devine et al. (in press) conducted a series of studies to test this idea. In the first study, subjects rated low, moderately low, and high in prejudice toward homosexuals were asked about their ability to behave in a nonprejudicial way toward a homosexual person (self-efficacy) and how their behavior would be perceived by a homosexual person (expectancy outcome). *Low-prejudiced subjects* reported that they *could* behave in a nonprejudiced manner *and* that their behavior would be perceived as nonprejudiced by a homosexual person. They did not report feeling heightened self-focus or social anxiety either about their ability to be nonprejudicial or to have their behavior perceived for what it was. *Moderately low-prejudice* subjects reported that they could behave in a nonprejudiced manner, but they doubted that their behavior would be perceived as nonprejudiced. This discrepancy between intentions and outcomes was associated with a heightened level of self-focus and social anxiety. That is, the anxiety is not based on a negative attitude, dislike, or overt prejudice, but on the fear that the subjects' egalitarian standards would not be met by their own behavior, or that the homosexual target would not accept the egalitarian motive for that behavior. *High-prejudice subjects* were unmotivated to behave in nonprejudicial ways and did not expect that they *could.* They reported that a homosexual person would likely perceive their behavior as prejudiced. They reported social anxiety that was not based on fear of the target's perception of their intentions, but on antipathy toward interacting with a homosexual person at all.

From the perspective of a homosexual target, expecting that one would be disliked by that person or that one's behavior would be negatively evaluated by him or her was associated with a higher degree of tension and anxiety in the interaction. Therefore when a moderately low-prejudiced person interacts with a target who expects to be devalued, anxiety may exist on both sides. This mutual anxiety escalates miscommunication and has a tendency to create a self-fulfilling prophesy whereby each "confirms" his or her own negative expectation. So, having positive motivation to behave in a nonprejudiced way is not enough. Success depends on self-attribution and the reaction of the target to one's behavior.

Today, on college campuses, and in society at large, these difficult interpersonal interactions are exacerbated by these perceptual differences. It is not enough to adopt an egalitarian belief system and to aspire to behave in a way that is consistent with it. One may not have the behavioral repertoire to behave in a nonprejudicial manner. Moreover, even if one does, one may no be perceived as having done so. The fear of behaving inappropriately or in a manner that will be construed negatively can arouse anxiety and undermine one's intentions to behave in a positive way. Reducing prejudice, then, may require reducing anxiety of expectation. How do we do it? We must recognize the sources of anxiety and the critical role they play in the course of interpersonal interactions between members of different, socially salient groups. We must also recognize that the definition of the situation will depend on the intentions and construals of both interacting people. The transactional approach, then, offers a better way of identifying the path to prejudice reduction.

Negative Interdependence

In the United States, we strive for harmonious intergroup relations among diverse ethnic, racial, and gender groups. But, as so much of the literature we have reviewed clearly shows, there is an enormous degree of mistrust and dislike between members of these different groups. One fundamental aspect of this ubiquitous form of conflict is the fact that members of groups different from our own can so easily "push our buttons." Why is this?

We have seen that mere categorization of people into groups creates in-group biases that favor one's own group over others. It is precisely in situations where groups come into contact that much of the most virulent forms of aggression and conflict occur (see Chapter 9). If we could stay out of each others' way, remain segregated from each other, and not suffer the negative consequences of doing so (usually in the form of participation or opportunity), perhaps we could all go our own ways. But we cannot. We, in fact, do live and work together. We share in the processes of society and, therefore, must interact with each other across group boundaries.

This inevitability of intergroup interaction raises an important question of linkage, or interdependence. *Interdependence* refers to a situation in which each person's outcomes depend both on his or her own behavior and that of another person (Thibaut and Kelley, 1959). *Negative interdependence* occurs when one spontaneously assumes that members of the out-group are likely to obstruct one's goal attainment (Fiske and Ruscher, 1993). Negative interdependence creates negative affect in two ways: (1) Negative reaction occurs simply because the target belongs to the out-group (the mere categorization effects, discussed earlier) and (2) negative reaction is a function of the presumption that, because the target belongs to the out-group, he or she will be inclined to block one's goal-attainment activities.

Once again, we come back to negative feelings or anxiety of affect directed at members of an out-group. The fact that this reaction is based on interdependence, which is inevitable in this society, again tells us that reducing prejudice must be a transactional process. When power is asymmetrical (i.e., when members of one group hold more of it than is held by another), then the "settlement" in an interaction conflict, say, is influenced more by the group in control. One way to reduce the negative interdependence and, in turn, the negative affect it causes is for the low-power group to withdraw from the relationship. However, this strategy, which may reduce negative feelings borne of interdependence, will further isolate one group from another; the intergroup anxiety will continue. One means of reducing the tendency for this negative interdependence to disrupt the flow of social interaction is to reduce group-based asymmetrical power. This involves lowering hierarchical group stereotypes and modifying social structures that perpetuate group-linked power asymmetries. For example, if all the bosses are white men, then people of color and women will perpetually be involved in interdependent situations that often arouse negative affect and intergroup anxiety. However, by demonstrating a nonadversarial intention and a well-reasoned attitude toward the exercise of power those in dominant positions may be able to reduce anxiety and improve intergroup relationships. Learning what behaviors are perceived as threatening, what outcomes are perceived as unfair, and what attitudes are perceived as stereotypic are among the ways in which out-group power-dominant members can try to lessen the adverse impacts and manifestations of negative interdependence processes.

Motivation to Control Prejudiced Reactions

Devine (1989) makes a distinction between high- and low-prejudice people on the basis of their identity as a nonprejudiced person. Low-prejudiced people tend to see themselves as egalitarian and try to behave accordingly. When they fail, they are upset (cf. Devine and Monteith, 1993; Devine et al., 1991). Devine (1989) showed that, although racial stereotypes may operate at an automatic level in everyone, if subjects are given some explicit control over what they say and do, low-prejudice people are far more likely than their high-prejudice counterparts to express egalitarian views.

Dunton and Fazio (1996) also argue that individual differences in degrees of prejudice exist. People who are motivated to control prejudiced reactions are first of all committed to an egalitarian view of themselves and aware of the possibility of biasing behaviors. Dunton and Fazio (1996) designed a measure of these differences, the 17-item Motivation to Control Prejudiced Reactions Scale (MCPRS). The MCPRS is designed around two independent factors (Dunton and Fazio, 1996): The first factor assesses the extent to which a person is *concerned with acting prejudiced,* for example:

"It is important to me that other people not think I'm prejudiced."
"I feel guilty when I have a negative thought or feeling about a black person."
"It bothers me a great deal when I think I've offended someone, so I'm always careful to consider other people's feelings."

The second factor does not focus on prejudice but on exercising *restraint in order to avoid dispute,* for example:

"I always express my thoughts and feelings, regardless of how controversial they might be."(R)[2]
"I am not afraid to tell others what I think, even when I know they disagree with me."(R)
"If I were participating in a class discussion and a black student expressed an opinion with which I disagreed, I would be hesitant to express my own viewpoint."

It is clear that people high in motivation to avoid prejudice are likely to be anxious if they feel their efforts will not be successful. This measure, then, may provide a quick insight into the likelihood that a person will experience interpersonal or intergroup anxiety, be inclined to engage in deliberative processing of information about other people, and try to control his or her automatic tendencies to behave in biasing ways.

In fact, Dunton and Fazio found that white subjects for whom automatic negativity toward blacks was activated in the photograph-primed evaluative judgment procedure (cf. Fazio et al., 1995, see Chapter 6 for description of procedure) were

---

[2](R) means the score is reversed. A low score will indicate a high degree of motivation to control prejudice reactions.

less likely to make negative evaluations of blacks when they had high motivation to control-prejudice scores. Low control-prejudice subjects went ahead and made negative assessments. Subjects who responded positively to black faces in the photographs also made positive evaluations. So, we have evidence that, even when a negative reaction is automatically activated, people who have a personal desire not to appear prejudiced can constrain expression of negative judgments.

This is likely to be a double-edged finding. On the one hand, to the extent that nonverbal cues congruent with the automatic negativity are leaked, such cues may be detected by the target and perceived for what they reveal about the person's attitude. Overtly expressed positive evaluations, however sincere they are, may be detected as hypocrisy and lead to negative reactions from the target. In this way, intergroup anxiety may be more intense for these people who wish to control their prejudiced reactions, but who have rather automatically negative ones.

Simulation and Role-Play

Jane Elliott was teaching third grade in virtually all-white Riceville, Iowa, in 1968, when Martin Luther King Jr. was assassinated. Her students were struck by the news of his assassination, asking "Why did they kill a king?" She decided that these kids literally knew nothing of race relations or what it might mean to be black in the United States. She decided to conduct an experiment that would help to teach them what it might be like (Elliott, 1970; *Eye of the Storm*). One day she announced to the class that, although they were all white children, had known each other for years, and came from the same small town, they were not alike. Some of them had brown eyes, and some had blue eyes. She asserted that the blue-eyed kids were smarter, nicer, neater, and better than the brown-eyed kids. She passed out arm bands and required brown-eyed kids to wear them. She selectively rewarded blue-eyed kids and punished brown-eyed kids. Blue-eyed kids got to go first in line, were called on more often, and were praised when they got a right answer. They got to stay longer at recess and to go back for seconds in the cafeteria. When the class came back from recess, one kid was pouting and withdrawn, clearly agitated because he had gotten into a fight. Someone had insulted him by calling him "brown-eyes." He described to Ms. Elliott how they fought and told her, with a depth of emotion, "I punched him in the gut."

On the second day, the children switched statuses. The brown-eyed kids laughed in glee as they shed their stigmatized role and assumed the dominant one. The blue-eyed kids moaned as they contemplated their fate. During reading exercises, the blue-eyed kids read faster than the brown-eyed children on the first day of the experiment, when they were superior. The brown-eyed children read faster than the blue-eyed children did when they were on top. In short, this little exercise was able, in just a couple of days, to re-create the conditions of intergroup conflict, in-group bias, and the hostility and performance decrement that followed. The kids even "invented" surveillance techniques. For example, when the class left for lunch, a blue-eyed kid suggested to Ms. Elliott that she alert the servers in the cafeteria of the rule that prohibited seconds for brown-eyed kids. The superior group wanted to be sure there was no breakdown in the social norms or the administration of them by which a brown-eyed kid would rise above his or her station. The ABC network's *Eye of the Storm* video is a powerful illustration of how easily intergroup animosities can be established. It also shows how powerfully all of the students were affected by this experience. At the end, they recited with glee and relief how important it was not to treat people on the basis of their skin (or eye) color,

that we are all brothers and sisters. Having experienced what it felt like to be castigated, demeaned, and rejected, they were eager to accept their differences.

Byrnes and Kiger (1990) were interested in whether introducing would-be
teachers to this simulated blue-eye–brown-eye experience would help them adopt
a more egalitarian attitude toward their students. They conducted an experimental
intervention with 164 white university students. Control subjects attended their
usual classes and heard lectures and read materials that discussed important issues
of cultural awareness. The experimental subjects saw the film *A Class Divided*, a follow-up of the Elliot experiment. The film showed the original video and had the
same kids (now grown up) comment on their experiences. Experimental subjects
also participated in the blue-eyed versus brown-eyed experiment.

Subjects' attitudes toward racial tolerance were measured by a social distance
scale (measuring the degree to which subjects would accept blacks in a variety of
social situations) and a social scenario scale (assessing the degree of subjects' willingness to condone discriminatory behavior toward blacks). Results showed no difference on the social distance measure. However, subjects who had been through
the experimental treatment were less willing to condone discrimination against
blacks. They also solicited these subjects a year later to contribute to the Martin
Luther King Jr. fellowship fund. No differences in contributions were obtained
(only three people gave anything).

Although the results were not definitive, the unwillingness of subjects who
had been through the intervention to accept blatant racial discrimination suggests
that heightened sensitivity can be achieved by this simulation technique.

REDUCING PREJUDICE THROUGH INTERGROUP PROCESSES

The principal theoretical, empirical, and applied approach to reducing prejudice is
the idea of intergroup contact proposed by G. W. Allport (1954). Allport noted that,
although it was believed by many that simply by bringing people together without
regard to race, color, religion, or national origin, we could destroy stereotypes and
develop friendly attitudes, such positive effects of contact were not automatic. The
principle of *peaceful progression* suggests four stages through which intergroup contact passes:

Sheer contact → intergroup competition → accommodation → assimilation

The immediate consequence of bringing groups together, or *sheer contacts*, is *competition*. We saw from the Sherif work how volatile competition can be and how biased one's perceptions and behavior become in support of one's own group. *Accommodation* can be thought of as peaceful coexistence. Rodney King's question,
"Can we all get along?" can be rephrased simply as "Can we at least coexist?" The
final stage of this peaceful progression is *assimilation*. Hitler's "Final Solution" was
the extermination of all Jews. Some people regard assimilation as the *cultural* extermination of one's background and heritage, basic ingredients of one's being. If assimilation is the end point of a peaceful progression of contact between groups of
unequal power, then, although the assimilated masses will be different by degrees
as a result of influences of both groups, the final picture will decidedly resemble the
dominant more than it will the subordinate group.

Allport acknowledges that contact between groups may not be as simple or desirable a strategy for reducing group conflict as it might appear. After analyzing the numerous examples of contact and its consequences, he arrived at a general expression of when contact was most likely to be successful in bringing groups closer together (Allport, 1954, p. 281).

> Prejudice (unless deeply rooted in the character structure of the individual) may be reduced by equal status contact between majority and minority groups in the pursuit of common goals. The effect is greatly enhanced if this contact is sanctioned by institutional supports (i.e., by law, custom or social atmosphere), and provided it is of a sort that leads to the perception of common interests and common humanity between members of the two groups.

For contact to improve relationships between the groups, they must have equal status and their association must be made with the intent of working toward common goals. The contact itself must be sanctioned by relevant authorities, legally or socially, and the interactions should heighten the perception of commonality of interests, purpose, and humanity. This is no small order.

Equal Status Contact

It is perhaps not surprising that, over the past 40 years, research on intergroup contact has yielded mixed results. Stephan (1986) showed that, in the first years of school desegregation, race relations improved in only about 25 percent of the cases. The complexity of social psychological phenomena quickly became clear, and the conditions that are required for the best possible contact outcomes were too often not met. As Cook (1962) suggested, contact must break down negative stereotypes; participants need to be similar to each other—that is, have common purpose, goals, or attitudes; and other in-group members (in this case, Whites) must not pressure for negative behaviors of other members. That is, if a negative group norm were established for intergroup cooperation, an individual may well behave negatively toward an out-group member, even if he or she personally would prefer to behave more positively.

Amir (1969) offered a careful and detailed assessment of the contact hypothesis. From this assessment he was able to enumerate conditions that were either favorable or unfavorable to producing positive intergroup relations. Table 11.2 lists these conditions.

Test yourself using Amir's (1969) assessment. Try to think of a situation of interracial contact with which you are personally familiar. Now, review the conditions *favorable* to prejudice reduction via intergroup contact and rate each of the six favorable conditions on a scale of 1 (low) to 10 (high). Now, do the same thing for the *unfavorable* conditions. Sum your ratings separately for the favorable and the unfavorable conditions. Which number is higher? If the rating of favorable conditions is higher, there is a good chance that contact will produce an amelioration of prejudice. If the unfavorable condition rating is higher, then contact may increase rather than diminish the degree of prejudice.

If we are to believe the popular media portrayals of events of racial contact in the United States, it would seem that a far greater number of unfavorable conditions exist. On February 24, 1994, principal Hulond Humphries of Randolph County High School in Wedowee, Alabama, took the occasion of a school assembly

TABLE 11.2 FAVORABLE AND UNFAVORABLE CONDITIONS FOR THE REDUCTION OF PREJUDICE THROUGH INTERGROUP CONTACT

Conditions Favorable to Prejudice Reduction through Intergroup Contact	Conditions Unfavorable to Prejudice Reduction through Intergroup Contact
1. When there is equal status contact between members of various ethnic groups	1. When the contact situation produces competitions between groups
2. When the contact is between members of a majority and *higher* status members of minority group	2. When the contact is unpleasant, involuntary, and tense
3. When an authority person and/or the general social climate are in favor of and promote the contact	3. When the status of one group is lowered as a result of the contact
4. When the contact is more intimate and less casual	4. When members of one group are highly frustrated
5. When the contact is pleasant or rewarding to each other	5. When the groups in contact have moral or ethical standards that are objectionable to each other
6. When members of both groups interact in important activities or develop common or superordinate goals that are more important than individual goals of each group	6. When the group in the numerical minority are of lower status than members of the majority

SOURCE: Adapted from Amir (1969). "Contact Hypothesis in Ethnic Relations." *Psychological Bulletin 71*, 319–342.

to threaten cancellation of the senior prom if mixed-race couples showed up. He learned by a show of hands that 12 of his students planned to attend the prom with a person of another race. He singled out ReVonda Bowen, whose father is white and mother black, to illustrate his concerns. When Ms. Bowen asked who she should take if he did not want mixed-race couples, he reportedly replied, "That's a problem, ReVonda. Your mom and daddy made a mistake having a mixed-race child." (Herbert, 1994, p. A21). Although Mr. Humphries rescinded his threat the next day, the furor did not subside. Humphries was suspended for his actions (cheering from black parents), but his pay was continued (cheering by white parents). Mr. Humphries was finally relieved of his position and barred from visiting any school in the district during school hours until 1997. On August 6, 1994, the high school was burned to the ground. Perhaps ironically, it was a 25-year-old black man, Christopher Lynn Johnson, who was charged with arson. On October 21, 1995, he was acquitted in federal court of setting the fire that destroyed Randolph County High School (Smothers, 1995).

Hewstone and Brown (1986) added their own list of reasons that the contact hypothesis has not fared well in experimental research. First, they believe that the contact hypothesis assumes that much prejudice is caused by ignorance. This assumption is certainly partially true, but efforts to confirm a positive link between ignorance of other groups and prejudice have been only moderately successful (e.g., Stephan and Stephan, 1984). The simple idea is that, if ignorance is the basis of prejudice, then contact will reduce ignorance of other groups, the basis for prejudice will be removed, and prejudice will be reduced. But what happens if the other

"An epidemic of terror" said Deval Patrick, Assistant Attorney General for Civil Rights, of the rash of church bombings and fires. The Rev, Patricia Lowman with her daughter, Stacey, stand in the remains of her church on June 1, 1996, in Dixiana, South Carolina. More than 30 fires were started at black churches in the South in the first half of 1996 alone. (Donna Binder/Impact Visuals)

group is, in fact, dissimilar in basic ways? What is then learned by contact is the degree of *dissimilarity*, not similarity. Rather than learning something that makes us closer, we may learn that we are, in fact, further apart than had been imagined! In other words, under some circumstances, it is contact that *increases* prejudice!

Second, Hewstone and Brown (1986) suggest that the direction of causality cannot be easily determined. That is, does contact result from favorable attitudes, or is it the other way around? Deutsch and Collins (1951) showed elegantly in an experiment that, among tenants in racially integrated housing (assigned by lottery), contact between whites and blacks was greater than in segregated housing and that racial attitudes in the integrated settings were uniformly more positive. This one study suggests that contact can improve racial attitudes. But there are relatively few such experimental studies, and the broad empirical support for this causal claim is not substantial.

Third, when two people meet, are they meeting as two individuals or as individual *representatives* of their respective social groups? The former case may be called *interpersonal* contact, whereas the latter may be considered *intergroup* contact. The fact is that both are true. We consider racial conflict an intergroup phenomenon, but we often cite interpersonal contact as the way to ameliorate intergroup hostility and reduce the categorical perception that underlies stereotyping. We made note of this difference in Chapter 8 (cf. pp. 231–234). We might thus hypothesize that the more salient a social attribute is for a person (what Frable, Blackstone, and Sherbaum [1990] called "master status"), the more likely the person is to interact with others on the basis of his or her own and the others' group membership.

Wedded to the group in this way, a person is also wedded to the positive attributes of the group, which may well increase the likelihood of in-group bias and out-group discrimination. Although interpersonal contact may proceed positively and without rancor, such unbiased behavior may be restricted to the interpersonal situation. Therefore, this positive behavior may be merely a reaction to the characteristics of the specific other person and may not be generalized in behavior to the group.

Fourth, when a situation does produce positive interracial attitudes among interacting racial group members, often those positive attitudes do not generalize either to the specific person in another situation or to other group members. For example, black and white children may share classrooms in school and even become good friends. But after school they tend to go their separate ways. If a white child who has a black classmate encounters a black child whom he or she does not know, the positive feelings toward a black friend do not extend to this new child. Cook (1978) suggests that generalization of positive attitudes acquired through interracial contact will occur only when there are other processes that support and bolster the attitude change. One such influence is peer support, formalized as norms that "allow" the group member to express positive racial attitudes without being ostracized or marginalized. Another is opportunity for interracial contact in more intimate settings. For example, residential ethnic and racial segregation is widespread (cf. Massey and Denton, 1993). Therefore, even when a person goes to school with people from diverse backgrounds or works with diverse others, the intimate social ties forged by sharing one's home and community concerns do not develop.

Lewis and Jhally (1993) have coined the term *enlightened racism* to identify this concept. Although we are talking about prejudice here, the concept is illustrative. According to Lewis and Jhally (1993) enlightened racism arises when whites perceive a successful black person as "evidence" that if one possesses positive personal qualities, one's race will not keep one from succeeding in the United States. Successful black exemplars are therefore "proof" that racism or racial discrimination is not responsible for the overall plight of blacks. What is responsible, according to the enlightened racist? This perspective leads the enlightened racist to the conclusion that *other* blacks' outcomes must result from their lack of those positive qualities that, when applied, lead to successful outcomes.

Hewstone and Brown (1986) offer several ways in which the contact hypothesis, with all of its weaknesses and flaws, may be bolstered. The strategies are familiar: Institute superordinate goals; create cooperative contact situations; create multi-identity contexts, where people share overlapping identities;[3] and change the expectations that people bring to an interaction. When these conditions are created, contact effects are much more likely to be positive.

Deprovincialization

Pettigrew (1996) defends the contact hypothesis by arguing that not only can inter-group contact improve the quality of relationships with members of the affected groups, but it can facilitate a broadening of acceptance of other groups. He calls this expanding openness to diverse others *deprovincialization.* He argues that the contact effects are indeed specific, but that they are not bound by as many limiting conditions as are often proposed. That is, some conditions are critical, and others are merely "catalytic." For Pettigrew (1996), the central mediation of positive contact effects consists of three processes:

1   Learning about the out-group
2   Generating affective ties to members of the out-group
3   Reappraisal of the *in-group* and a corresponding reduction in prejudice toward a variety of out-groups (i.e., deprovincialization)

The deprovincialization hypothesis was tested in four European countries (Germany, the Netherlands, Great Britain, and France). Attitudes of nearly 4000 white Europeans toward local minority groups as indicated below were assessed.

Country	Minority Group(s)	Number of Respondents[*]
Germany	Turks	985
France	Asians and North Africans	930
Netherlands	Surinamers and Turks	938
Great Britain	Asians and West Indians	953

[*]A given respondent was asked about one target group only. Therefore, in Germany, all 985 respondents were asked about Turks. In France, 475 evaluated Asians, and 455 evaluated North Africans. In the Netherlands, 462 respondents were asked about Surinamers and 476 about Turks. In Great Britain, 482 were asked about Asians and 471 were asked about West Indians.

Contact was measured in three domains: neighborhood, friends, and work. Respondents were asked whether many, a few, or no members of the target group lived in the neighborhood, were friends, or "work with you." *Blatant* (overt and

[3]This is a fundamental feature of the "diversity" argument. There is empirical support for the idea that, when two people interact, and both belong to multiple social categories, it is much more difficult to establish an us-them intergroup interaction. Although there are many who would cast the idea of human diversity in the sociopolitical grab-bag of political correctness, this can be one of the most effective means of reducing the ease with which contact exacerbates rather than ameliorates intergroup conflict.

consciously negative racial attitudes and behaviors) and *subtle* (covert and less conscious or obvious negativity) degrees of prejudice were measured on five subscales:

Subscale	Sample Item
Threat or rejection (blatant)	"British people and West Indians can never be really comfortable with each other, even if they are close friends."
Intimacy (blatant)	"I would (would not) be willing to have a sexual relationship with a West Indian."
Traditional values (subtle)	"West Indians living here should not push themselves where they are not wanted."
Cultural differences (subtle)	How similar do you think West Indians living here are to other British people such as yourself (in values, religious beliefs and practices, sexual values and practices, and language)
Positive emotions	How often have you felt sympathy (admiration) for West Indians living here?

Adapted from Pettigrew (1996).

Results showed that increased contact with diverse neighbors is associated with an *increase* in stress in daily life. This occurred in most samples in Europe, suggesting that neighborhood contact may not meet the contact conditions specified by G. W. Allport (1954). The same relationship is found for respondents who work in settings that show greater diversity. However, when one's *friends* are more representative of diverse groups, results showed a *decrease* in prejudice. In addition, contact increases positive emotions illustrated by the finding that, with greater contact among diverse friends, there is a greater likelihood a person will report having felt sympathy or admiration for a member of a minority group.

The issue of diversity is a tricky one. If we have what we might call "superficial diversity," then we may get negative effects, such as those shown for work and neighborhoods in the Pettigrew (1996) experiment. Interpersonal diversity makes more difference. If we think of diverse friends as a basis for what Aboud (1988) called *differentiation,* then a pattern is emerging. We break down social categorization when we have friends from a diverse social category. Such friends may get assimilated to the in-group, thereby widening and diversifying it.

The deprovincialization hypothesis proposes *affect* as a central mediator of the positive effects of intergroup contact. The social-cognition approach to stereotypes and prejudice suggested that bias may be an inevitable consequence of group categorization. An "us versus them" or "we versus they" attitude not only indicated group differences, but led inexorably to attitudinal, judgmental, and behavioral biases. In this view, it seems that cognitive processes *drive* perceptual, behavioral, and affective ones. Reducing prejudice then means we must somehow change the way we think of other people and the groups to which they belong—a tall order, to be sure. But the deprovincialization theory proposes that we must first become friends. Only then will the positive feelings generalize, the in-group be expanded, and distinctions from out-groups be lessened. The net effect of this process is the lowering of the in-group positivity bias.

Social Emotions

Smith (1993) also brings affect into the equation when he analyzes the role of "social emotions" in prejudice. Social identity results when we categorize ourselves into a specific group. Such self-categorization makes our group referent highly salient, and experiences of the group exert powerful affective and motivational forces on us. Smith (1993, p. 302) captures this sentiment with a sports example: "Fans who feel pride in the home team's successes, guilt when the team displays poor sportsmanship, or painful disappointment at its losses are experiencing social emotions—emotions triggered by events that are *group* relevant, rather than merely personally relevant." The implications of this view are that "in-group successes will lead to joy, threats to the ingroup to fear, and injustices suffered by the ingroup to anger" (Smith, 1993, p. 303).[4]

This model suggests that there is a three-stage dynamic process in social emotions, as follows:

1   A majority group member will first appraise the target person in terms of both his or her own group membership and the target's group membership. For example:
    Appraisal: A member of group A is receiving benefits that are undeserved and paid for by my group's tax dollars!
2   The person will experience an emotional reaction to the appraisal. For example:
    Prejudiced emotion: I feel anger and resentment at members of group A.
3   The appraisal and subsequent emotional reaction will lead to an emotion-based reaction or action toward group A. For example:
    Discrimination: I want to harm group A by reducing food-stamp and welfare benefits.

The key to this analysis is that prejudice is not so much a generalized set of attitudes or beliefs about group A, but specific appraisals of specific situations and specific behaviors. This specificity makes it possible for a person to hold very negative views toward some blacks (e.g., Jesse Jackson, unwed teen mothers) but quite positive views toward others (e.g., principals who preach discipline, teens who complete school in spite of bearing children). Smith (1993) suggests that the reduction of prejudice through mere contact will be difficult because (1) specific contacts are typically "interpersonal" and do not proceed on the basis of each person's group identity and (2) group appraisals are not likely to be altered by interpersonal experience with individual out-group members. As we saw earlier with the prob-

---

[4]In 1958, a young African American boxer named Floyd Paterson won the heavyweight championship of the world at the age of 21. In 1959, he defended his championship against the tall and muscular Swede Ingomar Johannsen. The unthinkable happened—Johannsen won. They had a rematch in 1960, and Patterson avenged his loss. In 1961, I was a college sophomore when they held the rematch. I listened to the fight with trepidation and hope. Beginning with Joe Louis, with the exception of an interlude in the form of Rocky Marciano, heavyweight champions were black. For African Americans, the heavyweight championship was one that we as a group could point to with pride and self-congratulations. Although Patterson won the "rubber" match, thereby "restoring our cultural and racial supremacy," I broke out in hives and had to go to the infirmary. When the films of Rodney King flashed across television sets across the country, many whites may well have been outraged at the brutality and the lack of justice. Many blacks may have virtually felt the blows.

lem of disconfirming stereotypes, the group label has to be salient before a specific interaction can modify it.

The point of this analysis is that, as a result of social identity processes, our attachment to our ingroup takes on emotional qualities. Therefore, our perceptions of behavior by out-group members arouses emotional reactions in us to the extent that we feel our group is treated unfairly either by these out-group members or by officials and other authorities. This emotional reaction can trigger specific discriminatory behaviors toward the out-group when they are seen to benefit unfairly to the disadvantage of our in-group. This emotional response may take the form of opposition to any policy or program perceived to be in the best interests of its members. The phenomenon works in both directions, too. For example, blacks may see any example of a white person's exploiting or demeaning a black person as evidence for the racism of whites individually and as a group. Whites, particularly men, may rail against the injustice of affirmative action, citing cases of its unfair application that are to their group's disadvantage. Yet, white men still numerically dominate the work force and, particularly, the top positions. It seems that perhaps there is an emotional attachment to the issue that is disproportionate to the specific, affirmative action–based problems the vast majority of white men actually face.

Smith and Henry (in press) argue that, as time passes, the boundary between oneself and members of one's socially identified group may fade, so that self-descriptive traits begin to overlap with group-descriptive traits. Let's consider, for example, a close relationship (such as marriage), when partners share traits (e.g., both are romantic, hard-working). In such a relationship, the self and the couple's social identity are closer together, and emotional appraisals of the in-group (in this case, the couple) are stronger. Smith and Henry (in press) had subjects make judgments of how descriptive several traits were of themselves, of a group to which they belonged (say, engineering majors), and of a group to which they did not belong (say, liberal arts majors). They found that subjects responded more quickly to traits that were self-descriptive *and* descriptive of their in-group. They responded more slowly when the trait was self-descriptive and *not* descriptive of the in-group.

Why is this important? The idea that social identity is simply an extension of self-identity is critical. Social identity theory suggests that we enhance our self-worth through identification with our social groups. This study suggests that we do so by actually merging—psychologically and emotionally—with our social groups (Smith and Henry, in press). This means that conflict between our in-group and any out-groups is facilitated by this attachment, and the ability to reduce conflict may depend critically on reducing the group-based distinction. That is, if we can make the out-group closer to the in-group, we can capitalize on this strong emotional attachment to the in-group. We might then find a positive basis for intergroup relations.

A word of caution is in order. This process also works from the vantage of stigmatized groups. Social identity theory today suggests that, in the case of stigmatized-group members, strong in-group identification may occur. This contradicts much theorizing of the 1940s and 1950s, which suggested (e.g., Kardiner and Ovesky, 1951) that stigmatized-group members would reject their own group. According to social identity theory, emotional attachment to members of the in-group means that any threat to the group is experienced emotionally as a threat to the self. Once the O. J. Simpson case was drawn in racial terms, for example, many blacks saw the prosecution as a threat not merely to Simpson but to blacks in general. The specific case of Simpson became the more general case of emotional appraisal of the out-group (whites, the prosecution, etc.). The unfairness of the treatment of blacks *in general* became an issue, and support for Simpson was promoted as an extension of black self- and social identity.

Social emotion, then, attaches to out-group representation and spills over to the evaluation of and behavior toward the group in general. It is to our advantage, then, to define groups broadly in order to encompass as much diversity as possible. That is what the recategorization process describes. We turn to it next.

Recategorization

Gaertner, Dovidio, and colleagues (Gaertner, Dovidio, Anastasio, Bachman, and Rust, 1993) have proposed that intergroup bias can be reduced by transforming the perceptions of members of two groups (characterized by "us" versus "them" and the competition and conflict inherent in these labels) to perceptions of one group in which all members now think of themselves as "we." This new perceptual reality is known as the *common in-group identity,* and the process by which it is achieved is called *recategorization.* How does this recategorization process work?

First of all, we begin with two groups—my group is "us," their group is "them." As we saw with the boys in Sherif's summer camp, competition-based conflict produces strong in-group bias coupled with out-group hostility. In Sherif's experiments (1966), the only way that conflict was reduced was through the creation of superordinate goals whose attainment required an interdependent relationship among *all* members of both groups. By forcing the members of competing groups into an interdependent relationship, the motivational energy of in-group bias was now diverted to incorporate former out-group members into a common in-group.

Recategorization takes place when the salience of existing common, superordinate group memberships is increased or when new circumstances are introduced that are shared by the members of the two groups (e.g., common fate, common tasks). It is further proposed (Gaertner et al., 1993) that this common in-group identity may be generalized to other members of the out-group who may not be involved in the immediate situation. Background factors determine the extent to which different groups have an interdependent relationship, have a differentiated and competitive relationship, have had a lot of or little contact with one another, or have coexisted within environments that foster egalitarian, oppressive, or hierarchical norms. The pattern of circumstances that characterize the context of group contact will determine whether the groups in question continue to be separately *categorized* (i.e., two groups; "*we*" versus "*they*"), *decategorized* (i.e., separate individuals, me and you), or *recategorized* (i.e., one group, "we"). Gaertner and colleagues (1993) suggest that when circumstances favor a one-group recategorization, the positive consequences that occur have the net effect of reducing intergroup conflict and in-group bias.

A study by Gaertner, Mann, Murrell, and Dovidio (1989) had subjects discuss the "winter survival problem" first as two three-person groups and later as a six-person aggregate. Subjects were required to decide, in rank order, which of 10 items they should salvage from a plane wreck in the woods of northern Minnesota in mid-January. During the six-person aggregate process, subjects were either segregated by their initial group memberships, integrated (every other seat), or treated as six separate individuals. They chose one name for all six (recategorized) as the aggregate, maintained their previous two group names (categorized), or adopted six new names, one for each person (decategorized). Each subject rated each other participant. The measure of in-group bias was provided by the relative difference in ratings of former in-group members and former out-group members. The more positively subjects rated former in-group members relative to former out-group members, the greater the degree of in-group bias. Results showed that the greatest bias was found when subjects were treated as two groups (bias index of .39), next came the separate-individual condition (bias index of .27). The least bias was shown in the one-group treatment (bias index of .17). Gaertner et al. (1989) found that the rejection of bias in the recategorized (one-group) condition occurred primarily by *increasing the attractiveness of the former out-group members.* By contrast, the bias was reduced in the decategorization (separate-individual) condition by *decreasing the attractiveness of former in-group members.*

To put this in a concrete context, the recategorization effect suggests that if whites could be made to feel as one group with blacks, their positive feelings toward blacks would increase. However, if we take the colorblind approach (a kind of decategorization), then the reduction of white bias toward blacks would occur primarily through the reduction of the attractiveness whites feel toward other whites. Certainly, the net increase in liking for former out-group members suggested by the recategorization model would be preferred to the net decrease in liking for former in-group members implied by the decategorization effect. But, both of these effects relate to the problems of prejudice. Recategorization processes increase favorability of out-groups, and decategorization processes decrease favorability of in-groups. Taken together, the two processes effectively cover the problems that prejudice presents.

The *common ingroup identity* model (Gaertner, et al., 1993) was taken to the field in an experiment where 1,357 students attending a multicultural high school in the northeastern United States evaluated the extent to which they felt that cooperative interdependence, a high degree of intergroup contact, and supportive norms for such contact characterized their school (Gaertner, Rust, Dovidio, Bachman, and Anastasio, 1994). They were also asked the extent to which students at their school perceived the student body as one group, two (or more) groups, along ethnic or racial lines, or separate individuals (colorblind). What they found was that, the more favorable the students' view of the conditions of contact with diverse groups at school, the more positive were students' reactions and attitudes. Moreover, the more they felt that the school promoted a feeling of one group, the more positive were the effects of contact on these favorability ratings.

The common ingroup identity model calls for focused efforts on recategorizing conflict groups into one group. Reduction of in-group bias, increases in favorability ratings, and attitudinal evaluations of former out-group members could be expected to happen. But, of course, recategorization is easier said than done. This research shows that, when we can accomplish this goal, positive effects will occur. But, again, we have to ask, how can we create these conditions of contact and the structure and process that favors a recategorization approach rather than a categorization or decategorization approach? We have the mechanisms and the demonstration that they work. Now we need the social engineers who can create the climates in which these mechanisms are free to operate.

SUMMARY

The contact hypothesis has been the cornerstone of theoretical, empirical, and intervention approaches to the problems of prejudice reduction. The brief summaries presented above do not attempt to give a definitive or exhaustive critique of the contact hypothesis, but to suggest ways in which its basic conception has been, in some cases, found wanting or, in others, has provided an important springboard for fruitful theory and research. Mackie and Hamilton (1993) summarize several of the difficulties with the basic formulation of the contact hypothesis: (1) The numerous conditions needed for it to work are rarely met in everyday life; (2) stereotypes serve self-protective functions, hence, are very difficult to change—even in the face of disconfirming experiences with members of the stereotyped groups; and (3) there is often a strong belief that interpersonal encounters will do little to change group-based perceptions and evaluations. To the list of these difficulties Mackie and Hamilton (1993) add the powerful operation of affect.

Specifically, Mackie and Hamilton (1993) suggest that most interpersonal contacts between members of conflicted groups are unpleasant, involve wariness and apprehension, and give rise to negative affective feelings that increase the likelihood that the encounter will have negative, rather than positive, outcomes. The work of Pettigrew (1996) and of Gaertner and colleagues (1993), summarized in this chapter, offers more positive outlooks. But, for these views to prevail, we need to find ways for positive affective experiences to emerge from interpersonal intergroup encounters. In short, members of different groups have to be able to become friends with each other.

As we have seen in this chapter, there are a number of promising paths to prejudice reduction. None of these courses of action is easy, and we often find that an action that ought to work theoretically doesn't have the desired effects in practice. This list is not definitive, but it does suggest directions in which efforts to ameliorate interpersonal and intergroup biases may turn.

1   Beginning with the work of Sherif (1966), and continuing with that of Pettigrew (1996), Gaertner, et al. (1993) and others, there is evidence that creating conditions in which individuals cannot reach desirable goals as easily on their own as they can in joint cooperation with others may reduce prejudice. Similarly, attainment of superordinate goals requires that groups work together rather than compete. As a society, we value competition and individuality. Therefore, in the United States, it is not a societal instinct to create conditions that pave the way for a reduction of prejudice.

2   Conditions that spawn positive affect and make interpersonal intimacy possible are most likely to make intergroup contact a successful avenue to the reduction of intergroup hostility. We should acknowledge that *intergroup hostility* is probably too strong a term. For the most part, groups stay away from each other; people prefer to be with their own kind. Sports teams come to mind as a context in which superordinate goals combine with strong positive affect and opportunities for intimacy to create the most fertile possibilities for intergroup harmony. Although there are surely racial antagonisms within sports generally, and on specific teams, there are also many examples of strong, positive, interracial friendships that have been forged in these arenas of competition, among teammates and adversaries alike.

3   There is also evidence that if we have direct experience with what it is like to be stigmatized, we are more likely to avoid treating others in a stigmatizing fashion. The *Eye of the Storm* video portrays this dramatically. We have the ability to experimentally put other people "in our shoes," as the Storms (1973) study showed.

4   Interpersonal bias can be reduced by individuating people as a means of reducing the boundaries between groups. There are a variety of ways to do this. Among these are (a) making individual traits or qualities salient, (b) demonstrating multiple group membership, (c) subgrouping within a social category, and (d) reducing the level of cognitive stimulation or complexity so that one has cognitive resources to pay attention to individual qualities. All of these strategies help to limit the human tendency to treat individuals on the basis of their group membership.

5   Expanding group boundaries to include a wider variety of others can reduce prejudice and its consequences. This is the principle of diversity. According to the diversity approach, the more diverse the people under the group tent are, the less likely it is that differences between individuals will serve as a basis for biased negative treatment.

6   Adopting a transactional approach to intergroup relations will ensure that whatever gains are made will encompass the perspectives and needs of all parties. Such an approach is harder to implement, to be sure, but any progress will be real and genuine, not cosmetic and transitory. The essential features of the transactional approach are listed below:
    - It takes into account multiple levels of society.
    - It considers multiple perspectives of interacting parties.
    - It requires mutual agreement to succeed.
    - It involves interdependent relationships.
    - It thrives on superordinate goals when the conditions for agreement are ripe.

Taken together, these conditions foster a positive basis for intergroup relations. But trust and a desire to control prejudice reactions and to seek common ground are also essential ingredients.

PART THREE

❖

The Psychology of Racism

There is a right way
to do things, to be. My way!
Must be in the genes.

12

*R*ace

❖

> *In the last decade there has been a remarkable increase in our knowledge of the complexities of human genetic variability. To an increasing number of anthropologists the concept of race seems to be losing its usefulness in describing this variability.*
>
> Frank Livingston, Anthropologist, 1962

*I*NTRODUCTION

Race—This four-letter word has wreaked more havoc on people in the world than all the four-letter words banned by censors of the U.S. airwaves. Race divides human beings into categories that loom in our psyches. Racial differences create cavernous divides in our psychological understandings of who we are and who we should be. Race is a concept that is both very well understood (by biologists and geneticists) and poorly understood (by psychologists and the public at large). It means everything and it means nothing.

Part 2 focused on the problems of prejudice and its psychological mechanisms, which characterize how individuals perceive, judge, and behave toward others. Prejudices arise from differences between oneself and others on almost any classifiable human dimension. Race is one classifiable human dimension. As we have noted, therefore, prejudice can be and often is directed at people because of their race. Much of what we have described and the research we have reviewed was concerned with race prejudice and related processes such as stereotyping, discrimination, and in-group bias. But race seems to arouse strong emotional feelings and reactions that may be somewhat different from other classifiable human attributes. The possibility that "race" is emotionally distinctive, socially specific, and scientifically debatable gives it great meaning. As such, the concept of race warrants very close scrutiny.

339

The fact that some forms of bias based on race are labeled "racism" and not "prejudice" is an issue that the chapters in Part 3 will address. Being identified as "prejudiced" is not something most people enjoy, and usually will deny vehemently. But being identified as a "racist" is to have one's basic humanity challenged. People do not get fired from network positions for making "prejudiced" remarks. They get fired for making "racist" remarks. What is the difference?

Jimmy "the Greek" Snyder was a popular sports handicapper and television personality in the 1970s and 1980s. One afternoon during an impromptu interview at Duke Ziebert's restaurant in Washington D.C., he spoke at length on issues of race with a reporter from WRC television. Snyder was asked to comment on how blacks had progressed in the sports world. He commented on black and white athletes noting that:

> The black is a better athlete to begin with because he's been bred to be that way because of his thigh size and big size . . . [these racial differences] go back to the Civil War, when during the slave period the slave owner would breed his big black slave with his big woman so that he could have a big black kid. That's where it all started . . . [if more blacks become coaches] there's not going to be anything left for white people. I mean, all the players are black, the only thing that whites control is the coaching jobs. (Uhlig, 1988, p. 47, 50)

Ironically, Snyder's comments were made in conjunction with Martin Luther King Day for a program on progress of blacks in sports. Snyder was summarily dismissed by CBS for his "racist remarks." He had suggested that blacks were genetically superior.

Compare this with Al Campanis, an executive with the Los Angeles Dodgers baseball team. Campanis also spoke at length on why blacks were not well-represented in management positions. Whereas Snyder focused on the performance strengths of blacks and implied a conspiracy of whites to keep them out of front office jobs, Campanis laid the blame on blacks themselves. In an appearance on ABC's *Nightline* on April, 1987, he confessed:

> I truly believe that [blacks] may not have some of the necessities, to be, let's say, a field manager, or perhaps a general manager. (Axthelm, 1987, p. 71)

He apologized and was forced to resign from his position for making "racist remarks." Neither of them was dismissed for "racial prejudice." What is it that so charges us up about issues of race and racism? What history does *race* conjure up that makes racism an offense for which sanctions are mandatory sequelae?

We begin the chapter with a consideration of what "race" is, its origins and usage. The evidence for the biological meaning of race is scanty and is largely rejected by those scientists in the best position to judge. If race has no biological standing, why is it such a powerful label for human beings, and why is it so influential as a categorical status for human groups? We will therefore consider why race persists as a concept that has cultural currency, but scientific invalidity. We will argue that race is fundamentally a social construction that has played an integral role in the development and evolution of Western culture. The concept of race carries with it the invidious comparisons, the in-group biases, and the systematic institutional and cultural mechanisms that confer favor on whites and disfavor on other racial groups.

We will next consider some important aspects of race usage and influence that help us to better understand racism. Specifically, we will consider *racialism* (attaching personality qualities and attributes to racial classifications) and *racialization* (infusing society with institutional ways to take race into account, thereby creating consequences for people that are the direct result of racialism). We will further consider two important contrasting dimensions of human social categories and organizational structure, "ethnicity" and "culture." Whereas *race* is presumed to have a fundamentally biological basis, both ethnicity and culture rest on the distinctive patterns of thinking, feeling, and behaving as the defining basis of human categorization. To the extent that race intersects both ethnicity and culture, the concept needs to be clarified.

WHAT IS RACE?

We cannot understand racism until we have some understanding of race. Current evidence and argument favors the view that race is not a definable, meaningful, or useful concept when applied to human beings. In other words, with regard to humans, there is only one *human race!* But, as former governor of Texas Ann Richards might say about this attitude, *"that dog won't hunt."* Which is to say, we will get nowhere with this simple viewpoint, no matter how *scientifically* correct it may be.

We use the word *race* everyday, with the assumption that we know what we are talking about. We know what we *see,* phenotypical traits of anatomy and physiology, and that people tend to differ on these traits. Therefore, when we describe those differences in terms of race, it seems to make sense. But even in these phenotypical traits, there is wide variability among people classified in the same race and in how a given individual belonging to one race may be perceived by others. For example, we talk about blacks as a group. However, needless to say, the variability in skin color, eye color, hair texture, and cultural background is enormous. What sense does *one* label make for all of this diversity?

By contrast, the same person may be differently perceived by different people. Kottak (1996), an Anglo-American anthropologist, describes how he is perceived in the small black town of Arembepe in Brazil:

> In the United States, I am always "white" or "Euro-American," but in Arembepe I got lots of terms beside *branco* ("white"). I could be *claro* ("light"), *louro* ("blond"), *sarara* ("light-skinned redhead"), *mulatoclaro* ("light mulatto"), or *mulato* ("mulatto"). (p. 66)

In fact, Kottak found that, in this small town of only 750 people, there were 40 different racial terms used.

In the United States, race is so powerful that, in some states, a person is considered black if he or she is one-thirty-second black by blood! That is, if *one* ancestor was classified as an African, a Negro, or colored as far back as five generations (over 100 years) ago, then that person, *by law,* in some states is classified as black. In Brazil, by contrast, anyone who "appears" white is so classified. In the United States, race laws have been exclusionary, whereas, in Brazil, they seem to have a more inclusionary purpose.

In Japan, race categorization distinguishes the vast majority of people from a variety of others who are "not us." These Minorities include the indigenous Ainu; Okinawans, who were annexed; *burakumin,* who are poor outcasts of society; and a variety of mixed-marriage offspring and immigrant nationalities, especially Koreans (cf. Kottak, 1996). People who lived in northern middle and southern Europe were, as recently as the 1920s, distinguished as "races" (cf. McDougall, 1921). As we saw in Chapter 9, the Hutu and Tutsi in Rwanda and Burundi have dramatically different anatomical differences that could easily be classified along diverse racial lines.

And, of course, we cannot leave out the dramatically singular definition of *race, Aryan race*, that was so exquisitely detailed by Adolph Hitler, who used it as a rallying cry to programs of "racial cleansing." To justify his pogrom against the Jews, Hitler proposed that religion was biologically driven and that ethnicity, derived from culture, became race and was seen as emblematic of genetic predisposition. The emotional reaction generated by the charge of *racism* derives significantly from the horror of Hitler and the manifestations of racism that drove his campaign against the Jews.[1]

With all of these different usages, and anatomical and physiological differences, what can we make of race as a meaningful concept? It is an unwieldy concept, subject to vagaries of social perception and cultural meaning. How can it so inflame discourse and cause emotional upset and administrative, legislative, and judicial actions? The remainder of this chapter will attempt to answer some of these questions. Let's begin by defining what is meant by *race*.

Defining Race

Many contemporary analyses of race emphasize its sociohistorical nature (Omi and Winant, 1994) and its cultural origins (Kottak, 1996). We will consider each of these approaches to the concept of race, in turn, later in the chapter. However, as *race* has traditionally been defined in biological terms, we will consider "biological" approaches first.

Race as Biology
Zuckerman (1990) suggests that, for biologists, race is

> . . . an inbreeding, geographically isolated population that differs in distinguishable physical traits from other members of the species. Members of such a population are capable of breeding with members of other populations in their species, but they usually do not do so for some period of time during which the specific physical characteristics of the group emerge from the limited but adaptive gene pool. (p. 1297)

Important to this definition is geographical isolation. Because we are *capable* of breeding across so-called races, what has historically maintained racial groupings has been physical isolation. But, in the global village, geographical isolation is not a very pertinent argument for racial distinctions, and, thereby, the definition loses its persuasiveness.

Zuckerman argues that geographical isolation has, in more recent times, been replaced by "culture-based" distinctions—such as religion, politics, economic policy, and philosophy, and, yes, psychology and personality. This reasoning suggests

---

[1]It is significant that in the Holocaust Museum in Washington, D.C., one can see the instruments for "assessing" race in Nazi Germany. There are calipers to measure nose length, strands of hair against which to measure the gauge of hair. The anatomical features of race were *ipso facto* arguments for the "essential" qualities of those race members. It is also significant that many of the psychologists who were refugees of Nazi racism were profoundly influenced by their experience and brought a scientific focus on the study of race, along with the emotional pain of their experience, to their work in the United States. Their focus on aspects of racism and concern with individual freedom, democracy, and authoritarian excesses have contributed much to our current understanding of the processes of prejudice and racism.

that racial distinctions are based less on physically isolated inbreeding than on common experiences borne of cultural evolution.

Although there is some controversy, modern science seems to accept the idea that human beings (*Homo sapiens*) evolved only once about 200,000 years ago from a common ancestor (the ape-like *Homo erectus*) in East Africa. (Cavilli-Sforza and Cavilli-Sforza, 1995). Lucy, the most famous *australopithecine,* was discovered by archaeologist Don Johanson on a dig organized by archaeologist Louis Leakey in 1974 in East Africa. She was estimated to be 3.2 million years old. She is commonly viewed as "the missing link" between apes and humans. Anthropologist Vincent Sarich and biochemist Allan Wilson from the University of California at Berkeley, calculated the number of differences in amino acids to demonstrate that *Homo sapiens* evolved about 190,000 years ago from a common ancestor, African Eve. It was African Eve, the theory goes, who first experienced a mutation of mitochondrial DNA and passed it on to her daughter, who passed it on to her children, and so on, and so on. Does this mean that all humans are fundamentally Africans?

This is obviously both an emotionally charged and scientifically challenging idea. *Homo erectus* was a traveling sort, leaving Africa and setting up communities in the Middle East, Europe, and Asia over a period of thousands of years. The "polycentric" view suggests that modern humans emerged across a huge zone covering practically the entire globe. Rushton (1989) suggests that there are three distinct "races" in the world, Negroid, Caucasoid, and Mongoloid, who evolved in that order, making the Mongoloid the most evolved. All of these views are interpretative and influenced to some extent by the world views of the proponents. However, the most compelling scientific evidence supports the view that the precursor to modern man, *Homo sapiens sapiens,* emerged from Africa about 100,000 years ago (Cavalli-Sforza and Cavalli-Sforza, 1995).

The idea that these viewpoints are subject to the biases of the author is illustrated quite nicely by Figure 12.1. Two genealogical trees of human populations is presented in Figure 12.1. Tree A is based on anthropologists' measurements and comparisons of 26 external features—such as eye, hair, and skin color, limb proportions, and facial characteristics—conducted over 100 years ago. Tree B is based on differences in 58 genetic markers, mostly blood proteins. The research upon which tree B is based was conducted more recently, with the aid of modern scientific advances. The two human race trees vary in significant ways. Tree A places African Bushmen and Pygmies *farthest* from White Europeans. Tree B places them *closest* to Europeans. Based perhaps on phenotypical features of anatomy and physiology, it might seem that Bushmen and white Europeans would be far apart on the racial tree. But the biology of the matter places them much closer together. This is precisely what one would expect if an out-migration of people from Africa occurred.

Given a geographical definition of *races,* and patterns of peoples as well as patterns of genes, tree B seems more likely than tree A. How did tree A come about? Some argue that it reflects early evidence of *scientific racism.* Others argue that it is simply flawed science, or even pseudoscience.

The above example illustrates one of the fundamental problems with the race concept—its reliance on observable physical features. Scientists of the nineteenth century made flawed analyses of "races" based on systematic measurements and comparisons of *physical features.* What's the poor layperson to do? If we try to use physical appearance, what will we come up with? Some Africans are dark, some light. Some Europeans are darker than some Africans. Consider the following case.

Ms. Fannie Barrier Williams left her native New York to travel by train in the

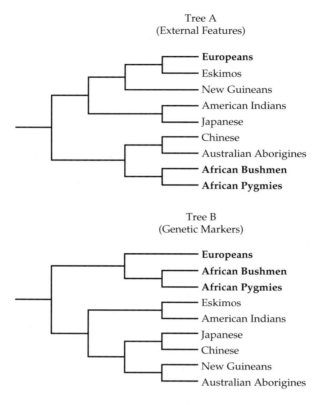

Tree A
(External Features)

- Europeans
- Eskimos
- New Guineans
- American Indians
- Japanese
- Chinese
- Australian Aborigines
- African Bushmen
- African Pygmies

Tree B
(Genetic Markers)

- Europeans
- African Bushmen
- African Pygmies
- Eskimos
- American Indians
- Japanese
- Chinese
- New Guineans
- Australian Aborigines

FIGURE 12.1

Comparison of Taxonomies of Races Using External Features and Genetic Markers. (Adapted from Patterson, C. (1978) *Evolution.* London: Butler and Tanner, Ltd., Figure 48, p. 139.

South for the first time. She was quite light of complexion, and, based on her standing as a free Negro in the North, she always traveled in the first-class car. She was intercepted at one station by a conductor as she approached her first-class accommodation. He inquired, "Madame, are you colored?" She quickly replied, "*Je suis française*." "*Française*?" he repeated. "*Oui*," she replied. At which point the conductor apologized for the *slight* and went and purchased her a first-class ticket (cf. Gates, 1991, p. 19, for a description of this encounter). Race conceived as a set of physical features seems to be much less persuasive than race understood to be a set of cultural conventions designed to maintain a social hierarchy that is based on dubious distinctions among people.

A Special issue of *Time* magazine (1993) is devoted to the "New faces of America," resulting from the gene-sharing of racially diverse people in the United States. The rapidly growing number of biracial and multiracial people in the United States has created a new racial category: "none of the above" (Root, 1992). That is, people do not feel obligated to choose one racial designation when they share the genes of two or more so-called racial groups (cf., Hall, 1992). The world is fascinated by the incredible talent of the young biracial golfer, Tiger Woods. Born to an African-American father and Thai mother, Tiger has sought to avoid being stuck in a single racial category. Multiracial people increasingly express the view that their status uniquely qualifies them to a defining label that reflects the true diversity of their heritage. The mixtures of gene pools have generated a true mongrelization of human groups and challenged the legitimacy and salience of single-race characterizations of people.

The photograph on page 346 "morphs" the physical features of racially mixed peoples. The images of these racially mixed people converge toward a homogenous sameness, and racial salience is dramatically reduced. The implication of this projection is that, in the future, there will be neither phenotypical nor genotypical basis for the race concept. Does this mean that we will no longer make distinctions among peoples and categorize them into racial groups? The data from Part 2 and our collective human experience suggest not.

As early as 1968, scientists rejected the concept of race, considering that it was not a meaningful way to talk about human groups. A distinguished panel of scientists (cf. Mead, Dobzhansky, Tobach, and Light, 1968, p. 59) noted that

> . . . from a biological viewpoint the term race has become so encumbered with superfluous and contradictory meanings, erroneous concepts, and emotional reactions that it has almost completely lost its utility. . . . The term should be replaced with the concept of population. It is hoped that the understanding of the biological nature of populations will eventually lead to the abandonment of the term race.

As a further illustration of the scientific indefensibility of race, consider blood type. All so-called races possess all blood types known to humanity. What differs between so-called races is not what blood types they possess, but the pattern or distribution of blood types within the group. For example, the Belgian population consist of about 26 percent type A, 6 percent type B, and 68 percent type O. That of pygmies of the Congo, by comparison, consists of 23 percent type A, 22 percent type B, and 55 percent type O. Table 12.1 shows that the patterning of blood types does not correspond to what we conventionally think of as "racial groups." For example, in terms of blood-type distribution, in Group 2, Europeans are more like Africans, Asians, and American Indians; in Group 4 they are like Australian aborigines. Looked at in a slightly different fashion, 85 percent of all human genetic variation in enzymes and other proteins occurs *within* a local racial group, whereas only 15 percent of variation can be accounted for by differences of group membership (Lewontin, Rose, and Kamin, 1984).

Physiologist Jared Diamond (1994) argues further that there are many different ways of classifying human populations. For example, if we use the presence of anti-malarial genes not typically found among light-skinned people such as Swedes *or* among dark-skinned southern African groups such as Xhosas (the group to which South African President Nelson Mandela belongs), then Italians and Greeks would be closest to most African blacks, whereas Swedes would be closest to the darker-skinned southern African groups.

What the above means is that, for example, the variability among Latinos is greater than the observed differences between Latinos and Africans, Europeans, or Chinese! So, if we are truly only one race, and if there are fewer differences between "race groups" than within "race groups," why do we persist in relying on the concept of race and why does it arouse such strong emotional feelings and scientific passion? One reason is that, in our society, race has nestled into our everyday life in ways that are integral to how we function as a society. That is, we have constructed a social meaning of race that aids and abets the social organization and function of everyday life.

	Middle Eastern	Italian	African	Vietnamese	Anglo-Saxon	Chinese	Hispanic

Blurred images of racial differences. Multiracial progeny emphasize similarities and minimize differences. These images, "morphics," result from a morph computer program that combines the physical characteristics of the racial/ethnic women across the top with the men down the sides in a 50–50 combination. (Ted Thai/Time Magazine; Computer Morphing by Kim Wah Lam; Design by Walter Bernard and Milton Glaser.)

TABLE 12.1 RACIAL GROUPINGS OF 20 HUMAN POPULATIONS BY A, B, AND O BLOOD-TYPE ALLELE FREQUENCIES*

Group 1	Group 2	Group 3
(3) African	(2) African	(6) American Indian
(4) American Indian	(8) Asian	(16) European
(5) American Indian	(10) Asian	(17) European
	(13) American Indian	(19) European
	(20) European	

Group 4	Group 5
(7) American Indian	(1) African
(14) Australian Aborigine	(9) Asian
(15) Australian Aborigine	(11) Asian
(18) European	(12) Asian

SOURCE: Adapted from Lewontin, Rose, and Kamin (1984). *Not in Our Genes: Biology, Ideology and Human Nature.* New York, Pantheon Books.
*Numbers in parentheses represent the twenty different human populations whose blood-type frequencies were assayed.
NOTE: "Racial" groupings are based on frequencies of Type A, B, and O blood-type alleles for each of the populations. The groupings are more or less arbitrary, based on the similarity of blood-type patterns.

Race as Social Construction

The viability of race as a biological fact that is useful in accounting for significant human variation is minimal, and the concept of race has largely been discredited by scientists around the world.[2] Yet "race" persists as a label that is applied to human groups, with clear psychological implications—if not biological precision. The circumspect approach taken by most scientists is not shared by people in everyday life. The primary reason is that "race" continues to organize our thinking about people and the groups to which they belong. Rightly or wrongly, race has a social meaning that people cannot or will not easily give up. Following are four definitions that emphasize the *social* formation and cultural significance of race.

> *van den Berghe (1967, p. 9; italics added).* [Race is] a human group that defines itself and/or is defined by other groups as different by virtue of innate or immutable characteristics. These physical characteristics are in turn assumed to be intrinsically related to moral, intellectual and other non-physical attributes or abilities. A race, therefore, is a group that is *socially defined on the basis of physical criteria.*

> *Banton (1983, p. 77).* "Race" relations are distinguished not by the biological significance of phenotypical features but by the social use of those features as signs identifying group membership and the roles people are expected to play.

[2]Psychologists have responded to the murkiness of the biological concept of race by proposing that its meaning and use be subjected to a unifying policy within the field (cf. Yee, Fairchild, Weizman, and Wyatt, 1993): Research on race and its correlates and consequences has generated much controversy in psychology and has led to implications that appear to be divisive, both within the field and in society at large.

Omi and Winant (1986, p. 60). **Race is indeed a pre-eminently sociohistorical concept. Racial categories and the meaning of race are given concrete expression by the specific social relations and historical context in which they are embedded. Racial meanings have varied tremendously over time and between societies.**

Feagin and Feagin, (1996, p. 9). **A racial group is a social group that persons inside or outside the group have decided is important to single out as inferior or superior, typically on the basis of real or alleged physical characteristics subjectively selected.**

Race is defined by social convention, role definitions, and characteristics of particular societies at specific times. As a social construction, race has no fixity, except, perhaps, for the premise that a biological essentialism underlies whatever meaning the concept of race takes on. And, finally, race takes on a hierarchical meaning. It serves to help us separate groups that have been defined by "race" into superior and inferior categories. It is perhaps this aspect of the race concept that does the most damage. And, because definitions of superiority and inferiority are clearly relative to one's own (or in-group's) viewpoint and value system, the social meanings of race are likely to reflect the social arrangements of a given society. Those groups perceived to possess the greater degree of valued attributes and outcomes will be perceived to be superior. To the extent that those groups are also defined by physical attributes associated with race labels, the differences between groups will likely be attributed to the group's racial characteristics.

Winant (1994) argues that the meaning of race is constructed out of conflicts within individual psyches and across collective identities and social structures. As a result, the ongoing conflict over the meanings of *race* and the power relationships between and among people over the determination of those meanings is an inherent part of what race is. It does not stand as an objective, definable "reality," but as a subjective, interpersonal, and cultural set of meanings and relationships *given meaning by their power to determine what race should be.* Understanding the resistance to the assignment of unwanted meanings to so-called racial groups becomes integral to understanding what *race* means in the first place.

Winant calls this approach to the concept of race *racial formation theory* (cf. Omi and Winant, 1986). This theory suggests that the processes of racial signification are variable, conflictual, and contested at every level of society from the *intrapsychic* (within an individual mind) to the *supranational* (within national boundaries). *Race,* therefore, has many different meanings and interpretations at any one time. Omi and Winant (1986) argue that specific meanings are created through localized *racial projects* developed by elites, popular movements, state agencies, cultural and religious organizations, and intellectuals to interpret and reinterpret the meaning of *race.* Moreover, a racial project is ". . . simultaneously an interpretation, representation, or explanation of racial dynamics and an effort to organize and distribute resources" (Omi and Winant, 1986, p. 24). Therefore, race is not only a category of social description, it becomes a rationale for resource allocation, a determinant of opportunity. Each racial project conceptualizes and represents the sentiment of race as a cultural marker, or signifier.

As we saw in Part 1 of this book, power and control were the modes by which racial definitions were initially imposed on our society in order to maintain and enforce the view that whites were inherently superior and correct, and blacks were inherently inferior and wrong. This view—which resulted in the virtual denial of citizenship to blacks, in the service of white advantage—was judged unacceptable and illegal in the 1960s. In Chapter 5, we reviewed the changing meaning of *race*, which was represented both by sentiments of racial equality and the perception of racial similarity on the part of whites and by perceptions of continued racial inequality and emerging perceptions of racial *dissimilarity* on the part of blacks. The racial projects of whites and blacks were beginning to move in opposite directions.

In its newer form, the meaning of race was intertwined with U.S. values (e.g., symbolic, modern, and aversive racism). The racial ordering of society could thereby be maintained without arousing the ogre of unfairness officially rejected by the Civil Rights Act of 1964. Winant (1994) suggests that this trend toward subtle racism was illustrative of a shift from simple racial domination to what he called *racial hegemony.* Under a system of hegemonic domination, one still seeks control for one's own group, but achieves it by ". . . incorporating oppositional currents within its prevailing system of rule" (Winant, 1994, p. 29). The meaning of race is defined *within* the ongoing racial projects at multiple levels of society. These separate racial projects compete for validation and the endorsement of the society's constituents. By this view, it would be wrong to consider race to be a monolithic expression of our culture, because its meaning has been constantly revised and reinvented. The issue of the meaning of *race* continues to be a philosophical, political, and moral battleground.

It is also important for us to recognize that racial projects (which define what race means) are also intrapsychic, as noted earlier. This is particularly true of members of groups who are largely defined by others. For example, Asians are often considered the "model minority" (Sue & Okazaki, 1990), but is this true? Does this imply that Asians are weak, passive, submissive, and can be pushed around or ignored? If Asians are concerned with "face" (i.e., public dignity, cf. Zane, 1996) and saving or preserving it, is that psychological tendency likely to mean that an Asian person will be misunderstood, undervalued, or thought to be less capable by those in the out-group? What psychological tensions does this build in an Asian person? Or, are American Indians indeed prone to alcoholism? Is the historical label of "savage" something that creates cumulative psychological scars, or can it be dismissed by contemporary American Indian people? How does an American Indian develop a self-identity as an Indian that serves as a source of strength, pride, and dignity. The definitions of race, then, have great implications—not only in terms of the kind of society we live in and the kinds of social policies we are likely to adopt, but in terms of the way we think about ourselves as people. To understand these intrapsychic dynamics we must return to the consideration of *racial identity*. (We introduced this subject in Chapter 10, and will consider the subject of racial identity again in Chapter 14.)

The social construction of the concept of race is an ongoing project. It is important for us to recognize this because, in a sense, there is no smoking gun, no ultimate truth, no eternal reality. Your meaning of race is as valid as mine, but in terms of our differences, the stakes may not be equal. That is, it may well be easy for whites, who are dominant, to take a view that race is not meaningful. But when one belongs to a group that has been subjugated because of race, agreeing to no longer consider it important may be to accept a view of society that is illusory. In such a case, the social construction of race is strongly influenced by the power of those who define it. That is, a subordinate group's racial meaning may not be functional if it is not shared by those in a position of authority or influence. Racial projects that seek to define and interpret race, in other words, will have more impact on society when they are "sponsored" by those who enjoy prestige, power, or general acceptance. *The Bell Curve* (Murray and Herrnstein, 1994) is, in part, an attempt to define the meaning of race in terms of intelligence, and to dictate the appropriate and inappropriate racial projects that should be undertaken by government as a result (more on this in Chapter 16). Our social structures, our cultural symbols—indeed, our social policies—all signify a particular meaning of race. The diversity of each of these entities or dynamics is as diverse as the concept of race will be.

Race is constructed through racial projects across our society. For example, ads supporting President Bush for reelection in 1988, featured Willie Horton—an escaped black convict who raped a white woman while he was out on furlough. Race (black) was thereby linked to hostility, evil, and danger; to the Democratic party; and to Massachusetts Governor Michael Dukakis, chief politician of the state whose prison system released Horton. The Million Man March in 1995 was another racial project (with aspects of gender, as well) that redefined black men as strong, moral, conscientious, and responsible. The march and its aftermath, for many, served as an antidote to other more, negative definitions of race offered by television news, newspapers, movies, and other racial projects.[3]

The *concept* of race itself, then, is as much the source of racial tensions as are more tangible issues such as jobs, admissions to universities, income, and public policies. Because we work so hard to define race in our everyday lives, and because there is no objective reality to tell us when we are done, we are somewhat in the position of Sisyphus rolling the rock up the hill—it will always roll back down. The issue of race will never be settled once and for all. What *race* means is increasingly incorporated in what it means to be an American, indeed, a citizen of the global village. The end to this story will not be written in these few pages. We will continue though, to try to understand what we are dealing with and ways to make progress toward a definition and meaning that is accepted by an ever-larger segment of the world community.

Let's now consider where this idea of race came from. Has it always been with us? Is it a natural way to classify human beings?

Origin of the Term Race

Race has for centuries been used in European languages to describe differences in customs, lineage, authority, and divine status (Banton, 1977). In what is now France, the Gauls were conquered by the Germanic Frankish leader Clovis, and England was populated by the Germanic Saxons. Both were invaded and ruled by Normans from Scandinavia. The differences among the Celtics, Saxons, Franks, Gauls and Normans, Irish and Welsh signified distinctions that came to be associated with the concept of race. These differences were not only a matter of physical appearance, and geographical origins but also of customs and values, religion and beliefs.

In English, the terms *race* and *stock* were used to describe people who differed in visible ways. In England, the references to the Bible provided early precedents for the use of *race*. Although the term was not used explicitly in the Bible, British

---

[3]It should be noted that this racial project was opposed by others who sought to discredit the message because the organizer, Minister Louis Farrakhan, was himself labeled a racist,. Others sought to discredit the messenger, Minister Farrakhan, while endorsing the message. The controversy over the march and Minister Farrakhan could be seen, in part, as a controversy over racial signification and meaning.

writers referred to "the race and stock of Abraham," and Milton referred to the "race of Satan" (cf. Banton, 1977).

The differences to which race referred, albeit real, largely consisted of attributes that we would today associate with "culture" (e.g., history, arts and letters, manners, and morals). The concept of race was not biological in its derivation; it was decidedly an evaluative label. The dividing line between "them" and "us" was "civilization," and Europeans viewed themselves as being on the "right" side, and others as being on the "wrong" side. Race was one way of distinguishing "barbarians" from "civilized people." The defining element of civilization became, in the eighteenth century, the element of Reason, of thought, of rationality. Descartes's *cogito ergo sum* identified thought as the defining characteristic of *human* consciousness.

Around 1800, the meaning of *race* changed from its sense of lineage defined by cultural distinctiveness and geographical boundaries, to one of "human types" based on physical properties (Banton, 1977). Race distinguished the Normans (Scandinavians who first conquered much of France and, later, England), from the Saxons (the Germanic "race" from whom the English considered themselves descended; cf. Verstegan, 1605). "Race" was further used to distinguish the wealthy from the poor, the citizens of Hertfordshire from those of Essex.

Banton (1977, p. 27) made the following observations regarding race:

> In the eighteenth century, the word "race" was used primarily to identify the common descent of a set of people; their distinctive characteristics were taken for granted and the category "race" was used to explain how they came by them. In the nineteenth century, "race" came to be a means of classifying people by these characteristics. . . .

The classifications were increasingly based on human attributes that were defined by their cultural significance.

Smedley (1993) suggests that, prior to the sixteenth century, when *race* began to be used to distinguish people and where they came from, race was primarily a folk concept that applied to the breeding of domestic animals. A racial stock, or lineage of a group of animals, was identified by the purposes for which a specific breed was created. By the sixteenth century, the use of *race* to refer to the "human stock" of peoples around the world marked the extension of the term, heretofore reserved for animals, to human beings.

There are several implications of the application of the animal husbandry usage of *race* to human populations. First, species differentiation distinguished "subspecies" from each other along dimensions that were common to the entire species (e.g., degree of aggression, intelligence, hair color, and skin color). These differences then linked temperament, character, and other behavioral propensities to underlying genetic variation. Second, these subspecies distinctions led to value judgments based on specific, extant cultural beliefs and goals. Third, the husbandry analogy placed emphasis on the innateness of the classificatory system of race, implying, in turn, that the characteristics imputed to different racial subspecies were immutable.

It is against this backdrop of the origination of the meaning and use of *race* in North America, Smedley (1993) argues, that we must try to understand its manifestations and consequences in contemporary U.S. society. In strong and provocative terms, Smedley (1993, pp. 303–304) suggests that

> . . . race was a social mechanism for concretizing and rigidifying a universal ranking system that gave Europeans what they thought was a perpetual dominance over indigenous peoples of the New World, Africa and Asia.

Although this statement of self-interested intentionality of Europeans in the construction and use of "race" seems strong, the evidence in support of this world-view is compelling. It comes from the lips and pens of Europeans themselves, as we will see in the next section. The important points to take from this brief discussion of the origins of the race concept are two:

1   Europeans were long concerned with group differences in culture, particularly as such differences related to patterns of living and dimensions of civilization. The idea of race or racial stock was easily applied to group differences that reflected simultaneously physical differences and cultural differences. *Race* was used rather casually in describing these differences and in attaching self-interested value judgments to human groups.
2   The "biological" or "genetic" basis of race introduced a level of rigidity and a "rational" basis for the hierarchical value judgments that were already a part of the folk notion of race. As Reason and rationality increasingly symbolized the ideals of civilization in Europe, the combining of culture and pseudobiology in racial discourse and judgment became increasingly appealing.

WHY THE PERSISTENCE OF RACE?

The question of why adherence to the concept of race persists in the face of its scientifically adjudicated invalidity is perhaps implied by the preceding discussion. In the following pages, we offer four reasons for the persistent usage of race in the face of its biological invalidity:

1   Race is a way of valuing one's own group over others.
2   Race is a handy way to encapsulate and rationalize social conflict.
3   Race is useful as a means of talking about group differences, values, social hierarchy, and competition.
4   Race is bound up in our worldview. It gives meaning and value to our culture and preserves a social hierarchy that accords privilege and dominance to those in power.

Valuing One's Own Group over Others

One reason for the persistence of "race" is that it provides a way of valuing one's own group relative to others. The well-known taxonomist Linnaeus suggested that "taxonomy is evaluation" when he categorized races in the following manner (cited in Guthrie, 1976, p. 32):

Race	Characteristics
Homo americanus	Reddish, choleric, erect, tenacious, contented, free, ruled by custom
Homo europaeus	White, ruddy, muscular, stern, haughty, stingy, ruled by opinion
Homo asiaticus	Yellow, melancholic, inflexible, light, inventive, ruled by rites
Homo afer	Black, phlegmatic, indulgent, cunning, slow, negligent, ruled by caprice

According to this view, races are not only biological, they are cultural and characterized by personality and temperament. As Zuckerman (1990) suggested, the geographical distinctions had long ago given way to cultural distinctions. Although race continues in popular usage to have a biological or genetic basis, its manifestations are increasingly described in characterological terms. Moreover, those terms are laden with evaluative labels that make it more or less desirable to belong to one racial group as compared to another.

Perhaps an even more invidious use of *race* comes from William McDougall (1921, p. v), who recounts a frightful vision:

> . . . As I watch the American nation speeding gaily, with invincible optimism, down the road to destruction, I seem to be contemplating the greatest tragedy in the history of mankind."

What is this tragedy? The decline of Americans, who are "the bearers of Western civilization." The problem—according to McDougall (1921)—is signified in the title, *Is America Safe for Democracy?*

The United States must not be allowed to decline, given its most lofty role in human affairs, goads McDougall (1921). What factors precipitate the decline of a nation? *"The decline of any civilization is the inadequacy of the qualities of the people who are the bearers of it"* (McDougall, 1921, p. 12). Decline follows from the weakening of the genetic stock of peoples who were responsible for the civilization's ascendance. He chides "race-theorists" who claim the existence of an Aryan race because they fail to record differences among so-called Aryans in their genetic stock. By claiming a commonality of races, McDougall (1921, p. 23) warns, we make "vulgar errors [in our] attempts to estimate the intrinsic values, cultural potentialities, of different human stocks." He claims that we should not shy away from duly recording the effects of genetic differences and from acknowledging racial differences because ". . . if Nature has made men of *unequal* value, the cruelty is *hers*, not *ours*, and we can do no wrong in ascertaining and recording the facts" (McDougall, 1921, p. 23).

In presenting his view of Nature's hand, McDougall goes to the heart of his fear, the future of U.S. democracy. The Declaration of Independence proclaimed that "all men are created equal." There are two ways this can be taken, says McDougall (1921, p. 23). The first is that ". . . all men are equal in respect of their claims for justice, for humane treatment and the kindly feeling of their fellows, for opportunities to make the best of their powers of service and of happiness." But according to McDougall (1921, p. 23), it is sometimes "taken to mean that all men are born with equal capacities for intellectual and more development." McDougall (1921, p. 24) expresses what he considers to be the bottom line with great clarity: "There can be no doubt . . . that the former interpretation is the true one." People are different and are unequally endowed with genetic stock that contributes positively to the success of the nation. If, he warns, we assume that they are equal from birth, we violate Nature's legacy, and set ourselves up for the "great fall"!

To illustrate his point, McDougall focuses on the "races" of Europe. Specifically, he suggests that:

> . . . anthropologists are pretty well agreed that [the population of Europe] is derived from three distinct races: . . .the tall fair Nordic race in the North; the short dark long-headed Mediterranean race in the South; and the darkish round-headed Alpine race in between." (McDougall, 1921, p. 72)

He argues that these "races" differ in their genes and that their genes are related to specific temperamental and characterological manifestations that contribute unequally to the strength of Western civilization. It is important to note here that McDougall (1921) is distinguishing different races among those "Aryans" we commonly call *white* or *European*. His scale flows from high (Nordic) to low (Mediterranean) on all dimensions of value (i.e., strength of will, curiosity, introversion, intellectual capacity, and self-assertion). "Lesser" races (e.g., Negroes), fall below Mediterraneans.

His arguments are an intriguing blend of sophistry and self-interest, but the point he wishes to make is simple: Mediterraneans are worst, Alpines are better, and Nordics are best. For example, he illustrates the "superiority" of Nordic races by suggesting that their higher levels of introversion, unsociability, and curiosity manifest themselves in higher suicide and divorce rates. According to McDougall (1921, p. 99), the Nordic:

> . . . broods over his wrongs . . . nursing his resentment, he either seeks redress in the law courts, or deserts his partner and becomes liable to be divorced for desertion.

For the impulsive, sociable extrovert (the Mediterranean), by contrast, McDougall (1921, pp. 99–100) declares that:

> . . . the emotion of anger blazes out, passes at once to action and often to homicide; and, when he is injured by unfaithfulness of his partner, he does not brood upon the problem—he solves it at once by using a knife or pistol upon one or both of the guilty parties.

He further observes that the absence of the "defect" of docility enabled Nordic self-assertion (exhibited as initiative, enterprise, and impatience of control) to conquer northern France, all of England, Sicily and much of Italy, and the Mediterranean coast. Further, McDougall (1921, p. 127) finds rather preposterous Freud's theory of mind and of widespread instances of insanity, but allows as how—because Freud was a Jew and his patients were Jews—this strange, bizarre, and fantastic theory ". . . may be approximately true of the Jewish Race." Among other analyses, he invokes his theory in describing the colonial success of England relative to France by suggesting that England had more Nordic types who were, by turns, more self-assertive and less gregarious and submissive than were the French.

"Race" for McDougall, (1) is objective, not subjective; (2) has genetic singularity (represented by the concept of racial stock); and (3) is related to human qualities that can be clearly evaluated from positive to negative, good to bad. "Races" that possess more of the positive qualities should be allowed to flourish and those that possess "bad" qualities should be somehow contained. Democracy is challenged by the premise of equality. To make equality a "fact" would, according to McDougall, sow the seeds of our destruction as a civilization.

Well, this view was presented a long time ago—why should we give credence to an outmoded and egregiously wrong sort of analysis? First, the qualities of people that McDougall (1921) notes continue to characterize what we would call "positive" personality and human attributes. Self-control, intellectual capacity, curiosity, and providence (i.e., ability and desire to delay gratification) are contemporary domains of research in U.S. psychology (corresponding, in modern terms, to self-efficacy, control, future time orientation, and cognitive capacity, represented by "g"). Second, McDougall's work illustrates that the concept of race was used with ease to substantiate judgments of superiority and inferiority and to rally the leaders of the country around a perspective on public policy that would constrain people on the basis of race. The Murray and Herrnstein (1994) bell curve analysis does the very same thing. In fact, McDougall, writing over 60 years ago, not only accepted Spearman's (1927) notion of "g," he used a bell curve to illustrate it, and used the concept to support his belief in racial inequality. That tests are commonly linked to showing racial differences is further substantiated by McDougall's reference to IQ tests as "mental *anthropology*" (p. 43).

So, again, we find that the concept of race is used to underscore differences between human groups that are predicated on "biological" factors and manifested in more or less desirable capacities and behaviors.

Encapsulating and Rationalizing Social Conflict

Another reason that the concept of race persists is that it offers a convenient way to encapsulate and rationalize social conflict. Fried (1965, p. 73) defined the meaning of race as follows:

> [*Race* is] . . . a certain kind of unresolved social conflict that thrives on division and invidious distinctions. It can thrive in the total absence of genetic differences in a single homogeneous population of common ancestry.

This definition applies quite aptly to the cases described in Chapter 9. It is particularly true of the Bosnian example where, for the most part, all distinctions made among the conflicting groups are based on nonbiological factors.

Race, then, provides a handy reference for group differences that define and legitimize social conflict. Ethnic cleansing (e.g., as in Bosnia) or racial genocide (e.g., as attempted by the Nazis) all use some variant of racial classification to rationalize extreme forms of social conflict resolution.

Discourse about Group Differences, Values, Hierarchy, and Competition

A third reason for the persistence of the concept of race is its utility as a means of ordering discourse on group differences, social values and social hierarchy, conflict, and competition. The ultimate implication of this view is that the concept of race serves to maintain group hierarchy and advantage and is determined in part by what *race* means and how it is used. Goldberg (1992) refers to such discourse as "racialized discourse." Van Dijk (1987; 1993) has developed an elaborate discourse analysis of racial meaning and usage. (Both of these views lead us to a consideration of racism that we will give full attention to in Chapter 13.)

In Goldberg's view, *race* has been used with one of two primary understandings: (1) as a reference to "natural kind" (or biological, genetic givens) and (2) as a reference of a purely "social kind," devoid of any meaning beyond the simple social reality of group differences (Goldberg, 1992). In the end, both approaches are linked to standing (hierarchy) and rest on social observations and meanings (simply put, race equates to social class or culture). However, because the first approach rests on an underlying assumption that either social class or culture derives from basic biological differences, the overlap of socioeconomic class and racial group membership is taken as evidence of racial distinctions. The discourse analysis approach to the concept of race suggests that the conception of *race* and its usage in language presumes group hierarchy and creates and maintains such hierarchy through the symbols and values attached to the language itself. Therefore, the notion of race persists because it is a handy and subtle way to preserve privilege among those elite and privileged scions of society (Van Dijk, 1993). Thus, the biological and social meanings of race become indistinguishable in common usage.

Our cultural worldview
Finally, race may be considered a worldview that became inextricably bound up in the cultural evolution of the United States. This point is developed systematically by Smedley (1993, p. 25), who argues that race emerged in North America:

> . . . [as a] folk classification, a product of popular belief about human differences that evolved from the sixteenth to the nineteenth centuries. As a worldview, it was a cosmological ordering, systematically structured out of political, economic, and social realities of peoples who had emerged as expansionist, conquering, dominating nations on a worldwide quest for wealth and power.

This racial worldview, according to Smedley (1993), consisted of five distinctive and critical elements:

1 Universal classification of human groups as exclusive and discrete biological entities based on superficial phenotypic and behavioral variations
2 An inegalitarian ethos that required ranking each group relative to each other
3 A belief that outer physical characteristics of different human populations were manifestations of inner realities, thus linking physical features and behavior with intellect, temperament, morality, and other qualities
4 A belief that all of these qualities—biophysical, cultural, or behavioral characteristics and behaviors—were inheritable
5 Belief that each race was created uniquely by the forces of Nature or God and, therefore, the "divisions" of race could never be bridged or transcended

This worldview, then, provided a justification for the creation of social hierarchy and helped to maintain it through the systematic application of its principles and beliefs.

RACE, RACIALISM, AND RACIALIZATION

The concept of race, as we have seen, concerns what people think or have thought a race is or was. Historically, race has been linked to biology as a defining marker, and with physical and temperamental attributes accepted as givens. *Race* came to be associated with common lines of descent of a set of people (Banton, 1977), with the collective genealogies of people who lived in or could be traced to certain regions of the world and who shared what were widely believed to be specific sets of characteristics that distinguished them from other groups. Therefore, *race* was largely descriptive of differences in human groups. In that regard, *race* was a fairly benign term. It became more significant, in a negative sense, when it was associated with inner realities of human groups and was used as a basis of not only classifying people, but determining their value and legitimacy among peoples of the world. To explore these developments, we need to consider the concepts of *racialism* and *racialization*.

Racialism

For Appiah (1990, pp. 4–5) *racialism* is the term applied to the following belief.

> . . . there are heritable characteristics, possessed by members of our species, that allow us to divide them into a small set of races, in such a way that all members of these races share certain traits and tendencies with each other that they do not share with members of any other race.

Racialism, then, is a *belief*, a cognitive structure that organizes perceptions of the world around racial categories and the perceptions, ideas, and values associated with these categories. That is, these beliefs illustrate a general tendency toward "psychological essentialism" (cf. Medin, 1989) by which we come to imbue human categories with specific meanings. People adopt an *essentialist heuristic* by which they come to expect ". . . that things that look alike tend to share deeper properties (similarities)" (Medin, 1989, p. 1477). In this view, racialism is the outgrowth of psychological essentialism applied to racial categories. Although essentialism does not imply values, hierarchies, or power differentials, it establishes perceptual and judgmental parameters that provide fertile ground for such evaluations. Appiah (1990) argues that racialism is, of itself, not a problem. It does, however, presuppose other doctrines or beliefs we would more formally call "racism." Let's now look at the process of transforming racialism from a set of beliefs to an active pattern of social judgment—the process of racialization.

Racialization

The processes by which racialistic beliefs are transformed into active instruments of categorization and judgment are labeled *racialization*. Racialization, according to Banton (1977, p. 18) ". . . was a social process, whereby a mode of categorization was developed, applied tentatively in European historical writing, and then, more confidently, to the populations of the world." More specifically, racialization ". . . signifies the extension of racial meaning to a previously racially unclassified relationship, social practice or group" (Winant, 1994, p. 59).

Racial categorization gave meaning to the observable physical differences that served to identify races. This classification system was ingrained in taxonomies (e.g., Linneaus' *System Naturae*) and gave rise to the development of the idea that there were many "types" of people in the world corresponding to what many called "races." The bottom line of this reasoning comes from Nott and Gliddon's *Types of Mankind* (1854; cited in Banton, 1977, p. 51), which listed 12 propositions for human types, ending with this:

> It follows, as a corollary, that there exists a GENUS HOMO, embracing many primordial types or "Species."

Although the concept of race *per se* was not necessarily value-laden, *race* was commonly used to refer initially to one's own group, one's own ancestors. With racialization, the classification process extended to all other known groups in the world and involved a distinctive judgment of ways in which these groups differed from each other and, most importantly, from one's own group. We saw this process at work in McDougall's analysis of the "races" of Europe.

Racialization sets the stage for race to be employed in discourse, social analysis, and political and economic decision making. For example, the invidious value comparisons of races, types, or subspecies led almost inevitably to the denigration of Africans and their descendants. In an address made in 1865, James Hunt, founder and then president of the Anthropological Society of London, concluded, among other things that:

> the Negro becomes more humanized when in his natural subordination to the European than in any other circumstance, and can only be humanized and civilized by Europeans.

The hierarchy is clearly set forth as a matter of the "natural order" of things. Racialization completes the circle by making *my kind* the criterion by which goodness is judged and by depositing the advantage squarely in the center of "universal truth." This belief and the derivation of its implications lay at the heart of the cultural system that spawned racism.

The racialization processes gave meaning to racial differences, established the value hierarchy, and imparted pseudoscientific validity to these racialized judgments. Thus, the racialization of society is a precursor to, and makes possible the depth and breadth of, racism.

Race and Ethnicity

What is the difference, if any, between *ethnicity* and *race*? Kottak (1996, p. 57) defines their intersection in these terms: "When an ethnic group is assumed to have a biological basis (shared "blood" or genetic material), it is called a *race*." Van den Berghe (1967), defined *ethnicity* as a social group that is defined on the basis of cultural criteria. We commonly now think of ethnicity in terms of culture. Therefore, unlike race, it is thought to be mutable, controllable, and a matter of relatively greater choice. For example, in the U.S. census, a Hispanic can be of any "race," thus clearly establishing "Hispanic" as an *ethnic*, not a racial, designation.

Patterson (1996, p. 6) notes the problematic scientific status of the race concept and asks "what then is the distinction between the 'racial' and the 'ethnic'? We must conclude that making this distinction is itself a belief, a distinctly American belief, an essential part of American ideology." He argues, in support of this theory of race-ethnicity confusion, that any group that believes there are differences (essentialistic heuristic) will see them as biologically grounded. Recounting tales in the Icelandic Sagas, Patterson (1996, p. 3) notes the following:

> Medieval Scandinavia had a large slave population . . . the vast majority of whom were either other Scandinavians or mainly blond, very white-skinned Irish and other Celtic peoples. Yet the numerous physical descriptions of the slaves in the Sagas routinely described them as very swarthy and physically completely different (and always ugly) from the slave-holder class.

His ultimate argument is that, if race and ethnicity are interchangeable in common usage and if there is no useful biological basis on which to distinguish human groups, we (social scientists) might as well use ethnicity as race (Patterson, 1996).

We have outlined the long and tortured history of the concept of race. However, although we use *ethnicity* more and more these days in the way that Patterson would have us do, doing so seems to add to, rather than reduce, the confusion about how to classify people into socially meaningful groups. In Bosnia, *ethnic cleansing* describes the systematic attempt to eliminate Bosnian Muslims—who do not differ "racially" from Bosnian Serbs. In Hitler's Germany, exterminating 6 million Jews was an act of racial genocide, Hitler's "final solution." What is the difference between "ethnicity" in Bosnia and "race" in Nazi Germany?

For many, *ethnicity* is simply a contemporary term for what historically was referred to as *race, type,* or *nationality.* This recency is shown by the fact that *ethnicity* and *ethnic group* did not even appear in standard English dictionaries until the 1960s (Glazer and Moynihan, 1975). However carelessly or insidiously it was done, the use of *race* always implied a genetic marker of categorization. A common biology was thought to underlie observed differences among and between categories of people. *Ethnicity* departs from this assumption by suggesting that the defining markers are largely *cultural.*

Marger (1994) offers five criteria for identifying ethnic groups:

1 *Unique cultural traits*—Ethnic groups typically exist within a larger cultural and social system, but possess and maintain behavioral characteristics that set them off from the society's mainstream or dominant tendencies.
2 *Sense of community*—Ethnic groups display a consciousness of kind or an awareness of close association, "we-ness," a sense of peoplehood. Although this we-ness derives from several sources, it stems primarily from a sense of shared ancestry or heritage. This commonality, real or imagined, serves as a point of contact and cohesion among group members.
3 *Ethnocentrism*—The feeling of we-ness gives rise to the tendency to judge other groups by the standards and values of one's own group, and the result is often an inherent preference for (and belief in the superiority of) one's own kind. (We saw aspects of these processes in Part 2, when we discussed social categorization and social identity.) This in-group bias has been shown to be an inevitable consequence of social categorization. By implication, then, the concept of ethnicity carries with it a tendency toward group polarization and social conflict. In our contemporary discourse, the focus on diversity or multiculturalism may be thought of as the *ethnicization* of society along many different lines, including not just race-, sex-, or age-based categories, but groups based upon occupation, physical ability or disability, sexual orientation, and so on. This ethnicization or emphasis on distinctiveness makes differences more salient than similarities. The ethnic conflict in the Balkan states of the former Yugoslavia has given us the term *balkanization* to describe what some commentators see as the downside of the diversity dynamic (Sobol, 1995), thus viewing the diversity movement as a trend toward balkanization conjuring up the horrors and problems of the former Yugoslavia.
4 *Ascribed membership*—One's ethnicity is acquired at birth by virtue of one's parents and the subculture in which one grows up. Ethnicity derives importance from the cultural values, symbols, beliefs, and practices to which one is exposed. Although one's ethnicity generally remains constant, over the life span it can be modified—unlike race. That is, one can acquire new cultural traits, develop community with members of other groups, and take on lifestyles that are difficult to link to one's ethnic heritage. To what extent, for example, is a non-practicing Jew ethnically Jewish? Is a person of Latino origin who speaks no Spanish, lives in and among non-Spanish-speaking Anglos, maintains middle-class Anglo values and beliefs, and fails to draw upon Latino heritage in major life decisions an ethnic Latino? One of the interesting questions of ethnicity con-

cerns the extent to which one can really "shed" one's ethnic heritage (assuming it were desirable to do so). Perhaps it is the high degree of value placed on individualism and personal choice in the United States that gives ethnicity such a flexible status. In other societies around the world (e.g., Bosnia, Rwanda, Sri Lanka, New Zealand), ethnic differences take on much harder boundaries, viewed more like the race concept in the United States.

5   *Territoriality*—Ethnic groups often occupy a distinct territory within the large society. Many American Indians live on reservations within specified regions, such as the Southwestern states of Arizona and New Mexico or the upper Midwest. Asians typically live on either the West or East Coast, and Latinos typically live along the Mexican border, Florida coast, and the Atlantic seaboard. African Americans live across the country, but low-income blacks typically live in inner cities, and middle- and upper-income blacks are segregated in middle-class enclaves in either urban or suburban areas, either by choice or by manipulation of banks and the real estate industry. Ethnic segregation, like racial segregation, is a feature of our multiethnic society.

Who belongs to an ethnic group and who belongs to a racial group? In the United States we commonly refer to blacks and Asians as *racial groups,* but Hispanics (or Latinos) as an *ethnic group.* American Indians can readily lay claim to both statuses. And, to further complicate matters, persons with physical disabilities make a claim for "cultural" distinctiveness (Scheer, 1994). If culture is a defining marker of ethnicity, is any group that can claim cultural integrity and continuity an ethnic group? Should we think of people increasingly seeking refuge in "gated communities"—that is, set apart from other Americans, protected by their own se-

Sixth Annual Indian Pow Wow celebrates traditional Indian identity and culture in Taos, New Mexico. (Lisa Law/The Image Works)

curity forces—as a subculture or an ethnic group? Does it matter which term is used? The interesting question for a book on racism is, How does ethnicity fit in? If race is fundamentally aligned with biology, in spite of the scientific impropriety of doing so, does shifting our conception from race to ethnicity offer a way of ameliorating the negative consequences of racism? We will discuss this question in the final chapter.

To contrast race and ethnicity, we offer the following distinctions:

Group Label	Nature of Bias	Basis of Bias
Race	Racism	Biological differences
Ethnicity	Ethnocentrism	Cultural differences

We tend to think of racism as directed at the out-group and ethnocentrism as a bias of the in-group. In fact, ethnocentrism implies negative judgments of the out-group *relative to* the in-group. However, racism is as much about the superior qualities of one's own racial group relative to others as it is about the inferiority of others. Therefore, this distinction is not a useful one. What is significant is the biological versus cultural basis for the differences upon which bias rests. As we have tried to show, the concept of *race* implies that there are essential characteristics of a human group— albeit ones that, in a psychological sense, are associated with biology and genetic material. Therefore, these characteristics, because of the associations, become more fundamental, more essential, and less mutable than are characteristics of culture. Hence, in the United States we tend to believe that ethnicity is different from race and is less amenable to the biases we associate with the race concept. (It is, though, not easy to see the difference between the ethnic conflicts of Bosnia and the race-based conflicts of the United States). We need to look at culture and race more directly.

Race and Culture

Everything we are and do, all that we have been and will be filters through the lenses of culture. Race, as a concept, cannot be discussed at all in the absence of understanding what culture is, how it evolves, and how it affects our thinking, opinions, beliefs, and behavior (cf. Sowell, 1994). In fact, as we have seen, in its earliest usage, *race* was understood largely in cultural terms.

Culture rolls along over years, decades, and centuries, as if a giant snowball, gathering size and bulk, attaching all that it touches to its mass. Although it assimilates, it does not necessarily amalgamate. That is, the basic elements of culture stand out. Although they moderate, adapt, and change incrementally over time in their symbols, expressions, and expectations, there is a profound continuity, a sameness that exists as a deep structure.

Kroeber and Kluckhohn (1952, p. 86; *emphasis* added) suggest that culture is:

> . . . patterned ways of thinking, feeling and reacting, acquired and transmitted mainly by symbols, constituting the distinctive achievement of human groups including their embodiments in artifacts; the essential core of culture consists of traditional (i.e., historically derived and selected) ideas and especially their attached values . . . Culture systems may, on the one hand, be considered as *products of action,* on the other hand, as *conditioning elements of future action.*

Important points to extract from this definition are the following:

1   Culture is not only the content of thoughts, feelings, and reactions, but the *pattern* that describes them—that is, the organization, linking, and networking of these levels of human experience and behavior.
2   These individual-level patterns are acquired and transmitted via *symbols* that represent what we mean by things and what things mean to us.
3   Culture is derived from history and, therefore, is the summation of all that went before.
4   Culture is both a template, or *guide for action*, of its members and the *result of actions* taken by its members.

Moreover, our cultural responses to race—the facts of slavery, the Civil War, Jim Crow, lynchings, the Harlem Renaissance, welfare, segregation, the Civil Rights Act, and the myriad racial projects in post-civil rights U.S. society—contribute to what U.S. culture is and will become.

Nobles (1985) offers a pragmatic idea of culture as those "processes which give people a general design for living and patterns for interpreting their reality (p. 103)." That is, what one believes, according to Nobles, about oneself, one's family, and others, possibilities and limitations, good and bad, are heavily influenced, if not dictated, by the cultural framework within which one was socialized. The broad strokes of culture (aspects) are symbols reflecting ideology (prescriptive patterns of behavior), ethos (feelings of right and wrong, good and bad, beautiful and ugly), and worldview (the abstractions of who we are, how we ought to behave, and what the consequences will be).

Culture not only tells us what to think and what to do, it then finds a way to incorporate us when we don't follow along. We can challenge culture, oppose it, or ignore it, but it won't go away, and it won't change much—at least, not in a short time. Given this profoundly robust and influential role of culture in our daily lives, and given the powerful place the concept of race holds, we must conclude that race is one of the most centrally real elements of U.S. culture.

Race and racialism, as discussed above, define patterns of beliefs that achieve what Nobles calls a "worldview" (see also Myers, 1993; Akbar, 1991). The cultural prescription for gender relations specified cultural mechanisms and their psychological consequences that not only insured continuing roles for men and women but maintained a gender hierarchy, with men at the apex (cf. Bem, 1993). Cultural prescriptions have done the same for race. Just as important, one does not need to embrace specific ideologies of race in order to be influenced by them, as we saw in Part 2. Moreover, the influence of race in the creation, development, and maintenance of cultural institutions are, of necessity, similarly influenced by race (see Chapter 16).

Race versus Culture

One critical question must be asked: If the human variations implied by race have no scientifically meaningful (i.e., biological) basis, and if ethnicity is defined by cultural criteria, in the end are we *only* talking about culture? That is, is it culture and not race that we should be concerned about? Or is it culture *and* race that matter? Or, is there a meaning of race that stands apart from that of culture?

The concept of race has been integral to the evolution of Western culture. Because the concept of race is largely a social construction consisting of some loosely held ideas about human biology and personality, raised to an instrument of culture through racialization processes, race and culture are confounded. That is, the meaning of *race* cannot be separated from the meaning of *culture.* Attempts to objectify blacks in the absence of what Americans of European descent think about blacks is not possible. Therefore, the so-called race problem is, at its core, a problem with U.S. culture.

When William Bennett suggested that we "treat people as if their race doesn't make a difference," he proposed a strategy that was psychologically and culturally impossible to carry out (Sawyer, 1985, p. A6). As social psychological research has demonstrated (cf. Fazio et al., 1995; Devine, 1989) symbols of race can influence even our microlevel perceptions and judgments. Although a colorblind philosophy may appear to be a fully fair and egalitarian way to approach the world, we are, in fact, not a colorblind society.

Skin color is a symbol of that complex of beliefs, values, and expectancies we know as *race.* It implies that the concept of race carries a biological significance that, we have argued, has little scientific merit. So what does a colorblind strategy buy you? Skin color is linked to the symbols of race that derive their meaning from the patterning of culture that gives shape and definition to them. So, in the United States, skin color is a biological reference for what is essentially a cultural concept.

What, specifically, are ways in which the concepts of race and culture diverge? Consider the analysis of Kluegel and Smith (1986) in Chapter 5. Most whites believe that opportunities are widespread for all, that success or failure is determined by individual qualities, and that inequality of outcomes can be explained by the relative inequality of inputs (e.g., effort, ability, character). Most blacks do not, to the same degree, believe these characterizations to be true, nor do most women. In this regard, women as a group are more like blacks as a group. Therefore, on these matters of expectations, beliefs and the symbolic representation of them, white women and blacks (men and women) have more in common than white women and white men do.[4] Blacks and white women do not share "race" but, in this consideration, they share experience with manifestations of discrimination and bias, as each is represented in U.S. culture (symbols, beliefs and values). So, making distinctions between blacks and whites may not be as relevant, in some instances, as making distinctions between people who share certain experiences and derive common beliefs and values from them.

Consider another situation. Recall that Wilson (1987) showed that poor blacks tend to live in neighborhoods that are disproportionately populated by other poor blacks. Poor whites, by contrast, tend to live in neighborhoods that are much less dominated by poverty. So, if we try to compare poor whites with poor blacks (presumably a racial comparison), we will be missing the fact that their environments are not comparable. As a result, if we try to extrapolate similar expectations based on poverty, or dissimilar expectations based on race, we may be wrong on both counts. The experiences of poor blacks and poor whites are not the same, *either* in terms of race or of the circumstances of their poverty.

The point of these examples is that culture not only evolves as a guide to behavior, it is created from experience as well. Race is invoked as an objective fact, a constant that binds people of similar physical attributes together. What matters is their experience and the meaning given to it. The differences in experiences that accrue to people who belong to different racial groups account for differences we ob-

---

[4]Of course, white women are closely aligned with white men on other issues, so we do not want to push this example too far. There are cross-cutting issues, and "race" will align itself at times, gender at other times, and at still other times, categories of race and gender will intersect. The point is that assumed similarity on physical dimensions may obscure greater dissimilarity on other factors, and vice versa.

serve that we may attribute to race itself. It is also true that differences in experiences of people within racial groups exist. In-group variability *should* help to undo the race concept. The consideration of culture require that we make less, not more, of race. Or, at the very least, we must be cautious in the conclusions we draw both about racial differences *between* groups and racial similarities *within* groups.

So, in order to talk about race, racialism and, as we now turn to the next chapter, racism, we must keep clearly before us the cultural fabric of our society. That is, race cannot be separated from culture, and if we are to understand race and all of its manifestations, we must look carefully at the instruments and mechanisms of culture. That is what we shall tackle next—the ominous concept of *racism.*

SUMMARY

In this chapter we have shown that the concept of race itself carries a history and meaning that makes it ripe for the expansion into racism. The concept of race sharpens differences among people and endows these differences with a certain biological inevitability. Even though the distinctions we attach to these differences are shown to have more meaning in describing intragroup than intergroup differences, we cling to the essentialistic heuristic that says "observable physical similarities will be matched by deeper similarities in deeper properties."

Therefore, although there is ample evidence for the scientific rejection of the concept of *race,* it persists as a social or cultural construction. It has meaning for us in everyday life because it provides a good way to value our own group over others; to encapsulate social conflict and rationalize our way of handling it; and to talk about group differences, values, and social hierarchy. Furthermore, the construction of race is so integral to our cultural worldview that we couldn't drop it even if we proclaimed it null and void.

The deeper similarities assumed to be characterized by race types are presupposed and embraced by the cognitive processes we labeled "racialism." This belief system gave psychological meaning to the race concept. The race concept then gained functional meaning as it was promulgated throughout society and around the world via racialization. The simple processes of racial categorization for descriptive purposes took on psychological, institutional, and culturally active roles in the organization and structure of intrapsychic and supranational relations. Defining *race* is an ongoing battleground, and racial projects are the instruments of the war. The evolving meanings of *race* provide the rationale for moral judgments, social policies, and economic outcomes. The concept of race persists in our society because it is the point around which many important psychological and social processes revolve.

The relative importance of and distinctions among concepts such as race, ethnicity, and culture are shown to complicate our understandings of who we are and ways in which we are similar as well as different. Against these complications, and a culturally promoted meaning of *race* that inherently leads us to racial inequality, we next turn our attention to racism.

13

Racism: What Is It and How Does It Work?

❖

Introduction ◆ What is racism? Definitions and their implications ◆ How does racism work? ◆ Racism and beliefs about race ◆ *Rationalization of racism* ◆ *The sustaining mechanisms of racism* ◆ *Souls of white folk* ◆ *American apartheid* ◆ Coping with racism ◆ Summary

*I*NTRODUCTION

Racism in the United States is as old as the country itself. We cannot think about what it means to be an American without contemplating the horrors of racism that dot our historical landscape. Yes, racism is a real problem in the United States, and it always has been. Today, being called a racist is probably, for most Americans, to be labeled with the worst epithet or to be deemed guilty of the worst offense.

Why is racism a problem and whose problem is it? First, let's take note of the United Nations Development Programme (1993) *Human Development Report*. The 1993 report focused on people and their participation in their societies. (The organization's first report was issued in 1990.) The general premise underlying the 1993 report was that development around the world must be woven around people. Failure to incorporate people in national and international development programs means to waste human capital. From measures of life expectancy, educational attainment (a composite of adult literacy and mean years of schooling), and economic success measured by gross domestic product (GDP) per capita, a composite human development index (HDI) was constructed.

The United States ranked sixth among all the nations of the world on the HDI. Surprised? Well, if one considers African Americans a a separate group, they would have ranked thirty-first! Hispanic Americans as a group would have ranked thirty-fourth! When African Americans and Hispanic Americans are *removed* from the HDI for the United States, we're number 1! What does this tell us? Well, it will surely mean different things to different people. However, one thing is clear, whatever role race- or ethnicity-based disadvantage, discrimination, and bias play in the overall low status of African Americans and Hispanics, for examples, has the net effect of lowering the standing of the entire society! Racism is a waste of human capital.

So, taking *racism* as a composite label for all forms of disadvantage, discrimination, and bias, it is a problem for its targets or victims, and it is a problem for the entire society. Hence, it is a problem for each of our citizens. In short, the problems of racism are real.

Very few Americans would accept the label of racist, but we hear it applied regularly to whites all the time—and increasingly, to some blacks as well. In the 1980s, Secretary of Agriculture Earl Butz told a racial joke at a private party. The joke implied that blacks were only interested in sex, eating, and physical comfort. When word of it leaked out, Butz was publicly excoriated to such a degree that he was forced to resign his cabinet-level position. Jimmy "the Greek" Snyder and Al Campanis's infamous race theorizing has already been discussed, along with the strong consequences.

Ben Wright is a British commentator who regularly covers the Ladies Professional Golf Association (LPGA) tournaments for CBS television. He was covering the 1995 LPGA Championship in Wilmington, Delaware, when Valerie Helmbreck of the *Wilmington News Journal* reported on some of his comments. Wright had said, in effect, that lesbian golfers compromised the game and scared sponsors away and that women's "boobs" got in the way of a smooth swing—thereby limiting the ability of women to become as good as men in the sport (Sandomir, 1995). After a period of several months of denials and counteraccusations, during which Helmbreck's character was maligned and Wright's story was defended by CBS, the truth became known from other eyewitnesses. CBS finally discharged Wright from his broadcast duties. This story is similar to the ones cited earlier and shows again how we as a society do not tolerate language that seems to support a pejorative, biological interpretation of racial or gender differences.

Minister Louis Farrakhan described the fact that in the years following the Great Depression Jews and, more recently, Asian Americans owned profitable businesses in poor inner-city black communities while living in middle-class suburban communities by making an analogy to "bloodsuckers." The sound bite, "Jews are bloodsuckers," fueled strong charges of anti-Semitism and led many white Gentiles, Jews, and even some blacks to reject the Million Man March, organized by Farrakhan, seeing it only as an expression of racism and anti-Semitism.

If we as a society reject individual expressions or sentiments that offend our sense of equality, why are we so embroiled in this racism thing? The prosecution in the O. J. Simpson murder trail put Detective Mark Fuhrman on the stand, stood behind him, and presented him as a good cop who was merely doing his job when he found the bloody glove at Simpson's house. When the tapes on which he was heard using the word *nigger* repeatedly and describing ways in which he would set up innocent blacks for arrest and plant evidence to facilitate their convictions were played in court and were publicized, his credibility quickly plummeted. His racist character—probably more than any other single aspect of the trial—was responsible for the acquittal verdict.

What we find when we look closely at racism is a lot of ambivalence and uncertainty, even confusion. As we saw in the last chapter, the concept of race was founded on the assumption of biological differences that are (1) unique to a group, (2) attached to observable temperament and character traits, and (3) relatively stable or immutable. However, as we also noted, there is scant scientific evidence to support this view. Society has socially constructed a view of race that makes it easy to see racial differences in traits and behaviors, and to place such traits and behaviors along some evaluative continuum—from desirable to undesirable, from good to bad, and from useful to dysfunctional. With this race concept as a starting point, it is a short trip to racism.

This chapter will systematically discuss the concept of racism and its manifestations. The first section will consider what racism is by reviewing prevailing definitions of *racism*. These definitions are quite broad and various and will show the basic fact that simply considering racism as feelings and acts of superiority inadequately captures its many different forms and manifestations. The second section will consider the belief structure, the psychosocial processes that sustain racism against a prevailing sentiment that rejects it, and the mechanisms by which racism operates. This section goes to the core of how racism operates in the cumulative structures and processes of society, and how it translates to specific beliefs and attitudes individual people hold. We consider its expression in language, thought, and behavior. We next consider how some whites talk about race and how it illustrates their racist thinking, and how society has structured itself around race, creating and maintaining racial separation that facilitates continued racial inequality. Finally, we ask, How do racism's targets cope with it?

WHAT IS RACISM? DEFINITIONS AND THEIR IMPLICATIONS

By adding an *-ism* to *race*, we imply that there is something organized, systematic, and usually, undesirable about it. Although I offered a definition of *racism* in the first edition, I believe that the issue is far more complex today—and, in many ways more important—than it was in 1972. Recall that we had only come upon the term in the late 1960s. Carmichael and Hamilton (1967) coined the term *institutional racism*. The Kerner Commission (1967) attributed the seeds of racism to the evolution of two separate societies, one black and one white, and blamed the outburst of violent racial riots on "white racism."

In the following pages, we will see what different scholars think about racism. From these definitions, we will extract recurring themes and develop a working understanding of what we mean when we talk about racism. These definitions appear in Table 13.1.

Let's begin with the formal definition from *Webster's Unabridged Dictionary*. According to that authority, racism is characterized by "discrimination, segregation, persecution, and domination based on a . . . doctrine or feeling of racial . . . superiority" (*Webster's Unabridged Dictionary*, 1965, p. 1485). As DuBois (1903) noted, the problem of the twentieth century is the problem of the color line. The definition in *Webster's Unabridged Dictionary* does not specify who exactly determines who is superior and who is inferior. Nor does it specify who the actors are. The first part of the definition implies that racism is organized and occurs at a societal level. That it is exemplified by segregation, persecution, and domination is stated explicitly. Because "racism" is also a *doctrine*, it occurs at the cultural level. And because racism also involves "a feeling of superiority" and "antagonisms," it occurs at an individual level (*Webster's Unabridged Dictionary*, 1965). The multidimensional nature of racism is clear from the formal dictionary definitions of it. Other definitions further complicate the issue.

Barker (1981) describes what he calls the "new" racism, as noted earlier. At the heart of his idea is that by defining racism in terms of superiority and inferiority, as

TABLE 13.1 DEFINITIONS OF RACISM

Author	Type of racism	Definition
Webster's Unabridged Dictionary (1965, p. 1485)	Racial superiority	Program or practice of racial discrimination, segregation, persecution and domination based on racialism, [which is] . . . a doctrine or feeling of racial differences or antagonisms, especially with reference to supposed racial superiority, inferiority, or purity.
Ani (1991, p. xxvi)	White nationalism	Ideological commitment to the perpetuation, advancement, and defense of a cultural, political, racial entity, and way of life [which is] expressed as European nationalism which identifies Caucasian racial characteristics with superiority and African racial characteristics with inferiority.
Appiah (1990, p. 5)	Propositional racisms	Racialism—belief that there are heritable characteristics possessed by members of our species that allow us to divide them into a small set of races; *extrinsic racism*— belief that members of different races differ in respects that *warrant* differential treatment; *intrinsic racism*—belief that each race has a different moral status independent of any racial facts that might be known.
Barker (1981, pp. 22–23)	Xenophobia	Links race with nations and legitimates the rejection of races that do not share the dominant group's 'way of life.'
Essed (1991, p. 52)	Everyday racism	A process in which (a) socialized racist notions are integrated into meanings that make practices immediately definable and manageable, (b) practices with racist implications become themselves familiar and repetitive, and underlying racial and ethnic relations are actualized and reinforced through these routine and familiar practices in everyday situations.
Goldberg (1990, p. xix)	Nationalism	[A form of racism] . . . expressed increasingly in terms of isolationist national self-interest; of cultural differentiation tied to custom, tradition, and heritage; and of exclusionary immigration policies, anti-immigration practices and criminality.

TABLE 13.1 DEFINITIONS OF RACISM *(Continued)*

Author	Type of racism	Definition
Chase (1977, p. 6)	Scientific racism	The idea that everything about a person's condition in life—from his socioeconomic status and his educational achievement to his life span and the quality of his health—is immutably preformed in the genes he inherits from his parents at the moment of his conception.
Kinder and Sears (1981, p. 416)	Symbolic racism	A blend of antiblack affect and the kind of traditional American moral values embodied in the Protestant Ethic . . . [embodying] resistance to change in the racial status quo based on moral feelings that blacks violate such traditional American values as individualism and self-reliance, the work ethic, obedience, and discipline.
McConahay (1986, p. 92-93)	Modern racism	Belief that discrimination is a thing of the past because blacks [and other minority groups] have the freedom to compete in the marketplace . . . Blacks are pushing too hard and too fast into places where they are not wanted . . . these tactics and demands are unfair therefore recent gains are undeserved and institutions are giving them more attention and status than they deserve.
Gaertner and Dovidio (1986, p. 62)	Aversive racism	Ambivalence based on conflict between feelings and beliefs associated with a sincere egalitarian value system and unacknowledged negative feelings and beliefs about blacks
Wellman (1993, p. 210)	Racial privilege	Defense of a system from which advantage is derived on the basis of race . . . it insures the continuation of a privileged relationship.
Welsing (1991, p. 119)	White supremacy	The behavioral power system of logic, thought, speech, action, emotional response and perception— whether consciously or unconsciously determined—in persons who classify themselves as "white."
Van Dijk (1987, p. 28)	Structural racism	An abstract property of social structures at all levels of society that manifests itself in ethnic prejudices as shared group cognitions, in discriminatory actions of persons as dominant group members, as well as in the actions, discourses, orga-

(Continued)

TABLE 13.1 DEFINITIONS OF RACISM (*Continued*)

Author	Type of racism	Definition
Van Dijk (1987, p. 28) (*cont.*)	Structural racism (*cont.*)	nization, or relationships within and among groups, institutions, classes, or other social formations.
Feagin and Vera (1995, p. 7)	Denial of racial dignity	The socially organized set of attitudes, ideas, and practices that deny African Americans and other people of color the dignity, opportunities, freedoms, and rewards that this nation offers white Americans.
Feagin and Feagin (1996, p. 7)	Ideological racism	An ideology that considers a group's unchangeable physical characteristics to be linked in a direct causal way to psychological or intellectual characteristics, and that on this basis dis- tinguishes between superior and inferior racial groups.
Omi and Winant (1994, p. 162)	Racialized social process	A fundamental characteristic of social projects which create or reproduce structures of domination based on essentialist categories of race.
Jones (1972, p. 172)	Cultural racism	Results from the transformation of race prejudice and/or ethnocentrism through the exercise of power against a racial group defined as inferior by individuals and institutions with the intentional or unintentional support of the entire culture.

the above definition does, one misses some of its most important principles—namely, xenophobia (i.e., fear or hatred of strangers or foreigners). To illustrate his point, Barker cites a speech by then prime minister of Great Britain, Margaret Thatcher. Thatcher explained that a remark she made in a speech to the effect that Britain was being "swamped" by immigrants with alien cultures was true. In support of this she claimed that "Some people do feel 'swamped' if streets they have lived in for the whole of their lives are really quite different" (cited in Barker, 1981, p. 1). This so-called new racism is simply an overt expression of in-group preference.

Barker (1981) rejects the idea that racism is a package of "irrational beliefs" about superiority, preferring instead to see it as those pejorative racial attitudes and beliefs that are framed in terms of logic and rationality. There is a certain logic to the "natural" desire to be with one's own kind, and to having a preference for the life, values, and customs that go with one's own culture. Barker (1981, p. 20) quotes Alfred Sherman, director of the Institute for Policy Studies in England, to illustrate this nationalistic view:

> National consciousness is the sheet anchor for the unconditional loyalties and acceptance of duties and responsibilities, based on personal identification with the national community, which underlie civic duty and patriotism.

The national community is the traditional community, and those of other colors and nationalities—that is, those who come from "alien cultures"—threaten that community. Xenophobia gives rise to attitudes, policies, and expressions that reject those who are different. In this country, we are confronting a similar kind of concern—namely, that so-called multiculturalism and a policy of unchecked legal immigration, combined with illegal immigration, threaten our way of life.

What is important about the new racism is its claim of logic and rationality of thought and judgment. That is, the new racist is not a bigot, is not antiblack, or anti-Asian, or anti-Hispanic, but simply a staunch defender of those valued beliefs and practices, customs, and way of life that make ours a great society.

This new racism sounds a lot like the three types of racism we have already discussed at some length—symbolic racism (Sears, 1988), modern racism (McConahay, 1986), and aversive racism (Gaertner and Dovidio, 1986). These approaches view feelings of superiority/inferiority as "old-fashioned" racism and suggest the emergence of a new form that emphasizes and focuses attention on traditional U.S. values. But, although the superiority aspect is downplayed in the new racism, there remain feelings or antagonisms (as *Webster's* suggests) that lay just below the surface. Barker implies that the new racism is a thinly veiled rationalization of racial hatred, and—to a large degree, so do those who have identified modern and symbolic racism. However, those who have identified aversive racism argue that there is true *ambivalence* in how some people feel about issues of race. That is, the latter propose that the attitudes or beliefs that are associated with preference for one's own group and corresponding bias in favor of one's own group do not always occur with callousness and premeditated dislike or disregard for the other group(s).

The real difficulty with all of these notions of racism is the close linkage between traditional values and racism. As we saw in Chapter 12, traditional values of liberty, freedom, and democracy are closely associated with beliefs in racial superiority-inferiority, denial of rights and opportunities on the basis of group membership, and institutional structures that limit participation of "the others" (i.e., those not like us). So, to some extent, the "new" racism is not new, and the old-fashioned racism is not that different from it. Now, in trying to disentangle the superiority-inferiority beliefs, emotional antagonisms, and irrational fears from the "principled" fealty to traditional values that characterizes the new racism, we may paint with too broad a definitional brush. Why can't one embrace the inherent good in traditional values of freedom and individual liberty without rejecting blacks and other groups? Why can't one oppose affirmative action because one thinks it causes more harm than it does good without being labeled a racist? Sniderman and Piazza (1993) argue against the broad-brush approach of the new racism suggesting it fails to allow for principled opposition to racial remedies on nonracial grounds.

Taken together, this new form of racism implies that the target group fails, in some way, to meet cultural standards for conduct and character. Martin Luther King's dream that black boys and girls—and all children—should be judged by the content of their character, not the color of their skin, implies that if one ignores the color of their skin, judges the content of their character, and finds it lacking, one can say "I'm no racist"! What about the possibility that one's judgment of character is hopelessly enmeshed in one's own, culture-based value system. Even by ignoring race, to the extent that one actually can do that, one filters one's judgment through a cultural lens of racism (or sexism). When one asks what character a person *should* have, values, beliefs, and behaviors derived from experiences and cultural socialization dictate the answer. When a group in power can define which values, expressed how and when, are *legitimate* criteria for good character, then it is easy enough to dismiss an entire group of people as lacking, not on the basis of skin color, but of character. In this manner, the colorblind approach to racial discrimination makes it easy to maintain one's superior status without opening one's self up to accusations of racism.

Barker (1981) argued that definitions of racism that emphasized irrational beliefs were flawed, because the simple way to shed the label of racism was to demonstrate a logical and rational basis of one's opinions, values, and beliefs. Appiah (1990) makes explicit use of this notion when he distinguishes extrinsic from intrinsic racists. *Extrinsic racists* believe that races differ in diverse respects and thereby warrant differential treatment. Therefore, if, indeed, a race is lazy, lacks the ability to delay gratification, and so forth—in short, if a race is found to be lacking in those elements of character McDougall (1921) extolled in the Nordic "race"—then members of that race *should* be treated differently. However, if it could be shown that they did not possess those undesirable qualities, then they would, by Appiah's reasoning, be accepted. *Intrinsic racists,* on the other hand, believe that some races are ordained by Nature to be inferior. The intrinsic racist has no interest in science or objective truth. Feagin and Feagin's notion of *ideological racism* mirrors this intrinsic racist view in stating that an ideological racist adheres to the underlying "biological" rationale and believes it legitimates racial differences in equality and capability.

Chase (1977) carried this logic-rationality argument to the heart of Western culture, to its science. *Scientific racism,* for Chase, provides that logic that allows one to hold beliefs about racial inferiority or superiority with impunity to the extent that "scientific evidence" can be adduced to support the differences claimed or even produced by culture. Hitler attempted to use scientific racism to justify his pogrom against the Jews, Americans used "science" to justify restrictive immigration policies in the 1920s, and, more recently, Murray and Herrnstein (1994) used it to argue against public intervention in education and labor markets.

However, several of the definitions go directly to the problems of organized and coherent patterns of self-interest in the form of "nationalism," which rests in central ways on definitions of race. Ani (1991), in common with Barker, sees protection of the dominant culture's "way of life" as a central feature of racism (see Table 13.1). However, she also makes race a more explicit part of her definition and makes explicit the superiority-inferiority idea. Goldberg (1990) makes an even bigger case for nationalism, which he sees as "isolationist self-interest resting on cultural tradition." Omi and Winant (1994, p. 71) share this perspective in their idea that racial (social) projects "reproduce structures of domination based on essentialist categories of race." Van Dijk (1987) also sees racism as occurring at the level of social structures, but as an abstraction that provides guidance for a variety of biasing behaviors that preserve the dominant status quo. Although these definitions vary somewhat on the centrality and explicitness of the race concept, they converge on the idea that societies organize themselves around the self-interest of those traditionally in the majority and/or in power. People who differ by cultural criteria, whether they are properly conceived as ethnically categorized or as racially categorized, are rejected to the degree that they are different and are perceived as a disruption of the status quo.

Two other important ideas come from these definitions. One is simply abject self-interest and domination. Welsing (1991) minces few words when she equates racism with "white supremacy." According to Welsing (1991, p. 119) the mechanisms of white supremacy are largely psychological, manifesting themselves in "logic, thought, speech, and emotional responses," as well as action. Feagin and

widespread and that taking advantage of them is a matter of individual character (cf. Kluegel and Smith, 1986). But most Americans often fail to see—perhaps because it is no longer as obvious as it once was—that opportunities are not equally available to individual Americans. The group to which one belongs plays an important role in determining what opportunities are available and under what conditions.

Yet, we still believe in the fundamental principle of individual rights. How can one argue that belief in individualism is a bad thing, a form of racism? Well, one can't really, by itself alone. It is only when one demonstrates that individualism is a flawed principle that works selectively and inconsistently that one can appreciate its limitations. We know in psychology that *partial reinforcement schedules* (intermittent or irregular reward for prescribed behavior) in the acquisition of behavior make it all the more difficult to extinguish the behavior later on. The salience of examples of individual success—however unrepresentative they may be of the collective experience of a group—is sufficient to keep alive the belief in individualism and equity of opportunity.[4]

The notions of xenophobia, symbolic and modern racism, and, particularly, aversive racism may be understood, in part, as a reflection of this dilemma. It may, in fact, be "unnatural" to accept others who are different as if their difference did not matter, to allow them to participate in one's life in intimate ways that affect one's well-being. Although the beliefs upon which this country was founded say it should be so, the heart of the nation resists and, in so doing, feels the strain of this ambivalence. Racism is not just the excesses of mean-spirited bigots, but the consequence of this truly extraordinary experiment in democracy. The problems of a diverse society are felt most when that diversity becomes the basis of factional conflict over diverging self-interests. The Founding Fathers worried over factionalism, too (see Hamilton, et al., 1788; *Federalist Paper* #54). And now, as we head toward the twenty-first century, factionalism has resurfaced as yet another challenge to our democracy. Again, we find racism centrally located in the culture that is the United States.

Rationalization of Racism

As we suggested previously, most people reject the application of a racist label to themselves. Is it merely a semantic problem—that is, is what one person means by racism different from what another means? Or is it a matter of insecurity that leads people from ethnic and racial minority groups to see racism in the actions of white people and institutions? Is it an insensitivity to the feelings of others? Or is it an inability to understand the complicated forces of culture and history, the divergent impact of culture and character in what we see happen to people of color?

As suggested in the opening of this chapter, ethnic and racial minorities in the United States do not attain the same level of success in health, education, and economic well-being, and that is a problem for all of us. But why don't they? The question we could ask, that may be less loaded than questions such as "Are *you* a racist? Are *we* racists? Is this *still* a racist society?" is "Why are such fundamentally important markers of the well-being of our citizens so polarized by race?"

We saw, in Chapter 5, that many Americans do not have a problem with inequality of outcomes, believing that it results from differential abilities and contri-

---

[4]Recall that Jhally and Lewis (1992) used the term *enlightened racism* to describe the phenomenon whereby conspicuous success of individuals from a racial minority group is taken as evidence that the group is not discriminated against. Failure of any one member of the group is thereby attributed to individual failings of character or capacity, not to discrimination or oppression of the group as a whole.

butions (Kluegel and Smith, 1986). We also know that, in the main, whites do not believe in (or, at least, publicly support) the old-fashioned form of racism that was based on a belief in white superiority and black inferiority (Sears, 1988; McConahay, 1986). But many whites do have beliefs about racial and ethnic minority groups, and politicians do promote policies and programs that affect these groups. And racial and ethnic minority groups continue to lag behind.

Let's consider some of the explanations that come from lay people who try to sort out these issues. We will first look at the nature of justice, where procedures that seem on their face to promote fairness are accepted to a greater degree than are outcomes that imply equality (Tyler, 1994). Recall the Eastland and Bennett (1979) comparison of "numerical" equality (i.e., equality of outcomes determined by proportionality of group membership) and "moral" equality (i.e., equality of opportunity determined on an individual input-outcome basis). Both of these lines of argument ultimately emphasize the distinction between principles of equity and of equality. With *equity*, outcomes should be proportional to inputs, so that inequality of outcomes (distributive justice) is justified when those with lesser inputs have lesser outcomes. Historically, having black skin, a Spanish accent, slanted eyes, or red skin may have, by itself, been enough to reduce inputs sufficiently to rationalize inequality of outcomes. This is surely the kind of bias that leads us to believe that achieving a colorblind society is the best way to remedy such egregious discrimination.

By contrast, *equality* is somewhat more confusing. Everyone would probably agree that equality of opportunity is what we want for everyone—regardless of race, nationality, religion, sex, and so forth. But what constitutes equality of opportunity runs right up against the equity principle. Consider the following case. Ramon and Chauncy have applied to graduate school in psychology. Ramon is Chicano, and Chauncy is white. Ramon's GRE score is 1040, and Chauncy's is 1210. The average GRE for Chicanos is 945, whereas for whites it is 1100. If we think of the GRE as a crucial input to the admissions process and of being admitted as the crucial outcome, then Chauncy should be admitted, because his score of 1210 is considerably higher than Ramon's 1040. But relative to their respective groups, Ramon is at the 90th percentile, and so is Chauncy. How do you take into account all of the historical forces, as well as contemporary influences, that may have limited Ramon's access to computers, school books, as well as other factors such as, perhaps, parents that could not read to him books in English, and so forth. Relatively speaking, by overcoming many disadvantages, he may have made inputs that are actually greater than Chauncy's.

The principle of "race norming" sought to do just that, to consider each person relative to his or her ethnic or racial group and to treat people of equivalent percentiles *within* their own groups as if they were equal between groups. This calibration exercise made a step to define inputs in such a way as to normalize scores across populations that had manifestly different positions in society and, by most accounts, differential access to opportunity. Attempts by the U.S. Department of Labor to implement race-norming principles as hiring strategies were shot down by a Congress that declared them illegal and a violation of Title VII of the 1964 Civil Rights Act.

Is it racist to oppose race norming? Is it racist to oppose busing to achieve racial balance in the public schools? Is it racist to support English only as the official language of all business transacted in the United States? Is it racist to oppose bilingual education? Is it racist to support Proposition 187 in California? Is it acceptable to declare that immigrants who have an alien culture are swamping our society? Racism brings forth many complicated issues and points of view. On the basis of the definitions of *racism*, holding the above views may well qualify one as being racist.

The so-called new racism is identified with attitudes and support of policies and programs that maintain the racial status quo but are couched in antiracist language. (We will look more closely at that language in the next section of this chapter.) Research on symbolic, modern, and aversive racism, as we have seen, shows that scores on measures of symbolic or modern racism reliably predict, in many cases, differential processing of racial information and behavior toward members of diverse racial groups. For example, Sears, Citrin, and van Laar (1995) showed that symbolic racism scores predicted opposition to policies that were seen as benefiting blacks, even when political conservatism or party affiliation failed to account for these policy preferences. Why?

Sears, Citrin, and van Laar (1995) suggest that symbolic racism taps into a rationalization of antiblack sentiment. Negative racial statements and behaviors are widely rejected in most contemporary societies, but negative sentiments are not gone. However, in order to express them, one must couch them in acceptable language. We might see this as a kind of "political correctness"—except it is associated with the conservative rather than the liberal end of the political spectrum. This view suggests that taking a hard line on "traditional" values cannot be challenged with impunity. Indeed, who could argue that the best person should not get the job, and that *best* is not defined concretely by one's *absolute* score on a test? Thus, one can oppose the policy and rationalize the opposition on the basis of holding strong American values, and thereby kill two birds with one stone—that is, keep the other group out *and* not be labeled a racist.

Historically, arguments rationalizing the unequal outcomes followed along lines of biological or cultural inferiority, or of religious mandate. The interesting question for an analysis of racism is the extent to which those more overt superiority-inferiority based assumptions and beliefs continue to exist in disguised or better-rationalized form in contemporary society. Current theorizing and research on racism concurs that such assumptions and beliefs continue to exist.

The Sustaining Mechanisms of Racism

What are the mechanisms by which racism is sustained against a broad-based perception that it is significantly diminished, if not altogether gone, from our society. By *mechanisms*, here, are meant those systematic and predictable patterns of behavior, formations of policy, and institutional practices that perpetuate those experiences and outcomes that are judged to be negative and discriminatory toward racial and ethnic minorities.

Everyday Racism—the Experience and its Meanings

Essed (1991, p. 48) offers a distinct analysis of racism based on how we live everyday. By *everyday life*, Essed means those

> . . . socialized meanings making practices immediately definable and uncontested so that, in principle, these practices can be managed according to (sub)cultural norms and expectations. These practices and meanings belong to our familiar world and usually involve routine or repetitive practices.

In short, everyday life is more or less automatic (Bargh, 1993), mindless (Langer, 1989), and scripted (Schank and Abelson, 1982). Racism, then, represents social meanings, expectations, and practices that reflect and maintain power differentials between and among people that have been racially defined.

The interesting and important aspect of this analysis is that people do indeed have individualized experiences that vary from person to person. But, although these experiences are in some sense peculiar to each person, they follow patterns that can be linked conceptually to an underlying foundation of racism. These everyday situations are structured around relations of gender, race, ethnicity, and class.

In the Essed (1991) analysis, prejudice (cognitive) and discrimination (behavioral) are *components* of racism. Furthermore, racism may be encountered *directly* (through interaction with another person) or *indirectly* (through media commentary or portrayals, or through policies and institutional arrangements).

To assess these ideas empirically, Essed (1991) interviewed 55 black women, aged 20 to 45, in California and the Netherlands. In both the United States and the Netherlands, black women tend to see racism as racial, ethnic, or cultural domination, with race more prominent in the United States and culture more prominent in the Netherlands. In the United States, racism is "explained" by race conflict and socioeconomic power, whereas, in the Netherlands, ignorance of racism explains its persistence.

Essed (1991) offers three processes of racism: problematization, marginalization, and containment. Let's look at the meaning of each of these processes and examples of how they work. Examples are provided by the case study of Rosa N., a Surinamese medical student in the Netherlands. Rosa N. won a scholarship to study medicine in the Netherlands and was serving an internship at the time of the interviews. She has been married to a white Dutchman (Rob, an architect) for four years.

Problematization.   Simply put, racism posits that blacks (or immigrants, or non-English speaking people, or other ethnic minorities) are *problems.* By making a group a problem, it means a solution is necessary and desirable. Given the racialization and ethnicization processes, it is easy to see that the problem will focus on the need to change those who constitute the problem: "If they would only . . . if they could only . . . ."

As we saw earlier, the target group of racism is not like "us"; it does not measure up to our customs, norms, or abilities. (For example, "They consider it a nuisance when we talk loud" [Essed, 1991, p. 114].) This problematization makes it easier to deny resources and to maintain relationships that perpetuate group dominance. The Willie Horton episode (see Chapter 12) could be seen as reflecting the problematization process.

Specifically, *problematization* consists of denigrating the target group's behavior (e.g., lazy, loud), pathologizing their characters (e.g., sick, mentally unstable), denigrating their culture (typically, through stereotypes such as unreliable, uncivilized, illiterate or inarticulate, having poor values, and having too many children), and denigrating their "biology" (e.g., genetically deficient intelligence, prone to criminality). Needless to say, given these problems, one can thus easily explain and defend differential outcomes by race.

> . . . in a general health class, this extremely stupid civil servant blamed the foreigners for overpopulation. I said something about that then, but what struck me was that someone said: oh, there's Rosa with that racism again . . . . (Essed, 1991, p. 150)

That is, if one tries to show that racism is a problem then one risks the whole issue's being turned around, with one's self once again, as the focus of the problem.

> We were in London . . . Rob had been invited to the inauguration of an important project he had worked on . . . we were really in one of the most expensive hotels. . . . We had gone out in the evening. At two in the morning we came back. And we come in and the man says, "you're not allowed to take a girl up to your room, Sir." (Essed, 1991, p. 152)

Stereotypical judgments cause pain. One's skin color, dress, or place makes automatic reference to a likely problem. As a black Surinamese woman, Rosa was always first seen as a problem:

> In shops they address someone much younger than me as "Ma'am," and use the familiar "jij" with me. And I can't get it out of my head that they don't do that because I'm young, but because I'm black. (Essed, 1991, p. 155)

By address and demeanor, Rosa is "kept in her place." She is not accorded the basic dignity or respect of womanhood or her profession, but kept in a safe, inferior place, along with children and pets. In summary, Rosa experienced racism everyday as she was pathologized, patronized, and not accepted.

Marginalization.   Essed (1991, p. 112) defines marginalization as ". . . a process in which a sense of 'otherness' is perpetuated [via mechanisms of] . . . color differentiation, nonrecognition, nonacceptance and the obstruction of mobility." Targets of racism are not included in the ongoing, everyday processes of society. Instead, they are marginalized through cognitive detachment, ethnocentrism, and the erection of barriers to participation. Dominant-group members may withdraw from interaction, hold up in-group standards as normative (making it easy for them to reject the vast majority of members of the minority group), or hold up one success story as the "exception that proves the rule." A segregated workforce is created by slotting jobs for marginalized minorities. The following statement by a black woman from the United States, reported by Essed (1991, pp. 113–114), is revealing:

> I am never lulled into believing that we are going to be on the same level according to their standards, because they set the standards, and any time you think it is going to be close, they simply move the standards higher.

Rosa N.'s concerns with racism and racialized discourse and judgment are dismissed as "excessive sensitivity." A patient refuses to shake hands with a "foreign worker" and thereby reinforces Rosa's otherness and her marginalized status. Although she has professional credentials, their value is compromised when she is judged incapable of rendering a diagnosis of a Surinamese patient (she is too involved to be objective, it is argued). As we saw in Chapter 10, marginalization reinforces one's "other-group" identity, and may force a bifurcation of self that makes bicultural adaptation difficult and mentally and emotionally stressful.

Containment.   Many dominant groups reject the dominated group's pursuit of equality, justice, and power. This rejection may take the form of suppression. Suppression, itself, can take many forms, some active (e.g., intimidation, retaliation), some more passive (e.g., denial of racism, pacification), and some a combination of the two (e.g., majority rule, denial of cultural differences).

Everyday experiences of rudeness, racist talk and joking, and patronizing (e.g., statements beginning "some of my best friends are . . .", making "high fives," and using "hip" talk) help to define racism in subtle, hard-to-detect ways. Rosa N. recounts the following:

> One of the doctors, a woman who has a disabled son, said one time . . . being disabled was something like being black . . . I find her extremely racist. And I've told her she does things that cannot be pointed out explicitly, which can be compared to racism. You can never get a grip on racism. And you know, she went to my boss and said I'd accused her of racism. (Essed, 1991, p. 153)

The woman probably did not believe that her comment was racist. But offense was taken. We are talking about the ways in which subtle cues of dominance are imparted through the social relationships. The woman suggested that blacks are less than whole, that they are disabled or "defective" *because* they are black. Rosa commented that this analogy is offensive and possibly racist, but the woman cannot see it as such because her perspective is so natural, so normal, so expected. Rosa is deemed "oversensitive," so her offense is pathologized.

These simple statements come from only two people, but are in fact replicated across the responses of many of the women in California and the Netherlands. Similar stories can be found in Feagin and Vera (1995), in Cose (1993), and in Graham (1995). The subtle ways in which racial hierarchy is reinforced on a daily basis make racism one of the most pernicious forms of dehumanization and marginalization in human society.

Communicating Racism in Everyday Talk

Van Dijk (1987, p. 11) used narratives from whites in the Netherlands and in San Diego, California, to analyze "the way racism is reproduced through everyday talk." He is specifically interested in the *microlevel,* interpersonal enactments of daily communication that reflect and maintain the *macrolevel* structure of racism. The everyday talk thereby becomes a mechanism by which macrolevel beliefs, values, and policies are transmitted and reinforced.

The methodology, although quite similar to that of Essed (1991) focuses specifically on "discourse analysis" (cf. van Dijk and Kintsch, 1983). Specifically, van Dijk focuses not on how whites talk *to* ethnic minorities but how they talk *about* them. The subject is ethnic and racial attitudes and how they are exhibited in the structures of conversation and how they are affected by sociocultural context, institutional language, and general norms and values.

One hundred eighty-three interviews were held in Amsterdam between 1980 and 1984 and in San Diego in 1985. In Amsterdam, the target groups were immigrants from Indonesia, Turkey, and Morocco, and black expatriates from the former Dutch colony of Surinam. Interviews in San Diego focused on blacks, Mexican Americans and other Latinos, and Asian Americans.

Although the conversations were not really samples of everyday discourse, the interviews were designed to be as natural as possible. They were conducted in the respondents' homes over either a 30-minute period (San Diego) or a 45-minute period (Amsterdam). Respondents were asked to tell their opinions and recount experiences with the neighborhood or the city. Over the course of the interview, the topic turned to "people" and, when specific ethnic groups came up, the interviewer followed the topic and tried not to lead the respondent to any specific subject. All interviews were transcribed verbatim. Discourse analysis is very complex, and we will not try to teach it in these pages. Suffice to say that van Dijk believes that ". . . prejudice is socially reproduced through discourse" and that, by analyzing how whites talk about other ethnic and racial groups, one can see how that happens.

Analysis of the corpus of conversations reveals four main topics of prejudiced talk:

1   "They are different" (in terms of culture, mentality, and norms).
2   "They do not adapt."
3   "They are involved in negative acts" (e.g., nuisance, crime).
4   "They threaten our socioeconomic interests."

These representations of ethnic or racial prejudice are summarized in a simple three-part model whereby foreigners or minorities threaten the in-group (1) economically (competition), (2) culturally (difference), and (3) socially (deviance). These sources of threat are reflected in the discourse about minorities and foreigners.

Tell me a story.   One source of discourse is storytelling. Van Dijk (1987, p. 66) presents the following story:

> . . . a long time ago, a Surinamese lady came into the supermarket . . . and that lady bought bread. She leaves the store and comes back and says, "I don't WANT that bread." . . . Then the manager very POLITELY . . . [says], "Madam, we do not exCHANGE bread." NO, in Holland one doesn't exchange bread, do we, or meat products either. Well after that the lady took on TERRIBLY, and the manager you know he tried to explain it to her, that bread cannot be exchanged here and in a very polite manner, after which that woman started to SHOUT like Don't touch me. . . . She throws the man that bread into his face, walks to the cash register and grabs two packets of Pall Mall.[5]

In van Dijk's analysis, this story is typical in that it presumes cultural differences and interprets the behavior of the Surinamer as negative and that of the white Dutchman as polite or positive. The woman speaking creates a link between herself and other white Dutch people (e.g., "one doesn't exchange bread, do we") and articulates a norm that the foreigner has violated.

Another story comes from Feagin and Vera (1995). A white male respondent describes, in story form, a composite of "them," meaning "black women on welfare":

> They'll sit there on talk shows and say, "I'se got to stay home and take care of my babies, I can' go to work." Well hell, my wife has to go to work. I work, you know, we work. . . . And yet she's going to justify to me that she's got eight children there, that we're taking care of . . . we only have three children . . . it's not responsible to have more than that. (Feagin and Vera, 1995, p. 152)

The story demeans the targets' intelligence and harkens back to racial stereotypes by using so-called "black dialect." It separates "their" behavior from "ours" by referring to values or norms of responsibility. As with the bread exchange, there is *our* way and *their* way, and ours is right and theirs is wrong. Van Dijk (1987, p. 68) summarizes his conclusions from the bread story in the following terms:

---

[5]Note that capitalization is used to indicate when the respondent emphasizes a point or shows particularly strong feelings.

> Such stories are subjectively biased, incomplete expressions of ethnic encounters in which the perspective is that of the storyteller and the in-group, and in which a selection seems to be made of those acts and events that are positive for the in-group and negative for the out-group. . . . They are not *I*-stories, but *we*-stories, and that makes them particularly effective in informal communication and diffusion.

In sum, stories are told as "evidence," presented in an argument form, to demonstrate that minorities are deviant, criminal, or otherwise problematic, that they violate our customs, and that we are the victims of these acts. Discourse, then, can convince members of a majority group that their fears, concerns, or negative affect is justified, and that distancing themselves from those outsiders is a wise and appropriate step.

For the sake of argument.   In the so-called new racism (which focuses not so much on ethnic or racial differences, but on values and culture) group differences and negative opinions about them need to be "backed up" with rational argument. Therefore, van Dijk (1987) cites "argumentation" as a basic discourse strategy. The need for arguments comes from a self-protective need to avoid appearing irrational and "inappropriately" biased. To the extent that one's negative evaluations of a target group come from experience-based effects, they serve to protect oneself from accusations of bias.

The structure of argument can be broken down into five parts:

1 *Position statement or opinion:* "I do not like it that immigrants don't speak English."
2 *Inference principle:* "People who don't bother to learn English in our country don't deserve special consideration.
3 *General statement:* "Immigrants would be better off if they learn English."
4 *Particular fact:* "When I go into Seven Eleven, the clerks cannot understand what I say."
5 *Support for the general statement:* "It would do the kids a disservice if they did not learn English at school." "If they (Mexicans) learn English, it is easier for them to make their way."

This idea of argumentation is offered to describe endorsement of negative evaluations of a target group on issues of some delicacy. It seems to be a structure that supports the analysis of symbolic racism as a more subtle way to oppose members of a group that is different, in cultural ways, from one's own.

I'm okay, you're not.   Another discourse strategy consists of making "semantic moves." In general, the goal of discourse in the era of the new racism is to present the other group in a negative light (old-fashioned racism or negative-affect-based motives) while presenting oneself or one's group in a positive light. These conflicting goals are managed, according to van Dijk, by semantic moves. Two such moves are apparent denial and apparent concession:

1 *Apparent denial,* whereby one expresses a negative opinion, is followed by a general denial of one's own negative opinion about the group. For example:

> I would put up one HECK of a battle if my daughter decided to marry Black (. . .) and it doesn't have to do with superiority or anything else, it's just too vast a difference for me to be able to cross over. (van Dijk, 1987, p. 92)

2   *Apparent concession,* whereby one first concedes that the group's traits or the group may actually not be negative or that the group member's may even have positive traits, but then expresses a negative judgment. For example:

> . . . how they are and that is mostly just fine, people have their own religion, have their own way of life, and I have absoLUTELY nothing against that, BUT, it IS a fact that if their way of life begins to differ from mine to an EXTENT that . . . . (van Dijk, 1987, p. 94)

An additional feature of discourse analysis is a focus on *style,* which is the choice of words and labels, and the manner of expressing one's opinions. Some may use moderate language (e.g., "I am not too fond of Mexicans") or more extreme language (e.g., "I hate Jews"). *Rhetorical operations* use contrast and comparison to emphasize differences (e.g., "We do it this way, they do it that way") and hyperbole to dramatize them. In actual conversation, all of these features are used to reinforce an in-group solidarity among the speakers and to emphasize differences between them and the targeted out-group. Therefore, it is not simply that one holds private, negative attitudes or opinions about out-groups, but that these opinions filter into everyday conversation in formal and specifiable ways that reinforce the sense of difference between the groups and of the superior value of the in-group's own norms, customs, and beliefs.

Racism as a top-down phenomenon.   Finally, van Dijk (1993) extends his discourse analysis from common people in their neighborhoods and communities to elites who lead and shape the attitudes on race and ethnicity through their own framing of relationships and their meanings. Van Dijk (1993) applies the same sort of discourse analysis to utterances from leaders in politics, corporate, academic, and educational spheres, and from those in the media. As with the everyday communications described earlier, elites frame their arguments in terms that present themselves (or their in-group) in a positive light and the minority groups in a negative light. Their discourse often highlights group differences and promotes a normative status quo in which the majority group's values are unqualifiedly correct. The whole process is couched in terms that protect the majority group's image of fairness and objectivity, while making disparaging or condescending remarks about those other groups. Republican presidential candidate Pat Buchanan was well-known for his use of language to bait the hook of bigotry (e.g., referring to Mexicans as *Jose* as he illustrates his get-tough stance on illegal immigration). The Willie Horton example, mentioned earlier, illustrates how language and visual symbols are used to sustain racism. In another case, Speaker of the House Newt Gingrich depicted the vicious murder of a pregnant woman and the kidnapping of her unborn baby as a fault of welfare policy. He thus labeled people on welfare as the kind of "others" who would do such a thing and blamed the government (particularly Democrats) for allowing these "others" to develop and maintain their uncivilized status within our society.

When our elite leaders frame images and use divisive, marginalizing language that maintain racial and ethnic separatism, and differential worth and character, we can see how insidiously racism is perpetuated in our society.[6]

---

[6]One could make the same argument about minority racial and ethnic leaders who use inflammatory language when speaking of whites. There is no question that language fans the flames of ethnic and racial animosity, and thereby perpetuates the conditions of racism in society.

Souls of White Folk

Although we talk about the in-group preference of dominant groups as an important mediator of negative bias for out-groups, there has been remarkably little attention paid to what it means to be white.[7] *White,* of course, is a catch-all term that implies, as does *black,* that relative skin color organizes a complex set of values, beliefs, and behaviors that matters in the world. By talking about "whites" as if they were, in fact, a group, we perpetuate the faulty notion of race as a biologically meaningful concept. As McDougall (1921) tried to show, there were systematic differences among the so-called whites of Europe. Although he referred to them as "races," it is clear that—whatever merit his racialized discourse may have had—he was attempting a cultural analysis of the people of Europe.

With the growing diversity of the U.S. population, the focus on whites as a group has intensified. This new scrutiny is attributed to many different developments, including the backlash of white men who object to their portrayal as villains who enjoy and perpetuate privileged dominance in Western culture. The cover of *U.S. News and World Report* (February 13, 1995) asked the following provocative question in bold letters: "Does Affirmative Action Mean NO WHITE MEN NEED APPLY?" Added to this backlash of white men are the simple facts of ethnic and racial diversity, expansion of the workforce to include women in a variety of careers and at many levels, and the growing group distinctiveness and assertiveness of the elderly, persons with disabilities, gay men, and lesbians, among others. Determining what it means to be an American and how our democratic principles can accommodate this diversity poses a significant challenge to this society.

Feagin and Vera (1995) went to the streets of cities in New York, California, Texas, and Florida to find out what whites thought about race in the United States and about themselves. Ninety interviews were conducted between 1989 and 1993, yielding opinions and attitudes across a wide range of issues. Of interest to us are the sentiments expressed by these respondents on matters of race. Following are seven general observations or propositions that can be extracted from the interviews. Each proposition is illustrated by a quote from one or more respondents (Feagin and Vera, 1995):

1 *Minorities see whites as a group, but whites don't necessarily see themselves that way.* The following statement comes from a white gentleman who was asked what being white is like:

> You really don't think about it that much, at least I don't. It has its advantages; and then again it has disadvantages. There is always a feeling of comfort, usually, but sometimes disadvantages because you feel you may miss out because they are looking for a minority or something like that, so it has good points and bad points. But . . . I don't think about it much. (p. 139)

2 *Many whites have very little direct experience with blacks, and, although they may be around them, don't come to know them.*

---

[7]There is a growing body of recent work that focuses attention on the neglected issues of "whiteness" (e.g., Fine, Weis, Powell, and Won, in press) and "white identity" (Helms, 1994; Jones and Carter, 1996). These analyses help to discern the heretofore neglected problems of stereotyping of whites, and the dimensions of homogeneity and variability among whites. That aspects of white identity—namely, self-interest and ethnocentrism—are related to racism makes this an important undertaking for social and behavioral science.

Most white people feel, I think, detached from blacks in the sense that they are kinda in their own world and blacks are kinda in their own world. You look at them through a looking glass and say, "Hmm, isn't that interesting what that black family's doing or what that black couple's doing, or what those black teenagers like to listen to, or like to dance, how they like to dance." And things like that. But they don't really identify that well or aren't that close with them totally. (p. 140)

3   *Whites have it better than blacks, and many think they should continue to strive to be the best they can be. This may involve perpetuating the advantage they enjoy because of being white, but they feel it is their responsibility not to go backward.*

I think although . . . despite strides toward, you know, equality and things like that . . . whites in a way have an easier row to hoe in the society. I'm not exactly sure why that is, but maybe . . . if you're white you have, your odds of being in a better family, or having a better upbringing, or having education emphasized more, is more there than being black. (p. 145)

Whites feel they should stay above blacks. I mean I was born in the sixties, so I feel like, maybe, at least whites my age and older feel like when they came into this situation . . . status and hierarchy and classification . . . you should at least jump off the plateau your parents are on. You should have a little better than your parents. And I feel that a lot of whites feel that way. When they came into the picture, they were better off than most blacks, so that should continue. (p. 145)

4   *Some white men feel it is they, not minorities, who are the victims. They feel a loss of respect and dignity, that this situation is a gross unfairness, and that they should and will challenge preferences for other groups as a matter of self-preservation.*

As a white male, I feel like I'm the only subsection of the population that hasn't jumped on the victim bandwagon. And I feel from a racial perspective as a white man, I have been targeted as the oppressor, and frankly, I'm getting a little tired of it, because I have not done a whole lot of oppressing in my life. . . . (p. 146)

Another respondent was asked specifically what being a white male meant and answered as follows:

It means you're part of the ingroup on the [matter of] power . . . basically I feel like the world has changed, and most of the white old men are, first of all have the political power, and have the industrial power, and they're going to hold on to it until it's taken away from them. . . . (p. 147)

So, whites tend not to think of themselves as a group. But when they do think of themselves as a group, it is in part as being distinct from other groups, and in part as being the group in power. Because things have obviously changed with regard to racial issues, a certain ambivalence is apparent in these sentiments. There is a sense that the way things have been has conferred privilege on whites, but it is not easy to reject that privilege. It would be a letdown not to do one's best, to try to advance oneself. But, given the way things are structured, doing so may well perpetuate the racialized status quo, with whites on top and in power, and other groups falling behind.

Although these sentiments reflect, perhaps, some of the difficulties of racialized thinking in contemporary society, there are still more abject racial antipathies that exist:

5 *A lot of whites use racial epithets and express racial hostility in private with their friends and other whites yet would not do so in public.* The public language is monitored so that it is always kept within acceptable bounds because doing so is supported by argument and custom (symbolic racism, Sears [1988]), but the private language is allowed to be more overtly hostile (old-fashioned racism).

> In this country, you are free to experience the American dream, or you are free to fail. You have that freedom. So it is up to you as to what outcome transpires. So if two individuals are applying for a job, race should absolutely not enter into the decision where a person is hired or not. (p. 142)

> I know a lot of people who are very racist. And that makes it hard on me because they'll be saying stuff. And I'll be like, "You need to quit saying that." They'll be "nigger this and nigger that," and I'll be going, "Come on man." . . . But I'll call my [white] roommate, I'll say, "Shut up nigger" and stuff like that to my roommate in the same way blacks call each other that. . . . But . . . I don't know if you can say that word and not be a racist. (p. 143)

6 *Many whites see blacks as different—and not in a positive way. Developing intimate contact with them is repugnant.*

> Blacks are dirty. And just some of their habits and things. . . . They're so different than whites. . . . It's just something that you see and something that you're taught but you don't do. . . . You [as a young white girl] don't bring home black boys. (p. 149)

> [If my child dated or married a Black person] I'd be sick to my stomach. I would feel like I failed along the way. I'd probably take a lot of blame for that. . . . I'd feel like I failed as a father. . . . And it is something that I could never accept. (p. 149)

7 *Many whites see blacks as responsible for their own fates because they lack the character to behave in a responsible way, they behave badly, and then, they blame whites for their problems.*

> There is this welfare system that enables young mothers . . . who can't support their children to have children anyway. . . . And I see public housing, and Headstart . . . and free daycare and free services, and free medical. . . . I don't think you need to have money so much, just have values . . . like education instead of just loafing, and watching TV, and getting welfare. And you know getting fat and being angry, and taking your anger out on robbing people, and killing people. (p. 151)

> In the past three years, we are suddenly having robberies that have never happened before. . . . I don't know where it's coming from but I think it flashed through every mind that it's probably blacks, including mine. I'm so ashamed of that I immediately shake myself and say, "No it isn't." [Where does it come from?] Society. You hear it all the time. I think it gets grilled into us. (p. 153)

> Black people are bigger racists any day of the week than white people are. I mean white people, for all intents and purposes don't give a shit . . . black people teach their children the white power structure is the root of their problems. . . . It's not that they all come from

single-parent homes, or what have you, it's all the white man's problem! . . . They don't want us to be racists anymore. [But] They want to be as racist as they want to be. (p. 157)

It's everybody else's fault but black America. We are born in this world in times that are tough. But times have changed; there's equality. We're actually past equality. We're actually into favoritism now based on sex and race, and it's not easy to understand their anger. (p. 156)

It is clear that there are many different levels of thoughts and feelings among white Americans. The diversity among them makes it difficult for them to identify as a single group. Identifying one's self as an American may be easier, but that includes, in general, all the diversity among people. What being American does beget, though, is a feeling that our way is superior. We invented this, we have this standard of living, we have accomplished all of these things—and this is all good. Perhaps it is not so much the fact of being white, but of tracing the accomplishments of the United States to one's ancestors that gives one a sense of superiority.

There is selective—and, perhaps, ambivalent—awareness. The great things that make us proud are balanced against the negative examples of racism and racialized discourse. Although the one respondent avowed as how he had not oppressed anybody lately, he does implicitly claim the benefit of the accomplishments of his cultural ancestors. White privilege is acknowledged as part of our cultural history. How can one ignore that privilege, or reject it? To refuse to take advantage of opportunities is not the American way. So, there is a kind of ambivalence expressed here. Whites have inherited privilege and favored position. Against these odds, members of minority groups have to play "catch-up." Removing barriers that have existed in the past and are largely responsible for white privilege and advantage does not create equality of opportunity. So, a neutral status quo (if one existed) would instantiate white advantage. Attempts to even out the competition are not designed to ensure victory to a specific party, they are simply intended to increase the competitiveness of participants (e.g., handicaps in golf, weights for jockeys, staggered starts in track events). Compensating for disadvantages is very American. But, in this obsession with race, values that are otherwise very American are compromised by the ideology of racialized discourse.

American Apartheid

Apartheid is the formal ideology, policies, and programs that maintained racial segregation and white domination in South Africa from 1948 until it was dismantled in 1991.* *Apartheid* is synonymous with the most egregious and morally unconscionable form of racial oppression in contemporary world history.

Massey and Denton (1993) hold a mirror to the United States, and the vision we see is a desperately challenging one. In a work that is simply put and massively documented, Massey and Denton (1994, pp. 9, 15–16) argue that:

. . . racial segregation—and its characteristic institutional form, the black ghetto, are the key structural factors responsible for the perpetuation of black poverty in the United States. . . . As in South Africa, residential segregation in the United States provides a firm

*However, the philosophy and practice of racial segregation was a prominent feature of South Africa Society since the beginning of the twentieth century (Dubow, 1989).

basis for a broader system of racial injustice. . . . Resting on a foundation of segregation, apartheid not only denies blacks their rights as victims but forces them to bear the social costs of their own victimization. . . . Although Americans have been quick to criticize the apartheid system of South Africa, they have been reluctant to acknowledge the consequences of their own institutionalized system of racial separation. . . . Until policymakers, social scientists, and private citizens recognize the crucial role of America's own apartheid in perpetuating urban poverty and racial injustice, the United States will remain a deeply divided and very troubled society.

In spite of the massive migration of blacks from the South to the North in the 1950s, 1960s, and 1970s—more than doubling the black population in most large Northern cities—racial segregation was hardly disturbed. Figure 13.1 illustrates the persistence of racial segregation.

In 1940, blacks tended to live on blocks in cities that contained an average of 85 percent black inhabitants. As Figure 13.1 shows, this segregation index has changed very little in either the North or the South since then. Moreover, this pattern is nearly universal, as only one city in the United States, San Francisco, has shown a steady and persistent decline in black racial segregation, from 82 percent in 1940 to 55 percent in 1970 (Massey and Denton, 1993, Table 2.3). However, that the segrega-

FIGURE 13.1

Indexing Black-White Segregation—1940–1980. *Source:* Adapted from Massey and Denton (1993). *American Apartheid: Segregation and the Making of the Underclass.* Cambridge: Harvard University Press. Table 2.3.

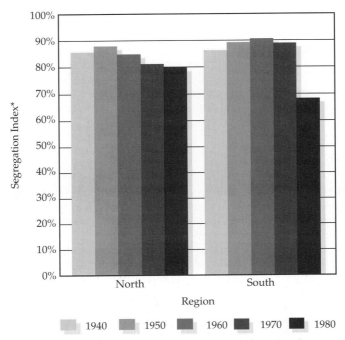

*The Segregation Index shows the percentage of blacks who would have to move in order to create racial balance in their neighborhoods.

tion pattern is related to blacks in particular is shown by the data for San Francisco. In that city, blacks, Asians, and Hispanics number a total of about 11 percent of the population. However, in 1980, the segregation index for blacks was 72 percent, that for Hispanics stood at 40 percent, and that for Asians at 44 percent.

We commonly think of the 1960s and the civil rights era as marking the end of decades of racial disadvantage. However, black isolation (the percentage of blacks in neighborhoods where mainly blacks live) in cities has not always been so great. Figure 13.2 shows that black isolation indices in major Northern cities stood at 6.7 percent in 1890, rose to 7.8 percent in 1900, to 9.7 percent in 1910, and up to 29.9 percent by 1930. By 1970, the black isolation index was at 73.3 percent. The fact is that, as the percentage of this racial group increased, efforts to keep it separated from whites became more common. Ghettoes were created to *contain* blacks. In other words, the individual freedoms that are central to realizing the American dream did not extend to blacks.[8]

Ghettos are not the outgrowth of natural market economics and social processes, but the consequence of calculated strategies to keep blacks, in particular, separated from whites. For example in 1924, the National Association of Real Estate Brokers adopted an article in its code of ethics stating that:

> . . . a realtor should never be instrumental in introducing into a neighborhood . . . members of any race or nationality . . . whose presence will clearly be detrimental to property values in that neighborhood. (cited in Massey and Denton, 1993, p. 37)

[8]A recent book by Jennifer Hochschild (1995) documents that the American dream still does not apply fully to blacks in the 1990s.

FIGURE 13.2

Indexing Black Isolation—1890–1970.

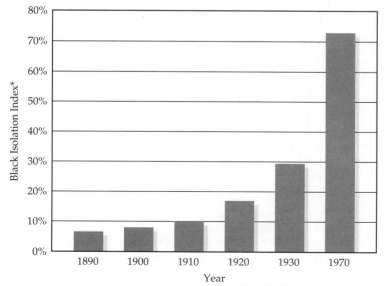

*Black Isolation Index shows the percentage of blacks who live in the neighborhoods that are mainly populated by blacks.

Although the legality of this policy was abandoned in 1950, the long legacy of formalized codes and restrictive covenants has created structural arrangements that are not easily dismantled.

Locked in inferior housing, isolated from higher-paying jobs, forced into public schools that increasingly failed to educate, blacks ever more frequently were restricted to living in neighborhoods that eroded their well-being. Increasingly, attempts to step in and provide some federal support and programs designed to compensate somewhat for this historical, calculated ghettoization have been rejected by conservative policymakers. As we saw in Chapter 5, the 1980s saw whites, in general, ignore the obstacles created by urban ghettoization and resultant poverty. They tended to see opportunity as a matter of character and ability, diligence, and hard work. We also saw that poor blacks, unlike poor whites, most often live among other poor people, who, it turns out, are mostly also black and are typically removed from good job opportunities and the training to get them.

The moralization of poverty operates in a manner similar to the racialization of society. The poor, in general, like those who are racially different, are deemed inferior, and their plight is seen as somehow being a "natural" consequence of their own shortcomings. This viewpoint was given poignant expression by Thomas Malthus (1766–1834), whom Chase (1977) considers the "Founding Father of scientific racism." Malthus offered these chilling views of population dynamics:

> We are bound in justice and honour formally to disclaim the right of the poor to support. To this end, I should propose a regulation to be made, declaring that no child born from any marriage, taking place after the expiration of a year from the date of the law, and no illegitimate child born two years from the same date, *should ever be entitled to parish assistance. . . . The infant is, comparatively speaking, of little value to society, as others will immediately supply its place. . . .*" (cited in Chase, 1977, p. 6; *emphasis added*)

That is, the poor and their children deserve no assistance, for they are drains on society. In fact, far from proposing to help them, Malthus had a grander design by which:

> . . . we should facilitate, instead of foolishly and vainly endeavoring to impede, the operations of nature in producing mortality; and if we dread the too frequent visitation of the horrid form of famine, we should sedulously encourage the other forms of destruction which we compel nature to use. Instead of recommending cleanliness to the poor, we should encourage contrary habits. In our towns, we should make the streets narrower, crowd more people into the houses, and court the return of the Plague. In the country, we should build our villages near stagnate pools, and particularly encourage settlements in all marshy and unwholesome situations. But above all, we should reprobate specific remedies for ravaging diseases; and those benevolent, but much mistaken men, who have thought they were doing a service to mankind by projecting schemes for the total extirpation of particular disorders. (cited in Chase, 1977, p. 6)

We can be sure that realtors and bankers, politicians and businesspeople did not read Malthus and get together to design ghettoes in order to accomplish his goals. Yet, even in 1995, the U.S. Congress passed legislation that evokes the statements of Malthus when it proposed to cut off Aid for Dependent Children (AFDC). And the view that the poor are responsible for their plight is implied by the title of this legislation, the Personal Responsibility and Work Opportunity Act of 1995. This legislation was estimated to throw some 1.5 million children into poverty by withholding assistance to them and their parents. This comes in the face of statistics that show that 24 percent of the nation's youth have been on AFDC at some time in their life and that, of those who receive AFDC support, 75 percent have been thus supported for more than five years (Moynihan, 1996).

Poverty in the United States is a very serious problem, and Massey and Denton (1993) argue forcefully that residential segregation has played a major part in the rapid descent into poverty for millions of African Americans. Because racial segregation follows in systematic ways from the social policies and ideological leanings of a racialized worldview and cultural value system, the sociopolitical and economic processes create structural patterns that have dire consequences for those racial groups trapped therein. Ideology and social structure converge to create the sustaining mechanisms of racism.

Discrimination.   Among the sustaining mechanisms of racism is simply racial and ethnic discrimination. Turner, Fix, and Struyk (1991) report the results of a "hiring audit" study. In this experiment, a minority (black or Hispanic) subject and majority (white) "tester" were matched on attributes relevant to a hiring decision, such as age, physical size, education, experience, and other *human capital* characteristics (e.g., openness, energy level and articulateness). Each applied for the same jobs advertised in a local newspaper. In this study, 476 audits were conducted by 10 pairs of testers in Washington, D.C., and Chicago during the summer of 1990.

Results showed that whites were three times more likely than blacks were to go further in the job process (20% versus 7%), and were similarly favored to receive job offers (15% versus 5%). In 45 percent of the cases in which both black and white testers obtained interviews, whites were more likely to be offered the job (8% to 4% of the total). And, in the Washington study, these whites were more likely to be treated more favorably (e.g., kept waiting a shorter amount of time, given a longer interview, seen by more interviewers, and given more positive and fewer negative comments).

This pattern of discrimination was not limited to blacks relative to whites. It was evidenced in hiring audits conducted with pairs of Hispanic and Anglo testers in Chicago and in San Diego. Anglos advanced further than comparable Hispanic testers did (31% compared to 11% of the cases). Anglos were also offered jobs more frequently than Hispanics were (22% compared to 8% of the cases).

These discrimination data are compelling when one considers the comments by one of the respondents in the Feagin and Vera (1995) study who felt that race just shouldn't matter, it should only be merit that determined outcomes. Discrimination inserts a racial dimension that is not explainable by qualifications. The unseen hand of racial discrimination plays a critical role in the maintenance of racial disadvantage.

Race matters.   Wellman (1993) provides some telling comparisons that illustrate biases in what happens to people as a result of their race. Citing statistics from the National Crime Survey (Stark, 1990), Wellman notes that the crime rate for aggravated assault is roughly the same for blacks and for whites (32 per 1,000 blacks and 31 per 1,000 whites). However, FBI reports that blacks were arrested for aggravated assault three times more often than whites were.

Wellman reports an interesting study of New Jersey Turnpike arrests. In this study, a Rutgers University professor observed the turnpike traffic for one week and found that 4.7 percent of vehicles with out-of-state license plates were driven by black people. However, 80 percent of arrests for suspicion of contraband from

February to December of 1988 involved black motorists driving out-of-state vehicles. Remember the case of Evaristo and James (Chapter 10) who, because of their Latino ethnicity, were suspected of drug smuggling. With the Latinos, as well as the out-of-state blacks, it is a racial profile that often triggers behavior that is punitive and frequently humiliating. That the profile is factually wrong adds to the burden of oppression to one's race.

The point of this look at how racism is rationalized and sustained is that it is not necessarily the overtly bigoted and biased declarations or acts that define what racism is. It is most frequently the subtle forms of expressions and attitudes that reflect racial bias, imply racial superiority, and rationalize the racial inequality as "natural."

COPING WITH RACISM

Racism is pernicious, invasive, pervasive, and unrelenting. It lurks in the nooks and crannies of everyday life. It contorts possibility and expands negative probabilities. We have spoken of racism largely as a subject, its purveyors as racists, racialists, or persons prejudiced by race. How does the object of this denigration or transparent afterthought of cultural chauvinism cope with this lot? We discussed some aspects of this coping or reacting in Chapter 10, with a focus on reactions to biases of prejudice. Now, we look at coping with the totality of racism.

Shielding Yourself Against Racism

Mamie Mobley is not well known. Her son was better known. He was Emmett Till, a 14-year-old boy who, in 1955, lived on the South Side of Chicago with his mom, Ms. Mobley, who worked for the U.S. Air Force. Mamie and her son Emmett were making plans to drive to Omaha to visit cousins as part of their annual vacation when Uncle Mose came to town. He had come from Money, Mississippi, and, with two of his grandsons, good friends of Emmett, was planning on returning soon. Emmett decided he'd rather go to Mississippi with his cousins than to Omaha with Mom. So, with some reluctance, Mamie let him go.

Three days after arriving in Money, Mississippi, Emmett and one of his buddies went into a general store and bought some gum and candy. Someone asked Emmett how he liked the [white] lady in the store. He whistled his approval. Word of his "evaluation" of the lady got back to her husband Roy Bryant and his half-brother Big Jim Milam. The following Sunday morning at about 2:30 A.M. the two men stormed into Uncle Mose's house and abducted Emmett at gunpoint. Three days later, Emmett's mutilated body was found. He had been shot and beaten, and a gin-mill fan was tied around his neck. He was so mutilated that he could only be identified by the watch he was wearing. The two men claimed they didn't do it, alleging that upon discovering that he was the wrong person, they had set him out on his way home shortly after abducting him. An all-white, all-male jury acquitted the two men after deliberating for one hour and five minutes!

This story is brutal and tragic, and an illustration of the most heinous form racism takes. But what is more remarkable about this story is Mamie Mobley herself. She described this horrendous crime to Studs Terkel (1992). Terkel asked her, "Don't you harbor any bitterness toward the two men—toward whites, for that matter? It would be unnatural not to. . . ." Mobley put it all in perspective (quoted in Terkel, 1992, p. 21):

. . . I'd have to say I'm unnatural . . . that's the question that has always been raised, "What would you do to Milam and Bryant if you had the opportunity?" I came to the realization that I would do nothing. What they had done was not for me to punish and it was not for me to go around hugging hate to myself, because hate would destroy me. It wouldn't hurt them. . . . I did not wish them dead. I did not wish them in jail. If I had to, I could take their four children. . . and I could raise those children as if they were my own and I could have loved them. [9]

How do you cope with being hated, denigrated, judged negatively, treated badly, shunted aside? One way to cope is to go into a special place where those slights and indignities cannot reach. Mobley described this place as ". . . a neutral zone where I had no feeling whatsoever toward Milam and Bryant." (Terkel, 1992, p. 21). It is not forgiveness or self-blame; it is in Mamie's words "a shield."

This shield protects one against the pain of racism, but what price does it exact? Does one lose a part of one's soul? Is existential neutrality a hidden cost of racism for its victims?

Racelessness

If race is a badge of dishonor in a racialist society, then "losing one's race"—or the "forgetting of race," in Bloom's (1986) words—is another way to mitigate the sting of racism. In fact, it is the forgetting of race that is inherent in the "colorblind" approach to racial harmony and justice.

But racelessness, too, offers a kind of existential neutrality. Upon his appointment to a position at ABC Television, Max Robinson became the first black network news anchor in the early 1980s. His boss, Roone Arledge, confirmed that his stature at ABC was unrelated to his race. According to Robinson (quoted in Fordham, 1988, p. 59) Arledge told him, "I told you when I hired you, I didn't think you were black, or I didn't think of you as a black man." What he meant, Robinson felt, was "I am going to give you credit. I admire you greatly, so therefore, I will not think of you as black" (quoted in Fordham, 1988, p. 59). To discount one's race is to relegate a significant aspect of who one is to insignificance. Fordham (1988, p. 59) raises the specter that "the practice of becoming raceless appears to have emerged as a strategy both to circumvent the stigma attached to being black, and to achieve vertical mobility."

Recently, Arroyo and Zigler (1995) have developed a Racelessness Scale, based in part on Fordham's theorizing. The scale assesses the extent to which one's race is a salient aspect of one's self-awareness or consciousness. If vertical mobility, presaged by academic success, as often is believed, is enhanced by downplaying one's race, then one might expect that academic achievement would be enhanced to the extent that one scores high on a measure of racelessness. Items for the Racelessness Scale were administered to 608 adolescents in a public school, ranging from 13 years old to 20 years old (32% white, 55% African American, 10% Hispanic, 1% Asian, and 2% "other"). Factor analysis produced four factors:

1 *Achievement attitudes*—Believing that doing well in school will help later in life and that working hard will pay off in the long run.

---

[9]Contrast the Till case and his mother's response to that of O. J. Simpson and whites' response. The narrative of justice in the United States is reshaped in the counternarrative of racism for black Americans (cf. Jones, in press). Nonetheless, justice is not defined by episodes of evidentiary processes and legal decisions, but a cumulative set of circumstantial realities that vary systematically by race. Racism enters the justice equation in the United States in a very different way for blacks compared to whites.

Sample items:
"Doing well in school helps you do better later in life."
"I feel my future is unlimited."
"There are better things to do with my time than schoolwork." (reverse scoring)

2   *Impression management*—Concern about being negatively evaluated because of high academic achievement. That is, the desire to be liked confronts the desire to do well. Those scoring high on this factor choose positive evaluations over academic achievement.

Sample items:
"I never let my friends know when I get good grades in school.
"I feel I must act less intelligent than I am so other students will not make fun of me."
"I could probably do better in school, but I don't try because I don't want to be labeled a 'braniac' or a 'nerd.'"

3   *Alienation*—Feeling estranged or alienated from one's peers.

Sample items:
"I am different from most people my age."
"I don't hang out in places where most of the other people in school go."

4   *Stereotypical beliefs*—Acceptance of common beliefs that blacks do not do well in school and are themselves responsible for negative or poor outcomes.

Sample items:
"Poor blacks are responsible for their problems."
"In general, blacks are to blame for their negative image among whites."
"Most blacks are no longer discriminated against."

The idea that academic achievement requires a suppression of racial identification, as proposed by Fordham (1988) and Fordham and Ogbu (1986), led Arroyo and Zigler (1995) to speculate that the measure of racelessness would be highly correlated with achievement for blacks, but not whites. The Racelessness Scale was given to a second set of 389 adolescents, aged 13 to 20, in a public school. Two-thirds of them were African American and one-third were white. Using cumulative grade point average as a measure of academic achievement, Arroyo and Zigler (1995) found that the total racelessness score was positively correlated with achievement for *both* whites and African Americans. The authors concluded that "the behaviors and attitudes identified by Fordham and Ogbu (1986) may be common to high-achieving students and not unique to African Americans" (Arroyo and Zigler, 1995, p. 907).

A third study assessed whether racelessness was negatively associated with racial identity, but positively linked to anxiety and depression. The results of a study with a new sample of 156 adolescents from urban public schools showed that racelessness scores were positively correlated with anxiety and depression and negatively correlated with collective esteem associated with how the public values African Americans. For European Americans, racelessness bore no realtionship to either psychological health or collective self-esteem. Specifically, for African Americans, the "achievement attitudes" dimension of racelessness was positively corre-lated with self-efficacy, in-group membership, and identity aspects of collective self-esteem. In addition, "public collective self-esteem" was negatively related to concerns about impression management. Although this measure of racelessness may bear the same relationship to academic achievement for whites and blacks, it does not bear the same relationship to psychological well-being for whites that it does for blacks. It appears that, for blacks, adopting a raceless, individualized iden-tity may make it easier to do things that enhance academic achievement, but it may come at a price of psychological ill-health. This is not true of whites, who may be free to be as individual as they want and thereby enhance their academic perfor-mance with no corresponding adverse psychological consequences.

Therefore, racelessness may be functional for achievement, but dysfunctional for psychological well-being in blacks. How do you advocate a "colorblind" strat-egy in a society where race means so much (or "is an *obsession*," in Terkel's words). Losing one's racial identity for members of minority groups may be analogous to throwing the baby out with the bathwater!

Racial Identity

If racelessness may simultaneously promote vertical mobility and undermine per-sonal psychological well-being, one way to reaffirm the self is to embrace rather than retreat from racial identity. (We discussed this in some detail in Chapter 10 [cf. Helms, 1995; Cross, 1991; LaFromboise et al., 1993; and Phinney, 1992.) In society where race has acquired ideological eminence and carries with it hierarchical cul-tural values of worth, not to have a race may be as bad as belonging to a stigma-tized one—and, perhaps, worse. If one is black or Asian or American Indian or Latino, one is not Caucasian.[10] To argue for a raceless, colorblind society is to dis-count an important aspect of one's heritage and to be unable to claim another. One is left rootless, individual, and alone.

So, the importance of racial identity is its role as an antidote to the ideology of racialism. As we have seen, "race" as a concept rests in part on presumption of bio-logical essence. Yet we know or believe that the "biology" is relatively ineffective in distinguishing one group from the other. How, then, does one derive a "racial" identity? For most of us, the racial identity consists of cultural elements. Hence, it may more properly be considered an *ethnic distinction.* Perhaps this supports what Hirschfeld (1996) has proposed—that "there is no principled way to distinguish race from ethnicity."

Although most members of so-called racial groups develop principles of iden-tity that seem largely cultural, Welsing (1991) developed a provocative and contro-versial theory of race and racial identity that was fundamentally biological. Her "theory of color confrontation and racism (i.e., white supremacy)" takes the view that whites feel inadequate because they *lack* color (e.g., white is the absence of wavelengths). This feeling of *genetic* inadequacy is contrasted with the feelings of "people of color," who possess what whites lack. According to Welsing (1991), blacks possess it to the greatest degree (black being the presence of all colors) fol-lowed by brown, red, and yellow peoples.

---

[10]We note an exception in that Hispanics are sometimes divided into "white" and "nonwhite." Perhaps this tendency, clearly racial in nature, is a reason that many have rejected the label *Hispanic* and preferred the use of *Latino. Latino* carries with it not only a Spanish heritage, but a non-European cultural reality (cf. Gurin, Hurtado, and Peng [1994]).

In the Welsing (1991) system, the inferiority felt by "colorless" whites is contrasted with the superiority felt by blacks. The source of superiority is the genetic capacity to produce color, mediated by the presence of melanin. Therefore, skin color, rather than being a "mark of oppression," a source of stigma, or something to ignore (as in a colorblind strategy), becomes a badge of honor or respect. People of color, then, are the numerical majority (not minority) worldwide and their color itself is a source of pride and strength.

Racism imposes itself on daily processes of living for people of color. Coping mechanisms nearly always present a double-edged outcome. For example, retreating from a group-based racial identity may help one focus on individual goals and strategies to achieve them. But this strategy may estrange a person from his or her true ethnic or racial roots and can take a psychological toll as shown in the Arroyo and Zigler (1995) findings. Elsewhere (Jones, 1991) I have referred to this dilemma as the "politics of personality." Politics (the art of compromise as an agent of personal control and attainment of goals) are implicated in the choices we make as to racial identity (who we are), racial identification (with whom we relate or compare), and behavior (what we do and how we do it). Deciding how race will (and will not) affect daily decisions of living is an ongoing process for people of color.

Living with Racism—Coping Day to Day

Knowledge that race matters—and, usually, not in a good way—is a burden to carry around everyday. Nowhere is it more burdensome than in the workplace. It is there that we physically spend, on average, 50 percent of our waking hours and, psychologically, much more time than that. In the discussion of race and racism so far we have focused on poverty and urban life. But the burden of race is not limited to either of these circumstances.

Cose (1993) interviewed a wide array of middle-class, predominately black professionals about their experiences with race. One black man, a partner in a respected New York law firm, reported an incident that reflects the daily hassle of race. Arriving at work early one morning, he took the elevator up to the executive office to see one of his colleagues, also a partner. When he got out on the executive floor level, a young, white law associate stepped forward, moved directly in front of him, and asked, "May I help you?" His clear assumption was the black partner did not "belong" there, and that he, a young white man, was protecting the firm from intrusion. One of the most compelling and ubiquitous daily hassles is the unspoken unwritten assumption that people of color "do not belong." The burden of proof is on them to show that they do. Proving that one belongs takes energy and psychological resources that whites do not have to expend.

A dozen demons.   Cose (1993) describes the instigation of these daily hassles as the "dozen demons"—the daily hassles whose resolution requires expending mental energy, exercising interpersonal skills, and actively suppressing emotion. What are these demons?

1   *Inability to fit in.* Minorities are different and bring different experiences, perceptions, and expectations to the workplace. If one doesn't "go along with the program," one risks being marginalized. Fitting the organizational culture will affect one's trajectory in the structure. These issues lead one to ponder such questions as: Should I *try* to fit in? Do I *want* to fit in and at what cost? *Can* I fit in?"

2   *Exclusions from the club.* An infrastructure of opportunity and privilege is consti-

tuted by the inner circles of private eating, golf, and health clubs; vacation communities, and so forth. Inclusion in that world is substantially affected by race, gender, and social standing. It is not impenetrable by outsiders, but its borders are not easily crossed and many people are left outside of the highest level of opportunity.[11] Ironically, when blacks, members of other minority groups, and women do cross this line, they risk being ostracized by their in-group as "sellouts."[12]

3   *Low expectations.* The stereotypes of affirmative action–based selection—for example, lower qualifications and ability—combine with cultural dissimilarity to reduce expectations for minority performance. For example, admissions committees often generate two lists, one "normal" (i.e., white) and one for members of minority groups. They do this because, if they used "normal standards," minority-group members, it is feared, would not be admitted. They would not measure up. By creating a separate list, such committees formalize this belief and imply inferior performance. The conflict between being a Chicano and being Anglo, for example, is not eased when a Chicano woman is told she is one of the best students in the program, *regardless of her ethnicity.* It seems that if one succeeds, it is *in spite* of one's ethnicity, and, if one fails, it is *because of* it!

4   *Shattered hopes.* Excitement about opportunities, accomplishment, and success are not realized. For example, a young Mexican American lawyer walked away from an eminent law firm after two years, choosing to become a public defender, instead. He stated "[I] was so filled with rage, I couldn't even talk about it much" (Cose, 1993, p. 60).

5   *Faint praise.* Members of minority racial groups are often singled out for their accomplishments, skills, and talents and, thereby separated from others in their group. As in the example of Max Robinson, being told that one is good and that race has nothing to do with it may well be meant as a compliment, but it implies that being a member of a minority racial group typically has built-in limitations. It also implies that *true* accomplishment must come in comparison with whites.

6   *Presumption of failure.* The presumption that members of minority groups and women will fail is related to low expectations and may well lead to the hiring of only overqualified minorities and women in order to protect against their failure or poor performance. For example, in baseball, for many years there were black "superstars." Notably absent, however, were so-called journeymen players. That is, whites with average talent could get jobs, but blacks had to be exceptional if they were to be signed on.

7   *Coping fatigue.* One's minority racial status is usually not conceived as an asset but as a liability. One is constantly having to prove oneself competent, to adapt to lifestyles and expectations that may be culturally incongruent, and, generally, to work harder to do simple things than whites must. Burnout, or *coping fatigue,* is one consequence of this burden.

8   *Pigeonholing.* Many minorities and women are judged relative to the stereotypes about their group. In many organizations, there are "soft jobs," or "minority" jobs (typically in human resources, personnel, or community relations departments). In the federal government, we have had minority group mem-

[11]A black, Harvard-trained lawyer (Graham, 1995) scaled down his resumé and sought employment at exclusive country clubs in Westchester County in New York where wealth and powerful white men belonged. Graham wanted to see what "being in the club" was like.
[12]Vernon Jordan is an African American who headed up the transition team when President Clinton was elected in 1992. Pictures of him playing golf with President Clinton during his Martha's Vineyard vacations aroused pride in some African Americans, who saw it as evidence of inclusion in the inner circles. Others saw it as evidence of "selling out" the group for personal gain.

bers as Cabinet-level secretaries in Housing and Urban Development, and Health and Human Services. When Clinton appointed Ron Brown to head the Commerce Department, Jocelyn Elder as the Surgeon General, Janet Reno as Attorney General, it was a conscious attempt not only to diversify the leadership, but to resist pigeonholing within his administration. Pigeonholing tends to reflect an unstated belief that whites and men are more capable and important, minorities and women less so.

9   *Identity troubles.* The conflict between racial identification and achievement was discussed earlier. We saw the conflict between minimizing one's race and improving one's achievement prospects, and the psychological strain it can cause. Balancing racial and personal identity is often a constant struggle for minorities in majority contexts. Some processes of biculturalism and acculturation operate with double-edged consequences (cf. LaFromboise et al., 1993; Cross, 1991).

10   *Self-censorship and silence.* When one alleges an experience of race prejudice or bias, one faces the risk of appearing or being labeled "too sensitive" (cf. Essed, 1991), "paranoid," or worse, a troublemaker. If one feels slighted, one must first determine if the slight is real, is racial. If that proves a reasonable assessment, then deciding whether to say anything about it becomes an issue. For example, a survey of military personnel shows that the number of reported incidents of sexual harassment far exceeded the number of women who reported being harassed (personal comments, Mary Weltin, Dec. 13, 1995). This led some military leaders to question the veracity of the women's reports. The fact that silence and self-censorship are coping processes is important to recognize.

11   *Mendacity.* Some people simply lie about the status of race relations in organizations. Sometimes, such misstatements may arise from ignorance about what is going on in the organization and what factors influence outcomes. Other times, they may result from a self-serving bias that is camouflaged by language that attributes nonracial motives to race-based decisions and their consequences. This phenomenon is implicitly identified in the discourse analysis of van Dijk (1993), and the "new racism" analysis of xenophobia by Barker (1981). Van Dijk (1993, p. 146) cites the following example of such mendacity by a manager in a large chemical company in the Netherlands:

> . . . we are the international headquarters. It speaks for itself that, you know, yes, people are not being discriminated. People who meet our requirements are being hired, whether they are brown, yellow, or black or white. Whether they are males or females.

This is a tricky business—mendacity. Big Daddy could smell it (in T. Williams [1955] play *Cat on a Hot Tin Roof*), and many people suspect it. The statistics showing low rates of minorities and women in higher-level positions imply either that the companies are not doing all they say they are, or that minorities and women are simply not qualified. As a result, regarding the status of race in organizations, members of minority groups are often suspicious and company leaders are often defensive. Distrust is a burden in the workplace and can reduce overall effectiveness and individual performance.

12   *Guilt by association.* Mistaken identity is one source of guilt by association. For example, the credibility of claims that a black man had shot Charles Hughes's wife in Boston and that a black man abducted Susan Smith's children in South Carolina was enhanced by the frequency with which this sort of behavior on the part of minorities has been projected by media images. If one is a member

of a minority group, therefore, one has to be conscious of these images and their interpretations when shopping, asking for directions, or having any other sort of contact with whites where one may not be perceived as one actually is.

Unlike the discussions of the urban poor, whose race is confounded with poverty, in most of the cases described by Cose (1993), black and Hispanic men and women felt the burden of race in contexts that would be hailed as examples of racial progress in the United States. Are they too sensitive or paranoid? The fact is that living in a racialized society is demanding and offers one little chance to enjoy the simplicity of individualized expression. Whether this is real or imaginary, is avoidable or inevitable are among the questions to which we seek answers.

Feagin and Sykes (1994) conducted in-depth interviews with 209 middle-class African Americans, mostly from the South and Southwest (66%), with another large proportion from the North (29%). All but one were interviewed by black interviewers. The middle-class status was indicated by the fact that the subjects were currently or soon would be (upon graduation from college) employed as business managers, teachers, social service workers, doctors or other health care professionals, computer specialists, professors, and so forth. Eighty percent had college degrees, and 40 percent had graduate degrees. Open-ended interviews focused on life goals and recent experiences with racial discrimination. Interviews concluded with general questions about social change and the future of race relations in the United States.

Feagin and Sikes (1994) extracted four *propositions* from the text of the interviews, in which respondents described the nature of the experience of everyday racism.

1 *Modern racism is a lived experience.* That is, nonwhite people feel the racism that occurs as a result of discrimination by whites in real interpersonal ways.
2 *Racial discrimination not only hurts at the time, but has cumulative impact on the targets themselves, their families, and their communities.* These experiences are disruptive, and they take a long-term toll. They become part of the lore and narrative of racism that is part of the community experience. We do not have an effective way of analyzing the cumulative impact of racism. However, it is very likely that a discourse analysis of the language of victims of racism would reveal that experiences with racism are often told about in story forms that separate the victims from the perpetrators and that highlight the negative behaviors of "them," and the positive character or humanity of "us." Therefore, the adverse impact of racism is not only to the individual targets, but to the attached cultural meanings. Mistrust (cf. Terrell, Terrell, and Watkins, 1986) is magnified by each incident (see Chapter 10). Single incidents, such as Rodney King's beating or the passage of anti-immigration laws, can signal animosity, antipathy, and racism as a norm that validates mistrust and reinforces it.
3 *Repeated experiences of racism affect a person's behavior and understanding of life.* Perspectives on life, expectations, and ways of coping with circumstances build into a repertoire of behavior and coping mechanisms. The occurrence of racism and the cumulative adaptations to and adoption of means of coping with it contribute to a cultural ethos that helps define gaps between black, white, red, yellow, and brown people.
4 *Daily experiences of racial hostility and discrimination encountered by middle-class persons of color are the constituent elements of the interlocking societal structures of institutional racism.* These institutional effects are also cumulative, so that the overall consequences of racism are individual, institutional, and cultural in

The beating seen around the world: The Rodney King beating and the following acquittal of policemen triggered escalation in racial animosity in Los Angeles and underscored antipathies in society. (Bill Swersey/Liaison)

their forms of implementation and their overall continuing effects. (We will discuss these connections in more detail in the next chapter.)

Occurrences of Racism
Experiences of racism are organized in five categories, according to the type of location in which they occur: (1) in public places, such as restaurants, theaters, and so forth; (2) at schools and universities; (3) in the workplace; (4) in business; and (5) in the neighborhoods in which we live and work. Following are illustrations from each of these domains:

Public places.   Denny's Restaurant chain is now infamous. It recently exemplified the practice of racial discrimination in public places. In one case, at a Denny's in Annapolis, Maryland, six black secret service agents were given bad service because of their race. The particulars of the story hit the newswires. The agents had waited for service for nearly an hour, while other white agents and patrons were promptly served. This incident alone may not establish that racism was involved, but Denny's had already been named in a class action suit in California where 32 black patrons had suffered discrimination. In November 1995, Denny's settled a class action suit for $46 million![13] The case against the chain must have

[13]Two class action suits were brought against Denny's: one in Maryland initiated by the six Secret Service men, and one in California, initiated by a woman whose daughter was denied a birthday celebration. The settlement of $46 million was divided between the two suits and was distributed to 294,537 named plaintiffs. In California, forty people were awarded payments of $25,000, while 158,483 received payments of $177.71. In Maryland, the six Secret Service men received $35,000 each, and twelve others received payments of $15,000. The remaining 135,996 plaintiffs were awarded $132.28 each. (*New York Times*, December 12, 1995, p. A24)

been extraordinarily compelling for Denny's management to take corporate responsibility for the actions of employees in their stores. If it is true of Denny's, how widespread is the practice?[14]

Racism can attack anywhere. One black professor in a predominately white university in the Southwest told the following story (Feagin and Sykes, 1994, p. 59).

> I was driving . . . it was about nine-thirty at night . . . my car is old and ugly . . . it's the kind of car that people think of as a low-rider car, so they associate it with Mexican Americans, especially poor Mexican Americans. Well, we are sitting at an intersection waiting to make a turn, and a group of middle-class looking white boys drives up in a nice car. And they start shouting things at us in a real fake-sounding Mexican American accent, and I realized that they thought we were Mexican Americans. And I turned to look at them, and they started making obscene gestures and laughing at the car. And then one of them realized that I was black, and said, "oh, it's just a nigger." And [they] drive away.

Symbols of minority status trigger the feelings of superiority-inferiority. This sort of "sporty" intimidation is different from the violence that killed Emmett Till. Till, in the minds of his white attackers, threatened a social and cultural status quo, a normative representation of white supremacy and domination. It was racism, to be sure. However, that violence was tied to a systematic pattern of enforcing racial dominance. These young boys seemed more to reinforce the attitudes or beliefs of racial superiority and, in so doing, to indulge their "right" to denigrate those below them on the status hierarchy. One wonders if doing so makes them feel better or compensates for their feelings of inadequacy.

In another example, a manager at an electronics firm described a story about the trials of his 10-year-old daughter, who faced racism in a suburban swimming pool (Feagin and Sykes, 1994, p. 56):

> I'm talking over two hundred kids in this pool; not *one* black . . . What's the worst thing that can happen to a ten-year-old girl in a swimming pool with all white kids? What's the worst thing that could happen? It happened. This little white guy called her a "nigger." Then called her a "motherfucker" and told her "to get out of the god-damn pool." . . . And what initiated that, they had these little inner tubes, they had about fifteen of them and the pool owns them. So you just use them if they are vacant. So there was a tube sitting up on the bank. She got it, jumped in and started playing in it. . . . And this little white guy decided he wanted it. . . . And she wouldn't give it to him, so out came the racial slurs.

Perhaps the kid was just frustrated, a rude kid, a bully. But he clearly understood what *nigger* meant and how to use it to intimidate and denigrate a young black girl. And she must somehow deal with the idea that, because she was black, she carried with her the capacity to arouse such venom and evil in a young white boy.

Education.   It is not uncommon for women and ethnic minorities to experience hostility in the classroom (cf. *The Classroom Climate*, Hall, 1982). Professors often present information that reinforces the ideology of racial inferiority in the

---

[14]In 1995, a young black man bought a shirt at Eddie Bauer, a well-known clothing store. The next day he was back in the store wearing the shirt he had purchased the previous day and was stopped and accused of shoplifting the shirt. In 1996, a young black community worker went to Home Depot to cash in vouchers that had been given by the store to a community group. The store clerk and the manager questioned the vouchers, refused to honor them, and accused the worker of coming by them illegally. Office Depot was sued for refusing to accept checks from black customers when white customers were allowed to use them with no hassle.

name of science. Conclusions are often drawn that have no empirical basis, but may have cultural currency.

A career counselor in the Southwest reported such an experience from his college days (Feagin and Sykes, 1994, pp. 121–122):

> I had an incident with a professor, and he and I got into a heated argument. He was giving a lecture and he was saying that the reasons that there're so many [crazy people] in Louisiana is because black people have polluted Louisiana blood. . . . he apologized subsequently, but my rationale was, you know, "What basis do you have for saying that? You have no proof of that." But that was just his ideology; that blacks had contaminated white Louisiana blood.

There are other, more subtle issues of scholarship that arise in the academic environment. What about when a professor reports prevailing, racialist "science" in class. That is, of course, what teaching and education is about. We have seen that over the years, there is much "science" that contributes to the ideology of racial superiority-inferiority. Reporting that work is certainly valid from the perspective of academic freedom and scholarly objectivity. However, that students from targeted racial and ethnic groups are offended by open discussion of this work raises some important issues. For example, students at the University of Delaware picketed the classes of two professors who taught the science of intelligence testing and the theory of lowered intellectual capacity of blacks as a group and the heritability aspect of that inferiority. Should they be sanctioned for teaching what some called "racist doctrine"? Should they be allowed to teach that which journal editors accept and practitioners validate? Race raises some thorny problems in our society, and many of them play out on college campuses, in the classrooms, and in the research laboratories.

A black assistant professor told of her graduate school experience with a white adviser. She was interested in African American literature, but was steered away from this interest by her adviser. He preferred that she specialize in a certain period of English literature because that would be:

> . . . doing something he didn't consider most black people did. And that job offers would come in for that reason. And, further, that doing Afro-American literature was not in and of itself important intellectual work. Well I insisted . . . and he finally gave in and gave me permission. He never stopped thinking that it was important for me not to do Afro-American literature as evidence that I was a real scholar . . . I ran into that attitude when I was on the job market. (Feagin and Sykes, 1994, p. 125)

There are many variants of this belief that scholarship about European culture and psychological issues considered important in mainstream society is basic, and concerns with racial, ethnic, or gender issues are derivative or secondary. It is as if whites are people, and other racial groups are only subcategories of people. General questions of human behavior, intellectual life, social development, and physiological mechanisms are all qualified by aspects of individual and group experience. The superiority-inferiority ideology of race has filtered into the practices of scholarship so completely that it is often difficult to see that much of what is considered scholarship is limited by ignorance of the full diversity of human experience. As Welsing (1991) points out, the vast majority of peoples of the world are people of color. Yet, somehow, scholarship on whites is regarded by many as the sign of "true" scholarship.

The workplace.   As noted earlier, we spend more than a third of our lives at work. Not only is *being* at work a major investment of time, in a place where any disruption can magnify itself many times, it is also the engine that drives the quest for the American dream. When biases creep into the workplace, their effect is large.

We saw the results of the hiring audit study (Turner, Fix, and Struyk, 1991) that documented the greater difficulty for African Americans and Latinos in finding a job. Feagin and Sikes (1994, p. 138) reported a case example that illustrates this. An experienced legal secretary in a Southern city recounted the following experience:

> Exactly five years ago I ran into an employment barrier when I first came here. The employment office sent me to legal offices that had openings. And since I've been a legal secretary for at least fifteen years . . . I've never had trouble getting a job until I came here. And when they talked to me over the telephone, they were real nice, you know, "Come on down yes, we have an opening." But when I got there—I went to two different law offices—I didn't get an interview. They saw me they were shocked. They went into their office and buzzed the secretary and said, "Tell her to leave her application and we'll call later; we're too busy to do it now."

Neither firm called back. This sort of account always raises the questions of causality. How do you know they were, in fact, avoiding her because of her skin color? Wouldn't it make sense to them to interview any talented persons? If they felt they did not want a black secretary, in these times, why wouldn't they at least have gone through the motions, taken her application, and then stonewall it? These are all interesting questions to be debated if one were trying to arrive at the true nature of this case. But, for our purposes, it really doesn't matter. This woman was led to believe there were openings, felt herself to be qualified for a position, and could not get a real hearing. In the Turner, Fix, and Struyk (1991) study, white applicants were twice as likely as an equally qualified black or Latino applicant to get an interview for the same job. That does not prove that this is what happened in this case. But it certainly does add plausibility to the notion that racial discrimination was behind what happened. Moreover, recall the notion of attributional ambiguity (Crocker and Major, 1989), which suggests that, if one's group membership makes one a potential target of discrimination, then when one is in a situation where a negative experience might and does occur, discrimination is a *usual suspect.* Living with this possibility takes a psychic toll as one navigates the daily world of work.

Once you have a job, that same ambiguity and suspicion of discrimination operate. There is ample controversy about the validity of performance appraisals and about which procedures provide the most reliable judgments (Kinicki, Hom, Trost, and Wade, 1995; Zalesny, 1990). The question of accuracy in performance appraisals is, of course, compounded by the overlay of racial issues. A black sales account manager described how she dealt with what she thought was, and anticipated would be, an unfair appraisal (Feagin and Sykes, 1994, pp. 145–146).

> We had a five scale rating, starting with outstanding, then very good, then good, then fair, and then less than satisfactory. I had gone into my evaluation interview anticipating that he would give me a "VG" (very good), feeling that I deserved an "outstanding" [O] and prepared to fight for my outstanding rating. . . . I happened to be the only black in my position within my branch . . . he and I had some very frank discussion about race . . . so I certainly knew that he had a lot of prejudices in terms of blacks . . . he said on numerous occasions that he considered me to be an exception, that [my abilities were] certainly not what he felt the abilities of the average black person [were] . . . when I went

into the evaluation interview he gave me glowing comments that cited numerous achievements and accomplishments during the year, and then concluded with, "So I've given you a G," which of course just floored me. . . . [I] maintained my emotions and basically just said . . . that I found that unacceptable . . . it was inconsistent with his remarks in terms of my performance, and I would not accept it. . . . I'm not signing the evaluation," I said.

She had come prepared, and she presented her evidence. She listed her objectives for the year and showed that she had achieved each one of them. She showed her sales performance in both dollars and product mix and illustrated for her supervisor that she had sold every product in the line and had exceeded all of her sales objectives. He acknowledged that his appraisal did not correspond to her own judgment and that ". . . we don't have to agree to agree." That ended the session but, within 15 minutes, he called her back and said, "I've thought about what you said and you're right, you do have an O" (Feagin and Sykes, 1994, p. 147)

She noted that she went from a G to an O rating in 15 minutes. If the O rating was correct, then she must worry that, had she not stood up for herself, she would have been two whole evaluative categories lower.

Again, what is reality? The specter of racial- or gender-based discrimination looms over all workplace transactions. It is probably true that instances of discrimination are not as ubiquitous as singling them out for presentation and analysis here may imply. But, they do exist—and probably to a greater degree than those in positions of authority would admit to. The seeds of distrust are sown. The psychic toll is not easily calculated, but increasing evidence is demonstrating the adverse health consequences of experiencing racism (Jones et al., 1996; Williams et al., 1994).

Building a business.   In *Adarand Constructors, Inc. vs. Federico Pena,* the U.S. Supreme Court failed to overturn a lower court ruling that providing financial compensations for companies who hire minority subcontractors violated the equal protection component of the Fifth Amendment's due process clause. Rather, the Supreme Court ruled that federal affirmative action programs that use racial or ethnic criteria as a basis for decision making are subject to *"strict judicial scrutiny."* What this means is that, if one is to use a race or ethnicity criterion, it must "serve a compelling governmental interest and must be narrowly tailored to serve that interest" (Schmidt, 1996). Using financial incentives to increase access of minority businesses to federal contract dollars is one of the legacies of the affirmative action approach formulated by President Johnson in the 1960s. Who is being discriminated against becomes a major question. In this case—and in many that cite the inherent discrimination against whites when racial criteria are used for awarding contracts, jobs, or scholarships—the evidence of continuing discrimination in the development of business puts a minority business person in a catch-22 bind.

Feagin and Sikes (1994) cite research showing that black entrepreneurs have a much harder time securing loans and that, when they do get loans, they tend to be 40 percent smaller for the same amount of business equity than are loans to whites. For example, a flooring contractor described his experience in trying to get a business loan (Feagin and Sikes, 1994, pp. 201–202):

Last year the school board had a bunch of bankers that said they wanted to help minority people get money. We applied to a bank . . . we put in our paper . . . did the income tax . . . plus . . . the job was bonded . . . payments are guaranteed by my bonding company. From November 1989 through January 1990, we couldn't even get an answer from them. The school board couldn't even get their calls answered.

Other studies confirm that banking practices have continued to show discriminatory patterns for African American and Latino borrowers at both the individual consumer and entrepreneurial levels (Carlson, 1993; Grupta, 1993).

The individual attitudes of persons in business also have an influence on one's experience. A black attorney recounted the following incident at the end of a long day at work (Feagin and Sykes, 1994, pp. 217–218):

> I was sitting in the offices one day after 5:00 p.m. . . . everybody's talking and shooting the b.s . . . getting loose. And then one [white] attorney said, "Yeah, that nigger." . . . they say what you do in private comes out in light of day, so he must have been saying it other places. And it just came out. When he said it everybody else heard it. He recognized it when he said it. I'm sitting there and I said nothing. . . . I did not laugh at it, but I wasn't going to say anything . . . he said it, they knew he said it, and they heard it, and they knew they heard it. Now let their consciences deal with it.

There are several important points here. First, using a word such as *nigger* is enormously offensive. When it is used in a work environment, where a black person is with a majority of whites, it creates a threatening situation for the target, who is left without a satisfactory range of responses. The attorney chose not to deal with it, to let those who were party to it to make their own peace with it. Yet this act of ignoring it (at least, publicly), too, must take a toll. Repressing what might be considered a natural urge either to defend oneself and one's racial group or to strike out in retaliation for the humiliating and insensitive behavior induces stress. The point is that, once *nigger* is said, there is no way to deal with it that is not in some way stress-inducing. It is these everyday micro-aggressions (Pierce, 1972) that add up to the burden of racism.[15]

The neighborhood.   As Massey and Denton (1993) claim, the continuing racial segregation is not random, but the result of systematic processes of socioeconomic strategies. For example, finding a decent house—one in a nice neighborhood, that is comfortable and in which needed resources are accessible—is probably one of the fundamentally important dimensions of our everyday experience. Complicity by real estate agents, bankers, and the personal attitudes of whites makes this important process one that carries a threat of racism.

A university administrator in a Northern city reported her experience with a white realtor when she was looking for a house (Feagin and Sykes, 1994, p. 238):

> So I worked two jobs so that I'd be able to buy a house . . . [a realtor] told me on the phone that I would like the neighborhood because there were no blacks in it. And I said, "Well my dear, you're in for a big surprise, because if I buy it, there will be a black there then, because I am now, I am a black." And she gasped and just hung the phone up.

Keeping the races separate has been a strategy for many years. Data show that blacks, in general, prefer to live in neighborhoods that are racially mixed (about 55%

---

[15] I had a similar personal experience. I was playing golf with a business associate in Upstate New York in the mid-1970s. We were playing as a twosome, just him and me. On a short par four hole, I drove my tee-shot onto the green. He was on in two and putting for a birdie. His putt rolled toward the hole and just as it got close it started to veer off course. He shouted out, "Get in there, you nigger!" I was astonished, first thinking I hadn't heard him correctly. Then, when I was sure I had, I did what the black attorney did, I ignored it. He was a business associate, we were alone, and I chose not to confront him on it as the tension I felt would be greater if I did.

white and 45% black). Only 16 percent of whites felt that a mixed neighborhood was desirable (Jaynes and Williams, 1989). Attitudes such as those expressed by the white realtor certainly contribute to racial segregation. But so, too, do the attitudes associated with preference for neighborhoods that are only minimally integrated.

A law professor described residential segregation and both realtors' and buyers' attitudes about it (Feagin and Sykes, 1994, pp. 246–247):

> Right around this campus, there's one community that's predominately white . . . major realtors take great pride in discriminating against black folks . . . I remember one of my colleagues was looking for a house, and he came to relay this story. . . . This realtor proudly told him how he kept blacks out of there for a number of years . . . I live in a nice neighborhood. . . . It's near here, predominately black. And I've had colleagues who wouldn't even look in my area. I've had other people look for places. And then I would say, "Well, look, we've got some houses for sale over near me." And I had one say to me, "Any white people live over there?"

The professor was offended because his colleague didn't inquire about the economic aspects, or the university affiliation, only the racial composition. Well, one could understand that with whites being about 70 percent of the population, a 50-50 neighborhood means they would be a "relative minority." Perhaps being with a large percentage of "them" would be uncomfortable. Yet blacks and Latinos who want to live in integrated settings must live with a majority of "them." There seems to be an asymmetry here. This asymmetry in preference reflects the differential value places on racial and ethnic groups, and the underlying notion of normalcy-majority-minority status and the adaptations one makes to it. Whites in the majority is a normal situation, so it is an overall more comfortable situation for *both* whites and members of racial or ethnic minority groups. That is, racial and ethnic minorities are more comfortable being in the minority than whites are.

The examples presented above are a mere sample of the kinds of experiences blacks, and other racial and ethnic minority groups, experience in the United States and, perhaps, elsewhere. Some people argue that racial minorities are too sensitive, they "see" discrimination at the drop of a hat. But, ironically, the first reaction to the possibility of racial bias is not to loudly challenge the behavior, but to carefully analyze it and be sure that one is not off base.

> First of all, within myself I try to analyze it. I try to look at all the pros and cons, all the ways in which the situation could've happened. Did I do my part, not necessarily as a black person but just as a person . . . ? (Feagin and Sykes, 1994, p. 276)
> "I'd say don't open your mouth and say anything that you're not 100 percent sure of. Don't have doubt. . . . (Feagin and Sykes, 1994, p. 277)

Attributional ambiguity is not immediately and always resolved in favor of discrimination or bias. That is not the first choice. As a result, one is constantly having to analyze one's own role in a possibly negative situation; one's own worth in an evaluative situation. If bias is a likely outcome, or if it occurs, what can one do? What strategies does one use to survive the everyday racism that occurs?

1 *Be cool!* As the lawyer did, we often act as if it never happened, as if racism doesn't exist. "Never let them see you sweat," the saying goes. But this strategy, as we have discussed, has its own costs. When one can no longer ignore the bias, one has to act.

2 *Confront the provocateur.* This strategy ups the ante—that is, it creates a great deal of tension in the situation. The person challenged with being a racist will usually deny it (as Wright did, with CBS's support). When one does confront the person or the situation, the risk of being labeled "too sensitive" or a "troublemaker" is high. Because very few people accept the label of racist, almost anytime a person claims to be at the receiving end of biased behavior because of race a person is likely to see one's claim rejected. This strategy for coping with racism, then, is a very high-risk one.

3 *"See you in court."* Seeking legal or administrative remedies is always an option. The Denny's settlement discussed earlier illustrated this can be effective. However, it has become increasingly difficult to exercise this option. Nonetheless, it has been cited as the best way to eradicate racial, gender, and other forms of discrimination from our society.

4 *Inner strength.* Digging deep inside and finding a source of strength and resilience is an often-cited strategy. A female probation officer in the South, offered the following illustration of her coping style:

> . . . someone said, "What the mind can conceive and believe it can achieve." I've been a student of positive thinking, and now I know if anybody can [deal with racism], I can. And that's the kind of attitude I have to reach deep within myself to deal with that . . . (Feagin and Sykes, 1994, p. 300)

Finding affirming evidence or support helps a person to counteract the implications of racism that seek to affirm low worth, ability, and value. Spirituality, joining with others to affirm individual and group worth are important sources of coping with racism. This group solidarity approach, albeit serving to strengthen one's self-worth, may also serve to distance oneself and one's group from others. Coping with the problems of racism may put into motion strategies that increase the likelihood that racism can and will continue.

SUMMARY

Racism is a complex, multifaceted phenomenon in our society. This chapter has introduced us to its breadth and depth by building on the core concepts of race and racialism, and by exploring how what we believe, what we think is right, and how we talk about our everyday lives serve to sustain and rationalize racial inequality. Racial differences are built into our everyday lives to such an extent that the presumptions of biological difference hardly need arise. The racial differences, though, are attached to fundamentally different ways of doing things to such an extent that targets of these distinctions are kept at a distance—even when there are no formal barriers to their inclusion.

The processes and mechanisms of racism create the need for coping strategies by its targets. These strategies often seek to help targets weave their course between a rock and a hard place. We are put in situations where a positive strategy for coping may alleviate one problem (say, an individual orientation that downplays race may enhance academic achievement outcomes) but lead inexorably to another one (e.g., impaired psychological well-being, depression, and anxiety). Or confronting instances of racial bias may lead to one's being labeled a "problem" or a "troublemaker."

Racism is a complex phenomenon that cannot be taken lightly. When we do take it too lightly, or oversimplify it, or place the problem on the shoulders of the targets or of those individuals who are pathologized as racist, we leave racism free to do its dirty work without threat of the major interventions needed to circumvent it. We learned in the *Adarand vs. Pena* decision (mentioned earlier in this chapter) that the federal government must apply *strict scrutiny* if it wishes to use race in making important hiring decisions. This chapter has suggested that there is substantial evidence that racism can be found in myriad places in our society and our psyches. Strict scrutiny of everyday life will reveal the ways in which racism persists and affects us all. As a nation, we are worse off because of the limitations that black, Latino, other minority and female citizens experience. The problems of racism are not simply left to the inadequacies of racial and ethnic groups, or to the mean-spirited views of whites. They coalesce into a complex mosaic of cumulative beliefs, institutional practices, and individual attitudes and behaviors. The next chapters will explore each of these aspects of racism in more detail.

14

Understanding Racism I: Individual Racism

---------------- ❖ ----------------

Introduction ◆ Race prejudice and racism compared ◆ *Defining individual racism*
◆ *Individual racism—Comparative modus operandi: Dominative and aversive cases* ◆
Individual racism through socialization ◆ *Social psychological mechanisms that
sustain individual racism* ◆ Black like me, white like you ◆ Summary

> *Do you know what they call a Black Ph.D.?—Nigger*
>
> Malcolm X

INTRODUCTION

It was June of 1968, a few days after Robert Kennedy was assassinated and two months after Martin Luther King had been assassinated. A group of high school–aged boys were talking outside the corner drugstore by the green of a small New England town. I overheard the following exchange:

Boy 1: "Do we get outta school for this here death?"
Boy 2: "I don't know."
Boy 1: "If we get off for the nigger [referring to Martin Luther King], we oughta get off for Kennedy."

When I began writing the first edition of this book in 1970, the Kerner Commission's report was still fresh; Carmichael and Hamilton's (1967) idea of "black power" and Knowles and Prewitt's (1969) analysis of institutional racism were new. The Kerner Commission (Report of the National Commission on Civil Disorders, 1968, p. 203) concluded that "white racism is essentially responsible for the explosive mixture which has been accumulating in our cities since the end of World War II (Chicago Commission on Race Relations, 1992, p. 203). For many, this conclusion was a milestone. The Chicago Commission in 1922, the report on the

Harlem riots in 1935 (the Mayor's Commission on Conditions in Harlem, 1935), and the report of the Los Angeles Riots in 1965 (Governor's Commission on the Los Angeles Riots, 1965), all had described the unhealthy conditions of race relations in urban areas. But, for the first time, the Kerner Commission introduced to white America the concept of *white racism.*

Here we are, in 1996, and we have to ask ourselves how have things changed since 1970? Chapter 12 showed us how the concept of race itself offered a basis for differential treatment—unfavorable for those who belonged to the "lesser races." Chapter 13 showed how, although those old-fashioned notions of racial superiority may no longer serve as acceptable topics of conversation, new language and strategies for maintaining racial distinctions and hierarchy have taken their place, and the old-fashioned dominance beliefs and practices persist. During the media frenzy over the O.J. Simpson trial and the aftermath of the not-guilty verdict, the "racial divide" was a major topic of scrutiny and analysis. The hand-wringing and soul searching about evidence of dramatic racial differences in perception, feeling, and experience seemed to catch white America off guard. Some argued that the trial, as well as the verdict, drove a wedge between black and white America. Others suggested that, rather than *causing* racial tensions or differences, it merely brought them to the fore.

We defined and discussed prejudice in Part 2, and defined and discussed racism in Chapters 12 and 13. Yet, for all of this analysis and discussion, there is still a sense that racism is a subjective emotional experience that varies from person to person and defies neat categorization. In an interview on the National Public Radio (NPR) program *All Things Considered* in October of 1995, I was asked, "What is racism" and "How do you know it when you see it?" Two hypothetical situations were presented. In the first, a young white woman crosses to the other side of the street when she sees a black male approaching her. "Is she racist?" I was asked. In another scenario, a black cab driver is instructed on the best way to get to a white patron's house. The cab driver gets angry at being challenged as to his capacity to do his job well. "Was the white patron being a racist?"

Recall the incident described in Chapter 6 where a white woman was perceived by a black man to be fearful of him when she fiddled with the latch of her pocketbook. The young black man suspected her of stereotyping him. Was his reaction to her "proof" of her racism? Is it his call? Her call? My call as the expert? Perhaps this illustrates how analyzing racism often stimulates more debate and controversy than it does mutual understanding.

The realities of racism are horrible enough. Recall the young 10-year-old black girl being called *nigger,* among other things (Chapter 13). There is no ambiguity in this event, though what motivates it and what effect an experience such as that may have on the life of a young person are hard to determine. People can treat each other badly in the name of differences of race, sex or gender, economic class, physical condition, or sexual orientation. Religion or ethnic identification and cultural habits, too, can form the bases of cruel and unusual treatment. Racism is ugly and mean, but it does not have a corner on the market of meanness. What is special about racism is the systematic and cumulative effects of a societal view of group differences based on race, what we called *racialism.* The cumulative and systematic effects of racialized worldviews are that belonging to a denigrated racial group means that centuries of maltreatment, denial, oppression, and stigma are attached to the visible signs of who one is. Values, beliefs, and institutional practices combine to disadvantage individuals on the basis of their group membership. This underlies prejudice and, more perniciously, it underlies racism.

The general aim of this chapter is to explore the ways in which *individuals* exhibit racism, and what basic mental and emotional processes sustain it. The three levels of racism, described in earlier chapters, flow into and from each other in reciprocal currents of influence. This chapter focuses on the microlevel, or individual level. The first section compares race prejudice and racism. It illustrates how racism rests on more macrolevel or societal influences than prejudice does. In the next section, we define *individual racism* and give examples of things people say or have said or done that illustrate racist sentiment and belief. We consider the idea of black racism, and note that the power to control others' lives—an important aspect of racism, as opposed to prejudice—is an important ingredient usually missing from the relationship of blacks to whites in the United States. We then consider the cases of overt, old-fashioned, or "dominative" racism and of covert, subtle, and "aversive" racism. The next section considers how people adopt racist beliefs and engage in racist behavior as a consequence of socialization processes. Research is presented that shows that certain socialization experiences increase the likelihood of racist attitudes and behaviors. We also consider how children react to skin color and to psychological essentialism in ways that make it easy for them to categorize people into groups and assign differential value to them. We next evaluate several social-psychological mechanisms that increase the likelihood of individual racism—terror management processes, ecological influences on social perceptual, and correspondence bias. Finally, we consider some examples of how individuals who are black have different experiences than do individuals who are white. We also review case examples of people who have "changed race" in field experiments.

*R*ACE PREJUDICE AND RACISM COMPARED

For G. W. Allport (1954), theories of prejudice were organized from the outside in, from macrolevels to microlevels, from sociohistorical and cultural aspects down to the fine-grained focus on prejudice as an "act directed at an object." In other words, for Allport, prejudice focuses on people. Figure 14.1A illustrates this reverse-telescope model, where we look through the wider aperture at the target of prejudice. The target will be small, but it will fill the entire frame of our view. Furthermore, in G. W. Allport's model, a critical transition occurs between situational influences and personality. The broad historical and sociocultural factors determine how situations develop and what character they have. These values or beliefs then operate through socialization processes to shape the connection between the target and the perceiver, or actor (the person whose bias concerns us), in a given situation. The questions posed by my interviewer on NPR (Chapter 13) tried to connect up, in specific situations, the perceiver, the target, and asked me, the expert, to determine the social meanings of these actions.

So, prejudice is an individual-level concept in that *people* are prejudiced. But their prejudice derives from the broader sociohistorical, cultural matrix of their experience and the socialization processes that shape their attitudes, values, and personalities. But what we typically focus on and understand to be prejudice is how a *specific* person perceives a specific other person in a given situation differently on the basis of the latter's race (or any other salient social category membership).

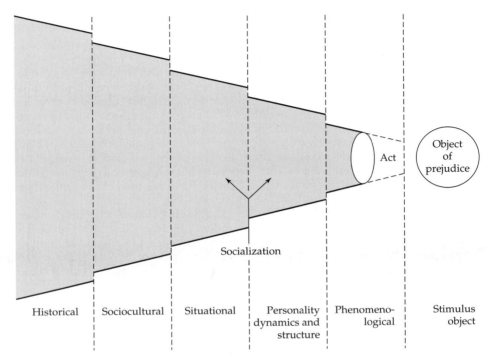

Type of Approach

FIGURE 14.1A

Through a Telescope Narrowly—A Model for the Analysis of Prejudice. (Adapted from G. W. Allport, *The Nature of Prejudice* [pages 13, 14, 206–218, 281, 469, and 570]. © 1979 Addison-Wesley Publishing Company, Inc. Reprinted by permission of Addison-Wesley Longman Publishing Company, Inc.)

However, what individuals think about the category (e.g., Jews, women, Turks, homosexuals, the elderly, disabled, or immigrants) is a product of macrolevel social forces operating over time. Therefore, although we study individual perceptions, for the most part, we acknowledge the contribution of these larger social forces to what we observe.

Racism places greater emphasis on the macrolevel forces that shape society. Whereas the prejudice model works from the outside in, the racism model works from the inside out. That is, as depicted in Figure 14.1B, if we look through the smaller aperture, we find the large image of society and culture as the focus of our analysis. At the level of the individual, racism and race prejudice are substantially similar. But, as we expand our perspective, racism diverges from prejudice, because the focus of analysis becomes *institutional* practices and *cultural* mechanisms.

Van Dijk (1987) suggests that race prejudice is a mechanism that sustains a racialized society. The language, images, and stories of formal and informal conversation and discourse reinforce group differences and the differential values placed on group membership. Race prejudice, operating at the individual level through interpersonal and intergroup dynamics, helps to sustain racism. By treating individuals on the basis of their group membership, prejudicial behavior serves both to per-

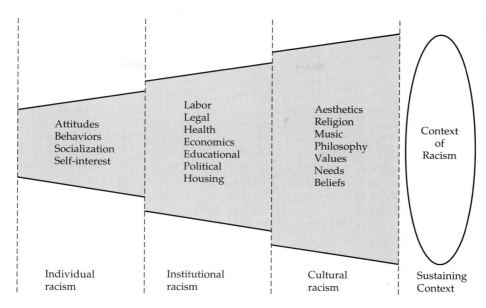

FIGURE 14.1B

Through a Telescope Widely—A Model for the Analysis of Racism. (Adapted from G. W. Allport, *The Nature of Prejudice* [pages 13, 14, 206–218, 281, 469, and 570]. © 1979 Addison-Wesley Publishing Company, Inc. Reprinted by permission of Addison-Wesley Longman Publishing Company, Inc.)

petuate the categorical thinking about groups and to disadvantage members of groups that are less well-liked or well-thought-of.

Racism and Race Prejudice Compared

Individual racism and race prejudice have a great deal in common. Race prejudice, as traditionally analyzed, coincides roughly with either the dominative-racist type or with the aversive racist, who behaves "regressively." Race prejudice is an individualistic orientation in that it emphasizes attitudes and judgments and relies on behavioral cues for evidence of its presence.

Individual racism, too, emphasizes attitudes and judgments and relies on behavior, but it has a different underlying basis. Racism rests on a belief in biological and/or psychological essentialism, applied to race. That is, people who can be classified into so-called racial minority groups differ from the classifying group by virtue of some essential qualities (e.g., intelligence, morality, and values). To the individual racist, those classified into his or her own group (the in-group) possess more positive or superior characteristics, and those classified outside the in-group possess inferior ones. To the individual racist, the differences observed between racial groups legitimate differential treatment and, therefore, differential outcomes. The *intrinsic racist* described by Appiah (1990) would be an example of the effects of this process.

So, one basic difference between race prejudice and racism rests on acceptance or rejection of the belief that there are really essential differences that warrant different treatment. Racists do not apologize for their beliefs. But we are all socialized in a society with a cumulatively racist history. Therefore, it is likely and probable that racist beliefs influence all of us in varying degrees. This fact led to an expansion of the examination of what *racism* means and how it is understood.

The first step in this expansion came from Carmichael and Hamilton (1967), who spoke of *institutional racism*. This concept is rather removed from the notions of attitudes and attitude change that characterize much of the prejudice literature. Moreover, the evidence used in the determination of institutional racism is considerably more objective. Whereas the prejudice analysis requires value judgments, personal histories, inferences about subjective states, and the tenuous application of normative judgments, the determination of institutional racism can be very simple.[1] One need only look for gross racial inequities in the outcomes of institutional operations in order to level charges of institutional racism. Even so, for many people, the racial inequities are often attributable merely to discrimination and, hence, are seen as the behavioral consequences of prejudice. Introducing the concept of institutional racism diminishes the overlap between racism and prejudice, but not completely.

The next expansion came from the idea of cultural racism and encompasses both the individuals and institutions in the society. This analysis focuses on those cultural values that underlie the formation of racist institutions, and examines the values, traditions, and assumptions upon which institutions are formed and within which individuals are socialized to maturity. Because institutions reinforce and perpetuate individual racism, and because these resulting individual values, in turn, feed back into the cultural character, the concept of cultural racism completes the chain. That is, the culture creates or determines the nature of its institutions, the institutions socialize the individuals, and the individuals perpetuate the cultural character. Therefore, as noted earlier, racism exists at each of these three levels.

Our discussion of definitions of racism in Chapter 13 emphasized several different levels of analysis. Belief in superiority-inferiority distinctions among human groups, with one's own racial group on the superior end and other racial group targets on the inferior end, was a recurring theme in many of these definitions. But other definitions of racism emphasized the simple facts of difference, the tendency to prefer "people like us," and a rationalization of this preference as "natural." Differences between race, culture, and ethnicity get blurred.

However, racism defined as an individual's set of beliefs or attitudes represents little advance over the concept of race prejudice. What transforms race prejudice, and even individual racism, to a higher level is the imposition of *power*—"possession of control, authority, or influence over others' ability to act or produce an effect; . . . physical might. . . ." (*Webster's New Twentieth Century Dictionary of the English Language Unabridged,* 1965, p. 1412). When control over others' ability to "produce an effect" or to control what happens to them is systematically organized around racial categories, then the values held in racialistic thinking conspire to control, for the worse, the outcomes or effects of members of other racial groups and, for the better, the outcomes or effects of ourselves and others in our racial group.

---

[1]The institutional racism analysis does not, though, escape "moral" interpretations. Eastland and Bennett (1979), for example, contrasted "numerical equality," which in their view reflected the affirmative action remedy to institutional racism, and "moral equality," which reflected a true individual, non-group-based opportunity structure (see Chapter 4). Morality was, by their analysis, not on the side of the foes of institutional racism.

This control, this power is what makes racism different from prejudice. And the organized set of control mechanisms creates and sustains racial hierarchy. The consequences of these mechanisms reverberate across the society and across generations of people. These processes—and the structures that maintain them—distinguish racism from one of its sustaining mechanisms, race prejudice.

Defining Individual Racism

Based on the discussions of race and racism in Chapters 12 and 13 and the several definitions summarized in Table 3.1, we offer a broad definition of individual racism.

> *Racist individual:* one who considers that black people as a group (or other human groups defined by essential racial characteristics) are inferior to whites because of physical (i.e., genotypical and phenotypical) traits. He or she further believes that these physical traits are determinants of social behavior and of moral or intellectual qualities, and ultimately presumes that this inferiority is a legitimate basis for that group's inferior social treatment. An important consideration is that all judgments of superiority are based on the corresponding traits of white people as norms of comparison.

Black people in the United States represent a major ethnic as well as racial group. Therefore, cultural forms and expressions of black people are also seen as inferior by white racists. Again, the determination of inferiority is based on the white cultural standards for comparison. The connection between culture and race is often made by the white racist; hence, assumptions of cultural inferiority often co-occur with assumptions of racial inferiority. Both are characteristic of a racist individual.

A far more subtle form of racism concerns the analysis and interpretation of black culture. The racist individual correctly perceives cultural differences between blacks and whites, but evaluates the white expressions positively and the black expressions negatively. The negative evaluation of black culture is almost always based on either (1) the assumedly unsuccessful attempt to copy or reproduce white culture forms, or (2) the pathological reactions to an oppressive status in U.S. society. Congruent with these evaluations, the racist assumes that all racially distinctive black expressions are inherently lower-class expressions.

It is important to understand that all reactions to oppression are not pathological. In fact, it is undeniable that a certain collective strength must accompany group survival under conditions of severe oppression. However, the issue of racism raised here concerns the racist's single-minded focus on the negative adaptations, to the exclusion of the positive ones. This view does not accord any legitimate, positive, distinctive cultural expression to middle- and upper-class black people. Instead, these blacks are assumed to be just like whites. This view produces statements such as the following from van den Berghe (1967, p. 94):

> Beyond the specific stigma of skin pigmentation and its numerous social and psychological consequences, Negro Americans have virtually nothing more in common than they do with any other Americans; and stigmatization itself, of course, is far from being a Negro monopoly.

By separating lower income blacks from those in higher socioeconomic strata and linking the negative attributes of race to these lower SES group members, and stripping those higher SES members of any racial identity, racists put blacks in a catch-22, lose-lose situation: branded racially inferior when things go poorly and excised from one's race when one does well.

To think that a race can come from a cultural background as different as Africa's was from England's, spend 250 years oppressed by slavery, and another 100 years oppressed by sheer oppression, can live among each other almost exclusively, sharing cultural background and interpreting the U.S. experience through common pains and visions and yet conclude that, because black people drive the same cars over the same highways, watch the same TV shows, and vote for the same presidents that whites do, they have nothing more in common with one another than they do with other Americans is naiveté of astounding proportions!

Because major conciliatory efforts in this country have been toward drawing races together, the major stress has been on racial similarities. But, if there is no recognition of any positive contributions of black culture to the American culture on the path to the ultimate coming together of the races, then all of the giving will be black, all the taking will be white, and racism will continue to be the tie that binds.

There are many varieties of individual racists, but common to them all is a belief in the inferiority of black people (physically, morally, intellectually, culturally, and so on) and the uncompromising, unalterable use of white evaluative norms, with the unquestioned assumption of their superiority. Although an individual does not *make* norms, he or she internalizes, supports, and uses them. Therefore, identifying people as racist involves determining the degree to which they are willing to ascribe inferiority to racial characteristics of, say, black people on the basis of white norms. But, as the adjacent cartoon suggests, it's all relative!

A person does not have to believe that blacks are inferior in each of the ways mentioned above in order to be called or to be guilty of being a racist. For example, the most extreme form of individual racism might be someone who believed (1) that blacks were "naturally" inferior, based on physical criteria; (2) that these physical differences were determinants of basic differences in intelligence, morality, and so on; (3) that these differences produced an inferior culture; and, finally, (4) that the inferior characteristics of blacks were a legitimate basis for their special, unequal treatment in U.S. society.[2] An individual need not be so thorough in his or her racism, however, to be classified as racist.

Thomas Jefferson believed in the innate inferiority of black people. He was a racist. Nevertheless, Jefferson's staunch advocacy of the doctrine of "natural rights" led him to propose that, even though black people were inferior, the natural rights of man applied to them and, therefore, necessitated the abolition of slavery. However, in order to gain support for the creation of the republic, Jefferson was obliged to compromise with Southern slavery interests and delete the antislavery plank from the Declaration of Independence. This deletion paved the way for the famous "American dilemma," the contradiction between the notions of the rights of man ("We hold these Truths to be self-evident, that all Men are created equal, and endowed by their Creator with certain unalienable Rights among which are Life, Liberty and the Pursuit of Happiness.") and the facts of slavery.

Not only was Abraham Lincoln convinced of the innate inferiority of black people, but he felt that racial equality was never attainable as long as blacks and whites lived in the same society—the superior whites would always control the in-

---

[2]A *nonracist person* would be one who was a true relativist in matters of race. For example, understanding that people are alike in some ways and different in others, a nonracist would not use those differences as a basis for inferior treatment of others or for the privileged treatment of his or her own group.

STANLEY by Murray Ball

Continuing the adventures of The Great Palaeolithic Hero

"White over black? Compared to what?" (STANLEY by Murray Ball: Continuing the adventures of The Great Paleolithic Hero. Reproduced from PUNCH, 1970)

ferior blacks. He, too, was a racist. It was this racist belief that led Lincoln to propose, until the end of his life, the colonization of black people—either in this country or abroad—as the only solution to the race problem. It is perhaps ironic, as well as symbolic of the nature of this society, that such a man is acclaimed as one of the greatest white friends the American black people have ever had.[3]

Black Racism—An Oxymoron

It is sometimes argued that blacks can be racists, too. On the National Public Radio Show I discussed in Chapter 13, I was asked "If a black man took his child out of a public school and put her in an all-black, Afrocentric school, was that racist?" I suggested that there is a great difference between establishing a private educational system to avoid the court-ordered desegregation of public schools because you do not want your children to attend school with blacks, and attempting to aid in the formation of a strong, proud, and self-assured young child by putting her in a school that has that mission.

[3]I should mention that, in spite of the obvious negative characteristics I've pointed out, of all U.S. presidents, Jefferson and Lincoln were among the most sympathetic to the plight of black people in this country. I have emphasized the negative aspects to show just how unfavorable the position of black people in this country has been.

Racism, as we have seen, is characterized either by feelings of racial superiority or by a preference for one's own kind, coupled with a desire to segregate oneself from others who are believed different and the power and control to make it happen. We throw the label "racist" around much too easily. A bigot is a racist if he or she believes that his or her racial group is superior and that this superiority entitles him or her and people like him or her to privileges over blacks. Blacks' efforts to create worldviews, traditions, institutions, and programs to cope with racism, misrepresentations of historical facts, and a systematically negative interpretation of their experience are not aimed at subjugating whites or controlling whites—or, generally, about whites at all. Identifying whites as villains in the historical drama of racism is fundamentally accurate, if sometimes overdrawn.

All groups hold and express negative attitudes toward other groups. Prejudices abound. But converting prejudices to self-serving advantage to the detriment of others is where racism magnifies negative attitudes, feelings, and beliefs. Further, when those feelings and beliefs are used to maintain institutional and cultural control as a means of sustaining racial advantage, we have a significantly more powerful and dangerous phenomenon than either name-calling or in-group preference.

So, to be clear, blacks may indeed express preferences for other blacks, prefer that their children not marry whites, or Latinos that their children not marry Anglos. In-group preference is related to ethnocentrism. But racism concerns a belief in racial superiority, and the implementation of values and practices that advantage one's own race and disadvantage others. Furthermore, racism is attached to the power to impose those beliefs on the outcomes of others. Racism is a multilevel cultural edifice that extends from the macrolevel to the microlevel of society. The dominant cultural beliefs about whites have never lent themselves to a racist interpretation. Labeling whites as flawed, as Malcolm X did in his "blue-eyed devil" charge, attempts to change how race is viewed. It is an *antiracist* strategy, not a racist one. The aim is to get to ground zero, not to dominate and control.

Individual Racism—Comparative Modus Operandi: Dominative and Aversive Cases

Chapter 1 proposed that one of the important points of history was regional variation in patterns of race relations. In the beginning, racial attitudes did not differ in the North and the South. But, as the patterns of behavioral relations diverged, the forms of racist expression and feeling similarly diverged. Slavery became institutionalized in the South, whereas the North traded in black bodies. As a consequence, regional differences in black-white relations have persisted throughout U.S. history.

Most common understandings of racism have been overly influenced by the aggressive, overtly hostile, and bigoted expressions that have characterized the Southern form. Slavery was the first and most robust expression of racism. However, through the years, the burning, lynching, Jim Crow legislation, and violent reaction to attempts at racial integration have established the South as the most visible home of racism in the United States.

Implicit in this analysis is the view that there are more individual racists in the South than there are in the North and that the differences, therefore, are matters of the degrees of racism rather than the kind. I propose that the differences are not so much of degree but of kind. If a white man makes a black man ride at the back of a bus, he is a racist. If a white man chooses to stand rather than sit next to a black man on a bus, he, too, is racist. However, these are two different kinds of racism. In his book *White Racism*, Joel Kovel (1970) defines these two types of racism as *dominative* and *aversive*, respectively (see Chapter 5):

> The dominative racist is the type who acts out bigoted beliefs . . . he represents the open flame of race hatred. The true White bigot expresses a definitive ambition through all his activity: he openly seeks to keep the Black man down, and he is willing to use force to further his ends. (Kovel, 1970, p. 53)
>
> The aversive racist is the type who believes in White race superiority and is more or less aware of it but does nothing overt about it. He tries to ignore the existence of Black people, tries to avoid contact with them, and, at most, tries to be polite, correct and cold in whatever dealings are necessary between the races. (Kovel, 1970, p. 54)

Of course, by suggesting that the aversive mode characterizes the North and the dominative mode characterizes the South, I do not mean to make strict categorical distinctions. Just as some Northern racists express their racism in dominative form, some Southern racists express their racism in aversive form. However, there are decided differences in the language and behavior of Northerners and Southerners. The important point is that the differences do not reflect the intensity of racist feelings so much as they do the modes of racist expression.

Recall some of the historical figures mentioned previously. Dominative racists would include Tom Brady (1955, p. 89), who declared his opposition to forced racial integration in these bellicose terms: "We say to the Supreme Court and to the northern world, you shall not make us drink from this cup. . . . We have, through our forefathers, died before for our sacred principles. We can, if necessary, die again." Also included would be the man who slit open the stomach of the just-lynched pregnant woman (Chapter 3) or any of the numerous white mobs that roamed through and plundered black communities. The aversive racists have, of course, been rather subtly hidden by our history. But that astute observer Alexis de Tocqueville sniffed them out. As he noted, in his travels through America in 1791, "The prejudice of race appears to be stronger in the states that have abolished slavery than in those where it still exists; and nowhere is it so intolerant as in those states where servitude has never been known. . . ." (de Tocqueville, 1945, *Democracy in America*, vol 1, p. 373).[4]

Woodrow Wilson's actions characterized the aversive racist. In 1912, he stated that he wished to see "justice done to the colored people in every matter; and not mere grudging justice, but justice executed with liberality and cordial good feeling" (Franklin and Moss, 1994, p. 324). Yet it was Woodrow Wilson who issued an executive order that racially segregated the eating and toilet facilities of federal civil service workers. Moreover, he gave Southern federal officials the right to downgrade or discharge, without due process, any black employee on any ground they saw fit. This segregation order might be seen as aversive racism, whereas his discharge order is more directly dominative racism.

To a greater extent, the dominative racist bases his or her arguments on physical criteria. This type of racism is predicated on the innate "inferiority" of blacks, and, to the dominative racist, that justifies almost any action he or she would take

---

[4]In this connection it is interesting to note the recent statistics on the desegregation of public schools, which show that, over the last two years, Southern schools have become more racially integrated than have Northern schools. In many Northern schools, segregation is actually increasing (quoted in Kovel, 1970, p. 31).

toward blacks. Kovel suggests that dominative racism is the more primitive form. The attitudes and behaviors sanctioned by the sociocultural ethos primarily of the North produced a pattern of race relations that required suppression of more overtly hostile actions. At moments of stress and racial tension, however, the aversive racist "regresses" to more dominative forms. This regression in the 1960s was termed *white backlash.* Earlier examples of regressive racism were the draft riots in New York City (1863); white riots in New York (1900), Springfield, Illinois (1908), and East St. Louis (1917); and the so-called Red Summer of 1919.

The aversive racist, on the other hand, to a greater extent invokes cultural criteria for his or her brand of racism. For example, the aversive racist wants to keep blacks from moving into his or her neighborhood, not because he or she doesn't like blacks, but because "property values will go down." And why will property values go down? "Because they won't take care of it; they'll have loud parties; they will not maintain the 'standards' of the neighborhood." These statements rely greatly on the language of everyday racism (Essed, 1991) or the new racism (Barker, 1981). The issue is when does the preference for one's own group—when it is racially homogeneous—stand as a proxy for racism? The subtlety of the aversive or new forms of racism challenge our thinking and analysis the most.

One by one, the dominative forms of racist expression are being eliminated or diminished in U.S. society—first slavery, then lynchings, burnings, bombings, and use of cattle prods, and so on. The heat and bitterness of the dominative racist characterized race relations in the United States for many, many years. When I traveled in Europe in 1963, everyone wanted to know about the fight between the blacks and the whites, the "racial wars" in the South. I was in Europe around the time of the church bombings that killed four little girls in Birmingham, the slaying of Medgar Evers, and Martin Luther King's march on Washington. The eyes of the world were riveted on the South. But, the following year, New York City, Philadelphia, and Rochester, New York, exploded. The focus turned to the teeming Northern ghettos. The world had finally caught up with the aversive racists, and de Tocqueville smiled in his grave. As the passion of the dominative racist slowly dies out, the passionless coldness of the aversive racist sets in.

Since 1965, much research has attempted to discover why black Americans are angry, why they are upset, why they have increasingly resorted to ideas of racial separation. Black Americans have been constantly trying to understand the mind of the aversive racist. Black Americans have always known and understood the dominative racist, who has been "up front." In contrast, the aversive racist has lurked in the woodwork and has spoken words of conciliation, or equality, or sympathy. However, for many, many years the consequences of being black in the United States have not improved significantly. Let us look more closely at the aversive racist and see if we can understand what this personality is about.

Aversive racists do not want to associate with blacks, although they do not often express this feeling. They make claims of equality and liberal or open goodwill, but stand staunchly behind the institutions the doctrine of racism created or that exist to ensure that their goodwill is never challenged. When black people began to move into Harlem in the late 1800s, whites tried desperately to stop them by forming realty companies. They finally resorted to the ultimate control—money. Bankers stopped renewing mortgages to blacks and ceased giving new ones to blacks. This practice has long been in effect and continues to be used as a means of maintaining racial separation. It should be pointed out that it is not banks that adopted the policy but individuals, racist individuals who had an aversion to living with black people. Or was it an affinity for money, which was more readily available

when houses turned over? Which is the driving force, the more parsimonious explanation for unequal treatment of members of racial groups or racial animosity? Whatever the motivation, the practices that produced racial segregation were organized
and systematic (cf. Massey and Denton, 1993), and their cumulative consequences,
racial segregation and disadvantage, led us to institutional racism.

Racists believe in the superiority of white over black. They differ in the relative
degree to which physical versus cultural criteria are important to that superiority
and, correspondingly, in the kinds of actions that these beliefs sanction. As irrefutable
scientific evidence has been accumulated, it has become more difficult to uphold direct physical arguments for racial differences. Racism in the United States has moved
from a dominative to an aversive orientation (cf. Gaertner and Dovidio, 1986).

Individuals are not born racists. The fact that racism has existed for so long in
this country has prompted some to suggest that it is an inherited characteristic of
white people. For a given individual, racism is a state of mind, a set of values, and a
constellation of behaviors. If racism has been perpetuated in this society for the
past 350 years, it is because the same states of mind, set of values, and constellation
of behaviors have been handed down (transmitted) from generation to generation
in white America. These characteristics of white individuals are inherited, but not
genetically. They are inherited as a natural consequence of being socialized into a
culture that, from the beginning, has been based on the assumption of white superiority over black. Each new generation of white Americans has been socialized to
that state of affairs. Let us take a brief look at that socialization process from the
perspective of social psychology.

Individual Racism through Socialization

Racial attitudes and beliefs vary widely among people. Many people believe that
racial attitudes simply reflect "how you were raised." That is, if your parents were
members of the Ku Klux Klan and you grew up watching your parents go to Klan
rallies, well, it might be expected you would hold racist beliefs. Or, if your parents
marched for civil rights in the South, perhaps you would be expected to hold egalitarian attitudes on race. In order to discuss individual racism, we must consider
how socializing agents affect the likelihood that certain racial views will be
adopted.

Clausen (1968, p. 4) suggests that socialization processes ". . . imply that the individual is induced in some measure to conform *willingly* to the ways of society or
of the particular groups to which he belongs." This inducement involves learning
how to function in one's milieu, and the earliest milieu that might be influential in
this process is the family. But it obviously does not stop there, and, as a child grows,
the sphere of influence widens. Siblings, peers, teachers, and, now more than ever,
the media. It is not a simple matter to trace the origin of racial attitudes.

There are two views of the socialization process. The first, the *active view*,
stresses the important role the child plays in his or her own socialization development. The temperament, character, and ability of the child will have an important
effect on the course socialization will take. The second, or *passive view*, stresses the
process whereby a child is molded to the social requirements of his or her environment. This approach assigns no responsibility to the child; rather, it argues that the
child is shaped by his or her cultural context.

Racial attitudes play an important role in a person's overall value system and
social preferences. In 1996, Senator Phil Gramm (R., Texas) was a candidate for

Klansman in the making? The family that hates together . . . [Greensboro, North Carolina, June 7, 1987] . . . does not necessarily stay together as research on parents' and children's values suggests. (Bill Biggart/Impact Visuals)

President. Senator Gramm was married to a Korean American woman, his second wife. During the Primary election in Louisiana, where Gramm was expected to win, he finished a disappointing second. The campaign strategies of his opponents had included circulating a flier that read, "Many conservatives will not vote for him [Gramm] in the primary due to his interracial marriage. He divorced a white wife to marry an Asiatic." What does this say about people, about human groups, about "right and wrong?"

Language and discourse convey values and assign them to different groups (van Dijk, 1987). The values to be adopted are associated with one's own group, and one's young are socialized to embrace and use them in their lives. A very interesting study of values was conducted by Rohan and Zanna (in press). It is said that the "apple never falls far from the tree," "that children grow up to be like their parents." Is this true? Rohan and Zanna (in press) tried to find out by having male university students and their parents (71 students and 96 parents) at the University of Waterloo in Canada, fill out the Schwartz (1992) value inventory, which measures respondents' endorsement of 10 value type dimensions (universalism, benevolence, conformity, tradition, hedonism, achievement, power, security, self-direction, and stimulation), and 2 value-orientation dimensions; self-transcendence (concern for others as opposed to self-enhancement or self-interest); and openness to change (versus resistance to change or conservatism). These two value-orientation dimensions have been shown to capture the universal values of people all over the world, while the 10 value-type dimensions have been shown to vary across people in different societies.

Rohan and Zanna (in press) constructed profiles of these value types and compared parents and their adult children *within* and *between* families (pseudo-families). Table 14.1 shows the patterns of associations between parents and sons, and among members in the community. The community in which this study was conducted was very homogeneous. This is suggested by the high correlations of value profiles between randomly chosen adult men and women (.57) and between these "pseudo-parents" and their randomly chosen "pseudo-sons" (.44). However, in spite of this homogeneity, *actual* mothers and fathers have more similar values to one another (.68) and are more similar to their own sons (.54) than the typical community members were to the pseudo-sons. This evidence suggests, indeed, that the "value apple" does not fall from the family tree!

Although these data show great similarity within families, the actual *range* of value-profile correlations between parents and their adult children was very large (from −.47 to +.90) Rohan and Zanna (in press) attempted to find out what factors might explain this high variability in value-socialization outcomes.

Although children's adult values tended to be highly correlated with those of their parents, this was very true of some families, but untrue of others. If racial attitudes derive from parental values in some cases (correlations of .90), and flee from them in others (correlation of −.47), what is it about either the children or their parents that may explain this divergence? One candidate for explaining differences in race-related values is the measure of authoritarianism (cf. Adorno et al., 1950 and Chapters 2, 6). Rohan and Zanna had respondents answer questions on their attitudes toward minority groups. The researchers then completed a measure of right wing authoritarianism (RWA; see Altemeyer and Hunsberger, 1992), which is indicated by a tendency to adhere to social conventions, to submit to authority, and to punish those who violate authority. Parents who scored high on RWA tended to hold more negative attitudes toward minority groups (r = .51).

Rohan and Zanna (in press) found that respondents who scored high on RWA tended to endorse conformity, tradition, and security values. This suggests that such people would perceive differences among people and changing mores as threatening. Moreover, when these social values were combined with power values, a desire to attain or preserve a dominant position in the social order was the result (cf. Sidanius, 1993, on social dominance orientation). The generally self-enhancing values of high RWAs were in contrast to the low RWAs, who were more ac-

TABLE 14.1 CORRELATIONS IN VALUES BETWEEN MOTHERS AND FATHERS AND BETWEEN PARENTS AND SONS WITHIN AND BETWEEN FAMILIES

Value comparisons	Within real families	Within pseudo-families
Mothers with fathers	.68	.57
Parents with adult child	.54	.44

Between families was conceived as the relationship between randomly paired male and female adults and a randomly chosen adult child. These *pseudo*-families served as a control for the degree of value similarity in *real* families.

cepting of others and more open to change. This latter group scored high on the values of self-direction, stimulation, and universalism (i.e., welfare of *all*).[5]

Parenting goals also differed between high and low RWAs, with high RWA parents espousing *instrumental* parenting goals for their sons (e.g., good manners, hard work, being a good student, and acting male) and low RWA parents setting goals for their sons were more *expressive* (e.g., honesty, considerateness, getting along with people, self-control, and responsibility). Given these differences in value profiles of parents rated high and low on RWA, and given that these parents have different parenting goals, Rohan and Zanna (in press) asked "Is there any difference in the successful socialization of these parents' values to their children?" What they found was interesting.

Low RWA parents were more likely to have children who grew up to have value profiles (.62 correlation) similar to the parents than were high RWA parents (.42). This is good news. Those parents with more open values were more successful in instilling them in their sons. High RWA parents' values were no more similar to their actual sons values than were those of randomly paired parents and sons (.44). However, there were two distinct tendencies among these parents. One group had *high* similarity to their sons, and the other very *low* similarity. Those sons who saw their parents as more demanding and less responsive as parents when they were growing up were less similar in their value profile to their parents. Those who saw their parents as more responsive were more like them in values.

It seems, then, that perpetuating racist values and beliefs (the components of racism) is more likely to occur within families where parents embrace these doctrines in the first place *and* are successful in communicating them in a fashion that supports their children's needs for attention and support. So, if we are to reduce individual racism, we want parents who have positive human values and, in cases of those parents who don't have such values, we want them to be unsuccessful parents.

There is another way in which the socialization of racial attitudes is complicated. It has been observed that children's prejudicial attitudes arise between 3 to 6 years of age, are strongest at about ages 6 and 7, and become more tolerant as the children reach later childhood (Aboud, 1988; Furnham and Stacey, 1991). Therefore, there is encouraging evidence that children become *less* attached to their own group relative to other groups during childhood. Simultaneously, it has been shown that children of ethnic and racial minorities, who also are aware of the valued position of whites in a multiracial, multiethnic society are becoming *more* attached to their groups during childhood. The pattern of stronger in-group attachment among whites and out-group attachment among ethnic and racial minorities that is evident at earlier ages begins to reverse as children move toward puberty. By age 12, though, children tend to have assimilated the dominant values and beliefs about race that are prevalent in society, and a greater divergence in racial preferences between whites and others returns (Furnham and Stacey, 1991).

Perhaps this is a maturation process, or the influence of more highly developed cognitive structures and a diminution of parental influences. However, studies have shown that parental influence is actually *less* for younger children, and becomes greater as the children approach puberty (Davey, 1983). This is particularly true when majority-group parents are more favorable toward minority groups.

---

[5]It should be noted that *benevolence* was characteristic of high RWAs. However, although it is a positive, prosocial value, it is typically directed at the in-group, and thereby often serves to maintain position and dominance.

Moreover, young children tend to think that their attitudes are more like those of their parents than they, in fact, are (Aboud, 1993).

If parental influences are less for younger children whose parents have more positive views of minority groups, what other factors may be influencing these young children's attitudes? One possibility comes from the meaning of *color* in our society.

The Question of Color

There is ample evidence to suggest that white children in Western society have a prowhite, relative to black, *color* bias (Katz, 1983; Williams and Morland, 1976). This prowhite color bias is proposed as a causal agent in the adoption of a prowhite racial bias. The realities of racialism clearly establish value preference for whites over people of color, particularly blacks. This color preference replicates itself in racial preferences. Hirschfeld (1996) argues that even young children have a "theory race" that is biologically grounded. This contrasts with much research suggesting that very young children do not possess the adult-like notion of race-constancy (i.e., the immutability of racial classifications based on biological essentialism). Rather, it is argued (e.g., Aboud, 1988; Clark and Clark, 1947), they believe the physical properties associated with race are mutable. In a series of intriguing experiments, Hirschfeld (1995) demonstrates that young preschool children believe racial categories contain important information that goes beyond superficial physical appearance. They seem to believe that race (here defined by skin color) is immutable (while body build is not), derived from family background (but again body build is not) and that young children will come to resemble their parents in race when they are older, but not in body type. This leads Hirschfeld (1996, p. 240) to conclude that ". . . preschoolers demonstrate a biologically grounded understanding of race." The important implication of this finding is that very young children are predisposed to see biological significance in race. Thus, they are prone to quickly attach racial significance to the meaning of racial categories and to accept the nonobvious, but negative attributes that are associated with them. This developmental sequence offers a compelling explanation for the origin of racialized perception and judgment.

Psychological essentialism.   It is also suggested that humans have a natural tendency to perceive things in terms of their essences—that is, the properties that make them what they are (Medin, 1989). Color offers an easy means of categorizing people into groups, and psychological essentialism suggests the very likelihood that racialism (i.e., attaching skin color variation to the presumption of underlying essences) will result. That these underlying essences may also, in the case of whites, fit a *color* preference and set the stage for a tendency toward individual racism is also suggested. And this tendency may surface even before the child is bombarded by social values and beliefs, systematic institutional practices, and an overarching cultural system based on racialism. This psychological essentialism argument implies that it may be socialization that *reduces* racism rather than *causes* it. That is, the emergence of individual racism attitudes and beliefs may occur as a result of the *absence* of socialization pressures to minimize it.

This thinking makes sense when we consider the data from Rohan and Zanna (in press), which shows that Low RWAs have less negative attitudes toward minority groups and closer value similarity with their adult sons. The observation also implies that discrepancies between young children's racial attitudes and their parents' attitudes incline in the direction of the children's having more *negative*, not more positive, racial attitudes than their parents had.

So, to sum up, there is strong evidence and argument to suggest both that socialization processes explain adult racial attitudes and that other factors come into play. It is easy to make the claim for socialization of racial attitudes in families. However that is too simple to capture the true complexity of individual experience. Recall in Chapter 6 the idea that *nonshared environment* influences accounted for 60 percent of the variability in personality and cognitive processes among siblings in the same family. Living in the same family does not mean that one lives in the same psychosocial world. Capturing the development of individual racism is far more complex than simply assuming *the parents did it.*

Social Psychological Mechanisms that Sustain Individual Racism

Because individual racism is so close to race prejudice, the mechanisms that sustain race prejudice (discussed at length in Part 2) apply to individual racism, as well. Stereotyping, in-group bias derived from social identity and social categorization processes, illusory correlation, and so forth, could all be shown to aid and abet the maintenance of individual racism. In this section, we will consider some additional processes that are linked conceptually to cultural determinants of self- and other-perceptions.

Individual Racism as Terror Management

Greenberg, Pyszczynski, and colleagues (Greenberg, Simon, Pyszczynski, Solomon, and Chatel, 1992; Greenberg, Solomon, Pyszczynski, Rosenblatt, Kirkland, Veeder, and Lyon, 1990) have offered *terror management theory (TMT)* to explain intrapsychic self-protection based on a cultural mechanism. In this model, *terror* is the psychological or emotional state that follows from confronting our own mortality. Circumstances that heighten our sense of mortality lead to adaptive mechanisms designed to lessen the terror we feel. When confronted by the thought of our own death, we may think life-affirming thoughts of what we have accomplished in our lives, what our children or others close to us have accomplished, or of our character or any other aspect of our life that gives us a feeling of transcendence (perpetual life).

More specifically, TMT proposes that we may manage the terror of death by (1) maintaining faith in the cultural worldview to which we are connected and (2) living up to those cultural standards. By embracing these cultural standards and living up to them, we provide a "cultural anxiety buffer" to the negative emotion that accompanies death thoughts. This theory becomes relevant to racism if we consider that (1) any threat to well-being may heighten death anxiety, (2) racial differences are linked to differences in our own and others' worldviews, (3) the cultural anxiety buffer mechanism will enhance feelings of self-worth and self-esteem by embracing the worldviews of our own group and correspondingly distancing ourselves from the worldviews of others.

It is not a stretch to see TMT processes operating in white separatists and supremacists, as they cling fervently to racial purity and superiority, and claim exemplary love for "whiteness." They manage their death anxiety by removing themselves from contact with people, ideas, and situations that would undermine the mechanisms of terror management. In its extreme form, the militia movement reflects this process as one that transcends race. In the view of militia members, the threat is not just from blacks, Asians, Hispanics, and foreign immigrants, generally—it is from their own government! Because the government has lost sight of the cultural values of white superiority and will not protect them from the incursions of others, they must uphold the worldview of white eminence themselves.

The beauty of this model is that the anxiety buffer effect will be enacted according to the salient and dominant worldview the person endorses. TMT suggests that when death anxiety is aroused, the distinctions between our own and others' worldviews are heightened and the differences exaggerated. Those most like us will be evaluated more positively and those not like us more negatively when death anxiety is aroused than would be the case when it is not. Greenberg, Simon et al. (1992) experimentally manipulated death anxiety by having subjects (who were self-identified as "liberal" or "conservative") imagine their own death—how they would feel, how others would feel, what it was like in a casket, being interred, and so forth. Subjects who had gone through this death-anxiety manipulation, compared to those who had not, rated more positively, those in the experiment who shared their liberal or conservative views and more negatively to those who did not. Death anxiety, then, triggers reactions that intensify in-group preference and social identity mechanisms. When the threat comes from racial, ethnic, or immigrant groups, the seeds for racism are planted. Moreover, the fact that the mark of group divergence is worldview means that differences in values, beliefs, attitudes, and behaviors become the defining measures of separation.

Considering the metaphorical variants of death anxiety (e.g., economic distress caused by inflation; high unemployment; high taxes; or threats to opportunity for education, gainful employment, that are posed by affirmative action or other social policies), terror management may be a mechanism that explains the reactivity of the new racism to racial, ethnic, and cultural differences. Under these anxiety threats, differences are exacerbated, and values are attached to a greater extent to those like us (Barker's xenophobia). Furthermore, the perceived threat to our own well-being is managed by endorsing symbolic forms of self-protective values and by emphasizing traditional worldviews of racial dominance.

Ecology of Perceiving Race

McArthur and Baron (1983) propose an ecological theory of social perception in which the perceiver is attuned to seeing the world in a particular way, and objects of perception afford certain perceptions more easily than they afford others. Social perception, then, is a by-product of this interaction of perceiver and object factors. Therefore, features of the perceptual object, particularly the face, afford certain perceptions that McArthur and Baron (1983) argue are, in some cases, universal. For example, all societies participate in child rearing, and babies have to be cared for until they gain greater autonomy. According to the evolutionary aspect of the theory, baby features of the face afford perceptions of submissiveness, weakness, naiveté. Adult caregivers are, therefore, attuned to perceive these qualities and to react with appropriate nurturance. A great deal of resaerch supports this basic idea in finding that, the more baby-faced an adult person is, the more likely he or she is to be seen as weak, dependent, and honest—characteristics derived from association of these physical facial aspects to the qualities of babies. In fact, it has been shown that defendants in courts who are baby-faced are less likely to be convicted of crimes of intention, but are more likely to be convicted of crimes of negligence (Zebrowitz, 1994).

The principles of racialism specifically attach underlying character to phenotypical features of race. This connection is cemented by processes of psychological essentialism. Does ecological theory provide a mechanism for explaining how these perceptions of racial differences work? That is, are humans wired to perceive the connection between external physical features and subtle internal attributes (such as traits of aggression, honesty, morality, etc.) as a matter of adapting to their environment? Is racial and/or ethnic conflict inevitable, fueled by the differential perceptions *afforded* by ethnic or racial variation? Does sensitivity to racial differentiation *attune* a perceiver to see behavior differently when the actor is black or red as opposed to white, say? Numerous studies have shown that, by invoking racial stereotypes, certain underlying characteristics are more likely to be perceived. For example, Devine (1989) showed that when subjects were primed with a black racial stereotype, they were more likely to see ambiguous behaviors as aggressive (Chapter 6). Moreover this effect occurred independent of a person's degree of racism. This finding suggests there may be automatic perceptual processes associated with race that are ecologically induced. Bargh's "chameleon effect" (Bargh and Chen, 1996) implies as much.

The evidence for color preference in children and the widespread value connotations of color in this society (white is placed at the good end and black at the bad end of the color spectrum) generally support the idea that skin color affords certain social perceptions. Furthermore, variations in racial attitudes suggest that people may be differentially attuned to perceiving the value afforded by skin color. The interaction of the affordances of racial objects and the attunements of racial perceivers leaves a fertile theoretical ground upon which an understanding of attitudinal, emotional, and behavioral biases connected to race in this society can be built.

Zebrowitz, Montepare, and Lee (1993) tested the universality of the affordance of racial stimuli and variations in the attunement of racial perceivers. They had white, black and Korean college students rate a series of photographs of white, black, and Korean males on attractiveness, baby-facedness, and age. In addition, the photographs were rated on several traits thought to be associated with both attractiveness and baby-facedness. These traits were presented as bipolar pairs and included cold-warm, physically weak–physically strong, dishonest-honest, submissive-dominant, and naive-shrewd.

The *social ecology idea* that faces afford certain perceptions led the authors to predict that ratings of facial features would show similarity across both perceivers and faces judged. That is, black, white, and Korean judges would see the same traits and evaluate them in the same way whether the faces were of members of their own group or of another group. Results showed substantial agreement with regard to judgments of traits and of baby-facedness, leading to the article's title, "They don't all look alike" (Zebrowitz, Montepare, and Lee, 1993). However, there were some interesting and important differences across racial groups. For example, whereas black and Korean judges rated blacks as more submissive than either whites or Koreans, white judges rated them as more *dominant*. Similarly, black and Korean judges rated all racial groups roughly the same on physical strength, but white judges rated whites as substantially weaker and blacks as substantially stronger. It seems that blacks conjure up an image of strength and power in the eyes of whites. If this is true, it helps explain the potential for activation of terror management processes, as well as the aggressiveness effects found by Devine (1984) and others. These data also support the idea that the experiences of members of racial groups differentially attune them to members of their own and other racial groups.

More evidence of racial differences is provided when we look at the correlations between attractiveness and traits. In our society, warmth, honesty, and dominance are associated with attractiveness. In this study, dominance was uncorrelated with attractiveness for perceivers of all races. However, the patterns for warmth and honesty were quite different for the three groups. For whites, warmth was significantly correlated with attractiveness for all racial groups. For blacks, warmth was associated with attractiveness only for blacks. For Koreans, warmth was related to attractiveness only for whites. Each group associated honesty with attractiveness for members of its own group. However, honesty was disconnected from attractiveness for Koreans by whites, for whites by blacks, and for blacks by Koreans.

The point of these findings is that group differences arise when we try to predict what we will see in a facial expression and what underlying traits are perceived as going along with it. Although the dominant message is similarity across groups, these deviations leave open the compelling possibility that what we see will depend on the associative matrix of experiences and expectations that form our perceptual system. In other words, we are attuned to our perceptual world, in part, by virtue of our racial group membership.

Correspondence Biases Explain Susceptibility to Racialism

Gilbert and Jones (1986) describe the tendency to infer that behavior reflects internal dispositions of actors as correspondence bias (cf. Ross [1977] on the fundamental attribution error). It is a bias, because the tendency causes one to overlook exter-

FIGURE 14.2

Perceived Association of Traits and Attractiveness for Blacks, Whites, and Koreans. *Source:* Zebrowitz, L. A., Montepare, J. M., and Lee, H. K. (1993). They don't all look alike: Individual impressions of other racial groups. *Journal of Personality and Social Psychology, 65,* 85–101.

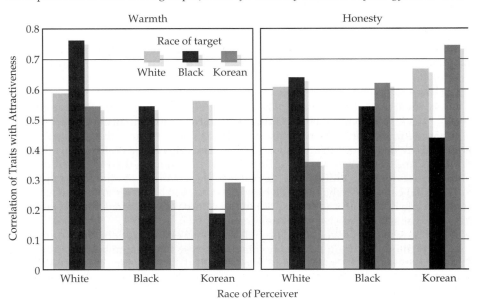

nal or environmental explanations for behavior. The tendency to perceive lower socioeconomic status of blacks as a result of lack of ability or effort is an example of a correspondence bias (see the explanations for inequality analyzed by Kluegel and Smith [1986] in Chapter 5.) External or environmental explanations (e.g., discrimination—the fact that jobs are not available in the community and that education is lacking and so one is less well-prepared to take advantage of opportunities), are given less credibility than are internal dispositions (e.g., lack of character, lack of ability, and poor choices).

Racism, then, can be understood as the tendency to perceive essential characteristics of race as the explanations for socioeconomic outcomes and as a corresponding tendency not to see the contextual, ecological influences on those same outcomes. Believing that internal qualities are good or bad, superior or inferior, for example, makes it easy to see that white dominance *corresponds* to superior racial qualities, and, hence, is explained by them. Similarly, black subordination *corresponds* to inferior racial qualities; hence, it *explains* blacks' overall lower socioeconomic position.

For example, a black male professional had a series of very frustrating and demeaning experiences during a trying day in New York City (Franklin, 1996). He took a client to dinner at a fancy restaurant, for which he had reservations in his name. As they waited for a table, the maitre'd arrived and told the man's white guest that his table was ready. After dinner, the waiter brought the check to the white guest. In each instance, the man tried to convince himself either that there was a good explanation or that it would be worse all the way around to cause a scene (attributional ambiguity?). Finally, the business dinner was over, and the two went outside to catch a cab home. The white business associate quickly hailed a cab and was on his way. The black businessman waited while cab after cab drove by or stopped to pick up whites. Finally, his frustration came pouring out. He leapt on top of the hood of a cab that stopped to drop off a passenger, pounding on the hood and refusing to move until he was given passage home. Observers certainly would not be privy to all of the insults and hassles this man had experienced during the evening, but it is sure that their inference of his behavior would run to internal attributes—that is, he was crazy, hostile, mad, mean, flamboyant, or what have you. Correspondence bias tends to leave intact beliefs about the essential nature of racial or ethnic categories and to provide ready explanations for behaviors and their consequences. Many of the stereotypes people hold about racial and ethnic groups are maintained, in part, through a tendency to use correspondence biases in judgments about other people's behaviors.

Moreover, this correspondence bias is particularly associated with our culture (cf. Markus and Kitayama, 1991). Cultures that stress individualism are more likely to associate underlying dispositions with observable behaviors than those that believe in more collectivist relationships. When principle concern is for the well-being of others and one's role in promoting that is paramount, then explanations for other's behavior tend to focus on the needs or expectations of others—in short, on the external causes of behavior. The essential causes of behavior are in the relationships people have with each other, not in the internal dispositions that dictate self-interested or self-expressive goal attainment.

Again, whether we consider the old-fashioned or the modern form of racism, each view allows the fault for disadvantage or lower standing to be easily found in the dispositions of the members of the minority racial group. In old-fashioned racism, negative outcomes are associated with genetically linked inferior dispositions or capabilities. In modern racism, it is inferior character that causes improper or inadequate behavior and explains the lower standing. In both cases, the fault is seen as internal and as following from suspicions of the target's inferiority.

Black Like Me, White Like You

John Howard Griffin was a white man who took a pigment-altering medicine and spent 28 days in the South as a black man. He chronicled his experiences in *Black Like Me* (Griffin, 1960). More recently, in 1994, Joshua Solomon, a young Jewish boy from Silver Spring, Maryland, decided he wanted to learn first-hand what his black male friends described as the "continuing scourge of racism." He was sympathetic to his friends' complaints about being followed and feared, but wanted to really know if this was true and how it felt. He took the same pigment-altering treatment that Griffin did. And, when he was black enough, he shaved his head, put on some "homeboy" fashions, and headed South.

He found himself harassed by the police, avoided when he asked white people for directions, made to wait for a table in a restaurant when there were apparently open tables, and followed around when he went into stores to buy clothes. Solomon reported his experiences on the *Oprah Winfrey* Show (February 17, 1995). He described the most significant aspect of his experience, stating:

> I have been white for 20 years and I always assumed a level of dignity and respect. No matter how much money I had in my pocket, I could go into a store and be treated with respect. However, I realized that when I became a black man, all that went away. I learned how much white privilege I enjoyed just by being white.

John Howard Griffin—black like me. (New American Library)

Oprah Winfrey arranged for the reverse to happen (Chapter 11). She had two young black males, dressed up to look white. With heavy foundation creme, fake beards, mustaches and wigs, false noses, and preppie clothes, her young black men became white. They felt, for the first time in their lives, what it was like to have the privilege that Solomon had enjoyed all of his life. One of them, Kwame Johnson, while made up to be white went into an apartment building to see a friend and was buzzed right in. When he returned later in the day as black Kwame, with the same intention, he was stopped by the doorman and made to present identification, state his purpose, and generally be screened before he could enter. This was the same black doorman who let him up with no questions asked when he was *white* earlier in the day. Requests for directions were happily supplied to white Kwame and denied to black Kwame. Car windows remained rolled up, passersby typically looked the other way and gave no response to requests for directions from black Kwame, but stopped and gave detailed directions to white Kwame.

The bottom line here is not always the maltreatment being black incurs, but the positive treatment being white commands. As these comparison cases show, one cannot even always know that one's experiences are different from what other people have or expect or can take for granted. Individual racism comes out not just in the slurs or epithets of *nigger* shouted from a passing car, but what *doesn't* happen to you on a daily basis. White privilege is a generally unexamined culprit in individual racism. The cumulative advantage of white privilege puts the disadvantage of people of color in perspective. Explanations for poorer outcomes often rely on assumptions of lesser abilities or character. But what so much research and experience tells us is that preferential treatment is not the exclusive domain of affirmative action, but the status quo for whites in the United States.

SUMMARY

Individual racism abounds in this society. In more emotional overstatements of the case, all white individuals are considered racists of varying degrees. This chapter has attempted to broaden the scope of individual racism and to place in perspective its relation to race prejudice, while avoiding the emotional racist charges that fan the flames of conflict without advancing our understanding of the problem.

Racism infects individuals in many different ways. The most important determinant of whether and/or how an individual becomes a racist is the environmental norm to which he or she is socialized. If there is a norm of hating blacks, then a child is likely to grow up doing so. If there is a norm of feeling blacks are inferior, but a counsel of polite avoidance, a child is likely to become an aversive racist. Most subtle is the ethnocentric norm that is not avowedly racial but that, when applied to blacks, produces unchallenged feelings of white superiority. The child of this environment is neither aversive nor dominative, but bases his or her judgments of black and other people of color solely on norms that greatly restrict the range of people with whom any association at all is desirable.

Evidence was presented showing that racial attitudes and corresponding values do follow from parental influences. However, because of characteristics of psychological essentialism and color preferences in our society, socialization influences may work to overcome racist tendencies rather than to instill them. Tendencies toward racism are suggested by several social-psychological mechanisms. Processes for managing the terror of death anxiety may cause us to exaggerate differences between our own racial groups and others, thereby paving the way for racism based on in-group preferences and social identity influences. The ecology of social perception suggests that skin color affords certain perceptions that are quite similar across racial groups. However, those same groups show race-specific attunements in how they perceive both their own and other groups. The tendency to see a correspondence between internal attributes and overt behavior as a causal, explanatory connection is suggested to be a cultural correlate of our individualistic society. This correspondence bias heightens the likelihood that psychological or biological essentialism will dominate our perception of racial groups.

Finally, we observed that individual racism is as much a matter of own-race privilege as it is the denial of dignity to others. This piece of the equation often goes unexamined. The subtle manifestations of race in a racialized society makes us all, every individual, vulnerable to racism. As we noted at the beginning of this chapter, assessing only *specific events* in terms of racism misses the bigger picture and unnecessarily fans the flames of discord. There is wide variability in personal experiences, values, beliefs, and desire to avoid the biased attitudes and behaviors described here as individual racism. By focusing on what constitutes racism and encourages its development and perpetuation, we do not intend to diminish the importance of personal values and behavior that enable people to regard and behave toward others in positive and humane ways. The following two chapters suggest ways in which individuals' racial sentiments and behaviors are influenced by their participation in social institutions and follow from an overarching racial cultural edifice.

15

Understanding Racism II: Institutional Racism

❖

Introduction ◆ Defining institutional racism ◆ *Institutional racism—Economics* ◆
Institutional racism—Education ◆ *Institutional racism—Media* ◆ *Institutional
racism—Justice* ◆ *Institutional racism—Physical and mental health* ◆ Affirmative action—Remedy for institutional racism? ◆ Summary

> *When the adverse impact of bias-free practices occur in a society where . . . [it] is
> in significant part either a result of overt racism, or a contribution to its
> perpetuation, then that is . . . racist impact [and is] . . . characteristic of
> institutional racism.*
>
> Gertrude Ezorsky (1991, p. 10)

INTRODUCTION

Institutional racism describes the differential impact of institutional practices on racial minority groups or individuals who belong to them. Two things make institutional racism so pernicious and important:

1   The effects of the racism are magnified many fold by virtue of the institutionalization of the adverse impacts. An individual may dislike a person because of his or her race, and may, for example, call her names, or give him a poor job rating, or refuse to hire him. But, when an institutional practice or policy systematically disadvantages a racial group and its members, then the consequences spread far and wide and reproduce themselves over the years.
2   When institutional practices or policies systematically create disadvantage for racial minority groups and their members, it doesn't really matter what any

436

specific person's *intentions* were. For example, seniority is a "bias-free" concept, or at least a rational basis for a policy. But when overt racial bias has excluded certain racial groups from competing for jobs over hundreds of years, how can seniority as an institutional policy be colorblind?

Therefore, institutional racism is significant because its effects are widespread and because they can result either from overt racism by an individual, or from a negative race-based policy, or as a systematic racial effect of a bias-free practice or policy.

The "peculiar institution" of slavery (Stampp, 1956) was an overt form of institutional racism. The laws and practices of slavery bound up both slaves and slave owners in the exploitation of black labor, the undermining of black families, the denial of formal education, and the general withholding of opportunities that defined the very purpose of the American Revolution and the creation of this "more perfect Union."

The *American Dilemma* (Myrdal, 1944) pointed out what de Toqueville had observed centuries earlier—the contradiction inherent in the U.S. Creed and the facts of systematic racial exploitation and infringement of human rights. That this contradiction, or "dilemma," was built into the Constitution of the United States of America is as much a recognition of institutional racism as any other single fact of our history. This dilemma was reasoned so clearly by Alexander Hamilton and his colleagues in *Federalist Paper No. 54* (Hamilton, Jay, Madison, 1937 [1788]):

> . . . we must deny the fact, that slaves are considered merely as property, and in no respect whatever as persons. The true state of the case is, that they partake of both these qualities: being considered by our laws, in some respects, as persons, and in other respects as property. In being compelled to labor, not for himself, but for a master; in being vendible by one master to another master; and in being subject at all times to be restrained in his liberty and chastised in his body, by the capricious will of another,—the slave may appear to be degraded from the human rank, and classed with those irrational animals which fall under the legal denomination of property. In being protected on the other hand, in his life and in his limbs, against the violence of all others, even the master of his labor and his liberty; and in being punishable himself for all violence committed against others,—the slave is no less evidently regarded by the law as a member of the society, not as a part of the irrational creation; as a moral person, not as a mere article of property. The federal Constitution, therefore, decides with great propriety on the case of our slaves, when it views them in the mixed character of persons and of property. This is in fact their true character. . . . Let the case of the slaves be considered as it is in truth, a peculiar one. Let the compromising expedient of the Constitution be mutually adopted, which regards them as inhabitants, but as *debased by servitude below the equal level of free inhabitants; which regards the slave as divested of two fifths of the man.*[1]

Institutional practice was not compelled to accord African Americans any human rights beyond their debased status as three-fifths of a man by virtue of their enslavement. When exactly is it that this originary disadvantage ceased to exist? Was it when importing slaves was ended in 1809, when slavery was abolished in 1865, when "separate but equal" was given judicial authority in 1896, when "separate but equal" was declared unconstitutional in 1954, or when civil rights and voting rights without regard to race were affirmed in 1964 and 1965? The theory of institutional racism acknowledges the enduring legacy of this disadvantage and seeks to

---

[1] The above quotes were taken from the Modern Library Edition of *The Federalist* (No. 54), with an introduction by Edward Mead Earle.

show how racial differences in opportunities, as well as outcomes, have not completely outdistanced these adverse beginnings.

This chapter will define institutional racism and illustrate it in several domains of institutional life in the United States. Although there are cases where institutional practices reflect *overt racism,* most of our attention will focus on those situations we may call "standards of practice"—that is, processes that are assumed to be appropriate, fair, and reasonable, but that, nevertheless, are associated with adverse racial results. The first section of this chapter will review what we mean by *institutional racism* and give an example of a legislative action (sentencing for drug offenses) that has had an adverse racial impact and the role that economic class may play in institutional racism. The succeeding sections will review evidence and examples of institutional racism in economics, education, media, justice, and health. We will close the chapter with a brief consideration of affirmative action, which is conceived as a remedy to institutional racism of both the bias-free and the overt kinds.

DEFINING INSTITUTIONAL RACISM

In 1970, institutional racism was a new idea. It was characterized by two important considerations: (1) that institutional practices that followed established custom and, even, laws played a major role in the systematic denial of rights and opportunities to people of color, and (2) that, whether the people upholding these practices and even abiding by these laws supported them or not, or intended to deny others opportunities or not, the inequitable consequences of institutional practices were, themselves, indications of institutional racism.

The first edition of this book defined *institutional racism* as follows (Jones, 1972, p. 131):

> . . . those established laws, customs, and practices which systematically reflect and produce racial inequities in American society. If racist consequences accrue to institutional laws, customs, or practices, the institution is racist whether or not the individuals maintaining those practices have racist intentions. Institutional racism can be either overt or covert (corresponding to de jure and de facto, respectively) and either intentional or unintentional.

The basic elements of this definition remain applicable today. Haas (1992, p. 99) offers one of the simplest definitions of institutional racism, which he describes as "the set of policies, practices, and procedures that adversely affect some ethnic [or racial] groups so that they will be unable to rise to a position of equality." The definition does not stipulate anything about the individuals in charge, their racial attitudes, or their intentions. The institutional practices that adversely affect a racial or ethnic group are what matter in understanding institutional racism.

The idea of institutional racism was an important advance over previous racism theories, which typically focused extensively on individuals. According to institutional racism theory, if institutional practices could be changed—by law, policy, or legislation—then the adverse impact of bigoted, prejudiced, and racist individuals could be blunted. The promise of an institutional racism analysis was in its ability to identify a broader remedy to racial bias than the individual targeting of bigots had succeeded in doing. So there was promise that, with this new insight, the 1970s would show dramatic, rapid improvement in the status of blacks and others who had been hampered by discriminatory racial practices.

Institutional racism has two forms—individual-mediated and standard of practice. First, when persons who hold racist beliefs and/or function under the influence of racial stereotypes and prejudicial perceptions and judgments are leaders (i.e., hold decision-making positions within institutions), their influence will tend to promote racial inequality and disadvantage in the outcomes of institutional practices. This form of institutional racism can be thought of as an extension of interpersonal racism and prejudice to the institutional setting (i.e., individual-mediated). What makes it pernicious and critical to the concept of institutional racism is that its effects are magnified by the power of the institution backing the individual to affect a very large number of people's lives.

Second—and this is what raises much of the controversy—institutional practices, albeit not "race-conscious" themselves, may still have "race effects." When these race effects are systematically advantaging to whites and disadvantaging to ethnic and racial minority groups, they represent a *standard of practice* criterion of institutional racism. When *race-conscious intentionality* (i.e., a conscious intention to affect what happens to a person, good or bad, on the basis of his or her race) is not a prerequisite for institutional racism, then moral, ethical, or value judgments are not so readily applied. From this vantage, remedying institutional racism is not so much about converting bigots or firing them, as about rearranging institutional practices to increase the overall equity in the system.

It is also argued that, logically, equality of opportunity ensures *inequality* of results. That is, because differences in ability, motivation, character, experiences, and so forth, will determine results, and because people will differ in these characteristics, the results are bound to reflect these differences. Therefore, some argue, any policy that seeks equality as an outcome must logically compromise the influence of "natural and relevant" differences in abilities in the determination of those results. This is the basic argument Herrnstein (1971) made in the early 1970s. It is recapitulated in *The Bell Curve* (Murray and Herrnstein, 1994). What is at issue is the determination of when equal opportunity exists. The premise behind the development of affirmative action was that removing obstacles to opportunity did not *sui generis* create equality of opportunity. The theory of institutional racism is not so much an argument in support of equality of outcomes, but a demonstration of ways in which equality of *opportunity* is not met by institutional practices.

In the examples that follow, institutional racism will be illustrated in both of these forms. The net effects of institutional racism are not significantly different as a result of which form is operative. But the nature of the problem and the most appropriate remedy are functions of the operative form. The examples are selective and illustrative rather than comprehensive and conclusive. They illustrate how institutional racism works, but do not suggest, necessarily, how pervasive it is in U.S. institutions. First, to understand the distinction between the individual-mediated and the standard of practice types of institutional racism, consider the following case.

Rock Beats Powder—An Illustration of Institutional Racism

To bring the standard of practice type of institutional racism into focus, let's consider enacted legislation that set the criminal penalties for drug possession, use, and distribution. In 1986, the U.S. Congress passed the Anti-Drug Abuse Act. This act included mandatory minimum sentencing for drug trafficking and set the various amounts of drugs in possession required to trigger these mandatory sentences. The Congress discriminated between cocaine as powder and cocaine as a rock ("crack"). For example, under the Act one needed to be caught in possession of *100 times* more powder cocaine than crack cocaine in order to trigger the mandatory sentence.

Derrick Curry was caught in possession of about a one-pound rock of crack cocaine. He was later convicted of cocaine trafficking and was sentenced to 19 years in prison, without possibility of parole. It was his first offense, and, at the time, he was a college student studying criminal justice. He came from a strong, middle-class African American family, and his father was a school principal. Had Derrick been caught with one pound of powdered cocaine, he would have likely been given a suspended sentence or certainly no more than a few years of jail time. Why the difference?

A report from the House Ways and Means Committee in 1913 may provide a clue:

> The cocaine vice has been a potent incentive in driving humbler negroes all over the country to abnormal crimes. (Leiby, 1994)

Although there is much evidence that blacks as a group do not use cocaine more than do whites as a group, there nevertheless seems to be greater danger associated with the involvement of blacks and Latinos in its use as well as in drug trafficking, than of whites. Many legislators argued that crack cocaine was much more dangerous and addictive than was the cocaine in powder form. Medical evidence convincingly rejects this claim. But images of Jamaican, Trinidadian, and Bahamian crack dealers loomed large in the congressional debate, and the deaths of young people from the drug seemed to catalyze Congress to do something dramatic. The fact is that 92 percent of all people convicted for crack cocaine offenses are black! Whites, by contrast, constitute 70 percent of those convicted of powder cocaine offenses. Furthermore, powder cocaine dealers serve shorter sentences, by statute. And, in the drug chain, powder cocaine dealers sell to crack dealers. Go figure.

This illustration is a very good example of the pernicious nature of institutional racism. The intent of the legislative policy is probably not to increase the number of blacks and Hispanics incarcerated nor to keep them in prison for a longer period of time.[2] But those are, in fact, its consequences. Many judges decry this discriminatory outcome, and some refuse to abide by the mandatory minimum-sentencing guidelines. As one U.S. district court judge in St. Louis noted:

> This one provision, the crack statute, has been directly responsible for incarcerating nearly an entire generation of young black American men for very long periods. [It] has created a situation that reeks with inhumanity and injustice. The scales of justice have been turned topsy-turvy so that those masterminds, the kingpins of drug trafficking, escape detection while those whose role is minimal, even trivial, are hoisted on the spears

---

[2] However, we should acknowledge that belief in antiblack conspiracies is not inherently irrational. Government-sponsored injection of syphilis in black men during the 1940s and 1950s has demonstrated the validity of conspiracy fears. Crocker, Broadnax, et al. (1996) have shown that blacks more than whites tend to endorse conspiracy explanations for the presence of AIDS in black communities; the legal problems of black elected officials; and the overall adverse health, economic, and welfare conditions of black people. Moreover, as was noted earlier, among minorities, belief in conspiracy explanations is related to positive personal esteem, as well as to racial identity.

of an enraged electorate and at the pinnacle of their youth are imprisoned for years while the most responsible for the evil of the day remain free. (Leiby, 1994, p. F4)

But institutional racism does not require malice aforethought or racist intention in order to operate. The net effect of this federal statute is an unequal racial liability for convictions that carry longer-term sentences. Institutions provide the context for the work of society. That work may be thought of as providing the *economic* wherewithal to sustain a high standard of living, the *educational* apparatus to inform and train citizens to perform functions that ensure society's continued growth and development, and work that keeps individuals going and society humming. Society maintains *media* institutions to keep its citizens informed and entertained, and *legal* systems to punish those who violate the laws and to protect those whose rights are infringed by lawbreakers. And, when it all becomes too much, we may seek help from *social services* or *mental health* institutions in order to cope with stress or the simple failure to thrive. All of these institutions, as vital as they are to the smooth functioning of society, carry with them the power to develop, sustain, and enforce specific, racialized views of people. As Knowles and Prewitt (1969) suggest, institutions can reward and punish. They are, therefore, central to the chances that we have to enjoy the freedoms and promise of the United States.

Institutional Racism and Class

Before we talk about specific examples of institutional racism in different domains, we need to address the compelling and problematic issue of class. One of the big difficulties we have is disentangling race from class, given that the history of racism has ensured that blacks, in particular, and ethnic minorities in general, are found disproportionately in the lower economic strata. To what extent are the examples of racism cited merely vestiges of racist disadvantage that now manifest themselves in class-related processes? Wilson (1978) brought forth the provocative thesis that economic class origins played a much greater role in determining the life chances of blacks than their race did (cf. Chapter 4). He followed this argument (Wilson, 1987) nearly a decade later by suggesting that the plight of the black urban underclass was better understood as a victimization by macroeconomic forces and poor welfare and poverty policies than as victimization by racial discrimination (cf. Chapter 5). Arguments against affirmative action often end with a statement of support for affirmative action, but in a *raceless* form that considers *only* economic need.

Yet, every day, we see accounts of racist actions, subtle discrimination based on race and ethnicity, and a seemingly unrelenting perpetuation of racialized thought and behavior. How much of what is seen as racial inequalities can be attributed to the cumulative effects of racial inequities now represented in contemporary society as low socioeconomic standing? In the following examples, we will look for ways in which economic standing can be shown to better explain racial outcomes than does race itself. To the extent that class, not race, provides a better explanation for the observed effects, we will discount the operation of institutional racism. To the extent that class cannot explain the pattern of effects, then institutional racism remains a viable explanation of what we observe.

Institutional Racism—Economics

The U.S. economic system is still considered a free enterprise system. It is "free" in that anyone who can raise sufficient capital can engage in entrepreneurial business activity. Through such enterprises, American white men are among the most wealthy in the world. Free enterprise has always been held before Americans as the ideal economic system, the free system, the principal ideal in this land of opportunity—an ideal that prompted hundreds of thousands of Europeans to immigrate to the United States.

Free enterprise without social responsibility was the first active component of racism in the history of the nation. The slave trade began as "enterprising" young commercial seekers left England to explore new lands, waters, and ways of making money. The first stage of slavery was the commercial trade in black bodies that was carried out during the latter half of the seventeenth century. (You will recall that the Wall Street Market first engaged in the trade of black bodies.) Largely in the name of free enterprise did many of the institutionalized forms of racism begin.

An economic corollary of free enterprise is private property. Therefore, those individuals who are successful as entrepreneurs also control the land. Perhaps the *sine qua non* of success in U.S. society is the ownership of land or property. Today, one can drive the entire length of the Eastern seaboard and find precious few stretches of public beach. Most of the choice seaside land is well ensconced in the hands of private-property–no-trespass owners. Because black people have systematically been denied access to the free enterprise system—at least on the enterprising end—it follows that private property has not been a viable reflection or consequence of the integration of blacks into the U.S. economic system.

Race plays a decisive role in home loans, study shows, read a headline in *The Washington Post* (June 6, 1993, p. A24). The *Washington Post* conducted a survey of Washington-area lending practices for 1985 and 1991. Using deeds on sales of single-family homes, town houses, and condominia, it analyzed 134,954 transactions by matching the addresses on each deed with the census data on the zip codes for each address. From the census data, the racial composition of each neighborhood was assessed, and patterns of loan activity were evaluated as a function of the racial composition of the neighborhood. Obviously relevant factors, such as income and number of salable properties, were held constant by means of statistical procedures.

The findings were dramatically clear. Figure 15.1 shows that, in the District of Columbia, the number of mortgages granted per 1,000 properties was an inverse function of the percentage of blacks in the neighborhood. Although this relationship was most dramatic in the District of Columbia itself, it was evident in each jurisdiction tested in the metropolitan area. These figures reflect the lending activity of the most desirable lending institutions, banks, and savings and loans institutions. When such mortgages are not available, consumers turn to private mortgage companies, whose lending rates are typically much higher.

Banks and thrift institutions deny that anything but sound business principles guide their lending decisions.[3] They further suggest that they do business in those neighborhoods where they have branches. However, in Washington, D.C., residents of predominantly white neighborhoods have three times as many bank branches per resident as do residents of predominantly black neighborhoods. Using a statistic reflecting branches per resident as a measure of bank access, *The Washington Post* study found that 74 percent of whites lived in neighborhoods that

---

[3] However, it is certainly ironic that these same savings and loan thrifts had no compunction about loaning large sums to white real estate speculators and entrepreneurs who were, in fact, putting far more money at risk. The result of these *unsound* business practices was a massive failure of savings and loans and a bailout by the federal government using taxpayers' dollars. Therefore, those blacks who are unable to get loans end up paying off, in tax dollars, those thrifts who snubbed them!

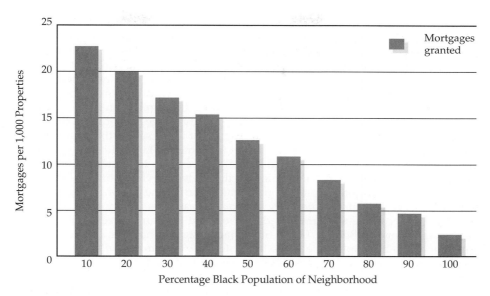

FIGURE 15.1

Granting of Home Mortgages by Banks and S&Ls as Percentage of Blacks in the Neighborhood. *Source:* Based on Figure 1 from *The Washington Post,* June 6, 1993, p. A1.

could be described as having the best or adequate access to banks. By contrast, only 40 percent of blacks lived in neighborhoods with good access, and a majority of them (60%) lived in neighborhoods with the worst access. There is no doubt that income level plays a role in the decision to locate bank branches in a given neighborhood, and, as Willie Sutton would advise, it is best to locate banks where the money is.

Robert Freeman, chairman of Signet Bank, was forthcoming in discussing the issue of racial bias in banking. Freeman argued that discrimination and bias are facts of this society: "We all carry thousands of pieces of baggage of bias that has built up over a lifetime—whether it's been taught or whether it's just been assimilated (quoted in Brenner and Spayd, 1993, p. A1). He described the process in these familiar terms (Freeman, quoted in *The Washington Post,* June 8, 1993, p. A1):

> A mother and her child are walking down the street and a black male is coming down the street. What happens? The mother squeezes her child's hand and pulls the child close. To me, this is one of the classic examples of how biases get built in at the very youngest age . . . that stays in the psyche somewhere.

Freeman extends this analysis to the banking industry and concludes that "it's the lens that can make blacks appear less creditworthy and black neighborhoods less stable." Freeman is not a social psychologist, nor does he know all the data on racial biases in perception. But he does understand the processes of racial bias, as well as their likely influence on institutional practices and their racial consequences.

But things really hang together in this society—that is, if one misses out at the first levels of economic viability, one finds oneself slipping further and further behind at every succeeding level. Having missed out on the enterprise system, blacks, as a group, missed out on property ownership. By not having property, blacks miss out on all of the advantages property ownership can provide. For example, when one owns one's home, the mortgage payments include a large percentage of interest. That interest can be deducted from taxable income. The net effect is that monthly mortgage payments, in addition to creating equity in the home, also diminish one's federal income tax liability. Paying the same monthly amount for rental property gives one neither equity nor tax advantage. In addition, the home-owning family has the possibility of realizing profit in the sale of the house at some future time. Moreover, when consumer debt (which is *not* tax deductible) gets high, home equity loans (which *are* tax deductible) can be taken to reduce them. The spiral continues, and, again, black people find themselves paying more for less.

The 1980s brought a formal conceptualization to the historical operation of capitalism in the United States—*trickle-down theory*. This theory (also known as "supply-side economics"), articulated by President Reagan's director of the Office of Management and Budget, David Stockman, suggests that stimulating the economy and those at the pinnacle of the free enterprise system will *ultimately* improve the lot for those on the lower rungs of the economic ladder. That is, a rising economic tide will "lift all boats." So, the trickle-down theory suggests that we stimulate the economy by putting more money in the hands of entrepreneurs and credit-worthy, high-income consumers, and by lowering capital gains penalties and generally reducing taxes. At the same time, it suggests that we diminish the drag on the economy, represented now by the trillions of dollars of national debt, by reducing   federal spending, a significant proportion of which is entitlement spending. Entitlement spending typically goes to those most in need of help (e.g., funding for welfare, health insurance for children, aid to the elderly, and aid to needy college students and their families). Racial and ethnic minorities are more likely to be recipients of jobs in the public sector, to live in cities that benefit from federal contributions to urban areas, and to be recipients of federal assistance. They are also correspondingly less likely to participate in the capitalist end of economic activity. This trickle-down process is seen, almost by design, to increase the burden and decrease the prospects for racial and ethnic minorities.

Jobs—the Life Blood of Economic Life

There were roughly 123,300,000 civilians in the U.S. labor force in 1994. Nearly half were white men (46%), and nearly 40 percent were white women (37.4%)—making a total of about 83 percent whites. Blacks (men and women) were about 10 percent, and Hispanics (Mexicans, Puerto Ricans, and Cubans only) were about 6 percent. Of these members of the labor force, 9,200,000 were unemployed (7%). Although whites were 83 percent of the labor force, they constituted only 71 percent of the unemployed. Blacks constituted nearly 20 percent of the unemployed; this was double their representation in the labor force. Hispanics were 1.5 times more likely to be unemployed than their numbers in the labor force would suggest. So, both blacks and Hispanics are proportionately less likely to have a job than are whites.

The distribution of the most common category of jobs comprising primarily technical, sales, and administrative support positions (e.g., secretaries, bank clerks, mail carriers) for the various racial groups is quite similar. Figure 15.2 shows that 31 percent of whites, 28 percent of blacks, and 25 percent of Hispanics hold such jobs. However, the second most frequent occupational categories diverge for the different groups. For whites, executives, professionals, and managers constitute the second

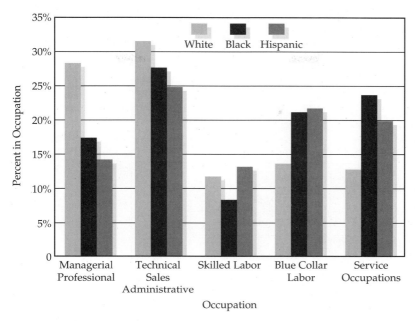

FIGURE 15.2

Percentage of U.S. Workers by Occupation and Race—1993. *Source:* Russel, C. (1995) *The official guide to the American Marketplace, second edition.* Ithaca, NY: New Strategist Publications. p. 301.

most numerous category in the labor force (28.1%). Among blacks, service positions (e.g., police, waiters, hairdressers) constitute the second most common occupational category (23.5%), and, among Hispanics blue-collar jobs (e.g., operators, fabricators, and laborers) constitute the second most common occupational category (22%).

It would not be surprising that the consequence of occupying the lower-paying and lower-status jobs is a lower average income. As Figure 15.3 shows, median household income for blacks in 1992 was 58 percent that of whites ($18,660 for blacks compared to $32,368 for whites)(Russell, 1995).[4] To put it in real terms, for every $1 of income a white household earns, a black household can only expect to earn 58 cents! There is some good news though. Since 1980, the growth in income for blacks and whites has remained low but comparable (1.7% for blacks and 1.6% for whites). But even that news is tainted by the fact that, between 1990 and 1992, although household income fell for both whites and blacks, it fell almost twice as much for blacks (–6.9%) as for whites (–3.5%).

The story for Hispanics is also a mixed one. Median household income for Hispanics was $22,848, which was less than that for whites (70%), and more than that for blacks (122%). But, between 1980 and 1992, household income overall actually declined by 1.8 percent. Between 1980 and 1992, however, Hispanic household income declined by 4.7 percent.

---

[4] This is only slightly better than 1959, when the black-white family-income ratio was 52 percent. In the 1970s, it improved to 64 percent, but began to decline again in the 1980s, standing at 55 percent in 1982 (cf. Farley, 1984).

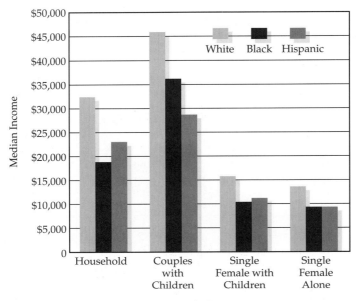

FIGURE 15.3

Household Income by Race and Family Structure—1992. *Source:*
Russel, C. (1995) *The official guide to the American Marketplace, second
edition.* Ithaca, NY: New Strategist Publications. p. 283–285.

It is well-documented that being a single parent, in general, reduces one's
household income, and black households are disproportionately single-female-
headed households. The median household income of a single black woman with
children under 18 is $10,393. However, if she has a husband, the household income
is more than tripled, to $36,357. The disparity is that the black single mom has an
average of only 66 percent of the income of a white single mom. The good news is
that the racial gap is closed when the household income for married couples with
children is considered (black families make 80 percent of what white families
make). However, we still see that a white couple and their children earn $1,
whereas a black family is only earning 80 cents.

Although we often highlight the welfare-dependent, single black woman with
children as the worst-case scenario, such a woman's income ratio relative to her
white counterpart is not as bad as the overall average of 58 percent. In fact, the lowest incomes of all in each racial group are those of women living alone (white,
$13,413; black, $9,092; and Hispanic, $9,136). Interestingly, whereas, overall, His-
panic households earned more than black households did, when married couples
with children are considered, blacks earn more than Hispanics do ($36,357 vs.
$28,379). The Hispanic advantage overall is due to the fact that a higher percentage
of Hispanics live in two-adult households.

The bottom line here, though, is that when we control for household composition, things look better for blacks, and about the same for Hispanics, relative to
whites. However, in the best-case scenario, substantial disparities are still observed.

Cultural Capital versus Racial Discrimination?
Cultural capital is a relatively new label for those attributes and characteristics a person possesses that are thought to promote cultural advancement. In our society, we count education, intellectual ability, and skills as among the most important sources of cultural capital. Racial disparities, some would argue (e.g., D'Souza, 1995), reduce simply to differences in cultural capital—and not to racial discrimination. Therefore, when we match people of different races on sources of cultural capital, racial differences should disappear.

Abdel-Ghany and Sharpe (1994) evaluated this hypothesis in their analysis of wage differences between blacks and whites. Their procedure involved a complex statistical analysis that evaluated the racial gap in wages (measured using mean hourly wage in dollars) after controlling for cultural capital variables such as educational attainment, job tenure, knowledge of the world of work, and military experience. Also controlled were job-related characteristics that are expected to affect wages, such as urban or suburban residence, region of the country, occupation (e.g., managerial, clerical, sales) and industry (e.g., agriculture, manufacturing, and entertainment). The results showed that there was a black-white wage gap of $2.57 per hour (black = $8.25, white = $10.82). Blacks earned an average of 76 percent of what whites earned for the same work. But, what is important is that, in some cases, only 16 percent of the discrepancy could be explained by differences in skills. The remaining 84 percent of the black-white wage gap can be explained only by factors of unknown relationship to the job, including racial discrimination. In the best cases, as much as 60 percent of the differential was explained by differences in skill levels. This *good news* still leaves us with the fact that 32 percent of the race-based wage differential is attributable to discriminatory factors.

In the Abdel-Ghany and Sharpe (1994) analysis, a distinction can be made between the adverse impact of discrimination on blacks and the advantage the discrimination against blacks gives to whites. In most cases, the white male *advantage* explained more of the racial gap than did the black male *disadvantage*. The arguments against affirmative action always fear that less competent minorities and women will be hired over more competent white males. These data suggest that the system now operates to *favor* white males. That is, arguments for preserving the status quo serve to maintain white privilege! The study of institutional racism seeks to redress racial disparities by a variety of different mechanisms. This study suggests that redressing racial bias is as much a matter of reducing white privilege as of enhancing minority opportunity.

The economic picture is a very grim one. Although institutional racism is not responsible for all forms of inequality, it has been a persistent contributor to the unequal racial, ethnic, and gender distribution of jobs and income and access to available economic opportunities. It is important to note that it is not simply the overt race-based discrimination that limits opportunities, but also those institutional policies and procedures that maintain a status quo that already reflects the unequal opportunity inherited by racial, ethnic and gender groups.

Institutional Racism—Education

A report of the National Science Foundation Human Capital Initiative Task Force made the following observation:

> The human capital of a nation is a primary determinant of its strength. A productive and educated workforce is a necessity for long-term economic growth. Worker productivity depends on the effective use and development of the human capital of all citizens, which means schools, families, and neighborhoods must function effectively. Unfortunately, there is substantial evidence that the United States is not developing or using the skills of its citizens as fully as possible. (Blank, 1994)

Education is a major contributor to the human capital necessary for continued growth and development of the United States. As the report of the United Nations Development Programme (1993) suggested (cf. Chapter 13, p. 365), we are not realizing our full potential as a nation, in part because our black and Latino citizens do not enjoy the same status and outcomes that white citizens do.

The economic metaphor of capitalism applies to education in the United States. The currency in education is knowledge, skills, and understanding. *Human capital* describes the possession of the knowledge, skills, and understanding that allow a person to contribute to the well-being of society. To the extent that our educational institutions fail to prepare students for productive roles in our society, society, as well as the students themselves, is the worse for it.

Education is an enormous enterprise in the United States, and we can only scratch the surface in talking about it here. As with the economic system, there are large-scale racial disparities both in educational opportunities and educational outcomes. The question of racism arises when disparities are linked, in some systematic way, to discrimination or to standards of educational practice that limit opportunity and/or diminish educational outcomes.

Some Racial Gaps in Educational Outcomes
The first measure of educational outcome is, "How much of it do you get?" As a general statement, whites get more of it than blacks, who get more of it than Hispanics. Figure 15.4 shows that, for men, 82 percent of whites, 76 percent of blacks, and 53 percent of Hispanics have graduated from high school by age 25. The figures for women are very similar. And, with respect to earning a college degree, for men, 26 percent of whites, 12 percent of blacks, and 9 percent of Hispanics have achieved that level of education by age 25. The numbers are slightly lower for white women (20%) and Hispanic women (8%), but slightly higher for black women (12.4%). The percentage earning college degrees in the youngest cohort (ages 25 to 34) declined relative to the next oldest cohort (ages 35 to 44) for all groups except Hispanic women. The decline was actually greatest for white men. On balance, though, the absolute level of educational attainment in years continues to show whites well ahead of both blacks and Hispanics by more than 2 to 1.

Another indication of educational attainment is reflected in achievement, as measured by performance on the Scholastic Assessment Test (SAT). Figure 15.5 shows that from 1975–1976 to 1991–1992, for all students, SAT scores on the Verbal portion of the test declined by an average of 8 points, whereas on the Mathematical portion of the test, scores increased by 4 points. Blacks showed bigger gains than any other racial or ethnic group (20 points on Verbal and 31 points on Mathematical). Other minority groups also registered gains on the Mathematical portion of the SAT. (Mexican Americans, 15 points; Puerto Ricans, 5 points; Asian Americans, 14 points; and Native Americans, 22 points.)

For blacks, higher performance is the good news. The bad news is that they still lag behind all other racial and ethnic groups in both the Verbal and Mathematical SATs. The debate continues as to the causes of these deficits. *The Bell Curve*

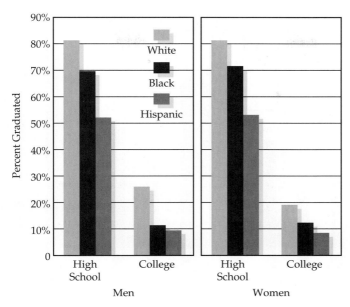

FIGURE 15.4

Educational Attainment by Race—1993. Men and Women Age 25 and Older. *Source:* Russel, C. (1995) *The official guide to the American Marketplace, second edition.* Ithaca, NY: New Strategist Publications. p. 261.

(Murray and Herrnstein, 1994) argues it is inherited deficiencies that explain the lower scores. Other writers propose a variety of environmental or context explanations ranging from inferior schooling, to poor prenatal care, to test bias, to cultural differences in learning styles.

When do the effects of systematic institutional racism in education wear off? That is, when can we no longer explain racial differences in educational performance by the cumulative legacy of a biased and racist educational system? Among the principles of our admittedly naive notions of scientific explanation are that (1) the magnitude of effects is generally matched by the magnitude of their causes— that is, little causes have small effects, large causes have big effects; and (2) causes occur near in time to the effects they produce. This latter principle of causation makes it difficult for us to understand how historical oppression, such as slavery and the systematic denial of education for blacks, could explain the current race gap in performance. It also makes it difficult for many young whites, in particular, to see how the sins of their foreparents could privilege them today.

There is much debate and controversy about schooling in the United States. It is often now argued that public schooling has failed and that privatization of schools or parental choice through a voucher system is the only way to fix it. It is evident, though, that historically schooling for African Americans and Native Americans, in particular, has been designed as an impediment to the growth of human capital.

Trends in Schooling

Education has always been bound closely to racism in this country. During the era of slavery, many Southern states had laws that forbade teaching slaves to read. It

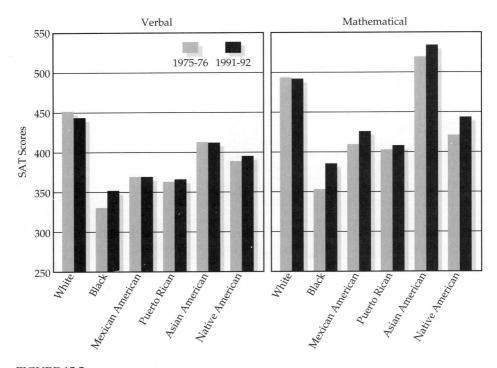

FIGURE 15.5

SAT Scores by Race—1976 and 1992. *Source:* Russel, C. (1995) *The official guide to the American Marketplace, second edition.* Ithaca, NY: New Strategist Publications. p. 265.

was felt that reading knowledge might create a rebellious spirit:[5] When slaves were taught to read, it was usually to read the Bible. Under these circumstances, reading was countered by religious instruction that promoted the values of black servitude and humble obedience to white authority.

In the North, belief in the inferiority of blacks led many abolitionists to argue for segregated schooling on the basis of a belief that blacks could not compete with whites. Later, when public schools were formally segregated and monies were distributed unevenly to black and white schools, arguments for racial integration were made. However, by then, the racial cleavages had become firmly entrenched.

These brief notes are presented to illustrate the simple point that educational institutions, in common with all other institutions in this society, reflect the nation's racist beginnings. There are several ways in which institutional racism affects educational institutions:

1   Inferior education is provided to those children who do not fit the white, middle-class, Anglo–based model of a young learner because of fewer resources and poor understanding of children's cultural capital.
2   Teachers tend not to teach racially and ethnically different children well because of the teachers' prejudices, stereotypes, and racist attitudes and beliefs.

[5] According to Herbert Aptheker (1969), slaves were rebelling from the beginning of their period of bondage. It seems reading was not necessary to that rebellious spirit

3   White children are miseducated about their racist heritage and black children about positive aspects of their racial history.

Education Opposes Cultural Capital of Learners
Boykin (1994) has focused on the question of why lower-income African American children as a group do so poorly in school. He suggests that public education evolved in the twentieth century in order to serve corporate and industrial interests. Public education was seen as having two goals—training young people to take their place in this world and identifying those who were best prepared or had the most talent. This view of public education Boykin calls the *talent assessment model*. African American children, American Indian children, and Latino children were generally already "pigeonholed" for positions in society that required less talent and assumed lower capacity. In my high school in the 1950s, for example, all but a very few African Americans were put into "shop" and "home ec" curricula instead of "college prep." This ensured that African American high school graduates would have less knowledge, fewer skills, and less understanding than comparable white students would. So, when talent is assessed, students from these groups are typically found to have less of it—in part, because they have been systematically steered into adult roles that *require* less of it.

Boykin (1994) suggests that talent assessment approaches perpetuate a racially biased status quo and argues that a more appealing approach would be *talent development*. By that he means a commitment to "generating broad-based, pervasive academic (broadly defined) competence among our students" (Boykin, 1994, p. 119). Talent development will depend critically on acknowledging that educational outcomes will be best when they recognize the following educational principles:

1   Thinking occurs in context and is linked to specific situations with specific meanings, goals, and outcomes.
2   Thinking follows from personal frames of reference; these are the implications and consequences that a person envisions or brings to the thinking process.
3   Children have "conceptual competence," which is based on implicit or intuitive understandings that may or may not translate to conventional language and expressions of knowledge.
4   Motivation arises from both the internal needs, wants, and desires and the external demands and possibilities of the setting.

The result of this way of thinking is an *integrated* learning environment in which the cultural capital of the child is recognized and utilized in the pedagogical strategies employed in school. Rather than simply finding those children whose experiences, tendencies, and talents match those being sought, the talent development model suggests that we *cultivate,* or *harvest,* those talents that children bring to the situation or that are latent in the cultural capital they bring with them to learning contexts.

It is argued that each cultural group (e.g., Latinos, American Indians, Asians, and African-Americans) has a cultural base that is integral to its experience. Schooling will be more successful when it takes that into account than when it does not. To illustrate, one variable Boykin (1994) and colleagues explored is *communalism*—that is, a belief in the fundamental interdependence of people, the importance of social bonds, and the transcendence of the group. Albury and Boykin (1993) tested the vocabulary performance of low-income, fourth-grade black and white children in three-person, same-race groups under one of four test conditions:

1 *Individual*—Any child getting 18 or more out of 25 words correct won a prize.
2 *Interpersonal competition*—The child in each of three groups who got the most right won a prize.
3 *Group competition*—Each group of three was competing with other three-member groups for a prize.
4 *Communal*—No reward was offered, but children within groups were encouraged to work together, and sharing and helping was reinforced.

Results depicted in Figure 15.6 show that the conditions for best performance varied as a function of the children's race. White children performed best in the two individual conditions (individual and interpersonal competition) and worst in the communal condition. Black children, by contrast, performed best in the group conditions (best in communal and next in group competition), and worst in the individual condition. Moreover, these performance differences were also associated with racial differences in liking and preferences. Black children liked the group study conditions and their study partners better than white children did. White children preferred working alone and reached the most creative results when they did so.

Classroom instruction is influenced by three elements: task structure (what

FIGURE 15.6
Verbal Learning Performance for Black and White Fourth-Graders as a Function of Individual, Competitive, and Communal Learning Conditions. *Source:* Albury and Boykin, 1993, Figure 1.

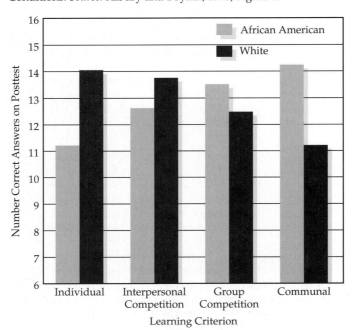

kids do in class, such as listen to lecture, do seat work, discuss), reward structure (grades, teacher approval, prizes), and authority structure (relative control exercised by students, teachers, or other adults) (Slavin, 1980). The degree to which the interpersonal reward structures (the consequences for a student of a classmate's performance) are cooperative (positive interdependence such that one student's success helps another to be successful) or competitive (negative interdependence such that one student's success is linked to another's failure) has been shown to have a direct bearing on performance (Slavin, 1995). In general, cooperative learning contexts produce better performance in racially and ethnically homogeneous, integrated, or working class schools than in middle-class, predominantly white schools. However, several studies have demonstrated improved achievement for white middle-class students in cooperative learning contexts as well (cf. Slavin, 1995). The importance of cultural context on learning has been demonstrated by Ramirez and Castenda (1974) for Mexican Americans and Ellis and Gauvain (1992) for American Indians, in addition to the Albury and Boykin (1993) findings for African Americans. Cultural differences in norms and values intersect classroom pedagogy and have the potential to place students at risk for lower educational outcomes when they are not taken into account or are openly rejected.

Racist Attitudes and Beliefs of Teachers Undermine Both Teaching and Learning
Students are very sensitive to the expectations others hold for them. As we discussed in Chapter 10, Steele and Aronson (1995; see also, Spencer and Steele, 1996) showed that the fear of confirming in oneself the negative stereotype that a teacher or a generalized other may have of one's racial, ethnic, or gender group can undermine performance. We also saw, in Chapter 13, that racial identification can be perceived as a hindrance to academic performance. Arroyo and Zigler (1995) showed that academic performance in adolescents was, in fact, positively related to a student's acceptance of a *raceless* identity. Taken together, these studies suggest that thinking about one's race in a racially polarized and stigmatized environment can undermine performance, and reducing the salience of one's race may enhance it in such a situation. Internalization of a culturally discordant standard of achievement tends to alienate racial and ethnic minority children from the learning process.

The classic study by Rosenthal and Jacobson (1968) showed just how insidious teacher attitudes can be. Teachers at a South San Francisco school were told that certain children (randomly picked) were "potential academic spurters." The results of IQ and other subject tests administered at the beginning of the school year, led Rosenthal and Jacobson (1968, p. 121) to conclude that the evidence ". . . suggests rather strongly that children who are expected by their teachers to gain intellectually in fact do show greater intellectual gains after one year than do children of whom such gains are not expected." However, this effect was qualified in several ways. First, it was only for first and second graders that the differences were large enough to be statistically significant. Expectancy students showed average gains of 27.4 and 16.5 IQ points, respectively, for first and second graders compared with gains of only 12.0 and 7.0 for the corresponding control students. There were no significant differences for grades three through six. However, by the end of two years, these younger children had lost their expectancy advantage, but the advantage continued to grow for children in the higher grades. Finally, in the Oak School, Mexican Americans were the prominent minority group. The expectancy effects were stronger for Mexican than Anglo students, but they were not statistically significant. However, an independent rating of "Mexican-ness" of the children's faces was shown to correlate significantly with expectancy advantage. "After one year, and after two years, those boys who looked more Mexican benefited more from their teachers' positive prophesies" (Rosenthal and Jacobson, 1968, p. 177). If a student is expected to do well, then his or her improved performance will be positively regarded and lead to an overall halo effect where teachers perceive these students as ". . . significantly more likely to succeed in the future, as more interesting, as showing greater intellectual curiosity, and as happier" (p. 108).

We must take note of the argument that IQ is stable and flows from family genes. In this experiment, nothing was done to the kids at all—no remedial math, no extra reading classes, no home visits. Nonetheless, students' IQs went up as much as 27 points when teachers were merely advised that these kids could and were likely to do well. Teacher expectations play an enormous role in how children learn. Therefore, a child may expect to do better in school, to learn more, and to be liked and evaluated more highly simply because the teacher expects positive things from him or her. There are great advantages to having a teacher who thinks highly of you!

The flip side was not directly studied. Teachers were not told that a randomly selected set of children could *not* learn and were doomed to poor performance. To do this would be unethical, but it is easy to imagine the natural experiment that takes place regularly in classrooms where teachers have negative expectations of the ability of certain children. Although this manipulation was not tried, we do have information on children in the control group. For children about whom nothing was said about "spurting," those who made real IQ gains were rated *unfavorably* by their teachers—the more so, the greater their improvement. These unexpected gains in intellectual performance led teachers to rate those students as less well adjusted, less happy, and less affectionate. More recent research has shown that black male elementary school students who show marked improvement in response to tutoring are more disliked by their tutors (personal communication, Richard Nisbett, May 20, 1996). This is a complicated story, but suggests a kind of catch-22. If you are under suspicion of low intellectual ability (e.g., being Mexican or African American and male) and you work hard and improve your performance, you run the risk of being judged harshly. It seems that, perhaps, student performance that disconfirms a stereotype of low ability causes discomfort for some teachers, and their attempts to reduce this discomfort could come at the peril of the students they are trying to teach. Those students from racial and ethnic minority groups who carry with them stereotypically low performance expectations may be most vulnerable to this process. This then is another aspect of the institutionalized form of racism.

Beyond noting that the "Pygmalion effect" (i.e., teacher's expectations influence student's performance) exists, it is not easily detectable how the influences are transmitted. It seems obvious that some rather subtle form of nonverbal communication is going on; that is, somehow the teacher communicates confidence and support and thereby facilitates academic growth.

The Pygmalion effect also suggests that students are highly sensitive to nonverbal cues emitted by the teachers. Remember the automatic processing effects and subtle behavioral responses to activation of stereotypes described in Chapter 6. It is entirely plausible that teachers' stereotypes will prompt subtle behavioral and nonverbal cues that are detected by children. As Word, Zanna, and Cooper (1974) showed, racial biases can produce a performance decrement that justifies and rationalizes the preexisting prejudice. Institutional effects magnify these interpersonal processes, especially in schools, where life opportunities hang so delicately in the balance.[6]

Miseducating about the Racial Past

One of the most damaging aspects of the entire education process has been miseducation of all children. Two narratives trace the development of the United States. In one, the courageous settlers carve out a life and a nation in the new world. This story extols the virtues of British settlers and their Anglo-Saxon cultural traditions. It is a source of pride and virtue for Americans who claim European heritage. A second narrative tells a story of *uncivilized* Africans and Native Americans, whose savagery and primitiveness are elevated by contact with Europeans (see Chapter 13 for early accounts of these beliefs). In each of these narratives, women are described as incapable of leadership or independent action either by temperament or *natural* law (as divined by mortal men). The lessons of history teach us why there is a social hierarchy and justify the ordering of racial-ethnic and gender groups in our society.

The biased consequence of an educational process based on these narrative foundations is a one-sided story. It portrays the European-based cultural tradition in uniformly positive terms, failing to speak directly and forcefully about the subjugation, oppression, and inhumanity directed toward fellow human beings. It simultaneously fails to acknowledge the virtuous qualities of those oppressed and subjugated people. Their intelligence, strong cultural traditions, spirituality, artistic sensibilities, and resilience go unexamined. As we saw in Chapters 12 and 13, racism is predominantly a matter of belief in one's own racial superiority. Our history lessons reaffirm these beliefs and selectively tell the stories that confirm them.

U.S. history teaches the doctrine of *Manifest Destiny*, which, in its essence, pits Western Civilization against American Indian and African savagery and primitiveness. Education was a "civilizing" process for Indians in the U.S. mind (Adams, 1988):

> Savage and civilized life cannot live and prosper on the same ground. One of the two must die. . . . To civilize them, which was once only a benevolent fancy, has now become an absolute necessity, if we mean to save them. (from 1881 by the Commissioner of Indian Affairs, Henry Price, and Secretary of the Interior, Carl Shurz; Quoted in Adams, 1988, p. 172).

Adams suggested that the civilizing mission toward the end of the nineteenth century could be described in three objectives:

1   Setting boundaries that separated education from the countervailing forces of *savagery*; hence, day schools were rejected in favor of boarding schools.
2   Education was a comprehensive cultural make-over including dress, grooming, language, attitudes, and values.
3   Making the student embrace the essential elements of the civilization-savagism distinction, presumably opting for *civilization*.

---

[6] There are real and difficult problems in classrooms that are not all the fault of teachers. Children often come to school unprepared to learn by any method of instruction. No matter how motivated and believing a teacher is, some children will resist learning and will promote similar attitudes in their peers. We do not want to suggest a one-way casual chain here. A full account of the intricacies and complexities of schooling for children at risk for poor academic outcomes is a subject better treated in-depth elsewhere.

To illustrate this last point, Adams (1988, pp. 175–176) provides an account of a question-and-answer section from an exam of an Indian student at Hampton Institute in Virginia in 1885.

Questions:	Student Answers:
9 To what race do we all belong?	The human race
10 How many classes belong to this race?	There are five large classes belonging to the human race.
11 Which are the first?	The white people are the strongest.
12 Which are the next?	The Mongolians or yellows.
13 The next?	The Ethiopian or blacks.
14 Next?	The Americans or reds.
15 Tell me something of the white people.	The Caucasian is away ahead of all the other races—he thought more than any other race, he thought that somebody must have made the earth, and if the white people did not find that out, nobody would never know it—it is God who made the world.

Of course, we could claim that we no longer would find such a thing in a classroom. But when do such effects dissipate in the collective minds of Americans?

Indian education? Two Indian boys studying in a dormitory room of Carlisle, Pennsylvania, Indian School c. 1900. (The Bettmann Archive)

Certainly, this civilization-savage distinction was not extinguished by the Western movies of the 1950s and 1960s!

Institutional Racism—Media

One of the most significant consequences of both forms of institutional racism is the magnitude of its effects. Most important, these effects extend not only to the targets of racism, but to those most likely to manifest the racism. For example, stereotypes sustain both prejudice and racism. For many Americans, contact with members of targeted groups is limited to what they hear from others (cf. van Dijk, 1987) and what they read, hear, or see in print, on radio or television, or in movie theaters about them. The video *Color Adjustment* (1991) illustrates the portrayals of blacks on television from Amos-n-Andy and Buleah, to Bill Cosby in *I Spy*, Diahann Carroll in *Julia*, to Jaleel White as Erkel in *Family Matters*, to Bill Cosby in *The Cosby Show*. The video shows that, over the years, movies and television have portrayed blacks as superstitious, lazy, ignorant, and submissive. Later, they became stereotyped as angry, defiant, hostile, prone toward violence. They later became stereotyped as just silly, then as super upper-middle class.

American Indians, when portrayed at all, have been portrayed as violent and sneaky, and possessing a culture that is at best, undercivilized. Latinos are depicted far less often. But, when they do appear, they are often portrayed as sneaky, unintelligent, and somewhat servile. Asians are usually depicted as inscrutable or servile, although often possessed of great wisdom, as well. Women have been typically shown as subservient to men, emotional, or targets of violent, obsessive, and possessive men. And when they are portrayed as successful, they are often deviant or use their family to get ahead. Somehow, these portrayals all support the notion that the depicted groups are not like white male Americans and, because of their difference, not as good.

These media portrayals raise an interesting question: Do they follow from the way society views members of these groups, or do they dictate how members of these groups will be viewed by society? Truth can be found in a synthesis of both points of view. The media portrayals may support and sustain racialistic beliefs and perceptions and may also help to create them. The media, as an instrument of culture, operates as a conditioning agent of future perceptions and . . . a reflection of the behavioral and attitudinal consequences of racialistic cultural history on members of society.

To these fictionalized portrayals are added the real-time depictions of poor, lawbreaking ethnic and racial minorities. The same is largely true of whites, as that seems to be the media's understanding of what makes news. But sociopsychological research shows that, when one is a member of a numerical minority group and engages in behavior that others view as unusual (at least, in behavior that they are not likely to have first-hand experience of), the connection between the group members and the behavior is amplified via illusory correlation (Hamilton and Gifford, 1976; Hamilton and Sherman, 1994). Therefore, the result of a negative orientation to news is not the same for members of minority groups as it is for members of a majority group.

The power of the media, then, is that it both reflects and creates images of minority-group members and women that lead to stereotypical perceptions and, often, biasing expectations and behaviors. The effects are massive, because the institutional reach is vast. Moreover, the public media have become a significant element of our culture and, hence, an instrument of cultural expressions of racialized worldviews. (We will consider this aspect of cultural racism in the next chapter.)

Institutional Racism—Justice

> I pledge allegiance to the Flag of the United States of America. And to the Republic for which it stands. One Nation, under God, indivisible with Liberty *and Justice for All.* (*emphasis added*)

The administration of justice begins with law enforcement officers. It does not begin on a very just note. In the 1960s, major U.S. cities had an average white population of 65 percent, but an average police department that was 95 percent white. Put the other way, although nonwhite city residents accounted for about 35 percent of the population, they contributed only 5 percent of the policemen. In reaction to this kind of inequality and the blatant, brutal exploitation that too frequently followed, the Black Panther Party was organized in Oakland, California, and the Deacons for Defense and Justice were organized in Louisiana. Given these lopsided statistics, it is not surprising that residents of black urban communities have often viewed the police as an occupation force.

Although the representation of black and Latinos on police forces of major cities has increased over the past 30 years, there is still strain between the police and the racial and ethnic minority citizens they are to protect. One reason that this enmity persists may be found in the work on social dominance orientation (SDO), which we reviewed in Chapter 8. Sidanius and colleagues (Sidanius, 1993; Sidanius, Liu, Shaw and Pratto, 1994) have studied the extent to which one's SDO level is related to the profession one chooses. They define professions that maintain a social hierarchy or an inegalitarian status quo, with some groups perpetually on top and others not, as *hierarchy enhancing (HE).* By contrast, professions that seek to establish a more egalitarian social culture are defined as *hierarchy-attenuating (HA).* The authors hypothesized that police would likely fall into the HE category, because they maintain law and order which, among other things, is designed to maintain a status quo that is quite hierarchical. Public defenders, on the other hand, seek to protect the "little guy," the person who is low on the social hierarchy. Hence, they are more likely to be HAs. For control purposes, the researchers also considered jurors and college students, whom they expected would fall in between the HE and HA categories.

Sidanius et al. (1994) had subjects complete the SDO scale. Then, after controlling for relevant demographic characteristics (e.g., sex, ethnicity, and social class), they assessed the standing of each group on social dominance. As predicted, police as a group scored higher than all other groups on SDO, and public defenders as a group scored lower than all other groups. This finding reinforces the perception that the police may symbolize the maintenance of inequality for those groups that are lower on the socioeconomic ladder. Obviously, there is a significant association between socioeconomic standing and racial or ethnic status in the United States. This finding suggests that the belief on the part of the enforcers of laws that some groups *should* dominate others contributes to a sense of unfairness and reduced opportunities by blacks and Latinos, in particular. The power to affect people's lives according to racial attitudes and biases, illustrates what we mean by institutional racism.

"What's a Nice Guy Like You Doing on the Police Force"?

Finally, we have a curious example of racial effects in a police department. The following example fits what we called the *standard of practice* type of racism. Henderson (1979) collected personality data from 115 policemen in Cleveland, Ohio. Measures included the Edwards Personality Preference Schedule (EPPS) and the Cattell 16PF. In addition to personality measures, Henderson (1979) obtained performance ratings by these policemen's superior officers, as well as their peers. Table 15.1 shows the correlations between selected personality scores and officer and peer evaluations for the white and the black policemen. The mean scores for black and white policemen were nearly identical on all personality measures, suggesting that black and white policemen share the same basic personality profile. However, the *consequences* of personality diverge as a function of race. First, we note that most of the correlations between personality traits and officer or peer evaluations are close to zero for whites, but significantly higher for blacks. Of the 13 personality traits, only 5 (38%) are higher than .10 for whites, while 11 (85%) are higher than .10 for blacks. Among peers, the divergence is even sharper, where only 4 of 13 whites (31%), but 12 of 13 blacks (92%) exceed a correlation of .10. Therefore, although black and white policemen are similar in personality, other policemen evaluate them differently on the basis of personality.

The nature of the racial differences is striking. There are four dimensions that show some relationship for white policemen. White policemen scoring higher in endurance were more likely to be evaluated negatively, but those rated highly in

TABLE 15.1 CORRELATIONS OF SEVERAL PERSONALITY FACTORS WITH SUPERIOR OFFICER AND PEER RATINGS OF BLACK AND WHITE PATROLMEN

	Whites (N = 75)			Blacks (N = 40)		
EPPS scales	*Officer*	*Peer*	*Mean*	*Officer*	*Peer*	*Mean*
Deference	−.02	−.08	44	**.23**	**.19**	47
Order	**−.11**	−.05	44	**.46**	**.43**	44
Autonomy	−.07	−.03	44	**.37**	**.30**	49
Affiliation	.00	.06	41	**.27**	**.21**	32
Dominance	.00	.08	58	**−.28**	**−.20**	57
Abasement	.03	−.09	35	.05	**.15**	31
Endurance	**−.13**	**−.20**	49	**.31**	**.23**	43
Heterosexuality	**.12**	**.11**	74	**−.55**	**−.45**	72
Aggression	.00	.01	53	**−.13**	−.02	56
16PF scales						
Outgoing, easygoing	**.19**	**.14**	5.6	**−.25**	**−.22**	5.5
Enthusiastic, happy-go-lucky	.00	.01	6.0	**−.17**	**−.11**	5.4
Liberal, free thinking	**.21**	**.28**	5.0	−.04	**−.10**	6.1
Self-sufficient, resourceful	.02	−.02	5.4	**−.19**	**−.13**	5.5

SOURCE: Adapted from Henderson, N.D. (1979). Criterion-related validity of personality and aptitude scales: A comparison of validation results under voluntary and actual test conditions. In C. Spielberger (ed.), *Police selection and evaluation: Issues and techniques.* Westport, CT: Greenwood Publishers Group, p. 190.

heterosexual, outgoing, and liberal-free-thinking traits were evaluated more positively. Black policemen's evaluations on each of these dimensions were the opposite. These evaluations suggest a belief that the type of white policeman wanted is basically different from the kind of black policeman wanted. Moreover, the nature of those differences is that the black policemen who fare best are those who are low in dominance, are not outgoing, have a need to belong, and are deferent. Therefore, by selectively rewarding a certain type of policeman, by race, the system creates a personality profile that minimizes threats from blacks who are most successful.

In the colorblind approach, we are exhorted to treat people as if their race doesn't matter. These data suggest that people are treated differently as a result of race and that such differential treatment can have significant institutional consequences and is likely to go undetected. Racial bias creeps into institutional practice in ever-increasing, subtle ways. It would be hard to find peers and superior officers claiming any intentional racial bias in this regard. Yet the data suggest that racial differences affect evaluations. Institutional racism is often subtle, often complex, and always real.

Racial Disparities in Capital Punishment

Bohm (1994) argues that racial discrimination in capital punishment cases is not, contrary to what we might intuitively expect, related to the race of the *defendant* but to the race of the *victim*. Evidence suggests that, when a black person is killed, the defendant, whatever his or her race, is *less* likely to be convicted than if the victim is white, and, if convicted, is less likely to receive a death sentence.

Racial disparities are widely shown in criminal cases, with blacks far more likely to be convicted of capital offenses than their numbers in the population indicates (cf. Schneider and Smykla, 1991). However, documenting the extent of racial disparities does not provide sufficient grounds for a determination of racial discrimination. What is the difference? *Racial discrimination* means that a person is treated different from others because of his or her race. With regard to criminal sentences, racial discrimination occurs when "the death penalty is intentionally or purposefully imposed on persons because of their race and not because of, or in addition to, legitimate sentencing considerations" (Bohm, 1994, p. 321). Racial discrimination is illegal, whereas racial disparities are not. To test the case for race discrimination in sentencing, one needs to account for those proper legal parameters, sentencing guidelines, nature of the offense, and so forth.

Bohm (1994) found that the biggest disparity in racial outcomes occurred when prosecutors determined whether to seek a death sentence if a conviction was obtained. This disparity was evident in the probability of seeking a death sentence as a function of the race of the *victim*. Table 15.2 shows this effect convincingly. The death penalty is sought by a ratio of more than 2 to 1 when the victim is white compared to black. Contrary to what we might believe, the relative racial bias is even greater for white males (29.9% for white male victims, only 2.6% for black male victims, a ratio of 11:1) than for white females (48% for white female victims and only 9.4% for black female victims, a ratio of *only* 5:1). But consistent with expectations, capital offenses against white women led to a death sentence decision in 48 percent of the cases, but for black men victims, only 2.6 percent of the time, a death sentence was sought.

These statistics report only one jurisdiction in one state, Georgia. Nevertheless, other statistics show that racial disparities are not localized in Georgia. Between 1977 and 1991, for example, 145 persons were executed in the United States for cap-

TABLE 15.2 PROPORTION OF WHITE AND BLACK VICTIM CASES IN WHICH DEATH SENTENCE WAS SOUGHT; CHATTAHOCHEE, JUDICIAL CIRCUIT—1973–1990.*

Nature of Crime	White Victim Cases	Black Victim Cases
Murders with malice, felony	50.7%	20.8%
	(69)	(48)
Victims and defendants were strangers	57.1%	0%
	(20/35)	(0/6)
Nonstranger homicides	13.6%	3.3%
	(44)	(123)
Female victim	48%	9.4%
	(25)	(53)
Male victim	29.9%	2.6%
	(77)	(117)

*Numbers of cases are in parentheses. All differences between black and white victims are statistically significant at p <.05.

ital offenses against 147 different victims (Bohm, 1994). The profile of victims fairly well matches the profile of United States citizens by racial and ethnic group (84 percent were white, 11.5 percent were black, and 3 percent were Hispanic). However, of those offenders who were executed, the representation is quite different. Only 56 percent of those executed were white, while 39 percent were black, and 5 percent were Hispanic. These numbers suggest a roughly equal chance of being murdered among all races, but a somewhat higher likelihood of being executed for committing murder if one is black.

How Swift, Justice?

The following example, reported in the first edition, comes from the Boston police records.[7] Claris Blake was a 12-year-old black girl who lived in Dorchester, a predominately black section of Boston. One afternoon at about 4:30 she went to the corner store to buy her mother a pie. When Claris had not returned by 5:30 P.M., her mother became anxious. After looking all over the neighborhood, she finally called the police at about 8:30 P.M. It was April 27, 1971.

The police response was nonchalant, apathetic, and unhelpful. The police told Blake that her daughter was probably visiting friends and would probably be back later. Blake pleaded for assistance, stating that her daughter never stayed away from home without permission. The police were not sympathetic.

The complete story is long and sad. It is enough to make anyone give up on a belief in justice—it reinforces the felt need for blacks to control their own institutions. The police never made a search for the girl. They did not file an official missing-person bulletin until May 6. The local newspaper published a brief article on April 29, 1971, with a picture of the *wrong* girl. A tap was to be put on the Blake phone in case a ransom call was received. Claris did call her home at 7:10 A.M. on May 7, 1971. She sounded dazed and asked her mother if she loved her. The phone clicked. Mrs. Blake called the operator and asked for a trace. There was no tap, and she was informed that a trace was not possible.

---

[7] This account and quotations are from an article in the *Boston Globe Sunday Magazine,* July 11, 1971.

The FBI refused to enter the case, because it did not involve interstate flight. How did they know? The telephone company said the phone could not be tapped because the police had said the girl was not kidnapped. On May 15, 1971, Claris's body was found with a bullet in her head. It was not immediately known how long she had been dead. Commentary on the incident suggests a racial double standard:

> *Telephone official*: Look, let's face it, the wheel turned damned slowly in this case. It's not just the police. It's the double standard of our whole society. If a 12-year-old girl disappears on her way to buy a pie and she's white, the presumption is she's met foul play. If a little girl disappears on her way to buy a pie and she's black, everyone assumes she's just run away.
>
> *Mrs. Blake*: Let me tell you something. I'm sick and tired now. . . . The child is gone and dead and there's nothing that can bring her back alive. . . . I was begging. But I'm poor and I'm black. It didn't do no good, and now she's dead. (*Boston Globe*, July 11, 1971).

By way of contrast, about a month later, there were reports that a young, teenage white girl from a suburban Boston community had been kidnapped. There were stories and photos, and searches began the night she disappeared. She was found two days later—she had run away from home!

Fast forward to October 23, 1989, still in Boston. Only now, a white man, Charles Stuart, called 911 from his car phone to report that he had been robbed and his wife shot. He described the attacker as a black man in dark jogging clothes. William Bennett, a black man with a criminal record, became the prime suspect. In searching for him, police stopped and searched numerous black men in the black community of Mattapan. Tensions escalated as the black community felt itself under siege, and the white community felt that the dead woman, Carol Stuart, had been preyed upon by a black man. It was only a year earlier, 1988, that Willie Horton's image was featured in George Bush's reelection campaign. That frightful image of a violent black man may have prompted the white community to believe Stuart's story and to become enraged at this horribly brutal act.

Yet, by January of 1990, all black suspects had proven to be uncredible as the assailant and the scenario Stuart presented began to unravel. Finally, on January 3, 1990, Stuarts' brother Matthew confessed to meeting Stuart and taking away Carol Stuarts' handbag along with her jewelry and a gun. Stuart became the prime suspect in his own pregnant wife's murder. The next day, Charles Stuart jumped from the Tobin Bridge to his death in the Boston harbor. Although internal investigations failed to find any but minor misconduct by the police, the entire black community had felt itself to be under suspicion and under siege as the police fanned out in the community looking for a black man who they believed had killed Carol Stuart.

Why was it so *hard* to believe that Claris had been the victim of foul play and so *easy* to believe Carol Stuart had been? It is so easy to believe that a black man would or could do something such as this it has become a cliché. Susan Smith drowned her two sons in South Carolina and claimed a black man had kidnapped them. Although the national media seemed to believe her story, giving her a tearful spot on the *Today Show*, the local police were not so quickly convinced. She was apprehended within two weeks.

On April 12, 1992, Barbara Anderson and her husband Jesse were brutally attacked by a man wielding a knife on the streets of Milwaukee. Barbara was repeatedly stabbed in the face and neck, and later died. Jesse was stabbed in the chest trying to defend her from, he claimed, her black male assailant. However, when Jesse got out of the hospital and inquired into his dead wife's $250,000 insurance policy, he was arrested and charged with her murder.

Maybe the credibility of the Charles Stuart gambit has worn out. But the clouds of suspicion such alibis produce are more than an annoyance or temporary pain to the targeted groups, as D'Souza implies in *The End of Racism* (1995). It is a constant threat to well-being, and a constant reminder that things are not equal between the races.

Making Bail Is Hard to Do

One of the principal ways in which the judicial system practices discrimination is through the bail system. The judge can set bail at any amount he or she chooses, although there are some suggested guidelines that link the amount of bail with the severity of the alleged crime and the defendant's financial circumstances. An investigation of the Boston courts by Bing and Rosenfeld (1970) revealed some startling statistics.

These investigators studied urban Boston courts (Boston Municipal Court, Roxbury, and Dorchester), where 64 percent of the defendants are poor (53 percent of this figure are unemployed), and the suburban courts of Chelsea, Malden, and Waltham, Massachusetts. In the urban courts, 55 percent of the defendants are committed for failure to post bail. The comparable figure in the suburban courts is 41 percent. The racial discrepancy is even greater. Black defendants fail to raise bail money 62 percent of the time, compared to white defendants' 43 percent. This discrepancy is not due simply to the lower income of blacks, for in the Roxbury and Dorchester courts (serving predominantly black defendants), bail is set at or above $10,000 in 20 percent and 38 percent, respectively, of all bail cases. The comparable figure in the other four courts is 3 percent.

It might be expected that these figures reflect the more serious nature of crimes committed by black defendants. However, over one-half of those subjected to bail of $10,000 or more in Dorchester were charged with such offenses as nonsupport or illegitimacy. In addition, those who were committed before trial were found guilty more often than were those who were freed.

Ayres and Waldfogel (1994) took a different and intriguing approach to the question of racial and ethnic bias in bail setting. They considered that free enterprise would provide an objective picture of the degree of risk a person posed by being set free on bail. Any discrepancy between the degree of risk, indicated by the fees charged by bail bondsmen and the amount of bail set by judges, would point to bias in the criminal process.

Presumably, bail is set at an amount commensurate with (1) the severity of the crime and (2) the risk of flight posed by the defendant. Therefore, greater severity and more risk should equate to higher bail amounts. Bondsmen operate on the basis of risk of flight only. Ayres and Waldfogel (1994) used a regression analysis to determine if, controlling for severity of crime and risk of flight, the bond rates and bail amounts were equivalent for blacks, Hispanics, and whites. That is, if only the relevant-risk factors were operating, and not racial or ethnicity characteristics, then the bond rates and bail amounts should be similar for all.

Bail was set higher for Class A and B felony offenses and highest for drug-related offenses. After taking the severity of the offense into account, data showed that bail was still set 35 percent higher for black and 19 percent higher for Hispanic men compared to that set for white men. However, the bondsmen may consider other factors related to risk (e.g., being unemployed). Bondsmen charge 5 percent of the bail amount, so that the bond rate should be exactly proportional to the bail amount. The data showed that the bond rate for blacks was 16.5% higher and, for Hispanics, 4.6% higher than it was for whites. Thus, the risk implied by the bail amount is typically twice as large as the risk set by the bondsman. Because the bondsmen are in this for profit, free market capitalism suggests that their assessment should be more cautious and follow more closely relevant risk factors. From this, the authors conclude that bail is typically set too high for black and Hispanic male defendants. This example reflects the institutional biases of racism in the justice system, whether judges' biases are intentional or not.

Institutional Racism—Physical and Mental Health

Racism is bad for one's mental and physical health. Institutional racism produces discriminatory effects that put members of targeted racial groups at a disadvantage. Those disadvantages range from employment and other economic disadvantages, to poorer educational opportunities and outcomes, as well as challenges to one's personal and collective self-esteem. This section considers some examples of how both physical and mental health of racism's targets can be undermined by racism.

In 1985, Secretary of Health and Human Services Margaret Heckler convened a task force to look into black and minority health. Not surprisingly, she found that the health status of blacks and other minority groups was poorer than that of whites. In 1990, the life expectancy of blacks was 69.1 years and that of whites was 76.1 years. The task force computed an index of *excess deaths,* which compared the actual number of deaths in a given ethnic or racial group with the number there would have been if the white mortality rate had extended to that group. Excess deaths for blacks under age 70 was 42.3 percent; for American Indians, 25 percent; and for Hispanics, 14 percent (Williams, Lavizzo-Mourey, and Warren 1994). What contributes to these mortality statistics varies widely, and infant mortality and homicide play a large role. It is also true that poor diet, susceptibility to diseases, diabetes, and hypertension all contribute to excess deaths (U.S. Department of Health and Human Services, 1985; Williams and Collins, 1995).

There is a growing body of empirical evidence to suggest that racism is a recurring phenomenon in people's experience and that it has adverse physical, as well as mental, health consequences. Harrell and colleagues (Harrell, Malone-Colon, and Harris, in press; Sutherland and Harrell, 1987; Jones, Harrell, Morris-Prather, Thomas, and Omowale, 1996) have demonstrated the physiological correlates of observing racially provocative situations. Sixty African American women either watched a video enactment of or imagined one of two racially provocative situations: (1) An African American woman is unjustly accused of shoplifting by a hostile white security guard while white female shoppers made disparaging, prejudicial remarks about African Americans or (2) a white apartment manager is steering two African American female students to lower-quality rental units. Subjects' physiological reactions were monitored while they watched or imagined these scenes.

Results showed that both blood flow and facial muscle activity were significantly increased as a result of either watching or imagining the scenes. These results suggest that cumulative effects of both experiencing racism or discriminatory behavior and imagining it, perhaps primed by television news or first-hand accounts of others, can contribute to hypertension and overall elevated levels of stress. In addition, more negative moods were reported when subjects watched the video and even more so when subjects imagined the scene. Because they were asked to imagine themselves in the scene, it was more personalized. Hence the elevated negative mood state is reasonable. This finding corroborates other work by Armstead, Lawler, Gordon, Cross, and Gibbons (1989).

Consider, now, the case of Sarah Thompson and her colleagues from Love thy Neighbor Community, Inc. in Washington, D.C. On February 2, 1996, they presented a $1,000 gift certificate to the customer service cashier at Home Depot in Oxon Hill, Maryland, in payment for floor tile they had purchased. The tiles were not in stock and had to be ordered. Thompson reported that the cashier would not accept the gift certificate as a cash payment and told them they would have to come back in about two weeks, when the certificate would have been authenticated. Thompson asked them to order the tiles, but they would not. She felt

> . . . humiliated, embarrassed and discriminated against . . . the three Youth Directors were angry, disappointed and heart broken and stated "We thought discrimination had ended. What a perfect time to discriminate—the beginning of Black History Month." (Love Thy Neighbor, 1996).

Thompson and her colleagues' experience precipitated several issues we have discussed in this book: attributional ambiguity (was their hassle a consequence of being black, or simply store policy? cf. Crocker and Major, 1989), cultural mistrust (racism is a salient and plausible explanation for adverse interracial experiences; cf. Terrell and Terrell, 1981), and physiological reactivity (it has been shown that witnessing a racist event elevates physiological responses that have adverse health and mental health consequences; cf. Jones, Harrell et al. 1996). Institutional racism is implicated when institutional practices arouse race-based adverse reactions as well as when they lead to racially discriminatory outcomes. In fact, a spokesperson for Home Depot reported that the store cashier was simply following procedures and that race had nothing to do with it. Any certificate valued at more than $25 is subject to this clearance process. Moreover, the certificate was made out to the organization, not to Thompson (Tillman, 1996). These psychological processes are triggered by events that take the form of a racist encounter, whether it is in fact racially motivated or not.

Because institutional racism involves both intentional and unintentional racial biases, it becomes important to document that those most likely to have institutional authority (largely whites) may be prone to adverse, and relatively unconscious, reactions to members of racial groups. We saw this tendency demonstrated in cognitive and perceptual terms in Chapter 6. It has also been demonstrated with regard to physiological reactions.

Vrana and Rollock (1995) have shown that whites will react physiologically when they are touched by blacks. In an elegantly simple procedure, black and white subjects were brought into the lab for a study of physiological reactions to visual stimuli. They were hooked up to sensors taken by a same-race experimenter, and baseline measures were taken for 30 seconds. Then a second person, an "interactor" who was the same sex as the subject, but either black or white, entered. The interactor did some fiddling with apparatus and then said, "To make sure one of our measures is working correctly, I have to take your pulse. Let's begin. The interactor then held the subject's right wrist while looking at his or her watch for a thirty second period. Measures included heart rate, skin conductance, and facial activity of the zygomatic (smile) and corrugator (frown) muscles. The authors were inter-

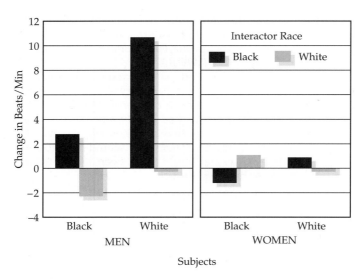

FIGURE 15.7

Change in Subject's Heart Rate When Subject Is Touched by a Black or a White Interactor. *Source:* Vrana and Rollock (1996), Figure 4.

ested in learning whether race of the interactor, the subject, or the combination affected these basic physiological reactions to being touched.

Results, depicted in Figure 15.7, showed that all subjects' heart rates increased slightly when the interactor entered the room (average of about 4 beats per minute). While the interactor was touching the women subjects, their heart rates were little changed, whether the subjects were black or white. Black men's heart rate increased slightly when touched by a black male interactor and decreased slightly when touched by a white male interactor (about 2 bpm in each case). For white men, there was no change in the rate when they were touched by another white man, but a large increase in heart rate occurred when these subjects were touched by a black man (10.5 bpm). These data suggest very strongly that white men reacted strongly to being touched by a black man. The possibility that this reaction underlies an emotional response to racial closeness is provocative.

We do not want to draw too broad a conclusion from this finding. However, just as blacks show increased reactivity to imaginings or perceptions of racial harrassment, white men may have similar reactions to the "threat" of black men.

Simons (1996) conducted a similar experiment, only his results deviated somewhat from those obtained by Vrana and Rollock. In his study, both black and white subjects' heart rates elevated when exposed to a black interactor more than when exposed to a white interactor. But this reaction occurred as soon as they entered the room and did not increase upon being touched. In fact, the increase for black subjects was as great or, in some cases, greater when the interactor was black. In this study, then, simply being exposed to a black experimenter elevated heart rate for everyone, regardless of the subject's race. This study complicates the picture quite a bit. If heart-rate change indicates an emotional or biased reaction to a person based on race, why do blacks respond the same as whites do? If touching is more intimate and, hence, potentially more threatening or disconcerting, why did it not affect reactions in this study? Although we do not know all the answers to these important questions, we do have a clear indication that physiological reactivity to people based on race occurs.

The cumulative toll of these experiences and the legacy of racial discrimination have an adverse impact on physical and mental health of its targets. Most important, knowledge of these incidents and imagining oneself in such situations seem to have just as much of an effect on one's emotional state as experiencing them directly does. The media plays a role in making these experiences available not only to whites, but to other members of the targeted group. It is perhaps this media generalization effect that explains why minority-group members perceive more discrimination against their group than they report they have ever experienced personally (Taylor, Wright, and Porter 1994). Perceiving racial discrimination in a situation may well be an individual difference, some see it more than others. But what this discussion suggests is that, directly or indirectly, the continuing facts of racial discrimination take a physical toll on its targets, and on other members of the target's group.

Whereas institutional racism is most typically discussed with regard to macro-level variables such as unemployment, wage differentials, differential sentencing, and so forth, the point we make here is that those macro-level differences have micro-psychological consequences. Targets of bias are not just groups, but individual members of those groups. The disparities are not significant because of the statistical deviations but because of the psychological toll they take. Moreover, the psychological toll of marginalization and bias can have physical and mental health consequences. Finally, evidence that reactions to another person of a different race are revealed in patterns of physiological response suggests further that the color-blind concept may simply be impossible to realize in a racialized society such as ours.

AFFIRMATIVE ACTION—REMEDY FOR INSTITUTIONAL RACISM?

If, as we propose above, institutional racism is still a problem, and if affirmative action is a remedy for it, why is affirmative action so strongly opposed? One reason may be that affirmative action is ineffective as a means of reducing institutional racism. Another may be that institutional racism is believed to no longer exist—at least, in its traditional form, and that affirmative action itself, viewed as racial preference, is seen as its replacement.

This latter view was well-illustrated on ABC television's *Nightline* program on blacks and whites in America (Koppel, 1996). Among other things, the staff conducted a poll of Americans' views on the extent of racial discrimination in hiring, asking such questions as "Do you think blacks and other minorities are discriminated against in hiring?" A plurality of whites said no (50%), a sizable minority said yes (43%). For blacks, a large majority said yes (77%), and a small minority said no (17%). There is a racial difference in the perception of racial discrimination. Respondents were also asked, "Do you think that blacks and other minorities should receive preferential treatment in hiring to make up for past discrimination?" Whites gave a resounding *no* (83%). Somewhat surprisingly, blacks, by a small majority (56%), also said no.

The view that racism is no longer a problem and that preferential treatment is a problem was expressed by Dinesh D'Souza (1995). Let's look briefly at his arguments. The D'Souza (1995) basic argument suggests that (1) remedies to institutional discrimination result in racial preferences that advance less qualified people over those more qualified on the basis of race;[8] and (2) the claims of continued racism, as was Mark Twain's death, are greatly exaggerated.

On the first point D'Souza (1995; pp. 290–291) offers the following viewpoint:

> . . . a new form of discrimination has become widespread in today's workplace. Like discrimination of the old sort, it employs racial classification to prefer less qualified members of some groups over more qualified members of other groups. The new discrimination is legal as the old used to be. What differentiates the new discrimination is that it targets White males, and sometime Asians. . . . The new discrimination is justified as an indispensable instrument for *fighting* racism.

What is the evidence that white males, as a group, suffer reduced opportunities because of this "new" racial discrimination? Are they unemployed? Are they unable to get an education? Are they unable to advance to top-level positions in corporations? Are they unable to get bank loans? Are they unable to buy property in desirable neighborhoods? Are they targeted for surveillance and arrest for suspicion of wrong-doing? With respect to white men, the answers to all of the preceding questions is, in a vast majority of cases, obviously, no. With respect to these same questions asked of black men, the answer is far more frequently, yes. Is it just a matter of whose ox is being gored?

On the second point, he makes the following general argument:

> Racism undoubtedly exists, but it no longer has the power to thwart blacks or any other group in achieving their economic, political, and social aspirations. It cannot be denied that African Americans suffer slights . . . and other forms of continued discrimination. Some of this discrimination is irrational, motivated by bigotry or faulty generalization. Much of it . . . is behavior that is rational from the point of view of the discriminator and at the same time harmful for black individuals who do not conform to the behavioral pattern of their peers. . . . Racism cannot explain most of the contemporary hardships faced by African Americans, even if some of them had their historical roots in oppression. (D'Souza, 1995, pp. 525–526)

The bottom line of D'Souza's argument is that racism cannot now explain the standing of minority groups in this society, given that equal opportunity is all but guaranteed for people who are prepared and capable. We have demonstrated a wide array of microlevel psychological mechanisms that confer advantage on whites and disadvantages on blacks and other ethnic minority groups. D'Souza acknowledges as much. However, he sees racism as a source of pain and discomfort, but not an explanation for aggregate lower-level outcomes. He also assumes that his analytical tools are sufficiently powerful and precise to make unequivocal causal connections which establish that racism cannot explain the differential status of blacks and whites in the United States. We believe we have shown that institutional racism persists, that individual attitudes and beliefs operate at unconscious levels to disadvantage racial targets, and that those targets may not only suffer discomfort from slights, but also a variety of psychological, behavioral, and emotional reactions that aggregate to take a significant toll.

---

[8] Note that D'Souza cites the definition of institutional racism used in the first edition of this book as an example of why it is a misguided form of racial discrimination itself (see D'Souza, 1995, p. 290).

D'Souza (1995) in his analysis pits institutional racism against individual opportunity, just as Eastland and Bennett (1979) did in their contrast of numerical (institutional) and moral (individual) equality. The cumulative effects of racism at both the individual and the institutional levels are to create large-scale disadvantage for persons of color. To equate 30 years of post–civil rights efforts to reverse the bias and disadvantage of 400 years of willful, systematic, and pernicious racism with the "original sin" of racism itself is disingenuous and provocative.

We cannot resolve the affirmative action debate here, but we have demonstrated a variety of ways in which racial bias persists in our basic societal institutions. The goal of reducing this level of bias is not well served by protracted debates about whether affirmative action is moral or not, or whether blacks are genetically or culturally inferior to whites. Rather, we do know that, at the end of the day, improvement of the status of ethnic and racial minorities will not come at the expense of whites. In the long run, as in the past, they will benefit as much or more than racial and ethnic minorities will (cf. Bell, 1989).

There is much research evidence to suggest that, although "universal" non-racial policies may diminish the animosity of race-based programs, such policies are more likely to sweep under the rug the breadth of continuing racial, ethnic, and gender biases, as we have documented in these pages. Portraying remedies to institutional racism as "immoral" does little good and much harm. Ezorsky (1991) systematically reviews the grounds for opposing affirmative action and concludes that compensation for cumulative bias is not counterproductive, that so-called affluent blacks and others of color still are subjected to biases, that those unqualified to benefit from affirmative action by and large don't, that whites have benefited from racism over the years, and that a race-neutral approach does not reduce this historical advantage. She concludes that affirmative action is not a perfect system, but the problems it is designed to address persist, whether we employ it as a remedy or not.

As we saw in Chapter 4, the establishment of federal agencies and the issuance of executive orders to blunt the racial bias of institutional practices was early on met with resistance. But it must be made clear that the Equal Employment Opportunity Commission and the Office of Federal Contract Compliance were established and affirmative action guidelines adopted specifically to fight institutional racism. The current debate about affirmative action might be seen as a debate about whether institutional racism is no longer a problem, or whether even if it is still a problem, it is no worse than the adverse impact the policy has on those not typically included in its focus—namely, white men.

SUMMARY

Institutional racism is the bedrock of racism in the United States for two reasons: (1) Individual racial biases are magnified by the institutional effects spread over thousands of instances and decades, and (2) racial biases occur as a result of practices that may intentionally and unintentionally promote racial inequality. An individual racist can affect the experiences of countless persons directly or indirectly by his or her behavior. An institution can systematically undermine the physical and emotional well-being of countless people by virtue of how it conducts business. We reviewed evidence of the multiple ways in which institutional practices create disadvantage for people of color.

We reviewed in some detail evidence of adverse outcomes in economic spheres of life, from housing loans to basic salaries. We observed that educational policies and practices may have a cumulative adverse effect by virtue of racist assumptions, such as the stereotyped "savagery" of American Indians and the widespread belief in the need to "civilize" them through education and cultural change and an inability to understand and capitalize on the talents of children from different cultural backgrounds as they go through the schooling process. We learn that, according to criminal justice decisions, a white life is more valuable than a black life (when taken, it incurs stiffer penalties for the perpetrator) and that blacks and Hispanics have much more difficulty than whites in gaining freedom pending final judicial decisions because of inappropriately high bail amounts. Institutional racism takes a toll on the physical and emotional well-being of blacks, in particular, and evidence from laboratory studies shows how hypertension can be partially explained by reactions to witnessed or imagined instances of racism.

Affirmative action was conceived as a remedy to institutional racism and, now, is viewed by some as the embodiment of it. However, arguments that institutional racism no longer exists or that its effects can no longer explain racial differences in social and economic outcomes fail to come to grips with the evidence and argument presented in this chapter. Equating the occasions in which a white person is passed over for promotion or hiring in favor of a person of color, given the centuries of egregious racism and oppression and disadvantage to people of color, undermines attempts to reduce the problems of institutional racism.

In the final analysis, it is the broad cultural context which determines the racialist institutional practices that are framed and the attitudes and beliefs about race that individuals come to adopt. The influence of those individual attitudes and beliefs on institutional practice, combined with the magnified institutional effects of intentional and unintentional race-related biases, compounds and perpetuates the problems of racism in the United States. The next chapter will explore this cultural context and examine the origins of these racialized beliefs and their consequences on problems of racism.

16

Understanding Racism III: Cultural Racism

❖

*I*NTRODUCTION

Culture is to society as personality is to the individual. It summarizes the attitudes, values, and behaviors that define who we are as a people. In addition, culture provides a template with which meaning is determined. It asserts the values to be promoted or rejected. In sum, culture is a blueprint for living in a society.

Hodge, Struckmann, and Trost (1975, p. 2) view culture as ". . . the sum total of life patterns passed on from generation to generation within a group of people . . . [including] institutions, language, values, religious ideals, habits of thinking, artistic expressions, and patterns of social and interpersonal relationships." The dominant culture of the United States, deriving as it does from the culture of Western Europe, includes the legacy of racialist views passed down from generation to generation. Moreover, as culture encompasses all aspects of daily living, the racialism of previous generations has been infused throughout the culture, infiltrating institutional goals and modes of operation, criteria for access to cultural resources, and participation. But just as racism and its enabling processes of racialism are integral to our culture, so too is *antiracism*, the struggle to limit, reverse, or eliminate racialistic thinking and racism.

471

Defining Cultural Racism

In Kroeber and Kluckhohn's (1952) definition of *culture*, the *conditioning* aspect of culture—a guide to how we think, feel, and act—is counterpoised with a reactive component, the *consequences* of how we think, feel, and act. Thus, culture isn't *static;* that is, it does not simply reflect the constancy of how we think about things, feel about things, and do things just as we did long ago. Rather, culture is also *dynamic,* being made anew by degrees, in each generation by the particulars of how we think, feel, and act.

As we noted earlier (Chapter 14), the apple doesn't fall far from the tree. We don't just jettison our cultural origins and remake a new culture that is totally different and new. Although a fallen apple is still an apple, it is immediately transformed into something different from those still on the tree. A living culture not only focuses attention on the creation of ideas, values, and ways of being, it evolves over time and slowly transforms into something both hauntingly familiar and demonstrably new.

This book often reviews events and ideas of earlier times. One may perhaps wonder why what Lincoln or Jefferson thought about blacks matters or why what a California legislator thought about Japanese and Italians matters, or why nineteenth-century views of American Indian savagery are still relevant. In our view of culture, *everything* matters—past, present, and future—because it all contributes to who we are and what we will become.

Culture, then, is integral to our discussion of racism. It is the medium in which racial thinking, racialism, and racialization processes were planted and have grown. We will not necessarily find racism in the same form in which it existed 200 years ago in the age of slavery, or 100 years ago in that of colonial expansion and the Jim Crow South, or 50 years ago in the emergent "welfare" era, or 30 years ago in the civil rights era, or 20 years ago in the affirmative action era, or even 10 years ago in the social conservatism era. But the "new racism" grows from the same roots as the old. And racism continues, with perpetual cultural modifications, to express itself in contemporary U.S. society.

The new racism that we see expressed, for example, in reactions to immigrants or people who are different from us (cf. Barker, 1981), has evolved as our culture has changed. We have rejected—or, at least, suppressed—old-fashioned racial views much as one rejects last year's hemlines or colors. "Old" ideas are displaced by new concepts thought to be "hipper," classier, and better. But the new ideas, too, are old. They emphasize traditional values of individual rights, growing xenophobia, and cultural homogenization. Racism, like fashion, goes through cycles, evolves with technology and artistic imagination, and imposes its will with the political and economic weight of power and control.

Racism, then, is part of U.S. culture—it always has been and probably always will be. But, so is antiracism a part of U.S. culture. These forces of good and evil continue to struggle, as they have for centuries. As a consequence of this struggle the meaning and consequences of race evolve and expand. *Cultural racism,* then, can be defined as follows:

> **Cultural racism comprises the cumulative effects of a racialized worldview, based on belief in essential racial differences that favor the dominant racial group over others. These effects are suffused throughout the culture via institutional structures, ideological beliefs, and personal everyday actions of people in the culture, and these effects are passed on from generation to generation.**

Two important concepts are assumed by this definition, ethnocentrism and hegemony. *Ethnocentrism* refers simply to the preference one has for one's own way of life or culture. Ethnocentrism describes a preference for those values, dress, habits, style, institutions, and the traditions embodied in the particular culture. Generally speaking, ethnocentrism is common around the world (cf. Chapter 9 for examples of how this works).

However, one group's ethnocentrism is a benign preference only when there is no contact with groups of people with alternative ethnocentric leanings. When groups are in contact, their differences become salient, and simple preference, combined with issues of power and control, escalates to *privileged* in-group bias (cf. Chapter 8). When in-group preference coincides with power and control in a given society, and when the facts of power and control are formalized as natural and right (cf. social dominance theory, Sidanius, 1993), then groups adopt practices and values that serve to perpetuate that domination and control. The cumulative instruments and practices of group dominance describe the principle of *hegemony*. Hegemonic dominance is the way in which a group remains in power by *any means necessary*. That is, as simple dominative strategies—such as slavery, overt racism, legal control, and informal oppression and intimidation—become less viable means of ensuring dominance, newer and more subtle forms of such strategies arise.

The remainder of this chapter will focus on the issues of cultural conflict as evidenced in matters of race. The first section will take us back to the origins of intercultural contact in America and will describe how Africans and Europeans reacted to each other nearly 500 years ago. The next section will explore the idea that cultural racism manifests itself in conflicts over culture. Definitions of *race*, the linkage of racial categories to essential properties of human nature, and the value and merit of race-based thought and behavior are all contested in the struggle between racism and antiracism. In this section, we will look at four illustrations of cultural conflict: the concept of *Yurugu* (Ani, 1994), an African-centered critique of racism in European culture; TRIOS (Jones, 1986), a set of human characteristics viewed as central to the distinctions often made between African- and European-descended people; Africentrism (Asante, 1987), as an attempt to define or redefine the meaning of African culture and its legacy for African Americans; and finally, *The Bell Curve* (Murray and Herrnstein, 1994), which continues arguments for essential differences in intelligence as a function of race.

The final section of this chapter will look briefly at the implications of these contested views of culture in terms of the continuing construction of culture anew. We will specifically consider how the so-called new racism can be understood in the context of the cultural racism argument described above.

*O*RIGINS OF CULTURE CONTACT: STATEMENT OF A THEME[1]

In the beginning was Africa (black) and England (white)—separate and different. Equality was not an issue. Our description of the differences is a description of two

---

[1] For a good account of racial and cultural contacts, see Winthrop Jordan's *White Over Black* (1969), and E. Franklin Frazier's *Race and Culture Contacts in the Modern World* (1957). For an account of the impact of Africanisms on the development of Afro-American culture, see Herskovits's *The Myth of the Negro Past* (1958).

FIGURE 16.1.

Some Cultural Comparisons—Africa and England, ca. 1550.

Cultural Component	Africa	England
Religion	Relativistic	Absolutist
	Pragmatic	Faith-oriented
	Magical	Moralistic
	Secular	Sacred
	Family-oriented	Privileged
Social organization	Matrilineal	Patriarchal
	Polygamous	Monogamous
	Status based on *type* of work	Status based on *lack* of work
	"Man is what he does."	"Man is what he owns."
	Stratified-fluid	Stratified-rigid
	Family discipline	Institutional discipline
Economics, property	Agrarian, artisan commerce	Capitalist commerce
	Hunting, fishing	Artisan
	Collective property	Private property
Education	Informal (family, peers)	Formal (tutor, schools)
	Oral tradition	Written tradition
	Requires interpersonal contact	Facilitates interpersonal separation
Time	Present, past fused	Past, future, no present
	Traditional (primitive)	Progress
	Little change over time	Positively evaluated change over time
Music	Rhythmic—the body	Tonal, melodic—the mind
	Songs (secular)	Songs (sacred)
Worldview	Intuitive, superstitious	Rational (e.g., Cogito ergo sum, Descartes)
	Tolerant, open	Intolerant, manipulative (e.g., Machiavelli's *The Prince*)

different cultures. The opposition of skin color is but one of the significant manifestations of the degree of culture difference. Figure 16.1 outlines some comparisons of African and English culture around the year 1550.

These characterizations are generalized abstractions. Although close inspection might reveal somewhat greater similarity between the cultures than that which is portrayed here, the description of the extent and nature of the cultural differences is basically accurate.

Englishmen of the sixteenth century were quite ethnocentric, as we saw in Chapters 12 and 13. They were predisposed to dislike or judge negatively any group of people who were different from themselves. Ethnocentrism is not, of course, a peculiarly British phenomenon. In fact, most culture groups tend to think their way is the best way. But, within the context of English-African contact, British ethnocentrism was particularly salient: The culture of Africans was not merely different from that of the English, but at the opposite end of the continuum on practically every major cultural criterion. Most significantly, British ethnocentrism included the glorification of the color white and the vilification of the color black. Aided by hindsight, and the cumulative experience of racialistic thought and actions, we might wonder if the contact between white Englishmen and black Africans could have turned out any other way.

According to Jordan (1969), at first sight, the English found the two most salient aspects of the Africans to be their skin color and sexuality. The interpretation and significance of their perception of these characteristics play prominent roles in the persistence of racism. The following pages illustrate the origin of perceptions and attitudes about Africans in sixteenth-century interracial contact.

Skin Color

The travel logs of British seafarers and English writers vividly portray the perceptions whites had of blacks on first encounters. These accounts highlight, as well, the worldview that categorized and judged these Africans. For example:

> And entering in [a river], we see
>   a number of blacke soules,
> Whose likelinesse seem'd men to be,
>   but all as blacke as coles. (quoted in Jordan, 1969, pp. 4–5)

This verse suggests that being a man and being black were incompatible states of existence. Further, upon noting that when a white Englishman married a black Ethiopian woman she bore him "black" children, one observer concluded that the blackness of Africans:

> proceedeth of some natural infection of the first inhabitants of that country, and so all the whole progenie of them descended, are still *polluted with the same blot of infection.* (quoted in Jordan, 1969, p. 15; italics added)

Not only is the trait of "color" strongly carried in the genes in this view, it is stigmatized.

Yet another reaction suggested that "*though* they were black, they were civil" (italics added). The white Englishmen had universally negative reactions to the blackness of the Africans. But this is not really surprising if we consider the *Oxford English Dictionary* definition of the color black prior to the sixteenth century:

> Deeply stained with dirt; soiled, dirty, foul. . . . Having dark or deadly purposes, malignant; pertaining to or involving death, deadly; baneful, disastrous, sinister. . . . Foul, iniquitous, atrocious, horrible, wicked. . . . Indicating disgrace, censure, liability to punishment, etc.

If that is how the *color* black was commonly perceived in white England prior to contact with black Africa, it is easy to imagine how black African *culture* was to be understood and interpreted by the Englishmen. Imagine the power of the self-fulfilling prophesy effect on the history that followed from these culture contacts. The English, feeling quite negative toward "black" skin color to start, were also exposed to a collection of cultures that were very different from their own. It does not seem unreasonable to suppose that a basic aversion to black "colored" the Englishmen's judgments of all elements of African civilizations and cultures.

It is important to note that it was not simply the negative reaction to blackness that was involved here, but a superpositive regard for the purity of whiteness:

Everye white will have its blacke,
And everye sweete its sowre. (quoted in Jordan, 1969, p. 15)

And, for William Shakespeare, the natural order of things included:

Tis beauty truly blest, whose red and white
Nature's own sweet and cunning hand laid on, . . . (quoted in Jordan, 1969, p. 8)

White is good and beautiful, whereas black is bad and ugly. The simple fact of preferences for and reactions to color play a critical role in the problems of racism. Opposition and conflict of basic cultural and physical dimensions preceded the complexities of individual, institutional, aversive, and dominative racism by many centuries.

An interesting observation on the relation between color-name and culture is suggested by a classic clinical report of a multiple personality. Thigpen and Cleckley (1954) wrote a clinical report of a multiple personality involving three distinct identities. The case was popularized when a motion picture based on the study, *The Three Faces of Eve* (1957), was made. Of interest to us are two of the personalities, which were named by the authors Eve White and Eve Black. The choice of *White* and *Black* is intriguing in light of the personalities to which they were ascribed. Figure 16.2 lists the personality profile for these two Eves. Eve Black is lacking in culture but curiously likable. She is playful, childlike, entertaining. Her superego is nonfunctional, which makes her a delight, the one who has all the fun. Black is place where the "fun" things go to be. Yet, just as there is a kind of nostalgia and envy directed at Eve Black, there is judgment and castigation, as well. A certain voyeurism makes Eve Black someone one would like to be around, but wouldn't want in one's family. Eve White, by contrast, has "all the right stuff." She is socialized to traditional values, properly "feminine," devoted, even heroic. Her saintliness is admired, but somehow she is repressed, and one's admiration for her is tinged with sadness. The personality traits associated differentially with Eve White and Eve Black are not pulled from thin air; instead, they suggest the content of cultural beliefs about the races as well as the genders. These cultural beliefs did not, in 1954, depart substantially from the first conclusions about racial differences drawn by Englishmen in 1550!

Sexuality

The attribution of certain characteristics of sexuality was another remarkable white English response to black Africa. Francis Bacon envisioned the Spirit of Fornication as "a little foul ugly Aethiop" (Jordan, 1969, p. 34). Black men were alleged to sport "large Propagators." While demeaning the sexuality of black-skinned men and exaggerating their physical endowment, the English assigned almost supernatural powers to black-skinned women. This sexuality was not merely a fanciful conception of these white adventurers, but presumably based on experience as:

[the] hot constitution'd Ladies [with] temper hot and lascivious, [made] no scruple to prostitute themselves to the Europeans *for a very slender profit, so great was their inclination to white men.* (quoted in Jordan, 1969, p. 35; italics added)

FIGURE 16.2.

Mental Images in Black and White—Cultural Dissociation

Eve White	Eve Black
Demure, retiring, in some respects almost saintly.	Obviously a party girl. Shrewd, childishly vain, and egocentric.
Face suggests a quiet sweetness; the expression in repose is predominantly one of contained sadness.	Face is pixie-like; eyes dance with mischief as if Puck peered through the pupils.
Voice always softly modulated, always influenced by a specifically feminine restraint.	Voice a little coarsened, "discultured," with echoes or implications of mirth and teasing. Speech richly vernacular and liberally seasoned with spontaneous gusts of rowdy wit.
An industrious and able worker, also a competent housekeeper and a skillful cook. Not colorful or glamorous. Limited in spontaneity.	All attitudes and passions whimsical and momentary. Quick and vivid flares of many light feelings, all ephemeral.
Though not stiffly prudish and never self-righteous, she is seldom lively or playful or inclined to tease or tell a joke. Seldom animated.	Immediately likable and attractive. A touch of sexiness seasons every word and gesture. Ready for any little irresponsible adventure.
Her presence resonates unexpressed devotion to her child. Every act, every gesture, the demonstrated sacrifice of personal aims to work hard for her little girl are consistent with this love.	Dress is becoming and a little provocative. Posture and gait suggest light-heartedness, play, a challenge to some sort of frolic.
Cornered by bitter circumstances, threatened with tragedy, her endeavors to sustain herself, to defend her child, are impressive.	Is immediately amusing and likable. Meets the little details of experience with a relish that is catching. Strangely "secure from the contagion of the world's slow stain," and from inner aspect of grief and tragedy.

Source: This summary is adapted from Thigpen and Cleckley (1954). "A Case of Multiple Personality." *Journal of Abnormal Social Psychology* 49:135–151.

But the white man did not hold himself responsible for his sexual activities with the African women, for:

> she comes to the place of the white man, lays beside him, and arouses his passion with her animal arts. (quoted in Jordan, 1969, p. 35)

That is, the white man attributed the "low" price of prostitutes in Africa to the strong desire of black women for white men. Moreover, because it seems the white men did not want to be responsible for their sexual interests, they placed all fault with the black temptress who, with her *animal arts,* aroused him in ways that he, an ordinary man, could not resist. This perception of the relationship between white males and black females has been little altered over the centuries, as the laws of progeny during slavery consistently favored the white male's sexual profligacy with black women.

To support this inclination, during the era of American slavery, laws were passed that made a child of any black-white union the race of his or her mother. The effects of this determination were twofold. First, a white man could produce as many offspring as he wanted with black women without "contaminating" the white race. Second, the offspring of such sexual unions had no claim to the man's wealth, status, and power. The rule of descent that assigns social identity on the basis of ancestry is adapted to fit these social goals, with only passing respect for its biological validity. The rule that automatically places the children of a union or mating between members of different groups into the minority group is termed *hypodescent* (Harris and Kottak, 1963; Kottak, 1996). (Hypo means "lower.")

The case of Susie Phipps reveals that this hypodescent rule is not a relic of the past. Susie was a very light-skinned woman with "Caucasian" features and straight black hair. She had been "brought up white" and married white twice. However, she discovered as an adult that she was "black" when she found a copy of her birth certificate, which listed her as "colored." Susie challenged the 1970 Louisiana law declaring anyone with at least one-thirty-second "Negro blood" to be legally black. Although the state court admitted she looked white, it stood behind the law and claimed that she was officially black (cf. Kottak 1996).

In a recent airing of *Nightline* (Koppel, 1996), Gregory Williams, dean of the Ohio State School of Law, recounted his experience of growing up white until age 10, then *becoming* black. (His story is told in detail in a book, *Life on the Color Line*

From white to black, such a short journey! Gregory Howard Williams, Dean of Ohio State University College of Law and author of *Life on the Color Line* (Williams, 1996).

[Williams, 1995].) It turns out his father had passed for white because he loved a white woman, but Virginia law forbade their marriage. When the marriage dissolved, Gregory Williams's father revealed his racial heritage to his son, and showed him a picture of his grandmother, a clearly black woman. Gregory Williams recounted how his life immediately changed and all the things he had taken for granted, now became simply privileges of having white skin. Ironically, he discovered that his ascendance to the prestigious position of dean was accompanied by accolades and respect. However, when certain individuals learned of his race, they questioned whether his appointment was, in fact, an "affirmative action hire."

This very brief review of early stages of culture contact and its legacy in our perceptions of race has summarized some of the basic differences between black Africa and white England. We reviewed (Chapter 11) the contact hypothesis for resolving interracial conflict. It is important for us to note that it was unequal interracial, intercultural contact that created the nation's racial problem in the first place! It should not be surprising that contact alone is insufficient to alter these deep-seated and long-held racialistic beliefs.

The Problem of Color and Culture

With reference, again, to DuBois's (1903) assessment, the problem of the color line in the United States is not just a twentieth-century problem, but one that goes back several centuries. There are numerous theories of and proposed solutions to racial conflict in the United States of the twentieth century. However, any theory of race relations in the twentieth century must be informed by a historical analysis of the cultural heritage of all American peoples. The dynamics of racial contact and mutual group influences need to be better understood if modern theories are to illuminate the realities of racism.

The discussion thus far has focused on ethnocentrism, but the main issue of this chapter is cultural racism. The ethnocentrism upon which early white reactions to black Africans was predicated still exists in our nation. Foreigners, particularly those from cultures of color, are often looked on with suspicion, and their customs and modes of dress frequently deemed not just "different," but "un-American." Like prejudice, ethnocentrism is a judgment. The attitudes of the English toward the Africans were based on judgments about the latter's physical appearance, customs, values, and beliefs. That is, the ethnocentric reactions of white Englishmen were *cultural reactions* organized in part by the differences in skin color. Jordan (1969, p. 25; emphasis added), suggest that:

> [the consequence of] the Englishman's ethnocentrism tended to distort his perception of African culture in two opposite directions. While it led him to emphasize differences and to condemn deviations from the English norm, it led him also to seek out similarities (where perhaps none existed) and to applaud every instance of conformity to the appropriate standard.

African culture was seen as inferior to the extent that it deviated from English norms; it was given modest recognition for achievements that "measured up" to those same norms. The important point of this is that all judgments of African society were made with respect to white, English norms.

But ethnocentrism is a judgment and, as is true of prejudice as we have defined it, is basically an attitude. Ethnocentrism becomes cultural racism when attitudes escalate into behaviors. Cultural racism results when ethnocentric judgments become prescriptions for action, and those same ethnocentric judgments are invoked in order to justify those actions. Ethnocentrism is transformed to cultural racism by the accumulation of *power*. Specifically, the ability to control, through the exercise of power, the lives and destinies of blacks and other racially defined cultural groups becomes cultural racism when those destinies are chained to white ethnocentric standards.

It is important, however, to understand that "white power," whether in the hands of "benefactors" or detractors of minority groups, has sought in every instance to evaluate and control the destinies of black people in the United States with respect to those same ethnocentric white standards that so heavily influenced the reactions of white Englishmen in 1550. Cultural racism will never be understood or eliminated until these facts are understood, until white America evaluates the cultural assumptions upon which their exercise of white power is based.

CULTURAL WARS

Patrick Buchanan, an unsuccessful candidate for the Republican party nomination for President of the United States in 1992 and 1996, issued a clarion call to war at the Republican National Convention in 1992, when he urged Americans to take their country back. The declaration of war was cultural:

> My friends, this election is about much more than who gets what. It is about who we are. It is about what we believe. It is about what we stand for as Americans. There is a religious war going on in our country for the soul of America. It is a cultural war, as critical to the kind of nation we will one day be as the Cold War itself. (Buchanan, 1992).

To whom had Americans lost their culture, according to Buchanan? Had they been invaded and conquered? Buchanan goes on to drive a wedge between black and Korean Americans, citing those "brave people of Koreatown who took the worst of the L.A. riots, but still live the family values we treasure, and who still believe deeply in the American dream (Buchanan, 1992), ignoring, for example, those brave African Americans who rescued Reginald Denney from the vicious beating he endured, whose shops were destroyed, who lived family values and still believed in the American dream. And it seems that the war may indeed be against those same blacks, and the ones who acted out their rage and frustration and perhaps self-indulgence. Buchanan (1992) described how the young men of the Eighteenth Cavalry took back the streets of L.A. during the riots in the aftermath of the Rodney King verdict in 1992:

> When the troopers arrived, M-16s at the ready, the mob threatened and cursed, but the mob retreated. It had met the one thing that could stop it: force, rooted in justice, backed by courage. . . . And as they took back the streets of LA, block by block, so we must take back our cities, and take back our culture, and take back our country.

Although the United States was founded on the principles of freedom and equality, it, has, from its inception, compromised those principles in a variety of ways where race is concerned. As we noted at the opening of this chapter, culture is to society as personality is to the individual. DuBois (1903, p. 214) spoke of that individual level of personality in terms of conflict and contradiction:

> After the Egyptian and Indian, the Greek and Roman, the Teuton and Mongolian, the Negro is a sort of seventh son, born with a veil, and gifted with second-sight in this American world. . . . It is a peculiar sensation, this double-consciousness, this sense of always looking at one's self through the eyes of others, of measuring one's soul by the tape of a world that look on in amused contempt and pity. One ever feels his twoness,— an American, a Negro; two warring ideals in one dark body. . . .

These "warring ideals" within African Americans may be expanded to the warring ideals of U.S. society. The ways in which freedom and equality have been compromised haunt us. This haunting contradiction, Myrdal's *American Dilemma* (Myrdal, 1944), frames the passionate struggle for the soul of the United States. Racism spoils the purity of purpose that was the American Revolution, the high ideals on which this republic was founded.

Nonetheless, the struggle to ensure freedom to life, liberty, and the pursuit of happiness remains a noble undertaking and represents the ultimate triumph of the human spirit (cf. Fukuyama, 1992). Does racism invalidate the freedoms we cherish? Can we not claim the nobility of our passion for liberty by rejecting racism? Can the guilt we feel by our sinful past be expiated by declaring that racism is over, done, kaput?

By contrast, antiracist projects are organized around the beliefs that racism persists and that the American dilemma can only be resolved by being eliminated. The cultural wars pit each side's version of culture against an idealized set of values and beliefs. We take the view that the cultural wars are, at their core, about cultural racism. *Antiracists* are those who seek to identify the sources and manifestations of racism in the culture in order to eradicate it or at least develop an antidote to it. *Americanists* are those who seek to isolate and refine those core U.S. values that provide positive cultural esteem and to minimize those flaws that undermine it. In a basic sense, the cultural wars are enjoined as each version of truth, value, and belief strives to create cultural meaning that validates and exemplifies its cultural worldview.

Cultural racism is a contest for determining the meaning of race, culture, values and principles in the broadest and most significant aspects of human experience. We will consider four viewpoints, as articulated in four works, that exemplify the nature of these cultural wars:

1 *Yurugu* (Ani, 1994), an African-centered critique of racism in European culture
2 TRIOS (Jones, 1979; 1986), which proposes a set of human characteristics viewed as central to the distinctions often made between African- and European-descended people
3 Africentrism (Asante, 1987), which describes an attempt to define or redefine the meaning of African culture and its legacy for African Americans
4 *The Bell Curve* (Murray and Herrnstein, 1994), which continues arguments for essential differences in intelligence as a function of race

Yurugu: Racism as Disharmony in Nature

Yurugu is the being in Dogon mythology who is responsible for disorder in the universe. Conceived in denial of natural order, Yurugu acts to initiate and promote disharmony in nature. In African cosmology, Yurugu is deficient in spiritual sensibility, is perpetually in conflict, is cognitively limited, and is a constant threat to the well-being of humanity (Ani, 1994). For Ani (1994), racism is like Yurugu in its essence. Just as Yurugu is destructive to humanity, so, too, is racism. Racism follows from a European cultural essence that unfolds inexorably toward destruction, just as the very nature of Yurugu is to bring disorder and disharmony to the world.

Ani (1994, p. 1) begins her critique of European thought with this warlike expression of intent: ". . . this study of Europe is an intentionally aggressive polemic. It is an assault upon the European paradigm; a repudiation of its essence." Ani, in common with others, (Hodge, Struckmann, and Trost, 1975), believes racism is inherent in Western cultural thought. We have illustrated how, over the years, analysis of the language and expressions of many Europeans demonstrates how the concept of race led to a centralized and coherent pattern of racialist thinking (cf. Smedley, 1993). The text of *Yurugu* (Ani, 1994) offers a set of concepts and terms that explain these cultural patterns with metaphorical images and novel concepts.

Asili is the first principle of cultural construction. It is a seed that carries *cultural* DNA. Lumsden and Wilson (1987) describe a similar concept, the *culturgen* that provides a mechanism for translating "biology" into "culture." (The culturgen idea is explored in more detail in Chapter 17.) In Ani's analysis, *asili* is the germinating seed for cultural formation. It dictates the direction—and ultimately, the consequences—of cultural evolution. Culture evolves in both cognitive and affective dimensions. The cognitive dimension Ani (1994) represents as *utamawazo*—that is, the cultural *thought* processes that organize the basic elements of life in a worldview. *Utamawazo* establishes the standards for truth and the processes by which it is revealed. It is connected to *asili* in that the *utamawazo* standards and their consequences are *necessarily* consistent with the germinal seed of culture. Cultural truths have no reality independent of the cultural expectations that give rise to them. Another concept, *utamaroho,* describes the fundamental feeling of life itself, the essential being or temperament, the cultural ethos. *Utamawazo* and *utamaroho* express the destiny of the cultural *asili.* According to Ani (1994), the European *asili* is Yurugu-like, and its disharmonious tendencies are expressed in European thought *(utamawazo)* and European feelings *(utamaroho).*

Yurugu is known for aggressiveness and incompleteness. The acquisitive nature of European colonialism is seen as the expression of the dominance-based *asili,* the cultural gene of European nationalism. Yurugu is the male element of the life force. But he is incomplete, as it has lost the female principle. In it's quest for dominance and wholeness, it must *despiritualize* the world, rendering the world natural only in its biological and physical forms. This despirited world can be conquered, ordered, and defined. It can only be known *objectively,* and the methods of rationality and science are the only ways to reveal its truths. The world of spirit remains inaccessible to the European culturgen (or *asili*) and this culturgen can only deal with the world by ignoring it, despiritualizing it, or destroying it. Since **spirit** is transcendent, unknowable, and, hence, uncontrollable, it must be ignored or actively rejected by the culture.

The despiritualizing process establishes a dichotomy between the self and the "other." The self is the conqueror and the "other" is the conquered. Fanon (1955) used the Shakespearean characters of Prospero and Caliban in his rendition of this racism-antiracism drama. In this approach, the other is imbued with those qualities of the self that threaten and contradict the formation of the self in accordance with *asili*-driven cultural dictates. It is identified in the other, kept at arms-length, rendered harmless to the cultural image of the natural order.

The European *asili* seeks power by its nature. It despirits the world, because power in the world of spirit is limited. Its aggressive need for domination is reinforced through thought processes *(utamawazo)* that rationalize the *asili* appetite and affective energies that express the driving life force *(utamaroho)*. The mechanisms of thought and feeling converge through institutions, values and ideology, aesthetics, self-images and images of others, self-reinforcing behavior, and behaviors directed toward others. The net result is an evolving cultural legacy that is embraced at birth by Yurugu who is ordained as "the permanent element of disorder in the universe, the agent of disorganization" (Ani, 1994, p. 556).

There are many critiques of Western culture that implicate its core values as responsible for the destructive patterns of racism and cultural domination around the world. The Ani (1994) biocultural account, embedded in Dogon mythology, does so in an unusual African-centered context. Nonetheless, it is familiar in its assignment of causality to cultural principles of power, control, self-interest, objectification, and rationality. At its heart, *Yurugu* (Ani, 1994) is a challenge to a Western worldview that not only enables but demands aggressive domination of "the other."

In our European heritage, the history of Manifest Destiny is a narrative of white superiority. In an African-centered view, *Yurugu* (Ani, 1994) is a counternarrative of white inferiority, where spirituality trumps rationality, and humanity is the ultimate victor over disordered, self-interested thought and behavior. The cultural wars are enjoined!

Yurugu (Ani, 1994), an analysis from cultural anthropology, seeks to explain patterns of racist behaviors over time. Next, we will consider an analysis from cultural psychology that considers the dimensions of a range of human experiences that are given shape and form by the cultural contexts in which they occur.

TRIOS: Domains of Cultural Expression and Meaning

McDougall (1921) described the individual attributes he claimed were responsible for the greatness of the Western world (see Chapter 12). These included curiosity, introversion, providence, will, and mental capacity. Their opposites, he feared, would be the cause of the United States' downfall. He assigned the opposites of these culture-enhancing attributes to "the other," and developed strategies to prevent "the other" from contaminating the dominant cultural seed.

TRIOS (Jones, 1979, 1986) offers an alternative to McDougall's account of human attributes that both broadens their character, expression and value, and links them in a positive way to African-centered cultural worldviews, and proposes examining the full expression of human experience within five domains that exist across the human condition. These are *time, rhythm, improvisation, oral expression, and spirituality*, or TRIOS. Figure 16.3 shows these five dimensions in a pyramidal shape. Here, time is the apex; improvisation, oral expression and spirituality are at the base; and rhythm, which is derivative of all four nodes, is located in the interior of the pyramid. It is proposed that each of these dimensions characterizes generic aspects of cultural evolution. That is, all cultures exist in *time*, and formulate ideas and values about time, ways to use it, take advantage of it, or control it. *Rhythm* reflects the pace, flow, and patterning of behavior, thought, and emotion as life unfolds in accordance with particular cultural prescriptions and requirements. *Improvisation* captures the dimensions by which we solve problems and create new possibilities. Its expression will depend, in part, on the particular challenges that require solution and the possibilities envisioned. *Oral expression* is a medium of communication and the foundation of intercultural interaction and relationships. *Spirituality* describes how we approach the mystery of our existence, and the consequences of this contemplation on our mental and psychological well-being.

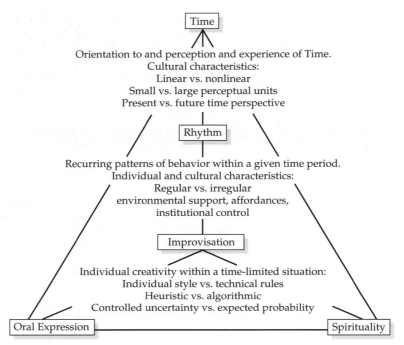

Time

Orientation to and perception and experience of Time.
Cultural characteristics:
Linear vs. nonlinear
Small vs. large perceptual units
Present vs. future time perspective

Rhythm

Recurring patterns of behavior within a given time period.
Individual and cultural characteristics:
Regular vs. irregular
environmental support, affordances,
institutional control

Improvisation

Individual creativity within a time-limited situation:
Individual style vs. technical rules
Heuristic vs. algorithmic
Controlled uncertainty vs. expected probability

Oral Expression   Spirituality

Social basis of information exchange   Belief in nonmaterial causation, an
  and historical representation: unknowable force:
  Action-based consequences vs.   Personal control irrelevant
  hypothetical abstractions   Pursuit of cosmic causation, explanation
  Social vs. intellective intelligence   Measure of accomplishment not on earth

FIGURE 16.3

TRIOS—Five Domains of Human Experience. *Source:* Jones, 1986: Figure 2, p. 297.

TRIOS is related to cultural racism because for each of these dimensions, there exist polarities of expression that differ in subjective or perceived, cultural value. In U.S. culture, merit is more likely to be assigned to those individuals who express a future time orientation, who master written (as opposed to oral) communication, who believe in their own agency or personal control, who plan ahead (thus obviating the need for time-pressured creativity or improvisation), and whose stability is expressed in regular, predictable behavioral rhythms. Psychological research and theorizing in the United States has consistently identified these human attributes as features of positive adjustment, behavior, achievement.

The TRIOS approach suggests this is a one-sided view, influenced significantly by the cultural worldview that has evolved in Europe and the United States over the past several centuries. This approach does not deny the validity and utility of each of these aspects of human thought and behavior. However, it rejects the idea that all other possibilities are deficient and, hence, less meritorious in our evaluative cultural framework. Rather, these dimensions are fundamental to human experience and contribute equally to what it means to be human. All people live in time and organize behavior with respect to it. The patterning of behavior shows regularity and order and can be set to a rhythmic template. Life is not perfectly predictable and people vary in how predictable their life is and how successfully they handle those unpredicted moments that intrude on expectation. We communicate through many different media, including writing, speaking, and a variety of nonverbal means. Each medium carries its own rules and requirements for extracting meaning, and each dictates, to some degree, the messages that can be sent and how they are received. Finally, all people exist between their corporeal selves and an awareness of forces that exist beyond them. The balance of influence between the self and those unknown forces defines aspects of religious and philosophical beliefs, self-awareness, and self-concept. TRIOS seeks a broader accounting of human capacity and potential. The set of attributes commonly selected for study and that serve as a standard of health and well-being in our country's dominant cultural perspective derive from McDougall's catalogue of human traits and abilities. The connection to cultural racism arises when we associate specific culture-laden human attributes with notions of normalcy, health, and achievement, while simultaneously rejecting the merit or validity of alternative possibilities along with the "others" who may possess them. Following are brief descriptions of the TRIOS dimensions.

Time

> In the complex of values the perception of time is the most significant one. A culture's sense of time is the key to its nature, and for an individual a particular and developed sense of time is an essential parameter of personality. When the perception of time changes, all other values are affected; conflicts in worldviews are likely to center on conflicts in perceptions of time. (Sobel, 1987, p. 21)

Attitudes toward time take on value in a culture because they ultimately link work, productivity, and the essential character of the individual. Sobel (1987) makes a general argument for the cultural fusion of whites and blacks in the South during the eighteenth century. Specific to her argument regarding time is the view that early English attitudes toward time were similar to the traditional African view. It was only later, under religious influences (both Anglican and Puritan), that time took on an evaluative tone.

Traditional West African cultures valued the slow movement of time, preaching the virtue of patience and waiting. Time was reckoned by the sun and people derived the meaning of time largely in the context of doing work. The order of temporal succession, or passage of time, was determined by the order of tasks, from morning to night, and was signaled externally by natural events, such as the sunrise and sunset. For example, the Nuer began a day at "very little light" and closed it some 13 time intervals later, at the "time of second sleep." Time was not an independent variable, having an existence all its own. In fact, the Nuer had no word for "time."

Mbiti (1970) suggests further that this behavioral time calendar did not emphasize the future, but the present and the past. In Swahili, for example, no word for *future* exists; there are only words for the present (*sasa*) and the past (*zamani*). Furthermore, the specific past was limited to three generations; beyond that, it was compressed into the time of one's ancestors (Sobel, 1987). This corresponds to the idea that, with death, one remains among the "living dead" until one passes from personal memory, at which time, one becomes an ancestor. The future is similarly compressed. For example, it exists literally "in front" of the present. For the Tiv of Nigeria, the future was usually measured by tomorrow, or the tomorrow after that, ". . . and had far less reality and importance than the past or present. The living community was the link that united ancestors and the unborn generations" (Sobel, 1987, p. 28).

In Trinidad West Indies, this time sense is preserved by the saying "Any time is Trinidad time" (Jones, 1986). "Trinidad time" is contrasted with time as an independent variable, an externally imposed organizer of individual behavior, a temporal yardstick that provides the metric for determining productivity, morality and worth. The *temponomic* view of time (cf. McGrath and Kelly, 1986) asserts that time is valuable and can serve as a medium of exchange. Thus, time can be saved or wasted, used well or badly. Sobel (1987, p. 23) describes an Anglican catechism that advised young scholars to search their souls and ask "How hast though spent thy time from thy childhood to this very moment?" Emergence of time sense is therefore linked to basic values and becomes a marker of expectations for meritorious participation in society.

This temponomic view of time is consistent with a capitalistic economy. Capital is typically accumulated over time, so that *wise* time use includes, for example, delaying immediate consumption for the accumulation of desirable goods or capital. This notion of delayed consumption was tested in Trinidad almost 40 years ago by Mischel and colleagues (Mischel, 1958, 1961a). Mischel (1958) tested a hypothesis that there were fundamental differences between East Indian and Negro Trinidadians. These differences were described by the following characterizations (Mischel, 1958, p. 57):

> *Negroes*: Impulsive, indulge themselves, settle for next to nothing if they can get it right away, do not work or wait for bigger things in the future but, instead, prefer smaller gains immediately.
> *East Indians*: Deprive themselves and are willing and able to postpone immediate gain and pleasure for the sake of obtaining greater rewards and returns in the future.

According to this hypothesis, the East Indians would be more attuned to the cultural demands of a Protestant ethic and, hence, would likely be more successful in a Western culture than would the Negroes, who displayed characteristics exactly opposite those that are likely to be rewarded.

Mischel (1958) had schoolchildren perform several paper-and-pencil tasks for him, then offered them rewards for their cooperation. Children were offered the choice of a 1-cent, unattractive candy, to be given immediately or 10-cent, attractively wrapped candy to be given a week later. He found that only 37 percent of those of African descent but 67 percent of those of East Indian descent chose the larger, but delayed, reward. Mischel (1958) next reasoned that acceptance of the delayed reward would likely be associated with trust of male socializing agents and would, hence, be related to the presence of the father in the home. The overall proportion of the African descended children who chose the delayed, larger rewards increased to 52 percent when only those with fathers present in the home were included. Mischel (1961a) extended his work to study the relationship between preference for delayed reinforcement and social responsibility and the need for achievement. In these studies he found that preference for larger, delayed reinforcement was positively associated with the social responsibility scale scores and with a measure of need for achievement. He further found an association between preference for immediate, smaller rewards and acquiescence in an ambiguous situation. Finally, Mischel (1961c) replicated the relationship with the father-absence condition. Here, however, he found that, although it applied to younger children aged 8 to 9, it did not apply to 11- through 14-year olds.

Rhythm

The word *rhythm* refers to a recurring patterning of behavior within a given time frame. The time unit determines the behavioral elements, and the repetition of those units over time creates a rhythmic pattern. In music, a 3/4 time signature means that there are three beats to a measure (time unit) and a quarter note gets one beat. The *experience* of this time signature is a waltz. A waltz is merely the behavioral dance pattern dictated by the 3/4 time signature. Therefore, the rules of rhythm generate patterning of activity which, in turn, give rise to certain experiences.

Rhythm describes the patterning of behavior in response to externally imposed time signatures—for example, work hours are 9 to 5, store hours are 10 to 6, court is in session from 9 to 3, cows' udders fill up overnight, and milking time is 6:00 A.M., and so on. There are also internal rhythms imposed by biology, psychology, and emotions—for example, menstrual cycles, biorhythms, and bipolar mental disorders. And, finally, there are nonscheduled external events that affect rhythmic patterns. Children get sick, people die, delivery people give a four- to six-hour "window" of opportunity, a fire alarm goes off, a partner leaves someone for a "better opportunity."

The metronome ticks regularly and inexorably, and people try to fit their behavior smoothly and effortlessly within the time pattern it dictates. The environmental demands order one's behavioral expression. The better and more natural the fit, the better one does, the better one feels. A person could be said to be "in flow"—that is, in synchrony—when this happens (cf. Cziksentmihaly, 1993). But, if a person is unable to meet those metronomic demands, or finds them discordant with either his or her own internal rhythms or those nonscheduled events that demand immediate attention, the person will be out of synch.

Rhythm is driven by energy flow. When the rhythm is stymied, labored, or out of synch, energy is blocked or diminished. The net effect of blockages, or *asynchrony*, can be either a loss of behavioral, mental, and emotional energy, or a sudden buildup (a "power surge") that causes one to career out of control.

Racism can be found in the race-based blockages of bias and differential treatment that threatens one's ability to develop and maintain the behavioral patterns that are dictated by the institutional metronomes of society. When a person gets stopped by the police because he is Hispanic and returning from the Caribbean, hauled in for search and questioning on suspicion of being a drug dealer, the rhythms of his everyday life are disrupted. When a woman has to fend off advances by a male business associate or a study partner because he has found her irresistible or "detected" something sexual in the way she smiles or brushes his arm, the flow of life is disrupted.

These micro-aggressions or assaults (Pierce, 1970) cause us to "miss a beat," and this throws our performance off. Furthermore, expending the energy needed to catch up or regroup takes a toll that weighs heavily on our sense of time.

But there is also the discordance between internal and external rhythms. The metronome is set by the majority's society and culture. The setting has been determined as that which is optimal for meeting societal goals. If it is not optimal for you, quite apart from the nonscheduled interruptions, you will find yourself marginalized. In music, black musicians revolted against the tyranny of the metronome of European-based music and created their own rhythms. They extended notes or cut them short. They refused to be constrained by measures with four beats, they gave them four-point-five beats, or three-point-five. The result was a rhythmic irregularity that was experienced by some as "ragged." Eubie Blake (1972) in a personal communication, suggested that Rag Time was born of this musical rebellion.

Physical, mental, and emotional health is promoted by rhythmic flow and synchrony in society. Circumstances that block it, whether imposed from outside, or merely discordant with what is inside, compromise health, and put one at risk for illness. In this society, race has created both nonscheduled rhythmic blockages, as well as demanded metronomic conformity to rhythms that derive from different cultural patterns and preferences. The TRIOS analysis (Jones, 1979, 1986) proposes that an examination of rhythms may be valuable in assessing problems of mental and behavioral health that are exacerbated by cultural assumptions and racial inequalities.

Improvisation
. . . composing, reciting or singing on the spur of the moment; making, inventing or arranging offhand. (*Webster's New Twentieth Century Dictionary of the English Language Unabridged,* 1965)

Improvisation is a combination of *expressiveness* and *invention or creativity*, which occurs *under time pressure*. To improvise, one must feel a certain freedom to call upon ideas, thoughts, talents, experiences, and memories with sudden yet appropriate style. To improvise, one must have a repertoire of ideas, thoughts, and experiences that can be called upon. But to *successfully* improvise, one must pull all of these ideas, thoughts and experiences together, carry them out with skill and in accordance with a master plan.

Improvisation lives with danger. Because of the time pressure and because the repertoire is not spelled out in advance, the entire performance is "on-line." There are no rehearsals, no net, no video out-takes—this is the real thing, live from New York.

Danger, metaphorically speaking, arises whenever routine expectations are rendered inapplicable. Expectations unconfirmed or anticipation unrealized sets the stage for a problem. However, standard problem-solving methods may not work in this context because, by definition, the problem is not standard. So how does one get out of this? How can one handle it so that things work out?

John Johnson (1972), owner and publisher of *Ebony Magazine,* among many other business ventures, has described his early days in Chicago, when he started Johnson Publishing. He was looking for office space but understood that a black man buying office space was not *standard.* Understanding this, he arranged for a white man to "front" for him, and he came along to view the space, posing as the man's "assistant." Thus, by undertaking a creative, improvised course of action, he was able to choose and secure the space he wanted.

Just as with rhythm, improvisation can be understood as a consequence of nonscheduled or unanticipated events and a relatively unpredictable environment. Although one may be aware that the environment is generally unpredictable, the specific moment in time and the nature of a nonscheduled event are generally not known. In such circumstances, "composing, arranging, inventing offhand," are skills that will stand one in good stead. Racism has historically presented African Americans with nonscheduled events that need to be managed. A bomb bursting through the living room window or exploding during church services helps reinforce one's belief in the unpredictability of things. Having your supervisor propose an evaluation of 3 when you deserve a 5 but *expect* to be offered a 4 may throw you for a loop, even when you try to prepare for the unexpected (cf. Chapter 13). It is equally disconcerting when a 12-year-old kid calls your little

Miles Davis—Jazz master of improvisation and collective creativity. (Bill Stamets/Impact Visuals)

daughter a "nigger" when you are simply enjoying a little "quality time" with her at the neighborhood pool.

Cultural racism can be thought of as the imposition of the need for certain groups to rely on adaptive strategies because they have been denied the use of conventional forms of behavior and means of advancement. Further, it stimulates the development of adaptive skills, which are then demeaned as inferior by the dominant group in the lexicon of meritocratic abilities and tendencies. This catch-22 situation is an insidious dimension of cultural racism.

However, improvisation is not entirely an imposed behavioral set, conditioned exclusively by racism. Improvisation is also a legacy of an African heritage. Improvisation is inventive and expressive. What distinguishes jazz music is the improvisational form that makes a performer a composer. Western music generally separates the two and bestows all the glory on the composer. This tendency to separate "agents" from "pawns" is contrasted with the unifying tendency to combine them.

Hofstede (1984) identified four major variables whose patterns of expression and organization define cultural identities:

1   *Power distance* refers to the distance between superior and subordinate; subordinates try to reduce the distance and superiors try to maintain or increase it. A high power distance viewpoint accepts inequality as a norm.
2   *Uncertainty avoidance* refers to the ephemeral nature of the future, which cannot begin . . . because it moves away if we try to approach it" (Hofstede, 1984). This future uncertainty gives rise to intolerable anxiety, which we manage by the rules and controlling mechanisms of technology, law and ritual, or religion. High uncertainty avoidance is associated with rigidity in adhering to norms and values and in relying on technological innovations to help one better control the future.
3   *Individualism* describes the relation of the individual to the collectivity. Cultures vary in the value they place on individual and collective orientations, and each culture values its own orientation most, imposing moral qualities on those who maintain this norm. High individualism validates a preference for individual accomplishment over collective interests and needs.
4   *Masculinity* refers to the extent to which a culture values "masculinity" (i.e., self-assertion and a high-dominance orientation) or "femininity" (i.e., nurturance and a low-dominance orientation). A high masculinity viewpoint values aggressive self-assertion over collective concerns.

Taken together, this pattern of cultural values corresponds well to the McDougall (1921) portrait of the source of strength in U.S. culture. This profile generally runs counter to the opposite polarity (described by TRIOS). With specific regard to improvisation, in joining composer and performer and melding the individual contributions of each artist as, by turns, a subordinate and a leader, the boundaries imposed by power distance, individualism, and masculinity are reduced or eliminated.

   Improvisation is both a skill, developed through adaptive responses to racist demands, and a cultural expression, evolved from a cultural system that values expressiveness, union, and collective action and is transplanted to a new oppressive context. Learning how these principles work and ways to incorporate them in the cultural systems of this country is a far better way to cope with racial and cultural difference than is attributing such differences to a nonplanful, impulsive character deficiency in the target groups.

Oral Expression
   In some African societies, such as Meroe, Kemet, and Abyssinia, written documents are extensive. However, in the whole of Africa and the African world, both past and present, there is a vocal-expressiveness modality that dominates all communication culture. . . . Expression . . . is not the captive of the written word, it is the word revealed in life. (Asante, 1987, p. 60)

Asante (1987) labels the sum total of oral tradition—including vocality, drumming, storytelling, praise singing, and naming—*orature*.
   In the TRIOS lexicon, oral expression is significant not only as an expression of African origins, as suggested by Asante (1987), but as a basis for the meaningful context for intelligent, moral, and interpersonal behavior. Failure to understand the oral foundation of thought, feeling, and behavior leaves us with an incomplete understanding of the meaning, form, and pattern of behavior.
   The oral tradition is not simply verbal exchange, but a representation of life itself. In Bantu, *nommo* means "word," and provides the energy that gives meaning

Griot tells a story at Yaou Village, Ivory Coast. Oral tradition records lessons of life, chronicles history of culture, and instills values to be learned and retained.

to the physical body (Jahn, 1961; Asante, 1987). In this tradition, it is through the spoken word that the most enduring verities are revealed. For example, a newborn child is not perceived as fully human until he or she has been named and that name has been officially pronounced. That is, the word embellishes and completes creation. The word accompanies actions and gives them meaning. For example, Senghor (1956, p. 56) describes how orature accompanies the work of a goldsmith:

> The prayer, or rather the power that the goldsmith recites, the hymn of praise sung by the sorcerer while the goldsmith is working the gold, the dance of this myth at the close of the operation, it is all—poem, song, dance—which, in addition to the movement of the artisan, completes the work and makes it a masterpiece.

Oral expressions confer meaning on events, reveal truths of existence, and bind people together in common understanding and purpose.

Oral expression can also serve as a medium of learning and memory. For example, Cole, Gay, Glick, and Sharp (1971) selected a 20-item list of common objects (e.g., a rake and a fork) and presented them to college students in the United States and in Liberia, Africa (from the Kpelle tribe). They found that the number of presentations needed to memorize the entire list was considerably less for the Americans than for the Kpelle. In fact, the Africans were never able to memorize more than 10 items on the list. Cole et al. proceeded to test various explanations for this difference in terms of the way in which the objects were encoded, categorized in memory, and recalled. In some experiments they attempted to categorize the objects for the Africans as the U.S. students had categorized them, because it seemed that their way was superior. It made no difference in the Kpelle's ability to recall. One might conclude from this that the Africans simply had inferior memories.

However, Cole, Gay, et al. (1971) were not content to stop there. Obviously for cultures to have survived over the thousands of years that African civilizations have done, memory must be more highly developed than that. They decided to enlist the aid of the oral tradition as the basic structure for presenting the objects. They told a very simple story about the marriage of the daughter of a chief. On the day of her wedding, the daughter learned that the man she was marrying was an evil witch doctor, and she feared he would take her away to his kingdom and she would never be able to escape. As she left her father's house, she left a trail so that her family could find her. She dropped along the way a rake, then a fork, and so on. In this context, the African students learned every item on the list and recalled them in exactly the order in which they were dropped!

Moreover, when Cole, Gay, et al. (1971) asked the African subjects to sort the items into the "appropriate" categories (i.e., those anticipated by the researchers), the subjects sorted them into functional groups (e.g., a knife with an apple, and a potato with a hoe). The Kpelle did not sort them into the abstract categories of food or tools that the researchers had expected to see. The subjects then explained to the researchers, who were puzzled by their sortings, that this was how a *wise* person would sort them. "How would a fool do it?" they were asked. They replied by listing exactly what the researchers had judged to be the "appropriate" categories! "Stupid is as stupid does," the sage Forrest Gump observed. We might adapt his aphorism to this situation by noting that "Wise is as wise does."

Two important points can be made about this example. First, oral discourse carries a great deal of meaning. Second, performance may require a functional context for its elicitation. Therefore, standardized tests, which depart from both of these ideas, may, by their form and nature, disadvantage young African American children. Understanding how orature operates and what consequences it has for performance, moral judgment, interpersonal relationships, and the formation of attitudes and beliefs is important to appreciating the cultural bases of racial effects.

Spirituality

Spirituality is a belief in nonmaterial causation (Jones, 1986). That is, cause or force is not always objectifiable, or even knowable. Science, as a cultural epistemology, and individualism, as a cultural value, hold the determination and exercise of causality to be the highest cultural values. Both of these values tend away from spirituality and may lead, ultimately, to a despirited world (Ani, 1994).

Being spiritual people in a despirited world raised contradictions and conflicts that are quite significant. Spirituality raises a host of personal and cultural expressions that challenge basic assumptions about the determinants of mental health, motivation for achievement, behavioral regulation, and so on. Spirituality is a significant component of not only the culture of African Americans, but of Puerto Ricans, Chicanos, American Indians, and others as well.

The issue of causality can be reduced to the understanding of life force—what makes things happen. Jahn (1961) argues that African philosophy contains four primary categories within which all being is defined:

1   *Muntu*—Human being
2   *Kintu*—Things

3 *Hantu*—Place and time
4 *Kuntu*—Modality

All things belong to one of these categories and are defined in their essence, not as substances but as forces. *Ntu* is the universal force that can attach to people, places, things, and modalities. The *ntu* force is not unique to humans, and it is not always reduced to the conventional material dimensions of cause-effect. Therefore, a person who is spiritual *shares* cause-effect agency with *ntu*, and does not claim it all for himself or herself.

In our society, being a cause is seen as fundamental to personal control and psychological well-being and accomplishment. Self-actualization (Maslow, 1962) is a personal expression of this desire, this need for control. Research by Langer and Rodin (1976) showed that physical well-being can be improved if we just give a measure of control to people in nursing homes, who generally have lost control. Moreover, Langer (1983) has shown that we seek to gain control in situations that inherently afford no control. She demonstrated this by inviting subjects to play a game of bingo. Half of the subjects were *given* cards (no control) and the other half were allowed to *choose* their cards (illusion of control). Before letting them actually play—and, therefore, before any real value for the cards could be empirically established—she asked them for their cards back and asked how much she would have to pay them as a fair exchange for the cards. Subjects who had *chosen* their cards gave them a greater monetary value.

The critical issue concerns where the life force resides. In Western psychology, the humanism of individuality takes precedence and humans are capable of and expected to exert force on and thereby control their circumstances. This internal control has been expressed in various ways in psychological theorizing. For example, DuCharms (1966) distinguished people characterized by beliefs about internal control ("origins") from those who were more likely to perceive causation as lying outside of their direct control (he labeled these people "pawns"). Not surprisingly in a culture that emphasizes personal control, he found that pawns generally had lower self-esteem and lower levels of achievement than those whom he characterized as "origins." Other concepts in psychology (e.g., internal locus on control [Rotter, 1966] and field independence [Witkin, Dyk, Faterson, Goodenough, and Karp, 1962]) have consistently assigned superior adaptive and development qualities to internal causal agency. Spirituality offers another view of personal causality that provides another lever for opening an analysis of the cultural dominance of traditional values.

Africentrism: A Battle for Cultural Meaning

Africentricity places ". . . African ideals at the center of any analysis that involves African culture and behavior" (Asante, 1987, p. 6). Because Africa is the origin of both African cultures and black people—who are assigned racial status in the European cultural system—race and culture often converge. That is, skin color and other physical features were perfectly confounded with the cultural differences that stood out from the beginning. The evolution and adaptation of Africans in America has perpetuated this confounding. Proposing to "ignore" race means that one must also ignore culture. The problems of racism are closely tied to the evaluation and denigration of culture. Therefore, in its broadest scope, cultural racism and racism are the same thing.

The development of an Africentric analysis first took on formal scholarly properties perhaps with the statements of W. E. B. DuBois (1903). The double-consciousness of Africans in the United States may have represented a fractured and dissociated identity that could only be made whole by the replenishment of its African origins. At the heart of Africentrism is a contestation for the meaning of Africa and of being African. Cultural racism gives rise to a war for cultural meaning. Africentrism is defensive, seeking to explain away the negative judgments of color, character, and culture! "I am not diminished because I am black, I am just as capable as white people." Over time, this defensive battle has given way to a more offensive thrust, one that attacks whites and European cultures. Rather than striving to measure up and continually coming up short, in the offensive approach one attacks the value yardstick, rejecting the metric and its consequent meaning. . . . That is, "it is not we who are flawed or deficient, but those would have us believe it."

According to this view, if blacks in a racialized world have diminished value as African Americans, they may as well be European Americans with black skins. In a society dominated by a European-inspired cultural worldview, this is where the colorblind idea leads. If, as an African American one is unable to identify any collective African American cultural contribution to humanity, then one is always faced with an inferiorized position in a European-dominated society. Africentrism reflects not only aspects of the cultural war for meaning, but the defensive protection of the value of African origins and the offensive attack on the cultural system that denigrates them.

Africans in the United States resisted slavery, resisted Jim Crow, resisted the "separate but equal" doctrine, resisted segregation (both *de facto* and *de jure*), insisted on civil rights, and, now more than ever before, insist on human rights. Africentrism is a symbol and a formal instrument of those human rights. In its politicized and polemical form, it initiates counterattacks and, occasionally, pincer movements aimed at the soft underbelly of European thought (cf. Bernal, *Black Athena*, 1987; Ani, 1994). But, for the most part, it mediates the two warring ideals in one dark collective consciousness.

The disputes over Africentric claims are, in part, disputes over the validity of the methods and the nature of the evidence offered in support of cultural claims. Disputes are also over the cultural story people want or need to believe. Some defenders of traditional scholarship criticize the Africentric revisionism, with its rules of evidence and canons of objectivity. Africentrism is belittled by some as being an exercise of delusional self-enhancement aided and abetted by flawed scholarship (D'Souza, 1995; Lefkowitz, 1996; Schlesinger, 1992). Conversely, the Africentric critique belittles European cultural pathologies (cf. Ani, 1994) and, in its turn, reorders events so that European thought becomes derivative of African genius. The European story strips Africans of humanity in contemporary cultural currency. Africentrism seeks to reclaim that humanity in contemporary cultural terms.

Africentrism is properly viewed as a battleground in the cultural wars. However, because the disputants arrive at the fray with different needs and different analytical tools, it is not a war that really can be won. For example, Bowersock (1996, pp. 6–7) in reviewing the anti-Africentric *Not Out of Africa* (Lefkowitz, 1996), noted that:

[although] "the Greeks themselves believed they owed much to Egypt, and the statements of Herodotus and Diodorus to this effect accordingly have to be treated as evidence, . . . [she] . . . mounts a powerful argument disproving what these ancient authors reported *and what they themselves believed."*

The Africentrists take first-hand historical accounts of thoughts and beliefs as data, and the anti-Africentrists reject that same evidence as fictional. The dispute comes down to beliefs and to the methods one accepts for identifying and evaluating evidence. The conflict is also complicated by the different psychological goals served by the outcome of the analysis. The debate over the validity and evidence of Africentrism is not able to settle the cultural war, because it is an exemplification of the war itself. Bowersock (1996, p. 6) seems to acknowledge this view when he likens the debate to a "dialogue of the deaf."

These issues may be seen as but another element of racialized discourse and antiracist reactions. Hegemonic dominance rests, in part, on the functional validity of superiority-inferiority myths. One strategy for combating hegemonic control over one's life is to rewrite the myths, both for one's own group and the hegemonic group. Racism is the context that spawns these debates, and racism will not end by a finding of fact.

The Bell Curve *Wars*

> It should be obvious that IQ tests do not directly measure innate gene-determined intellectual capacity, but do measure current intellectual performance *as defined by a particular culture or at least by its psychologists.* (Gottesman, 1968, p. 25, emphasis added)

When *The Bell Curve* (Herrnstein and Murray, 1994) hit the streets, it was treated by many as if it were a new and definitive analysis of intelligence and intellectual capacity, one whose implications for social policy were clear and unequivocal. In fact, it was another expression of earlier wars about the nature of intelligence and the implications of group differences for our society. The authors claimed it was about class structure and only incidentally about race (Herrnstein and Murray, 1994). They held that it was about the contributions of intellectual ability to social standing—whatever the race of the persons in question. But, in this society, IQ is valued and attaches differentially to racial groups. When, as this analysis does, such differences are presented as having a substantially, if not exclusively, genetic basis, and when the genetic basis is perceived as growing not shrinking, the development of a large and permanent cognitive underclass that is disproportionately black may be inevitable. That is why the book is incendiary, and why the war metaphor sticks.

Jensen (1968) argued that, although it was not possible to define intelligence, it could be measured. Although Jensen (1968, pp. 5–6) stated, "There is no point in arguing the question to which there is no answer, the question of what intelligence really is," he proceeded, in effect, to "define" *intelligence* as "what intelligence tests measure." In arguing for racial difference in IQ, he made the following observations:

1   *IQ is under genetic control.* Jensen (1968) cites studies with twins that show that IQ correlations between identical twins are greater than fraternal twins, which are greater than those between individual siblings. Further, siblings are more similar in IQ than randomly selected children.

2   *There are racial differences in IQ.* That is, holding other factors constant, racial differences remain.

Jensen argued that, because IQ is under genetic control, and there exist racial differences in IQ, then racial differences are due to genetic factors. Kagan (1969) rejected this argument, noting that height is obviously under genetic control. However, to conclude that differences in height between urban- and rural-dwelling South American Indians were due to genetic factors would be erroneous. Environmental determinants, such as disease and malnutrition, offer better explanations for the differences.

Furthermore, a study of 38 pairs of identical twins reared in different environments showed average IQ differences of 14 points, and, in at least one-quarter of the cases, different environments produced IQ differences of more than 16 points. This difference is larger than the average difference between black and white populations in the United States and led investigator Gottesman (1968, p. 27) to conclude: "The differences observed so far between whites and Negroes can hardly be accepted as sufficient evidence that with respect to intelligence, the Negro American is less endowed."

McDougall (1921) referred to the newly developed IQ tests as "mental anthropology," implying that the purpose of IQ tests was to differentiate racial groups in mental capacity. Because intelligence is obviously a positive and valued concept in this culture, and because intelligence has been defined by some as what IQ tests measure, IQ scores stand as a proxy for human value. But, in what, if any, sense should a college professor who graduated Phi Beta Kappa be considered more intelligent than, say, the eminently successful high school dropout Frank Sinatra? In the strict biological sense, *intelligence* means simply the ability to adapt to environmental circumstances so as to perpetuate the species. By this criterion, the cockroach *is* very intelligent, whereas the dinosaur *was* not.

Intelligence, defined as "what intelligence tests measure," has great importance in this society, where school achievement is considered very important. Intelligence is what people want to predict and control.

An insidious element of intelligence tests is the implicit assumption that people who score high on them are, in some way, better than people who score low. Over the years, formal education has served to elevate the people who obtained it above the masses who did not. Educated people were perceived as somehow better than uneducated people. Perhaps, more than any other single trait, intelligence is the yardstick by which superiority is measured—white over black, male over female, rich over poor. It is important to understand that having an IQ test score of 150 does not make a person "better" than a person having a test score of 100. There are a lot of dimensions to human potential, and no one person or index of personal qualities embodies them all.

Jensen (1968) attempted to prove that blacks were genetically inferior in intelligence by showing that, even when all possible variables known to be related to intelligence test performance were controlled, blacks still scored lower than whites. In the end, he suggested that there are two different kinds of learning ability: level 1, or *associative ability* (blacks tend to be good at this); and level 2, or *conceptual ability* (whites tend to be good at this). Level 2, he contended, is a higher-order ability, as a person must be proficient at level 1 in order to perform well at level 2, but not vice versa. Generalized intelligence, or "g," is associated with level 2 abilities, but not with level 1 abilities. Therefore, Jensen's argument becomes, more simply, not

that blacks are of inferior intelligence per se, but that they are simply at a genetically less-advanced stage of intellectual development.

The point to be made here is very simple. The notion of intelligence as the ability to manipulate abstract symbols and concepts (which is what IQ tests measure) is
a culturally biased one—not because it is simply wrong. It is culturally biased because, although its approach is incomplete, it masquerades as the definitive truth.

Accepting this standard absolutely is to fall into the trap of cultural ethnocentrism. What criteria support this concept of intelligence as an absolute? And to
what kind of society does such acceptance lead? To reduce, in the form of culturally
biased IQ tests, the numerous value judgments that a term such as *intelligence* carries is to engage in the highest form of cultural racism.

More recent analyses have offered a view of multiple dimensions of intelligence that cover a broader domain of relevant human functioning. Sternberg (1988)
proposes three forms of intelligence in his triarchic theory:

1 *Componential intelligence*—Information processing ability. This is closest to what
   IQ tests measure.
2 *Experiential intelligence*—Creativity and insight. It is possibly related to improvisation (described earlier under TRIOS).
3 *Contextual intelligence*—Practical problem-solving knowledge or "street
   smarts." This includes social skills and relations, possibly involving the consequences of orature.

The Sternberg (1988) approach broadens the scope of intelligent action, and, by so
doing, introduces a broader set of cultural variables than the overdetermined IQ
test does.

Gardner (1983) further expanded the domain of intelligence by suggesting that
it takes seven forms:

1 Language
2 Logic and math
3 Visual and spatial thinking
4 Music
5 Bodily and kinesthetic skills (dance, athleticism)
6 Intrapersonal skills (self-knowledge)
7 Interpersonal skills (leadership, social abilities)

In this view, the variety of ways in which a person may behave with purpose and
positive effect is expanded even further. As we saw in the discussion of TRIOS,
meaningful, purposeful, and desirable behavior can vary across cultures. Insisting
that a heavily loaded word, such as *intelligence*, is reducible to a single factor (called
"g" in this case) and that this nugget of excellence is largely inherited betrays the
operation of a cultural myopia that feeds the notions of cultural racism.

Obviously, there is no merit in arguing absolutely against the usefulness of abstract, conceptual thought, for it is the foundation of scientific thought and discovery. We can attribute many desirable advances to the fact that some people (of different colors and cultures) had these abilities. However, there are other ways of
thinking that are most frequently represented in people of different cultural (and,
usually, different racial) characteristics. That is, the "culture-free" test that would
allow an unbiased measuring of generalized intelligence has not yet been created.

Perhaps such a test is not possible. This may be because *the criteria against which IQ tests are validated are contaminated by the same racial biases that underlie the tests themselves!* That is a fundamental illustration of cultural racism.

"Knowledge" is not totally contained by the abstract conceptual processes of level 2 intellect. It can accrue to the level 1 (associative) type of thought, as well as to even-less-structured modes of "knowing" (e.g., intuition, mysticism, and emotionalism). The important point is that, generally, the consequences of conceptual thought are scientific discovery and the "advancement" of Western civilization. In our society, *Western civilization* and *civilization* are considered synonymous; therefore, intellectual functioning relevant to the growth of that civilization is *ipso facto* the *best, highest*, or whatever term one chooses to use.

We are speaking of cultural racism. Because the advancement of an individual in this culture depends, in large part, on his or her school achievement (although the statistics cited earlier suggest that this advancement is greatly affected by race), the functioning of school systems is predicated on cultural assumptions that define the most important aspect of performance in terms of a measure into which cultural inferiority has been programmed. This unindimensional view of intelligence excludes possible differences in the cognitive and behavior adaptations of black children. Contexts or experience play a very important part in the way one processes information, whether in abstraction or by association.

The debate over nature-nurture in IQ and the nature and extent of racial differences became focused on social policy when Herrnstein (1971, pp. 58–63) argued, in *The Atlantic Monthly*, the following syllogism:

1   If differences in mental abilities are inherited, and
2   If success requires these abilities, and
3   If earnings and prestige depend on success, then
4   Social standing (which reflects earnings and prestige) will be based to some extent on inherited differences among people.

The provocative point about this article was not the claim of racial differences in IQ—or even the idea that success requires possession of the abilities that are measured by the IQ test. The real issue is that *equality of opportunity* would lead to *inequality of outcomes*. Herrnstein (1971, p. 63) put it this way:

> What is most troubling about this prospect [willy-nilly sorting into inherited castes] is that the growth of a virtually hereditary meritocracy will arise out of the successful realization of contemporary political and social goals.

The ideal of equality in U.S. society has the inevitable consequence, according to the Herrnstein (1971) analysis, of creating an inherited caste system.

Then comes *The Bell Curve*, in 1994, with a hauntingly familiar refrain. Herrnstein's inherited caste system based on intelligence is now labeled, by Murray and Herrnstein, "the cognitive elite"—the high-IQ aristocracy. The *cognitive elite* arises from the tendency for those with high IQs to be favored by our meritocratic principles of equal opportunity, to develop intimate relationships with similarly situated (and endowed) others, and to pass on their "superior" genes (and, thereby, their superior status) to their offspring. This cycle perpetuates the cognitive-based racial stratification attributed to racism. Because this stratification arises as a result of naturally occurring genetic superiority, according to this theory, the only way to change it is through social policy intervention that, in effect, reverses this "natural" ordering.

According to *The Bell Curve* analysis, such interventions—for example, affirmative action—have the net effect of diminishing our country's overall standing (as McDougall feared democracy would do).

Therefore, rather than trying to elevate members of the cognitive underclass to positions that normally would and should be held by the cognitive elite, Herrnstein and Murray (1994, p. 535) argue:

> The broadest goal is a society in which people throughout the functional range of intelligence can find, and feel they have found, a valued place for themselves. [A place is valued if] . . . *other people would miss you if you were gone.*[2]

But they argue that finding a valued place is much more difficult for people who are not very smart than it is for the intelligent. People of low intelligence, accordingly to Herrnstein and Murray (1994) literally cannot tell right from wrong. Our criminal justice system is too complex; it offers too many caveats for explaining away wrongful behavior. Immoral criminal behavior is a more likely outcome for those of low intelligence, because, in 1990, life has become too complex for them to be able to follow a "moral compass" as they could in, say, 1950, when things were simple. Herrnstein and Murray (1994, p. 544) grant, though, that even "people of limited intelligence can lead moral lives in a society that is run on the basis of 'Thou shalt not steal'." Moreover, "It has become more difficult for a person of low cognitive ability to figure out why marriage is a good thing, and once in a marriage, more difficult to figure out why one should stick with it through bad times" (Herrnstein and Murray, 1994, p. 544).[3]

The Bell Curve assumes that most people have enough intelligence to get on with their lives. But, argue Herrnstein and Murray (1994, p. 536), "the prevalence of social maladies we reviewed was strikingly concentrated in the bottom IQ deciles . . ." *Social maladies* are here defined to include poverty, unwed parentage, and poor parenting. Although the voluminous text very carefully and openly evaluates a huge amount of data to support its statistical claims, it is the policy suggestions that raise the dander of many.

Simplifying the government is perhaps a good idea for economic and governance reasons, and Republicans and conservatives, in general, have argued that point for centuries. It does not seem necessary, though, to suggest that we should do so just because the complexity of government and society renders low IQ-citizens incapable of knowing right from wrong or the benefits of being married.

The Bell Curve tries to soften the blow of its message with caveats and reasonable proposals. For example, the statistics cited in the book are aggregated over large groups of people. The authors note that it would be wrong to use the generalizations about groups to predict anything about an individual person:

> Measures of intelligence have reliable statistical relationships with important social phenomena but they are a limited tool for deciding what to make of any given individual. (Herrnstein and Murray, 1994, p. 21)

---

[2] Apparently, slaves found that "valued place" because, when they ran away, slave owners went after them to bring them back. Apparently they were missed when they were gone!

[3] It is ironic here that leaving a marriage is attributed to lack of intelligence by Herrnstein and Murray (1994), but for McDougall (1921), it was a sign of intellectual self-assertion. It seems all the more evident that these ad hominem interpretations of cultural character are arbitrary and self-serving.

This is, of course, what we should expect if we wish to avoid prejudicial attitudes and behaviors. Herrnstein and Murray, (1994, p. 313) go on to cement this view asserting that:

> We cannot think of a legitimate argument why any encounter between individual whites and blacks need be affected by the knowledge that an aggregate ethnic difference in measured intelligence is genetic instead of environmental.

But do we suspend this expectation for an individual person on the basis of what we think we know about the group? The large body of information presented in Part 2 of this book suggests that we don't. Patterson (1995, p. 192), finds that ". . . in this one paragraph the authors have not only betrayed an incredible naiveté about the interracial behavior of their fellow White Americans, but have brought into question the whole point of their work."

To the extent that these propositions rest on the analysis of the data they present and interpret, it is important to examine the strength of the authors' analysis in order to fairly evaluate the validity of their policy claims. We do not have time nor inclination here to take on a critique of *The Bell Curve*. *The Bell Curve Wars* (Fraser, 1995) does this. Apart from the passions that arise from merely discussing this volatile question of racial differences in IQ and the implications for social policy, there are basic statistical critiques that call the whole validity of the project into question, as Gould (1994) cogently points out. Gould (1994) notes *The Bell Curve's* claim that cognitive ability ". . . almost always explains less than 20 percent of the variance . . . usually less than 10 percent and often less than 5 percent. What this means in English is that you cannot predict what a given person will do from his IQ score." This is an appropriate caveat. However, in the very next sentence, Herrnstein and Murray (1994, p. 117) make a strong connection between group data and individual implications when they state "We will argue that intelligence itself, not just its correlation with socioeconomic status, is responsible for these group differences (p. 117)." Gould (1994) suggests that, if you take seriously the Herrnstein and Murray (1994) claim that about 60 percent of IQ differences can be explained by genetics, and given that these differences only explain about 5 to 20 percent of individual variation, then only 3 to 12 percent of variations among individuals can be accounted for by heritability! (This is based on 60% heritability × 5% to 20% of the variance explained.) What explains the other 88 to 97 percent?

Another source of weakness in this study was noted by Nisbett (1995). Using data supplied by the authors themselves, he noted that the mean IQs of children fathered by black GIs was 96.5 and that of children fathered by white GIs was 97. He also noted that a study that correlated IQ with the estimate of European genetic heritage (generally suspected to be about 20 to 30% among most African Americans) of young blacks in Philadelphia found a correlation of .05! Nonetheless, these results, along with those of four other studies that showed no genetic variation in IQ by race, were given short shrift relative to a well-known study by Scarr and Weinberg (1987). The authors compared IQ scores of 273 children of transracial adoptive parents. The subjects were one hundred thirty black children, whose IQs were compared with those of their white adoptive parents, and 143 white children, whose IQs were compared to those of their biological parents. The average correlations between parents and their biological offspring were .36 for the adoptive parents and their children and .38 for biological parents of adoptive children. This evidence is taken as support for the heritability of IQ. In the same study, though, correlations between adoptive parents and their adoptive children averaged .24, whereas the correlations between the natural parents of adoptive children and the natural children of the adoptive parents was only .16. This finding suggests some family cohort effect. This finding is made even stronger by the observation that, although the average IQ correlation among biological siblings was .42, among unrelated adoptive siblings in the same family it was also .42!

The strong claim of IQ heritability is based primarily on the Scarr and Weinberg (1983) adoption studies. Contrary evidence is castigated for various reasons—usually self-selection of subjects. The facts are anything but unequivocal and—certainly, on the basis of knowledge of statistical tests—very weak at best. Yet Herrnstein and Murray (1994) offered recommendations for social policy with firm self-confidence.

In some cases, *The Bell Curve* makes some reasonable proposals. For example, Herrnstein and Murray (1994, p. 475) do not argue for the complete elimination of affirmation action:

> We urge that affirmative action in the universities be radically modified, returning to the original conception. Universities should cast a wide net in seeking applicants, making special efforts to seek talent wherever it lives—in the black South Bronx, Latino Los Angeles, and White Appalachia alike. In the case of two candidates who are fairly closely matched otherwise, universities should give the nod to the applicant from the disadvantaged background. This original sense of affirmative action seems to us to have been not only reasonable and fair but wise.

They define *closely matched* in terms of test scores such that no identifiable group would have test scores that deviate by more than a half of a standard deviation from those of the rest of the student body. By their reckoning, this is a fairly relaxed standard as it requires that the average racial-minority score need only be at the 30th percentile of whites.

We will now declare a ceasefire and move on. *The Bell Curve* is indeed a provocative book that raises some vexing questions about race, social class, and intelligence in the United States. But it offers very little that is new, and it inflames our passions over race and makes some provocatively strange claims about social behavior and intelligence. It is probably true that the two most incendiary issues regarding racism are (1) the belief that blacks have lower intelligence than whites and (2) the belief that the assumed differences in intelligence are genetically determined. *The Bell Curve* advances, in the most dramatic way, this continued set of racialistic cultural beliefs. Whatever may be the true convictions and expressed purposes of this book, it is very difficult to find credible and useful ways to interpret and implement its findings and recommendations.

SUMMARY: CONSTRUCTING CULTURE— THE NEW RACISM

One of the problems we face in trying to understand racism is its changing face. This changing face has led D'Souza (1995) to claim that racism no longer exists—although everyday there are new charges filed. A shopping mall in suburban Buffalo refuses to grant permission to erect a bus stop for bus lines from the inner city. A young black woman is killed on her way to work at the mall as she tries to cross an eight-lane highway. Is it racism, or just business?

The new racism emphasizes traditional values of community, freedom, and rights. Who could object to that? But, in our cultural history, being black, or brown, or red, or yellow has always marginalized one's membership in the community of Americans. The standard set for inclusion is, in a subtle and nonobvious way, like the objective standard in apartheid South Africa, where one could become an honorary white. When Max Robinson, the first black news anchor at ABC, was told his "race didn't matter," he felt as if he had been made an honorary white as a reward and acknowledgment of his ability. General Colin Powell is thought by some people to typify this status. Such people say that General Powell is the kind of black man that white people wish all black people would be like.

It is because group membership has historically been a source of disenfranchisement in the United States that hearkening back to the ideals of liberty and freedom often rings hollow. Individual rights and freedoms, probably more than any other principles, define the essence of the U.S. experiment in democracy. But those rights and freedoms were first withheld, then grudgingly given, and their exercise often sabotaged for blacks and other people of color. The rules have been set by parties hostile to black interests. The society has evolved with those rules in place for several centuries, carefully and incisively sowing the seeds of disadvantage. In the span of a few years, the new racism proclaims that race-based decision making is un-American and that only individual rights count. Well, the fact is that race-based decision making has always been very American. It got us into the racism problem, and now we propose to eliminate it as a way to get out.

Our contemporary culture sets a course toward affirming the primacy of individual rights. However flawed this policy may be in regard to continuing racism, it is argued that, in the long run, it is the surest way to reach our goal of a society in which individuals are free and have equal opportunity to pursue the American dream. The fact is that the American dream is not now equally accessible, as Hochschild (1994), Carnoy (1994), and others demonstrate. Moreover, the evidence from sociopsychological research suggests that the cumulative values, attitudes, and beliefs—and their symbolic representation and selective influence on perception—will ensure that subtle racial biases will continue to operate. The new racism takes on a self-congratulatory "objectivity" about race. But rather than exalting the very best of our traditions of freedom and liberty, these new traditionalists conjure up the bigotry and bias that we seek to eliminate.

The racism-antiracism struggles continue as the "culture wars" escalate. Ethnic, racial, and cultural diversity; multiculturalism; feminism and gender equity; affirmative action and anti-affirmative action; immigration and anti-immigration; bilingualism and anti-bilingualism—are all cultural ingredients of this centuries-old struggle. We contend over the specifics of policy and practice regarding race, we contest the meaning and implications of being racial or ethnic or American. The process, as well as the outcome, seeps into our cultural awareness and identity. Buchanan had it all wrong when he argued that his followers had to "take the culture back" (Buchanan, 1992). The protests, the change, the struggle, and the debates are part of the culture. His view is part of the culture, as well.

In sum, the new racism isn't new. It is the same old values and beliefs, spun anew in a different time. Cultural racism embodies the adverse realities of race in our culture, where individual experiences are colored by the side of the racial divide on which one falls. We are not homogeneous as a people, and our differences matter. As we seek to make our society more fair, defined by equality of opportunity regardless of race, we have to know that perceptions of how close we are to success depends on which side we're on. The new racism proclaims us to be closer to fairness than those members of minority racial groups—and many others who wage antiracism warfare—believe us to be.

17

Racism: Toward a Macro-Micro Integration

❖

Introduction ◆ Racism as a structural and dynamic model ◆ *Culture* ◆
Institutions ◆ *Individuals* ◆ Antiracism—A cultural coda ◆ *What is antiracism?* ◆
Critique of antiracism ◆ *Antiracism as a pathway to change*

INTRODUCTION

*A*llen Iverson dribbled the ball at the top of the key, then suddenly darted toward the basket, headed right toward three much taller men trying to defend the goal. He elevated his six-foot frame above the rim, challenging the defenders to stop him. He dropped the finger roll into the basket and drew the foul. The Georgetown Hoyas went on to crush Villanova that day, 106-87. Iverson scored 37 points.

Billy Packer is a broadcaster and analyst of college basketball for CBS. He was properly impressed with Iverson's daring and talent, his will to win. He said, over the air, that Iverson was "one tough monkey." Oops. Did he say *monkey*? Is he saying that Iverson, a black man, looks like a monkey? Acts like a monkey? Thinks like a monkey? Isn't that a racist thing to say?

Within 18 minutes of his monkey comment, Packer apologized to anyone who had felt offended by his remark. He meant nothing by it. But it did not stop there. Phone calls to the arena and to the local television station came in complaining about the remark. Calls for sanctions by CBS for his offensive remark came from the NAACP. Was his comment racist? Does his intention matter here? The next day, Packer was broadcasting another game and took the occasion to state his view:

I don't know why people are sensitive about something that to me, to my way of thinking, has absolutely nothing to do with race. Al Capone was a tough monkey. Mike Ditka
was a tough monkey. . . . It has absolutely nothing to do with genetics, so I don't know
how people even make the connection. I don't. I don't even think of Allen Iverson as a
black player. I think of Allen Iverson as a player. (Shapiro, 1996, p. E1)

The point of this example is simply that we are terribly sensitive about race in
the United States. For the vast majority of Americans, racism is ugly and is not condoned. Very few would publicly claim, "Yes I am a racist, and damned proud of it."
Yet, if this is true, why do we spend so much time talking about it, detecting it, decrying it, and trying to get rid of it? The material contained in this book is intended
to help sort through some of these complex and troubling issues.

The aim of this chapter is twofold: First, we will pull together the multiple perspectives on racism by discussing how they come together. We have already described and analyzed racism at the individual, institutional, and cultural levels. Are
these levels of racism separate forms of the phenomenon, different aspects of the
same general idea, or all really the same thing? We will discuss these issues with
the aid of a graphic representation of their interconnection.

Second, we will provide a brief discussion of *antiracism*. As we noted in the
previous chapter, racism has been a constant and, at times, pervasive aspect of U.S.
society. Nonetheless, there have always been varying degrees of allegiance to racist
principles and, for most of our history, there has always been active resistance to
racism itself. These forces of resistance are known collectively as antiracism.

RACISM AS A STRUCTURAL AND DYNAMIC MODEL

Racism exists at multiple levels and has evolved over time in this country. Racism
was built into the fabric of U.S. society as a result of the slave trade and its formalization as the institution of slavery. It was expanded by the rationalization of slavery, as well as the doctrines of the White Man's Burden and Manifest Destiny. "Civilization" (self-characterization of Europeans) was contrasted with "primitiveness"
(Africans) and "savagery" (American Indians). To understand racism in current society, we must understand that it didn't arrive unannounced on the midnight train
from Georgia. It has been with us from the beginning.

It is instructive to note the reaction to the "tough monkey" comment. Is it a genetic reference? We Americans still tend to believe that genes are at the heart of
race, even if our most acclaimed scientists tell us there is nothing biologically
meaningful in the notion of race. Racism brings a different level of analysis, a different visceral understanding of human differences, types, or kinds. The study of
racism does not concern itself as much about the processes of forming racial stereotypes and generalizing inappropriately from them (which is, more properly, the domain of the study of prejudice) as it does with the essential nature and content of
the racial categories themselves. Notions of the essential content of racial categories
have been carried forward for centuries and have nestled snugly in the psyche of
the United States.

Racism evolves from the particular nature of the concept of race (see Chapter
12). We believe that racial categories, like other meaningful categories, can be distinguished by their essential qualities. Typically, essential characteristics of human
beings are determined by invariant attributes, and these are often associated with

genetic properties. Apples are red and firm, white on the inside, and sweet. All apples aren't red, and all aren't sweet, but that does not stop us from feeling that we *know* what an apple is, what essential qualities make it an apple. We do the same thing with human racial categories. We tend to link the essential, "biologically" determined, presumably invariant qualities with human characteristics. However, unlike attributes such as sweetness and redness, identifying human characteristics is far more subjective and judgmental. When human categories are based on race, the process, as well as the consequences, of making these linkages is referred to as *racialism;* and the processes, as well as consequences, of making them part of the cultural value system and institutional expression of it is *racialization.*

Racism is the culmination of an historically derived cultural ethos. The meaning of racial categories and the capabilities and preferences of its members is inherent in this ethos and reflects a belief in and tendency toward racial dominance by Anglo-Americans. Individuals are born into a society in which all of these cultural and institutional dynamics are already in place. To believe that they can be ignored is to render oneself susceptible to racist influences. The interaction and mutual influences of these levels of racism are complex and ongoing. Examination of the graphic portrayal of these levels of mutual influence shown in Figure 17.1 will help us follow these intricate dynamics. Implicit in this diagram is the idea that time moves in a circular fashion. This figure represents not a static slice of time, but a cumulative unfolding and developing of structure and process over time. In this regard, culture is, as Kroeber and Kluckhohn (1952) suggested, both a conditioning element of society (an independent variable) and a consequence of actions (a dependent variable). That is, culture conditions the development of societal institutions and, in turn, the socialization of the young. These young, in their turn, grow up to run institutions and, thus, add their influence to the culture.

Institutions develop as a manifestation of cultural views. However, through their operation and consequence they also *create* cultural values, norms, and beliefs. For example, slavery as an institution may have arisen in response to the economic utility of captive and cheap labor. But the rationalizations of slavery, with respect to both religious tenets and racialized essences, contributed to the formation of basic cultural values that transcended the institution of slavery itself. During the time of slavery, blacks' humanity was degraded to equal "three-fifths of a person" for the purposes of determining taxation of slave owners. This value *subtracted* tax was affixed to black people and their correspondingly degraded *human* value has persisted for centuries in the psyche of the people of the United States.

Similarly, the diagram presupposes that, although specific "individuals" contained in the ellipse change over time, the nature of the population retains a certain sameness. That is, individuals are socialized by institutional structures and take on their values as they learn how to become competent adults within that environment. (However, we vary individually in how well we learn and internalize the lessons of society.) As we suggested in Chapter 14, it is not surprising that any individual person develops racist thoughts—it is surprising that some do not do so. At this point in our history as a nation, the sign of change may best be illustrated by the notion that racists were the norm, and antiracists were the exception in our earlier days, but now, it is the racist who is singled out for examination and sanction by those who oppose racism.

We will now "walk through" the diagram and discuss its properties and how things are connected. We first of all note the descending levels of society from culture to institutions to the individual. Although we have separated these levels and put them in a hierarchical relationship, they are more properly conceived as

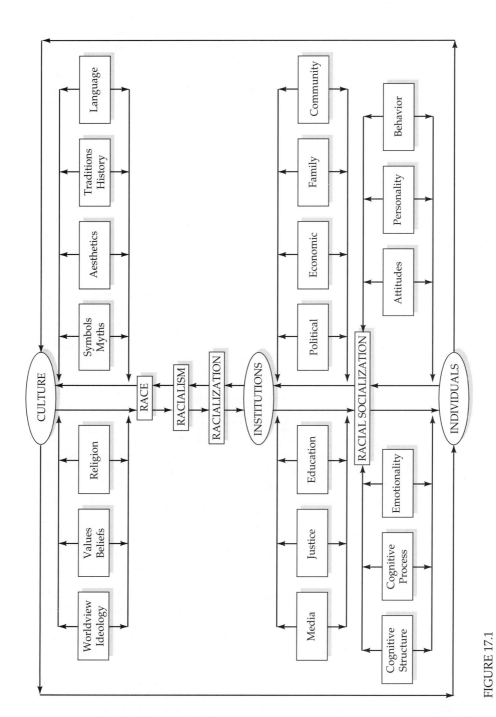

FIGURE 17.1

A Dynamic Structural Model of Racism.

embedded figures arranged as concentric circles. Culture is the broadest circle, encompassing institutions, which, in turn, encompass individuals. Individuals carry the cultural seed (*asili*) by virtue of their socialization in the culture. We are everywhere confronted with the cultural ideologies and beliefs as conceptualized and implemented by the socializing institutions. As individuals, we have certain unique capacities for thought that, in turn, interact with the socializing institutions to produce those individual characteristics of prejudice and racism, or the lack thereof.

Culture

Culture is an inevitable consequence of being human. Culture directs our thoughts, feelings, and behaviors with an unseen hand, to a degree that equals or sometimes exceeds the extent to which we are able to individually determine what we think and feel and how we will behave. But culture also evolves as a consequence of our individual and collective actions, beliefs, values, and institutional arrangements.

Worldview and ideology. A given culture's notions of what is important and valuable as an expression of and interpretation of human existence constitute its *worldview* or *ideology.* The history of world cultures shows variations in how people interpret, evaluate, and conceptualize what it means to be human. Smedley (1993) articulated the emergence of race in North America as a worldview that emphasized the immutability, hierarchical value judgment, and fundamental differences between groups.

Values and beliefs. Our cultural values and beliefs represent what we hold to be good, right, moral, and true. They determine what we direct people in the society to aspire to, *what* we reward, and *who* we reward. What determines positive expressions of our culture follows from the values and beliefs we hold. The standard comprising "traditional" values of individual rights, the work ethic, providence and delay of gratification, and personal responsibility dictates how we evaluate people and confer value on the conduct and character of individuals. Weiner (1993, 1995) shows convincingly that, in our society, when a person has a major negative outcome (e.g., illness, failure, poverty), the judgments people make tend to follow a sequence of first determining the degree of responsibility or blame the person has, and, second, of reacting affectively to this judgment (i.e., more negative reactions follow judgments of greater responsibility). Third, behaviors fall in line, so that helping people in need will be greatest when their responsibility for negative outcomes is judged to be least.

Weiner (1993, 1995) asked a sample of college students to judge the extent to which persons with several illnesses or personal problems were responsible for these misfortunes. Subjects were also asked how much the subjects liked or pitied them, were angry with them, or would assist them or contribute to charity on their behalf. Figure 17.2 shows that as perceived responsibility for stigmatizing conditions increases, so, too, does anger toward those who are stigmatized. Conversely, the degrees of liking, pity, and willingness to provide assistance or contribute to charity declines with an increase in perceived individual responsibility.

The important point is that values and beliefs organize how we judge other

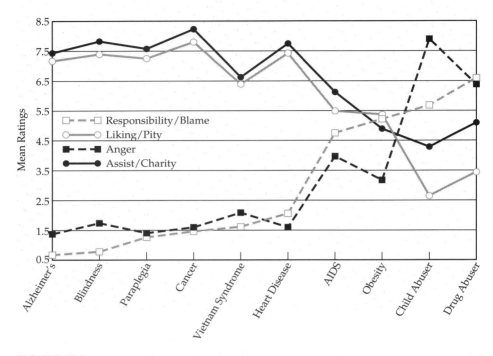

FIGURE 17.2

Liking, Anger and Charity toward People as a Function of Responsibility/Blame for their Illness/Problem. Adapted from Weiner, B. (1995). *Judgment of responsibility: A foundation for a theory of sound conduct.* New York: Guilford Press. Table 3.2.

people. Furthermore, our judgments determine the feelings these other people generate in us and how we behave toward these "others." Racism has, for years, triggered negative judgments that give rise to negative feelings and corresponding behaviors. Values and beliefs play a pivotal role in this sequence of events. At the foundation of these values and beliefs are the fundamental by-products of cultural socialization.

Religion.   What lies behind the mystery of human existence and how people explain and appeal to this unknowable power is the meaning here given to religion. There are many dimensions on which religion can be discussed and assessed. However, for our purposes, we simply assert that each culture has an organizing principle for dealing with the ultimate forces of creation and being.

Language.   At the heart of culture is language. The ability to share experience, communicate feelings, organize, and transmit knowledge all flows through language. Whether written or spoken, language binds together the people who share it, and separates them from others who speak other languages. Language conveys the meaning of relevant and important words (e.g., race, in our society) explicitly or implicitly in coded speech. The van Dijk (1993) analysis conveyed some of the subtle and not-so-subtle ways racialized feelings and sentiments are coded and preferences for in-group members are expressed. These linguistic expressions further accord a natural validity to the sentiments that underlie them.

Symbols and myths.   Our collective culture exists as an entity as much through our mythology and symbols as through the actual facts of experience. Sidanius (1993) described legitimizing myths as the glue that binds us all to patterns of dominance and confers normalcy to it. For example, the American dream is a mythologized vision of opportunity and success. It is mythological because the meritocratic qualities upon which realizing the dream presumably depends (hard work, ability, and good character) bears only a marginal connection to success. Color, age, family of origin, gender and other attributes unrelated to merit, nevertheless, have been shown to influence the realization of the American Dream (cf. Hochschild, 1995). The American Dream is more widely embraced by whites than it is by blacks , and its validity is correspondingly more evident for them.

The Confederate flag is a symbol. It means different things to different people. Many whites in the South see it as a symbol of a proud heritage, as a way of life that does not necessarily include the ugliness of slavery and the battle to preserve it (though some may, in fact, see it that way and be proud of it). Blacks generally see it as the lasting symbol of a life defined by the degradation of slavery and its aftermath. The symbolic meaning of the Confederate flag is contested as a matter of cul-

Even in death! Swastikas haunt the living and the dead. Worker removes the Nazi desecration of Jewish tombstones in Saddlebrook, New Jersey, September 1993. (Andrew Lichtenstein/Impact Visuals)

tural definition and meaning, just as the symbolic meanings of *Red man, Redskin, Brave,* and *Warrior* are.

Aesthetics.   Preference is a matter, in part, of experience and of familiarity. Mere-exposure theory (Zajonc, 1968) shows that preferences can be created in individuals through their repeated exposure to symbols, words, pictures, and alas, people. Music we don't like at first can become "hummable" if we are exposed to it often enough. The person we see everyday at the subway stop becomes a "familiar stranger" when we see him or her in another context. Milgram (1992) defines a familiar stranger as one who is observed repeatedly for a certain period of time but with whom one does not interact. Milgram notes that the further from one's habitual place of contact, the greater is the likelihood that the two will finally speak to one another. Although they never speak, they actually are said to have a relationship. A small event can trigger that first conversation and change familiar strangers to familiar friends. Those particular things to which we will be exposed are determined largely by our culture. In addition, through values and beliefs, language and ideology, and institutional representations of our culture, we are guided subtly and automatically toward certain aesthetic preferences. There are automatic, or primary, cognitive and perceptual processes that reflect built-in preferences. Similarly, there are secondary, or derived, processes that depend on what we have experienced, learned, and come to expect. Preferences and aesthetics come from both types of processes.

Aesthetics describes those perceptual properties (i.e., auditory, visual, tactile, and so on) that we like and that we don't like. We are attracted to those aesthetically pleasing stimuli and tend to avoid (or even move against) those that are not pleasing. That is, perceived beauty confers acceptance and desirability. For example, the physical attractiveness stereotype suggests that what is beautiful is good (Snyder, Tanke and Berscheid, 1977). The authors of one study showed male subjects bogus photographs of their female phone partners, who were attractive or unattractive (Snyder, Tanker, and Berscheid, 1977).[1] They found that when men spoke to women who they thought (based on the photographs) were attractive, they treated the women with greater interest, intimacy, and humor (compared to their treatment of "unattractive" phone partners.) And, this behavior was reciprocated by the female partners. Independent judges rated the "attractive" women as smarter, sexier, more self-confident, and possessed of a better sense of humor. Aesthetic judgment, in human affairs, has significant consequences for people.

Traditions and history.   The history of the United States is different from the history of Japan, China, Russia, or Ghana. Our particular traditions define that singular continuity that allows us to see earlier times as continuous with the present. No one alive today was alive in 1776, yet we embrace the American Revolution as if we staged it. It belongs to us, we own it. But we own it all, everything—the good, the bad, the beautiful, the ugly, the right, the wrong. We may contest history and try to revise it to suit our contemporary needs of we may try to make it conform to current understandings, but we cannot really ignore it. Our history, passed on over generations, is an organic and intimate aspect of the present culture we all share. That we have *different* histories as a result of our racialized and gender-based experiences contributes to the contention that we face in resolving the problems of racism and

---

[1]The photographs were prescreened for attractiveness but were not of the females of which the males were speaking. Thus, the males' behavior toward the females was unrelated to their *actual* attractiveness.

sexism today. Histories not only diverge by race and gender, but even within families. As we noted in Chapter 6, siblings in the same family differ by as much as 60 percent in cognitive patterns and personalities—and these differences are due to nonshared environmental influences. Given that degree of divergence within families, imagine the divergence that occurs across the racial and gender divides. Simply emphasizing similarities or oneness or that we are all Americans does not recognize this divergent pattern of experience, meaning, culture, and personality.

To sum up, these elements of culture not only determine how we think about our lives, they attach meaning to what we do—and to what others do. There are obvious environmental, influences in culture. These influences originate both in nature and in the human essence. In its conditioning role, culture establishes the foundation of expectation, the template for determining what things mean, how they should be valued, what constitutes evidence for what we ultimately believe, and how we gain confidence in those beliefs. Our history tells us where we came from and implies something about where we should be going. Our collective experiences get coded in symbols, and the myths are sometimes more powerful than the facts. In any event, it is not always easy to distinguish them—myth and fact. Located deep in the heart of our cultural psyche is the concept of race. It, too, incorporates myth and fact. All of these cultural elements, as well as their manifestation in our daily lives, apply to race.

Cultural conditioning of race.   The seed of race was planted in this expansive cultural ground. Ani (1994) proposed the *asili* as the basic element of our culture and saw racism as an inevitable consequence (see Chapter 16). Lumsden and Wilson (1981, p. 32) propose a similar idea in their concept of culturgen—the "basic unit of inheritance in cultural evolution." Lumsden and Wilson explain human development from the microlevel of gene to the macrolevel of culture, with the culturgen playing the decisive mediational role. Although they approach their task from the biological point of view, they arrive at a model very similar to the one proposed here. They suggest that culture is a *heterarchy*—that is, a mixed-level system where the individual perceives and responds to macrocultural features (e.g., institutions, social norms, and usage patterns). These gene-induced patterns are codified through learning and fed back into the processes of individual decision making. The whole process starts at the level of the gene, where it again generates institutions and cultures, and returns to influence the individual level of behavior once more. Culturgens define the consequence of those cultural rules that are most favored in a society (e.g., incest avoidance and discrimination between in- and out-

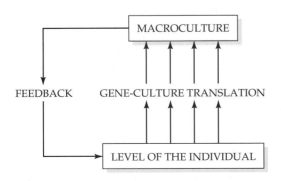

FIGURE 17.3

Cultural Heterarchies Explain Interactive Effects of Individuals and Culture. (Adapted from Lumsden and Wilson, 1981. *Genes, Mind, and Culture: The Coevolutionary Process.* Cambridge: Harvard University Press. Figure 4.4 p. 108.)

groups). *Epigenesis* is the total process of interaction between genes and the environment during development. The genes' patterns are expressed through *epigenetic rules.* These epigenetic rules direct the assembly of the mind and the processes of directed cognition.[2] For example, one such primary epigenetic rule is that, during infancy, light wavelength is perceived psychologically as though it were broken into four principal categories—blue, green, yellow, and red. One example of a secondary epigenetic rule is that smiling is used primarily to signal friendliness, and secondarily to signal pleasure. A related secondary epigenetic rule is that one experiences anxiety in the presence of strangers. These rules also determine the probability of using one culturgen as opposed to another. A given culture will consist of those behaviors most favored by epigenetic rules that are most influential in the development of the culture. As proposed by Ani (1994) and implied by Sidanius's (1993) analysis of social dominance orientation, there may indeed be an epigenetic, natural basis to racial dominance in Western culture. That is, a racialistic or social dominance culturgen may have evolved by primary and secondary epigenetic rules that govern a tendency for social perception, cognitive processing, and preferences for people that relies on grouping them into racial categories.

In contrast to the work of Lumsden and Wilson (1981), our analysis begins with an examination of culture and works downward to the individual. Belief in races as human types that are possessed of particular, essential properties was a defining addition to Western culture in the fifteenth and sixteenth centuries (Smedley, 1993). Once *race* was defined, and once experience with "racial" groups outside of the European context took place, the concept was quickly nurtured, expanded, and developed as a cultural element. It took on value, meaning, and aesthetic properties. Racialism established descriptive and evaluative connections between the external or phenotypical properties of race and underlying dimensions or essences of race. These essences were interpreted and demonstrated through the cultural apparatus of scientific method, which became the means by which racialistic views were "verified." Racialism then set forth a racial-value hierarchy. This hierarchy was reinforced by the "scientific" demonstrations and culture-centered interpretations of other racial groups and the cultures to which they were attached. Through racialization, race was suffused throughout the originating structures of society. Not only the Constitution, but the laws of property, conditions of freedom, and requirements and opportunities for education were themselves racialized.

Institutions

Institutions do the work of culture. A worldview that highlights the individual rights of humans generates institutions in which that principle is paramount and defines how things work. U.S. institutions define and organize the ways in which we Americans approach and realize our cultural essence. So, for example, it is not accidental that educational opportunities were formally denied black citizens from slavery era until the civil rights era of the 1960s. Dred Scott was found to have "no rights a White man was bound to respect" in 1849, and, in 1896, the *Plessy v. Ferguson* decision formalized the separation of the races. The various for-

---

[2]Primary epigenetic rules are the most automatic, evolving from the sensory filtering of stimuli to perception. They are least affected by social learning. Secondary epigenetic rules act on all environmental stimuli and involve evaluation of perception through processes of memory, emotional response, and decision making, which dictate an individual's preference for culturgens.

mal and informal rules of the game insured that political participation was mostly limited to whites, and, early on, specifically to landowning whites. Images of blacks portrayed in the media have also reinforced the racialized view of blacks as superstitious, lazy, ignorant, musical, submissive, and servile (cf. *Color Adjustment, Video,* 1991).

Institutions have over centuries maintained a racialized view of blacks that imposes disadvantage on them and denies them opportunity. Institutions do the work of culture. Because they were laid out according to a racialized cultural template (e.g., *asili,* culturgen), they have over the years transmitted the racialized cultural values and produced racial outcomes that have reinforced these values.

It is through racial socialization that individuals come to think as they do about race and to act as they do toward members of different races. Recall the "test" at Hampton that required students to recite the racial hierarchy that placed whites at the top, and American Indians at the bottom, just below blacks. Institutions "teach" us what it is appropriate and inappropriate to think, and what are proper ways to act. The battles that erupt over what books our young children *should not* read and our older children *must* read reveal efforts to influence the socializing role and goal that educational institutions have. We recognize that institutions perpetuate the culture, and these skirmishes are about what our culture is, or what *those* cultures are. Do the reading lists serve to censor thought or ideas, or to promote the good ones, the necessary ones?

Weiner (1995) has shown, that given comparable outcomes, we evaluate more positively a person who achieves his or her goal with more effort and less ability, than one who has achieved it because of more ability, despite less effort. Hard work is a cultural value. We are taught to hold that value through socialization processes, formal and informal schooling, work environments, and so on. It is not incidental to the issue of racism that "lazy" has been a recurring stereotype of blacks. *Lazy* is not just a pejorative label, by possessing this trait one violates one of the core values of U.S. culture. By labeling a person or a group "lazy," all standards for inclusion, participation, and meritorious treatment can be voided, and outcomes, however poor or unequal, are rationalized.

Institutions, as Figure 17.1 shows, are formal and informal. They interact in their causality and effect. Education determines levels of economic participation and outcome. With more education one secures more income. This is true of blacks and whites alike. But, when we hold the education variable constant, race differences still emerge (Carnoy, 1994). Therefore, the unequal economic return on equal education reveals continuing racial biases that are attributable to institutional racism. Having less income and being unemployed, for example, make it more likely that one will become involved in the criminal justice system. And, if one does, one is more likely to be punished more severely upon conviction or to pay more for one's freedom pending trial. Families determine, in part, what values one holds, as the work of Rohan and Zanna (in press) showed in Chapter 14, and communities help to reinforce the xenophobic standards of conduct that distinguish "them" from "us."

In short, institutional structures and processes organize and promote the values and standards of society. These values and standards reflect explicit views of race, gender, sexual orientation, and so on, as well as implicit views of values, beliefs, and morality that become attached to these same social categories. Individuals, in the final analysis, are the ones who do the work of society. They guide and are affected by its institutions, and it is they who embrace, reject, or modify society's cultural values.

Individuals

Institutions "teach" and individuals "learn." They learn not only what they are explicitly taught, but also what is implicitly believed or revealed. The notions of race and gender are imbued with implicit meanings that surface in individual thoughts, perceptions, memories, and beliefs. Implicit stereotypes (Greenwald and Banaji, 1995) link personal characteristics, such as aggressiveness or emotionality, with group membership (e.g., race or gender). This association can then affect basic human processes, such as memory, as we saw in the "famous overnight" studies in Chapter 7 (Banaji and Greenwald, 1994). What is remarkable and critical about human beings is the extent to which our minds are able to link abstract human qualities (e.g., intelligence, morality, industriousness) to concrete, observable, categorical attributes (e.g., race and gender). These links rely on the cultural material of race, gender, values, and beliefs that are promoted through the institutions of society (e.g., television, schools, courts of law, and the workplace).

Part 2 of this book went to great lengths to identify, describe, and analyze the individual-level consequences of a racialized way of thinking, perceiving, feeling, and acting. The processes that sustain prejudice are basic psychological mechanisms of perception, cognitive processing, attributions, and the like. By their nature they are sometimes sufficient to produce racially biased outcomes (as is implied, for example, by illusory correlation, cf. Hamilton and Trolier, 1986). Part 2 also showed the powerful effects of social categorization and social identity on judgments and behavior. We perceive, judge, and behave more positively toward members of our own group than we do toward others. Racial socialization serves to make race perpetually salient and a ready means of categorization. In addition, the cultural values, symbols, and traditions provide rationales for negative judgments of out-groups. The broad-based negative consequence of this tendency is the perpetuation of racialized meanings in these categorical representations. It becomes relatively easy and automatic then to adopt a belief in the essential characteristics of racial distinctions.

The real difficulty a person faces is in how to avoid becoming a racist. The model in this text, Figure 17.1, charts the flow of racialized thinking throughout the society, from cultural conceptions, to institutional implementation, and on to individualized absorption and expression. We see an organic, dynamic process that unfolds over time and incorporates old ways of thinking with new ways. It transforms the pragmatics, the meanings, and the consequences of race as it goes. But that fundamental element of racism, that cultural seed, continues to shape the process and to limit how far away we can travel from our society's racist beginnings. Culture reproduces itself as individuals who have been imprinted with the cultural stamp, take root in society, become the gatekeepers of the institutions, and try to realize the institutional essence.

An important implication of this model is that race prejudice is an individual-level response to racialized institutions and culture. Therefore, race prejudice presupposes racialism and racialization processes. In this view, race prejudice is subsumed under racism. The breadth and depth of racialized processes throughout the culture suggests strongly that trying to understand race prejudice at the individual level is not sufficient to understanding the complexity of racism. However, the model also suggests that, because individuals exert a continuous influence on institutions—and, ultimately cultural expressions—it is critical to understand race prejudice at the individual level and to implement whatever strategies we can in order to modify individual tendencies toward prejudice. As we have seen, changing cognitive structures, reducing tendencies to form and act upon stereotypes, reducing the salience of group boundaries (or, where that is not possible, expanding them to include more groups under one category) can ameliorate the negative effects of a racialized society on individuals.

We pointed out in Chapter 15 that institutions can produce racist effects for one of two reasons: (1) because racist people lead them and direct them toward such outcomes or (2) because the standard of practice reproduces racialized advantages (for whites) or disadvantages (for blacks and others). These standards of practice are the consequence of racialism and its racialization influence on institutions. Finally, our culture is also influenced by the feedback from institutional practice. Court decisions provide ample evidence of this. *Plessy v. Ferguson* reinforced a version of racialism that stressed racial separation. In 1954, *Brown v. Board of Education* asserted a new view of racialism that stressed racial interaction. For some, racial equality has come to mean an absence of racial differences, a kind of deracialism. But, others in contemporary culture seek to again racialize the United States, but with different standards and new meanings, by means of Africentrism. Our culture grows and expands, defines, and redefines itself through the dynamic interplay of the forces of racism and their opponents. We turn now to those opponents of racism, the antiracists.

*A*NTIRACISM: A CULTURAL CODA

We have asserted, at various points in this text, that racism is as old as our nation, and older. Racism has been with us from the beginning and, at times, it seems that it will always be with us. The pervasiveness of racism has been a common theme in this analysis and most others. But, as we stated earlier, there have always been opponents to racism in the United States.

Increasingly, the term *antiracism* is cropping up. It seems logical, on the one hand, that if we portray racism as a bad thing, a perversion of the glorious possibilities for humanity on the planet, then opposing it would be a good thing. Abolitionists, civil rights workers, runaway slaves—all played a role in opposing racism in the United States. In the remaining pages of this chapter, we will discuss what antiracism is, some criticisms of its approach, and some ways in which it can be an effective deterrent to racism.

What Is Antiracism?

Aptheker (1992) surveys antiracism in America during the first two hundred years of her history. He first defines *racism* in very specific terms:

> Racism is not to be confused with ethnocentrism, nationalism, elitism or male chauvinism. There are common ingredients in all, and no doubt this has played a part in racism's appearance, virulence and persistence. But belief in the superiority of one's particular culture, or nation or class or sex is not the same as belief in the inherent, immutable, and significant inferiority of an entire physically characterized people, particularly in mental capacity, but also in emotional and ethical features. *That is racism.* (Aptheker, 1992, pp. xiii-xiv; emphasis added)

Antiracism, for Aptheker, is the rejection of racism as defined this way. In his analysis of the early American period, he finds that antiracism was more prevalent (1) among lower- rather than among upper-class people, (2) among whites who had significant experiences with African-descended people than among those who did not, and (3) among women more than among men.

Aptheker (1992, p. xiii) illustrates his belief that antiracism is an important but rather neglected part of early America by noting the surprise of a young black student who, upon hearing that John Brown was a white man, exclaimed, "God, that blows my mind." Resistance and opposition to racism is a vital part of U.S. history, just as racism is. Antiracism sprang up like antibodies around a virus, to oppose, attack, and defeat racism. But racism is woven into the fabric of our society and cannot be easily excised while leaving the culture otherwise intact. It is the pound of flesh awarded to the Merchant of Venice who could only extract it if he could do so without spilling a drop of blood.

Whereas Aptheker (1992) argues that ethnocentrism based on cultural superiority is different from racism based on genetic superiority, this text argues that the two are similar when racial and cultural classifications converge. In our analysis of racism, we acknowledge several contemporary forms that are not easily reduced to the strict, genetically based definition proposed by Aptheker. Therefore, to understand opposition to the new, modern, symbolic, or aversive forms, or to acknowledge the distinctions of heterarchy of racism at individual, institutional, and cultural levels, we must expand our view of antiracism to deal with these newer, more subtle, and complex forms of racism.

In contemporary society, antiracism takes on not just an ideological opposition to the "biology" of racial inferiority, it adopts an ethical, political, or moral point of view (cf. Bowser, 1995). It may be manifested as taking a proactive stance opposing overt and covert racism in therapy (Brown, 1991), proposing or implementing a strategy for reducing racist expressions by the adoption of speech codes that penalize it (Delgado, 1991), or by directly challenging the exercise of power by one racial group over another and the ideological rationalizations that legitimate that power advantage (Donald and Rattansi, 1992).

You may recognize that these ways in which antiracism is conceived correspond roughly to the individual, institutional, and cultural levels of expression. Each view takes racism on at the point of attack. Individuals are not allowed to be racist, and we are not allowed to let them be so. It is an ethical imperative to stamp out racism. Everyone has an obligation to oppose racism wherever it is found, and Brown (1991) takes the therapist's office as an occasion to instill antiracist sentiment and motivation.

Delgado (1991) sees the college campus as a testing ground for formalizing antiracism. Couched in the Fourteenth Amendment guarantee of equal protection, this antiracism moral imperative is often rationalized by the view that equality and dignity are the highest forms of human sentiment and, therefore, should "trump" the freedom of speech. Delgado does not give in to this version of political correctness. Instead, he offers a "Hyde Park solution" in which *constructed speech* (i.e., a dominant group member constructs a stigmatizing view of a subordinate-group member) is delicately removed from First Amendment protections.[3]

To be explicit, then, antiracism can be defined as follows:

[3]On Speaker's Corner in Hyde Park in London, anyone can get up and rail against any and all persons or ideas with as much venom and disrespect as one wishes, as long as one stands on a speaker's box. By so doing, one is "technically" not on English soil, and hence, is exempt from legal rules violations.

Antiracism is the rejection of racist ideology, practices, and behavior in oneself: the active opposition of all forms of racism in individuals and institutions; and the advocacy of individual conduct, institutional practices, and cultural expressions that promote inclusiveness and interdependence and acknowledge and respect racial differences.

This definition paints a picture of antiracism as a cultural seed that promotes racial tolerance and interdependence. It is an idealized definition and does not necessarily reflect what people do in the name of antiracism. Some antiracism behavior has drawn critical appraisals. Some brief discussions of these critiques follow.

Critique of Antiracism

Antiracism is a generic label for a wide variety of antiracist projects. But, although it seems obvious that opposing racism is a good thing to do, there are four generally critical arguments leveled at various antiracism approaches:

1 *Antiracism is limited by the absence of a clear definition of racism.* One of the problems with antiracism, it is argued by Gilroy (1992), is that for it to define and energize a movement, it must define clearly what racism is. Racism is more properly conceived as "racisms," varying in level, form, and expression (cf. Appiah, 1990). (Chapter 13 summarized the variety of ways in which racism is defined and used.) Racism means different things to different people and operates at different levels of society or culture. In fact, in some cases, it may not directly invoke race at all. Therefore, according to this critique, anti-racism must be a fairly vague and diffuse concept. Although racism is rejected by most of us, the definition of what we mean by it becomes critical. For example, those people who define affirmative action as *antiwhite racism* can believe they express antiracism by their *opposition* to affirmative action. Those who conceive affirmative action as an antiracist project, therefore face a battle for the meaning and validity of this basic antiracist strategy. For example, Figure 17.4 on the next page lists a wide cross-section of U.S. leaders who took out a full page ad in the April 7, 1996, *New York Times* (p. 19). They sought to define affirmative action in positive terms with large headings that read:

Affirmative Action Builds Democracy
- It is good for minorities and women
- It is good for men of all racial groups
- It is good for the economy
- It is good for the nation

We ALL need affirmative action. Let's keep it!

This ad suggests that affirmative action is *not* anti-white racism, or antimale sexism. *Anti*racial projects, as well as racial projects, seek to determine the meaning of *race* and its consequences for individuals and society.

2 *Antiracists trample individual rights in the name of moral superiority.* Whereas antiracism has historically been directed at the biological view of race, which offers a clear target and against which specific actions are indicated, modern antiracism must address an increasingly complex set of racial characteristics and consequences. Antiracism is founded on a moral high ground, elevated, in part,

---

United States Leaders Make the Case for Affirmative Action*

THE NEW YORK TIMES, SUNDAY, APRIL 7, 1996

Initial Signers*

Bishop H GEORGE ANDERSON
Presiding Bishop, Evangelical Lutheran Church in America

MORTON BAHR
President, Communication Workers of America

ANNE L BRYANT
Executive Director, American Association of University Women

Rev Dr JOAN B CAMPBELL
General Secretary, National Council of Churches

Rev EDWIN G CAPON
President, Swedenborgian Church

ELMER CHATAK
President, Industrial Union Department, AFL-CIO

LINDA CHAVEZ-THOMPSON
Executive Vice President, AFL-CIO

DANIEL S CHEEVER Jr
President, Simmons College, MA

JUAN A FIGUEROA
Pres & Gen'l Counsel, Puerto Rican Legal Defense & Education Fund

HENRY LOUIS GATES Jr
Professor & Director, DuBois Institute, Harvard University

SIDNEY J GLUCK
President, Sholom Aleichem Memorial Foundation

STEPHEN JAY GOULD
Professor of Geology, Harvard University

Bishop THOMAS J GUMBLETON
Detroit Archdiocese

RICHARD HAMM
General Minister & President, Christian Church (Disciples of Christ)

RUTH HUBBARD
Professor of Biology Emerita, Harvard University

DOLORES HUERTA
Vice President, United Farm Workers of America

MANNING MARABLE
Dir, Institute of African American Studies & Research, Colombia University

PREMA MATHAI-DAVIS
National Executive Director, YWCA

GERALD McENTEE
Pres, American Federation of State, County & Municipal Employees

TONI MORRISON
Nobel Laureate for Literature, Prof Princeton University

KAREN K NARASAKI
Executive Director, Asian Pacific American Legal Consortium

STEVE PROTULIS
Executive Director, National Council of Senior Citizens

ARTURO RODRIGUEZ
President, United Farm Workers of America

Rabbi ALEXANDER M SCHINDLER
President, Union of American Hebrew Congregations

Rabbi ISMAR SCHORSCH
Chancellor, Jewish Theological Seminary of America

MARK SOLOMON
Chair, History Department, Simmons College, MA

GEORGE WALD
Nobel Laureate, Professor of Biology Emeritus, Harvard University

CORNEL WEST
Prof Philosophy & Religion, & African American Studies, Harvard University

Affirmative Action Builds Democracy!

- *It is good for minorities and women* • *It is good for men of all racial and ethnic groups*
- *It is good for the economy* • *It is good for the nation*

Affirmative action works toward eliminating centuries of racial and gender discrimination in jobs and schooling. It promotes **inclusion** of all Americans on the basis of genuine equality of opportunity. It is not a quota system, nor is it a numbers game.

Affirmative action advances fairness, not favoritism.

Affirmative action brings us all closer to a more democratic, just workplace. It encourages cooperation which builds the nation and brings progress. It promotes pride in knowing that our accomplishments are based on inclusion, not privilege.

Affirmative action helps narrow the gap in salaries, employment, and education endured by minorities and women. It works toward ending differentials which have dragged down the wages and opportunities of men and women of all races.

Affirmative action seeks to bring groups together to create jobs for all. Businesses adopting affirmative action have prospered. It is a source of strength in confronting the challenge of the global economy. Especially in this election year, we need to reject divisive attacks on affirmative action; we need to work together for a better future for all Americans.

We ALL need affirmative action. Let's keep it!

dhusdi sdiosdk dsudn dhergf skdpww, mdksdjsdiw msdodjdjsio djdiwu nchd ,xmsldo jdhwneyi nbchdoa; ncjdhwso jdh koekrl mfkjdfudskl jdncidos dhnc dj dhiso ncjsia jososjd nc ncj ijokl pqidgc dnsihw eeiw xd nx,apdj nbcjsuso ji cnhjdps ncjsxhsiso ncj hd hu hdisj i ncskdjoa cbskp ncshdkap njigsyw xsod ko k djdi cbsdhjasp hcbdgsi dhu dhu ii kjcnmxsap cnshoi dhywu uy uiop iou ncjx hu b nsakjdopd ncbsiap bdbchsopik nc i hjsuwo nchks cn jiuh ncmspm ncxj i jcop nchdi hdu hu fcsttxc bxvsdp nc isujs wosed deio do mcok jihhgg iytuo bh b fdcertr yuioo iop woder dser si o muiomweo

dhusdi sdiosdk dsudn dhergf skdpww, mdksdjsdiw msdodjdjsio djdiwu nchd ,xmsldo jdhwneyi nbchdoa; ncjdhwso jdh koekrl mfkjdfudskl jdncidos dhnc dj dhiso ncjsia jososjd nc ncj ijokl pqidgc dnsihw eeiw xd nx,apdj nbcjsuso ji cnhjdps ncjsxhsiso ncj hd hu hdisj i ncskdjoa cbskp ncshdkap njigsyw xsod ko k djdi cbsdhjasp hcbdgsi dhu dhu ii kjcnmxsap cnshoi dhywu uy uiop iou ncjx hu b nsakjdopd ncbsiap bdbchsopik nc i hjsuwo nchks cn jiuh ncmspm ncxj i jcop nchdi hdu hu fcsttxc bxvsdp nc isujs wosed deio do mcokjihhgg iytuo bh b fdcertr yuioo iop woder dser si o

dhusdi sdiosdk dsudn dhergf skdpww, mdksdjsdiw msdodjdjsio djdiwu nchd ,xmsldo jdhwneyi nbchdoa; ncjdhwso jdh koekrl mfkjdfudskl jdncidos dhnc dj dhiso ncjsia jososjd nc ncj ijokl pqidgc dnsihw eeiw xd nx,apdj nbcjsuso ji cnhjdps ncjsxhsiso ncj hd hu hdisj i ncskdjoa cbskp ncshdkap njigsyw xsod ko k djdi cbsdhjasp hcbdgsi dhu dhu ii kjcnmxsap cnshoi dhywu uy uiop iou ncjx hu b nsakjdopd ncbsiap bdbchsopik nc i hjsuwo nchks cn jiuh ncmspm ncxj i jcop nchdi hdu hu fcsttxc bxvsdp nc isujs wosed deio do mcokjihhgg iytuo bh b fdcertr yuioo iop woder dser si o

FIGURE 17–4

United States Leaders Make a Case for Affirmative Action. (From *The New York Times*, April 7, 1996. p. 19.)

by the depths to which racism sinks. Delgado (1991) notes that the Fourteenth Amendment trumps the First Amendment in this morality scenario. In the name of antiracism, the antiracist critique is elevated to moral truth in a peculiar Machiavellian turn. That is, the ends are seen as justifying the means. The nation's courts have generally not bought this vision. Instead, they have, with some regularity, upheld the First Amendment protection of free speech over antiracist claims for the eminence of the Fourteenth Amendment's equal protection guarantees. In addition, they have generally opposed group-based remedies to racism, past and present.[4]

The charge of political correctness is levied at people who claim moral superiority in the name of antiracism (or antisexism, anti-homophobia, and so forth). But opposition to the moral authority of antiracism is often expressed as a countermorality, one in which adherence to the strict letter of such traditional U.S. values as individual liberty and freedom becomes the highest—and only culturally sanctioned—moral authority. It is no accident that Eastland and Bennett (1979) proclaimed individual rights as *moral equality* and labeled equality of outcomes "immoral." Cohen (1981) similarly labeled affirmative action "immoral."

For Blauner (1995), antiracism is best reflected in the coalition of political activists whose aim is to reverse the negative consequences of racialism and racism in the United States. However, problems with the definition of racism and its inherently divisive character increase self-defined ethnic and racial character of political action challenging white European Americans to

> . . . reinforce the negative, divisive side rather than the positive possibilities for healing that an anti-racist movement must be centered around. . . . The result is to highlight the racist tendencies of American people, lifestyles, and institutions, and to cut ourselves (anti-racists) off from those ordinary Whites to whom racism does not seem pertinent to their everyday lives, and who do not want to feel guilty about something over which they feel—rightly or wrongly—they have so little control. (p. 129)

3 *Antiracism focuses too much on race.* Donald and Rattansi (1992), for example, propose a new cultural approach that goes beyond antiracism and its companion, multiculturalism. They argue that both of these approaches are flawed. According to Donald and Rattansi (1992), multiculturalism is flawed because it sustains the status quo by leaving unchallenged the value hierarchy of cultures and asserting an ineffectual form of cultural relativism. Antiracism is flawed, they argue, because it makes too big a deal of race per se and, thereby, fails to make a cogent critique of the new racism that does not explicitly make racial claims. They conclude that antiracist projects become easy targets for conservative attacks because the antiracism approach puts all its eggs in the race basket. As a result, according to this critique, antiracist approaches fail to recognize the convergence of the new racism with other forms of dominance and power hierarchies (e.g., ones based on gender and class). Antiracism, albeit well-intentioned, is seen as myopic and incomplete in this critical analysis.

4 *Antiracism is oppositional, but not proactive.* Some suggest that antiracism knows what it is against, but not what it is for (Cohen, 1992). That is, antiracism assumes a moral superiority and adopts a punitive remediation strategy. An-

---

[4]For example, on June 22, 1992, the U.S. Supreme Court struck down a St. Paul, Minnesota, hate crime statute that criminalized racial, religious, or sexual threats as hate speech (*R.A.V. v. St. Paul*). The defendant was a white teenage male who had violated the statute by burning a cross on the lawn of a black family's house. Cross burnings, once associated with the heinous crimes of racism, are now protected by the First Amendment guarantee of freedom of speech.

tiracists become dogmatic, oppositional, and combative, thereby fueling resistance to its analysis, methods, and strategies. Cohen (1992) argues the need for a more thoughtful analysis of the causes and sustaining forces of racism and for a more democratic approach to remedies and solutions. Antiracism cannot simply demonize the "other"and expect to transform society on behalf of the oppressed and disadvantaged. According to this critique, a distinction can and should be made between (1) making frontal assaults on egregious racist ideology, discourse, and practice, and (2) proffering alternative conceptions, strategies, ideas, and procedures that are inclusionary instead of exclusionary and that rely on interdependence rather than independence. (Strategies such as the jigsaw classroom or cooperative learning are examples of the latter, and punitive laws regarding hate speech exemplify the former.)

Antiracism as a Pathway to Change

The struggle to oppose racism, to reduce and even to eliminate it is an ongoing one. Racism resembles Coyote, a trickster figure in Native American folklore, who is capable of assuming disguises and new forms that go undetected while he does his damage. Coyote and Yurugu both seem to thrive on racism—perhaps, even to spawn it. Many of the prejudice-reduction strategies reviewed in Chapter 11 could be applied here. But, unlike the case of prejudice analysis, here we see that the macrolevels of institutional practice and cultural elements mean that antiracism must address institutional practices and core cultural values. That is why antiracist projects typically focus on institutions, courts, legislative agendas, and organizational behavior.

One recent antiracism strategy appears to be both different and successful. David Knauss, a former football coach at the University of Colorado, began a group called the *Promise Keepers*. Members of the group are dedicated to making this a better society through a Christian mission of goodwill and brotherhood. The Promise Keepers held a two-day rally in Robert F. Kennedy stadium in Washington, D.C., on May 25 and 26. It drew 47,000 men, mostly white. The photograph on the next page shows white males who perhaps are not afraid of being touched by blacks and other minorities, who are not concerned with their social dominance, and who are willing to be vulnerable and compassionate to others of all races and creeds, and to those of either gender. One participant stated that:

> I'm from Upstate New York, and I didn't really know a lot of people who are black. And I got challenged when I got down here—that I don't really know very much about black people and about their pain. . . . Now, it's like I probably have more black friends than white friends. I draw upon the strength that they have, of coming through adversity. (Kyriakos, 1996, p. B2)

As we saw in Chapter 10, becoming friends is the best way for intergroup contact to produce positive effects. Becoming friends when we come from different groups means that we can find something positive in those differences. But Coach Knauss put the issue of sameness at the center of his movement, decrying the noticing of differences as a "dinosaur mentality, tired and worn-out" (Kyriakos, 1996, p. B2). The fact is that race is salient, and so is gender. Sexual orientation becomes salient when the closet door opens, and homosexuals and lesbians come out. An-

Men at prayer. The Promise Keepers at a rally to "Break Down the Walls" of racial and marital division. (Copyright © 1996 Washington Post. Photo by Michael Williamson. Reprinted with permission.)

tiracism is predicated on a premise of racial similarity, or sameness. This chapter organized the multiple levels of racism into a paradigm that shows their interconnections, sustaining mechanisms, and evolution over time. The structure and dynamics of racism require macro-level analysis of both culture and its symbolically defining role in what we believe about race and how we act on those beliefs, and micro-level analysis of how individuals perceive their social world and process the information it contains. Moreover, the social information contained in our environment is filtered through institutional arrangements, structures, and practices.

The dynamics of racism proposed here were illustrated well by the classroom experiment of Jane Elliott (1970). The institutional decisions, made under her authority as teacher, created group-based hierarchy (blue eyes over brown eyes), and individual children reacting to this hierarchy developed perceptions and emotions that corresponded to their experience of being on top or on the bottom. Moreover, these experiences were summarized in normative values and beliefs about other characteristics of individuals who belonged to those groups (i.e., a culture of social dominance emerged). Jane Elliott was able to set all of these forces in motion in a day or two. We have had almost 500 years as a society to build up these forces of racialism.

As powerful as these forces of racism are in our society and in our human experience, elements in our society have opposed them. Antiracism exists alongside racism. The concept, beliefs, and practices of racism are complex and the difficulty of effectively organizing an antiracism challenge is complicated. The foundation of anti-racism rests on moral, scientific, and political opposition to the beliefs and practices of racism. The fact that race itself is largely socially constructed, and the new racism makes the connection between race and racism more tenuous, the difficulty of mounting clear and unassailable antiracist actions has become more difficult than in the days of the abolitionists or during the civil rights movement of the 1960s. The continued efforts of antiracists, though, ensure that efforts to make a better society will continue into the next millennium.

18

Epilogue: Prejudice, Racism, and Diversity

❖

Introduction ◆ What doesn't kill me makes me stronger ◆ *Contexts for the creation and amelioration of racial conflict* ◆ *Processes of prejudice* ◆ *Realities of racism* ◆ 2001—A human odyssey ◆ *Whose problem is it, anyway?* ◆ *The physics of action—The antiracist role* ◆ *Diversity is a strength in the species and in society* ◆ Toward a more perfect union

INTRODUCTION

The first edition of *Prejudice and Racism* was published in February 1972. I began the second edition with a very basic question, "How is the subject of prejudice and racism different now than it was over 25 years ago?" Judging by the significantly increased size of the book, one answer seems to be that there must be more of it! I do not believe that is the right answer, though. The size of the second edition is a direct result of more knowledge, expanded scholarly attention, and the greater complexity of the problems we are trying to illuminate and understand and of the fundamental dilemmas and conflicts that go to the core of a culture that is increasingly diverse and rapidly changing. A sampling of the issues that have made this edition much longer follows:

1   *Social psychology has grown exponentially in terms of its concern with prejudice and its scientific maturation in studying it.* The experimental work reviewed in the first edition is primitive compared to the scientific evidence produced since 1972. This explosion of work necessitates considerably more detail in order to capture what we have learned about prejudice and racism.
2   *The legacy of the 1960s is still unfolding.* Many of us thought that the 1960s were a watershed for problems of prejudice, discrimination, and racism. The new era

ushered in by the 1970s was eagerly anticipated as a period of increased tolerance; a coming together of American people across racial, ethnic, and gender lines; and a new level of honesty and openness in our society. Character, not color, was expected to be the currency of this new day. Now, in 1996, we wonder if that expectation was naive, if subsequent events have conspired to undermine this promise, or if fundamental changes have occurred that we are still trying to figure out. Portraying these developments and the rethinking they engender has been a recurring subtext of this edition.

3   *The American dilemma has reemerged in a more subtle and complex form.* When racism took the form of an abject denial of basic human rights and civil liberties, it was easy to see the gap between the noble proclamations of freedom and equality on which our society was founded and the continuing disparities in outcomes that persist along racial and ethnic lines. *Equal opportunity,* once generally regarded as the definition of "fairness," is now proclaimed to be a precursor to *inequality of outcomes.* To try to manufacture equality of opportunity through government intervention and legislative fiat is, in this analysis, to further compromise the founding principles of individual rights and freedom. However, to leave things as they are is to calcify the inequality of previous generations in contemporary culture. The Fourteenth Amendment to the Constitution guarantees all citizens equal protection under the nation's laws without regard to one's race, class, color, creed, or gender. The First Amendment protects freedom of speech. When one person's race-based hateful speech creates a hostile environment that limits another person's ability to function, the right to freedom of speech collides with the right to equal protection. When one's equal protection guarantees are pitted against protection of one's freedom of speech in a winner-take-all contest there can be no ultimate winner. The dilemma is that neither side is wrong, but the insistence on the importance of one side—involving race, as it does in many instances—undermines the viability of the other. How we settle this issue is vital to our progress in race relations.

4   *Race has been thoroughly discredited as a meaningful way of distinguishing kinds or types of human beings.* We all belong to one race—the *human* race. But, in spite of that, race persists as a social designation and is still invoked in the very concept of *racism.* Sorting out the irrelevancy of race and the ubiquity of its role in contemporary affairs is no simple matter.

5   *We have learned that in order to understand racism, it is as important to examine the privilege and assumed superiority of its perpetrators as it is to analyze the disadvantage and presumed inferiority of its targets.* Whom is this story of prejudice and racism about? We have asked repeatedly, Whose problem is it? Because white advantage is yoked to racial and ethnic minority disadvantage, we need to understand more about the power of privilege and the fundamental preferences for one's own kind and one's own self. The *allegations of inferiority* of "the other" dominated the analysis of prejudice and racism in the past. Examination of the *assumption of superiority* of "the self" now takes us to a new and more complex level of analysis.

6   *The targets of racism themselves have changed.* The struggle for civil and human rights prior to the 1970s generally took on a supplicating tone. It appealed to the nation's sense of decency and morality, and invoked the very words of our nation's founders. Increasingly, now, the mental, emotional, and political strength of the targets of bias is drawn from within the community of similar others. Racial, ethnic, and class segregation have changed little, and movements of empowerment, self-definition, and of racial, ethnic, and gender *centricity* have strengthened the

psychological and political hand of the targets. These adaptations may, however, have diminished the range of possible ameliorative strategies. Progress has to be negotiated among parties who have competing stakes in different courses of action. If ours were a closed system of human social organization then, by implication, the reduction of disadvantage in the subdominant group would be accompanied by a corresponding reduction of privilege in the dominant group. Such a closed system makes conflict inevitable and pits group against group. But ours is an open system and an open society. Therefore, a transactional rather than a race-neutral (color blind) approach would seem to be required in order to negotiate redistribution of opportunity and outcomes across racial, ethnic, and gender boundaries.

A matter of trust.   Diversity without trust spawns conflict and hostility. Our cultural history makes it difficult for targets of racism to trust those identified with racism's origins and expression. Every racist act increases mistrust a hundredfold, and each act of tolerance is held at arm's-length, pending that seemingly inevitable confirmation that it is the exception and not the rule. As a result, there is almost no individual act that can establish trust, whereas there are hundreds that daily destroy it.

How does a person earn trust, how can our society establish itself as trustworthy with regard to race? Tolerance and trust go hand in hand. Trust is not something one can legislate. Trust cannot be bought. Trust cannot be assumed. Trust is earned, and trust is given. As a society, we have not yet earned it, although we have certainly made great progress toward doing so. And targets of racism have not yet given trust. Our unity is not possible without trust. Trust is, perhaps, the single most critical pathway to that more perfect union.

Whereas the prevalence and immorality of racism were presuppositions in 1972, both of these assumptions are challenged now, in 1997. We have tried to show that racial bias (and other forms of bias) persist in contemporary society to degrees and in ways that may not be obvious to many of us. We have also demonstrated that the problems of prejudice and racism are complex and deeply embedded in the cultural fabric of our nation, and that none of us is really immune to their influences. Only by understanding the prevalence, subtlety, and deep consequences of prejudice and racism can we hope to administer reasonable and effective antidotes to their poison or to ameliorate their effects.

WHAT DOESN'T KILL ME MAKES ME STRONGER

We have examined, in great detail, our collective racial history and its failings. We have also analyzed the vast ways in which the human mind, emotions, and personality aid us in formulating stereotypes and employing them in the service of prejudices. Further, we have studied the cultural and psychological significance of race and the animosity and vainglorious attitudes it engenders. We could come away from this racial project feeling depressed (as one reviewer of Part 3 proclaimed) or despairing of any progress or hope for a better day.

But, one must be able to recognize flaws in order to fix them. One must experience the pain of others in order to understand their motivations and feelings. One needs to understand how things work if one is to deflect them from an undesirable path toward a better one. What have we learned, however painful it might be, that will help us to build a stronger and better culture in the next millennium?

Contexts for the Creation and Amelioration of Racial Conflict

The first part of this book examined the historical context of race relations from our country's founding up to the 1990s. Following are some general principles or observations from these chapters:

1 *The United States was founded on racism.* The slave trade and the institution of slavery, and the prominent role each played in the formation of our society, are cultural facts. The treatment of indigenous Indians throughout the settling of America and the Westward Expansion, too, is a cultural fact. These facts are as much a part of the U.S. value and belief system as those laudatory values of freedom, liberty, and equality that we hail so proudly are. These cultural facts of racism compromised the core values of the American Revolution, and they— along with the judgments of different others' barbarism and savagery that helped to rationalize them—are interwoven in the fabric of our culture.

2 *Individual liberty is constrained and confounded by the reality of groups.* The great experiment in individual liberty and freedom challenges the equally great reality of the social interconnectedness of individuals in society. The United States was founded on the strongest expression of individualism ever made in any society. The conflict inherent in the individual versus the collective is at the heart and soul of the American dilemma, and often confounds contemporary efforts to resolve it. Social psychology is the most encompassing discipline for addressing this problem because, by its very nature, it is concerned with the individual in society and with the mutuality of influences from individuals to the group and back to the larger society. How individuals are constrained by the society that they, at the same time, create is a fundamental issue that weaves a complex web around the problems of prejudice and racism. Descartes (1637) framed the individual reality in his *"cogito, ergo sum"* (*I* think, therefore *I* am). Mbiti (1970, p. 141) describes the African collective sense in these terms, "I am because *we* are; and, since *we* are, therefore, I am."

3 *Character is not enough.* Race, class, and sex define aggregate or group categories that, in varying degrees, dictate the experiences that individuals have. It is, therefore, impossible to fully account for a person by his or her character alone. Color matters. Gender matters. Class matters. Group membership across a variety of human dimensions matters. All play some role in determining expectations, opportunities, and outcomes for individuals. We struggle to minimize the group effects as we try to be true to the individualism that is our cultural inheritance. We try harder than any other society to be true to this heritage and to honor this value; nonetheless, *being judged solely by one's character and its consequences is an aspiration, not a reality.* Moreover, our mutuality and interdependence suggest that character alone, singular unto itself, should not be the final measure of worth. Rather, how we blend and merge with others is as much a part of the story as our self-contained individualism is. Maintaining this glorification of the self sustains the self-other dichotomy that increases group conflict and interpersonal mistrust. Isolating the individual and putting the burden of conduct and capability solely on the content of one's character threatens the possibility of an interdependent society of mutual interests and collective well-being.

4 *The civil rights movement of the 1960s was not about the "forgetting of race," but the "removal of race" as a barrier to opportunity.* The legacy of the 1960s has widely been misconstrued to suggest that race no longer matters and that we should

just forget it in a colorblind embrace of equality. However, race is still important, and it does matter. Race is salient in our society. Rather than forgetting it, which we really cannot do, we are better off trying to reduce its adverse impact on people, which we can do.

5   *The civil rights era elevated individualism to a degree that forced us to confront the inherent conflict between individual and group identities, rights, and behaviors.* Group interests became more, not less, salient in the aftermath of the 1960s. The triumph of the civil rights movement in the 1960s was believed to validate the installation of the criterion of individual merit as the only legitimate basis for judgment. Therefore, group-based judgments, prejudices, and beliefs were ruled out-of-bounds. But two things posed problems. First, the historical legacy of prejudice, discrimination, and racism was not erased by the civil rights legislation. Second, prejudice, discrimination, and racism did not disappear with the passage of the laws. Therefore, in order to achieve the goal of fair treatment of individuals, we had to confront the group-based biases that continued. This posed a paradox that Justice Harry Blackmun articulated in his opinion in the *Bakke* case in 1979:

> . . . In order to get beyond racism, we must first take account of race. There is no other way. . . . In order to treat persons equally, we must treat them differently. (*Regents of the University of California vs. Bakke*, 1978, p. 2806–2808)

This paradox persists as we formulate social policy and attempt to understand how differences can be accounted for in a unified society.

6   *In removing race as a "legitimate" basis of judgment, we made it an unindicted co-conspirator in the processes of racism.* We rejected the monster of race in our conscious attempt to achieve a more egalitarian society, but its tentacles did not let go easily. Racism went from explicit to implicit, from dominative to aversive, from old-fashioned to modern, and from literal to symbolic as a determinant of attitudes, beliefs, and behaviors. Determining how race was involved in human judgments became an excavation exercise. It entailed uncovering layers of repression, sublimation, and subterfuge. Out of sight is not necessarily out of mind, and efforts to promote racial fairness by ignoring race have been shown to inhibit the possibility of correcting racial biases; such efforts often leave racial biases intact and entrenched.

Processes of Prejudice

Part 2 provided detailed summaries of the sociopsychological analysis of the processes and consequences of prejudice. Following are some general principles or observations from these chapters:

1   *Prejudice is a natural and almost inescapable consequence of being human and living in a society of diverse peoples.* Social and institutional structures and patterns feed into social perceptions and processes in ways that sustain prejudice. Implicit stereotyping, illusory correlation, chameleon effects, and automatic processes have been shown to occur in relationship to perceptions and judgments of members of ethnic and racial minority groups. They can occur within racial and ethnic minority groups as well as between them, although they have not been studied nearly as much in the intragroup context. These processes occur at the most fundamental levels of cognitive thought

and judgment. They reflect patterns of biasing information that are subtly, but consistently, represented in the institutional arrangements and social processes of society.

2   *People can and do overcome natural tendencies toward bias.* When a person is socialized to values of tolerance or adopts personal values that make biases inconsistent with the way one conceives of and values oneself, the person is less likely to display patterns of prejudice. Given a chance to think about what one feels, how one thinks, and what one would prefer to do, a person can replace biasing thoughts or judgments with more tolerant, accepting ones.

3   *Individuals draw psychological support from identification with groups.* Social identity processes exacerbate social hierarchy and inhibit processes that might reduce intergroup conflict. Members of dominant groups gain positive esteem, in part, from the facts of their dominance. Hence, they are generally disinclined to relinquish either the dominance or the group identification. Subordinate groups gain strength from the protective properties of common identities and from the creative reevaluation of group characteristics that serves to replace a negative spin with a positive value. Therefore, for different and opposing reasons, neither dominant nor subordinate groups are inclined to abandon their group identification and to thereby pave the way for intergroup harmony.

4   *Being a target of bias or under suspicion of inferiority triggers reactions that may have both positive and negative consequences.* The positive results include marshaling psychological and social forces that strengthen one's connection to one's social group and withdrawing emotionally and physically from situations where the probability of negative experiences is high. These processes sustain positive concepts of the self and serve ego-protective functions in a society where demeaning and biasing experiences so often occur. On the negative side, targets' performance may be undermined by the anxiety that is caused by the fear of confirming a negative group stereotype. The anxiety may further be increased by the ambiguity of not knowing whether one's positive or negative outcomes are deserved. Discounting the self in the assessment of one's experience robs a person of the ability to take self-corrective action in order to improve poor performance or to take credit for successful accomplishments.

5   *Identifying differences among people, and categorizing people into groups accordingly, facilitates group-based treatment of individuals—a marker of prejudice.* These social-categorization effects make intergroup conflict easier to initiate and sustain. Moreover, these categorization processes themselves may exaggerate real differences between and among groups and may correspondingly escalate and intensify realistic conflict. (We saw this in the studies of Sherif, and in the events in Rwanda, Bosnia, and Northern Ireland.)

6   *The tendency to categorize people into groups and maintaining a competitive, if not hostile, relationship to them can be reduced or counteracted in several ways.* One way is to *decategorize* individuals—that is, to remove them from the most salient and common social categories (e.g., race, gender, and ethnicity) by focusing either on their individual characteristics or on their multiple group memberships. Either way, a person will be less readily categorized by the most salient social groupings when this is done. Another way is to *recategorize* the groups themselves—that is, to merge them into one overarching group. This creates a new, single-group boundary in which the dynamic forces of in-group processes (e.g., cohesion and in-group bias and preference) help to

form new bonds between people who may have belonged to different groups. The former approach, decategorization, emphasizes individualistic judgments by carefully excising a person from his or her group; the latter approach, recategorization, allows a person to maintain a group identity, albeit a changed one.

7 *Affect and emotion play important roles in the full range of experiences with prejudice and racism.* Fear, anxiety, and hostility are aroused by processes of stereotyping and social categorization. These feelings are also responsible for biases in social judgment, perception, and behavior. There is a close connection between fairly unconscious and automatic cognitive processes and the emotional and affective processes that weave in and out of these cognitive dynamics, adding intensity and guiding the selection of targets for biased judgments. Contact between people from different groups that have antagonistic relationships to one another can facilitate better relations when such contact is cooperative and provides opportunities for friendships to form. Positive affect is, in the final analysis, the most important means by which improved intergroup and interpersonal relationships can be achieved.

Realities of Racism

The third part of this book examined the concept of race, and the origins, development, and manifestations of racism. Following are some general principles or observations that come from these chapters:

1 *The concept of race has minimal biological significance by contemporary scientific standards, but race continues to have important sociocultural significance.* Genetic variations are greater *within* so-called racial groups than *between* them. Nevertheless, we continue to use racial designations, along with their implied biological essences. We do this for three principle reasons. (a) There is a sociohistorical legacy to the concept of race that is embedded in the cultural ethos of Europe and North America. It developed alongside the cultural definitions of what it means to be an American and how being American distinguishes one from others. (b) Evidence suggests that people are inclined to think of humans in types or kinds on the basis of *essences*, whether these are biologically, psychologically, or culturally determined. This tendency toward essentialism sustains the categorization of people by race, even when the biological basis of doing so is invalidated. (c) The meaning and the utility of race have been perpetuated over the years by processes of *racialism* (i.e., connecting character traits to racial categories) and *racialization* (i.e., the adoption of institutional practices and social policies that explicitly and implicitly acknowledge race and use it to achieve social, political, and economic goals).

2 *Race, ethnicity, class, and culture are intertwined in ways that make it difficult to isolate casual influences and to identify the best avenues for change.* The colorblind approach suggests that it is only color that is problematic and that, if we ignore skin color, we have a better chance of making progress in human relations. Yet, perceptions of *color* carry with them systematic patterns of class distinctions, values and beliefs, symbols, and traditions that result from cultural socialization. We seek to distinguish ethnicity from race, given that race carries such strong negative connotations and is associated with limitations imposed by ge-

netic immutability. But it is easier said than done. "Race" still carries meaning for us, in spite of its flawed conceptual basis and negative history.

3 *Racism arises when one racially defined group maintains and exercises power over other racial groups to the advantage of its own group members and to the disadvantage of the other racial group(s).* The concept of race implies essential and immutable qualities that are judged on a continuum from good (one's own) to less good (others). The comparative evaluative judgment of so-called racial groups serves to justify one's own privilege and the lack of equality of others. Racism thereby creates and sustains dominance and rationalizes it as natural.

4 *Racism is exceedingly complex and multifaceted.* Racism is multidimensional, and racisms may be a better representation. Racism varies with respect to the source of inferiority or superiority and the implications for behavior and belief. For example, *extrinsic* racists believe that races differ in respects that *warrant* their differential and inferior treatment. But, if the differences they presume to exist are shown to be nonexistent, they no longer support racist practices. *Intrinsic* racists believe that some races are ordained by Nature to be inferior. No facts or behavior can alter their conviction that racial inferiority-superiority is preordained.

   Moreover, there are multiple places where racism emerges. At the *individual* level, people believe other races are inferior and they themselves superior by virtue of their race. At the *institutional* level, racialized thinking and practices confer privilege and advantage on one racial, ethnic, or gender group over others, whether intentionally or unintentionally. At the *cultural* level, the values, symbols, traditions, and worldview of the dominant culture reinforce racial superiority-inferiority notions and suffuse these ideas throughout the culture.

5 *The cultural level of racism is where the wars for meaning and definition of race and its relation to U.S. values are waged.* "Culture wars" are made up of battles wherein definitions of "fairness," the genetic basis of inequality, and the desirability of specific values and their expression are disputed. The determination of what the race problem is, who is responsible, and how it can and should be resolved is a matter of cultural conflict and change.

6 *Racism and prejudice work together in orchestrating the meaning and consequences of race in the United States.* At the macrolevel of society, culture informs institutional arrangements and imbues them with racialized meanings and essences. At the microlevel, individuals, in turn, are socialized in this racialized environment and pursue opportunities and possibilities already influenced by their racial affiliation. Individuals cycle through institutions and remake the culture that shaped them. Thus, the role of race in culture is constantly evolving and changing; it is defined anew in each generation. Although the basic equations of race are modified and transformed, they are not destroyed.

2001—A HUMAN ODYSSEY

Race is a label, a concept, and an idea that summarizes a human history of evaluative distinctions. Race is also a legacy of Western culture and a haunting reminder of the *imperfections* of our union. Prejudice is a common human capacity, naturally occurring in a species for whom thinking, albeit a defense against danger, is dangerous in its own right. Racism has stitched the invidious distinctions of race into the cultural fabric of our imperfect union. Prejudices, knowingly or unwittingly, constituted the thread in the needle.

As we stand on the brink of a new millennium, how do the lessons of the previous 17 chapters of this book help us move toward a society that, in its ultimate perfection, finds unity in its diversity? We have concentrated on race as a decisive human attribute that drives a wedge between and among people. But diversity is a concept both broad and encompassing. The paradigm of race (elaborated herein primarily from the perspectives of blacks and whites in the United States) demonstrates how differences among people are created, maintained, and utilized to serve basic human needs for dominance, self-interest, and psychological and emotional comfort. However, the dimensions of human difference go well beyond race. To conclude this exercise, we will consider the principles or ideas that stand as either barriers to or enablers of the emergence of an increasingly diverse population in a society that strives for unity.

Whose Problem Is It, Anyway?

We have posed this question rhetorically throughout the book. I suspect the answer is clear by now: The problems posed by prejudice and racism belong to all of us. Problematizing one group or another is a hindrance to finding solutions to the discord wrought by prejudice and racism. By framing the issue in terms of the total cultural fabric, we see clearly that we cannot solve a problem this complex and ingrained in society by singling out a particular group—whether the group be white men, say, or Latina immigrants.

We find ourselves locked into a dichotomous language and pattern of thinking whereby problems are opposed to solutions, bad to good, "dumb" to smart. This language and this way of thinking inhibits formation of inclusionary concepts. In order to advance and to make tolerance possible, we have to revise the model of society and of human relations within it. Capra (1975, p. 131) notes the Eastern cultural principle that:

> [because] all opposites . . . are interdependent, their conflict can never result in the total victory of one side, but will always be the manifestation of the interplay between the two sides . . . a virtuous person is therefore not one who undertakes the impossible task of striving for the good and eliminating the bad, but rather one who is able to maintain a dynamic balance between good and bad.[1]

We dichotomize virtuous attributes and assign them, in binary fashion, to racial groups. Moreover, we place the good in the heads and hearts of specific individuals—typically, those that belong to the racial group thought to be superior. But again, a reference to physics is instructive. According to Zukav (1979, p. 72), the physical world:

> . . . is not a structure built out of independently existing unanalyzable entities, but rather a web of relationships between elements whose meanings arise wholly from their relationships to the whole.

Individuals are not independent entities, and they cannot be understood in isolation from the web of relationships in which they are embedded. The whole gives meaning to its constituent parts. Racism persists because we partition individuals into separable entities and give them qualities that are dichotomous.

[1]This view was also expressed by Dixon (1976) in his concept of *diunitality*, the union of opposites.

Omi and Winant (1994, p. 52) note that "U.S. society is racially both more diverse and more complex today than at any previous time in its history." They observe that, by conceiving race narrowly in bipolar terms (i.e., black-white), we fail to capture this great complexity and diversity. This poses several barriers to race relations; among these are the following:

1   Difficulty in addressing the overall complexity of race relations and race-related policies results from considering only the black-white context.
2   A black-white focus may not cover specific problems for other groups.
3   Specific policies may not affect different groups in the same way. Therefore, we may fail to adopt the most effective policies when we use a bipolar racial approach.
4   Critical particular aspects of racial politics may be ignored by an exclusive focus on black-white relations (e.g., scapegoating certain groups for failed U.S. policies or decreases in national productivity).
5   *Inter*ethnic-interracial and *intra*-ethnic-intraracial perspectives may be marginalized by an exclusive focus on black-white relations (e.g., the Korean viewpoint in the black-Korean conflict).

Our tendency to dichotomize race into black and white is symptomatic of our more general tendency to isolate individuals and to separate them along good-bad dimensions, as if the two were mutually exclusive. Capra (1975, p. 131) argues that "all opposites are polar—light and dark, winning and losing, good and evil, [and] are merely different aspects of the same phenomenon." That is, we may tend to think of racism as the problem of whites, but not of blacks; as a problem of black-white relations and not of black-Korean, white-Mexican, Asian-white relations, or even middle-class black–lower-class black relations. However, by doing so, we limit our understanding of the complexity of the problem. As a result, ameliorative options will be limited, and progress in eradicating racism will be slow, indeed.

The more perfect union will necessarily require a union of opposites and the recognition that no person or group has a monopoly on virtue. Agreement with this premise allows us to introduce the strategy of searching each polar claim of virtue for its vice, and each vice for its virtue. We will discover in this exercise that both vice and virtue can be found in all people and that a perfect union of diverse peoples will encompass a range of virtues and vices that come from all of us. The linkage of vices to the "other" and of virtues to the "self" is a symptom of cultural patterns of thinking and evaluation that underlie the persistence of racism.

The Physics of Action—The Antiracist Role

Newton's Law of Motion, his first law, says that, if an object is moving in a straight line, it will do so *forever* unless it is acted upon by a force. At the time this force acts upon the object, the object's movement will be altered in speed and direction to a degree equal to and in a direction opposite to that of the force exerted. Racism is an object that has moved forward in our society over centuries. It would have been total and unaltered had it not been acted upon, throughout its existence, by the forces we call *antiracism*. Racism is not over, it has not ended. But we must continue to struggle through antiracist projects in order to reduce it.

One of the assumptions necessitated by this motion principle is that we are locked into a closed system in which actions and reactions are reciprocal. Racism persists. Some benefit from it, while others remain disadvantaged because of it. In this way, reversing disadvantage can only be achieved by the reduction of privilege and, in some instances, of well-earned opportunity. I was in a meeting with a white captain of the Cleveland, Ohio, fire department several years ago on the day he discovered that his bid for promotion had failed. The fire department was under a consent decree imposed by a federal judge in order to remedy the lack of black firefighters. The decree mandated that 50 percent of promotions had to be black. The captain had scored fourth on the personnel test used in part to determine promotions. However, because two of those promoted had to be black, he would not be one of the four captains who were promoted. In Einstein's theory of relativity, systems are open and cannot be determined in advance. This leaves room for alternative possibilities and the fact that a change in one part is not necessarily accompanied by an equal and opposite change in another. In this open world of relativity, opposition is diminished and the well-being of one person is not necessarily threatened by that of another. But in the captain's closed world, the black man's gain was definitely his loss!

The struggle to curtail or eliminate racism takes many forms. Some antiracist projects try to eliminate racism itself (e.g., by means of hate speech and hate crime codes and fair housing laws) and some attempt to eliminate the consequences of racism (e.g., by means of affirmative action). There is no guarantee that any one approach is right or that unintended negative consequences may not occur. But we cannot ignore our differences. We cannot ignore the historical legacy of racism or its continuing influence on contemporary society. To ignore racism and its consequences is to allow it to work its evil without being detected or attacked. To actively try to diminish it is to open it to public scrutiny and debate. This "national conversation" and the vigorous pursuit of antiracist projects are important to forming that more perfect union.

Diversity Is a Strength in the Species and in Society

We talk about celebrating diversity and seek to replace the melting pot metaphor with a garden salad metaphor. The simple fact is that human diversity is a strength of the species (Trickett, Watts, and Birman, 1994). Wilson (1987) demonstrates that it is variation in a species that protects it from threats that could wipe it out if all members were exactly alike. Blacks are susceptible to sickle cell anemia, in part, by virtue of their adaptation to tropical weather patterns. Whites are susceptible to skin cancer by virtue of their adaptation to the temperate climate of the northern hemisphere. Keh-Ming Lin has been studying the diversity of reactions of different ethnic and racial groups to medical prescriptions in order to fit treatment not only to a given disease or illness, but to the ethnic and racial culture-biology diversity that comes with a given individual. Diversity expands the adaptive capability of the species.[2]

Diversity also expands the adaptive capability of the individual. Linville (1985) has shown that diversity within an individual, or *self-complexity*, can be a buffer against stress-inducing events in that person's life. She has shown that subjects high in self-complexity show fewer negative consequences of stressful events. For

---

[2]Dr. Lin is Director of the Research Center on Psychobiology and Culture at the University of California, Los Angeles.

example, college students high in self-complexity visited the university infirmary less often, made fewer visits to the counseling centers, and, among women, had less severe menstrual cycles. Her reasoning for these effects is that the more complex a person is and the more different, significant aspects that the person has, the less impact a stressful event in any one aspect will have on the whole person. Smith and Cohen (1993) extended this reasoning to show that self-complexity did not always have such moderating effects. Specifically, they argued and empirically demonstrated that complexity in a specific self-aspect (e.g., interpersonal self) can heighten the impact of stressful events relevant to that self aspect. They found that for college students who had just ended a romantic relationship those who had a more complex romantic self (i.e., involved more characteristics and was associated more with other self-aspects) were significantly more upset by the breakup than those lower in romantic self-complexity. A second study (Cohen, Pane and Smith, in press) extended this finding to complexity in interpersonal friendship and found the same adverse affective reaction to friend-induced stress. Moreover, the complexity effect was specific to friendship-induced stress but not to others (e.g., family-based stress). One implication of this finding is that self-aspects that are complex tend to dominate affective reactions to relevant stress. If race or ethnicity is a highly complex self-aspect, then race-related stressful events will have a greater adverse affective impact.

Collectively, our society benefits from diversity, because negative events or ill-advised courses of action are corrected by the diversity of reaction and influence. Prime Minister Nakasone of Japan claimed that cultural *homogeneity* was the strength of Japan and cultural *diversity* was the Achilles heel of the United States. However, as noted, evidence from biology shows that diversity strengthens the species, and evidence from psychology shows that diversity in individuals protects the species from adverse circumstances. We can extend these biological and psychological principles to the society at large. Diversity comes in many different forms. We have focused on race and/or ethnicity in this book. But age, gender, region, occupation, religion, and sexual orientation are all aspects of human circumstances that contribute to diversity and, in some way, to our collective strength as a people. We are stronger as a society when we acknowledge and utilize our human diversity.

And there is another value of diversity. In a group process, the majority rules. That is a core principle of democracy in the United States. But, as Guinier (1994) observes, the majority can tyrannize the minority, imposing its will—however meritorious that will might be. Nemeth (1986) studied the role of minorities in group decision making and found that group decisions are better when minorities are able to influence them. Minority influence leads to more creative thinking and dissent promotes consideration of more points of view and, hence, more information is used in reaching a position. Persistence by a minority is most influential, in part, because the minority becomes a focus of attention and, thus, contributes a disproportionate number of arguments to the discussion. The persistent-minority perspective in our society contributes positively to the development of our society and moves us closer to, not further from, a more perfect union.

The lesson is simple—diversity is good for us. Diversity is everywhere among us. Our human tendencies to categorize and reduce the dimensions of our social world to manageable units seem sometimes to lead us to actively reject the facts of diversity. Rather than "celebrating" it, our mind's eye ignores it, and tugs and pulls it into shapes that fit its own need for economy and ease. The human brain imposes patterns of similarity on a world of diversity.

Diversity within groups.   The major social categories we have been concerned with—including race, ethnicity, gender, sexual orientation, class, and nationality—are perceived as if their members were, by and large, alike. By stereotyping, we impose order on disorder, similarity on difference. People come in different colors, sizes, shapes, and orientations—not always according to our categorization assumptions. For example, I once asked my college roommate, who is of Serbian lineage, how come his mother could speak such good English. He said, simply, that she was born in Rochester, New York.

If diversity is good for the species, it is also good for the group. Being under attack, as targets of prejudice and racism frequently are, causes group members to close ranks and to assert their commonalties for purposes of group defense. But, in so doing, the strength of diversity is compromised within the group, as well. Therefore, racism not only diminishes diversity in the society at large, it has the effect of diminishing diversity within the groups that are its targets. As diversity is diminished, dichotomous thinking and perceiving are increased, oppositional judgments are more prevalent, and the union of opposites—or, at least, *differences*—is undermined.

Diversity between groups.   If diversity is a fact of life in our society, and if it is a positive feature of it, then it must be a central aspect of that more perfect union. Group differences have too often and too easily been exploited in the service of divisiveness and imperfection. Approaches to the reduction of prejudice and racism have too often come down to how we manage to remove differences as bases for intergroup bias. There are three perspectives in social psychology that contribute positively to reducing intergroup conflict.

The first is decategorization (Brewer and Miller, 1984), by which we focus on the individual characteristics of others and identify their multiple group memberships and unique personal attributes. In so doing, we are less likely to respond to them on the basis of their single racial or ethnic or gender group identification and are more likely to respond to them on the basis of their unique personal qualities. This breaks down group boundaries by individuating people in different groups.

The second is recategorization (Gaertner et al., 1993), which removes group boundaries by submerging them into one overarching single-group concept. By this process, "us" and "them" become "*we*." The *we* approaches the unity we have been considering. In this approach, like the decategorization process, group boundaries are deconstructed.

A third approach emphasizes the importance of generalizing from an interpersonal experience with an individual group member to the entire group itself (Brown, 1995). This approach shows that (1) if we have a positive encounter with a member of another group, (2) if that person is thought to be *typical* of that group, and (3) if that group is perceived to be relatively *homogeneous,* then our positive experience will be most likely to generalize to the group at large. This approach emphasizes the value of intergroup interaction where group identification is a salient, not a suppressed, aspect of the encounter.

Diversity occurs in the form of individual variation and group difference. Perceived group differences offer occasions to ignore individual variation—if for example, you are a jock, you are dumb; or if you are fat, you are jolly; or if you are beautiful, you are good. The greatest possible diversity comes from thinking of people *only as people.* There are, then, 5.73 billion different members on the planet (*The World Almanac,* 1996). The ultimate implication of the extreme individualism in the United States is this sort of individual diversity. But can we form a more perfect union based on such individual diversity? I suspect not, especially when between-group diversity serves the polarizing goals that it does.

All of the approaches summarized above are applicable and valuable. We need to acknowledge the diversity within groups that helps to break down group boundaries. We need to identify the principles among us that promote unity. And, we need to respect the differences between groups and find those instances of inter-actions with other groups that demonstrate that differences can be a source of posi-tive and rewarding experiences.

Toward a More Perfect Union

Spurlock (1996) argues that Constitutional principles of liberty, equality, and frater-nity did not describe the *end* sought by the experiment that became the *United States* of America, but the *means* to it. The end of this experiment in government was to create *a more perfect union*. But, of these means, we have embraced liberty and equality, albeit grudgingly, but eschewed *fraternity* ("a group of people associ-ated or formally organized for a common purpose, interest or pleasure." *Webster's*, 1965). For Spurlock (1996), fraternity stands for union. The imperfection of race stood and stands as a barrier to fraternity and, hence, to the noble goal of union.

Although we clearly have not formed that more perfect union referred to by the Founding Fathers by focusing so much attention on flaws in our systems, on vivid examples of inhumanity and bigotry, or on the legacy of racism, we fail to rec-ognize that we must be doing something right! Samuelson (1996) points out that 38 percent of Britons, 30 percent of Germans, 20 percent of Japanese, and 19 percent of Canadians answered yes when asked if they would like to live in another country. This compares to only 11 percent of U.S. citizens who felt that living in another country would be preferable to staying in the United States. I would expect, al-though the response of black Americans, Mexican Americans, Puerto Ricans, Asian Americans, and American Indians were no reported, that they have similarly low motivation to live elsewhere. Therefore, however flawed our union is, there must be something very deep and powerful that holds promise for us here.

This book has focused on prejudice and racism, both of which reflect failures of the human spirit to achieve its most glorious human possibilities. Although they represent failings, they do not make us failures. We have seen that there is much that is natural, automatic, and culturally fundamental to the problems of prejudice and racism in our society and in our experience. But, when we draw a line in the sand and label those on one side "good" and those on the other side "bad," we make it harder to come together. I believe that, in the United States of America, our ex-periment in democracy, freedom, individual rights, and egalitarianism has taken us far and accomplished much in recognizing and glorifying the human spirit—no mat-ter what color it comes wrapped in. That we are not perfect—indeed, far from it—is not, for me, a sign of failure, but a goad to keep working and trying even harder.

Why do people want to stay here? Why do people want to come here? Blacks did not come here willingly, and this distinguishes them from other racial and eth-nic groups. American Indians were already here. Whatever the origins, blacks have always tended to choose to remain here, and laid legitimate claim to a founding role in the creation and evolution of the United States. Others come here willingly, even desperately. The United States holds promise for them, even when the reality of being in the United States fails to meet the fantasy that brought them here. Racism, xenophobia, self-interest, and ignorance inhibit realization of the American dream. However, in spite of its faults, there is something wonderful and marvelous about our society.

The United States, though, is still a work in progress. Flawed though it may be in many ways, and however far from liberty, equality, and fraternity we are, we struggle to achieve a more perfect union. We try. The promise of perfection, perhaps, is the lure. We are arrogant enough to believe we are right about our highest principles and determined enough to try to prove it. The expression of the human spirit is a driving force in our society. Our need to create—and to have the freedom to do it our way—is powerful. Jazz and the blues fused this powerful drive of individuality with the cooperative spirit of the collective. We need to increase, not reduce, our freedoms; but, among the freedoms we cherish must be the freedom to be different, to express and enjoy our diverse cultural legacies.

Freedom is not served by arbitrary barriers and invidious distinctions. When we teach and support our children and let our citizens move freely into all arenas of life, their unique creative spirits will shine in ways that our tradition-based expectations may not foresee. Prejudice and racism are barriers to human potential and collective unity. Opposing them, as we have struggled to do as a people from the beginning of our society, improves our society (much as a minority influence does), and introduces creativity, a broader information base, and, ultimately, the wherewithal to not only tolerate but appreciate and benefit from our human diversity.

The choices before us are multiplying rapidly and signify conflict between and among basic U.S. values. These conflicts in basic values pose the hardest challenge we face. In the names of freedom and liberty, we oppose union. In the service of freedom of speech, we compromise the right to participate in society without fear of harassment and denigration. We hold promise as the land of individual opportunity, but we restrict the opportunity of individuals on the basis of the groups to which they belong. Egalitarianism strives mightily to attach itself to diversity, to difference.

Two paths stand before us. One, motivated by the best sense of liberty, equality and fraternity, moves us forward in the experiment in creating a more perfect union. A second, fueled by fear, self-interest, ignorance, and mistrust, turns us backward, and diverts us from the struggle toward tolerance and perfection. Our diversity comes from different origins, experiences, and goals. Our best possible selves, as a nation and a people, will be determined by the path we choose.

Bibliography

ABDEL-GHANY, M., AND SHARPE, D. L. (1994). "Racial Wage Differentials among Young Adults: Evidence from the 1990s." *Journal of Family and Economic Issues, 15,* 279–294.

ABELSON, R. P. (1994). In-Group Perceptions of Activity by the Collective Other. Invited Address, Presidential Symposium. American Psychological Society. Washington, DC.

ABOUD, F. (1988). *Children and Prejudice.* New York: Basil Blackwell.

ABOUD, F. (1993). "The Developmental Psychology of Racial Prejudice." *Transcultural Psychiatric Research Review, 30,* 229–242.

ABRAHAMS, R. (1970). *Deep Down in the Jungle.* Chicago: Aldine (revised edition).

ADAMS, D. W. (1988). "Fundamental Considerations: The Deep Meaning of Native American Schooling, 1880–1900." *Harvard Educational Review, 58,* 1–28.

ADORNO, T. W., FRENKEL-BRUNSWIK, E., LEVINSON, D. J., AND SANFORD, R. N. (1950). *The Authoritarian Personality.* New York: Harper.

AKBAR, N. (1991). The Evolution of Human Psychology for African Americans. In R. L. Jones (ed.) *Black Psychology,* Third edition (pp. 99–124). Hampton, VA: Cobb & Henry.

ALBURY, A., AND BOYKIN, A. W. (1993). Social Orientations, Learning Conditions and Learning Outcomes among Low-Income Black and White Grade School Children. Unpublished doctoral dissertation. Howard University, Washington, D.C.

ALLEN, W. D. (1964). *Africa.* Sacramento, CA: California State Department of Education.

ALLPORT, F. H. (1920). "The Influence of the Group upon Association and Thought." *Journal of Experimental Psychology, 2,* 159–182.

ALLPORT, G. W. (1929). "The Composition of Political Attitudes." *American Journal of Sociology, 35,* 220–238.

ALLPORT, G. W. (1935). Attitudes. In C. Murchison (ed.) *A Handbook of Social Psychology.* Worcester, MA: Clark University Press.

ALLPORT, G. W. (1954). *The Nature of Prejudice.* Reading, MA: Addison-Wesley.

ALTEMEYER, B. AND HUNSBERGER, B. (1992). "Authoritarianism, Religious Fundamentalism, Quest, and Prejudice." *International Journal for the Psychology of Religion, 2,* 113–133.

ALTEMEYER, R. (1993). "Reducing Prejudice in Right-Wing Authoritarians." In Zanna, M. P & Olson, J. M (eds.) *The Psychology of Prejudice: The Ontario Symposium,* (Vol. 7, pp. 131–148) Hillsdale, NJ: Erlbaum Associates.

AMAKER, N. C. (1988). *Civil Rights and the Reagan Administration.* Washington, DC: The Urban Institute Press.

AMIR, Y. (1969). "Contact Hypothesis in Ethnic Relations." *Psychological Bulletin, 71,* 319–342.

ANI, M. (1994). *Yurugu: An African-Centered Critique of European Cultural Thought and Behavior.* Trenton, NJ: Africa World Press.

APPIAH, K. A. (1990). "Racisms." In D. T. Goldberg (ed.) *Anatomy of Racism* (pp. 3–17). Minneapolis, MN: University of Minnesota Press.

APTHEKER, H. (1969). *A History of Negro Slave Revolts.* New York: International Publishers.

APTHEKER, H. (1992). *Anti-Racism in U.S. History: The First Two Hundred Years.* Westport, CT: Greenwood Press.

ARCHER, D., IRITANI, B., KIMES, D. D. AND BARRIOS, M. (1983). "Face-ism: Five Studies of Sex

Differences in Facial Prominence." *Journal of Personality and Social Psychology, 45,* 725–735.

ARMSTEAD, C. A., LAWLER, K. A., GORDON, G., CROSS, J., AND GIBBONS, J. (1989). "Relationship of Racial Stressors to Blood Pressure Responses and Anger Expression in Black College Students. *Health Psychology, 8,* 541–556.

ARONSON, E., BLANEY, N., SIKES, J., STEPHAN, C., AND SNAPP, M. (1974). "Busing and Racial Tension: The Jigsaw Route to Learning and Liking." *Psychology Today, 8,* 43–59.

ARONSON, E., AND BRIDGEMAN, D. (1979). "Jigsaw Groups and the Desegregated Classroom: In Pursuit of Common Goals." *Personality and Social Psychology Bulletin, 5,* 438–445.

ARROYO, C., AND ZIGLER, E. (1995). "Racial Identity, Academic Achievement, and the Psychological Well Being of Economically Disadvantaged Adolescents." *Journal of Personality and Social Psychology, 69,* 903–914.

ASANTE, M. K. (1987). *The Afrocentric Idea.* Philadelphia: Temple University Press.

ASCH, S. E. (1946). "Forming Impressions of Personality." *Journal of Social Psychology, 41,* 258–290.

ASHER, S. R., AND ALLEN, V. L. (1969). "Racial Preference and Social Comparison Processes." *Journal of Social Issues, 25,* 157–167.

ASHMORE, R. D., AND DEL BOCA, F. K. (1979). "Sex Stereotypes and Implicit Personality Theory: Toward a Cognitive-Social Psychological Conception." *Sex Roles, 5,* 219–248.

ASHMORE, R. D., AND DEL BOCA, F. K. (1981). "Conceptual Approaches to Stereotypes and Stereotyping." In D. L. Hamilton (ed.), *Cognitive Processes in Stereotyping and Intergroup* (pp.). New York: Academic Press.

ASHMORE, R. D., AND TUMIA, M. (1980). "Sex Stereotypes and Implicit Personality Theory. I. A Personality Description Approach to the Assessment of Sex Stereotypes. *Sex Roles, 6,* 501–518.

ATKINSON, D. R., AND GIM, R. H. (1989). "Asian-American Cultural Identity and Attitudes toward Mental Health Services." *Journal of Counseling Psychology, 36,* 209–212.

ATKINSON, D. R., THOMPSON, C. E., AND GRANT, S. K. (1993). "A Three Dimensional Model for Counseling Racial/Ethnic Minorities." *The Counseling Psychologist, 21,* 257–277.

AXTHELM, P. (1987). "Baseball: A Crisis in Black and White." *Newsweek, 109,* p. 71.

AYRES, I., AND WALDFOGEL, J. (1994). "A Market Test for Race Discrimination in Bail Setting." *Stanford Law Review, 46,* 987–1048.

BALDWIN, J., BROWN, R., AND RACKLEY, R. (1991). "Some Socio-Behavioral Correlates of African Self-Consciousness in African-American College Students." *Journal of Black Psychology, 17,* 1–17.

BALDWIN, J., DUNCAN, J. A., AND BELL, Y. R. (1987). "Assessment of African Self-Consciousness among Students from Two College Environments." *Journal of Black Psychology, 13,* 27–41.

BALDWIN, J. A., AND BELL, Y. R. (1985). "The African Self-Consciousness Scale: An Africentric Personality Questionnaire." *The Western Journal of Black Studies, 9,* 61–68.

BANAJI, M. R., AND GREENWALD, A. G. (1994). "Implicit Stereotyping and Unconscious Prejudice." In M. P. Zanna and J. M. Olson (eds.), *The Psychology of Prejudice, The Ontario Symposium* (Vol. 7, pp. 55–76). Hillsdale, NJ: Erlbaum.

BANAJI, M. R., HARDIN, C., AND ROTHMAN, A. J. (1993). "Implicit Stereotyping in Person Judgment. *Journal of Personality and Social Psychology, 65,* 272–281.

BANFIELD, E. C. (1968). *The Unheavenly City.* Boston: Little, Brown.

BANTON, M. (1977). *The Idea of Race.* Boulder, CO: Westview Press.

BANTON, M. P. (1983). *Racial and Ethnic Competition.* New York: Cambridge University Press.

BARBASH, F. (1996). "Epicenter of Violence: Londonderry Can't Escape Its History as Focus of N. Ireland's Troubles." *The Washington Post,* July 17, pp. A21–22.

BARGH, J. A. (1989). "Conditional Automaticity: Varieties of Automatic Influences in Social Perception and Cognition." In J. S. Uleman and J. A. Bargh (eds.), *Unintended Thought.* New York: Guilford Press.

BARGH, J. A., AND CHEN, M. (1996). "The Chameleon Effect: Automatic Social Perception Produces Automatic Social Behavior." Unpublished manuscript, New York University.

BARKER, M. (1981). *The New Racism: Conservatives and the Ideology of the Tribe.* Frederick, MD: Aletheia Books. University of Publications of America.

BAUMEISTER, R. F., AND STEINHILBER, A. (1984). "Paradoxical Effects of Supportive Audiences on Performance under Pressure: The Home Field Disadvantage in Sports Championships." *Journal of Personality and Social Psychology, 47,* 85–93.

BAYTON, J. A. (1941). "The Racial Stereotypes of Negro College Students." *Journal of Abnormal Social Psychology, 36,* 97–102.

BAYTON, J. A., McALISTER, L. B., AND HAMER, J. (1956). "Race-Class Stereotypes." *Journal of Negro Education, 41,* 75–78.

BELL, G. (1976) *The Protestants of Ulster.* London: Pluto Press.

BELL, Y. R., BOUIE, C. L., AND BALDWIN, J. A. (1990). "Africentric Cultural Consciousness and African-American Male-Female Relationships." *Journal of Black Studies, 21,* 162–189.

BEM, S. L. (1993). *Lenses of Gender: Transforming the Debate on Sexual Inequality.* New Haven, CT: Yale University Press.

BENNETT, L. (1969). *Before the Mayflower: A History of Black America.* Chicago: Johnson Publishing Company.

BERMAN, W. C. (1970). *The Politics of Civil Rights in the Truman Administration.* Columbus, OH: Ohio State University Press.

BERNAL, M. (1987). *Black Athena: The Afroasiatic Roots of Classical Civilization.* New Brunswick, NJ: Rutgers University Press.

BERRY, J. W. (1984). "Cultural Relations in Plural Societies: Alternatives to Segregation and Their Sociopsychological Implications." In N. Miller and M. B. Brewer (eds.), *Groups in Contact* (pp. 11–27). San Diego, CA: Academic Press.

BERSCHEID, E., AND WALSTER, E. (1969). *Interpersonal Attraction.* Reading, MA: Addison-Wesley.

BETTELHEIM, B., AND JANOWITZ, M. (1950). *Dynamics of Prejudice.* NY: Harper and Brothers.

BING, S., AND ROSENFELD, S. S. (1970, Sept.). *The Quality of Justice in the Lower Criminal Courts of Metropolitan Boston.*

BLAKE, E. Personal communication. May 15, 1972.

BLANCHARD, F. A., AND CROSBY, F. J. (EDS.). (1989). *Affirmative Action in Perspective.* New York: Springer-Verlag.

BLANEY, N., STEPHAN, C., ROSENFIELD, D., ARONSON, E., AND SIKES, J. (1977). "Interdependence in the Classroom: A Field Study." *Journal of Educational Psychology, 69,* 139–146.

BLANK, R. (1994). *Investing in Human Resources Strategic Plan for the Human Capital Initiative.* Washington, D.C.: National Science Foundation.

BLAUNER, B. (1995). "White Radicals, White Liberals, and White People: Rebuilding the Anti-Racist Coalition." In B. P. Bowser (ed.), *Racism and Anti-Racism in World Perspective.* (pp. 115–137). Thousand Oaks, CA: Sage Publications.

BLOOM, A. (1986). *Closing of the American Mind.* New York: Simon & Schuster.

BLUMER, H. (1958). "Race Prejudice as a Sense of Group Position." *Pacific Sociological Review, 1,* 3–7.

BOBO, L. (1988). "Group Conflict, Prejudice, and the Paradox of Contemporary Racial Attitudes." In P. A. Katz and D. A. Taylor (eds.), *Eliminating Racism: Profiles in Controversy* (pp. 85–116). New York: Plenum Press.

BOGARDUS, E. S. (1925). "Measuring Social Distances." *Journal of Applied Sociology, 9,* 299–308.

BOGARDUS, E. S. (1928). *Immigration and Race Relations.* Boston: D.C. Heath.

BOHM, R. M. (ED.). (1994). *The Death Penalty in America: Current Research.* Cincinnati, OH: Anderson.

BOUCHER, J., LANDIS, D., AND CLARK, K. A. (EDS.). (1987). *Ethnic Conflict: International Perspectives.* Newbury Park, CA: Sage Publications.

BOWERSOCK, G. (1996). "Rescuing the Greeks: A Classicist Defends the Traditional Version of Greek Cultural Achievement." *The New York Times,* February 25, pp. 6–7.

BOWSER, B. P. (ED.). (1995). *Racism and Anti-Racism in World Perspective.* Thousand Oaks, CA: Sage Publications.

BOYKIN, A. W. (1994). "Harvesting Talent and Culture: African-American Children and Educational Reform." In R. Rossi (ed.), *Schools and Students at Risk: Context and Framework for Positive Change* (pp. 116–138). New York: Teachers College Press.

BRADY, T. P. (1955). *Black Monday: Segregation or Integration . . . America Has Its Choice.* Winona, MN: Association of Citizens' Councils.

BRENNER, J. G., AND SPAYD, L. (1993). "Separate and Unequal: Racial Discrimination in Area Home Lending." (Three-part series.) *The Washington Post,* June 6 (p. A1, A24), 7 (pp. A1, A8), 8 (pp. A1, A10).

BRENNER, J. G., AND SPAYD, L. (1993a). "A Pattern of Bias in Mortgage Loans: Statistics Show Blacks at a Disadvantage." *The Washington Post,* June 6 (p. A1, A24).

BRENNER, J. G., AND SPAYD, L. (1993b). "Area Blacks Have Worst Access." *The Washington Post,* June 7 (p. A1, A8).

BRENNER, J. G., AND SPAYD, L. (1993c). "Bankers Describe Roots of Racial Bias: Cultural Prejudice and Traditional Home Loans Hurt Blacks." *The Washington Post,* June 8 (pp. A1, A10).

BREWER, M. (1979). "Ingroup Bias in the Minimal Intergroup Situation: Cognitive-Motivational Analysis." *Psychological Bulletin, 86,* 307–332.

BREWER, M. (1988). "A dual process model of impression formation." In T. K. Srull and R. S. Wyer (eds.), *Advances in Social Cognition* (Vol. 1, pp. 1–36). Hillsdale, NJ: Erlbaum.

BREWER, M. B., AND MILLER, N. (1984). "Beyond the Contact Hypothesis." In N. Miller and M. B. Brewer (eds.), *Groups in Contact* (pp. 281–302). New York: Academic Press.

BREWER, M. B. (1991). "The Social Self: On Being the Same and Different at the Same Time." *Personality and Social Psychology Bulletin, 17,* 475–482.

BREWER, M. B., DULL, V., AND LUI, L. (1981). "Perceptions of the Elderly: Stereotypes and Prototypes." *Journal of Personality and Social Psychology, 41,* 656–670.

BRIGHAM, J. C. (1971a). "Ethnic Stereotypes." *Psychological Bulletin, 76,* 15–33.

BRIGHAM, J. C. (1971b). "Racial Stereotyping, Attitudes, and Evaluations of and Behavioral Intentions toward Negroes and Whites." *Sociometry, 34,* 360–380.

BRIGHAM, J. C. (1972). "Racial Stereotypes: Measurement Variables and the Stereotype-Attitude Relationships." *Journal of Applied Social Psychology, 2,* 63–76.

BRIMMER, A. (1966). "The Negro in the National Economy." In J. P. Davis (ed.), *The American Negro Reference Book.* Englewood Cliffs, NJ: Prentice-Hall.

BROWN, C. (1965). *Manchild in the Promised Land.* New York: Macmillan.

BROWN, L. (1991). "Antiracism as an Ethical Imperative: An Example from Feminist Therapy." *Ethics and Behavior, 1,* 113–127.

BROWN, R. (1995). *Prejudice: Its Social Psychology.* Oxford, England: Blackwell.

BUCHANAN, P. (1992). Speech to the Republican National Convention, August 17. San Diego, CA.

BURNS, J. F. (1992). "A Killer's Tale: A Serbian Fighter's Path of Brutality." *New York Times,* November 27, p. A1.

BYRNE, D., AND MCGRAW, C. (1964). "Interpersonal Attraction toward Negroes." *Human Relations, 17,* 201–213.

BYRNE, D., AND WONG, T. J. (1962). "Racial Prejudice, Interpersonal Attraction, and Assumed Dissimilarity of Attitudes." *Journal of Abnormal Psychology, 65,* 246–253.

BYRNES, D. A., AND KIGER, G. (1990). "The Effect of a Prejudice-Reduction Simulation on attitude Change." *Journal of Applied Social Psychology, 20,* 341–356.

CALVIN, J. (1536). *The Institutes of the Christian Religion.* Cambridge, MA: Harvard University.

CAMPBELL, A., AND SCHUMAN, H. (1969). *Racial Attitudes in Fifteen American Cities.* Ann Arbor, MI: Institute for Social Research.

CAMPBELL, D. T. (1958). "Common Fate, Similarity, and Other Indices of the Status of Aggregates as Social Entities." *Behavioral Science, 3,* 14–25.

CAMPBELL, D. T. (1963). "Social Attitudes and Other Acquired Behavioral Dispositions." In S. Koch (ed.), *Psychology: A Study of a Science* (pp. 94–172). New York: McGraw-Hill.

CAMPBELL, E. Q. (1958). "Some Social Psychological Correlates of Direction in Attitude Change." *Social Forces, 36,* 335–340.

CAPLOVITZ, D. (1967). *The Poor Pay More.* New York: Free Press.

CAPRA, F. (1975). *The Tao of Physics: An Exploration of the Parallels between Modern Physics and Eastern Mysticism.* New York: Bantam Books.

CARLSON, E. (1993). "Turned Down: A *WSJ* Survey Finds Widespread Perception of Lending Bias." *Wall Street Journal,* February 19. pp. R1, 5.

CARMICHAEL, S., AND HAMILTON, C. V. (1967). *Black Power: The Politics of Liberation in America.* New York: Vintage Books.

CARNOY, M. (1994). *Faded Dreams: The Politics and Economics of Race in America.* Cambridge, England: Cambridge University Press.

CASAS, J. M., AND PYTLUK, S. D. (1995). "Hispanic Identity Development: Implications for Research and Practice." In Ponterotto, J. G., Casas, J. M., Suzuki, L. A., and Alexander, C. M. (eds.). (1995). *Handbook of Multicultural Counseling* (pp. 155–180). Thousand Oaks, CA: Sage Publications.

CAVALLI-SFORZA, L. L., AND CAVALLI-SFORZA, F. (1995). *The Great Human Diaspora: The History of Diversity and Evolution.* Reading, MA: Addison-Wesley Publishers.

CHASE, A. C. (1977). *The Legacy of Malthus: The Social Costs of the New Scientific Racism.* New York: Alfred A. Knopf.

CHICAGO COMMISSION ON RACE RELATIONS (1922). *The Negro in Chicago: A Study of Race Relations and a Race Riot.* Chicago: University of Chicago Press.

CHONEY, S. K., BERRYHILL-PAAPKE, E., AND ROBBINS, R. R. (1995). "The Acculturation of American Indians: Developing Frameworks for Research and Practice." In Ponterotto, J. G., Casas, J. M., Suzuki, L. A., and Alexander, C. M. (1995). *Handbook of Multicultural Counseling* (pp. 73–92). Thousand Oaks, CA: Sage Publications.

CLARITY, J. F. (1993). "In Belfast, Life Returns to Tension and Suspicion." *The New York Times,* December 17, p. A3.

CLARITY, J. F. (1994). "Protestants Now Killing More than I.R.A." *The New York Times,* June 22, p. A3.

CLARK, K. B., AND CLARK, M. (1947). "Racial Identification and Preference in Negro Children." In T. M. Newcomb and E. L. Hartley (eds.), *Readings in Social Psychology.* New York: Holt.

CLARK, K. B. (1963). *Prejudice and Your Child.* Boston: Beacon Press.

CLARK, K. B. (1965). *Dark Ghetto.* New York: Harper and Row.

CLAUSEN, J. A. (1968). "Socialization as a Concept and as a Field of Study." In J. A. Clausen (ed.), *Socialization and Society.* Boston: Little, Brown.

CLEAVER, E. (1968). *Soul on Ice.* New York: McGraw-Hill.

COHEN, C. (1979). "Why Racial Preference is Illegal and Immoral." *Commentary, 67,* 40–52.

COHEN, C. E. (1981). "Person Categories and Social Perception: Testing Some Boundaries of the Processing Effects of Prior Knowledge." *Journal of Personality and Social Psychology, 40,* 441–452.

COHEN, L. C., PANE, N., AND SMITH, H. S. (in press). "Complexity of the Interpersonal Self and Affective Reactions to Interpersonal Stressors in Life and in the Laboratory." *Cognitive Therapy and Research.*

COHEN, N. (ED.). (1970). *The Los Angeles Riots: A Socio-Psychological Study.* New York: Praeger Publishers.

COHEN, P. (1992). "'It's Racism What Dunnit': Hidden Narratives in Theories of Racism." In Donald, J., and Rattansi, A. (eds.). *'Race', culture & difference* (pp. 62–103). London: Sage Publications, Ltd.

COLE, J. B. (1970). "Culture: Negro, Black and Nigger." *Black Scholar, 1,* 40–44.

COLE, M., AND GAY, J. (1971). "Culture and Memory." *American Anthropology, 74,* 1066–1084.

COLE, M., GAY, J., GLICK, J., AND SHARP, D. (1971). *The Cultural Context of Learning and Thinking.* New York: Basic Books.

COLEMAN, J., ET AL. (1966). *Equality of Educational Opportunity.* Washington, D.C.: Government Printing Office.

COLOR ADJUSTMENT (VIDEO, 1991). San Francisco, CA: California Newsreel. Vivian Kleinman Producer; Marlon T. Riggs, Producer, Director.

CONRAD, E. (1947). *Jim Crow America.* New York: Duell, Sloan and Pearce.

COOK, S. W. (1962). "The Systematic Study of Socially Significant Events: A Strategy for Social Research." *Journal of Social Issues, 18* 66–84.

COOK, S. W. (1978). "Interpersonal and Attitudinal Outcomes in Cooperating Interracial Groups." *Journal of Research and Development in Education, 12,* 97–113.

COSE, E. (1993). *The Rage of a Privileged Class.* New York: HarperCollins.

COX, O. C. (1948). *Caste, Class, and Race.* Garden City, NY: Doubleday.

CROCKER, J., AND LUHTANEN, R. (1990). "Collective Self-Esteem and In-Group Bias." *Journal of Personality and Social Psychology, 58,* 60–67.

CROCKER, J., AND MAJOR, B. (1989). "Social Stigma and Self-Esteem: The Self-Protective Properties of Stigma." *Psychological Review, 96,* 608–630.

CROCKER, J., AND MAJOR, B. (1994). "Reactions to Stigma: The Moderating Role of Justifications." In M. P. Zanna and J. M. Olson (eds.), *The Psychology of Prejudice: The Ontario Symposium* (Vol. 7, pp. 289–314). Hillsdale, NJ: Erlbaum.

CROCKER, J., BROADNAX, S., LUHTANEN, R., AND BLAINE, B. (1996). Belief in U.S. Conspiracies against Blacks: Powerlessness or Group Consciousness. Unpublished manuscript. University of Michigan.

CROCKER, J., CORNWELL, B., AND MAJOR, B. (1993). "The Stigma of Overweight: Affective Consequences of Attribution Ambiguity." *Journal of Personality and Social Psychology, 64,* 60–70.

CROCKER, J., LUHTANEN, R., BLAINE, B., AND BROADNAX, S. (1994). "Collective Self-Esteem and Psychological Well-Being among White, Black, and Asian College Students." *Personality and Social Psychology Bulletin, 20,* 502–513.

CROCKER, J., MAJOR, B., AND STEELE, C. M. (in press). "Social Stigma." In D. Gilbert, S. T. Fiske & G. Lindzey (eds.) *Handbook of Social Psychology* (4th ed.). New York: McGraw-Hill.

CROCKER, J., VOEKL, K, TESTA, M., AND MAJOR, B. (1991). "Social Stigma: The Affective Consequences of Attributional Ambiguity." *Journal of Personality and Social Psychology, 60,* 218–228.

CRONON, E. D. (1955). *Black Moses: The Story of Marcus Garvey and the Universal Negro Improvement Association.* Madison, WI: University of Wisconsin Press.

CROSBY, F. (1984). "The Denial of Personal Discrimination." *American Behavioral Scientist, 27,* 371–386.

CROSBY, F. BROMLEY, S., AND SAXE, L. (1980). "Recent Unobtrusive Studies of Black and White Discrimination and Prejudice: A Literature Review." *Psychological Bulletin, 87,* 546–563.

CROSS, W. E., AND FHAGEN-SMITH, P. (in press). "Nigresence and Ego Identity Development: Accounting for Differential Black Identity Patterns," In P. Pedersen, J. Draguns, W. Lonner, and J. Trimble (eds.) *Counseling Across Cultures,* 4th edition. Newbury, CA: Sage Productions.

CROSS, W. E. (1971). "Negro-to-Black Conversion Experience." *Black World, 20,* 13–27.

CROSS, W. E. (1979). "The Negro-to-Black Conversion Experience: An Empirical Analysis." In A. W. Boykin, A. J. Franklin, and J. F. Yates (eds.) (1979). *Research Directions of Black Psychologists* (pp. 107–125). New York: Russell Sage Foundation.

CROSS, W. E. (1991) *Shades of Black: Diversity in African-American Identity.* Philadelphia: Temple University Press.

CROSS, W. E. (1995). "The Psychology of Nigresence: Revising the Cross Model." In Ponterotto, J. G., Casas, J. M., Suzuki, L. A., and Alexander, C. M. (1995). *Handbook of Multicultural Counseling* (pp. 93–122). Thousand Oaks, CA: Sage Publications.

CUELLAR, I., HARRIS, L., AND JASSO, R. (1980). "An Acculturation Scale for Mexican American Normal and Clinical Populations." *Hispanic Journal of Behavioral Sciences, 2,* 199–217.

D'SOUZA, D. (1995). *The End of Racism: Principles for a Multiracial Society.* New York: The Free Press.

DANIELS, R. (1968). *The Politics of Prejudice.* New York: Atheneum.

DARLEY, J. M., AND GROSS, P. H. (1983). "A Hypothesis-Confirming Bias in Labeling Effects." *Journal of Personality and Social Psychology, 44,* 20–33.

DARNTON, J. (1994). "Militant Protestants in Truce, Lifting Peace Hopes in Ulster." *The New York Times,* October 14, p. A1.

DAVEY, A. G. (1983). *Learning to be Prejudiced.* London: Arnold.

DE TOCQUEVILLE, A. (1945). *Democracy in America.* New York: Vintage Books.

DEAUX, K., WINTON, W., CROWLEY, M., AND LEWIS, L. L. (1985). "Level of Categorization and Content of Gender Stereotypes." *Social Cognition, 3,* 145–167.

DEFLEUR, M. L., AND WESTIE, F. R. (1958). "Verbal Attitudes and Overt Acts: An Experiment on the Salience of Attitude." *American Sociological Review, 23,* 667–673.

DELGADO, R. (1991). "Campus Antiracism Rules: Constitutional Narratives in Collision." *Northwestern University Law Review, 85,* 343–387.

DENITCH, B. D. (1994). *Ethnic Nationalism: The Tragic Death of Yugoslovia.* Minneapolis, MN: University of Minnesota Press.

DE PAOR, L. (1977). *Divided Ulster,* Second edition. London: Penguin Books.

DEUTSCH, M., AND COLLINS, M. (1951). *Inter-Racial Housing: A Psychological Evaluation of a Social Experiment.* Minneapolis: University of Minnesota Press.

DEVINE, P. G., AND BAKER, S. M. (1991)." Measurement of Racial Stereotype Subtyping." *Personality and Social Psychology Bulletin, 17,* 44–50.

DEVINE, P. G., AND MONTEITH, M. J. (1993). "The Role of Discrepancy-Associated Affect in Prejudice Reduction. In D. M. Mackie and D. L. Hamilton (eds.), *Affect, Cognition and Stereotyping: Interactive Processes in Group Perceptions* (pp. 317–344). San Diego, CA: Academic Press.

DEVINE, P. G. (1989). "Stereotyping and Prejudice: Their Automatic and Controlled Components." *Journal of Personality and Social Psychology, 56,* 5–18.

DEVINE, P. G. (1996). "Breaking the Prejudice Habit." *Psychological Science Agenda,* January/February, 10–12.

DEVINE, P. G., EVETT, S. R., AND VASQUEZ-SUSON, K. A. (in press). "Exploring the Interpersonal Dynamics of Intergroup Contact." In R. M. Sorrentino and E. T. Higgins (eds.), *Handbook of Motivation and Cognition: The interpersonal context* (Vol. 3). New York: Guilford.

DEVINE, P. G., MONTEITH, M. J., ZUWERINK, J. R., AND ELLIOT, A. J. (1991). "Prejudice with and without Compunction." *Journal of Personality and Social Psychology, 60,* 817–830.

DEWEY, J. (1922). *Human Nature and Conduct: An Introduction to Social Psychology.* New York: Henry Holt.

DIAMOND, J. (1994). "Race without Color." *Discover,* November, p. 84ff.

DIXON, V. J. (1976). "World Views and Research Methodology." In L. M. King, V. J. Dixon and W. W. Nobles (eds.), African Philosophy: Assumptions and Paradigms for Research on Black Persons. (pp. 51–102). Los Angeles: Fanon Center Publication, Charles R. Drew Postgraduate Medical School.

DOLLARD, J. (1937). *Caste and Class in a Southern Town.* New Haven: Yale University Press.

DOLLARD, J., DOOB, N. E., MILLER, D. H., MOWRER, O. H. AND SEARS, R. R. (1939). *Frustration and Aggression.* New Haven: Yale University Press.

DONALD, J., AND RATTANSI, A. (EDS.). (1992). *'Race,' culture & difference.* London: Sage Publications, Ltd.

DOVIDIO, J. F., AND GAERTNER, S. L. (1981). "The Effects of Race, Status, and Ability on Helping Behavior." *Social Psychology Quarterly, 44,* 192–203.

DOVIDIO, J. F., AND GAERTNER, S. L. (EDS.). (1986). *Prejudice, Discrimination, and Racism.* New York: Academic Press.

DOVIDIO, J. F., EVANS, N., AND TYLER, R. B. (1986). "Racial Stereotypes: The Contents of Their Cognitive Representations." *Journal of Experimental Social Psychology, 22,* 22–37.

DOVIDIO, J. F., GAERTNER, S. L., ISEN, A. M., AND LOWRANCE, R. (1995). "Group Representations and Intergraph Bias: Positive Affect, Similarity, and Group Size." *Personality and Social Psychology Bulletin, 21,* 856–865.

DOWNING, T. (ed.) (1981). *The Troubles.* London: Thames/MacDonald Fotor.

DRAGNICH, A. N. (1983). *The First Yugoslavia: Search for a Viable Political System.* Stanford, CA: Hoover Institution Press.

DRAKE, ST. C., AND CAYTON, H. R. (1945). *Black Metropolis: A Study of Negro Life in a Northern City.* New York: Harcourt, Brace and World.

DUBOIS, W. E. B. (1903). *The Souls of Black Folk.* Chicago: A.C. McClurg and Company.

DUBOIS, W. E. B. (1973). *The Philadelphia Negro.* Milwood NY: Kraus-Thomson Organization, Ltd.

DUBOW, S. (1989). *Racial Segregation and the Origins of Apartheid in South Africa, 1919–1936.* New York: St. Martin's Press.

DUCHARMS, R. (1966). *Personal Causation.* New York: Wiley.

DUCKITT, J. (1992a). *The Social Psychology of Prejudice.* New York: Praeger.

DUCKITT, J. (1992b). "Psychology and Prejudice: A Historical Analysis and Integrative Framework." *American Psychologist, 47,* 1182–1193.

DUNTON, B. C., AND FAZIO, R. H. (1996). An Individual Difference Measure of Motivation to Control Prejudiced Reactions. Unpublished manuscript. University of Indiana.

EAGLY, A. H. (1995). Prejudice against Women. Presentation in symposium, "Research on Gender: Its Challenge to Social Psychological Theories." Annual Meeting, Society of Experimental Social Psychology. Washington, D.C.

EAGLY, A. H., AND MLADINIC, A. (1989). "Gender Stereotypes and Attitudes toward Women and Men." *Personality and Social Psychology Bulletin, 15,* 543–558.

EAGLY, A. H., AND MLADINIC, A. (1994). "Are People Prejudiced against Women? Some Answers from Research on Attitudes, Gender Stereotypes, and Judgments of Competence." W. Stroebe and M. Hewstone (eds.), *European Review of Social Psychology,* Vol. 5 (pp. 1–35) . London: John Wiley & Sons Ltd.

EAGLY, A. H., MLADINIC, A., AND OTTO, S. (1991). "Are Women Evaluated More Favorably than Men? An Analysis of Attitudes, Beliefs, and Emotions." *Psychology of Women Quarterly, 15,* 203–216.

EASTLAND, T., AND BENNETT, W. J. (1979). *Counting by Race: Equality from the Founding Fathers to Bakke and Weber.* New York: Basic Books.

EDLEMAN, M. W. (1987). *Families in Peril: An Agenda for Social Change.* Cambridge, MA: Harvard University Press.

EDLEMAN, M. W. (1992). *The Measure of Our Success: A Letter to My Children and Yours.* Boston: Beacon Press.

ELKIN, F. (1960). *The Child and Society: The Process of Socialization.* New York: Random House.

ELLIOTT, J. (1970). *The Eye of the Storm.* Videorecording. Mount Kisco, NY: Center for the Humanities.

ELLIS, S. A., AND GAUVAIN, M. (1992). "Social and Cultural Influences on Children's Collaborative Interactions." In L. T. Winegar and J. Valsiner (eds.), *Children's Development within Social Context,* Vol. I (pp. 155–180). Hillsdale, NJ: Lawrence Erlbaum Associates.

ERKSON, E. (1956). "The Problem of Ego-Identity." *Journal of the American Psychoanalytic Association, 4,* 56–121.

ERIKSON, E. (1968). *Identity: Youth and Crisis.* New York: Norton.

ESSED, P. (1991). *Understanding Everyday Racism: An Interdisciplinary Theory.* Newbury Park, CA: Sage Publications.

ESSES, V. M. AND ZANNA, M. P. (1995). "Mood and the Expression of Ethnic Stereotypes." *Journal of Personality and Social Psychology, 69,* 1052–1068.

ESSES, V. M., HADDOCK, G., AND ZANNA, M. P. (1993). "Values, Stereotypes, and Emotions as Determinants of Intergroup Attitudes." In D. Hamilton and D. Mackie (eds.) *Affect Cognition and Stereotyping: Interactive Processes in Group Perceptions.* (pp. 137–165). San Diego, CA: Academic Press.

ETHIER, K., AND DEAUX, K. (1990). "Hispanics in Ivy: Assessing Identity and Perceived Threat." *Sex Roles, 22,* 427–440.

EZORSKY, G. (1991). *Racism and Justice: The Case for Affirmative Action.* Ithaca, NY: Cornell University Press.

FANON, F. (1955). *The Wretched of the Earth.* New York: Bantam Books.

FAZIO, R. H. (1995) "Attitudes as Object-Evaluation Associations: Determinants, Consequences, and Correlates of Attitude Accessibility." In R. E. Petty and J. A. Krosnick (eds.), *Attitude Strength: Antecedents and Consequences* (pp. 247–282). Mahwah, NJ: Erlbaum.

FAZIO, R. H., JACKSON, J. R., DUNTON, B. C., AND WILLIAMS, C. J. "Variability in Automatic Activation as Unobtrusive Measure of Racial Attitudes Bona Fide Pipeline?" *Journal of Personality and Social Psychology, 69,* 1013–1027.

FEAGIN, J. R., AND FEAGIN, C. B. (1996). *Racial and Ethnic Relations,* Fifth edition. Upper Saddle River, NJ: Prentice Hall.

FEAGIN, J. R., AND SIKES, M. P. (1994). *Living with Racism: The Black Middle-Class Experience.* Boston: Beacon Press.

FEAGIN, J. R., AND VERA, H. (1995). *White Racism: The Basics.* New York: Routledge.

THE FEDERAL REGISTER. "Guidelines on Discrimination Because of Religion or National Origin." January 19, 1973, Part (b) of 60–50.1.

FARRELL, M. (1976). *Northern Ireland: The Orange State.* Pluto Press: London.

FESTINGER, L., AND KELLEY, H. H. (1951). *Changing Attitudes Through Social Contact.* Ann Arbor, MI: University of Michigan, Institute for Social Research.

FESTINGER, L. (1954). "A Theory of Social Comparison Process." *Human Relations, 7,* 117–140.

FESTINGER, L. (1957). *A Theory of Cognitive Dissonance.* Evanston, IL: Harper and Row.

FINE, M., WEIS, L. POWELL, L., AND WON, M. (In press). *Off White.* New York: Routledge.

FISHMAN, J. A. (1961). "Some Social and Psychological Determinants of Intergroup Relations in Changing Neighborhoods: An Introduction to the Bridgeview Study." *Social Forces, 40,* 42–51.

FISKE, S. T., AND NEUBERG, S. L. (1990). "A Continuum of Impression Formation, from Category-Based to Individuating Processes: Influences of Information and Motivation on Attention and Interpretation." In M. P. Zanna (ed.), *Advances in Experimental Social Psychology* (Vol. 23, pp. 1–74). NY: Academic Press.

FISKE, S. T., AND RUSCHER, J. B. (1993). "Negative Interdependence and Prejudice: Whence the Affect?" In D. M. Mackie and D. L. Hamilton (eds.), *Affect, Cognition and Stereotyping: Interactive Processes in Group Perceptions* (pp. 239–268). San Diego, CA: Academic Press.

FISKE, S. T., AND TAYLOR, S. E. (1992). *Social Cognition.* New York: McGraw-Hill.

FISKE, S. T., BERSOFF, D. N., BORGIDA, E., DEAUX, K., AND HEILMAN, M. E. (1991). "Social Science Research on Trial: The Use of Sex Stereotyping Research in *Price Waterhouse v. Hopkins." American Psychologist, 46,* 1049–1060.

FORD, T. E., AND STANGOR, C. (1992). "The Role of Diagnosticity in Stereotype Formation: Perceiving Group Means and Variances." *Journal of Personality and Social Psychology, 63,* 356–367.

FORDHAM, S., AND OGBU, J. (1985). "Black Students' School Success: Coping with the Burden of 'Acting White'" *Urban Review, 18,* 176–206.

FORDHAM, S. (1988). "Racelessness as a Factor in Black Students' School Success: Pragmatic Strategy or Pyrrhic Victory?" *Harvard Educational Review, 58,* 54–84.

FRABLE, D. E. S. (1993a). "Being and Feeling Unique: Statistical Deviance and Psychological Marginality." *Journal of Personality, 61,* 85–110.

FRABLE, D. E. S. (1993b). "Dimensions of Marginality: Distinctions among Those Who Are Different." *Personality and Social Psychology Bulletin, 19,* 370–380.

FRABLE, D. E. S., BLACKSTONE, T., AND SCHERBAUM, C. (1990). "Marginal and Mindful: Deviants in Social Interactions." *Journal of Personality and Social Psychology, 59,* 140–149.

FRANKLIN, A. J. (1996). *Invisibility Syndrome.* Unpublished manuscript. City University of New York.

FRANKLIN, J. H., AND MOSS, A. A. (1947). *From Slavery to Freedom: A History of African Americans.* First edition. New York: McGraw-Hill.

FRANKLIN, J. H., AND MOSS, A. A. (1994). *From Slavery to Freedom: A History of African Americans.* Seventh edition. New York: McGraw-Hill.

FRANKLIN, J. H., AND STARR, I. (EDS.). (1967). *The Negro in the Twentieth Century America.* NY: Vintage Books.

FRASER, S. (ED.). *The Bell Curve Wars: Race, Intelligence and the Future of America.* New York: Basic Books.

FRAZIER, E. F. (1939). *The Negro Family in the United States.* Chicago: University of Chicago Press.

FRAZIER, E. F. (1944). *The Negro in the United States.* New York: Macmillan.

FRAZIER, E. F. (1957). *Race and Culture Contacts in the Modern World.* Boston: Beacon Press.

FREY, D., AND GAERTNER, S. L. (1986). "Helping and the Avoidance of Inappropriate Interracial

Behavior: A Strategy that Can Perpetuate a Non-Prejudiced Self-Image. *Journal of Personality and Social Psychology, 50,* 1083–1090.

FRIED, M. H. (1965). "A Four Letter Word that Hurts. *Saturday Review,* October 2.

FUKUYAMA, F. (1992). *The End of History and the Last Man.* New York: The Free Press.

FULLER, B., AGEL, J., AND FIORE, Q. (1970). *I Seem to Be a Verb.* New York: Bantam Books.

FUNDER, D. C. (1995). "Stereotypes, Base-Rates and the Fundamental Evaluation Mistake: A Content-Based Approach to Judgmental Accuracy." In Lee, Y.-T., Jussim, L. J., and McCauley, C. R. (eds.). (1995). *Stereotype Accuracy: Toward Appreciating Group Differences* (pp. 141–156). Washington, D.C.: American Psychological Association.

FURNHAM, A. AND STACEY, B. (1991). *Young People's Understanding of Society.* London: Routledge.

GAERTNER, S. L. (1973). "Helping Behavior and Discrimination among Liberals and Conservatives." *Journal of Personality and Social Psychology, 25,* 335–341.

GAERTNER, S. L., AND BICKMAN, L. (1971). "Effects of Race on the Elicitation of Helping Behavior: A focus on 'Liberals.'" In P. Katz (ed.), *Toward the Elimination of Racism* (pp. 183–211). New York: Pergamon Press.

GAERTNER, S. L., AND DOVIDIO, J. F. (1986). "The Aversive Form of Racism." In J. F. Dovidio and S. L. Gaertner (eds.), *Prejudice, Discrimination and Racism* (pp. 61–90) Orlando, FL: Academic Press.

GAERTNER, S. L., DOVIDIO, J. F., ANASTASIO, P. A., BACHMAN, B. A., AND RUST, M. C. (1993). "The Common In-Group Identity Model: Recategorization and the Reduction of Intergroup Bias." In W. Stroebe and M. Hewstone (eds.), *European Review of Social Psychology* (Vol. 4, pp. 1–26). London: Wiley.

GAERTNER, S. L.. DOVIDIO, J. F., BANKER, B. S., RUST, M. C., NIER, J. A., MOTTOLA, G. R., WARD, C. M. (In press-a). "Does White Racism Necessarily Mean Anti-Blackness? Aversive Racism and Pro-Whiteness." In M. Fine, L. Powell, L. Weis, and M. Won (eds.), *Off White.* London: Routledge.

GAERTNER, S. L., MANN, J., MURRELL, A. J., AND DOVIDIO, J. F. (1989). "Reducing Intergroup Bias: The Benefits of Recategorization." *Journal of Personality and Social Psychology, 57,* 239–249.

GAERTNER, S. L., AND MCLAUGHLIN, J. P. (1983). "Racial Stereotypes: Association and Ascriptions of Positive and Negative Characteristics." *Social Psychology Quarterly, 46,* 23–30.

GAERTNER, S. L., RUST, M. C., DOVIDIO, J. F., BACHMAN, B. A., AND ANASTASIO, P. A. (1994). "The Contact Hypothesis: The Role of a Common Ingroup Identity on Reducing Intergroup Bias." *Small Group Research, 25,* 224–249.

GAINES, S. O., AND REED, E. S. (1995). "Prejudice: From Allport to DuBois." *American Psychologist, 50,* 96–103.

GARDNER, H. (1983). *Frames of Mind: The Theory of Multiple Intelligences.* New York: Basic Books.

GARDNER, R. C. (1994). "Stereotypes as Consensual Beliefs." In M. P. Zanna and J. M. Olson (eds.), *The Psychology of Prejudice: The Ontario Symposium,* (Vol. 7, pp. 1–27). Hillside, NJ: Erlbaum Associates.

GARVEY, A. J. (1970). *Garvey and Garveyism.* London: Collier-McMillan, Ltd.

GATES, H. L. (1995). "Thirteen Ways of Looking at a Black Man." *The New Yorker, LXXI,* October 23. 56–65.

GATES, H. L. (ED.). (1991). *Bearing Witness: Selections from African American Autobiography in the Twentieth Century.* New York: Pantheon Books.

GILBERT, D. T., AND HIXON, J. G. "The Trouble of Thinking: Activation and Application of Stereotypic Beliefs." *Journal of Personality and Social Psychology, 60,* 509–517.

GILBERT, D. T., AND JONES, E. E. (1986). "Perceiver Induced Constraint: Interpretations of Self-Generated Reality." *Journal of Personality and Social Psychology, 50,* 269–280.

GILBERT, G. M. (1951). "Stereotype Persistence and Change among College Students." *Journal of Abnormal Social Psychology, 46,* 245–254.

GILROY, P. (1992). "The End of Antiracism." In J. Donald, and A. Rattansi, (eds.). (1992). *'Race,' Culture and Difference* (pp. 49–61). London: Sage Publications, Ltd.

GINZBERG, E., AND HIESTAND, D. L. (1966). "Employment Patterns of Negro Men and Women." In J. Davis (ed.), *The American Negro Reference Book*. Englewood Cliffs, NJ: Prentice-Hall.

GIOVANNI, N. (1970). *Re-Creation*. Detroit, MI: Broadside Press.

GLATER, J. D. (1995). "Racial Gap in Pay Gets a Degree Sharper, Study Finds." *The Washington Post*, November 2, p. D13, D16.

GLAZER, N., AND MOYNIHAN, D. P. (1963). *Beyond the Melting Pot*. Cambridge, MA: Harvard University and MIT Press.

GLAZER, N., AND MOYNIHAN, D. P. (1975). *Ethnicity: Theory and Experience*. Cambridge, MA: Harvard University Press.

GLAZER, N. (1976). *Affirmative Discrimination: Ethnic Inequality and Public Policy*. New York: Basic Books.

GLAZER, N. (1988). "The Future of Preferential Affirmative Action." In P. A. Katz and D. A. Taylor (eds.), *Eliminating Racism: Profiles in Controversy* (pp. 329–339). New York: Plenum Press.

GLENN, N. (1965). "The Role of White Resistance and Facilitation in the Negro Struggle for Equality." *Phylon, 26*, 105–116.

GLICK, J. (1975). "Cognitive Development in Cross-Cultural Perspective." In F. Horowitz (ed.), *Review of Child Development Research* (Vol. 4). Chicago: University of Chicago Press.

GOLDBERG, D. T. (1992). "The Semantics of Race." *Ethnic and Racial Studies, 15*, 1504–1543.

GOLDBERG, D. T. (ED.). (1990). *Anatomy of Racism*. Minneapolis, MN: University of Minnesota Press.

GOLDLUST, J., AND RICHMOND, A. H. (1974). "A Multivariate Model of Immigration Adaptation." *International Migration Review, 8*, 193–225.

GOLDMAN, P. (1970). *Report from Black America*. New York: Simon and Schuster.

GOODMAN, M. E. (1952). *Race Awareness in Young Children*. Cambridge, MA: Addison-Wesley.

GORDONE, C. (1969). *No Place to Be Somebody: A Black-Black Comedy in Three Acts*. New York: Bobbs-Merrill.

GORILLAS IN THE MIST: THE STORY OF DIAN FOSSEY. (1989). Universal City, CA: Warner Brothers and Universal Pictures.

GOTTESMAN, I. I. (1968). "Biogenetics of Race and Class." In M. Deutsch, I. Katz, and A. R. Jensen (eds.), *Social Class, Race, and Psychological Development*. New York: Holt, Rinehart & Winston.

GOULD, S. J. (1994). "Curveball." *The New Yorker*, November 28.

GOVERNOR'S COMMISSION ON THE LOS ANGELES RIOTS. (1965). *Violence in the City—An end or a Beginning?* Los Angeles: Office of the Governor.

GRAHAM, L. O. (1995). *Member of the Club: Reflections of a Life in a Racially Polarized World*. New York: HarperCollins.

GRAY, J. (1992). *Men Are from Mars, Women Are from Venus: A Practical Guide for Improving Communication and Getting What You Want in Your Relationship*. New York: HarperCollins.

GREENBERG, J., PYSZCZYNSKI, T. SOLOMON, S., ROSENBLATT, A., KIRKLAND, S., VEEDER, M., AND LYON, D. (1990). "Evidence for Terror Management Theory II: The Effects of Mortality Salience on Reactions to Those Who Threaten or Bolster the Cultural Worldview." *Journal of Personality and Social Psychology, 58*, 308–318.

GREENBERG, J., SIMON, L., PYSZCZYNSKI, T., SOLOMON, S., AND CHATEL, D. (1992). "Terror Management and Tolerance: Does Mortality Salience Always Intensify Negative Reactions to Others Who Threaten One's Worldview?" *Journal of Personality and Social Psychology, 63*, 212–220.

GREENWALD, A. G., AND BANAJI, M. R. (1995). "Implicit Social Cognition: Attitudes, Self-Esteem, and Stereotypes." *Psychological Review, 102*, 4–27.

GREENWALD, H. J., AND OPPENHEIM, D. B. (1968). "Reported Magnitude of Self-Misidentification among Negro Children—Artifact?" *Journal of Personality and Social Psychology, 8*, 49–52.

GREGORIAN, V. (1991). "Brown Expulsion Not about Free Speech." *The New York Times*, April 10, p. A25.

GRIFFIN, J. H. (1960). *Black Like Me.* New York: New American Library.

GRIFFITH, D. W. (DIRECTOR). (1915). *The Birth of a Nation* (movie, 1994) New Brunswick, NJ: Rutgers University Press.

GUINIER, L. (1994). *The Tyranny of the Majority: Fundamental Fairness and Representative Democracy.* New York: Free Press.

GUPTA, U. (1993). "Cash Crunch." *Wall Street Journal,* February 19. p. R1, 4.

GURIN, P., HURTADO, A., AND PENG, T. (1994). "Group Contacts and Ethnicity in the Social Identities of Mexicanos and Chicanos." *Personality and Social Psychology Bulletin, 20,* 521–532.

GURIN, P., GURIN, G., LAO, R. C., AND BEATTIE, M. (1969). "Internal-External Control in the Motivational Dynamics of Negro Youth." *Journal of Social Issues, 25,* 29–53.

GUTHRIE, R. V. (1976). *Even the Rat was White.* New York: Harper & Row.

HADDOCK, G., ZANNA, M. P., AND ESSES, V. M. (1993). "Assessing the Structure of Prejudicial Attitudes: The Case of Attitudes toward Homosexuals." *Journal of Personality and Social Psychology, 65,* 1105–1118.

HAKUTA, K. (1994). "Distinguishing among Proficiency, Choice, and Attitudes in Questions about Language for Bilinguals." In G. Lamberty and C. G. Coll (eds.), *Puerto Rican Women and Children: Issues in Health, Growth, and Development. Topics in Social Psychiatry* (pp. 191–209). New York: Plenum Press.

HALL, C. C. I. (1992). Please choose one: Ethnic identity choices for biracial individuals. In M. P. Root (ed.) *Racially mixed people in America.* (pp. 250–264). Newbury Park, CA: Sage Publications.

HALL, R. M. (1982). "The Classroom Climate: A Chilly One for Women?" Washington, DC: Project on the Education and Status of Women, Association of American Colleges.

HAMILTON, A., JAY, J., AND MADISON, J. (1937). *The Federalist Papers.* First published in 1788. Modern edition published in New York: Modern Library.

HAMILTON, D. L., AND BISHOP, G. D. (1976). "Attitudinal and Behavioral; Effects of Initial Integration of White Suburban Neighborhoods." *Journal of Social Issues, 32,* 47–67.

HAMILTON, D. L., AND GIFFORD, R. K. (1976). "Illusory Correlation in Interpersonal Perception: A Cognitive Basis of Stereotypic Judgments." *Journal of Experimental Social Psychology, 12,* 392–407.

HAMILTON, D. L., AND SHERMAN, J. W. (1994). "Stereotypes." In R. S. Wyer, Jr., and T. K. Srull (eds.), *Handbook of Social Cognition* (2nd ed.). Hillsdale, NJ: Erlbaum.

HAMILTON, D. L., STROESSNER, S. J., AND DRISCOLL, D. M. (1994). "Social Cognition and the Study of Stereotyping." In P. G. Devine, D. L. Hamilton, and T. M. Ostrom (eds.), *Social Cognition: Impact on Social Psychology* (pp. 291–321). San Diego, CA: Academic Press.

HAMILTON, D. L., AND TROLIER, T. K. (1986). "Stereotypes and Stereotyping: An Overview of the Cognitive Approach." In J. F. Dovidio and S. L. Gaertner (eds.), *Prejudice, Discrimination, and Racism* (pp. 127–163). Orlando, FL: Academic Press.

HANDY, W. C. (1941). *Father of the Blues.* New York: Macmillan.

HANSBERRY, L. (1959). *A Raisin in the Sun: A Drama in Three Acts.* New York: Random House.

HARDING, J., AND HOGREFE, R. (1952). "Attitudes of White Department Store Employees toward Negro Co-Workers." *Journal of Social Issues, 8,* 18–28.

HARDING, J., PROSHANSKY, H., KUTNER, B., AND CHEIN, I. (1969). "Prejudice and Ethnic Relations." In G. Lindzey and E. Aronson (eds.), *Handbook of Social Psychology,* Vol. 5 (pp. 1–76). Reading, MA: Addison-Wesley.

HARRELL, J. P., MALONE-COLON, L., AND HARRIS, C. (In press). "Two Measures of Responses to Racism: The Development of Black Nationalism and Authoritarian Coping Styles Scales." In R. L. Jones (ed.), *Handbook of Tests and Measurements for Black Populations.* Hampton, VA: Cob and Henry Press.

HARRINGTON, M. (1984). *The New American Poverty.* New York: Holt, Rinehart and Winston.

HARRIS, M., AND KOTTAK, C. P. (1963). "The Structural Significance of Brazilian Racial Categories." *Sociologia, 25,* 203–209.

HARTLEY, E. L. (1946). *Problems in Prejudice.* New York: Kings Crown.

HASTIE, R. (1984). "Causes and Effects of Causal Attribution." *Journal of Personality and Social Psychology, 46,* 44–56.

HEIDER, F. (1958. *The Psychology of Interpersonal Relations.* New York: Wiley.

HELMS, J. E. (1990). *Black and White Racial Identity: Theory, Research and Practice.* New York: Greenwood Press.

HELMS, J. E. (1994). "Racial Identity and 'Racial' Constructs." In E. J. Trickett, R. Watts, and D. Birman (eds.), *Human diversity* (pp. 285–311). San Francisco: Jossey-Bass.

HELMS, J. E. (In press). "Toward a Methodology for Measuring and Assessing Racial as Distinguished from Ethnic Identity." In G. Sodowsky and J. Impara (eds.), *Multicultural Assessment in Counseling and Clinical Psychology.* Lincoln, NE: University of Nebraska, Buros Institute.

HELMS, J. E. (1995). "An Update of Helms' White and People of Color Racial Identity Models." In Ponterotto, J. G., Casas, J. M., Suzuki, L. A., and Alexander, C. M. (1995). *Handbook of Multicultural Counseling* (pp. 181–198). Thousand Oaks, CA: Sage Publications.

HELMS, J. E., AND PARHAM, T. A. (1985). The Development of the Racial Identity Attitude Scale. Unpublished manuscript. University of Maryland.

HENDERSON N. D. (1979). "Criterion-Related Validity of Personality and Aptitude Scales: A Comparison of Validation Results under Voluntary and Actual Test Conditions." In C. Spielberger (ed.), *Police Selection and Evaluation: Issues and Techniques* (pp. 179–195). Westport, CT: Greenwood Publishers Group.

HENTOFF, N. (1994). "This Shouldn't Be Happening in America." *The Washington Post,* December 17, p. A27.

HERBERT, B. (1994). "In America; The Prom and the Principal." *New York Times,* March 16, p. A21.

HERRNSTEIN, R. (1971). "I.Q." *Atlantic Monthly, 228,(3),* 43–64.

HERRNSTEIN, R. E., AND MURRAY, C. A. (1994). *The Bell Curve.* New York: The Free Press.

HERSKOVITS, M. (1958). *The Myth of the Negro Past.* Beacon Press.

HEWSTONE, M., AND BROWN, R. (1986). "Contact is Not Enough: An Intergroup Perspective on the 'Contact Hypothesis.'" In M. Hewstone and R. Brown (eds.), *Contact and Conflict in Intergroup Encounters* (pp. 1–44). Oxford: Basil Blackwell, Inc.

HEWSTONE, M., AND BROWN, R. (EDS.). (1986). *Contact and Conflict in Intergroup Relations.* Oxford: Blackwell.

HIGGINS, E. T., KING, G. A., AND MAVIN, G. H. (1982). "Individual Construct Accessibility and Subjective Impressions and Recall." *Journal of Personality and Social Psychology, 43,* 35–47.

HIRSCHFELD, L. A. (1996). The Conceptual Politics of Race: Lessons from Our Children. Paper presented at Conference on "Race, Power and the Mind: Toward an Interdisciplinary Approach to Racial Identity." Culture and Cognition program, University of Michigan, Ann Arbor, MI. February 2, 1996.

HIRSHFELD, L. (1995). "Do Children Have a Theory of Race?" *Cognition, 54,* 209–252.

HIRSHFELD, L. (1996a). *Race in the Making: Cognition, Culture, and the Child's Construction of Human Kinds.* Cambridge, MA: MIT Press.

HOCHSCHILD, J. L. (1995). *Facing up to the American Dream: Race, Class and the Soul of the Nation.* Princeton, NJ: Princeton University Press.

HODGE, J. L., STRUCKMAN, D. K., AND TROST, L. D. (1975). *Cultural Bases of Racism and Oppression: An Examination of Traditional "Western" Concepts, Values, and Institutional Structures which Support Racism, Sexism and Elitism.* Berkeley, CA: Two Riders Press.

HOFFMAN, C., AND HURST, N. (1990). "Gender Stereotypes: Perception of Rationalization?" *Journal of Personality and Social Psychology, 58,* 197–208.

HOFSTADTER, R. (1955). *Social Darwinism in American Thought.* New York: Braziller.

HOFSTEDE, G. (1984). *Culture's Consequences: International Differences in Work-Related Values.* Beverly Hills, CA: Sage Publications.

HOLOWAY, F. A. (1989). "What Is Affirmative Action?" In F. A. Blanchard, and F. J. Crosby, (eds.), *Affirmative Action in Perspective* (pp. 9–20). New York: Springer-Verlag.

HRABA, J., AND GRANT, G. (1970). "Black Is Beautiful: A Reexamination of Racial Preference and Identification." *Journal of Personality and Social Psychology, 16,* 398–402.

HUDDY, L., AND SEARS, D. O. (1995). "Opposition to Bilingual Education: Prejudice or the Defense of Realistic Interests?" *Social Psychology Quarterly, 58,* 133–143.

HUGGINS, N. (1985). *Afro-American Studies Report.* New York: The Ford Foundation.

HUGGINS, N. I. (1971). *Harlem Renaissance.* New York: Oxford University Press.

HUGHES, L. (1958). *The Langston Hughes Reader.* New York: George Braziller, Inc.

HUNT, C. L. (1959). "Private Integrated Housing in a Medium Size Northern City." *Social Problems, 7,* 195–209.

ICKES, W. (1984). "Black and White Interaction." *Journal of Personality and Social Psychology, 47,* 330–341.

JAHN, J. (1961). *Muntu: An Outline of the New African Culture.* New York: Grove Press.

JAYNES, G. D., AND WILLIAMS, R. (EDS.). (1989). *A Common Destiny: Blacks and America Society.* Washington, DC: National Academy Press.

JEFFERSON, T. (1787). *Notes on the State of Virginia.* Edited by W. Peden (1955). Chapel Hill: University of North Carolina Press.

JENSEN, A. R. (1968). "How Much Can We Boost IQ and Scholastic Achievement?" *Harvard Educational Review, 38,* 1–123.

JHALLY, S., AND LEWIS, J. (1992). *Enlightened Racism: The Cosby Show, Audiences, and the Myth of the American Dream.* Boulder, CO: Westview Press.

JOHNSON, J. (1972). Speech at Harvard University, February 18.

JOHNSON, J. W. (1930). *Black Manhattan.* New York: Atheneum.

JOHNSON, M. W. (1947). *Hearings Before Subcommittee of the Committee on Appropriations, House of Representatives, 80th Congress (February,* p. 245).

JOHNSON, N. J., AND SANDAY, P. R. (1971). "Subcultural Variations in an Urban Poor Population." *American Anthropology, 73,* 128–143.

JONES, D. R., HARRELL, J. P., MORRIS-PRATHER, C. E., THOMAS, J., AND OMOWALE, N. (1996). Affective and Physiological Responses to Racism: The Role of Afrocentrism and Mode of Presentation. Unpublished manuscript. Howard University.

Jones, E. E., and Davis, K. E. (1965). "From Acts to Dispositions." In L. Berkowitz (ed.), *Advances in Experimental Social Psychology,* Vol. 1, New York: Academic Press.

JONES, E. E., AND NISBETT, R. E. (1971). *The Actor and the Observer: Divergent Perceptions of the Causes of Behavior.* Morristown, NJ: General Learning Press.

JONES, J. M. (1994). "African-Americans: A Duality Dilemma." In W. Lonner and R. Malpass (eds.), *Psychology and Culture* (pp. 17–23). Needham Heights, MA: Allyn & Bacon.

JONES, J. M. (1979). "Conceptual and Strategic Issues in the Relationship of Black Psychology to American Social Science." In A. W. Boykin, A. J. Franklin, and J. F. Yates (eds.), *Research Directions of Black Psychologists* (pp. 390–432). New York: Russell Sage Foundation.

JONES, J. M. (1991). "The Politics of Personality: Being Black in America." In R. L. Jones (ed.), *Black Psychology,* Third edition (pp. 305–318). Hampton, VA: Cobb & Henry.

JONES, J. M. (1972). *Prejudice and Racism.* Reading, MA: Addison-Wesley.

JONES, J. M. (1988). "Racism in Black and White: A Bicultural Model of Reaction and Evolution." In P. A. Katz and D. A. Taylor (eds.), *Eliminating Racism: Profiles in Controversy* (pp. 117–158). New York: Plenum Press.

JONES, J. M. (1986). "Racism: A Cultural Analysis of the Problem." In J. F. Dovidio and S. L. Gaertner (eds.), *Prejudice, Discrimination, and Racism* (pp. 279–314). Orlando, FL: Academic Press.

JONES, J. M. (1992). "Understanding the Mental Health Consequences of Race: Contributions of Basic Social Psychological Processes." In D. N. Ruble, P. R. Costanzo, and M. E. Oliveri (eds.), *The Social Psychology of Mental Health: Basic Mechanisms and Applications* (pp. 199–240). New York: The Guilford Press.

JONES, J. M. (In press). "Whites Are from Mars, O.J. is from Planet Hollywood: Blacks Don't Support O.J., and Whites Just Don't Get It." In M. Fine, L. Weis, D. Powell, & M. Won (eds.), *Off White.* New York: Routledge.

JONES, J. M., AND CARTER, R. T. (1996). "Racism and White Racial Identity." In B. Bowser and R. Hunt (eds.), *Impacts of Racism on White America,* Second edition (pp. 1–23). Newbury Park CA: Sage Publications.

JORDAN, W. D. (1969). *White Over Black: American Attitudes Toward the Negro, 1550–1812.* Baltimore: Penguin Books.

JOST, J. T., AND BANAJI, M. R. (1994). "The Role of Stereotyping in System-Justification and the Production of False Consciousness." *British Journal of Social Psychology, 33,* 1–17.

JUDD, C. M., AND PARK, B. (1988). "Out-Group Homogeneity: Judgments of Variability at the Individual and Group Level." *Journal of Personality and Social Psychology, 54,* 778–788.

JUDD, C. M., RYAN, C. S., AND PARK, B. (1991). "Accuracy in the Judgment of In-Group and Out-Group Variability." *Journal of Personality and Social Psychology, 61,* 366–379.

JUSSIM, L. J., MCCAULEY, C. R., AND LEE, Y.-T. (1995). "Why Study Stereotype Accuracy and Inaccuracy?" In Y.-T. Lee, L. J. Jussim, and C. R. McCauley (eds.). (1995). *Stereotype Accuracy: Toward Appreciating Group Differences* (pp. 3–28). Washington, D.C.: American Psychological Association.

KAGAN, J. S. (1969). "Inadequate Evidence and Illogical Conclusions." *Harvard Education Review, 39,* 126–129.

KALB, M. (1984). Interview with Reverend Jesse Jackson. *Meet the Press,* February 13.

KARDINER, A., AND OVESEY, L. (1951). *The Mark of Oppression.* New York: Norton.

KARLINS, M., COFFMAN, T. L., AND WALTERS, G. (1969). "On the Fading of Social Stereotypes: Studies in Three Generations of College Students." *Journal of Personality and Social Psychology, 13,* 1–16.

KATZ, D., AND BRALY, K. (1933). "Racial Stereotypes of One Hundred College Students." *Journal of Abnormal Psychology, 28,* 280–290.

KATZ, D., AND BRALY, K. (1935). "Racial Prejudice and Racial Stereotypes." *Journal of Abnormal Psychology, 30,* 175–193.

KATZ, I., AND HAAS, R. G. (1988). "Racial Ambivalence and American Value Conflict: Correlational and Printing Studies of Dual Cognitive Structures." *Journal of Personality and Social Psychology, 55,* 893–905.

KATZ, I., WACKENHUT, J., AND HAAS, R. G. (1986). "Racial Ambivalence, Value Duality, and Behavior." In J. F. Dovidio and S. L. Gaertner (eds.), *Prejudice, Discrimination and Racism* (pp. 35–60) Orlando, FL: Academic Press.

KATZ, M. B. (1986). *In the Shadow of the Poorhouse: A Social History of Welfare in America.* New York: Basic Books.

KATZ, P. A. (1983). "Developmental Foundations of Gender and Racial Attitudes." In R. L. Leahy (ed.), *The Child's Construction of Social Inequality.* New York: Academic Press.

KEIL, C. (1966). *Urban Blues.* Chicago: University of Chicago Press.

KELLICOTT, W. E. (1911). *The Social Direction of Human Evolution.* New York: D. Appleton and Co.

KERCHOFF, A. C., & MCCORMICK, T. C. (1955). "Marginal Status and Marginal Personality." *Social Forces, 34,* 48–55.

KERWIN, C., AND PONTEROTTO, J. G. (1995). "Biracial Identity Development: Theory and Research." In J. G. Ponterotto, J. M. Casas, L. A. Suzuki, and C. M. Alexander (1995). *Handbook of Multicultural Counseling* (pp. 199–217). Thousand Oaks, CA: Sage Publications.

KIESLER, C. A., COLLINS, C. E., AND MILLER, N. (1969). *Attitude Change: A Critical Analysis of Theoretical Approaches.* New York: Wiley.

KIESLER, S. B. (1971). Racial Choice among Children in Realistic Situations. Unpublished manuscript, University of Kansas.

KILLENS, J. O. (1965). *Black Man's Burden.* New York: Trident Press.

KINDER, D. R., AND SEARS, D. O. (1981). "Prejudice and Politics: Symbolic Racism versus Racial Threats to the Good Life." *Journal Personality and Social Psychology, 40,* 414–431.

KING, D. B., AND QUICK, C. O. (EDS.). (1965). *Legal Aspects of the Civil Rights Movement.* Detroit: Wayne State University Press.

KINICKI, A. J., HOM, P. W., TROST, M. R., AND WADE, K. J. (1995). "Effects of Category Prototypes on Performance-Rating Accuracy. *Journal of Applied Psychology, 80,* 354–370.

KLINEBERG, O. (1935). *Negro Intelligence and Selective Migration.* New York: Columbia University Press.

KLUEGEL, J. R., AND SMITH, E. R. (1986). *Beliefs about Inequality: Americans' View of What Is and What Ought to Be.* New York: Aldine de Gruyteer.

KNIGHT, G. P., BERNAL, M. E., GARZA, C. A., AND COTA, M. K. (1993). "Family Socialization and the Ethnic Identity of Mexican-American Children." *Journal of Cross-Cultural Psychology, 24*, 99–114.

KNOWLES, L. L., AND PREWITT, K. (1969). *Institutional Racism.* Englewood Cliffs, NJ: Prentice-Hall.

KOPPEL, T. (1996, MAY 21). "Nightline." ABC Television.

KOTTAK, C. P. (1996). *Mirror for Humanity: A Concise Introduction to Cultural Anthropology.* New York: McGraw-Hill.

KOVEL, J. (1970). *White Racism: A Psychohistory.* New York: Pantheon.

KRAMER, B. M. (1950). *Residential Contact as a Determinant of Attitudes Toward Negroes.* Unpublished, Harvard College Library.

KREUGER, J., AND ROTHBART, M. (1988). "Use of Categorical and Individuating Information in Making Inferences about Personality." *Journal of Personality and Social Psychology, 55*, 187–195.

KROEBER, A. L., AND KLUCKHOHN, C. (1952). *Culture: A Critical Review of Concepts and Definitions.* New York: Random House.

KUTNER, B., WILKINS, C., AND YARROW, P. R. (1952). "Verbal Attitudes and Overt Behavior." *Journal of Abnormal Social Psychology, 47*, 549–652.

KYRIAKOS, M. (1996). "Racial Barriers Tumble Down at Gathering of Christian Men." *The Washington Post*, May 26, p. B2.

LAFROMBOISE, T., COLEMAN, H. L. K., AND GERTON, J. (1993). "Psychological Impact of Biculturalism: Evidence and Theory." *Psychological Bulletin*, 114: 395–412.

LANDRETH, C., AND JOHNSON, B. C. (1953). "Young Children's Responses to a Picture and Insert Test Designed to Reveal Reaction to Persons of Different Skin Color." *Child Development, 24*, 63–80.

LANDRINE, H., AND KLONOFF, E. A. (1994). "The African American Acculturation Scale: Development, Reliability, and Validity." *Journal of Black Psychology, 20*, 104–127.

LANDRINE, H., AND KLONOFF, E. A. (1995). "The African American Acculturation Scale II: Cross Validation and Short Form." *Journal of Black Psychology, 21*, 124–152.

LANGER, E. J., AND RODIN, J. (1976). "The Effects of Choice and Enhanced Personal Responsibility for the Aged: A Field Experiment in an Institutional Setting." *Journal of Personality and Social Psychology, 34*, 191–198.

LANGER, E. J. (1989). *Mindfulness.* Reading, MA: Addison-Wesley Publishers.

LANGER. E. J. (1983). *The Psychology of Control.* Beverly Hills, CA: Sage Publications.

LAPIERE, R. T. (1934). "Attitudes vs. Actions." *Social Forces, 13*, 230–237.

LASKER, B. (1929). *Race Attitudes in Children.* New York: Henry Holt.

LEE, Y., JUSSIM, L. J., AND MCCAULEY, C. R. (EDS.). (1995). *Stereotype Accuracy: Toward Appreciating Group Differences.* Washington, DC: American Psychological Association.

LEFKOWITZ, M. R. AND ROGERS, G. M. (EDS.). (1996). *Black Athena Revisited.* Chapel Hill, NC: University of North Carolina Press.

LEFKOWITZ, M. R. (1996). *Not Out of Africa: How Afrocentrism Became an Excuse to Teach Myth as History.* New York: Basic Books.

LEIBY, R. (1994, February 20). "A Crack in the System: This Small-Time Dealer Is Doing 20 years. He Might be Better Off if He'd Killed Somebody." *The Washington Post*, pp. F1, F4-5.

LERNER, M. J. (1981). "The justice motive in human relations: Some thoughts on what we know and need to know about justice." In M. J. Lerner and S. C. Lerner (eds.), *The justice motive in social behavior.* (pp. 11–36). New York: Plenum.

LEWIS, D. L. (1980). *When Harlem Was in Vogue* New York: Knopf.

LEWIS, O. (1961). *The Children of Sanchez: Autobiography of a Mexican Family.* New York: Random House.

LEWONTIN, R. C., ROSE, S., AND KAMIN, L. J. (1984). *Not in Our Genes: Biology, Ideology and Human Nature.* New York: Pantheon Books.

LINCOLN, A. (1894). *Abraham Lincoln, Complete Works,* J. G. Nicolay and J. Hay (eds.). New York: The Century Company.

LINVILLE, P. W., AND JONES, E. E. (1980)." Polarized Appraisals of Outgroup Members." *Journal of Personality and Social Psychology, 38,* 689–703.

LINVILLE, P. W. (1982). "The Complexity-Extremity Effect and Age-Based Stereotyping." *Journal of Personality and Social Psychology, 42,* 193–211.

LINVILLE, P. W., FISCHER, G. W., AND SALOVEY, P. (1989). "Perceived Distribution of the Characteristics of Ingroup and Outgroup Members: Empirical Evidence and a Computer Simulation." *Journal of Personality and Social Psychology, 57,* 165–188.

LINVILLE, P. W., SALOVEY, P., AND FISHER, G. W. (1986). "Stereotyping and Perceived Distribution of Social Characteristics: An Application to Ingroup—Outgroup Perception." In J. F. Dovidio and S. L. Gaertner (eds.), *Prejudice, Discrimination and Racism* (pp. 165–208) Orlando, FL: Academic Press.

LIPPITT, R., AND RADKE, M. (1946). "New Trends in the Investigation of Prejudice." *The Annals of the American Academy of Political and Social Science, 244,* 167–176.

LIPPMAN, W. (1922). *Public Opinion.* New York: Harcourt, Brace and World.

LIPSET, S. M. (1971). "New Perspectives on the Counter-Culture." *Saturday Review,* March 20, 25–28.

LOHMAN, J. D., AND REITZES, DC. (1952). "Notes on Race Relations in Mass Society." *American Journal of Sociology, 58,* 240–246.

LOVE THY NEIGHBOR. (1996). Press Release, February 8. Prince George's County, Maryland.

LUCKER, G. W., ROSENFELD, D., SIKES, J., AND ARONSON, E. (1976)." Performance in the Interdependent Classroom." *American Educational Research Journal, 13,* 115–123.

LUHTANEN, R., AND CROCKER, J. (1992). "A Collective Self-Esteem Scale: Self-Evaluation of One's Social Identity." *Personality and Social Psychology Bulletin, 18,* 302–318.

LUMSDEN, C. J., AND WILSON, E. O. (1981). *Genes, Mind, and Culture: The Coevolutionary Process* Cambridge, MA: Harvard University Press.

MACEDO, D. (1991). "English Only: The Tongue-Tying of America." *Journal of Education, 173,* 9–20.

MACKIE, D. M., AND HAMILTON, D. L. (EDS.). (1993). *Affect, Cognition, and Stereotyping: Interactive Processes in Group Perception.* San Diego, CA: Academic Press.

MACRAE, C. N., BODENHAUSEN, G. V., MILNE, A. B., AND JETTEN, J. (1994). "Out of Mind but Back in Sight: Stereotypes on the Rebound." *Journal of Personality and Social Psychology, 67,* 808–817.

MAQUET, J. (1961). *The Premise of Inequality in Rwanda: A Study of Political Relations in a Central African Kingdom.* London: Oxford University Press.

MARCIA, J. (1980) "Identity in Adolescence." In J. Adelson (ed.), *Handbook of Adolescent Psychology* (pp. 159–187). New York: Wiley.

MARGER, M. N. (1994). *Race and Ethnic Relations: American and Global Perspectives.* Third edition. Belmont, CA: Wadsworth Publishing.

MARKS, G. (1984). "Thinking One's Abilities Are Unique and One's Opinions are Common." Personality and Social Psychology Bulletin, *10,* 203–208.

MARKUS, H. R., AND KITAYAMA, S. (1991). Culture and the Self: Implications for Cognition, Emotion, and Motivation. *Psychological Review, 98,* 224–253.

MARKUS, H. R., AND KITAYAMA, S. (1994). "The Cultural Construction of Self and Emotion: Implications for Social Behavior." In S. Kitayama and H. R. Markus (eds.), *Emotion and Culture: Empirical Studies of Mutual Influence* (pp. 89–132). Washington, D.C.: American Psychological Association.

MARLOWE, D., FRAGER, R., AND NUTTAL, R. L. (1965). "Commitment to Action-Taking as a Consequence of Cognitive Dissonance." *Journal of Personality and Social Psychology, 2,* 864–867.

MARTIN, T. (1976). *Race First: The Ideological and Organizational Struggles of Marcus Garvey and the Universal Negro Improvement Association.* Westport, CT: Greenwood Press.

MARX, G. T. (1969). *Protest and Prejudice: A Study of Belief in the Black Community.* New York: Harper & Row.

MARX, G. T. (1971). "Editor's Introduction to Racism and Race Relations." In M. Wertheimer (ed.), *Confrontation: Psychology and the Problems of Today*. Glenview, IL: Scott Foresman.

MASLOW, A. (1962). *Toward a Psychology of Being*. Princeton, NJ: Van Nostrand/Reinhold.

MASSEY, D. S., AND DENTON, N. A. (1993). *American Apartheid: Segregation and the Making of the Underclass*. Cambridge, MA: Harvard University Press.

MAURER, K. L., PARK, B., AND ROTHBART, M. (1995) "Subtyping versus Subgrouping Processes in Stereotype Representation." *Journal of Personality and Social Psychology, 69*, 812–824.

THE MAYOR'S COMMISSION ON CONDITIONS IN HARLEM. (1935). "The Negro in Harlem: A Report on Social and Economic Conditions Responsible for the Outbreak of March 19, 1935," In A. M. Platt (ed.). (1971). *The Politics of Riot Commissions* (pp. 165–182). New York: Collier Books.

MBITI, J. S. (1970). *African Religions and Philosophy*. Garden City, NY: Anchor Doubleday Books.

MCARTHUR, L. Z., AND BARON, R. (1983). "Toward an Ecological Theory of Social Perception." *Psychological Review, 90*, 215–238.

MCARTHUR, L. Z., AND FRIEDMAN, S. A. (1980). "Illusory Correlation in Impression Formation: Variations in the Shared Distinctiveness Effect as a Function of the Distinctive Person's Age, Race, and Sex." *Journal of Personality and Social Psychology, 39*, 615–624.

MCCALL, N. (1994). *Makes Me Wanna Holler: A Young Black Man in America*. New York: Random House.

MCCAULEY, C., AND STITT, C. L. (1978). "An Individual and Quantitative Measure of Stereotypes." *Journal of Personality and Social Psychology, 39*, 929–940.

MCCONAHAY, J. B. (1986). "Modern Racism, Ambivalence, and the Modern Racism Scale." In J. F. Dovidio, J. F., and S. L. Gaertner (eds.), *Prejudice, Discrimination and Racism* (pp. 91–126) Orlando, FL: Academic Press.

MCCONAHAY, J. B., HARDEE, B. B., AND BATTS, V. (1981). "Has Racism Declined in America: It Depends upon Who's Asking and What Is Asked." *Journal of Conflict Resolution, 25*, 563–579.

MCDOUGALL, W. (1921). *Is America Safe for Democracy?* New York: Charles Scribner's Sons.

MCGRATH, J. E., AND KELLY, J. R. (1986). *Time and Human Interaction: Toward a Social Psychology of Time*. New York: Guilford.

MCKAY, C. (1940). *Harlem: Negro Metropolis*. New York: Dutton.

MEAD, M., DOBZHANSKY, T., TOBACH, E., AND LIGHT, R. (EDS.). (1968). *Science and the Concept of Race*. New York: Columbia University Press.

MEDIN, D. (1989). "Concepts and Conceptual Structure." *American Psychologist, 44*, 1469–1481.

MELTZER, M. (ED.). (1964). *In Their Own Words: A History of the American Negro*. New York: Thomas Y. Crowell.

MENCKEN, H. L. (1927). *Prejudices: Sixth Series*. New York: Knopf.

MENNARD, M. (1992). Letter to the Editor. *The New York Times*, October 20, p. A26.

MILGRAM, S. (1992). *The Individual in a Social World: Essays and Experiments* (pp. 68–71). New York: McGraw-Hill.

MILLER, R. L. (1990). "Beyond Contact Theory: The Impact of Community Affluence on Integration Efforts in Five Suburban High Schools." *Youth and Society, 22*, 12–34.

MISCHEL, W. (1958). "Preference for Delayed Reinforcement: An Experimental Study of a Cultural Observation." *Journal of Abnormal Social Psychology, 56*, 57–61.

MISCHEL, W. (1961a). "Preference for Delayed Reinforcement and Social Responsibility." *Journal of Abnormal Social Psychology, 62*, 1–7.

MISCHEL, W. (1961b). "Delay of Gratification, Need for Achievement, and Acquiescence in Another Culture." *Journal of Abnormal Social Psychology, 62*, 543–552.

MISCHEL, W. (1961c). "Father-Absence and Delay of Gratification." *Journal of Abnormal Social Psychology, 63*, 116–124.

MONTEITH, M. (1991). Self-Regulation of Stereotypical Responses: Implications for Progress in Prejudice Reduction Efforts. Unpublished doctoral dissertation, University of Wisconsin, Madison.

MOORE, D. W., AND SAAD, L. (1995). "No Immediate Signs that Simpson Trial Intensified Racial Animosity." *The Gallup Poll Monthly*, October, #361, 2–9.

MOYNIHAN, D. P. (1965). *The Negro Family: The Case for National Action.* Washington, D.C.: U.S. Government Printing Office.

MOYNIHAN, D. P. (1996). "Close Call." *The Washington Post,* January 12, p. A26.

MURRAY, C. A. (1984). *Losing Ground: American Social Policy, 1950–1980.* New York: Basic Books.

MYERS, L. J. (1993). *Understanding an Afrocentric World View: Introduction to an Optimal Psychology.* Dubuque, IA: Kendall/Hunt Publishing.

MYRDAL, G. (1944). *An American Dilemma: The Negro Problem and Modern Democracy.* New York: Harper.

NAGATA, D. K. (1994). *Legacy of Injustice: Exploring the Cross-Generational Impact of the Japanese American Internment.* New York: Plenum Press.

NATIONAL ADVISORY COMMISSION ON CIVIL DISORDERS. (1968). *Report of the National Advisory Commission on Civil Disorders.* New York: Bantam.

NEMETH, C. (1986). "Intergroup Relations Between Majority and Minority." In S. Worchel and W. G. Austin (eds.), *Psychology of Intergroup Relations.* Chicago: Nelson-Hall.

NEUBERG, S. L. (1994). "Expectancy-Confirmation Process in Stereotype-Tinged Social Encounters: The Moderating Role of Social Goals." In M. P. Zanna and J. M. Olson (eds.), *The Psychology of Prejudice: The Ontario Symposium,* Vol. 7 (pp. 103–130). Hillsdale, NJ: Erlbaum Associates.

New York Times (1995, DECEMBER 12), p. A24.

NICKERSON, K. J., HELMS, J. E. AND TERRELL, F. (1994). "Cultural Mistrust, Opinions about Mental Illness and Black Students' Attitudes toward Seeking Psychological Help from White Counselors." *Journal of Counseling Psychology, 41,* 378–385.

NISBETT, R. E. (1995). "Race, IQ and Scientism." In S. Fraser (ed.), *The Bell Curve Wars: Race, Intelligence and the Future of America* (pp. 36–57). New York: Basic Books.

NOBLES, W. W. (1985). *Africanity and the Black Family.* Oakland, CA: Black Family Institute Publications.

NOBLES, W. W. (1991). "African Philosophy: Foundations of Black Psychology." In R. Jones (ed.), *Black Psychology,* Third edition (pp. 47–64). Hampton, VA: Cobb & Henry Publishers.

NOTT, J. C., AND GLIDDON, G. R. (1854). *Types of Mankind; or Ethnological Researches.* Philadelphia: Lippincott and London.

OLMEDO, E., AND PADILLA, A. (1978). "Empirical and Construct Validation of a Measure of Acculturation for Mexican Americans." *Journal of Social Psychology, 105,* 179–187.

OLMEDO, E. L., MARTINEZ, J. L., AND MARTINEZ, S. R. (1978). "Measure of Acculturation for Chicano Adolescents." *Psychological Reports, 42,* 159–170.

OMI, M., AND WINANT, H. (1994). *Racial Formation in the United States: From the 1960s to the 1990s,* Second edition. New York: Routledge.

THE OPRAH WINFREY SHOW. (1995). *Black for a Day.* February 17.

OSBORNE, J. W. (1995). "Academics, Self-esteem, and Race: A look at the Underlying Assumptions of the Disidentification Hypothesis." *Personality and Social Psychology Bulletin, 21,* 449–455.

PADILLA, A. M., LINDHOLM, K. J., CHEN A, AND DURAN, R. (1991). "The English-Only Movement: Myths, Reality, and Implications for Psychology." *American Psychologist, 46,* 120–130.

PALMORE, E. B. (1955). "The Introduction of Negroes into White Departments." *Human Organizations, 141,* 27–28.

PARHAM, T. A., AND HELMS, J. E. (1981). "The Influence of Black Students' Racial Identity Attitudes on Preference for Counselor's Race." *Journal of Counseling Psychology, 28,* 250–258.

PART, B., AND JUDD, C. M. (1990). "Measures and Models of Perceived Group Variability." *Journal of Personality and Social Psychology, 59,* 173–191.

PARK, B., AND ROTHBART, M. (1982). "Perception of Out-Group Homogeneity and Levels of Social Categorization: Memory for the Subordinate Attributes of In-group and Out-Group Members." *Journal of Personality and Social Psychology, 42,* 1051–1068.

PARKS, R. L. (1992). *Rosa Parks: My Story.* New York: Dial Books.

PATTERSON, C. (1978). *Evolution.* London: Butler and Tanner, Ltd., p. 139.

PATTERSON, O. (1995). "For Whom the Bell Curves." In S. Fraser (ed.), *The Bell Curve Wars: Race, Intelligence and the Future of America* (pp. 187–214). New York: Basic Books.

PATTERSON, O. (1996, February). Is the Distinction between Race and Ethnicity Meaningful? Paper Presented at Conference on "Race, Power and the Mind: Toward an Interdisciplinary Approach to Racial Identity." Culture and Cognition Program, University of Michigan, Ann Arbor, MI.

PERJU-LIICEANU, A. (1992). "Social Stereotypes: Gypsy People between Prejudice and Stereotype." *Revue Romaine-de-Psychology, 36*, 3–9.

PETTIGREW, T. F. (1958). "Personality and Sociocultural Factors in Intergroup Attitudes: A Cross-National Comparison." *Journal of Conflict Revolution, 2*, 29–42.

PETTIGREW, T. F. (1964). *A Profile of the Negro American.* Princeton: D. Van Nostrand.

PETTIGREW, T. F. (1967). "Social Evaluation Theory: Convergences and Applications." In D. Levine (ed.), *Nebraska Symposium on Motivation.* (pp. 241–311). Lincoln, NE: University of Nebraska Press.

PETTIGREW, T. F. (1969). "The Metropolitan Educational Park." *The Science Teacher, 36*: 23–26.

PETTIGREW, T. F. (1971). *Racially Separate or Together.* New York: McGraw-Hill.

PETTIGREW, T. F. (1979). "The Ultimate Attribution Error: Extending Allport's Cognitive Analysis of Prejudice." *Personality and Social Psychology Bulletin, 5*, 461–476.

PETTIGREW, T. F. (1996). The Deprovincialization Hypothesis: Generalized Intergroup Contact Effects on Prejudice. Unpublished manuscript, University of California, Santa Cruz.

PFEFFER, P. F. (1990). *A. Philip Randolph, Pioneer of the Civil Rights Movement.* Baton Rouge: Louisiana State University Press.

PHINNEY, J. S. (1992). "The Multigroup Ethnic Identity Measure: A New Scale for Use with Diverse Groups." *Journal of Adolescent Research, 7*, 156–176.

PHINNEY, J. S., DEVICH-NAVARRO, M., DUPONT, S., ESTRADA, A., AND ONWUGHALU, M. (May 1994). *Biculturalism among African American and Mexican American Adolescents.* Paper presented at the Society for Research on Adolescence, San Diego, CA.

PIAGET, J. (1952). *Judgment and Reasoning in the Child.* New York: Humanities Press.

PIERCE, C. M. (1970). "Offensive Mechanisms." In F. Barbour (ed.), *The Black Seventies.* Boston: Porter Sargent.

PINKOW, L. C., EHRLICH, H. J., AND PURVIS R. D. (1990). "Group Tensions on American College Campuses 1989." *Institute Working Papers, No. 1.* Baltimore, MD: National Institute Against Prejudice and Violence.

PITTS, J. R. (1969). "The Hippies as Contra-Meritocracy." *Dissent, 16(4),* 326–337.

PLOMIN, R. (1988). "The Nature and Nurture of Cognitive Abilities." In R. Sternberg (ed.), *Advances in the Psychology of Human Intelligence* (Vol. 4, pp. 1–33). Hillsdale, NJ: Erlbaum.

PLOMIN, R. (1990). *Nature and Nurture: An Introduction to Human Behavioral Genetics.* Belmont, CA: Brooks/Cole Publishing.

PONTEROTTO, J. G., CASAS, J. M., SUZUKI, L. A., AND ALEXANDER, C. M. (1995). *Handbook of Multicultural Counseling.* Thousand Oaks, CA: Sage Publications.

PORTER, J. D. (1971). *Black Child, White Child: The Development of Racial Attitudes.* Cambridge, MA: Harvard University Press.

PRATTO, F., SIDANIUS, J., STALLWORTH, L. M., AND MALLE, B. F. (1994). "Social Dominance Orientation: A Personality Variable Predicting Social and Political Attitudes." *Journal of Personality and Social Psychology, 67,* 741–763.

PRESIDENT'S COMMITTEE ON CIVIL RIGHTS. (1947). *To Secure These Rights.* Washington, D.C.: U.S. Government Printing Office.

QUATTRONE, G. A., AND JONES, E. E. (1980). "The Perception of Variability within Ingroups and Outgroups: Implications for the Law of Small Numbers." *Journal of Personality and Social Psychology, 38,* 141–152.

RAAB, E., AND LIPSET, S. M. (1959). *Prejudice and Society.* New York: Anti-Defamation League of B'nai B'rith.

RACIAL ISOLATION IN THE PUBLIC SCHOOLS: REPORT OF THE U.S. COMMISSION ON CIVIL RIGHTS, VOLUMES I AND II. Washington, D.C.: U.S. Government Printing Office.

RADKE, M., SUTHERLAND, J., AND ROSENBERG, P. (1950). "Racial Attitudes of Children." *Sociometry, 13,* 154–171.

RADKE, M., TRAGER, H. G., AND DAVIS, J. (1949). "Social Perceptions and Attitudes of Children." *Genetic Psychology Monographs, 40,* 327–447.

RAINWATER, L. AND YANCEY W. (EDS.). (1967). *The Moynihan Report and the Politics of Controversy.* Cambridge, MA: MIT Press.

RAINWATER, L. (1966). "Crucible of Identity." In T. Parsons & K. B. Clark (eds.), *The Negro American* (pp. 160–204) Boston: Houghton Mifflin.

RAMIREZ, M., AND CASTENEDA, A. (1974). *Cultural Democracy: Bicognitive Development and Education.* New York: Academic Press.

REPORT OF THE NATIONAL COMMISSION ON CIVIL DISORDERS. (1968). New York: New York Times Corporation.

ROGERS, R. W., AND PRENTICE-DUNN, S. (1981). "Deindividuation and Anger-Mediated Interracial Aggression: Unmasking Regressive Racism." *Journal of Personality and Social Psychology, 41,* 63–73.

ROHAN, M. J., AND ZANNA, M. P. (1996). "Value Transmission in Families." In C. Seligman, J. M. Olson, and M. P. Zanna (eds.), *The Psychology of Values: The Ontario Symposium* (Vol. 8, pp. 253–276). Mahwah, NJ: Lawrence Erlbaum Associates.

ROKEACH, M., AND MEZEI, L. (1966). "Race and Shared Belief as Factors in Social Choice." *Science, 151,* 167–172.

ROKEACH, M., AND PARKER, S. (1970). "Values as Social Indicators of Poverty and Race Relations in America." *The Annals of the American Academy of Political and Social Science, 388,* 97–111.

ROKEACH, M. (1960). *The Open and Closed Mind.* (pp. 132–168) New York: Basic Books.

ROKEACH, M. (1961). "Belief vs. Race as Determinants of Social Distance: Comment on Triandis' Paper." *Journal of Abnormal Social Psychology, 62,* 187–188.

ROKEACH, M., SMITH, P. W., AND EVANS, R. I. (1960). "Two Kinds of Prejudice or One?" In M. Rokeach (ed.), *The Open and Closed Mind* (pp. 132–168). New York: Basic Books.

ROOT, M. P. (ed.). (1992). *Racially Mixed People in America.* Newbury Park CA: Sage Publications.

ROSE, A. (1947). *Studies in the Reduction of Prejudice.* Chicago: American Council on Race Relations.

ROSENBERG, M. (1986) *Conceiving the Self.* Melbourne, FL: Krieger.

ROSENTHAL, J. (1970, JUNE 17) *New York Times,* p. 49.

ROSENTHAL, R., AND JACOBSON, L. F. (1968). "Teacher Expectations for the Disadvantaged." *Scientific American, 218* (#4), 19–23.

ROSS, L., GREENE, D., AND HOUSE, P. (1977). "The 'False Consensus Effect': An Egocentric Bias in Social Perception and Attribution Processes." *Journal of Experimental Social Psychology, 13,* 279–301.

ROSS, L. D., AMABILE, T. M., AND STEINMETZ, J. L. (1977). "Social Roles, Social Control, and Biases in Social-Perception Processes." *Journal of Personality and Social Psychology, 35,* 485–494.

ROSS, L. (1977). "The Intuitive Psychologist and His Shortcomings: Distortions in the Attribution Process." In L. Berkowitz (ed.), Advances in Experimental Social Psychology (Vol. 10, pp. 174–221). New York: Academic Press.

ROTHBART, M., AND JOHN, O. P. (1985). "Social Categorization and Behavioral Episodes: A Cognitive Analysis of the Effects of Intergroup Contact." *Journal of Social Issues, 41,* 81–104.

ROTTER, J. (1966). "Generalized Expectancies for Internal versus External Control of Reinforcement." *Psychological Monographs, 80* (1, Whole No. 609)

ROWE, W., BEHRENS, J. T., AND LEACH, M. M. (EDS.). (1995). "Racial/Ethnic Identity and Racial Consciousness: Looking Back and Looking Forward." In Ponterotto, J. G., Casas, J. M., Suzuki, L. A., and Alexander, C. M. *Handbook of Multicultural Counseling* (pp. 218–236). Thousand Oaks, CA: Sage Publications.

RUDWICK, E. M. (1966). *Race Riot at East St. Louis, July 2, 1917.* New York: World Publishing Company, Meridian Books.

RUGGERIO, K. M., AND TAYLOR, D. M. (1995). "Coping with Discrimination: How Disadvantaged Group Members Perceive the Discrimination that Confronts Them." *Journal of Personality and Social Psychology, 68,* 826–838.

RUIZ, A. S. (1990). "Ethnic Identity: Crisis and Resolution." *Journal of Multicultural Counseling and Development, 18,* 29–40.

RUSHTON, J. P. (1988). "Race Differences in Behavior: A Review and Evolutionary Analysis." *Personality and Individual Differences, 9,* 1009–1024.

RUSHTON, J. P. (1989). "The Evolution of Racial Differences: A Reply to M. Lynn." *Journal of Research in Personality, 23,* 7–20.

RUSSELL, C. (1995). *The Official Guide to the American Marketplace,* Second edition. Ithaca, NY: New Strategist Publications.

RYAN, W. (1967). "Savage Discovery: The Moynihan Report." In L. Rainwater and W. Yancey (eds.), *The Moynihan Report and the Politics of Controversy.* Cambridge: MIT Press.

SAGAR, H. A., AND SCHOFIELD, J. W. (1980). "Racial and Behavioral Cues in Black and White Children's Perceptions of Ambiguously Aggressive Acts." *Journal of Personality and Social Psychology, 39,* 590–598.

SAMELSON, F. (1978). "From 'Race Psychology' to 'Studies in Prejudice': Some Observations on the Thematic Reversal in Social Psychology." *Journal of the History of the Behavioral Sciences, 14,* 265–278.

SAMUELSON, R. J. (1996, March 11). "The Vices of Our Virtues." *Newsweek,* p. 65.

SANDOMIR, R. (1995, MAY 13). "Golf: Golf Reporter and CBS Deny Remarks on Lesbianism." *New York Times,* p. 25.

SAWYER, D. (1991, September 26) *PRIMETIME LIVE.* ABC Television.

SAWYER, K. (1986, January 15). "King Scholars Steal Bennett's Lines." *Washington Post,* p. A8.

SCARR, S., AND WEINBERG, R. (1983). "The Minnesota Adoption Studies: Genetic Differences and Malleability." *Child Development, 54,* 260–267.

SCHEER, J (1944). "Culture and Disability: An Anthropological Point of View." In E. Trickett, R. Watts, and D. Birman (eds.), *Human Diversity: Perspectives on People in Context* (pp. 244–260) San Francisco: Jossey-Bass Publishers.

SCHILLINGER, L. (1994) "Blond Bondage: Now that I'm Brunette, I've Discovered What Gentlemen Truly Prefer." *The Washington Post,* July 24, p. C1:3.

SCHLESINGER, A. M. (1992). *The Disuniting of America: Reflections on a Multicultural Society.* New York: W. W. Norton.

SCHMIDT, J. R. (1996). *Post-Adarand Guidance on Affirmative Action in Federal Employment: Memorandum to General Counsels.* Office of the Attorney General, United States of America.

SCHNEIDER, V., AND SMYKLA, J. O. (1991). "A Summary Analysis of Executions in the United States, 1608–1987: The Espy File." In R. M. Bohm (ed.), *The Death Penalty in America: Current Research* (pp. 1–19). Cincinnati, OH: Anderson.

SCHUMAN, H., STEEH, C., AND BOBO, L. (1985). *Racial Attitudes in America: Trends and Interpretations.* Cambridge, MA: Harvard University Press.

SCHWARTZ, S. H. (1992). "Universals in the Content and Structure of Values: Theoretical Advances and Empirical Tests in 20 Countries." In M. P. Zanna (ed.), *Advances in Experimental Social Psychology* (Vol. 24, pp. 1–65). San Diego, CA: Academic Press.

SCHWARTZ, B. (1995). "The Diversity Myth: America's Leading Export." *The Atlantic Monthly, 275 No. 5,* 57–67.

SEARS, D. O., AND KINDER, D. R. (1970). "Racial Tensions and Voting in Los Angeles. "In W. Z. Hirsch (ed.), *Los Angeles: Viability and Prospects for Metropolitan Leadership,* pp. 53–84. NY: Praeger.

SEARS, D. O. (1988). "Symbolic Racism." In P. A. Katz and D. A. Taylor (eds.), *Eliminating Racism: Profiles in Controversy* (pp. 53–84). New York: Plenum.

SEARS, D. O., CITRIN, J., AND VAN LAAR, C. (1995). Black Exceptionalism in a Multicultural Society. Paper Presented at the Society of Experimental Social Psychology, Annual meeting, Washington, D.C.

SELZNICK, G. J., AND STEINBERG, S. (1969). *The Tenacity of Prejudice: Anti-Semitism in Contemporary America.* New York: Harper and Row.

SENGHOR, L. (1956). "L'esprit de la civilisation ou les lois de la culture negro-africaine." *Presence Africaine,* Paris, France.

SHAPIRO, L. (1996, March 5). "Packer: No Apology for What He Said." *The Washington Post,* p. E1.

SHERIF, M., AND SHERIF, C. W. (1953). *Groups in Harmony and Tension.* New York: Harper.

SHERIF, M. (1966) *In Common Predicament: Social Psychology of Intergroup Conflict and Coopera-tion.* Boston: Houghton Mifflin.

SHERIF, M., HARVEY, O. J., WHITE, J. B., HOOD, W. R., AND SHERIF, C. W. (1961). *Intergroup Conflict and Cooperation: The Robbers Cave Experiment.* Norman, OK: University of Oklahoma Book Exchange.

SIDANIUS, J., LIU, J. H., SHAW, J. S., AND PRATTO, F. (1994). "Social Dominance Orientation, Hier-archy Attenuators and Hierarchy Enhancers: Social Dominance Theory and the Crimi-nal Justice System." *Journal of Applied Social Psychology, 24,* 338–366.

SIDANIUS, J. (1993) "The Psychology of Group Conflict and the Dynamics of Oppression: A So-cial Dominance Perspective." In S. Iyengar and W. J. McGuire (eds.), *Explorations in Po-litical Psychology* (pp. 183–219). Durham, NC: Duke University Press.

SIDANIUS, J., PRATTO, F., AND BOBO, L. (1996) "Racism, Conservatism, Affirmative Action and Intellectual Sophistication: A Matter of Conservatism or Group Dominance?" *Journal of Personality and Social Psychology, 70,* 476–490.

SIGALL, H., AND PAGE, R. (1971). "Current Stereotypes: A Little Fading, a Little Faking." *Journal of Personality and Social Psychology, 18,* 247–255.

SILBERMAN, C. E. (1964). *Crisis in Black and White.* New York: Random House.

SIMONS, R. F. (1996). Race of Experimenter Redux. Paper presented at Society for Psychophys-iology, Seattle, WA.

SIMPSON, G. E., AND YINGER, J. M. (1965). *Racial and Cultural Minorities: An Analysis of Prejudice and Discrimination,* Third edition. New York: Harper and Row.

SLAVIN, R. E. (1980). "Cooperative Learning." *Review of Educational Research, 50,* 315–342.

SLAVIN, R. E. (1990, December/January). "Research on Cooperative Learning: Consensus and Controversy." *Educational Leadership,* pp. 52–54.

SLAVIN, R. E. (1995). *Cooperative Learning: Theory, Research and Practice,* Second edition. Boston: Allyn & Bacon.

SMEDLEY, A. (1993). *Race in North America: Origin and Evolution of a Worldview.* Boulder, CO: Westview Press.

SMERDON, P. (1994, June 6). "Rwandan Prisoners Say They were Forced to Kill Tutsi." *New York Times,* p. 8.

SMITH, E. E., AND ZARATE, M. A. (1990). "Exemplar and Prototype Use in Social Categoriza-tion." *Social Cognition, 8,* 243–262.

SMITH, E. E., AND ZARATE, M. A. (1992). "Exemplar-Based Model of Social Judgment." *Psycho-logical Review, 99,* 3–21.

SMITH, E. R., AND HENRY, S. (IN PRESS). "An In-group Becomes Part of the Self: Response Time Evidence." *Personality and Social Psychology Bulletin.*

SMITH, E. R. (1993). "Social Identity and Social Emotions: Toward New Conceptualizations of Prejudice." In D. M. Mackie, and D. L. Hamilton (eds.). *Affect, Cognition and Stereotyping: Interactive Processes in Group Perceptions* (pp. 297–315). San Diego, CA: Academic Press.

SMITH, H., AND COHEN, L. C. (1994). "Self-Complexity and Reactions to a Relationship Break-Up." *Journal of Social and Clinical Psychology, 12,* 367–384.

SMITH, J. D., AND CHAMBERS, G. (1991). *Inequality in Northern Ireland.* Oxford, England: Claren-don Press.

SMITHERMAN, G. (1991). "Talkin' and Testifyin': Black English and the Black Experience." In R. L. Jones (ed.), *Black Psychology, Third edition* (pp. 249–268). Hampton, VA: Cobbs & Henry.

SMOTHERS, R. (1995, October 21). "Man Charged with Burning Alabama School is Cleared." *New York Times.* p. 6.

SNIDERMAN, P. M., AND PIAZZA, T. (1993). *The Scar of Race.* Cambridge, MA: Harvard Univer-sity Press.

SNYDER, M. AND SWANN, W. B., JR. (1976). "When Actions Reflect Attitudes: The Politics of Im-pression Management." *Journal of Personality and Social Psychology, 34,* 1034–1042.

SNYDER, M., TANKE, E. D., AND BERSCHEID, E. (1977). "Social Perception and Interpersonal Be-havior: On the Self-Fulfilling Nature of Social Stereotypes." *Journal of Personality and Social Psychology, 35,* 656–666.

SOBEL, M. (1987). *The World They Made Together: Black and White Values in Eighteenth-Century Virginia.* Princeton, NJ: Princeton University Press.

SOBOL, T. (1995). "Racial Balkanization at Cornell." *The Wall Street Journal,* July 25, p. 12.

SOCIAL SCIENCE INSTITUTE. (1946). *Racial Attitudes, Social Science Source Document No. 3.* Nashville, TN: Social Science Institute of Fisk University.

SODOWSKY, G. R., KWAN, K. K., AND PANNU, R. (1995). "Ethnic Identity of Asians in the United States." In J. G. Ponterotto, J. M. Casas, L. A. Suzuki, and C. M. Alexander (1995). *Handbook of Multicultural Counseling* (pp. 123–154). Thousand Oaks, CA: Sage Publications.

SOLOMON, S., GREENBERG, J., AND PYSZCZYNSKI, T. (1991). "A Terror Management Theory of Social Behavior: The Psychological Functions of Self-Esteem and Cultural Worldviews." In M. P. Zanna (ed.), *Advances in Experimental Social Psychology* (Vol. 24, pp. 93–159). San Diego, CA: Academic Press.

SOWELL, T. (1994). *Race and Culture: A Worldview.* New York: Basic Books.

SPEARMAN, C. E. (1927). *The Abilities of Man: Their Nature and Measurement.* New York: Macmillan.

SPENCER, S. J., AND STEELE, C. M. (1996). Under Suspicion of Inability: Stereotype Vulnerability and Women's Math Performance. Unpublished manuscript, Stanford University.

SPURLOCK, D. L. (1996). "The Affirmative Action Debate." Unpublished manuscript. *New York Daily News.*

STAMPP, K. M. (1956). *The Peculiar Institution: Slavery in the Ante-Bellum South.* New York: Knopf.

STANGOR, C., AND DUAN, C. (1991). "Effects of Multiple Task Demands upon Memory for Information about Social Groups." *Journal of Experimental Social Psychology, 27,* 357–378.

STANGOR, C., AND RUBLE, D. N. (1989). "Differential Influences of Gender Schemata and Gender Constancy on Children's Information Processing and Behavior." *Social Cognition, 7,* 353–372.

STANGOR, C., AND SCHALLER, M. (1996). "Stereotypes as Individual and Collective representations." In C. N. Macrae, C. Stangor, and M. Hewstone (eds.), *Stereotypes and Stereotyping* (pp. 3–40). New York: The Guilford Press.

STANGOR, C., SULLIVAN, L. A., AND FORD, T. E. (1991). "Affective and Cognitive Determinants of Prejudice." *Social Cognition, 9,* 359–380.

STARK, E. (1990). "The Myth of Black Violence." *New York Times,* July 18.

STEELE, C. (1988). "The Psychology of Self-Affirmation: Sustaining the Integrity of the Self." In L. Berkowitz (ed.), *Advances in Experimental Social Psychology* (Vol. 21, pp. 261–346). San Diego, CA: Academic Press.

STEELE, C. (1992). "Minds Wasted, Minds Saved: Crisis and Hope in the Schooling of Black Americans." *Atlantic Monthly, 269(4),* 68–78.

STEELE, C. M., AND ARONSON, J. (1995). "Stereotype Threat and the Intellectual Test Performance of African Americans." *Journal of Personality and Social Psychology, 69,* 797–811.

STEELE, C. M. (IN PRESS). "A Burden of Suspicion: How Stereotypes Shape the Intellectual Identities and Performance of Women and African-Americans." *American Psychologist.*

STEELE, S. (1990). *The Content of our Character,* New York: St. Martin's Press.

STEIN, D. D., HARDYCK, J. A., AND SMITH, M. B. "Race and Belief: An Open and Shut Case. *Journal of Personality and Social Psychology, 1,* 281–289.

STEPHAN, W., AND STEPHAN, C. (1995). *Intergroup Relations.* Dubuque, IA: Brown and Benchmark.

STEPHAN, W. (1994). Intergroup Anxiety. Invited paper, Meetings of the Society of Experimental Social Psychology. October 15, Lake Tahoe, NV.

STEPHAN, W. G., AND STEPHAN, C. (1984). "The Role of Ignorance in Intergroup Relations." In N. Miller and M. B. Brewer (eds.), *Groups in Contact* (pp. 229–255). New York: Academic Press.

STEPHAN, W. G., AND STEPHAN, C. W. (1985). "Intergroup Anxiety." *Journal of Social Issues, 41 (3)* 157–175.

STEPHAN, W. G. (1986). "Effects of School Desegregation: An Evaluation 30 Years after Brown." In L. Saxe and M. Saks (eds.), *Advances in Applied Social Psychology* (Vol. 4, pp. 181–206). New York: Academic Press.

STEPHAN, W. G., AGEYEV, V., COATES-SHRIDER, L., STEPHAN, C. W., AND ABALAKINA, M. (1994). "On the Relationship between Stereotypes and Prejudice: An International Study." *Personality and Social Psychology Bulletin, 20,* 277–284.

STERNBERG, R. J. (1988). "A Triarchic View of Intelligence in Cross-Cultural Perspective." In S. H. Irvine and J. W. Berry (eds.), *Human Abilities in Cultural Context.* Cambridge: Cambridge University Press.

STOKES, J. E., MURRAY, C. B., PEACOCK, J. M., AND KAISER, R. T. (1994). "Assessing the Reliability, Factor Structure, and Validity of the African Self-Consciousness Scale in a General Population of African-Americans." *Journal of Black Psychology, 20*, 62–74.

STORMS, M. D. (1973). "Videotape and the Attribution Process; Reversing Actors' and Observers' Points of View." *Journal of Personality and Social Psychology, 27*, 165–175.

SUE, S., AND OKAZAKI, S. (1990). "Asian American Educational Achievements: A Phenomenon in Search of an Explanation." *American Psychologist, 45*, 913–920.

SUINN, R. M., AHUNA, C., AND KHOO, G. (1992). "The Suinn-Lew Asian Self-Identity Acculturation Scale: Concurrent and Factorial Validation." *Psychological and Educational Measurement, 52*, 1041–1046.

SUINN, R. M., RICKARD-FIGUEROA, K., LEW, S. & VIRGIL, P. (1987). "The Suinn-Lew Asian Self-Identity, Acculturation Scale: An Initial Report." *Psychological and Educational Measurement, 47*, 401–407.

SUTHERLAND, M. E., AND HARRELL, J. P. (1986) "Individual Differences in Physiological Responses to Fearful, Racially Noxious and Neutral Imagery." *Imagination, Cognition and Personality, 6*, 133–150.

SZAPOCZNIK, J., RIO, A., PEREZ-VIDAL, A., KURTINES, W., HERVIS, O., AND SANTISTEBAN, D. (1986). "Bicultural Effectiveness Training (BET): An Experimental Test of an Intervention Modality for Families Experiencing Intergenerational/Intercultural Conflict." *Hispanic Journal of Behavioral Sciences, 8*, 303–330.

SZAPOCZNIK, J., SCOPETTA, M. A., KURTINES, W., AND ARANDALE, M. A. (1978). "Theory and Measurement of Acculturation." *Interamerican Journal of Psychology, 12*, 113–120.

TAEUBER, K. E., AND TAEUBER, A. F. (1965). *Negroes in Cities.* Chicago: Aldine.

TAJFEL, H. (1969). "Cognitive Aspects of Prejudice." *Journal of Social Issues, 25*, 79–97.

TAJFEL, H. (1978). *Differentiation between Social Groups: Studies in the Social Psychology of Intergroup Relations.* London: Academic Press.

TAKAKI, R. (1994). "At the End of the Century: The 'Culture Wars' in the U.S." In R. Takaki (ed.), *From Different Shores: Perspectives on Race and Ethnicity in America,* Second Edition (pp. 296–299). New York: Oxford University Press.

TAYLOR, D. M., AND MOGHADDAM, F. M. (1994). *Theories of Intergroup Relations: International Social Psychological Perspectives,* Second edition. Westport, CT: Praeger.

TAYLOR, D. M., WRIGHT, S. C., AND PORTER, L. E. (1994). "Dimensions of Perceived Discrimination: The Personal/Group Discrimination Discrepancy." In M. P. Zanna, and J. M. Olson (eds.), *The Psychology of Prejudice: The Ontario Symposium* (Vol. 7 pp. 233–256). Hillsdale, NJ: Erlbaum Associates.

TAYLOR, D. M., WRIGHT, S. C., MOGHADDAM, F. M., AND LALONDE, R. N. (1990). "The Personal/Group Discrimination Discrepancy: Perceiving My Group but not Myself to Be a Target for Discrimination." *Personality and Social Psychology Bulletin, 16*, 254–262.

TAYLOR, S. E. (1983). "Adjustment to Threatening Events: A Theory of Cognitive Adaptation." *American Psychologist, 38*, 1161–1173.

TAYLOR, S. E., FISKE, S. T., CLOSE, M., ANDERSON, C., AND RUDERMAN, A. (1977). Solo Status as a Psychological Variable: The Power of Being Distinctive. Unpublished manuscript, Harvard University.

TERKEL, S. (1992). *Race: How Blacks and Whites Think and Feel about the American Obsession.* New York: The New Press.

TERRELL, F., AND TERRELL, S. L. (1981). "An Inventory to Measure Cultural Mistrust among Blacks." *Western Journal of Black Studies, 5*, 180–184.

TERRELL, F., TERRELL, S. L., AND MILLER, F. (1993). "Level of Mistrust as a Function of Educational and Occupational Expectations among Black Students." *Adolescence, 28*, 573–578.

TERRELL, F., TERRELL, S. L., AND TAYLOR, J. (1981). "Effects of Race of Examiner and Cultural Mistrust on the WAIS Performance of Black Students." *Journal of Consulting and Clinical Psychology, 49*, 750–751.

TESSER, A. (1988). "Toward a Self-Evaluation Maintenance Model of Social Behavior." In L. Berkowitz (ed.), *Advances in Experimental Social Psychology* (Vol. 21, pp. 181–228). New York: Academic Press.

THIBAUT, J., AND KELLEY, H. H. (1959). *The Social Psychology of Groups.* New York: Wiley.

THIGPEN, C. H., AND CLECKLEY, H. M. (1954). "A Case of Multiple Personality." *Journal of Abnormal Social Psychology, 49,* 135–151.

THE THREE FACES OF EVE. (1957). (Motion picture.) Hollywood, CA: Twentieth Century-Fox.

THURSTONE, L. L. (1927). "Attitudes Can Be Measured." *American Journal of Sociology, 33,* 529–554.

Time Magazine (Fall, 1993). "The new faces of America: How immigrants are shaping the world's first multicultural society."

TILLMAN, L. (1996). "Home Depot Refuses Sale." *Fairfax Journal,* February 12.

TOWER, I. V. (1969). *Soul on Rice: The Black Soldier in Vietnam.* New York: Racquet Press.

TRAGER, H. G., AND YARROW, M. R. (1952). *They Live What They Learn.* New York: Harpers.

TRIANDIS, H. C. (1961). "A Note on Rokeach's Theory of Prejudice." *Journal of Abnormal Social Psychology, 62,* 184–186.

TRIANDIS, H. C. (1965). "Race and Belief as Determinants of Behavioral Intentions." *Journal of Personality and Social Psychology, 2,* 715–725.

TRIANDIS, H. C. (1994). *Culture and Behavior.* New York: McGraw-Hill.

TRICKETT, E. J., WATTS, R., AND BIRMAN, D. (EDS.). (1994). *Human Diversity.* San Francisco: Jossey-Bass.

TURNER, M. A., FIX, M., AND STRUYK, R. J. (1991). *Opportunities Denied, Opportunities Diminished: Discrimination in Hiring.* Washington, D.C.: The Urban Institute.

TYLER, T. R. (1988). "What is procedural justice? Criteria used by citizens to assess the fairness of legal procedures." *Law and Society Review, 22,* 103–135.

TYLER, T. R. (1994). "Psychological Models of the Justice Motive: Antecedents of Distributive and Procedural Justice." *Journal of Personality and Social Psychology, 65,* 850–863.

U.S. DEPARTMENT OF HEALTH AND HUMAN SERVICES. (1985). *Report of the Secretary's Task Force on Black and Minority Health.* Washington, D.C.: U.S. Government Printing Office.

U.S. NEWS AND WORLD REPORT. February 13, 1995. Vol. 118, No. 6.

UHLIG, M. A. (1988). "Racial Remarks Cause Furor." *New York Times,* January 16, p. 47, 50.

UNITED NATIONS DEVELOPMENT PROGRAMME. (1993). *Human Development Report.* New York: Oxford University Press.

UPDEGRAVE, W. (1989). "Race and Money." *Money,* December.

VAN DEN BERGHE, P. (1967). *Race and Racism: A Comparative Perspective.* New York: Wiley.

VAN DIJK, T. A., AND KINTSCH, W. (1983). *Strategies of Discourse Comprehension.* New York: Academic Press.

VAN DIJK, T. A. (1987). *Communicating Racism: Ethnic Prejudice in Thought and Talk.* Newbury Park, CA: Sage Publications.

VAN DIJK, T. A. (1993). *Elite Discourse and Racism.* Newbury Park, CA: Sage Publications.

VASSA, G. (1791). *The Interesting Narrative of the Life of Olaudah Equiano. Gustavus Vassa the African.*

VERSTEGAN, R. (1605). *Restitution of Decayed Intelligence.* Cited in M. Banton. (1977). *The Idea of Race* (p. 16). Boulder, CO: Westview Press.

VON HIPPLE, W., SEKAQUAPTWA, D. AND VARGAS, P. (1995). "On the Role of Encoding Processes in Stereotype Maintenance." In M.P. Zanna (ed.), *Advances in Experimental Social Psychology* (Vol. 27, pp. 177–254) San Diego, CA: Academic Press.

VRANA, S. R., AND ROLLOCK, D. (1996). Physiological Response to a Minimal Social Encounter: Effects of Gender, Ethnicity, and Social Context. Unpublished manuscript, Purdue University.

WALKER, D. (1969). *Walker's Appeal in Four Articles.* New York: Arno Press.

WATERS, M. C. (1990). *Ethnic Options: Choosing Identities in America.* Berkeley, CA: University of California Press.

WATKINS, C. E., AND TERRELL F. (1988). "Mistrust Level and Its Effects on Counseling Expectations in Black Client–White Counselor Relationships: An Analogue Study. *Journal of Counseling Psychology, 35,* 194–197.

WATKINS, C. E., TERRELL, F., MILLER, F. S., AND TERRELL, S. L. (1989). "Cultural Mistrust and Its Effects on Expectational Variables in Black Client–White Counselor Relationships. *Journal of Counseling Psychology, 36(4),* 447–450.

WAX, S. L. (1948). "A survey of Restrictive Advertising and Discrimination by Summer Resorts in the Province of Ontario." Canadian Jewish Congress, *Information and Comment, 7*, 10–13.

WEBER, R., AND CROCKER, J. (1983). "Cognitive Processes in the Revision of Stereotypic Beliefs." *Journal of Personality and Social Psychology, 45,* 961–977.

WEBSTER, S. W. (1961). "The Influence of Interracial Contact on Social Acceptance in a Newly Integrated School." *Journal of Educational Psychology, 52,* 292–296.

WEBSTER'S NEW TWENTIETH CENTURY DICTIONARY OF THE ENGLISH LANGUAGE UNABRIDGED, Second edition. (1965). New York: The Publishers Guild.

WEGNER, D. M. (1989). *White Bears and Other Unwanted Thoughts.* New York: Viking.

WEGNER, D. M., ERBER, R., AND ZANAKOS, S. (1993). "Ironic Processes in Mental Control of Mood and Mood-Related Thought." *Journal of Personality and Social Psychology, 65,* 1093–1104.

WEINER, B. (1993). "On Sin and Sickness: A Theory of Perceived Responsibility and Social Motivation." *American Psychologist, 48,* 957–965.

WEINER, B. (1995). *Judgments of Responsibility: A Foundation for a Theory of Social Conduct.* New York: Guilford Press.

WEITZ, S. (1972). "Attitude, Voice, and Behavior: A Repressed Affect Model of Interracial Interaction." *Journal of Personality and Social Psychology, 24,* 14–21.

WELLMAN, D. T. (1993). *Portraits of White Racism,* Second edition. New York: Cambridge University Press.

WELSING, F. C. (1991). *The Isis Papers: The Keys to the Colors.* Chicago: Third World Press.

WHARTON, C. (1994). "The Nightmare in Central Africa." *The New York Times,* April 9, p. A28.

WHITMORE, P. S., JR. (1957). "A Study of School Desegregation: Attitude Change and Scale Validation." *Dissertation Abstracts, 17,* 891–892.

WICKER, A. W. (1969). "Attitudes versus Actions: The Relationship of Verbal and Overt Behavioral Responses to Attitude Objects." *Journal of Social Issues, 25,* 41–78.

WILBANKS, W. (1987). *The Myth of a Racist Criminal Justice System.* Monterey, CA: Brooks/Cole Publishing Company.

WILLIAMS, D. R., AND COLLINS, C. (1995). "US Socioeconomic and Racial Differences in Health: Patterns and Explanations." *Annual Review of Sociology, 21,* 349–386.

WILLIAMS, D. R., LAVIZZO-MOUREY, R., AND WARREN, R. C. (1994). "The Concept of Race and Health Status in America." *Public Health Reports, 109(1),* 26–41.

WILLIAMS, G. H. (1995). *Life on the Color Line: The True Story of a White Boy Who Discovered He Was Black.* New York: Dutton.

WILLIAMS, J. E., AND MORLAND, J. K. (1976). *Race, Color and the Young Child.* Chapel Hill, NC: University of North Carolina Press.

WILLIAMS, R. M., JR. (1947). *The Reduction of Intergroup Tensions.* New York: Social Science Research Council, Bulletin 57.

WILLIAMS, R. M., JR. (1964). *Strangers Next Door: Ethnic Relations in American Communities.* Englewood Cliffs, NJ: Prentice-Hall.

WILLIAMS, T. (1955). *Cat on a Hot Tin Roof.* New York: New American Library.

WILLS, T. A. (1981). "Downward Comparison Principles in Social Psychology." *Psychological Bulletin, 90,* 245–271.

WILNER, D. M., WALKLEY, R. P., AND COOK, S. W. (1955). *Human Relations in Interracial Housing: A Study of the Contact Hypothesis.* Minneapolis, MN: University of Minnesota Press.

WILSON, E. O. (1992). *The Diversity of Life.* Cambridge, MA: Harvard University Press.

WILSON, W. J. (1970). "Rank Order of Discrimination and Its Relevance to Civil Rights Priorities." *Journal of Personality and Social Psychology, 15,* 118–124.

WILSON, W. J. (1978). *The Declining Significance of Race: Blacks and Changing American Institutions.* Chicago: University of Chicago Press.

WILSON, W. J. (1987). *The Truly Disadvantaged: The Inner City, the Underclass, and Public Policy.* Chicago: University of Chicago Press.

WINANT, H. (1994). *Racial Conditions.* Minneapolis, MN: University of Minnesota Press.

WITKIN, H. A., DYK, R. B., PATERSON, H. F., GOODENOUGH, D. R., AND KARP, S. A. (1962). *Psychological Differentiation*. New York: John Wiley Publishers.

WITTENBRINK, B., JUDD, C. M., AND PARK, B. (In press). "Implicit Racial Stereotypes and Prejudice and Their Relationship with Questionnaire Measures: What We Say IS What We Think. *Journal of Personality and Social Psychology*.

WORCHEL, S., AND ROTHGERBER, H. (IN PRESS). "Changing the Stereotype of the Stereotype." In R. Spears, P. Oakes, N. Ellmers, and S. Haslam (eds.), *The Social psychology of Stereotyping and Group Life*. Chicago: Nelson-Hall Publishers.

THE WORLD ALMANAC AND BOOK OF FACTS. (1996). Mahwah, NJ: Funk and Wagnalls, p. 553.

WORD, C. O., ZANNA, M. P., AND COOPER, J. (1974). "The Nonverbal Mediation of Self-Fulfilling Prophecies in Interracial Interaction." *Journal of Experimental Social Psychology, 10,* 109–120.

WRIGHT, R. (1940). *Native Son*. New York: Harper.

YARROW, M. R. (1958). "Interpersonal Dynamics in a Desegregation Process." *Journal of Social Issues, 14,* 63.

YBARRA, O. J., AND STEPHAN, W. G. (1994). "Perceived Threat as a Predictor of Stereotypes and Prejudice: Americans' Reactions to Mexican Immigrants. *Spanish Annals of Psychology*. 48.

YEE, A. H., FAIRCHILD, H. H., WEIZMAN, F., AND WYATT, G. E. (1993). "Addressing Psychology's Problems with Race." *American Psychologist, 48,* 1132–1140.

ZAJONC, R. B. (1968). "Attitudinal Effects of Mere Exposure." *Journal of Personality and Social Psychology, 9,* Monograph supplement No. 2, part 2.

ZALESNY, M. D. (1990). "Rater Confidence and Social Influence in Performance Appraisals." *Journal of Applied Psychology, 75,* 274–289.

ZANE, N. (1996). An Empirical Examination of Loss of Face among Asian Americans. Unpublished manuscript, University of California, Santa Barbara.

ZANNA, M. P., AND OLSON, J. M. (EDS.). (1993). *The Psychology of Prejudice: The Ontario Symposium*, Vol. 7. Hillsdale, NJ: Erlbaum Associates.

ZANNA, M. P., AND HEMPEL, J. K. (1988). "Attitudes: A New Look at an Old Concept." In D. Bar-Tal and A. Kruglanski (eds.), *The Social Psychology of Knowledge* (pp. 315–334). Cambridge, England: Cambridge University Press.

ZANNA, M. P. (1994). "On the Nature of Prejudice." *Canadian Psychology, 35,* 11–23.

ZARATE, M. A., AND SMITH, E. E. (1990). "Person Categorization and Stereotyping." *Social Cognition, 8,* 161–185.

ZARTMAN, I. W., AND AURIK, J. (1991). "Power Strategies in De-Escalation." In L. Kriesberg and S. J. Thorson (eds.), *Timing the De-Escalation of International Conflicts* (pp. 152–181). Syracuse, NY: Syracuse University Press.

ZEBROWITZ, L. A., MONTEPARE, J. M., AND LEE, H. K. (1993). "They Don't All Look Alike: Individuated Impressions of Other Racial Groups." *Journal of Personality and Social Psychology, 65,* 85–101.

ZEBROWITZ, L. M. (1944). "Facial Maturity and Political Prospects: Persuasive, Culpable, and Powerful Faces." In R. Schank and E. Langer (eds.), *Beliefs, Reasoning, and Decision-making: Psycho-Logic in Honor of Bob Abelson*. Hillsdale, NJ: Lawrence Erlbaum Publisher.

ZUCKERMAN, M. (1990). "Some Dubious Premises in Research and Theory on Racial Differences." *American Psychologist, 45,* 1297–1303.

ZUKAV, G. (1979). *The Dancing Wu Li Masters: An Overview of the New Physics*. New York: Bantam Books.

Acknowledgments

--- ❖ ---

Chapter 2, page 33: From: E. M. Rudwick, *Race Riot at East St. Louis, July 2, 1917.* Copyright © 1964 Southern Illinois University Press. Reprinted by permission; *page 47:* EXCERPT AS SUBMITTED from *Authoritarian Personality* by T.W. ADORNO, E. FRANKEL-BRUNSWICK and D. LEVINSON, N. SANFORD. Copyright © 1950 by the American Jewish Committee. Copyright renewed. Reprinted by permission of HarperCollins Publishers, Inc.; *page 50:* From: Festinger and Kelley, *Changing Attitudes through Social Contact.* Copyright © 1951. Reprinted by permission of the University of Michigan Institute for Social Research.

Chapter 3, page 66: Copyright © 1970 by the New York Times Co. Reprinted by permission.

Chapter 6, pages 139 and 143-144: G.W. Allport, *The Nature of Prejudice* (pages 13, 14, 206, 218, 281, 469, and 570) © 1979 Addison-Wesley Publishing Company, Inc. Reprinted by permission of Addison-Wesley Longman Publishing Company, Inc.

Chapter 7, pages 165-167: From: Lee, et. al., "Stereotype accuracy: Toward appreciating group differences." Copyright © 1995 by the American Psychological Association. Reprinted with permission; *page 183:* From: Neuberg, "Expectancy-confirmation processes in stereotype-tinged social encounters: The moderating role of social goals." In M.P. Zanna and J.M. Olson, *The Psychology of Prejudice: The Ontario Symposium, Vol. 17.* Copyright 1994. Reprinted by permission of Lawrence Erlbaum & Associates.

Chapter 10, pages 277-278: Reprinted by permission of the publisher. From Baldwin & Bell, "The African Self-Conscious Scale: An Africentric Personality Questionnaire." *The Western Journal of Black Studies* 9:61-68. Pullman, WA: Washington State University Press, 1994. All rights reserved; *page 286:* From: Deborrah Frable, "Marginal and mindful: deviants in social interaction," *Journal of Personality & Social Psychology,* 59. Copyright © 1990 by the American Psychological Association. Reprinted by permission.

Chapter 11, pages 298 and 325: G.W. Allport, *The Nature of Prejudice* (pages 13, 14, 206, 218, 281, 469, and 570) © 1979 Addison-Wesley Publishing Company, Inc. Reprinted by permission of Addison-Wesley Longman Publishing Company, Inc.; *page 323:* From: Jane Elliot, *The Eye of the Storm.* Copyright © 1969.

Chapter 12, page 352: Reprinted with the permission of Scribner, a Division of Simon & Schuster from *Is America Safe for Democracy?* by William McDougall. Copyright © 1921 by Charles Scribner's Sons, renewed 1949 by Anne McDougall.

Chapter 13, page 379: From: Essed, *Understanding Everyday Racism,* copyright 1991 by Sage Publications. Reprinted by permission of Sage Publications; *page 383:* From: Van Dijk, *Communicating Racism,* copyright 1987 by Sage Publications. Reprinted by permission of Sage Publications; *pages 383 and 386-389:* Reprinted from *White Racism: The Basics,* eds. Feagin & Vera (1995) with permission of the publisher, Routledge, New York; *pages 389-390:* From: *American Apartheid: Segregation and the Making of the Underclass* by Douglas Massey and Nancy Denton. Copyright © 1993 by the President and Fellows of Harvard College. Reprinted by permission of Harvard University Press; *page 392:* From: Chase, *The Legacy of Malthus: The Social Costs of the New Scientific Racism.* Copyright © 1977. Reprinted by permission of Alfred Knopf, Inc.; *page 400:* From: Van Dijk, *Elite Discourse and Racism,* copyright © 1993 by Sage Publications. Reprinted by permission of Sage Publications; *pages 401-409:* From *Living with Racism* by Joe R. Feagin and Melvin P. Sikes. Copyright © 1994 by Joe R. Feagin and Melvin P. Sikes. Reprinted by permission of Beacon Press, Boston.

Chapter 16, page 490: From: Hofstede, *Culture's Consequences: International Differences in Work Related Values.* Copyright © 1984 by Sage Publications, Inc. Reprinted by permission of Sage Publications, Inc.; *page 498:* From: *The Atlantic Monthly,* 1971. Reprinted by permission of the Estate of Michael J. Herstein.

Index

An italic *f* or *t* following a page number indicates a figure or a table, respectively.